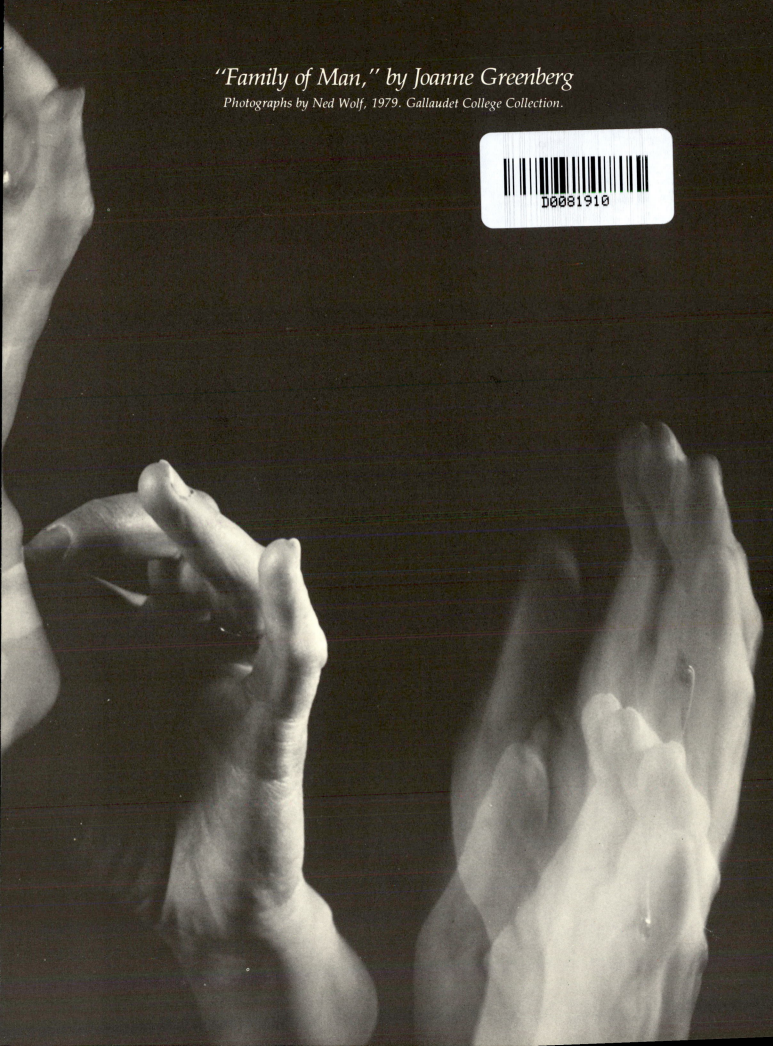

"Family of Man," by Joanne Greenberg

Photographs by Ned Wolf, 1979. Gallaudet College Collection.

Deaf Heritage

This book was made possible through the joint efforts of Gallaudet College and the National Association of the Deaf.

photo by Charles Shoup/Gallaudet College

iii

Deaf Heritage
A Narrative History of Deaf America

Jack R. Gannon

Best wishes, June.

Jack Gannon

7/10/81

Edited by JANE BUTLER and LAURA-JEAN GILBERT
Layout by ROSALYN L. GANNON

NATIONAL ASSOCIATION OF THE DEAF

Published by the National Association of the Deaf,
814 Thayer Avenue, Silver Spring, Maryland 20910.

ISBN 0 913072 39 7 Hard Back Edition
ISBN 0 913072 38 9 Soft Back Edition
Library of Congress Catalog Card Number: 80-82031

Published 1981

Printed in the United States of America

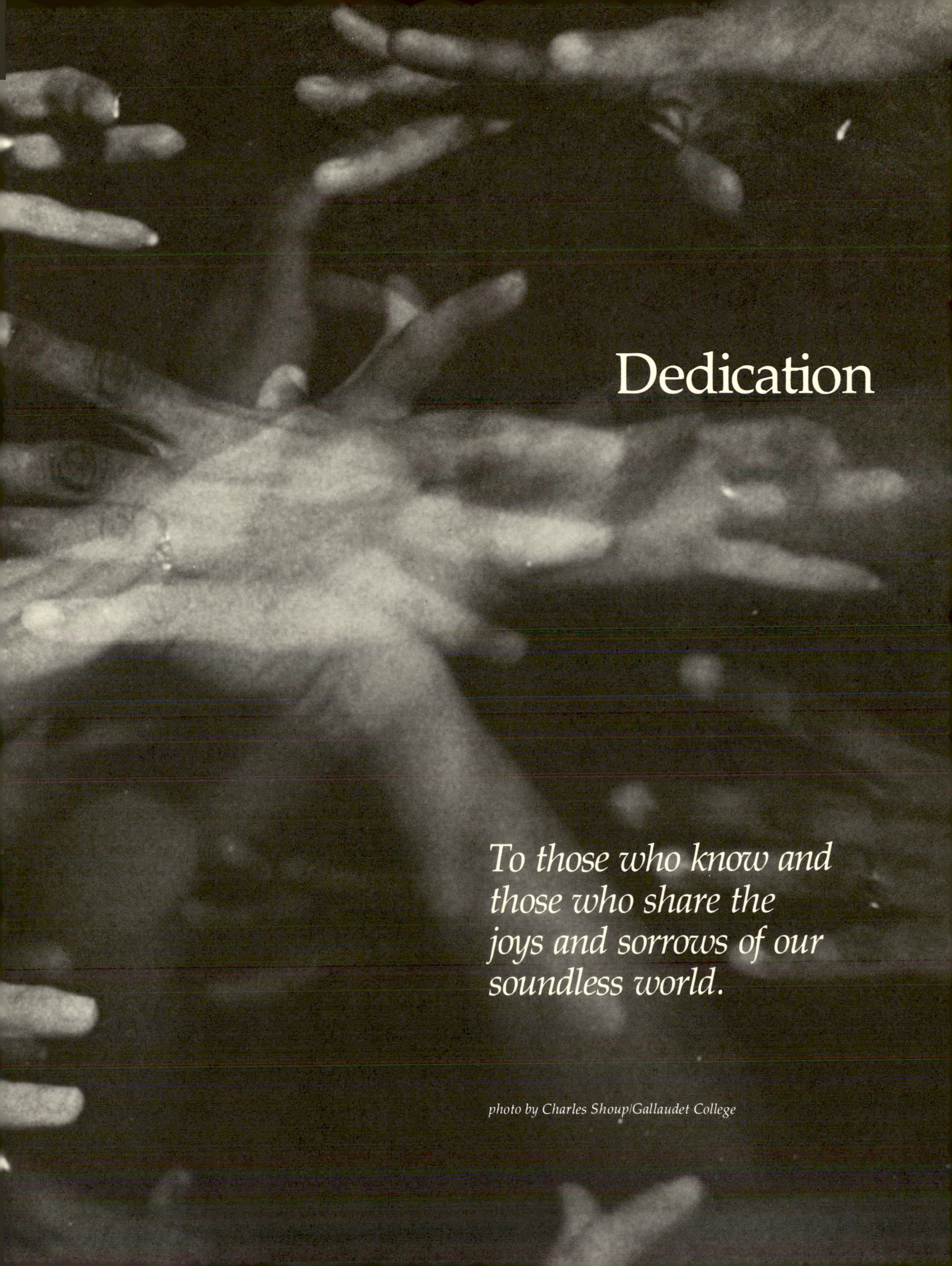

Dedication

To those who know and those who share the joys and sorrows of our soundless world.

photo by Charles Shoup/Gallaudet College

Contents

DEDICATION ix

FOREWORD xv

ACKNOWLEDGMENT xvii

INTRODUCTION xix

PROLOGUE xxi
    A Journey Begins . . .

CHRONOLOGY xxv

CHAPTER 1—The Early Years 1

    Early Attempts to Educate Deaf Children . . . Causes of Deafness . . . Deaf Teachers
    . . . Deaf Black Teachers . . . "What Hath God Wrought" . . . Deaf Smith . . . Denom-
    inational Schools . . . More Schools . . . Mr. Bartlett's School . . . The Civil War . . .
    Sign Language Saves a Life . . . Deaf Soldiers . . . Birth of a College . . . Oral Education
    Arrives in America . . . The Post-War Years . . . Schools for Deaf Blacks . . . Mr.
    Knapp's School . . . McCowen's Voice and Hearing School . . . The Trend Changes
    . . . John Carlin . . . Schools for the Deaf . . . School Seals and Logos . . . Schools
    Founded by Deaf Persons.

CHAPTER 2—The 1880s 59

    A Beginning . . . Birth of the National Association of the Deaf . . . Robert P. McGregor
    . . . Meeting at Milan: An Infamous Resolution . . . Edwin A. Hodgson . . . "If You
    Seek His Monument" . . . Edmund Booth . . . *The Raindrop* . . . The Decade . . . Job
    Turner . . . James H. Logan . . . George M. Teegarden . . . Train Deaths . . . John J.
    Flournoy . . . Intermarriages . . . Milestones . . . Annual Staff and Teacher's Salaries.

CHAPTER 3—The 1890s 75

    Dr. Bell's 'Deaf Variety of The Human Race' . . . The Volta Bureau . . . Albert Ballin
    . . . Albert Ballin Describes Bell . . . Bell on Speech and Sign Language . . . The Debate
    over Technical Education for the Deaf . . . The Fifer Cadets of Illinois . . . The Silent
    Wheelmen of the '90s . . . Valentine's Day, 1890 . . . Occupations . . . The Arrival of
    the Linotype . . . The Racycle . . . The Decade . . . Voices, Voices . . . Early Cures.

CHAPTER 4—Artists 93

Hillis Arnold . . . David Bloch . . . Morris Broderson . . . John Brewster . . . John Carlin . . . John L. Clarke . . . Theophilus d'Estrella . . . Robert J. Freiman . . . Louis Frisino . . . Eugene E. Hannan . . . Regina Olson Hughes . . . Felix Kowalewski . . . Frederick LaMonto . . . Charles J. LeClercq . . . Betty G. Miller . . . Ralph R. Miller . . . Henry H. Moore . . . Granville S. Redmond . . . William B. Sparks . . . Kelly H. Stevens . . . Douglas Tilden . . . Cadwallader L. Washburn . . . Tom Wood . . . Hilbert Duning . . . Olof Hanson . . . Thomas Marr.

CHAPTER 5—The 1900s 157

Birth of a Fraternal Insurance Society . . . Grand Presidents of the National Fraternal Society of the Deaf and Their Terms in Office . . . National Fraternal Society of the Deaf Hall of Fame . . . Frater of the Year . . . Division of the Year . . . Francis P. Gibson . . . The Decade . . . Orson Archibald . . . Homes for the Aged and Infirm Deaf . . . The Deaf Driver . . . Inventors . . . El Mudo.

CHAPTER 6—The 1910s 173

Preserving Sign Language . . . The Deaf Nurses of Mercy Hospital . . . The Gallaudet Airplane . . . Fifty Deaf Marksmen Dead . . . The Decade . . . Regulations.

CHAPTER 7—The 1920s 181

The Decade . . . Deaf Clergy . . . Episcopal . . . A Deaf Man's Prayer . . . Lutheran . . . The Deaf Minister . . . Methodist . . . Latter Day Saints . . . Baptist . . . John W. Michaels . . . Judaism . . . Catholic . . . Oralism and the Teaching of Religion . . . Interpreters . . . Laura C. R. Searing . . . Milestones . . . Deaf Pilots . . . Deaf Persons in the United States Who Have Earned a Pilot's License . . . Firsts Among Deaf Pilots.

CHAPTER 8—Humor 203

Our Deaf World . . . Classroom Humor . . . Hazards of Deafness.

CHAPTER 9—The 1930s 211

Labor Bureaus . . . A Tall Story . . . Hearing Aids . . . Lars M. Larson . . . Carnegie Medal Winners . . . Pest to Exterminate . . . Milestones . . . What Experience Taught Them . . . J. Schuyler Long . . . A Tragedy of Deafness . . . Hazards of Deafness.

CHAPTER 10—The 1940s 219

The Decade . . . Pearl Harbor . . . Joining Up . . . Soldiers on the Assembly Line . . . Doing One's Share . . . Gallaudet's "Five Iron Men" . . . The 'Most Misunderstood Sons of Men' . . . The U.S.S. *Thomas Hopkins Gallaudet* . . . Butch, the Little Lady Dog . . . The Post War Years . . . Edith Fitzgerald . . . G. Dewey Coats . . . Lawrence Yolles . . . *The Silent Worker* Revived . . . Toward a Greater Gallaudet.

CHAPTER 11—Publications of the Deaf 237

The 'Silent' Press . . . Ten Oldest Educational Publications of the Deaf Still Being Published . . . The Little Paper Family . . . Deaf Newspapermen . . . Proppaganda . . . Literary Efforts of Deaf Persons.

CHAPTER 12—The 1950s 255

"The Deaf Do Not Beg" . . . Profile of a Deaf Peddler . . . The Decade . . . Arthur L. Roberts . . . Advent of Television . . . "Operation Lipread" . . . The NAD Endowment Fund . . . Battling Misleading Claims . . . NAD Reorganization Plans . . . Turning Point at Fulton . . . Captioned Films for the Deaf . . . Emerson Romero . . . They Say I'm Deaf . . . On His Deafness . . . The Fifties . . . Milestones.

CHAPTER 13—Sports 271

Deaf Athlete's Contributions to the World of Sports . . . Milestones in Sports . . . Football . . . Inter-School Football Competition . . . State Football Champions . . . Undefeated Teams . . . Winningest Seasons . . . All-Americans . . . Professional Football . . . Undefeated Schools for the Deaf Football Teams . . . The Goodyear Silents . . . Bowling . . . Basketball . . . Regional Basketball Tournaments . . . School for the Deaf Basketball Teams Which Have Won 20 or More Games In a Season . . . All American Selections . . . Swimming . . . Wrestling . . . Gallaudet College Wrestling . . . National AAU Wrestling Champions . . . Deaf Professional Wrestlers . . . Professional Boxers . . . Baseball . . . "Dummy" Taylor Communicates . . . American Deaf Softball Guide . . . World Games for the Deaf . . . The American Atletic Association of the Deaf . . . American Athletic Association of the Deaf Hall of Fame . . . Helms Foundation Hall of Fame . . . Kitty O'Neil, Fastest Woman on Earth . . . S. Robey Burns . . . Deaf Coaches of Hearing Teams . . . Deaf Athletes on Hearing Teams . . . J. Frederick Meagher . . . Art Kruger . . . The Speed Demon . . . The A.A.A.D. Hall of Fame . . . Players . . . Coaches . . . Sports Leaders—Writers . . . Old Timers . . . Athlete of the Year . . . School Records.

CHAPTER 14—The 1960s 317

The Sizzling, Bountiful Sixties . . . Jr. National Association of the Deaf . . . Walter J. Krug . . . The Fort Monroe Workshop . . . Harley D. Drake . . . Honoring de l'Epée . . . The Telephone Arrives . . . Howard T. Hofsteater . . . Ten Fingers Have I . . . Now the Deaf Are Doing It! . . . Tom L. Anderson . . . Telecommunications for the Deaf, Inc. . . . Registry of Interpreters for the Deaf . . . The Mantle of Leadership Is Passed On . . . George M. McClure, Sr. . . . U.S. Navy and Space Experiments . . . On The Edward Miner Gallaudet Statue . . . Cued Speech . . . The Council of Organizations Serving the Deaf . . . Glad Recompense . . . Roy J. Stewart . . . The Christensen Case . . . Mary E. Switzer . . . Deaf Administrators . . . Bitterweed . . . "Greatest Cause on Earth" . . . Higher Education at the Crossroads . . . Gallaudet's Fourth President . . . The National Theatre of the Deaf . . . "My Third Eye."

CHAPTER 15—American Sign Language: Our Natural Language 357

"The Noblest Gift" . . . The War of Methods . . . The Controversy . . . Attempts to Suppress Sign Language . . . *The Deaf: "By Their Fruits Ye Shall Know Them"* . . . American Sign Language Comes Out of the Closet . . . Silent Homage . . . Sign Language Books . . . The NAD Communicative Skills Program . . . Total Communication Arrives . . . Manually Coded English Systems . . . And Interest Grows.

CHAPTER 16—The 1970s 377

The Decade . . . Shared Beauty . . . You Have to be Deaf to Understand . . . Robert M. Greenum . . . Petra F. Howard . . . Television and the Deaf Viewer . . . The Caption Center at WGBH-TV . . . National Captioning Institute . . . Other Developments in Television . . . Rock Gospel . . . Chair of Deaf Studies . . . Deaf Awareness Programs . . . More on Telecommunication . . . Hearing Ear Dogs . . . Recipients of Honorary Degrees . . . Seventh World Congress of the World Federation of the Deaf . . . P.L. 94-142 . . . National Center for Law and the Deaf . . . Deaf Ph.D.s . . . The White House Conference . . . Deaf Jurors . . . Spectrum, Focus on Deaf Artists . . . The Gee Jay Show . . . Milestones . . . Ben M. Schowe . . . *Deaf Like Me* . . . Offspring of Deaf Parents . . . The Reality of Deafness.

CHAPTER 17—The National Association of the Deaf 419

Frederick C. Schreiber . . . Presidents of the National Association of the Deaf . . . Highlights of the NAD Century . . . Miss Deaf America.

Appendix 437

Known Deaf Persons Who Have Been Ordained.
Known Deaf Persons with Earned Doctoral Degrees.

Special Acknowledgment 443

About the Author 444

Chapter Notes 445

Bibliography 449

Index 463

Foreword

Every book has a reason for coming into being. Basically, it is a response to a long-felt and oft-expressed need for a volume which deals with the contributions of deaf Americans to society.

The heritage was waiting to be recorded. For all its richness, the material on deaf people and deafness had not been tapped. The world of deafness has had its trail-blazers, innovators, statesmen, philosophers, writers, artists, politicians, and reformers. Throughout the years in our country, there have been events of import, deeds of courage, decisions of lasting influence, strokes of brilliance, works of high quality, and moments of glory—all created by deaf people. The need was to capture between the covers of a book as many of them as possible.

Many goals were envisioned for the book. Perhaps the most important one was to present in a cogent form the legacy left to us by the deaf people of generations gone by. It would remind our young deaf people that deafness need not be a barrier to what they can do to enrich the quality of life for deaf citizens everywhere. More importantly, it would make them aware of the rich heritage that has cumulatively been bestowed on them.

The book was sure to come sooner or later. The Centennial Convention is often cited as the reason that the book-writing project got moving. It wasn't. It did, however, provide a powerful impetus toward its development. Yet, the timing of the project couldn't be more favorable. It coincides with the National Association of the Deaf's Centennial Celebration in Cincinnati, Ohio, June 30-July 5, 1980.

It remained only for someone to undertake the monumental task of researching the innumerable gems of information and weaving them into the stir-ring and inspiring volume it finally became. The National Association of the Deaf selected Jack R. Gannon, Director of Alumni and Public Relations at Gallaudet College and Executive Secretary of the Gallaudet College Alumni Association for this job. For him, it was a labor of love. The document clearly reveals it. The National Association of the Deaf owes him a debt it cannot ever repay.

Mention must be made of Gallaudet College's contribution to the project. Although Gallaudet College and the National Association of the Deaf perform different roles in serving deaf Americans, they share some common goals. One of these is not only to promote respect for deaf individuals, but also to recognize the contributions of deaf Americans to society. The book is a tangible example of cooperation between the college and the Association. The National Association of the Deaf wishes to express its deep appreciation to Gallaudet College and Dr. Edward C. Merrill, Jr., its president, for providing the time and support for Mr. Gannon to write the book.

The National Association of the Deaf also wishes to express its gratitude to all who in any way, large or small, contributed to the development of the book.

The book is finally here. It has been worth waiting for!

Ralph H. White
President
National Association of the Deaf

Copyright Acknowledgments

The author wishes to express thanks and appreciation to the following for permission to use copyrighted material:

Abby Aldrich Rockefeller Folk Art Center, Williamsburg, Virginia, for use of John Brewster's work.

Alexander Graham Bell Association for the Deaf, Volta Bureau Library, Washington, D.C., for loan of photographs and for permission to use material appearing in the *American Annals of the Deaf*.

Chun Louie, New Carrollton, Maryland, for permission to reproduce his bumpersticker.

David O. Watson, Winneconne, Wisconsin, for use of material appearing in his book, *Talk With Your Hands*.

Gallaudet College Alumni Association, Washington, D.C., for use of photographs appearing in *Our Heritage, 1864-1964*, and for permission to use poetry appearing in *The Silent Muse, An Anthology of Prose and Poetry by the Deaf*.

Modern Signs Press for permission to reproduce the cover of *Signing Essential English*.

Helen Powers, Danbury, Connecticut, for quote appearing in *Signs of Silence*.

Joyce Media, Inc., Northridge, California, and Author Roy Holcomb, for use of material appearing in *Hazards of Deafness*.

National Geographic Society, Washington, D.C., for use of cover photograph taken by Koko which appeared on the cover of the *National Geographic Magazine*.

New Hampshire Historical Society, Concord, New Hampshire, for use of James H. Whitcomb's silhouette of his sister.

Rex Lowman, Riverdale, Maryland, for use of his poem appearing in *Bitterweed*.

Ripley International Limited, Toronto, Ontario, Canada, for use of their "Ripley's Believe It Or Not!" cartoons.

Thomas S. Spradley, James P. Spradley, and Random House, Inc., New York, for permission to reproduce the cover of *Deaf Like Me* and quote excerpts from the book.

Willard J. Madsen of Seabrook, Maryland, for permission to reprint his poem, "You Have to be Deaf to Understand."

Acknowledgment

The seed for this book was planted on a train ride from Washington, D.C., to West Trenton, New Jersey, in the winter of 1977. Gary Olsen and I were on our way to present a National Association of the Deaf and Gallaudet College-sponsored leadership training program for deaf adults at the Marie H. Katzenbach School for the Deaf in West Trenton. Gary was at that time chairman of the NAD Centennial Committee, and he was in the process of making plans for that forthcoming event. Among his many ideas, he said, he wanted a book about deaf America to record that century, and he was looking for someone to write it.

At that time I had been reading William Manchester's *The Glory and the Dream,* a fascinating historical account of America. The idea of writing a similar history of deaf America appealed to me. Not much time remained until the NAD Centennial when you think in terms of writing a book, but I agreed to submit an outline and a sample chapter for Gary's and the NAD Board's consideration. Having received them, Gary and the Board liked what they saw and, later, Gallaudet College, my employer, agreed to let me undertake the project on a part-time basis. Suddenly, I had what appeared to be an insurmountable task on my hands and realized—once again—what one gets into with a simple affirmative nod of the head!

Now, almost three years later, as I recall that trip to New Jersey, I also remember the many other trips I have taken in search of the deaf America story, and I am reminded of the many acquaintances I have made, all the letters I have written, and all the help I have received. I realize how fortunate I have been and how much I owe to so many in the production of this volume.

I wish to thank the National Association of the Deaf for the honor of being asked to write this book.

I am also grateful to Dr. Edward C. Merrill, Jr., president of Gallaudet College, for his sensitiveness to the need for this type of material, for permission to undertake this challenging project, and for his encouragement and support.

The time spent on this book was a long and difficult period for the members of my family and for that reason I have included a special acknowledgment to them. See page 441.

I owe so much to the members of my staff in the Office of Alumni/Public Relations at Gallaudet College for their patience, assistance, support, and understanding during my many absences. I would especially like to acknowledge the individual contributions of Evelyn Aker, Terri Baker, Gerri Born, Alice Bradfield, Gwen Brown, Donna Chitwood, Verna Domich, Georgette Lopes, Peter Moran, Joyce Moore, Dave and Polly Peikoff, Debbie Steffanic, and my supervisor, Barbara P. Harslem, for her support.

Mervin D. Garretson has been with this project from the very beginning. He is the type of person every author needs for a friend. He is very knowledgeable about the subject matter, and he served as an important sounding board and provided helpful input and encouragement. There were days when it seemed that this project would never end, but his faith in the finished project never faltered.

I also wish to thank:

Laura-Jean Gilbert and Jane Butler for their valuable assistance in editing this work.

Rosalyn L. Gannon, my wife, who did the layout, most of the indexing, and provided assistance where needed.

Byron B. Burnes for his assistance with the research, collection of material on the National Association of the Deaf, proofreading, and for his assistance with editing and indexing. His recollections of facts and sense of NAD history were invaluable.

For more than two years, Peggy Sugiyama filled a very important role by maintaining the voluminous files of all the material I collected. Her system made the information readily available and easy to find. Her husband, Bill, designed the manual alphabet artwork which begins each chapter.

Paul Wester represented Corporate Press, the printers of this book, and he is an important part of it. He displayed remarkable self-control when deadlines came and went . . . and nothing happened. His ideas and assistance and, especially, his familiarity with what an author must go through, and his encouragement, were most helpful. Bob Taylor worked closely with Paul, and he was responsible for overseeing the mechanical end of the production of this book. Both were a pleasure to work with.

Leon Auerbach and Jess Smith who reviewed the drafts and provided important input and helpful suggestions.

Betsey Cullen for her assistance with compiling information on the artists and for her assistance with the indexing.

Albert T. Pimentel, executive director of the National Association of the Deaf, for his confidence and support.

Fern Edwards, librarian, and Carolyn Jones of the Edward Miner Gallaudet Memorial Library and especially Corrine Hilton, archivist, and her assistants, David De Lorenzo and Mike Olsen.

Edith Kleberg, librarian at the National Association of the Deaf library, for her assistance in collecting photographs and information about the National Association of the Deaf.

The staff of the Aspen Hill Library in Rockville, Maryland, who so cheerfully and helpfully responded to my many requests for information over the tele-typewriter.

Art Kruger for his tremendous assistance with the sports section. Most of the material used in this chapter comes from Art's vast collection of sports records and stories which he has collected from over a half a century of sports writing.

Gilbert C. Eastman for the loan of his rare collection of material on the life of Laurent Clerc, and for the interest, enthusiasm, and encouragement he displayed in this book.

Wilbur Ruge for the special flavor he gave to the "deaf" cartoons found in the humor section.

The many writers, poets, artists, and photographers who have generously given me permission to include their work in this book. Their contributions are individually acknowledged throughout the book.

Anthony Papalia, editor of *The Washingtonian*, for the many items he sent or called to my attention.

To all the individuals in schools for the deaf who loaned me pictures, histories, and other documents and assisted with the compilation of the histories of the schools for the deaf.

Philip E. Cronlund, superintendent of the Marie H. Katzenbach School for the Deaf, initial publishers of *The Silent Worker*, and Jess M. Smith, editor of *The Silent Worker* and *The Deaf American*, for their permission to use much material appearing in that magazine.

And, the individuals, firms, and museums listed below, who provided their time and assistance in a variety of ways too numerous to list, but who were most helpful to the author in the compilation of information for this book:

Edna Adler □ E. Conley Akin □ Mildred Albronda □ Frank Almeida □ David Anthony □ Arrowhead Mills, Inc. □ Dallas Barker □ Louis Balfour □ Pat Banks □ R. Aumon Bass □ Carter E. Bearden □ James Beauchamp □ Edmund B. Boatner □ Bernard Bragg □ Joseph Bruce, C.J. □ Lupé Bryant □ Henry L. Buzzard □ Kathleen Callaway □ Edward C. Carney □ S. Mel Carter, Jr. □ Roger Claussen □ John Van Cleve □ Sara E. Conlon □ Clarence D. Connors □ Edward C. Corbett □ Thomas Coughlin □ Sam B. Craig, Sr. □ Alan B. Crammatte □ Florence Crammatte □ Albert Darby □ Deaf Smith County Chamber of Commerce □ Deaf Smith County Historical Society, Inc. □ Delbert Erickson □ Lance Fischer □ Alexander Fleischman □ Georgette Fleischman □ Natalie Gawdiak □ James Gillies □ Astrid Goodstein □ John A. Gough □ Gerilee Gustason □ David Halberg □ David Hays □ Barbara Heinrich □ Rance Henderson □ Herbert F. Hilmer □ Ben E. Hoffmeyer □ Elizabeth House □ Gerald Johnson □ Barbara Kannapell □ Stan Kelly □ Marcus Kleberg □ Ella Lentz □ Howard G. Mann □ William J. Marra □ Susan Marshburn □ William J. McClure □ Winfield McCord □ Arthur Merklin □ Tamsen Merrill □ Carol Moffett □ Fred R. Murphy □ Susan P. Neel □ Ralph Neesam □ North Carolina University Collection □ Malcolm J. Norwood □ Kathleen O'Leary □ Barbara Olmert □ James N. Orman □ Robert F. Panara □ Richard D. Reed □ Peter Ripley □ Hal Schwartz □ Rick J. Schoenberg □ Eldon Shipman □ Charlie Shoup □ Ausma Smits □ Archie Stack □ Bill Stark □ William C. Stokoe □ Barry Strassler □ Frank B. Sullivan □ Florence C. Taylor □ Frank R. Turk □ Andy Vasnick □ Angelia Watson □ David O. Watson □ Charlie Whisman □ Boyce R. Williams □ Edgar M. Winecoff □ James Woodward □ Joseph Youngs.

Admittedly, this book is but a scratch on the surface of the history of one of America's most overlooked minority groups. For me, the research and writing of this book has been a tough but fascinating experience. As I complete this final draft I do so knowing that I am a different person. For one thing, I am a much prouder deaf American.

May this book likewise influence your life.

Jack R. Gannon
Silver Spring, Maryland
December, 1980

Introduction

In the 1521 publication, *De Inventione Dialectica*, the pioneering humanistic educator Rudolf Agricola made the statement that deaf people can be taught a language. This is one of the earliest positive statements about deafness on record. Further back, in the shrouded mists of antiquity, references to deaf persons tended to be negative, as in the *Mishnah*, the collection of traditional rabbinical interpretations of Jewish law; in the writings of the Roman lawmaker Justinian; and in other works up through the Renaissance. The most vicious pronouncement probably is that attributed to Aristotle: "Those who are born deaf all become senseless and incapable of reason."

Practically all of these early discourses on hearing loss and on deaf persons were written by people who were themselves not deaf. It was not until the last 100 years or so that accounts written by a number of deaf persons appeared in print. These were shaped by actual experience and perception rather than by theory, assumption, and observation.

In *Deaf Heritage* Jack R. Gannon, profoundly deaf since the age of eight, has for the first time attempted to bring together a narrative of "the deaf experience" in the United States over the past century. Just what is "the deaf experience?" Hilde Schlesinger and Kathryn Meadow comment in *Sound and Sign*: "Profound childhood deafness is more than a medical diagnosis; it is a cultural phenomenon in which social, emotional, linguistic, and intellectual patterns are inextricably bound together."

Recognizing the need for some kind of documentation of the multi-faceted history of this unique minority group with its distinctive visual culture, three years ago the author began the formidable task of gathering materials relating to the origins of schools, programs, organizations, and events relating to deaf people in this country. Reviewing old and yellowed publications and photographs, meticulously following up on information tips and sources, interviewing old-timers and checking and verifying, Mr. Gannon continued to file, analyze, and classify and, in the process, found himself always learning something new.

Fascinated by this wealth of information about deaf persons and their environment, he soon confronted the twin constraints of time and space and the need to become selective if this introductory history were to be published during the centennial of the National Association of the Deaf. It is hoped that *Deaf Heritage* is but a beginning of a continuing compilation and closer examination of the impact of deafness on persons, their achievements, and their traditions. This valuable chronicle should prove helpful as a text in courses on deaf culture, in orientation-to-deafness seminars, in teacher and counselor preparation programs, as a reference source, and simply as interesting literature.

Mervin D. Garretson
Special Assistant to the President
Gallaudet College
Past President, National Association
  of the Deaf

xix

THE
ABBE SICARD,

SUCCESSOR OF THE ABBE DE L'EPEE,

And Director of the Institution for the Education of the

Deaf and Dumb,

IN PARIS,

PRESIDENT OF THE ROYAL INSTITUTE OF FRANCE, &c. &c.

IS ARRIVED IN THIS TOWN, ON HIS WAY FROM LONDON, TO PARIS,

And has the honour to inform the Nobility, Gentry, and the Public in general, that,
for the satisfaction of the inhabitants of this fashionable place,

he will give

A Public
LECTURE,

AT THE

OLD SHIP ROOMS,

Brighton,

On FRIDAY & SATURDAY next, the 28th and 29th
of July, instant,

TO COMMENCE AT ONE O'CLOCK IN THE AFTERNOON.

ADMISSION, 5s. EACH.

FLEET, PRINTER, BRIGHTON.

Prologue

A Journey Begins

 HE WIND billowed, filling the sails. The rigging snapped taut as the little wooden ship, the *Mary Augusta*, alternately floundering and plowing the seas of the Atlantic Ocean, made its way westward to the city of New York. Several days before, at high tide, on the afternoon of June 18, 1816, the *Mary Augusta* had left Le Havre on the northern coast of France. To the deaf people of America, this was a historic journey.

The vessel carried six passengers, a crew of twelve, and the ship's captain. Four of the passengers were Americans and the other two were Frenchmen, one of whom, Laurent Clerc, was traveling with one of the Americans—the Reverend Thomas H. Gallaudet.

In the beginning of the voyage, 30-year-old Laurent Clerc was something of an oddity to the other passengers. He was a deaf teacher of the deaf, coming from the National Royal Institution for the Deaf in Paris on a unique mission. He and his friend Gallaudet hoped to start a school for the deaf in America.

Clerc knew little English, and so he spent much of his time on the crossing learning the language from Gallaudet. In return, he taught Gallaudet the language of signs. He kept a diary of the trip, which lasted 52 days because of frequent calms and headwinds. Clerc recorded the events of each day, and then Gallaudet corrected his English. Afterwards, Clerc copied the corrected version in his stitched journal.

The long journey, Clerc wrote, "caused time to hang heavy on our hands," and the passengers despaired. Six hogs, several ducks, and chickens had been put on board, as Clerc explained, for their "daily nourishment." The Captain's dog have birth to a litter enroute. Some canaries had been brought along "to tickle the ears of the passengers by the agreeable sound of their singing. Ah, well!!!"

While sunning on deck one day, Clerc saw some mice scamper across the boards. A duck caught one and ate it. Clerc reasoned to himself that if ducks eat mice and people eat ducks, then people also eat mice. Thereupon, he informed the steward that he no longer desired to be served duck.

Laurent Clerc's journey to America had its beginnings in his childhood in the small French village of LaBalme. One day, when Clerc was a toddler, his high chair toppled into the open fireplace, and the right side of his face was badly burned. The accident was believed to have caused Clerc's deafness and the loss of his sense of smell. The resulting scar was the basis for Clerc's personal sign—closed index and middle fingers brushing downward across the right cheek.

Clerc's father, a notary public and mayor of LaBalme, learned about a school for the deaf in Paris and sent his son there. At this school, which had been founded by Charles Michel de l'Epée, Clerc studies and became a teacher. He and Gallaudet became good friends at this school. When Gallaudet was ready to leave for America, he asked Clerc to join him.

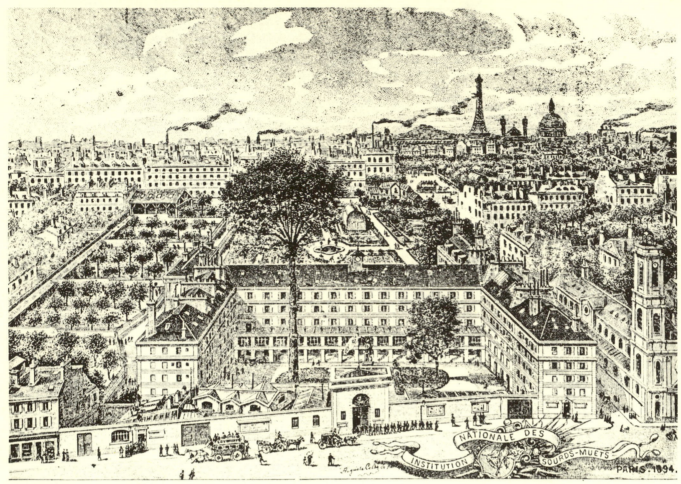

The school where Laurent Clerc taught before leaving for America.

As for Thomas Hopkins Gallaudet, his journey began one afternoon in the back yard of his Connecticut home. He was home from the seminary and he was watching his younger brothers and sisters play with some other children. He noticed that one young girl was not participating in the fun. He called one of his brothers to his side and asked about the girl. Her name was Alice Cogswell, and she was deaf. Gallaudet was intrigued. He approached Alice and tried to communicate with her. He taught her the word "hat" by pointing to his hat and writing the word with a stick in the sand. When Alice's father, Dr. Mason Cogswell, learned about the lesson he was thrilled. Cogswell, a prominent Hartford surgeon, spoke to Gallaudet about starting a school for the deaf in that city. After much consideration, Gallaudet agreed to take a trip to Europe to learn how to teach the deaf and how to start a school for the deaf in America.

Soon after their arrival in America, Clerc and Gallaudet set about raising funds for their new school. The following March, they announced the opening of Connecticut Asylum for the Deaf and Dumb, in Hartford. For a sum of $200, the offer read, the Asylum would provide each pupil with "board, lodging, washing, the continual superintendence of health, conduct, manners, and morals; fuel, candles, stationery and other incidental expenses of the school room. . . ." The notice added that in the event of sickness an extra charge would be made. It was requested that pupils applying be at least nine years old. The announcement was signed by Mason F. Cogswell and Daniel Wadsworth, members of the school's board. The formal education of deaf Americans had begun.

Alexander Graham Bell Association/The Volta Bureau

Laurent Clerc

Alexander Graham Bell Association/The Volta Bureau

Dr. Mason F. Cogswell

Alexander Graham Bell Association/The Volta Bureau

Rev. Thomas Hopkins Gallaudet

THE
DEAF AND DUMB ALPHABETS.
BY CHAS. PARKER.

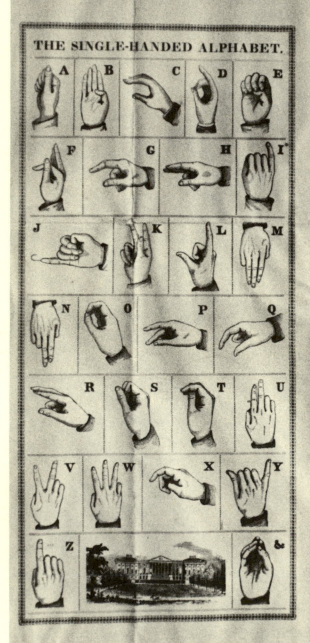

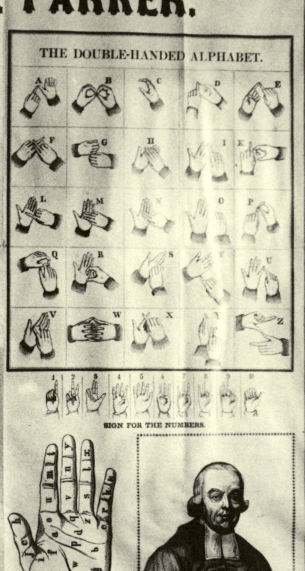

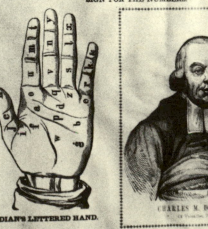

An early manual alphabet chart.

Chronology

355 B.C. — Aristotle says those "born deaf become senseless and incapable of reason."

721 — St. Bede writes about St. John of Beverly (d. 721) teaching a deaf-mute to speak.

1485 ca. — Rudolphus Agricola (1443-1485) writes about a deaf-mute who learns to read and write (1520-1584).

1500 ca. — Girolamo Cardano (1501-1576) is the first physician to recognize the ability of the deaf to reason.

Juan F. X. Navaretta (1525-1579) called El Mudo (the mute) serves as painter for Philip II of Spain.

Joachin Dubellay (1522-1560), a deaf poet, publishes *Hymn to Deafness*.

1550 ca. — Pedro Ponce de Leon begins teaching the deaf.

1575 ca. — Lasso, a Spanish lawyer, concludes that those who learn to speak are no longer dumb and should have right to progeniture.

1616 — G. Bonifacio publishes a treatise discussing sign language, *Of The Art Of Signs* (1579-1620).

1620 — Juan Pablo Bonet publishes first book on education of the deaf, Madrid, Spain.

1644 — John Bulwer (1614-1684) publishes *Chirologia* (The Natural Language of the Hand).

1648 — John Bulwer publishes *The Deaf And Dumb Man's Friend*.

1653 — John Wallis (1616-1705) publishes *De Loquela* (a method of teaching English and speech).

1661 — George Dalgarno of Scotland publishes *Art of Communication*.

1662 — Dr. John Wallis teaches D. Whaley to read and write (d. 1806).

1680 — George Dalgarno publishes *Deaf and Dumb Man's Tutor*.

1693 — DuVerney presents new Swiss resonance theory for hearing.

1700 — Johann Ammon (1669-1724) a Swiss medical doctor develops and publishes methods for teaching speech and lipreading to the deaf called *Surdus Laquens*.

1755(?) — Samuel Heinicke (1729-1790) establishes first oral school for the deaf in the world in Germany.

1755 — Charles Michel Abbe de l'Epée (1712-1789) establishes first free school for the deaf in the world, Paris, France.

1760 — Thomas Braidwood opens first school for the deaf in England.

1776 — Charles M. A. de l'Epée publishes *Instruction of Deaf and Dumb by Means of Methodical Signs*.

1777 — Arnoldi, a German pastor, publishes *Practical Instructions For Teaching Deaf-Mute Persons to Speak and Write*. Arnoldi believed education of the deaf should begin as early as four years.

1778(?) — Samuel Heinicke, the "Father of the German Method" (pure oralism), establishes a pure oral school at Leipzig.

1780 — Charles Green of Boston becomes one of the earliest deaf Americans to receive formal education overseas in Scotland.

1782 — R. A. Sicard (1742-1822) opens a school for deaf at Bordeaux: writes *Theorie Des Signes* (an elaborate dictionary of signs).

1784 — Abba Silvestri opens first school for the deaf in Italy in Rome.

1789 — Abbe de l'Epée dies.

1789(?) — Roch Ambroise Cucurran Sicard (1742-1822) succeeds Abbe de l'Epée.

1803 — Francis Green, father of Charles Green, publishes article recommending founding of a school for the deaf in America.

1807 — Rev. John Stanford discovers deaf children in New York City almshouse, later attempts to instruct them.

1812 — John Braidwood begins teaching private class of deaf children at Bolling Hall in Cobbs, Virginia.

1814 — Thomas H. Gallaudet meets Alice Cogswell.

1815 — Colonel Bolling opens the short-lived first school for the deaf in America at Cobbs, Virginia, to public.

Thomas H. Gallaudet departs for Europe to seek methods to teach the deaf.

1816 — Laurent Clerc returns to America with Thomas H. Gallaudet.

1817 — Connecticut Asylum for the Education and Instruction of Deaf and Dumb Persons, the first permanent school for the deaf in America, opens in Hartford on April 15.

1818 — New York School for the Deaf (Fanwood) opens.

1819 — Clerc marries Elizabeth Boardman.

First female teacher employed at the New York School.

1820 — School for the Deaf in Philadelphia (Pennsylvania Institution) opens.

1822 — American School for the Deaf adds vocational training to curriculum.

1823 — Kentucky School for the Deaf opens in Danville and becomes first state-supported school and first school for the deaf west of the Allegheny Mountains.

1825 — Central New York Asylum opens in Canajoharie, New York; merges with New York School in 1836.

1827 — Colonel Smith's School opens in Tallmadge, Ohio.

1829 — Ohio School for the Deaf opens.

1830 — Thomas Hopkins Gallaudet resigns as principal of the American Asylum for the Deaf.

Mason Fitch Cogswell (1761-1830) dies; his daughter, Alice, dies a few weeks later.

1837 — St. Joseph's School for the Deaf the first Catholic school for the deaf in the United States started in St. Louis, Missouri.

Perkins School for the Blind enrolls Laura Bridgman, one of the first deaf/blind persons to be formally educated in U.S.

1839 — Virginia School for the Deaf and the Blind becomes first school to serve both deaf and blind children.

1840 — Sisters of Loretto at the Foot of the Cross in Loretto, Kentucky, accept deaf girls in their school.

1864 — Melville Bell invents "Visible Speech."

1843 — Indiana School for the Deaf opens in Indianapolis.

1845 — Tennessee School for the Deaf opens.

North Carolina School for the Deaf opens in Raleigh.

1846 — Illinois School for the Deaf opens in Jacksonville.

American Annals of the Deaf begins publication at the American School in Hartford.

Georgia School for the Deaf opens.

1849 — South Carolina School for the Deaf opens.

The Deaf-Mute begins publication at the North Carolina School for the Deaf.

1850 — Convention of American Instructors of the Deaf holds first meeting at New York School.

School for deaf children is started in Clarksville, Arkansas.

1851 — Thomas Hopkins Gallaudet dies on September 10.

Missouri School for the Deaf opens in Fulton.

1852 — Wisconsin School for the Deaf opens in Delavan.

The Rev. Thomas Gallaudet starts St. Ann's Church for the Deaf in New York City, the first church for the deaf in U.S.

Louisiana State School for the Deaf opens.

Mr. Bartlett's Family School for Young Deaf-Mute Children opens in New York City.

1854 — Mississippi School for the Deaf opens in Jackson.

Michigan School for the Deaf opens.

Gallaudet Monument is dedicated in Hartford.

1855 — Iowa School for the Deaf opens in Council Bluffs.

1856 — Texas School for the Deaf opens in Austin.

J. B. Edwards' school opens in Lexington, Georgia.

P. H. Skinner's School opens in Washington, D.C.

P. H. Skinner's School for the Colored Deaf Children opens in Niagara City, New York.

1857 — Columbia Institution for the Instruction of the Deaf and Dumb (Kendall School) opens in Washington, D.C.

First special teacher of articulation employed by American School for the Deaf.

1858 — Alabama Institute for the Deaf opens.

Laurent Clerc retires from teaching at age 73.

1859 — St. Mary's School for the Deaf opens in Buffalo, New York.

Home for Young Deaf-Mutes (a shelter for preschool deaf children) opens in New York City; closes in 1862.

1860 — California School for the Deaf opens in San Francisco.

1861 — Kansas School for the Deaf opens in Baldwin.

Minnesota School for the Deaf opens in Faribault.

1864 — Congress authorizes the Board of Directors of the Columbia Institution to grant college degrees; President Lincoln signs charter on April 8.

1865 — Collegiate division named National Deaf-Mute College.

John Carlin and others organize Clerc Literary Society of the Deaf in Philadelphia.

1867 — Lexington School for the Deaf opens in New York City; first pure oral school in the country.

Clarke School for the Deaf, Northampton, Massachusetts opens.

1868 — Conference of Executives of American Schools for the Deaf organized at Gallaudet College in Washington, D.C.

Maryland School for the Deaf opens.

Melville Bell lectures about his work of teaching speech to the deaf in the U.S.

Presbyterian Mission Sabbath School becomes first day school for the deaf—later renamed the Pittsburgh School for the Deaf, then the Western Pennsylvania School for the Deaf.

1869 — Nebraska School for the Deaf opens in Omaha.

Horace Mann School opens in Boston.

North Carolina opens Institution for Colored Deaf and Dumb and Blind children.

St. Joseph's School for the Deaf opens in New York City.

Laurent Clerk dies July 18 at age 83.

1870 — West Virginia School for the Deaf and the Blind opens in Romney.

Oregon School for the Deaf opens in Salem.

1872 — Alexander G. Bell opens speech school for teachers of the deaf in Boston.

Rev. Thomas Gallaudet and others start Church Missions to Deaf-Mutes.

Rev. Thomas Gallaudet founds Home for Aged and Infirm Deaf in New York City.

Maryland School for the Colored Blind and Deaf opens in Baltimore.

1874 — First adult education program for the deaf starts in New York City.

Cincinnati Public School for the Deaf opens.

Chicago Day Schools for the Deaf open.

1876 — St. John's School for the Deaf opens near Milwaukee.

Bell gets patent for his telephone invention; exhibits it at Philadelphia Exposition that summer.

New England Industrial School for the Deaf-Mutes opens in Beverly, Massachusetts, (later renamed Beverly School).

1877 — Knapp School in Baltimore begins admitting deaf students in an integrated program setting.

1878 — Gallaudet Day School opens in St. Louis, Missouri.

E. Z. Westervelt introduces Rochester Method at New York School in Rochester.

First International Congress on Education of the Deaf meets in Paris, France.

1880 — National Association of the Deaf organizes in Cincinnati, Ohio.

Rochester School begins kindergarten for deaf children.

International Congress on Education of the Deaf meets at Milan, Italy and adopts infamous resolution banning the use of sign language in teaching deaf children.

1881 — Tennessee School for Colored Deaf and Dumb children opens in East Knoxville.

1883 — The Voice and Hearing School for the Deaf opens in Chicago, becomes one of first to accept deaf children as young as three years old.

Pennsylvania Oral School for the Deaf opens in Scranton.

1884 — Ephpheta Catholic School for the Deaf opens in Chicago.

Utah School for the Deaf opens in Salt Lake City.

Northern New York School for the Deaf opens in Malone.

1885 — Marie Consila Deaf-Mute Institution opens in St. Louis, Missouri.

New Mexico School for the Deaf opens in Santa Fe.

Florida School for the Deaf opens in St. Augustine.

1886 — St. Mary's School for the Deaf opens in St. Paul, Minnesota.

Evansville School for the Deaf opens in Indiana.

1887 — Texas Institute for Deaf, Dumb and Blind Colored Youth opens on a farm near Austin.

Women admitted to the National Deaf-Mute College.

Alexander Graham Bell establishes the Volta Bureau.

Home for Little Children Who Cannot Hear opens in Massachusetts.

1888 — The Kindergarten and Primary School for Hearing and Deaf Children opens in Washington, D.C.

Eastern Iowa School for the Deaf opens in Dubuque.

1889	— Albany Home School for the Oral Instruction of the Deaf opens in New York.
	National Association of the Deaf unveils memorial to Thomas Hopkins Gallaudet at National Deaf-Mute College.
	Gallaudet graduates organize alumni association.
1890	— North Dakota School for the Deaf opens in Devils Lake.
	Alexander Graham Bell founds and endows the American Association to Promote the Teaching of Speech to the Deaf (now the Alexander Graham Bell Association for the Deaf).
1891	— Teacher Training program begins at the National Deaf-Mute College.
	American Association to Promote the Teaching of Speech to the Deaf holds first convention at Lake George, New York.
1892	— Home for the Training in Speech of Deaf Children before they are of School Age opens in Philadelphia.
1893	— Cleveland Day School for the Deaf opens in Ohio.
	World Congress of the Deaf meets in Chicago.
1894	— Parents of deaf children organize association at the Sara Fuller School in West Medford, Massachusetts.
	National Deaf-Mute College becomes Gallaudet College.
	Wright-Humason School (later Wright Oral School) opens in New York City.
1895	— St. Joseph's (Catholic) School for the Deaf opens in Oakland, California.
	Minneapolis Day School for the Deaf opens in Minnesota.
	Military drill system for the deaf starts at New York School (Fanwood).
1897	— St. Francis Xavier (Catholic) School for the Deaf opens in Baltimore, Maryland.
1899	— Boston (Catholic) School for the Deaf opens.
1900	— Edith Fitzgerald develops the Fitzgerald Key.
1900-20s	— Day schools and classes for the deaf increase.
1900-30s	— Dr. Pintner becomes generally recognized as father of psychology of deafness.
1901	— Alumni of the Michigan School organize the Fraternal Society of the Deaf.
1902	— Helen Keller earns BA degree *cum laude* at Radcliffe College.

1905-07	— St. Olaf College in Northfield, Minnesota establishes a department for the deaf.
1908	— DePaul (Catholic) Institute for the Deaf opens in Pittsburgh, Pennsylvania.
1909	— Virginia State School opens in Hampton.
1910	— Edward Miner Gallaudet retires as president of Gallaudet College.
	Dr. Percival Hall becomes second president.
	The Volta Review begins publication.
1911	— Arizona School for the Deaf and the Blind opens.
1912	— Archbishop Ryan (Catholic) Memorial Institute for the Deaf opens in Philadelphia, Pennsylvania.
	Teacher Training program at Gallaudet College renamed Department of Articulation and Normal Instruction.
	Society for the Welfare of the Jewish Deaf (later New York Society for the Deaf) forms professional services in New York City.
1914	— Central Institute for the Deaf opens in St. Louis, Missouri.
	Dr. Harry Best publishes *The Deaf; Their Position in Society and the Provision for their Education in the U.S.*
1915	— St. Rita (Catholic) School for the Deaf opens in Wisconsin.
1917	— Edward Miner Gallaudet dies in Hartford.
1921	— Earl C. Hanson patents the first vacuum-tube hearing aid.
1922	— Alexander Graham Bell dies on August 2 in Nova Scotia, Canada.
1926	— Edith Fitzgerald publishes *Straight Language for the Deaf*.
1930	— U.S. Bureau of the Census does census of deaf people.
1931	— Convention of Executives of American Schools for the Deaf establishes teacher certification for teachers of the deaf.
1934	— Federal survey of the deaf and hard of hearing begins under U.S. Office of Education.
	New Jersey School hosts the International Congress on the Education of the Deaf.
1937	— Ernest Marshall produces a motion picture in sign language for deaf audiences.
1940	— Helmer Myklebust publishes *The Psychology of Deafness*.
	P.S. 47 in New York City (junior high school for the deaf) opens.
	First audiometers appear.

1941-45 — Individually and collectively deaf Americans make outstanding contributions to war effort and build excellent work records.

Clubs of the deaf flourish.

1942 — John Tracy Clinic opens in Los Angeles.

1943 — Harry Best's book, *Deafness and the Deaf in the United States* appears.

1945 — Deaf sportsmen organize American Athletic Association for the Deaf in Akron, Ohio.

Dr. Leonard M. Elstad succeeds Dr. Percival Hall as third president of Gallaudet College.

1947 — Rhulin Thomas flies solo across U.S.A.

1950 — First transistor hearing aid appears on market.

1954 — Second California residential school for the deaf opens in Riverside.

The Columbia Institution is renamed Gallaudet College by Act of Congress.

U.S. Supreme Court outlaws segregation forcing colored schools for the deaf to close and integrate with institutions serving white children.

1955 — Crotched Mountain School for the Deaf opens in New Hampshire.

1956 — NAD officials and state representatives meet at the Missouri School for the Deaf to reorganize the National Association of the Deaf.

Jewish leaders organize the National Congress of Jewish Deaf.

1957 — Wyoming School for the Deaf opens in Casper.

1958 — President Dwight D. Eisenhower signs P.L. 85-905 establishing Captioned Films for the Deaf.

1959 — Gallaudet College publishes *Occupational Conditions Among the Deaf*.

1960 — Riverside City College in California begins program for the deaf.

National Association of the Deaf forms the Junior National Association of the Deaf.

Federal government provides stipends for teacher training.

Northern Illinois University, DeKalb, Illinois, establishes program for speech and hearing impaired.

1961 — Gallaudet College sponsors Workshop on Community Development Through Organizations of and for the Deaf at Fort Monroe, Virginia.

Leadership Training Program in the area of the deaf begins at San Fernando Valley State College (California State University, Northridge).

Georg von Bekesy wins Nobel Prize for inner-ear research.

1963 — International Congress on the Education of the Deaf meets at Gallaudet College.

1964 — Registry of Interpreters for the Deaf organizes in Muncie, Indiana.

Alexander Graham Bell Association forms Oral Deaf Adult section.

National Workshop on Improved Opportunities for the Deaf meets in Knoxville, Tennessee.

Robert H. Weitbrecht invents a terminal unit which permits deaf people to use teletypewriters to send messages over the telephone.

State Technical Institute and Rehabilitation Center Plainwell, Michigan offers deaf services.

California State University at Northridge begins program for deaf students.

Gallaudet College observes centennial; Gallaudet alumni give college half million dollars in cash and pledges.

1965 — American Athletic Association of the Deaf sponsors 10th International Games for the Deaf in Washington, D.C.

Eastern North Carolina School for the Deaf opens in Wilson.

1966 — Professional Rehabilitation Workers with the Adult Deaf organize.

St. Petersburg Junior College, Clearwater, Florida opens program for the deaf.

National Theatre of the Deaf begins.

New York University in New York City opens Deafness Research and Training Center.

1967 — Council of Organizations Serving the Deaf incorporates under New York laws; Mervin D. Garretson is first Executive Director.

National Association of the Deaf begins Communicative Skills Program.

Educators and rehabilitation workers meet at Las Cruces Conference in New Mexico.

National Theatre of the Deaf goes on first national tour.

1968 — Community College of Denver offers program for the hearing impaired.

Alexander Graham Bell Association and National Association of the Deaf form Teletypewriters for the Deaf, Inc. in Indiana.

National Technical Institute for the Deaf opens on campus of Rochester Institute of Technology in Rochester, New York; Dr. Robert Frisina becomes first director.

Delgado Junior College, New Orleans, Louisiana begins offering programs for the deaf and the hard of hearing.

National Theatre of the Deaf forms The Little Theatre of the Deaf.

Congress authorizes the establishment of a Model Secondary School for the Deaf at Gallaudet College, Washington, D.C.

Utah State University, Logan, Utah, offers program for the hearing impaired.

Permanent Alumni Office opens on Gallaudet College campus; Jack R. Gannon becomes first Gallaudet College Alumni Association Executive Secretary.

1969 — Seattle Community College begins program for deaf students.

Dr. Edward C. Merrill, Jr. becomes fourth president of Gallaudet College.

Lee College, Baytown, Texas offers hearing impaired program.

National Theatre of the Deaf goes on first European tour.

Tennessee Temple School for the Deaf in Chattanooga, Tennessee opens.

St. Paul Technical Vocational Institute, St. Paul, Minnesota, opens program for deaf students.

Gallaudet College Alumni Association dedicates statue of Edward Miner Gallaudet.

1970 — Valley Vocational Adult School, Industry, California opens program for deaf students.

Kendall School becomes a national demonstration elementary school for the deaf.

Golden West College, Huntington Beach, California opens Hearing Impaired Program and Disabled Student Services.

1971 — Iowa Western Community College, Council Bluffs, Iowa starts program for the hearing impaired.

Portland Community College, Portland, Oregon opens special educational services.

Charles Stewart Mott Community College, Flint, Michigan, opens program for hearing impaired.

Johnson County Community College, Overland Park, Kansas establishes hearing impaired program.

Jefferson State Vocational Technical School, Jeffersontown, Kentucky, opens.

Tarrant County Junior College District,

Fort Worth, Texas opens service center for opportunities to overcome problems.

San Diego Community College, San Diego, California establishes Resources Center for the Handicapped.

1972 — Gallaudet College establishes Center for Continuing Education.

Gallaudet College becomes a member of the Washington Consortium of Universities and Colleges.

Ohlone College, Fremont, California establishes Department for the Hearing Impaired.

Pasadena City College, Pasadena, California begins Hearing Impaired Program.

University of South Florida, Tampa, Florida, opens program for the deaf.

College of Southern Idaho, Twin Falls, Idaho opens program for the deaf.

Waubonsee Community College, Sugar Grove, Illinois, establishes Waubonsee Hearing Impaired Program.

Eastfield College, Mesquite, Texas begins services for handicapped students.

Columbus Technical Institute, Columbus, Ohio adds technical education program for the deaf.

Community College of Philadelphia, Pennsylvania opens program for hearing impaired students.

North Central Technical Institute, Wausau, Wisconsin, opens program for the hearing impaired.

Ann Billington becomes first Miss Deaf America.

1973 — William Rainey Harper College, Palatine, Illinois starts hearing impaired program.

El Camino College, Torrance, California adds program for hearing impaired students.

National Theatre of the Deaf performs a Christmas special on CBS-TV—"A Child's Christmas in Wales."

New Hampshire Vocational Technical College, Clarement, New Hampshire adds program for the deaf.

Maryland opens second school for the deaf in Columbia.

1974 — Los Angeles Pierce College Woodland, California begins special services for the deaf.

National Association of the Deaf does census of deaf Americans; counts 13.4 million hearing impaired and 1.8 million deaf Americans.

Central Piedmont Community College, Charlotte, North Carolina offers post-secondary program for the deaf.

Chattanooga State Technical Community College, Chattanooga, Tennessee opens program for the hearing impaired.

Community College of Allegheny County, Monroeville, Pennsylvania, offers supportive services for deaf students.

1975 — Gallaudet College starts doctoral degree program.

World Federation of the Deaf meets in Washington, D.C.

"Spectrum, Focus on Deaf Artists" organizes.

Central School for the Deaf opens in Greensboro, North Carolina.

Congress passes P.L. 94-142 "The Education of All Handicapped Children" Act.

1976 — Federal Communications Commission authorizes reserving Line 21 on television sets for closed captions.

1977 — National Theatre of the Deaf holds first Deaf Playwrights Conference.

Dr. William Castle becomes second director of National Technical Institute for the Deaf.

1978 — Professional Rehabilitation Workers with the Adult Deaf becomes American Deafness Rehabilitation Association.

1979 — National Captioning Institute is formed to prepare captioned programs for television.

American Association of the Deaf-Blind, Inc. forms.

1980 — Sears, Roebuck and Co. begins selling decoders for closed captioning for television.

National Association of the Deaf observes centennial in Cincinnati.

Chapter 1

The Early Years

Early Attempts
To Educate Deaf Children

LMOST 200 years after the Pilgrims arrived in this country there were still no schools for deaf children. Dr. William Thornton, the first to head the U.S. Patent Office and also the architect of the U.S. Capitol, was the first to call the attention of the American press to the educational needs of deaf people. In 1793, his essay "On Teaching the Surd, or Deaf, and Consequently Dumb, to Speak" was published in the Transactions of American Philosophical Society magazine.

A decade later, Francis Green (1742-1809), the father of a deaf boy, made a census of deaf persons in Massachusetts with the assistance of local clergymen. He located about 70 deaf persons and using that figure estimated that there were approximately 500 deaf people in the United States. A Boston businessman, Green sent his son Charles to Thomas Braidwood's school in Edinburgh, Scotland, when Charles was eight. Green was eager to see educational opportunities for the deaf in America. He hoped that with his census data he would be able to convince the Massachusetts legislature of the necessity for a school for the deaf. He died in 1809 without realizing this dream.

About 1811, the Reverend John Stanford met several deaf children in the New York City almshouse where he preached. He was concerned because they could not receive religious training, and although he had no experience with deaf persons, he set about trying to teach them. He presented each with a slate and taught the children to write the names of objects.

Two years later, Colonel William Bolling of Virginia learned that John Braidwood, the grandson of the Edinburgh school founder, was in the Baltimore area. Bolling had two deaf brothers and a deaf sister who had attended the Braidwood School. Bolling sought Braidwood out and gave him the job of teaching Bolling's two deaf children, William and Mary, who became the first deaf children to receive formal classroom instruction in America.

Braidwood had tried unsuccessfully to start a school in New York and one in Baltimore. The Bolling school at Cobbs, Virginia also failed because Braidwood was undependable, "totally deficient in steadiness and moral principles." It was said that he was an alcoholic and that he "died a victim of the bottle."

The founding of the Connecticut Asylum for the Education and Instruction of Deaf and Dumb Persons in Hartford in 1817 was followed within a year by the establishment of the New York Institution for the Instruction of the Deaf and Dumb in New York City. Two years later, the Pennsylvania Institution opened in Philadelphia, and in 1823 the first state-supported school for the deaf—also the first one west of the Appalachian Mountains—opened in Danville, Kentucky.

The number of American children known to be deaf was so small at the time that the Connecticut Asylum

Connecticut Asylum in 1817.

opened that it was expected to accommodate them all. Accordingly, Congress granted the school 23,000 acres of land in Alabama, and the school's name was changed to the American Asylum. The lawmakers soon learned that this remedy was inadequate. The New York and Pennsylvania schools requested similar land grants. Congress refused. A request from Kentucky was granted because the Kentucky educators justified Congressional support with the argument that their school would serve all deaf children west of the Appalachian Mountains.

Men that are deaf are in all cases dumb; that is they can make vocal sounds, but they cannot speak.

ARISTOTLE
5TH CENTURY B.C.

Kentucky had difficulty securing a teacher for its school in Danville. The first teacher hired proved to be an impostor who faked deafness; he was discharged as incompetent. The school next hired DeWitt Mitchell, son of the president of the New York Institution. He also was a disappointment. The Board of Trustees then asked the advice of Thomas H. Gallaudet at the Hartford School. Gallaudet suggested that they recruit a nearby Centre College student. The Board approached John A. Jacobs. Jacobs was only 18 years old, but he was interested in the field of education of the deaf. In the summer of 1824, he saddled

up his horse, packed his things into the saddlebags, and took off on a 30-day jaunt to Hartford. His stay in Hartford was a busy one, spent learning how to teach deaf children. After hours, he studied the language of signs with Laurent Clerc, paying 40 cents an hour for the lessons. Little did Jacobs realize that his journey to Hartford would start a long tradition of Centre College alumni involvement in the education of the deaf.

Causes of Deafness

Most early school administrators kept careful records of the causes of the deafness of children entering their schools. Since this information came from parents or guardians rather than from medical sources, some inventiveness will be noted.

Spinal meningitis is a leading cause of deafness. The Illinois School for the Deaf reported meningitis as the cause of deafness in 333 of its students who had enrolled during the first fifty years of the school's existence. At the New York School for the Deaf 492 cases of deafness were attributed to scarlet fever. Other reports listed black tongue, sore eyes, summer complaint, nervous fever, sore mouth, fall into water, cramps, seasickness, cold water, sprain, clap of thunder, water on brain, lye, cold, fall on stove and salt in ear. Six cases of "sickness from fright" were listed. In Arkansas, eating buckeye was listed as the cause of one child's deafness, and another case was blamed on the "mother's conduct."

A swallow of tobacco "caused" one case, and a mother in New York claimed that during her pregnancy a servant's piercing shriek made her baby's ears close up. Teething and "impure blood" were listed among the causes at a Colorado school. Kentucky added the following: worms, morphine, sore head, lightning, fits, fright, lung fever, scrofula, cruelty, sores in head, swimming, white swelling and sand in

EDWARD STRETCH.
OBIIT 1874.

"It will take away half the bitterness of death to have been allowed to learn something."

Ohio Institution for the Education of Deaf and Dumb. Circa 1893.

Alexander Graham Bell Association Volta Bureau

ears. James Beauchamp, who has been associated with the Kentucky School as student, teacher, editor, and now board member, recalls the following story about the last cause: Two siblings overheard their parents talking about their younger brother. "Every time I tell him something, it goes in one ear and out the other." Puzzled, the two children took the little boy down to the creek, where they poured fine sand in one ear and then the other to see if it were true that what went in one came out the other.

Deaf Teachers

Teaching was becoming a promising career for deaf persons. Deaf teachers were in demand until the advent of the pure oral method, when the hiring of deaf teachers became unpopular, and only courageous administrators risked the practice. In 1850 36.6 percent of the teaching force in schools for the deaf in this country—excluding private and denominational schools—were deaf teachers. Eight years later, the ranks of deaf teachers peaked at 40.8 percent of the total. Within the next decade, the percentage fell to 30.9 percent, and the outlook was gloomy. By 1927—probably the height of pure oralism in this country—only 14.0 percent of the teachers were deaf. The prospects for deaf teachers were so bad that officials at Gallaudet College openly discouraged deaf students

from considering a teaching career. Today the percentage of deaf teachers in schools and programs for the deaf is estimated at 13.6 percent. In 1979 Ed Corbett, a doctoral student at Gallaudet College did a study of deaf teachers in educational programs with four or more hearing impaired students. His survey was sent to 848 programs and drew responses from 594. He found that of 4,887 teachers in the survey area, 663 were deaf (13.6 percent). It should be noted, however, that today deaf children receive a variety of services in different educational settings which may account for the lower percentage of deaf teachers.

Deaf Black Teachers

Most schools for the deaf were segregated by race during this early period in deaf America's history. The bill establishing the Texas Institute for Deaf, Dumb and Blind Colored Youth passed a few minutes before the adjournment of the Texas legislature in April, 1887. The bill appropriated $50,000 for grounds and buildings. The first deaf black teachers hired were Julius Carrett and Mrs. Amanda A. Johnson, products of the North Carolina School and H. L. Johns, a graduate of the Maryland School in Baltimore. Hiring these teachers, it was said, "creates self-respect and self-confidence and serves as an incentive for the students to aspire for greater achievement."

3

Erastus "Deaf" Smith, oil portrait by Thomas Jefferson Wright, San Jacinto Museum of History Association.

"What Hath God Wrought?"

In 1836 Samuel F. B. Morse invented the telegraph and indirectly began the chain of events that led to the founding of Gallaudet College, the only college for the deaf in the world.

Morse was married to a deaf woman. He spoke to her by tapping his fingers in her hands. Morse hired Amos Kendall to be his financial manager. When Morse was first experimenting with the telegraph, a line was strung from the Library of Congress in Washington to Baltimore. This line ran through Kendall's Northeast Washington estate. Over this line, on May 24, 1844, flashed the immortal words "What Hath God Wrought?" Both men became wealthy from the Morse Telegraph. Kendall donated much of his wealth to the interests of deaf people. He started the Columbia Institution for the Instruction of the Deaf and Dumb and Blind on his beautiful and spacious estate, offering some land and a building. Kendall also made a generous contribution to the construction of the Calvary Baptist Church in the city. For many years this church has had a class for deaf persons.

Deaf Smith

In what is now Texas, another kind of history was unfolding that year. Texas was fighting for its independence from Mexico. In April General Sam Houston, commander of the Texas Army, and his men met the Mexican Army commanded by General Antonio de Santa Anna in the crucial Battle of San Jacinto.

Erastus "Deaf" Smith, a Texas soldier, had been hand picked by Houston as his chief scout and spy. Smith's severe hearing impairment dated back to childhood. Born in New York in 1787, Smith grew up in Mississippi and moved to Texas in 1821. When

Five dollar Texas bill with Erastus "Deaf" Smith's portrait.

asked if his hearing impairment was an inconvenience, he responded: "No, I sometimes think it is an advantage—I have learned to keep a sharp outlook and I am never disturbed by the whistling of a ball (bullet)—I don't hear the bark till I feel the bite."

In the Battle of San Jacinto, Smith suggested destroying the bridge over Vince's Bayou, cutting off both armies and forcing them to fight to the finish. Houston agreed, and Smith, with a small band, proceeded to wreck the bridge. The outnumbered Texans won the battle and captured the Mexican general. Texas was independent, and "Deaf" Smith became a folk hero. A county in the panhandle was named Deaf Smith County. National brands of peanutbutter, pancake, waffle and biscuit mix made from wheat grown in the county carry his name. Smith's picture appeared on the Republic of Texas five dollar bill.

Deaf Smith is buried in Richmond, Texas. The inscription on his monument reads: "So valiant and trustworthy was he that all titles sink into insignificance before the simple name of 'Deaf' Smith."

Denominational Schools

In 1837 two Sisters of St. Joseph from Lyon, France, arrived in New Orleans. There they were met by the Right Rev. John Timon. Following a brief stay they took the boat up the Mississippi River to St. Louis. A year later, after the sisters had mastered enough English, the first Catholic school for the deaf opened at the convent in Carondelet in the St. Louis area. This school was called the Mariae Consilia Deaf Mute Institution. This school went through a number of name changes and merged with St. Joseph's School for the Deaf around 1910. In 1840, the Sisters of Loretto at the Foot of the Cross in Loretto, Kentucky began admitting deaf girls to their school. They were taught by a sister who had also been trained at a Catholic school for the deaf in France. This school was short-lived, however, and soon closed due to lack of funds and small attendance.

In 1859 the Sisters of St. Joseph opened the LeCouteulx St. Mary's School for the Deaf in Buffalo.

Minnesota Institution for the Deaf and Dumb. Circa 1893.

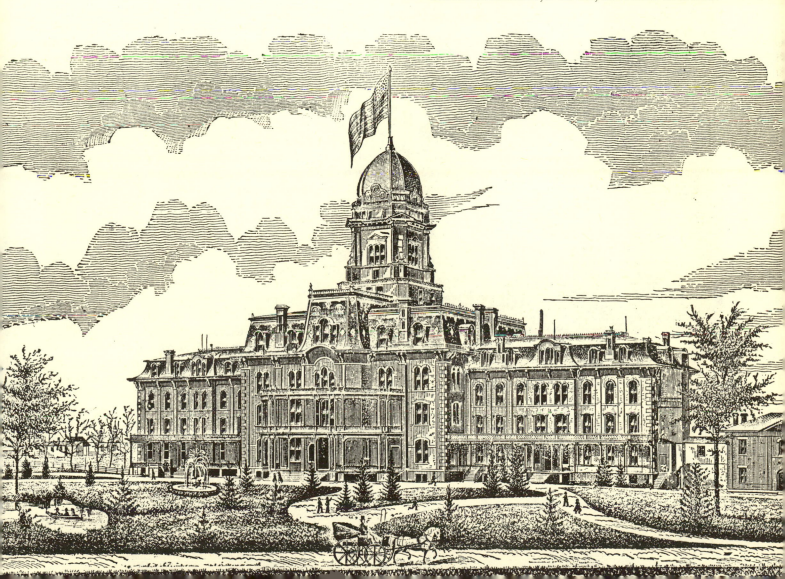

American School for the Deaf

Memorial to the Rev. Thomas Hopkins Gallaudet at the American School for the Deaf. Erected September 1854, in observance of the 100th anniversary of Gallaudet's birth.

Father Timon, who had met the first sisters to arrive in New Orleans, was instrumental in getting this school started. St. Joseph's School in New York City opened in 1869 and St. John's School near Milwaukee opened in 1876.

Nine other Catholic schools followed: Ephphetha School in Chicago (1884); St. Mary's School in St. Paul, Minnesota (1886; closed in 1893), Chinchuba Institution for the Deaf in Marrero, Louisiana (1890), St. Joseph's School in Oakland, California (1895; closed around 1939; reopened 1963); St. Francis Xavier School in Baltimore, Maryland (1897; closed around 1944), Boston School for the Deaf, Randolph, Massachusetts (1899), De Paul Institute in Pittsburgh, Pennsylvania (1908), Archbishop Ryan Memorial Institute in Philadelphia, Pennsylvania (1912) and St. Rita School for the Deaf in Lockland, Cincinnati (1915).

Other denominational schools followed. In 1873 the Lutheran Church of the Missouri Synod opened an orphanage near Detroit. A year later the orphanage was converted into the German Evangelical Lutheran Deaf-Mute Institution becoming the forerunner of Lutheran schools for the deaf. Today the school is known as the Lutheran School for the Deaf.

More Schools

In 1839 Virginia became the first state school to admit deaf and blind students. William Willard, a deaf man, started the Indiana School for the Deaf in 1843. Schools in Tennessee and North Carolina followed, opening within a month of each other.

The bill to establish the Illinois School was submitted to the Illinois Legislature by Orville H. Browning, who later became a Congressman, a U.S. Senator and Secretary of the Interior in President Johnson's cabinet. Browning had met an alumnus of the Kentucky School for the Deaf on a Mississippi River trip. He was impressed by the young man; the meeting kindled his interest in the needs of young deaf persons. The bill he introduced sailed through the Senate without a dissenting vote and passed the House by a large margin. Abraham Lincoln, then an Illinois legislator and a good friend of Browning's voted for the school, and his name is on the school charter. Later Lincoln added his name to another charter which resulted in the founding of a national college for the deaf in Washington D.C.

The Illinois bill appropriated a percentage of the funds in the state's educational fund to finance the school for the deaf, linking the school to the state's educational system. Despite this provision, seven years passed before the school opened. The state was heavily in debt; the hard times delayed all new state projects. The Illinois School for the Deaf was a new type of institution, one that the public was not prepared for, so its opening was delayed until 1846. Three members of the first Board became governors of the state.

Until 1846, Georgia had sent its deaf students to Hartford. In May of that year, a Department for the Deaf was set up in a log cabin behind the Hearn Manual Labor School in Cave Spring. Four students attended the first classes. The enrollment grew, and a new building replaced the log cabin in 1849. In 1854, school officials extended the maximum period of enrollment from four years to six, and in 1877, to seven.

Belle Missouri

by Howard Glyndon
(Laura C. R. Searing)

This poem, written by Laura Searing, was set to music and became the popular war song of the Missouri Union Army.

Arise and join the patriot train,
Belle Missouri! My Missouri!
They should not plead and plead in vain,
  Belle Missouri! My Missouri!
The precious blood of all thy slain
Arises from each reeking plain.
Wipe out this foul disloyal stain,
  Belle Missouri! My Missouri!

Recall the field of Lexington,
  Belle Missouri! My Missouri!
How Springfield blushed beneath the sun,
  Belle Missouri! My Missouri!
And noble Lyon all undone,
His race of glory but begun,
And all thy freedom yet unwon,
  Belle Missouri! My Missouri!

They called thee craven to thy trust,
  Belle Missouri! My Missouri!
They laid thy glory in the dust,
  Belle Missouri! My Missouri!
The helpless prey of treason's lust,
The helpless mark of treason's thrust,
Nor shall thy sword in scabbard rust!
  Belle Missouri! My Missouri!

She thrills! her blood begins to burn!
  Belle Missouri! My Missouri!
She's bruised and weak, but she can turn,
  Belle Missouri! My Missouri!

Some students were allowed an additional three years in a high class.

In the 1850s schools came into existence in Missouri, Wisconsin, Louisiana, Mississippi, Michigan, Iowa, Texas, Washington, D.C. and Alabama.

Mr. Bartlett's School

David Ely Bartlett, a hearing man who had taught for about twenty years at the Hartford School and the New York Institution, was concerned about the deaf children under 10 who were refused admission to many schools because of their youth. Bartlett believed that this was a waste of learning opportunities for these young children and decided to launch an experiment. He opened a school four doors west of the New York Institution in 1852, naming it "Mr. Bartlett's Family School for Young Deaf-Mute Children." Bartlett admitted students from the age of four and a half years to seven years old.

Bartlett also decided to teach deaf and hearing children in the same school, setting a precedent for the integrated or mainstreaming programs known today. He saw a mutual benefit in such arrangement and noticed that the hearing students encouraged verbal language among the deaf pupils while learning sign language and developing interpreting skills themselves.

Two notable men graduated from Mr. Bartlett's School: Henry W. Syle, who became the first deaf American to become an Episcopalian priest, and Gideon Moore, the first to earn a doctorate degree.

Bartlett's school was relocated four times. After the school was closed, largely due to financial problems, Bartlett returned to teaching at the American School in Hartford, where he died in 1879.

The Civil War

When the Civil War began in 1861, there were some 24 schools for the deaf in the country. The strife which followed touched many of the southern schools and forced them to close. The northern schools were less troubled.

One of the three teachers at the Kentucky School who resigned to join the Union Army was the son of Superintendent John A. Jacobs, who had hoped his son would succeed him as head of the school. The son did not return and grief at this loss left the elder Jacobs a broken man.

7

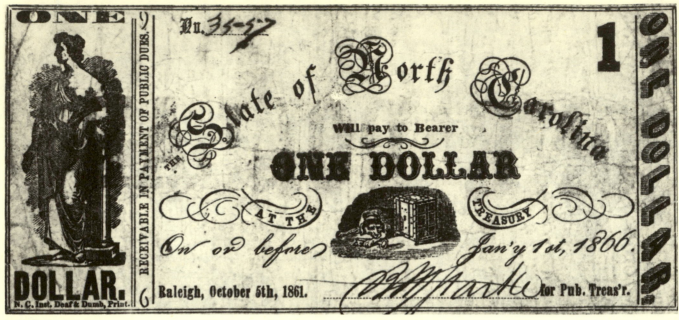

This one dollar bill was printed at the North Carolina Institute for the Deaf and Dumb during the Civil War. See lower left hand corner.

The Tennessee School closed when several members of the Board of Trustees and many employees left to join the Confederacy. In Washington, D.C., Dr. Alexander Y. P. Garnett, physician at the Columbia Institution for the Deaf and Dumb and Blind, also resigned to join the southern cause. He became Surgeon General of the Confederate Army and personal physician to Jefferson Davis.

> *. . . other institutions may, therefore, be established until at last, not a deaf and dumb adult in the United States may remain* **uneducated.**
>
> —LAURENT CLERC

Members of the Illinois School for the Deaf Student Military Company offered their services to Governor Richard Yates. He declined the offer but appointed them the Home Guard for the City of Jacksonville.

During the war teachers at the Wisconsin School continued working on reduced salaries. The *American Annals of the Deaf* suspended publication, and the 1861 Convention of American Instructors of the Deaf was cancelled. Currency for the state of North Carolina was printed at the North Carolina Institution for the Deaf and Dumb and Blind in Raleigh.

Shortly after the opening of the Arkansas School it was closed on account of the war. The same legislature which had incorporated the school voted to secede from the Union.

On September 2, 1861, 53-year-old John Barnes was returning to his Hatteras Island home on the Outer Banks of North Carolina when he was ordered by a sentry to halt. Barnes, who was deaf, continued on his way. The guard shot and killed him; Barnes was the sole casualty of the Battle for Hatteras Island.

As the strife continued, many school buildings were occupied by troops. These large buildings with residential facilities and equipment and spacious grounds were ideal sites for large numbers of soldiers. The Virginia, Louisiana, Mississippi, Georgia, Tennessee, and Missouri schools and the Columbia Institution were used by the armed forces.

Both armies occupied the Tennessee School, in turns, during the siege of Knoxville. At one time, the school was made into the Asylum General Hospital. This building, much later, became Knoxville's City Hall. Today it is a historical landmark.

Lack of money forced the Board of Commissioners of the Missouri School to close it. They auctioned furniture, bedding, and other household items to settle some of the school's debts. Union forces occupied the facilities and those of the neighboring state hospital for the mentally ill, then called the Lunatic Asylum, to use as barracks, stables, and a prison. They left the school in such a deplorable condition that it was years before it was fit for normal use.

Confederate Colonel E. R. Burt, who had introduced legislation founding the Mississippi School, was killed while leading his men on a charge near Leesburg. The school he had helped start fared little better. The buildings were leveled by the invading Northern Army.

Schools as far north as Washington, D.C. felt the presence of war. The school building at the Columbia Institution for the Deaf and Dumb in that city was used by soldiers from Rhode Island and Pennsylvania during the summer of 1861.

In March 1862 the Georgia School was forced to close when both male teachers resigned to join the Confederate cause. One of them later ended his army career in a Columbus, Ohio prison. Upon his release, following the war, he returned to the school and became principal.

As the war continued, the City of Danville, Kentucky, changed hands many times. The four-year-old school building was an ideal shelter in a prime location. Superintendent Jacobs refused to give it up. When first approached to turn over the facility, he took a firm stand. At each such request, Jacobs met the army representative on the front porch of the school and listened politely. Then he pointed to the door and said that the first soldier to cross that threshold would immediately be held responsible for all the deaf children in it, as all teachers and staff had sworn to resign the moment one soldier stepped through the door. No soldier did, and it is to Jacobs' credit that the Kentucky School was the only school in the southeast to remain open throughout the war.

Farmers in the vicinity of the Danville School were wary of giving their livestock to both armies because they realized that only one side was going to win the war and only one set of promissory notes could be collected. When word got out of Jacobs' resistance, the farmers asked Jacobs to shelter in the building what was left of their meager herds. Jacobs consented. It is said that when soldiers marched by the building and heard the bellowing of the cattle they wondered about the elocution lessons taught to the deaf children.

The building was threatened with destruction following the battle of Perrysville when a soundly defeated Southern army was retreating through Danville. While the Danville residents—most of whom were abolitionists—watched the retreat, a young girl from the town waved a Union flag from a window in the cupola. A group of angry Confederates decided to return to the building and burn it down, but were prevented by a young mounted officer. He told them that the building was a school for the deaf and that the young lady in the tower was not a deaf student. The young man's name was J. R. Dobyns. Years later he returned for a visit. He had become superintendent of the Mississippi School for the Deaf.

Sign Language Saves a Life

Eighteen-year-old Joshua Davis was squirrel hunting one day on his parents' southern plantation near Atlanta, Georgia during the Civil War. Suddenly he found himself surrounded by Union soldiers. Davis was deaf but he could tell that they were shouting at him.

No human condition can be imagined more deplorable than that of the uneducated deaf-mute.

—DR. ISAAC L. PEET

The soldiers were members of General Sherman's army which was marching to the sea destroying everything in its path.

Davis pointed to his ears and gestured that he was deaf but the soldiers did not believe him. They suspected that he was a spy and was trying to fool them by pretending to be deaf. They shoved and pushed the youth to a nearby house where a couple standing in front of it informed them that the youth was their son and that he was, indeed, deaf. The captors did not believe them either and they were looking for a rope to hang young Davis as a spy when a mounted officer rode up. The officer was informed that they had caught a spy who was "playing deaf." The officer rode over to the youth and fingerspelled to him: "Are you deaf?" The youth responded in signs, "Yes." "Where were you educated?" the officer asked next to which the young man told him at the school for the deaf in Cave Spring. With that information the officer ordered the youth's release and the family's house spared.

Greatly relieved at the unexpected turn of events the family invited the officer to dine with them. During the meal the officer and Joshua Davis conversed in sign language. The family learned that the officer had a deaf brother in Illinois who had taught him to talk with his hands.

Joshua Davis later moved to Texas, became a farmer and raised a family of seven. Five of his children were deaf and one was hard of hearing. He lived to the age of 84, never forgetting how close he came to being hanged when he was only 18.

Deaf Soldiers

Three or four deaf or hard-of-hearing men served in the war as soldiers. One was William Simpson, the hard-of-hearing brother of Delos and James Simpson, who were deaf. Delos was principal of the St. Louis (now Gallaudet) School and James was principal for 23 years at the South Dakota School. William decided to join the Northern cause during the outbreak of war. He realized that he and his hearing impairment were too well known in his hometown so he went to New York to enlist. He served throughout the war, then returned home to become a farmer.

One account tells of a deaf Confederate prisoner of war whose guard was also deaf. The two carried on a lively conversation in sign language. (If true, it is possible that the guard was William Simpson.)

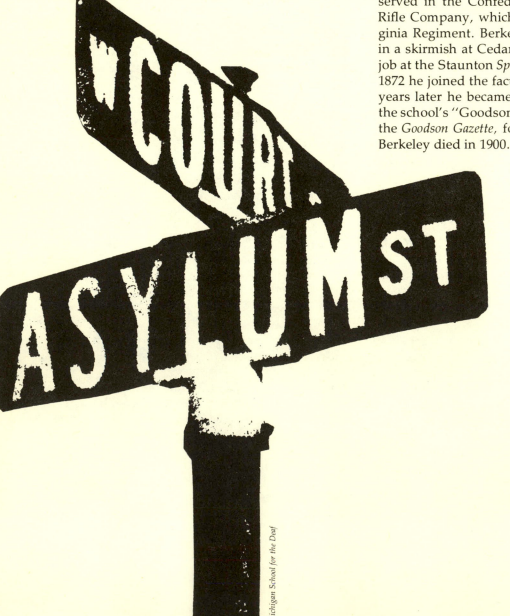

Michigan School for the Deaf

The institution is not intended as an Asylum where its objects are to pass their lives; but as a school where they are prepared to live.
—AMERICAN SCHOOL BOARD MINUTES
1818

Hartwell M. Chamberlayne was born deaf. He served in the Confederate infantry, cavalry, and artillery. The latter, no doubt, was ideal for him. He had been a student at the Virginia and New York Institutions, graduating from the latter. After the war he taught at the Virginia School from 1891 until his death in 1905. Chamberlayne's father, Dr. Lewis W. Chamberlayne, along with the Rev. William S. Plumer, had been instrumental in establishing the Virginia School.

According to Virginia School for the Deaf historian R. Aumon Bass, a man named William M. Berkeley "managed to get mixed up in the Civil War in spite of his deafness." Berkeley was born July 4, 1838, entered the Virginia School in 1848 and graduated in 1854. He served in the Confederate Army with the Augusta Rifle Company, which was attached to the 25th Virginia Regiment. Berkeley was wounded in the head in a skirmish at Cedar Mountain. He returned to his job at the Staunton *Spectator*, a weekly newspaper. In 1872 he joined the faculty of his alma mater, and two years later he became the first printing instructor in the school's "Goodson Printing Office" which printed the *Goodson Gazette,* forerunner of the *Virginia Guide.* Berkeley died in 1900.

Birth of a College

It was during the dark days of the Civil War that President Abraham Lincoln signed a charter authorizing the Columbia Institution for the Instruction of the Deaf, in Washington, D.C., to grant college degrees to deaf persons. This charter resulted in the founding of National Deaf-Mute College, which was renamed Gallaudet College in 1884. Laurent Clerc spoke at the college's first presentation day in 1864, along with John Carlin, who received the college's first honorary degree. Two years after Carlin received Gallaudet's first honorary degree, Melville Ballard of Maine, a graduate of the American School for the Deaf, earned the first bachelor of science degree.

Oral Education Arrives in America

Teachers at the New York School for the Deaf made early attempts to teach articulation to those deaf students who had some speech or hearing, but the results were unsatisfactory and the effort was abandoned. The early resignation of Dr. Harvey P. Peet, superintendent of the school may have resulted from his strong opposition to the oral method.

Few schools emphasized the teaching of speech to

Street signs stand near former site of the American School for the Deaf as mementos of the past.

The manual alphabet hand carved by a student at the Maryland School for the Deaf.

Richard J. Schoenberg

the deaf. Many were still called "manual schools." In some quarters, considerable hostility about the oral method existed: "It is absurd to speak of seeing sound or reading speech, as of hearing color. . . . As one who understands several languages will use the one which pleases and aids him most, so the deaf person will use such class of signs as is most satisfactory to him."

Two months after the founding of the National Deaf-Mute College in Washington in 1864 there arrived in New York City a man named Bernard Engelsman. Engelsman had been a teacher in Mr. Deutsch's Jewish School in Vienna. Within a month after his arrival he began teaching a deaf pupil by the "German Method," and before long he had a small school going. His clientele was largely of Jewish and German origin. Out of this school grew the New York Institution for the Improved Instruction of Deaf Mutes, which opened at 134 West Twenty-seventh Street on March 1, 1867. It was the first pure oral school in the United States. Ten pupils were in the first class. Within a decade the enrollment had grown to 117. Later the school was moved to Lexington Avenue, across the street from Hunter College, and its name was changed to the Lexington School for the Deaf.

In March 1864 Gardiner G. Hubbard—whose daughter Mabel later married Alexander Graham Bell—petitioned the Massachusetts legislature for a charter to establish a school where deaf children would be taught to speak and lipread. "This application," Hubbard later recalled, "was opposed by the friends of the American Asylum, on the grounds that it was a visionary project and attempting the impossible." After three weeks of hearings, the Committee on Public Charitable Institutions reported that the condition of state finances did not permit such an experiment. The Committee, however, expressed hope that private parties would give the plan a try and suggested that the Hartford School, where the Massachusetts deaf students were sent, install the German method. "More thorough trial of the method might, under their hands, be more successful, or at least forever settle the comparative merits of these different systems of teaching the deaf and dumb."

Nothing was settled. The controversy over the best method of teaching deaf children continues today.

Determined to convince the lawmakers that the new system was not merely a vision, Hubbard, with the assistance of a young teacher named Harriet B. Rogers, started a small school in Chelmsford, near Boston. He lined up powerful allies: Dr. Samuel G. Howe of the Perkins Institute, Dr. Thomas Hill, president of

Harvard College, and others. When Hubbard approached Massachusetts Governor Bullock for assistance, he learned that a wealthy Northampton resident named John Clarke had offered the state $50,000 for a school in Northampton. Governor Bullock supported the establishment of such a school.

A joint house committee visited the Chelmsford school and recommended the Northampton plan. Miss Rogers' school was moved to Northampton, where it became the core of the new school. The oral method has been used exclusively since.

The Post-War Years

The period after the war was a difficult time for the border states. It took special skill and tact to handle a

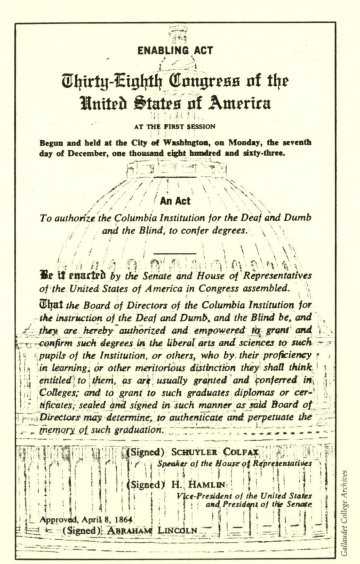

The charter establishing Gallaudet College.

Rose Cottage has been called "The Cradle of Gallaudet College." This frame house was used by Kendall School for two years (1857-59).

statewide program during these difficult times. In Kentucky, for example, the State Legislature declared every position in state-controlled institutions vacant with one exception—the position of superintendent of the Kentucky School for the Deaf held by John Jacobs.

Reverend Newton P. Walker established the South Carolina School for the Deaf and Blind on his own property. After the founder's death, the Board of Commissioners of the school reported to the South Carolina State Legislature that it had made no effort to fill the vacancy. "The Professors and their Assistants are connected by blood or marriage; the utmost harmony prevails, and each appears desirous of advancing the interest of the Institution; and the introduction of a stranger as Superintendent or governor would probably destroy that harmony which is necessary to success."

The South Carolina School for the Deaf and Blind shut its doors for a brief period after the Civil War because of unsettled financial conditions in the state. All pupils were sent home. The school reopened temporarily in 1866, closed again, and reopened in 1869 with J. M. Hughston, an alumnus of the school, as superintendent. When Hughston resigned in 1872, N. F. Walker became superintendent. The Walker family has administrated the school to this day.

In 1872-73, the school prepared a building for Negro students, whereupon the Board of Commissioners sent these requirements to the superintendent:

First. Colored pupils must not only be admitted into the Institution on application, but an earnest and faithful effort must be made to induce such pupils to apply for admission.

Second. Such pupils, when admitted, must be domiciled in the same building, must eat at the same table, and be taught in the same classrooms and by

---

Higher education of the deaf is useless and of little value.

CONGRESSMAN ELIHU WASHBURN

13

First national conference of heads of American schools for the deaf met on Gallaudet College campus in 1868. Picture taken in front of old Fowler Hall.

the same teachers, and must receive the same attention, care, and consideration as white pupils.

The superintendent, the officers and all the teachers at the school responded by resigning. The Board of Commissioners, unprepared, was unable to find qualified replacements to work on its terms. The school closed for three years. In 1876 N. F. Walker and most of his former staff gained permission to establish separate departments for black and white students, returned, and reopened the school.

Schools for Deaf Blacks

Following the Civil War schools for deaf and black children began to slowly emerge. In 1868 the North Carolina general assembly made provisions for the education of these children and became the first state to provide an institution for this race. The Colored Department, as it was then called, opened in January 1869 with 26 pupils. As this school began turning out graduates many of them found teaching positions in schools or departments for black students in other states.

In 1876 South Carolina opened a department for

black students and in 1882 Georgia did likewise. Other states followed.

Mr. Knapp's School

In 1877, a decade after the opening of the first two oral schools in this country, Frederick Knapp agreed to admit deaf pupils to his private school for hearing children in Baltimore.

Knapp was a German immigrant. His school offered courses in the German language and stressed academics. The school succeeded in educating over 17,000 children by 1893, not less than a hundred of them deaf.

Knapp believed in the integration of deaf and hearing students. He contended that "the more the deaf commingled with the hearing, the less they would notice their defect." Hearing children were forbidden to sign to deaf children lest they be guilty of reminding the deaf children of their affliction. The hearing children were admonished: "You can't read the lips, but that child can; speak to him therefore." Children, whether deaf or hearing, who broke the rule and used their hands wore gloves as "evidence of stupidity and punishment." Knapp believed that no school should admit more than 30 deaf pupils and that deaf students should live among hearing persons at all times.

The enrollment in Knapp's school declined with the addition of German to the curriculum of the Baltimore Public Schools.

McCowen's Voice and Hearing School

Mary T. McCowen, a teacher at the Nebraska School for the Deaf, experimented with audiophones, which she used in all her classes. She obviously believed in their use because this somewhat questionable statement appeared in one of the school reports: "During the latter part of the year the use of the audiophones was almost wholly discontinued from [sic] the fact that the pupils had discovered that without the audiophones they could *really hear. . . .*"

In 1883, McCowen left her position in Nebraska and moved to Chicago where she started a private school in her home, The Voice and Hearing School for the Deaf, later called the McCowen Oral School for Young Deaf Children.

The Trend Changes

In 1888 Sarah Fuller opened her Home for Little Children who Cannot Hear in West Medford, Massachusetts. The Kindergarten and Primary School for Hearing and Deaf Children opened in Washington, D.C. the same year. The trend was changing. Schools which had restricted the number of years a pupil could attend school because of limited funds were beginning to lower the age for admission. Another trend was influenced by the oral schools. The residential schools which for years had been considered manual schools because of their free use of the language of signs were feeling the pressure. They began to add teachers of articulation, and their annual reports began listing the number of students who were being taught to talk.

In 1889 the Albany Home School for the Oral Instruction of the Deaf opened in New York, and in 1892

John Carlin
(1813-1891)

John Carlin was an alumnus of the Pennsylvania Institution. He was a successful artist, poet, writer and leader. Guilbert Braddock called him a genius.

After graduating in 1825 he studied art locally and in London and Paris. In Paris he studied under Paul Delcaroche, eventually settling in New York City where he became a miniature portraitist. His painting of sailors making merry on a wharf with four-mast schooners in the background and entitled "After a Long Cruise" was a masterpiece. It was exhibited at the Detroit Institute of Arts.

Although born deaf he had amazed many with his talent for writing poetry, a feat which the editor of the *American Annals of the Deaf* compared to "a man blind [becoming] a landscape painter." Many of his poems and articles appeared in the *Pennsylvania Saturday Courier* and he wrote a book for children entitled "The Scratchsides Family." In 1851 when the teaching of articulation was largely unheard of he contributed an article to the *Annals* urging the teaching of speech and speechreading to deaf children although he could do neither. He considered the use of personal signs in lieu of fingerspelling a person's name "wholly nonsensical" and lazy.

Carlin was a leader in the deaf community. He had encouraged Edward Miner Gallaudet to start a college for the deaf. He raised $6,000 for St. Ann's Church, contributed a design for a panel for the Gallaudet monument in Hartford and chaired a fund raising committee for the Gallaudet Home for the Aged and Infirm Deaf.

Carlin's wife was related to William Seward, secretary of state in President Lincoln's administration.

Carlin died April 23, 1891.

The Home for the Training in Speech of Deaf Children Before They Are of School Age was formed in Philadelphia. Also, the Pennsylvania School for the Deaf at Mount Airy abandoned the use of sign language for the pure oral method in that year, becoming the first large residential school to do so and setting a precedent which many other residential schools would follow.

The teaching of speech and lipreading was called the "natural method" and was considered progressive. Deaf adults and the National Association of the Deaf referred to it as the "German Method" because it derived from the system used by Samuel Heinicke in Germany. The combined system was a result of the advent of pure oralism, before which it was thought impolite to sign and mouth words simultaneously.

Schools for the Deaf

American School for the Deaf
West Hartford

Opened: 1817

Founder: Thomas Hopkins Gallaudet, Laurent Clerc,* and Mason Cogswell

The American School for the Deaf is the first permanent public school for the deaf in this country and the first school for handicapped children in the Western Hemisphere. It is a privately endowed school. Originally named the Connecticut Asylum for the Education and Instruction of Deaf and Dumb Persons, the school was started in a small building on Prospect Street. It was later located on Asylum Hill in downtown Hartford and was moved to its present location in West Hartford in 1921.

Laurent Clerc, a deaf Frenchman and America's first deaf teacher of the deaf, was associated with this school. There were seven pupils in the first class ranging in age from 12 to 51 years. Four of them became teachers of the deaf. In the early years of education of the deaf in this country the American School served as a training center for many teachers of the deaf. *The American Annals of the Deaf*, the oldest educational periodical in this country, began publication at ASD in 1847. Except for a brief suspension during the Civil War it has been in continuous publication since.

A bronze bust atop a tall marble pedestal located in front of Gallaudet Hall and the Laurent Clerc Residential Hall memorialize Clerc's contributions to deaf America. Rockwell Gymnasium, Brewster Gymnasium, the Durian Vocational Building, and the Golladay Museum honor deaf men. Walter Rockwell, Walter G. Durian, and Loy E. Golladay were teachers at the school. John Brewster, Jr., an alumnus and a member of the first class, gained fame as a New England portraitist. His work is in the Abby Aldrich Rockefeller Folk Art Center and other collections.

John E. Crane, author of "Bits of History"; Louis C. Tuck, a writer and teacher; John B. Hotchkiss, a college professor; Wells Hills, a successful New England publisher; and George

*Deaf

American School for the Deaf, West Hartford, Connecticut.

Wing, inventor of Wing's Symbols, a system for teaching language to the deaf, were products of ASD.

New York School for the Deaf
White Plains

Opened: 1818

Founder: The Rev. John Stanford

The New York School for the Deaf, the second oldest in the country, began in an almshouse. The Rev. John Stanford, who had attempted to teach six deaf persons residing in the almshouse of which he was the chaplain, established the school. He took a census of the deaf in New York City and identified 66 deaf persons residing in the city. With that information he was successful in impressing prominent New York City citizens as to the need for a school.

The NYSD has been situated at several locations. The sites of the present day Saks Fifth Avenue store, St. Pat-

rick's Cathedral and Columbia College were the locations of the school. In 1856 the school was located on a 37-acre tract in Manhattan. This property was formerly owned by Colonel James Monroe, a relative of President James Monroe. Colonel Monroe had a daughter named Fanny and the woods surrounding the property became known as Fanny's woods. This name was shortened to "Fanwood" and the school has been known by that name ever since, although it has since moved to White Plains.

The first Convention of the American Instructors of the Deaf was held at the NYSD in 1850 under the leadership of Dr. Harvey Prindle Peet. In 1890 the school hosted the first International Congress of the Deaf in this country. In 1895 the pupils began wearing military uniforms, which were discontinued in 1952. In the early days the school had a 21-piece band.

Thomas F. Fox, a well-known educator of the deaf, president of the National Association of the Deaf and editor of *The Deaf-Mute's Journal* was a graduate of the school. He was principal of the Academic Department.

James N. Orman, principal of the Manual Department at the Illinois School for the Deaf for many years, was a Fanwood graduate. He served as president of the Gallaudet College Alumni Association for two terms and he was a member of the Executive Board of the National Association of the Deaf.

A more recent graduate of the Fanwood School was Bernard Bragg, the pantomimist and actor of international fame. He was one of the founders and organizers of the National Theatre of the Deaf.

Edwin A. Hodgson was the school's first printing instructor. The school acquired *The Deaf-Mute's Journal* which Hodgson published. It became the foremost publication of its kind. Hodgson was the second president of the National Association of the Deaf and was internationally known and respected as a leader.

In 1853 the school added a "High Class" to the regular program and extended the course of study three years for the more "academically inclined"

The Pennsylvania School for the Deaf, Philadelphia.

students. This High Class was comparable to a post-secondary program in those days before Gallaudet College came into existence. Many of the graduates of the High Class became teachers of the deaf and a number were involved in the establishment of schools for the deaf.

Brewster Gym, American School for the Deaf.

The Pennsylvania School for the Deaf
Philadelphia

Opened: 1820

Founder: David G. Seixas

When Thomas Hopkins Gallaudet and Laurent Clerc visited Philadelphia on December 7, 1816 in search of support for their school at Hartford, Connecticut, their visit aroused much interest in the education of the deaf. Early in 1819, David G. Seixas, a Jewish crockery merchant in the city, established a private school in his home on Market Street to instruct deaf waifs he found wandering the streets, feeding and clothing them with his own funds. Seixas acquainted himself with the methods used in Europe for educating the deaf, but used a self-invented sign language in instructing his pupils.

17

School seals and logos through the years

Alabama

American

Arkansas

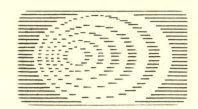
Clarke

Indiana

Katzenbach

Kendall

Model

Nebraska

New York

Ohio

Pennsylvania

Rochester

St. Mary's

Texas

Utah

Hampton

Western
Pennsylvania

CSUN

Gallaudet

NTID

Schools Founded By Deaf Persons

1817 American School for the Deaf
Laurent Clerc (and two others)

1843 Indiana School for the Deaf
William Willard

1850 Clarksville (Ark.) School of the Deaf*
J. W. Woodward

1861 Kansas School for the Deaf
Philip A. Emery

1868 Arkansas School for the Deaf
Joseph Mount

1870 Oregon School for the Deaf
William S. Smith

1875 New York School for the Deaf (Rome)
Alphonso Johnson (and two others)

1875 Chicago Day School for the Deaf
Philip A. Emery

1875 Cincinnati (Oh.) Public School for the Deaf
Robert P. McGregor

1878 Gallaudet (Mo.) School for the Deaf
Delos A. Simpson

1879 Beverly (Ma.) School for the Deaf
William B. Swett

1883 Pennsylvania School for the Deaf (Scranton)
Rev. Jacob M. Koehler

1884 Utah School for the Deaf
Henry C. White

1884 Northern New York School for the Deaf*
(Malone)
Henry C. Rider

1885 Florida School for the Deaf
Thomas H. Coleman

1885 New Mexico School for the Deaf
Lars M. Larson

1886 Evansville (In.) School for the Deaf*
Charles Kerney

1888 Eastern Iowa School for the Deaf*
William D. C. French

1890 North Dakota School for the Deaf
Anson R. Spear

1892 Cleveland (Oh.) School for the Deaf
John H. Geary

1895 Minneapolis (Mn.) School for the Deaf*
Anson R. Spear

1898 Oklahoma School for the Deaf
Mr. and Mrs. Ellsworth Long

1909 Virginia School for the Deaf (Hampton)
William C. Ritter

1911 Arizona School for the Deaf and the Blind
Henry C. White

*No longer in existence.

French

Geary

Koehler

Larson

All photos American Annals of the Deaf *except where noted.*

McGregor

Rider

Ritter

Spear

Willard

Seixas' school aroused a great deal of curiosity, and many benevolent Philadelphians became interested in his efforts and began to provide assistance. A group of such citizens met on April 12, 1820 in the Hall of the American Philosophical Society and established the Pennsylvania Institution for the Deaf and Dumb. Bishop William White of Revolutionary War fame was the school's first president. Laurent Clerc was "borrowed" from the American School in 1821 and served seven months as principal.

The school grew rapidly and soon outgrew its modest quarters at 11th and Market Streets. In 1824 the school was moved to a handsome, new structure at Broad and Pine Streets where it remained for 70 years. Articulation was introduced in the early 1870s and shortly afterward the main school established a day program at a different location in the city. This school used the pure oral method exclusively and was known as the "Oral Branch." The school's vocational program, begun in 1823, is recognized as the first of its kind among schools for the deaf.

The school continued its steady growth, and since the trustees considered further expansion in that part of the city both undesirable and impractical, in 1889 they purchased 62 acres in the northwest part of Philadelphia in an area known as Mt. Airy. The new plant was designed to provide four separate buildings, one each for the advanced, intermediate, primary, and oral departments. Each unit had its own dining room, dormitory, assembly room, playgrounds, and school building.

In 1934 the school's name was changed to The Pennsylvania School for the Deaf. The vocational training program was greatly expanded in 1962 with the construction of the new George W. Nevil Vocational School, which provided one of the finest such facilities for the deaf in the nation. In 1976 the first radio station for the deaf utilizing a radio-TTD connection was initiated and has become the prototype for other such installations.

Since the school was founded over 8,000 persons have studied there. The school has had two publications: *The Silent World* and *The Little World*. *The Silent World* continues publication today under the name of *The Mt. Airy World* and is one of the oldest school publications of its kind.

Albert Newsam (1808-1864), who at age 22 was recognized as one of the finest lithographic artists in the nation, was an alumnus of the school, as was John Carlin (1813-1891), the famous portrait artist who was also the first person to receive an honorary degree from Gallaudet College. Two more recent graduates of the school, Harvey J. Corson and Jay J. Basch, have earned doctorates. Corson is presently superintendent of the Louisiana School for the Deaf, and Basch is with the U.S. Department of Agriculture in Philadelphia.

Kentucky School for the Deaf
Danville, Kentucky

Opened: 1823

Founder: State Legislature

The Kentucky Asylum for the Tuition of the Deaf and Dumb became the first state-supported school for the deaf and the first such school west of the Allegheny Mountains when it opened its doors in Danville on April 11, 1823. A bill creating the school had been introduced in the Kentucky Assembly by General Elias Barbee, a state senator and the father of a deaf 19-year old daughter, named Lucy. The control of the school was placed under the direction of the Board of Trustees of Centre College. This arrangement continued until 1870 when the school was given its own board. This early relationship with Centre College no doubt accounts for the large number of Centre College alumni who have been involved in the field of education of the deaf. Dr. William D. Kerr, a Centre alumnus, was the founder of the Missouri School for the Deaf and the son of John R. Kerr, the first superintendent of the Kentucky School, who was also a Centre College alumnus.

A Centennial History of the Kentucky School for the Deaf, records the school's first century. It was written by Charles

Gallaudet Hall, Kentucky School for the Deaf.

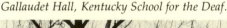

Chas. A. Thomas

Clerc Hall, Kentucky School for the Deaf.

Chas. A. Thomas

20

Uniforms worn by the students at the Missouri School long ago.

American Annals of the Deaf

American Annals of the Deaf

Carlin.) Barbee Hall is named for Lucy Barbee, the first student enrolled in the school. Fosdick Hall is named after a graduate, teacher and supervisor. Argo-McClure Hall, the boys' vocational building honors the former superintendent and George M. McClure, Sr. Charles A. Thomas Athletic Facility is the athletic complex built in 1973 and dedicated to Charles A. Thomas, a member of the Class of 1927. Thomas was printing instructor and school photographer. Beauchamp Hall honors James B. Beauchamp, an alumnus, teacher, editor of *The Kentucky Standard* and, following his retirement, a member of the KSD Advisory Board. He is now chairman of that Board.

Middleton Hall, the dormitory for older students, is named in honor of two KSD graduates. Daniel and Mildred Middleton were employees of the school for a total of 85 years. Both were houseparents.

George M. McClure, Sr. is the school's most well-known alumnus. He studied at Centre College and began teaching at KSD in 1880, the year the National Association of the Deaf was founded. His association with the Kentucky School spanned nearly eight decades. His wife also taught at the school and together they contributed a total of 125 years of service to KSD. McClure's son, William C., and grandson, William J., have continued the family's long tradition in education of the deaf. The elder McClure died in 1966 at the age of 105.

P. Fosdick, a KSD graduate and teacher at the school. In 1973 James Beauchamp wrote a second historical account as part of the school's observance of its Sesquicentennial. The title was *History of the Kentucky School for the Deaf, 1923-1973*. The March, 1923 issue ·of the *American Annals of the Deaf* has another interesting account of KSD written by George M. McClure, Sr., "The First State School for the Deaf."

Three of the school's superintendents were the sons of deaf parents. William K. Argo's parents were both deaf. His mother attended the Kentucky School. Charles B. Grow's mother was deaf. She was a product of the Missouri School for the Deaf where his father was a teacher. Both of Winfield McChord's parents attended the Kentucky School. Argo and McChord are distant cousins.

Many buildings on the campus pay tribute to the accomplishments of deaf persons. Clerc Hall, built in 1904 and since razed, was named for Laurent Clerc. (The school also has in its possession an oil portrait of Clerc painted by the well-known deaf artist, John

Military medals given to students at the New York School.

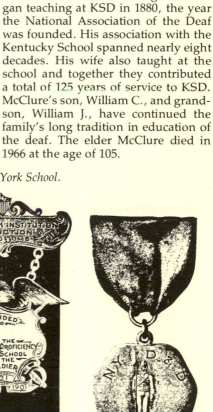

New York School for the Deaf

Ohio School for the Deaf
Columbus

Opened: 1829

Founders: Rev. James Hoge and State Legislature

The Rev. James Hoge was a member of the state commission responsible for the school system of Ohio. He was aware that other states had schools for the deaf, and he was determined that Ohio would provide the same educational opportunities for her children. He was able to persuade the governor and State Legislature of the need and a bill establishing the school was passed in January of 1827. The school was opened in a small frame house in Columbus, with one student, on October 16, 1829. By year's end there were ten pupils. Danford E. Ball, a graduate of the American School for the Deaf, joined the faculty the second year. He was the school's first deaf teacher.

In 1854 Ohio passed a law extending free education to all deaf children in the state.

Governor Rutherford B. Hayes was very interested in the education of the deaf. He presented the diplomas to the graduates at the first graduation ceremony held in 1869.

Robert P. McGregor and Robert Patterson were Ohio School students although neither stayed to receive his diploma. Patterson returned to the school to teach after his graduation from Gallaudet College. He was at the school a total of 51 years, 20 as teacher and 31 as principal. He served under four superintendents. His "Course of Instruction" went through five successive editions. During its heyday the Ohio School was one of the largest and most prominent schools for the deaf in the country.

McGregor founded the Cincinnati Day School for the Deaf and the Ohio Home for the Aged and Infirm Deaf. He was the first president of the National Association of the Deaf. He taught at the school from 1890 to 1921.

The Ohio School for the Deaf Alumni Association was organized in 1870 "to promote the general welfare of the mute community." In 1892 the members began a fund for a Home for the Aged and Infirm Deaf.

In the late 1940s, deaf people and their friends banded together to form the Ohio Federation of Organizations of the Deaf to persuade state officials of the need for a new school. Under the leadership of Hilbert C. Duning, a deaf architect and alumnus of the school, the group fought an uphill battle to persuade a governor and legislature which were determined to eliminate all "non-essential" expenditures from the budget of the need for a new school. They were successful in getting a limited construction budget and in the winter of 1951 construction began on a new school plant in the Columbus suburbs.

In 1949 Ralph E. LinWeber, an alumnus, compiled and published "The Graduation Classes of the Ohio School for the Deaf," which covered a span of 80 years and listed the names of 860 graduates of the school.

Virginia School for the Deaf and the Blind
Staunton, Virginia

Opened: 1839

Founder: State Legislature

The first effort to educate deaf children in Virginia began in 1812 when Colonel William Bolling started a school for his deaf children on his plantation. This school was short-lived and in 1839 the state opened a school for deaf and blind children in Staunton, Virginia. This was the first effort to educate deaf and blind children on the same campus at a state school.

The Rev. Joseph D. Tyler, an experienced teacher at the Hartford (American) School for the Deaf was retained as superintendent for an annual salary of $1,200 and board. Tyler had earned a Bachelor of Divinity degree at the Virginia Theological Seminary in Alexandria, Va., and bachelor and masters degrees at Yale University. In 1833, at the age of 29, he was stricken with a severe fever which left him deaf. His appointment to head the Virginia School was the first instance of a deaf man being hired to head a state school for the deaf as superintendent.

The first teacher Tyler hired was Job Turner who had been educated at the American School for the Deaf. Turner served the school for close to 40 years before leaving to become a missionary to the deaf.

In 1952 the school dedicated its new gymnasium to Thomas C. Lewellyn, a product, coach and teacher and an outstanding athlete at the school. Lewellyn was the "Father of the Mason-Dixon Basketball Tournament." Bass Hall, a dormitory on the campus is named for R. Aumon Bass and his wife, Mary, long-time teachers at the school. In 1949 Bass wrote a "History of Education of the Deaf in Virginia."

The School's main building is a national landmark. The school has fielded three undefeated football teams, 1938 (8-0), 1954 (9-0), 1969 (10-0).

William C. Ritter who founded the Virginia State School for the Deaf in Hampton, Edward C. Carney, director of Public Information at the National Association of the Deaf, and Thomas McCreery, who published the *Backhannon Banner* of Backhannon, West Virginia are alumni of the school. John Michaels, the first ordained deaf Baptist minister in the country, was another.

Race F. Drake has been principal of the Deaf Department since 1978.

A class in rhythm at the New York School in the 1930s.

22

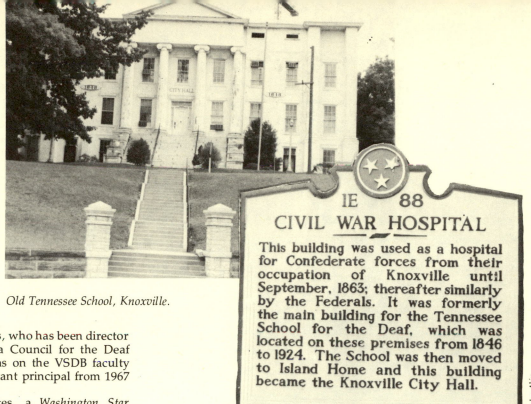

Old Tennessee School, Knoxville.

IE 88
CIVIL WAR HOSPITAL

This building was used as a hospital for Confederate forces from their occupation of Knoxville until September, 1863; thereafter similarly by the Federals. It was formerly the main building for the Tennessee School for the Deaf, which was located on these premises from 1846 to 1924. The School was then moved to Island Home and this building became the Knoxville City Hall.

E. Conley Akin

Fred P. Yates, who has been director of the Virginia Council for the Deaf since 1974, was on the VSDB faculty and was assistant principal from 1967 to 1974.

Leo A. Yates, a *Washington Star* printer and alumnus, was appointed to the school's Board of Visitors by Governor John N. Dalton in 1978.

Indiana School for the Deaf
Indianapolis

Opened: 1843

Founder: William Willard*

The first effort to educate deaf children in Indiana was made by James McLean, a graduate of the New York School for the Deaf. He started a small school with an enrollment of six in Parke County. The school closed after only a few months and nothing more was heard of McLean.

In the spring of 1843, William Willard, a deaf teacher from the Ohio School, arrived in Indianapolis and started a private school. A year later the Indiana Legislature made his school the state school for the deaf. Willard was hired as the first principal at a salary of $800 a year. In 1846, the legislature passed a law providing free education for deaf children in Indiana. School sessions ran from the first Monday in October to the last day in July. Students between the ages of 10 and 30 were admitted.

Willard was the school's first teacher and principal. He was principal for two years and then was succeeded by James S. Brown, a hearing man. Willard remained a teacher at the school

for twenty years, retiring in 1863 due to poor health.

The school probably had its greatest development during the administration of Richard O. Johnson, who became superintendent in July, 1889, and served for 30 years. It was during his administration that the school was moved to its present location. During World War I the school was closed one year when the U.S. Army took over the buildings. Johnson set up a correspondence course in hopes of keeping up the students' educational efforts.

The school has had eight name changes and has moved to five different locations. The former site of the school at State and Washington Streets is a city park named for Willard.

Memorials to deaf people on the campus include William Willard Unit, the intermediate primary building, the Ola Mary Brown Cafeteria, and the Lester C. Stanfill Vocational Building.

Tennessee School for the Deaf
Knoxville

Opened: 1845

Founder: General Assembly

In 1843 a bill was introduced in the Tennessee General Assembly calling for the establishment of a state school

for the blind at Nashville. General John Cocke, a member of the senate, secured an amendment as a rider to the bill appropriating $1,000 to start a school for the deaf at Knoxville. The bill passed and Governor James C. Jones set up a Board of Trustees to plan the operation of the school.

The Board employed the Rev. Thomas MacIntire, a teacher in the Ohio School, as principal and teacher. The school opened in June, 1845, an unusual date for the opening of school, in a rented residence. Six pupils were on hand for the first day but others soon enrolled. It was the eighth school for the deaf to be established in America.

North Carolina Schools for the Deaf
Morganton, Wilson, Greensboro

Opened: 1845, 1965, 1975

Founders: State Legislature and E. McKee Goodwin

In early 1845 the state of North Carolina hired W. D. Cooke, a hearing teacher at the School for the Deaf in Staunton, Virginia, to teach deaf children in the state. The school opened in rented quarters on May 1, 1845 in Raleigh, with seven pupils. Cooke ac-

quired some type, a printing press, wood working tools, and equipment for a shoe shop—all for $791—and started an industrial training program. The school remained open during the Civil War, and the students printed currency for the Confederacy. The school also printed the *American Annals of the Deaf* and began publication of the *Deaf Mute* in 1849, one of the earliest, if not the first, school for the deaf publications. The students also did Braille printing for the blind.

Following the Civil War the school suffered at the hands of political appointees, inept persons who had no knowledge nor experience in the education of the deaf or blind. The governing board, for example, had one member who could not even write his own name.

In 1891 the General Assembly voted to separate the deaf and blind pupils and move the school for the deaf to Morganton. Dr. E. McKee Goodwin was appointed superintendent of the new school. In 1893 the school started a teacher training program which later affiliated with Lenoir Rhyne College and Appalachian State University.

Around the turn of the century male students at the school wore uniforms as did students at a number of other schools for the deaf.

North Carolina was the first state to provide an institution for the education of black deaf children. The school opened in January 1869 and later became the Governor Morehead School. This school furnished deaf teachers to schools for black children in a number of other states.

In 1965 the Eastern North Carolina School opened in Wilson and in 1975 the Central School opened in Greensboro. In 1973 a preschool satellite program was begun in the state. These classes are located in the child's home area, serve deaf children in the 0-5 age range and operate out of the residential school nearest to them. All three residential schools are under the direction of the administrator of the Morganton school.

Three buildings on the campus of the Morganton school are named in honor of deaf persons. The Underhill Gym is named for Odie Underhill, a former teacher, coach, and editor of the school publication. The McCord Student Union Building is named for William S. McCord, a leader in the deaf community and a former member of the school's advisory board.

Main Building, North Carolina School for the Deaf, Morganton.

Crutchfield Hall, the vocational building, is named for the Crutchfield family, all members of which have been very active leaders in the school and deaf community.

The school at Morganton has a chapel on the campus which was financed by donations and state-appropriated funds. The school has had only four superintendents in its long history.

Illinois School for the Deaf
Jacksonville

Opened: 1846

Founder: State Legislature

The school opened in 1846 with four pupils. In little more than half a century the enrollment grew to 656 students, making ISD one of the largest residential schools for the deaf in the world.

The Illinois School was one of the first to employ female teachers (1856), and the first school to organize a Girl Scout troop (1919). Early in the 1920s, the school had a band, led by Frederick Fancher, who was himself hearing impaired.

Luther Taylor, a former New York Giants' pitcher, was a supervisor at ISD. He was instrumental in getting Richard Sipek into the major leagues.

The first officers of the Illinois School Alumni Association.

Sipek played briefly for the Cincinnati Reds.

The Molohon Vocational Building is named for Henry A. Molohon, who was connected with the school for 66 years as a student, houseparent, and instructor of woodworking. He died in 1957.

The Selah Wait Building is named after one of the founders of the ISD Alumni Association. Wait taught 34 years at the school. His four daughters

became teachers.

Charles Marshall, an outstanding athlete who played for the Goodyear Silents, was a physical education instructor at the school for 34 years. He was inducted into the American Athletic Association Hall of Fame in 1966.

S. Robey Burns, who was instrumental in starting the United States' participation in the World Games for the Deaf, was coach and athletic director at ISD. He was inducted into the

Illinois School faculty members between 1846 and 1900.

Georgia School, Cave Spring.

AAAD Hall of Fame in 1954.

The current superintendent, William P. Johnson, is hearing impaired.

(See Chapter 1, "More Schools" and Chapter 2, "The Fifer Cadets of Illinois.")

Georgia School for the Deaf
Cave Spring

Opened: 1846

Founder: O. P. Fannin

Prior to opening a school of its own, Georgia sent its deaf students to Hartford. In May 1846 a Department for the Deaf was opened in a log cabin behind the Hearn Manual Labor School in Cave Spring with four students in attendance. The cabin rented for two dollars a month. O. P. Fannin, an assistant principal in the Hearn School was employed to teach these deaf children. Out of this venture grew the Georgia School for the Deaf. Those log cabins were used until 1849 when a new school building was constructed on eight acres purchased from the Hearn School. In 1854 the duration the pupils were allowed to remain at the school was increased from four years to six. In 1877 that period was further extended to seven years and some students were allowed to remain an additional three years to study in the new "high class." In 1882 a department for colored children was started.

The school has two campuses and is located on 500 acres of land. At one time the school enrollment reached 600

students making the Georgia School the largest among schools for the deaf in the country.

Adjacent to the school campus is a cave from whence the town derives its name. The cave's spring supplies the school's and town's drinking water.

Shortly after introducing printing as a trade the students became so adept at it that a year later they were printing the town newspaper, *The Cave Spring Enterprise*.

John J. Flournoy, a deaf man of Huguenot ancestory, was one of the prime movers in the establishment of the school. In 1833 he presented a request to the state legislature for the establishment of a school but it remained for others to carry the project through to success.

In 1973 the state opened a second school in Atlanta. It is called the Atlanta Area School for the Deaf.

Ralph White, the 22nd president of the National Association of the Deaf is a graduate of the school.

Helen Muse, a deaf faculty member

of the school, is the author of *Green Pavilions*.

South Carolina School for the Deaf and the Blind
Spartanburg

Opened: 1849

Founder: The Rev. Newton P. Walker

In 1849 the Rev. Newton P. Walker, a Baptist minister, started a school with five deaf children in an old hotel building near Cedar Spring. The building was part of a resort area.

The South Carolina School has been administered by the Walker family for four generations.

The Cedar Spring post office is located in the school's Main Building. A cemetery where some students and former teachers are buried adjoins the school property.

(See Chapter 1, "The Post-War Years")

Arkansas School for the Deaf
Little Rock

Opened: 1850

Founder: Mr. and Mrs. Asa Clark

John W. Woodward, a deaf Virginian who had been educated in Paris, France, arrived at the Clarksville, Arkansas home of Augustus M. Ward in 1850. There were several deaf children in the area. Woodward began to teach them while working as a clerk at the county courthouse. The State of Arkansas provided Woodward with some funds for his school, but they were insufficient and the school soon closed. In 1860, Mr. and Mrs. Asa Clark, parents of a deaf girl, organized another school in their home at Fort Smith and hired Matthew Clark, an

Entrance to the Arkansas School in Little Rock.   *Arkansas School for the Deaf*

The Missouri School in the 1880s.

The Deaf-Mute Record

alumnus of the New York School to teach. The legislature incorporated this school and provided $2,000. Soon after this, however, the same legislature voted to secede from the Union. As a result, the school was open only ten months, from January 1861 to the following October, when it closed because of the war.

After the war, Joseph Mount, an alumnus of the Pennsylvania School (where he taught before becoming head of the Kansas School for the Deaf) persuaded the City of Little Rock to open a school for the deaf. The school was supported by the city and by contributions. It was incorporated as a state institution in 1868 and named "The Arkansas Deaf-Mute Institute." Mount was hired as principal, and Mrs. Virginia Woodward, widow of John W. Woodward, became the matron. The following February, Mount resigned abruptly, and at last report was editing

a newspaper called the *Sunny Clime* in Dallas, Texas.

By 1887 enrollment passed the 100 mark. That same year a separate building was erected for deaf black children. In 1899 the main building was destroyed by fire and in 1901 the legislature appropriated $80,000 to rebuild the school. In the early 1960s the school plant was completely rebuilt and only four older buildings were retained. The school was fully integrated in 1965.

John W. Michaels, Nathan Zimble and Robert T. Marsden were deaf administrators at the school. Zimble was principal of the school for 16 years. Marsden was vocational principal from 1959 to 1970.

When Zimble was at the school he coached the ASD wrestlers to 13 state Amateur Athletic Union championships. He also served as chairman of the state AAU Wrestling Committee. In 1949 the school's basketball team

won the State Class B championship.

Arthur Crow is one of the school's most outstanding alumni. He taught at the school for 50 years and was active in the community, in Scouting and in church work.

In 1969 the Arkansas Association of the Deaf presented the school a memorial garden in memory of former students of the school.

Missouri School for the Deaf
Fulton

Opened: 1851

Founder: William D. Kerr

The histories of the Missouri School for the Deaf and nearby Westminster College are closely intertwined. The cornerstones for the main buildings of the school and the college were laid on the same day, July 4, 1853, beginning

The Missouri School today.

a close working relationship between these two institutions that would span the century. Both buildings, ironically, were destined to be destroyed by fire. The MSD building caught fire in 1888, and within two decades the same fate struck the college's main building.

William Dabney Kerr, the founder of MSD, was the son of the Rev. John Rice Kerr, who served a tenure as superintendent of the Kentucky School. MSD was started on 40 acres of land that had belonged to the state asylum for the mentally ill located in the same town.

Westminster College was an outgrowth of Fulton College, which had also been established in 1851. In 1951 the college and the school observed joint centennials. (Westminster College is where Winston Churchill gave his famous "Iron Curtain" speech in 1946, a phrase that would become part of history. During Churchill's visit, the students of MSD gave him a gold engraved card with his name printed on it in Roman letters and in the manual alphabet. The gift was mentioned in the *London Daily Telegraph*.)

MSD and Westminster College are located in Callaway County, which is popularly known by local residents as "The Kingdom of Callaway," a name that originated during the Civil War. Residents of Callaway County were mostly supportive of the Southern

cause. When war came in 1861 and Missouri did not secede from the Union, the county seceded from the state and the Union!

Many of Westminster's students found employment at MSD and became interested in the education of the deaf. D. Robert Frisina, the first director of the National Technical Institute for the Deaf, graduated from Westminster. Other alumni of the college who went on to become administrators in a school for the deaf include Roy and Lloyd Parks, James N. Tate, William J. McClure, Eldon Shipman, and Robert D. Morrow. Close to a score of other school for the deaf superintendents were employed at one time or another at the Missouri School.

Shipman Field House, adjoining the football field, is named for Ernest Shipman, who was an outstanding athlete of the school. Shipman and his wife were long-time employees of the school and their sons, Eldon and John, became educators of the deaf.

The school's library is named for Grover C. Farquhar, a teacher, editor, and librarian. A graduate of the Texas School for the Deaf, Farquhar retired in 1963 after 42 years at the school. He was instrumental in encouraging many students to pursue a college education, including this author.

G. Dewey Coats was woodworking instructor and later vocational principal. He arranged the reorganizational conference of the National Association of the Deaf at MSD. This meeting resulted in changing the NAD into a federation of state associations, making it a much stronger national organization. Coats was an active leader in the deaf community up to the day of his death.

William C. McClure, MSD's sixth superintendent, was the son of deaf parents, Dr. and Mrs. George M. McClure, Sr., of Kentucky. William McClure was the father of William J. McClure, current superintendent of the Florida School.

Gross Hall, an intermediate boys' dormitory, was named for Henry Gross. Gross taught at the school and edited *The Missouri Record*. He wrote a history of the school in 1893.

Laura Searing, a graduate, became a successful newspaper reporter. She wrote under the pseudonym Howard Glydon. She was also a very good poet. One of her poems, "Belle Missouri," was used as the battle song of the Missouri Union Army. It appears in Chapter 1. Her name is one of those of the

few deaf persons included in the *Dictionary of American Biography* which was published in 1928.

George T. Dougherty also attended the Missouri School, although he enrolled in Gallaudet College before graduating. Dougherty made a name for himself as a chemist. He wrote many articles in his field. One of them on nickel in iron and steel found its way into a textbook.

Wisconsin School for the Deaf
Delavan

Opened: 1852

Founder: State Legislature

Prior to the opening of the Wisconsin School for the Deaf, the family of Ebenezer Chesboros moved to a farm near Delavan. They had a deaf daughter, Ariadna, who had attended the New York Institution for the Deaf and Dumb. Finding no school for deaf children in Wisconsin the Chesboros started a class on their farm and hired Miss Wealthy Hawes, a graduate of the New York Institution, to teach the class. John A. Mills, another graduate of that Institution later joined Hawes. As the class grew, financing became a problem, and the Chesboros and their friends petitioned the State Legislature for support. A bill incorporating the school passed on April 19, 1852. Twelve acres of land in Delavan were given to the State to be used for the school by the son of one of the founders of the city.

In 1861 the school graduated its first class, five boys. The first speech class, formed in 1868, was started the same year the Illinois School added articulation to its curriculum making these two schools the first in the west to teach speech to their students. Since its founding, the school has had 19 superintendents.

Ariadna Hall, a girls' dormitory, (razed in 1974) was named for the young woman who was instrumental in the establishment of the school. She is buried in the Spring Grove Cemetery, and her name on the headstone is enscribed in the manual alphabet.

Robinson Hall (razed in 1972) was named for Warren Robinson, a graduate of the school and Gallaudet College. Robinson was the school's first gymnastic instructor and a national proponent of industrial education for the deaf. Kastner Hall honors August C. Kastner, a product of the school, who was the boys' supervisor for nearly half a century. The athletic field is named for Frederick J. Neesam, a graduate of the school and Gallaudet College, who instituted the boys' athletic program and was coach for 41 years. The Neesam Sportsmanship Award, given annually, is also named for him. The school has a Wisconsin State historical marker which was financed by the school's chapter of the Jr. National Association of the Deaf.

The fence in front of the school campus once encircled the governor's mansion in Madison. It was made in 1872 and moved to the WSD campus in 1899.

Edith Fitzgerald, inventor of the Fitzgerald Key, Lars M. Larson, founder of the New Mexico School and the Wisconsin Association of the Deaf; J. Schuyler Long, a noted educator of the deaf and author of *The Sign Language, A Manual of Signs*, and Herbert

C. Larson, an administrator at California State University in Northridge were former teachers at the school.

Boyce R. Williams, Wilson H. Grabill, Edmund Waterstreet, John Kubis, Robert Horgen and the Rev. Arthur G. Leisman are graduates of WSD.

Louisiana State School for the Deaf
Baton Rouge

Opened: 1852

Founder: State Legislature

The State Legislature passed a bill in 1852 founding the school. It was named the Louisiana Institution for the Instruction of the Deaf and the Dumb and the Blind. J. S. Brown, the first superintendent, introduced vocational training in 1858.

Every two years the children and their blackboards were taken before the State Legislature where they performed classroom work "for the edifi-

cation of the legislators."

When the Civil War occurred, their learning was interrupted and all the children except the orphans were sent home. When fighting reached Baton Rouge, Federal gunboats steaming up the Mississippi River on their way from New Orleans, mistook the school buildings for Confederate Army headquarters and started bombarding them. One legend has it that one cannon ball fired at the school sailed through the wide hall without doing any damage. When the attack began the principal and the matron ran to the river and rowed to the flagship to inform the commander that the building was a school for the deaf and the blind. Firing immediately ceased. The school was later occupied and used as a hospital.

In the late 1860s fire destroyed an academy for men and the superintendent of the school for the deaf offered them temporary use of the school. This little academy grew into the Louisiana

Boys performing wood chopping and stacking chores at the Michigan School in Flint.

Bird's eye view of the Iowa School in Council Bluffs.

Romona Crookham

State University and crowded, first the blind, then the deaf from their own campus and took over the complete facilities. The school for the deaf moved to the heart of the city and from 1879 to 1887 carried on its programs in a small brick two-story building. When LSU became a land grant college it moved to another location and the deaf and blind boys and girls returned to their school. In 1898 the blind students were moved to their own school plant.

The school moved to a new plant in 1978.

The school's current superintendent, Dr. Harvey J. Corson, is a graduate of the Pennsylvania School for the Deaf at Mt. Airy.

Michigan School for the Deaf
Flint

Opened: 1854

Founder: State Legislature

The Michigan School was established by an act of the State Legislature in 1848 but it was not until six years later that it opened in a rented house at the corner of 8th and Church Streets.

The announcement of the school's opening read: "Candidates for admission must be thirty years of age, of sound mind, and susceptible of intellectual culture, free from infectious diseases, and of good moral character."

Barnabas M. Fay, a hearing instructor at the New York School for the Deaf, was hired as principal. He was the first of three generations of Fays to be involved in education of the deaf. His son, Edward A. Fay, was for 50 years editor of the *American Annals of the Deaf* and a professor and vice president at Gallaudet College. The Reverend's grandson also became a teacher of the deaf before his untimely death at the age of 43 cut short a promising career.

The Michigan School is the site of the founding of the National Fraternal Society of the Deaf. This organization was an outgrowth of a fraternal organization on the campus called "Coming Men of America."

In 1870 the school began a vocational program with courses in cabinet-making and shoemaking. Two years later printing was added.

Like many early residential schools, the Michigan School had difficulty correcting a misconception that the school was not an asylum or home or reformatory or a charitable institution. In 1917 the State Legislature recognized it as an educational institution similar to any public school in the state.

In 1971 the Mandatory Special Education Law was enacted in Michigan. It recognized the right of handicapped children to equal educational opportunities with the public schools and required state and school district officials to set up a plan to deliver special education programs for handicapped children. As a result of this law the school suffered an extensive loss of enrollment.

A number of the school's outstanding deaf teachers have been honored by having buildings named for them. Stewart Gynmasium is named for James Stewart, who taught in the school for 46 years. He was a graduate of the school and of Gallaudet College.

Stevens Hall, a residence building, is named for O. Clyde Stevens and his wife Ruth. He was another graduate of the school and of Gallaudet. He served the school for nearly a half century as teacher, houseparent, coach, and scoutmaster.

The Vocational Department was named by legislative act the Paul Zieske Vocational Wing, in honor of Paul Zieske, who was machine shop instructor for many years. The athletic field is named for Earl Roberts, teacher and coach. While at Gallaudet Roberts was a member of the only Gallaudet team that has ever won a basketball conference championship.

Mississippi School for the Deaf
Jackson

Opened: 1854

Founder: State Legislature and Col. E. R. Burt

Colonel Erasmus R. Burt, a member of the Mississippi House of Representatives, is called the father of the Mississippi School for the Deaf because of the leadership he provided in the State Legislature which led to the establishment of the school in 1854. Colonel Burt was killed during the Civil War when he led his regiment of 18th Mississippi Volunteers on a charge during the Battle of Leesburg and Edward's Ferry in October, 1861.

Jackson was selected as the site of the new school because of it's geographically central location in the state.

The first two administrators of the school were deaf men. John H. Gazly ran the school for one year, 1854-1855, and a Mr. Menfort (his first name does not appear in historical records) was head of the school the following year.

Before the school was established some of the deaf children from the state were sent to school in Kentucky and New York.

L. W. Saunders was the first pupil to enter the school. He was a popular and outstanding teacher for 41 years, until his accidental death.

During the Civil War, the school became a hospital for Confederate soldiers until the Federal troops arrived, "carrying the torch in one hand and the sword in the other," and burned the school to the ground. Construction of a new school was completed in 1871.

The Conference of Executives of American Schools for the Deaf met at the Mississippi School in 1888. The meeting was called "The Gallaudet Conference" in observance of the 100th anniversary of the birth of Thomas Hopkins Gallaudet, who had founded the first permanent school for the deaf in America.

In 1896, Mississippi appropriated $150 for tuition for students attending Gallaudet College. In 1897 MSD started a kindergarten class for children six and seven years old.

A fire completely destroyed the school on North State Street in 1902. A defective flue was blamed as the cause. There was no loss of life and, fortunately, the buildings were covered by insurance. Plans for a new school plant were drawn by Olof Hanson, the deaf architect, and the new school was built in 1904-05 at a cost of $141,195. Hanson, who worked out of a Seattle, Washington, office, was paid $500 for his work.

In 1953 the school's football team, coached by Cecil B. Davis, was undefeated in regular season play.

From 1937 to 1939 the school's basketball team, coached by Bilbo Monaghan, won three consecutive Southern Schools for the Deaf basketball titles. The 1939 team won 28 games while losing only 4.

In 1951 the school was moved to a new 51-acre campus with nine buildings.

Iowa School for the Deaf
Council Bluffs

Opened: 1855

Founder: State Legislature

The Iowa School for the Deaf became the second state residential school west of the Mississippi River when it opened its doors in 1855. That year the State Legislature incorporated a small private school which the Rev. W. E. Ijams had started in Iowa City. Prior to that some deaf children were sent to the Illinois School through the efforts of Edmund Booth, a deaf newspaper publisher. Ijams was a former teacher at the Illinois School. He had about 20 pupils and with state support his school grew rapidly.

In the 1870s the school was moved to an 80-acre site just outside the city of Council Bluffs and work began on a new main building. Before the work was completed, however, the structure caught fire and was destroyed. The following spring construction was resumed and as the building was nearing completion when a tornado struck, demolishing part of it. The building was finally finished only to be completely destroyed by fire in 1902.

The school held its first commencement in 1884 and that year graduated its most famous student—J. Schuyler Long. Long enrolled in Gallaudet College and graduated with the class of 1889. He taught briefly at the Wisconsin School before returning to his alma mater. He became principal in 1902 and held the post until his death in 1933. He was a widely respected editor of *The Iowa Hawkeye*. In 1914 Gallaudet College awarded him an honorary degree. During Long's tenure at the Iowa School, another deaf person who became well known was Tom L. Anderson, the school's vocational principal. Anderson, better known to many as "TLA," made his mark in the field of industrial training and vocational rehabilitation. He left the Iowa School to head a vocational rehabilitation program in Texas and later in California. Anderson was president of the National Association of the Deaf from 1940 to 1946. He received an honorary degree from Gallaudet College in 1939.

Norman G. Scarvie, a graduate of the school and Gallaudet College, succeeded Anderson as principal and held the position for a quarter of a century. He was instrumental in securing construction of the school's new vocational building.

Memorials have been established at the school honoring Anton J. Netusil,

Learning can get tiresome.

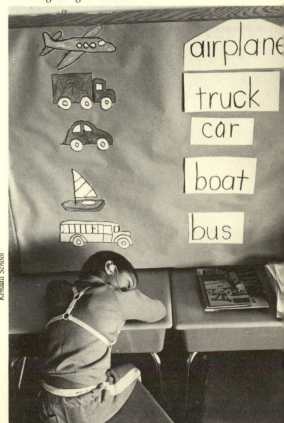

Kendall School

Kendall School students meeting President Richard M. Nixon at the White House.

instructor in upholstery and wood-work, and John J. Marty, an academic teacher, both of whom served the school for over 40 years. Netusil was a product of the Nebraska School and Marty was from the Iowa School.

Streets on the campus are named for illustrious persons in the field of education of the deaf. Dobson Street honors the Dobson family, all of whom, father, mother, and three children, attended the school. Two of them, Mary and Chester, became teachers, the former teaching in the Iowa School for 44 years. Other streets are named for Thomas H. Gallaudet, Alexander G. Bell, Laurent Clerc, and J. Schuyler Long.

Kendall Demonstration Elementary School
Washington, D.C.

Opened: 1857

Founder: Amos Kendall

The Columbia Institution for the Deaf, Dumb, and Blind opened its doors on June 13, 1857, with eight stu-

dents, four blind and four deaf. Amos Kendall, a philanthropist and postmaster general in the Jackson and Van Buren administrations, had come into contact with an undesirable character who was trying to exploit the handicaps of these children under the false premise of starting a school in their behalf. Kendall assumed responsibility for their care and education and opened a school for them on his estate in northeast Washington, D.C. He donated two acres of land and a building to start this school which, today, bears his name. Kendall next hired 20-year-

Deep in thought.

old Edward Miner Gallaudet of Hartford, Connecticut, as the first superintendent.

James Denison was the first teacher in the Columbia Institution, and he became the first principal of the Kendall School. Denison had a hereditary type of deafness. He was educated at the American School in Hartford where he met Edward Miner Gallaudet and where a friendship began that would span half a century. Denison and Gallaudet later became brothers-in-law. Following a year at the Michigan School, Denison accepted a position at Kendall and began a record-setting 53 years' association with the school. He invented the "Denison Fraction Teacher," a device to teach fractions. He was principal from 1869 to 1909. He never earned a college degree, and when offered a teaching position at the college he modestly declined on the ground that he had no degree. This did not, however, discourage Columbia University from giving him an honorary degree in recognition of his contributions to the education of deaf children. A house on the college campus

32

is named the Denison House in his honor.

Arthur L. Roberts, a member of the Gallaudet College class of 1904, was principal of the school from 1918 to 1921. Roberts left the field of education to accept a position with the National Fraternal Society of the Deaf in Chicago, where he built an illustrious career and became president of the Society. (See the 1950s.) Ronald E. Nomeland, a graduate of the Minnesota School for the Deaf and a member of the Gallaudet Class of 1958, was acting dean of the school for one year. In 1974 Robert Davila, a graduate of the California School for the Deaf at Berkeley and a 1953 graduate of Gallaudet, became dean of the school. Davila later became Gallaudet vice president for Pre-College Programs.

During the 1950s many deaf students who had taken the college entrance examinations and failed attended the Kendall School post-graduate program.

In 1970 legislation was passed changing the name of the school and its scope of responsibility. That year it became the Kendall Demonstration Elementary School and assumed the responsibility not only for teaching deaf children but also for testing, evaluating and developing educational materials, methods, and models and disseminating this information to other schools throughout the nation. In 1977 construction began on a new school plant to accommodate an enrollment of 300. These new facilities, in addition to meeting the needs of an expanded school program, include small live-in units for short-term occupancy by parents of children undergoing extensive educational diagnostic services, and by researchers and visiting professionals.

Kendall School has had many outstanding graduates who have gone on to work in a variety of fields. One family stands as an example: Gertude (Scott) Galloway, Meda (Scott) Hutchinson, and Roger Scott, sisters and brother. Galloway, president-elect of the NAD, will take office in 1980 to start the Association's second century. She is the first woman elected to the NAD presidency. Hutchinson was a mathematics instructor at Gallaudet College until her recent death. Scott is the first deaf foreman to be employed in the Government Printing Office.

Among the noted teachers at Kendall School was Ellen Pearson Stewart, wife of Roy J. Stewart. After graduating from Gallaudet she taught for a short time in South Dakota, then returned to Kendall School, where she was a member of the faculty for 37 years.

Texas School for the Deaf
Austin

Opened: 1857

Founder: State Legislature

The Texas School for the Deaf began in an old frame house, three log cabins, and a smokehouse. The three students and their deaf teacher, Matthew Clark, used the smokehouse as their classroom. Jacob Van Nostrand, a teacher from the New York School for the Deaf, was the first of 21 superintendents of the school.

Those early years were a constant struggle. That was the period of the Civil War and reconstruction. They were difficult times and the state treasury was depleted. For two years there were not enough funds to pay the teachers' salaries. Food was cultivated on the farm by the students and faculty, and sheep were shorn to make wool for clothing for some of the children. Unable to get sufficient money to hire enough teachers, the superintendent taught some of the classes.

In 1876 the school added a state printing office and two years later, a shoe shop. That year *The Texas Mute Ranger,* forerunner of the school's current publication, *The Lone Star,* appeared.

In 1851 the school was placed under the control of the State Board of Education. In 1954 the State Legislature voted a $2.5 million dollar reconstruction program. In 1965 the school acquired the campus of the Texas Deaf, Blind and Orphan School. The highest total enrollment of TSD was 750 in 1974-75, making the school the largest residential school for the deaf in the United States at that time. In 1973, legislation was passed dividing the state into five regions but TSD continued to serve as a state-wide educational program for deaf children.

A small bronze replica of the Thomas Hopkins Gallaudet and Alice statue (which is located on the Gallaudet College campus) is on display in the lobby of the school auditorium. The Lewis Literary Society, a literary-drama organization, and the Emily Lewis Dormitory are named for the first pupil of the school, who later became one of its teachers. A bronze plaque honors Louis Orrill, a graduate of the school, who was president of the Texas Association of the Deaf for 19 years.

Two of the school's alumni have become administrators of other schools. Roy Holcomb was head of the Margaret Sterck School for the Hearing Impaired in Delaware, and Larry Stewart founded and directed a model demonstration program for hearing impaired, developmentally disabled deaf children and adults in Arizona.

Kelly Stevens, a successful deaf artist, is a graduate of TSD.

The Mary L. Thornberry Speech and Hearing Center on the Gallaudet College campus is named for an alumna and former teacher of the school.

Alabama School for the Deaf
Talladega

Opened: 1858

Founder: Dr. Joseph Henry Johnson, Sr.

Dr. Johnson, a physician originally from Georgia, became interested in the deaf because he had a deaf brother whom he wished to assist in the pursuit of an education. He prepared himself as a teacher of the deaf and opened a school in his home. He continued his medical practice to help finance the operation of the school.

Dr. Johnson received from the state

The first group of boys to enter the "Branch House" at St. Mary's School, Buffalo.

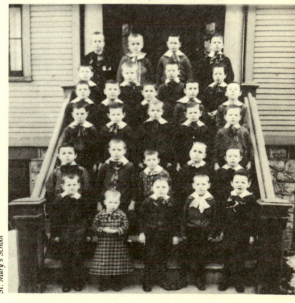

St. Mary's School

Dr. William Caldwell's class at the California School in 1900. The gentleman in front (white beard) is Dr. Warring Wilkinson, superintendent.

$240 per year for each pupil he taught when he started the school. In 1860 the legislature formally recognized the existence of the school, adopting an ordinance that established the Alabama Institution for the Deaf and Dumb, and appropriating $25,000 to erect suitable buildings. The Johnson home was purchased and became the central building on the campus.

In 1869 a department for the blind was added but in 1877 the blind pupils were removed to a campus of their own and the school became known officially as the Alabama School for the Deaf. The new school for the blind included a department for training the adult blind. One of its trainees was a former governor who was active in the establishment of the school and whose eyesight failed as he grew older.

In 1957 the school was practically rebuilt. Among the new buildings constructed was a modern library named for Harry L. Baynes, one of the school's noted deaf teachers. He served the school for almost 40 years as teacher, coach, athletic director, and counselor. He was an outstanding leader in activities among the deaf in the Southeast.

Another deaf teacher commanding nation-wide respect in the educational profession was John H. McFarlane. Originally from Gallaudet, McFarlane was a high school teacher and editor of the school publication. He was a gifted writer and poet and was one of the editors of *The Silent Muse,* an anthology of prose and poetry by deaf writers. The school's auditorium is named in his honor.

Among the graduates of the school are one of the nation's best known Episcopal ministers, the Rev. Robert Fletcher, and Byron B. Burnes, a former president of the National Association of the Deaf. Bill Sparks, the artist mentioned elsewhere, is a product of the school.

St. Mary's School for the Deaf
Buffalo, New York

Opened: 1859

Founder: Le Couteulx St. Mary's Benevolent Society for the Deaf

In 1836 a group of Sisters of St. Joseph arrived in New Orleans from France. They were met by Father John Timon. These sisters were destined for St. Louis, Missouri, where they started the first denominational school for the deaf in this country. Father Timon later invited the sisters to start a school for deaf children in New York and in 1859 the sisters opened a school in three small cottages on Edward Street in Buffalo, on property presented by Louis Le Couteulx, a Frenchman.

In 1862, Father Timon, who had become the first Bishop of Buffalo, had a four-story brick building erected at the school, and by 1880 additional wings had been constructed and the school had 130 pupils. Increasing enrollment soon caused over-crowding and property for a new school was purchased. By 1898 all the pupils had been moved to the new location, the present site of the school. The name was changed to St. Mary's School for the Deaf in 1936.

In 1927 St. Mary's began providing a full high school program, and in 1936 the school established a preschool class for three and four-year-olds.

Eugene E. Hannan, the deaf sculptor, attended St. Mary's. He was sculptor of the statue of de l'Epée, which the

34

National Association of the Deaf commissioned in observance of its 50th anniversary and unveiled in Buffalo in 1930.

Thomas Coughlin, the first deaf man to become a Catholic priest in the United States is a graduate of St. Mary's School.

In 1977, Karen Tellinghuisen, a pupil at the school, participated in the World Games of the Deaf in Romania and won a gold medal for the javelin throw.

(See Chapter 1, "Denominational Schools")

California School for the Deaf
Berkeley

Opened: 1860

Founder: Mrs. Pomeroy B. Clark and a group of women

The California School traces its origins to San Francisco where Mrs. Pomeroy B. Clark and a group of 23 ladies formed a Society for the Instruction and Maintenance of the Indigent Deaf and Dumb and the Blind in March 1860. Mrs. Clark had a deaf sister. The first teacher of the school was Henry B. Crandall, a graduate of the New York School for the Deaf. The school was moved across the bay to the foothills of Berkeley and ground was broken for a new school in 1867. At the cornerstone-laying program on September 26, 1867, the program included an ode written for the occasion by Bret Harte.

In 1875 fire destoyed the recently constructed school building and a new plant had to be built. Stone from the demolished structure was used to construct a wall around part of the campus.

Theophilus d'Estrella, Theodore Grady, Granville Redmond, and Douglas Tilden are among the school's more distinguished alumni. d'Estrella was one of the first pupils to enter the

Author

William Marra in the museum he started at the Kansas School.

school. Following his graduation from CSDB, he became the first deaf student to enroll in the neighboring University of California. He taught at CSDB for 53

The Kansas School in Olathe before the turn of the century.

years and was a successful photographer. The school's auditorium and the literary society which he helped start are named for him.

Theodore Grady was the first deaf person to earn a degree at the University of California. He also studied briefly at Johns Hopkins University. He studied law and was admitted to the California bar in 1897. He specialized in research and the preparation of briefs. He taught at CSDB, worked as a city and county tax collector and edited the *Oakland Daily Times*. The junior high school boys' residence is named for him.

Redmond became a successful landscape artist. His work has been exhibited at the Paris Salon, the St. Louis World's Fair, and the Alaska-Yukon-Pacific Exposition. The school has his painting "A Winter Scene on the Seine" which was one of 500 selected out of 6,000 entries for exhibit at the Paris Salon.

Douglas Tilden is CSDB's most widely-known graduate. He gained fame as a sculptor. Two works, "The Mechanics" and "California Volunteers," are located in San Francisco. Three others, "The Ball Player," "Father Junipero Serra," and "Admission Day," are on permanent exhibit in the Golden Gate Park. His "The Bear Hunt" is on the school campus.

In all, the California School has some ten buildings named for deaf persons. Crandall Hall, named after the first teacher, is the high school boys' residence. Winfield S. Runde Hall is named for the first CSDB graduate to enroll at Gallaudet College. Runde taught at the school for 25 years and was one of the founders of the school's Foothills Athletic Association. Frances Norton Hall, the elementary girls' residence, is named for Runde's wife. She was one of the first girls to enroll at Gallaudet College and she also taught

for many years at the school. The Annie Lindstrom Hall is named for the third CSDB student to graduate from Gallaudet College in the same class with the Rundes. The school's vocational building is named in honor of Douglas Tilden.

James Howson, another graduate of the school, earned a bachelor's and a master's degree from the University of California. He taught at the school and was an active leader in the deaf community. He was the first president of the California Association of the Deaf and held offices in the National Association of the Deaf and the National Fraternal Society of the Deaf. The school's gymnasium is named for him.

Vernon S. and Ruth Birck joined the CSDB staff in 1928 and gave long and dedicated service to the students. The lower school residences are named for them.

In 1960 Caroline Hyman Burnes and Catherine Marshall Ramger, two deaf staff members of the school, wrote *History of the California School for the Deaf, 1860-1960*. The book was printed by the students under the direction of John Galvan.

Leo Jacobs, the school's high school mathematics teacher, was the first holder of the Dr. Doctor Chair of Deaf Studies at Gallaudet College in 1972-73. The publication of *A Deaf Adult Speaks Out*, was the result of Jacobs' one year on the campus.

The California School moved to a new campus in Fremont in 1980.

Kansas State School for the Deaf
Olathe

Opened: 1861

Founder: Philip A. Emery*

Philip A. Emery moved to the Territory of Kansas with a group of people

who wanted to make Kansas a free state. Emery wanted to start a school for the deaf. The Kansas constitution, adopted in 1859, included provision for state support of a school for the deaf, but nothing was done until Emery's arrival.

Emery was born in 1830 in Ohio; his parents and grandparents were early Ohio settlers. When he was three years old his hearing was severely damaged by a bout with scarlet fever. He retained his speech, and people called him "a deaf but not mute gentleman." Emery was an excellent writer despite the fact that he had only a few years of formal education at the Indiana School for the Deaf. He taught four years, 1856-1860, at his alma mater before moving to Kansas.

When the Kansas School opened in 1861, Emery was hired as the first superintendent. He lived in a one-story frame house in Baldwin. The rent was five dollars a month. The first student to arrive at the new school was Elizabeth Studebaker. Her father could not pay for her tuition so he brought a wagonload of corn, ham, butter, and eggs.

Conditions were so bad during those early years—drought, famine, and the war—that Emery and his wife nearly starved to death. Emery's anti-slavery beliefs brought the rebels upon him, and on more than one occasion he had to hide and sleep in a cornfield.

The school was moved to Topeka in 1864, and Emery resigned, turning over the administration of the school to Benajah R. Nordyke, an Indiana schoolmate. Joseph Mount succeeded Nordyke in a year, making Kansas the only school to have three deaf administrators in a row. Emery moved to Illinois where he founded the Chicago Day School for the Deaf.

Roberts Hall, the Kansas school's academic building, is named for one of the school's most distinguished alumni, Arthur L. Roberts. Roberts was president of the National Association of the Deaf and a National Fraternal Society of the Deaf official from 1921 to 1957. The Marra Museum, one of the best collections of historical lore related to deafness in the country, is located in the basement of Roberts Hall. It is named for William J. Marra, an alumnus and teacher of the school, who has spent thousands and thousands of hours collecting and organizing the material. The school's football field is named for Paul D. Hubbard

Lauritsen Gym at the Minnesota School, Faribault.

Minnesota School for the Deaf

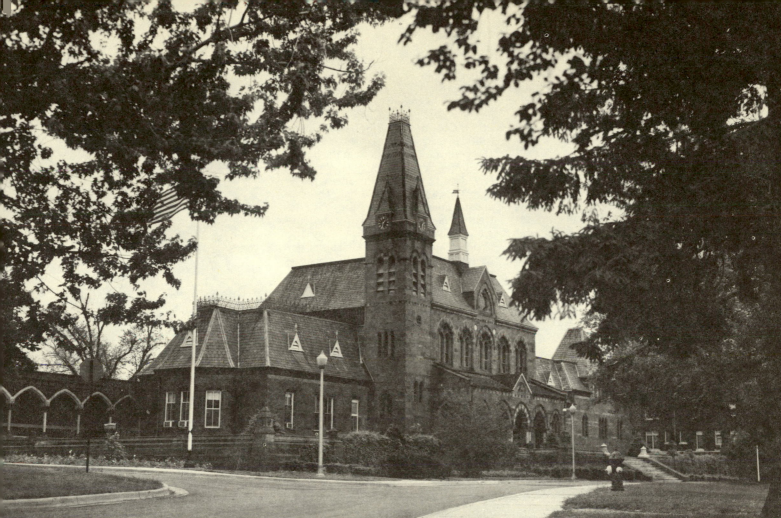

Chapel Hall on the Gallaudet College campus, Washington, D.C.

who is given credit for the invention of the football huddle. Emery Hall, the school's primary department, is named in honor of the founder.

The Kansas School takes pride in the fact that many of its alumni and employees have been enshrined in the American Athletic Association of the Deaf Hall of Fame. The list includes: Luther Taylor, Nathan Lahn, Frederick A. Moore, John Ringle, Edward S. Foltz, Paul D. Hubbard, Charles Bilger, Dalton Fuller, and Paul S. Curtis.

The school's gymnasium is named for Luther Taylor, the school's most famous athlete. Taylor spent nine seasons as a pitcher for the New York Giants baseball team.

For many years KSD has had an excellent Scouting program. The school has its own scout cabin, a gift of the Olathe Sertoma Club. Uel Hurd, who has been the scoutmaster for nearly half a century, was the first deaf Kansan to become an Eagle Scout. In 1943 he was awarded the Silver Beaver award, Scouting's highest honor.

The school is located on the Old Santa Fe Trail and a marker on the gymnasium wall records that fact.

Minnesota School for the Deaf
Faribault

Opened: 1863

Founder: State Legislature

When Minnesota became a state in 1858, action was taken by the legislature to start a school for the deaf. George E. Skinner, a representative from Faribault, urged the legislature to locate the school in his city and an offer of 40 acres was made but nothing happened for five years. The Civil War and Indian hostilities delayed action on the school. In 1863 Senator Berry of Faribault introduced a bill to establish the school. It passed in March and the school opened the following September in a building belonging to a Major Fowler in Faribault. Students between the ages of 8 and 30 were admitted. The name of the school was the Minnesota Institute for the Education of the Deaf and Dumb. The name was later changed to the Minnesota School for the Deaf in 1902.

Between 1915 and 1952 the male students wore military uniforms and practiced military drills and maneuvers. The young boys used wooden guns and the older boys practiced with Springfield rifles. In 1896 the school printed its first yearbook and in 1905 Minnesota began granting students attending Gallaudet College $300 a year in state aid. From 1916 to 1944 the school had a boys' band. In 1946 the Girls' Drum Corps performed before 16,000 basketball fans in a state tournament game between Ironton-Crosby and Minneapolis Marshall.

Military was taught by James H. Quinn, a Fanwood graduate. Quinn was drillmaster for two years. Wrote Superintendent Tate of the military training: "Since we have had the drill we notice that we have had comparatively little use for the hospital."

James L. Smith, a graduate of the school, taught at his alma mater for 50 years. In 1905-06 he was acting super-

37

intendent. Smith's family had moved to Minnesota in a covered wagon when he was three and a half years old. He had become deaf at eight years, entered MSD at eleven and graduated five years later. He earned his bachelor's and master's degrees from Gallaudet College. He was editor of the *Minnesota Companion*. Smith Hall, the school building is named for him.

Anson R. Spear was one of the school's most successful graduates. He entered the school in 1874 and graduated in 1878. He founded two schools, the North Dakota School for the Deaf and the Minneapolis Day School for the Deaf, and was a successful businessman and inventor. His son, Randy Merriman, was a popular television and radio personality in Minneapolis and New York City.

Minnesota has produced several well-known and successful alumni. Three, James L. Smith, Olof Hanson and Jay C. Howard, became presidents of the National Association of the Deaf. Two—Anson Spear and Anton Schroeder—were successful inventors.

The school's gymnasium is named for Wesley Lauritsen who was teacher and athletic director for over 40 years. He also edited the Minnesota *Companion*.

Gallaudet College
Washington, D.C.

Opened: 1864

Founder: Edward M. Gallaudet

In 1856 Amos Kendall, a well-known citizen of Washington, donated two acres of land in the northeastern part of the city to found a school for deaf and blind children. A year later, Congress incorporated the school as the Columbia Institution for the Instruction of the Deaf and Dumb and the Blind. Kendall hired Edward Miner Gallaudet, the son of Thomas H.

Gallaudet, to be the superintendent.

Edward M. Gallaudet's ambition was to build the Institution into a college for deaf students. In 1864 he induced Congress to authorize the Institution's Board of Directors "to grant and confirm such degrees in the liberal arts and sciences as are usually conferred in Colleges." President Abraham Lincoln signed the bill. The collegiate division became the National Deaf-Mute College, the blind students were transferred to a school for the blind in Maryland, and Gallaudet became president of the entire Institution.

In 1894 the name of the college division was changed to Gallaudet College, in honor of Thomas Hopkins Gallaudet. Women were first admitted in 1887, and in 1891 a department was established for training teachers of the deaf.

Edward M. Gallaudet retired in 1910. He had expanded the campus—called Kendall Green in honor of Amos Kendall—from the orginial two acres to 92 acres.

Dr. Percival Hall, a graduate of the teacher training department, became president upon Gallaudet's retirement and remained until 1945. He maintained an excellent teaching staff and kept the student body small, admitting students on a selective basis. During Hall's tenure as president the name of the Institution was changed to the Columbia Institution for the Deaf. It included Gallaudet College, Kendall School, and the teacher training program which was known as the Normal Department.

In 1945 Hall retired and Leonard M. Elstad became president. He had been superintendent of the Minnesota School for the Deaf and, like Dr. Hall, he was a graduate of the Normal Department.

During the Elstad administration the college underwent a multi-million dollar construction program. The entire corporation was renamed Gallaudet College and the Normal Department became the Graduate School. The enrollment quadrupled and the faculty increased. The college was accredited for the first time in 1957, and an alumni representative was added to the college Board of Directors.

When Elstad retired in 1969 he was named president emeritus. He was succeeded by Dr. Edward C. Merrill, Jr., dean of the College of Education at the University of Tennessee. The construction program continued under the Merrill administration, but the major thrust was in programs and services to deaf people. During Merrill's tenure as president, Gallaudet was reorganized to encompass five divisions: Pre-College, Academic Affairs, Research, Public Services, and Business Affairs. The academic affairs division was ex-

Author

Ed Corbett, assistant superintendent of the Maryland School, tries out a hearing device of yesteryear.

The Hessian Barracks at the Maryland School for the Deaf, Frederick.

Laura-Jean Gilbert

panded to include the School of Communication, the School of Education and Human Services, the College of Arts and Sciences, and the Graduate School. Special programs which have been developed within various of the five divisions include the International Center on Deafness, the National Center for Law and the Deaf, the College for Continuing Education, the National Academy, sign language programs, a National Information Center, and two national demonstration schools for the deaf.

There are many memorials to deaf people on the campus. The college has a Hall of Fame which enshrines the names of former faculty members and leaders. The list includes: Melville Ballard, Arthur D. Bryant, John Carlin, Laurent Clerc, Harley D. Drake, Amos G. Draper, Olof Hanson, John B. Hotchkiss, Frederick H. Hughes, Walter J. Krug, Thomas S. Marr, Edith M. Nelson, Richard M. Phillips, Henry Syle, George M. Teegarden, and Cadwallader Washburn.

Campus streets are named for Douglas Craig, Amos G. Draper and Alto M. Lowman. Buildings on the campus named for deaf people include: Drake House, Ballard House, Denison House, Washburn Arts Center, Hughes Gymnasium, Fowler Hall, Mary L. Thornberry Hearing and Speech Center, Krug Hall, Cogswell Hall and Clerc Hall. The Hotchkiss Athletic Field, the Agatha Hanson Plaza, and the Dr. Peter J. Fine Infirmary are also named for deaf persons.

Maryland School for the Deaf
Frederick

Opened: 1868

Founder: State Legislature

The Maryland School opened on September 25, 1868 in two old stone structures called the Hessian Barracks in the city of Frederick (formerly called Fredericktown). The history of these barracks dates back to the Revolutionary War. They were named the Hessian Barracks because they were used as a prison for those German soldiers who were paid by the British to fight against the Americans. Thirty-four students were in attendance on opening day—many of them barefoot.

One of the barracks was demolished to make room for a new Main Building. The other is now used as a museum.

Lewis and Clark had used these barracks as a supply depot before embarking on their famous expedition to the Pacific Northwest. These barracks were used as a school for seven years while a new school was being constructed.

George W. Veditz was a graduate and later a teacher at the school. Veditz founded the MSD alumni association. He became the school's first full-time vocational teacher. The Veditz Vocational Building is named for him.

The school's gymnasium is named for Harry Benson, who was connected with the school for 60 years as a student and teacher. The Bensons had two daughters, Mary and Elizabeth. Both became teachers of the deaf.

The Harry T. Creager Athletic Field is named for one of the school's outstanding athletes. Noah Downes, another outstanding MSD athlete, has been inducted into the Frederick Hall of Fame. Harry Baynes, an MSD graduate taught at the Alabama School for the Deaf. The ASD Library is named for him.

Rudoph Hines, a graduate of the school, has been a member of the school's 30-member Board of Visitors, which is appointed by the governor,

Archie Marshall of Missouri is one of a growing number of deaf persons serving on school boards.

since 1955.

The school has a bust of Laura Bridgman, the first deaf-blind person to be formally educated in this country.

The John A. Trundle Fellowship Fund at Gallaudet College is named for Trundle, who was an MSD student from the Eastern Shores.

In 1973 a second school was opened in Howard County. Called the Columbia Campus, it is located on 55 acres in Columbia, Maryland. The Frederick campus has 67 acres. Both schools are under the direction of the same superintendent. Gertrude Galloway, NAD president-elect, is assistant principal at the Columbia school.

Louis Frisino, an outstanding wild life artist, is an MSD graduate.

Western Pennsylvania School for the Deaf
Edgewood

Opened: 1869

Founder: The Rev. John G. Brown

In the summer of 1868 a little black boy was brought to the Mission Sabbath School, operated by the Presbyterian Church of Pittsburgh, Pennsylvania. The boy was deaf and his name was Henry Bell. A deaf graduate of the Pennsylvania Institute for the Deaf and Dumb, Philadelphia, agreed to teach the boy. The word spread that the school was teaching a deaf boy and soon other deaf children made their appearance.

The pastor of the church, the Rev. John D. Brown, felt that the children needed more education than they could be given in a Sabbath School, so he obtained a grant of $800 from the Board of Education along with the use of a schoolroom. In September, 1869, the school opened as the first day school for the deaf in the United States. Fourteen pupils were present.

Attending day school in those days was very difficult, so schoolrooms were found near a house where the children could live. The building soon overflowed and it was necessary to seek a new location. A wealthy citizen gave some land and pledged some money, and other citizens contributed. The Reverend Dr. Brown induced the legislature to make an appropriation. In 1876 the day school was closed. A building was erected and a new school was opened, to be known as the Western Pennsylvania Institution for the

Two Gallaudet College students enjoy a Coke in the 1940s. Note price.

perintendent of the school from 1946 to 1969. When he retired, he was succeeded by his son, Dr. William N. Craig.

West Virginia Schools for the Deaf and the Blind
Romney

Opened: 1870

Founder: State Legislature

Although the State Legislature is credited with the founding of the West Virginia Schools for the Deaf and the Blind, these two schools owe their existence to the efforts of Howard H. Johnson, a blind man. Prior to June 20, 1863 when West Virginia was admitted as the 35th state in the Union after being separated from Virginia during the Civil War, deaf and blind children were educated at the Virginia School in Staunton or in the neighboring states of Maryland and Ohio, but only those children whose parents could afford the traveling expenses were able to attend those schools.

Johnson was born with poor vision and eventually became totally blind. He attended the Virginia School for the Deaf and the Blind and became a teacher. Aware that there were no programs for the deaf or blind in his new home state, he struck up a correspon-

Deaf and Dumb. One of the new teachers was George M. Teegarden, a graduate of the National Deaf-Mute College (Gallaudet College). He remained at the school 48 years and became noted throughout the deaf world as a writer and poet.

Another deaf teacher who spent many years at the school was Bernard Teitelbaum. He was educated in the Colorado School and Gallaudet College.

This school could not permanently fulfill the need. It soon was crowded beyond capacity and plans were set in motion to build a new school. Land was purchased and some more was donated, and in 1884 the school moved to Edgewood, a suburb of Pittsburgh, where it still stands. New buildings, expansions in the program, and other improvements have come from time to time. In 1923 the name of the school was changed to the Western Pennsylvania School for the Deaf.

Dr. Sam B. Craig, a graduate of Centre College in Kentucky, was su-

C. Joseph Giangreco doing his practice teaching at the Kendall School. He later became superintendent of the Iowa School for the Deaf.

dence with recently-inaugurated Governor William E. Stevenson whom he found sympathetic and supportive. Johnson also canvassed the state seeking support for the school. A bill was introduced in the State Legislature to establish a school for the blind. At the last minute the bill was amended to include deaf students. It passed and became law on March 3, 1870. It was originally planned to locate the school in Wheeling, but legal complications came up and when the town of Romney offered the state a building known as Romney Classical Institute and 12 acres of land, the location was accepted. The White family donated more land. The building which was the home of Romney Classical Institute had been built in 1846. It still serves the WVSDB as the central part of an administrative building. Deaf and blind students shared the same dormitories until the 1920s when the buildings of the defunct Potomac Academy were deeded to the state for a separate school for the blind.

Seaton Hall on the campus was dedicated to Charles D. Seaton on June 1, 1955. Seaton was one of the school's best known deaf educators. He was treasurer of the Gallaudet College Alumni Association from 1917 to 1947.

A bronze plaque memorializes the contributions of other outstanding deaf teachers and includes the names of

"Oh, teach, do I halfta?"

E. L. Chapin, Holdridge Chidester, A. Dudley Hays, John A. Boland, and Maurice Relihan. August P. Herdtfelder, Mrs. Arietta Robertson Casey, Malcolm J. Norwood, Dean Swaim, and Marvin S. Rood were teachers at the school. Rood was one of the founders of the Jr. National Association of the Deaf and Norwood left the school to join the Captioned Films for the Deaf where he is presently chief of the branch.

Loy E. Golladay was a graduate of the school. He attended the school six years before enrolling at Gallaudet College where he graduated at the age of 20. He taught at the WVSDB and at the American School and was editor of *The West Virginia Tablet* and *The American Era*. On his retirement from the American School, Golladay joined the faculty of the National Technical Institute for the Deaf and rose to the rank of full professor.

Oregon School for the Deaf
Salem

Opened: 1870

Founder: William S. Smith*

The Oregon School for the Education of Deaf Mutes, opened in 1870, was established by William S. Smith, a product of the New York School for the

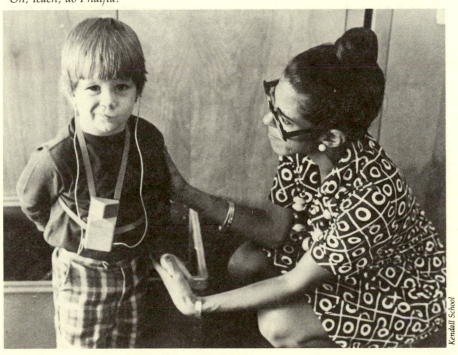

Deaf. With the assistance of other philanthropic individuals, he raised funds to begin the school and secured legislation making it a state institution. The State Legislature recognized the school and appropriated $4,000 for its support over the next two years. Smith taught at the school until 1876. He was principal from 1870 to 1874. Two other deaf men have been administrators there. Louis C. Tuck was acting principal from 1878 to 1880, and Thure A. Lindstrom served as acting superintendent in 1922 and again in 1926. Tuck graduated from the American School for the Deaf; Lindstrom from the Washington State School for the Deaf. Both were graduates of Gallaudet College. Lindstrom was honored by the college with a doctorate in 1955. A dormitory at the school is named for him.

In 1893 the school was placed under the State Board of Education. A new school was needed and land was purchased for that purpose. The school was at four different locations in and around Salem before the permanent site was acquired in 1910, closer to the center of town. Each move had been necessitated by increases in numbers of students and inadequacy of buildings and location. The first school had to close because the funds for rent ran out.

The superintendent with the longest tenure at the Oregon School was Dr. Marvin B. Clatterbuck, who retired recently after some 30 years in office. He received an honorary doctorate from Gallaudet College in 1968.

Thomas Ulmer, a teacher at the school for 40 years, is honored throughout the Northwest for his outstanding work with the Boy Scout troops at the School. He has trained 45 Eagle Scouts. A graduate of Gallaudet College, he is also a gifted poet.

Nebraska School for the Deaf
Omaha

Opened: 1872

Founder: State Legislature

The Nebraska School for the Deaf opened its doors in 1872, but education of the deaf was started earlier in 1867.

The Rev. H. W. Kuhns, the first Lutheran minister in Omaha, was a member of the local school board. He was approached by a Mr. Calhoun, who had a deaf daughter, with the request that he try to find a means of educating

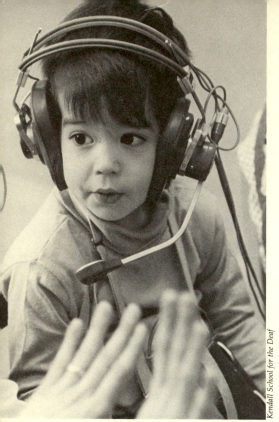

Kendall School for the Deaf

Randy Sugiyama listening for those elusive sounds.

the girl. The Rev. Mr. Kuhns made a study of the deaf and used his influence to have a house rented in 1867 for a school. William French, a deaf teacher, was appointed principal.

Kuhns approached the State Legislature for funds to build a suitable institution. The legislature adopted an act establishing the school but funds were not appropriated until 1869. The new school plant did not open its doors until 1872.

Professor French left before the new school opened but another deaf teacher, F. L. Reid, a graduate of the National College for Deaf-Mutes (now Gallaudet College), was a member of the new teaching staff. He was an outstanding teacher, and he sent the first Nebraska School graduate to college.

New buildings appeared from time to time as the school grew. It probably attained the height of its early development during the superintendency of Frank W. Booth (1911 to 1936). Booth was a son of Edmund Booth, one of the founders of the National Association of the Deaf. Among the deaf of Nebraska, though, he was considered something of a traitor to the environment which had nurtured him, for he installed a rigid oral method in the school. Before taking the Nebraska position he had been superintendent of the Volta Bureau in Washington.

In 1931 the school's basketball team made sports history by winning an all-classes state basketball championship, an achievement unequalled among schools for the deaf. To accomplish that feat, Nebraska a Class D school in sports competition, had to beat schools with much larger enrollments. The team was coached by Nick Petersen, a graduate of the school, who was well known in Nebraska-Iowa semi-pro circles as a baseball pitcher. The school won a state track title under Coach George Propp, and its eight-man football team coached by Jack R. Gannon was the first among schools for the deaf to post an undefeated season. Scott Cuscaden and Charles Marshall, who played for the Akron Goodyear Silents, were NSD graduates.

In the 1960s much of the school plant was rebuilt. The vocational education program during those years won a number of trophies and awards in state-wide competition.

George Propp, graduate of the school and former teacher, earned a doctor's degree from the University of Nebraska. He served one term as president of the Convention of American Instructors of the Deaf.

Lutheran School for the Deaf
Detroit, Michigan

Opened: 1874

Founder: The Lutheran Church

The Detroit Lutheran School for the Deaf had its beginnings in Royal Oak when a group of Lutheran Christians organized the German Evangelical Lutheran Orphans' Assistance Society to establish an orphanage.

The superintendent of the orphanage was a pastor named G. Speckhardt, who once had been a teacher of the deaf in Germany. When the orphanage opened, a number of orphans were received. Two of the children were not orphans. They were deaf girls, who had been brought by their parents in hopes that Pastor Speckhardt would teach them and prepare them for their confirmation.

Pastor Speckhardt accepted the two girls, and news spread that he was teaching them. Soon other deaf children were being sent to the orphanage. By the summer of 1874 there were 20 deaf pupils and only ten orphans. The church then ordered that the orphan-

age be converted to a "Christian school for the education of deaf children." In 1875 the school was moved to Detroit, where new buildings were erected, with accommodations sufficient for 112 pupils.

The school derives its financial support from fees paid by parents and in free-will offerings.

Colorado School for the Deaf and the Blind

Opened: 1874

Founder: Jonathan R. Kennedy

The snow-topped Rocky Mountains loom in the background of the Colorado School for the Deaf and the Blind, situated on a gentle slope just east of the city of Colorado Springs. The school opened its doors on April 8, 1874, as "The Colorado Institute for the Education of Mutes" in a frame structure on Cucharras Street. Ten acres of the present campus were donated by the Colorado Springs Land Company. The school moved to the site in 1876. Seven students enrolled on opening day and six more followed the first year. In 1877 a law was passed to admit blind students.

Jonathan R. Kennedy, who was instrumental in the founding of the school, was the father of three deaf girls. He had been steward of the Kansas School for the Deaf.

One of CSDB's pupils, deaf and blind Lottie Sullivan, participated in the 1904 World's Fair at St. Louis, Missouri, demonstrating the learning ability of deaf/blind students. The school and Lottie won gold medals for the demonstration. One of Lottie's teachers was Mrs. George W. Veditz.

George William Veditz, seventh president of the National Association of the Deaf, was connected with the school for many years. Tom L. Anderson, the fifth president, and Mervin D. Garretson, the 21st president, were graduates of the school, and Byron B. Burnes, 16th president, began his teaching career there.

Mrs. Ethel Taylor Hall, wife of the second president of Gallaudet College, was a graduate of CSDB.

In 1969 the deaf and blind students were separated but remained on the same campus.

For one of the smaller schools, the Colorado School has had an especially effective sports program. In 1971 and 1972, its football team was undefeated, and in 1977 it won the state Class A championship. Two of the school's outstanding athletes went on to Gallaudet College and later became nationally known as coaches. Louis M. Byouk was coach and counselor in the California School at Berkeley and Louis A. Dyer coached the Los Angeles Club for the Deaf team to a record number of American Athletic Association of the Deaf basketball championships.

Cincinnati Public School for the Deaf

Opened: 1875

Founder: Robert P. McGregor*

The Cincinnati Public School for the Deaf was organized in 1875 to serve those pupils whose parents did not wish to send to the Ohio School for the Deaf in Columbus. Robert P. McGregor was the first principal. For a few years the state appropriated funds to board students but this practice was dropped and the school continued as a day program.

McGregor was chairman of the first national convention of deaf persons which met in Cincinnati in 1880 and led to the founding of the National Association of the Deaf. McGregor was elected the first NAD president and served one term.

Deafened at the age of eight, McGregor was educated at the Ohio School for the Deaf and Gallaudet College, graduating in the same class as Amos Draper and Wells L. Hill, the Massachusetts newspaper publisher. McGregor left the Cincinnati School in 1881 and returned to his alma mater where he taught until 1920, retiring on a pension. He was struck and killed by an automobile on the rainy evening of December 21, 1926.

New York State School for the Deaf
Rome

Opened: 1875

Founder: Alphonso Johnson*, The Rev. Thomas Gallaudet, and 81 citizens.

The first steps toward the organization of a school for the deaf in Rome, New York, were taken when Alphonso

Perkins Hall at the Rochester School in New York.

Rochester School for the Deaf

Johnson appeared in Rome and proposed to establish a school. Johnson was a deaf man and a graduate of the New York School for the Deaf, where he had taught for some years.

Dr. Thomas Gallaudet assisted with Mr. Johnson's efforts. He was the eldest son of The Rev. Thomas Hopkins Gallaudet, and served as Episcopal missionary to the deaf in the northwestern area.

Mr. Johnson and the Rev. Gallaudet succeeded in gaining the interest of a number of the leading businessmen of Rome and a school was established in 1875. It was called the Central New York Institution for Deaf-Mutes. Dr. Gallaudet became the first trustee and Mr. Johnson the first superintendent.

In 1888, through the beneficence of the legislature of New York State, an appropriation of $40,000 was granted

43

the Institution for the erection of a main building, a hospital, a boiler house and a principal's residence.

In the 1960s the name was changed to the Central New York School for the Deaf, and finally to the New York State School for the Deaf.

It is said that the New York School organized the first deaf Boy Scout troop in the United States. The Rev. Silas J. Hirte is a member of the school's Advisory Board.

Rochester School for the Deaf
Rochester, New York

Opened: 1876

Founder: Mr. and Mrs. Gilman H. Perkins

The Rochester School for the Deaf owes its existence to Mr. and Mrs. Gilman H. Perkins, who had a deaf daughter. Mrs. Perkins engaged the services of a young Maryland School for the Deaf teacher, named Mary Hart Nodine, to tutor her deaf daughter. The Perkins later became acquainted with Zenas F. Westervelt, Miss Nodine's fiance, who was a teacher at the New York School for the Deaf (Fanwood). When the young couple married, the Perkins encouraged the Westervelts to start a private school in Rochester. The Perkins and others guaranteed its support.

Meanwhile, Westervelt, who had grown up on the campus of the Ohio School for the Deaf where his mother was matron, had done a survey of deaf children residing in the western part of the state who were not in school. He identified 112. These figures indicated a need for another school as NYSD was overcrowded. Rochester appeared the logical site for the school. A meeting was called by the mayor, and attended by interested citizens and the Rev. Dr. Thomas Gallaudet. Dr. Gallaudet, who was a member of the Board of Directors of NYSD, offered a resolution to found a school in Rochester to be known as the Western New York Institution for Deaf-Mutes. The school was recognized as part of the public school system of the state, but it was a private school and retained its eleemosynary character. In 1919 the school's name was changed to the Rochester School for the Deaf.

Westervelt was hired as the first superintendent. He believed that the continued use of signs interfered with deaf children's grasp and use of English. He introduced what was then referred to as "The Great Innovation," a system based on English, spoken, fingerspelled, and written. Westervelt's system became universally known as "The Rochester Method" and is still in use at the school today although it has been modified to meet the communication needs of individual students.

The school is situated on the eastern bank of the Genesee River. During its 100 years of existence it has had only five superintendents. In the mid 1960s the school underwent a multi-million dollar building program. Many of the buildings on the campus are named for benefactors or former superintendents.

Robert S. Menchel and Robert A. Bohli, two RSD alumni, are members of the school's Board of Directors.

Chicago Day Schools for the Deaf
Chicago

Opened: 1875

Founder: Philip A. Emery*

Philip A. Emery left the Kansas School, which he had founded, and moved to Chicago in the 1870s. Since David Greenberger's school for deaf children had been wiped out by the Great Chicago Fire of 1871, and Greenberger had dropped the idea of conducting a school, Emery petitioned the Chicago Board of Education for one. He argued that deaf children had a right to an education near their homes, a refrain still heard in modern times. The Board agreed with him. In January 1875, the Chicago Day School opened on Van Buren Street with Emery as principal. During the first years the school received state appropriations, but they were discontinued in 1887 and the Chicago Public School system assumed responsibility for support. At first there was one central school; later Emery started schools in districts near the pupils' homes with one central advance class. Emery resigned the principalship after seventeen years in 1892, but continued to teach several more years. Lars M. Larson, founder of the New Mexico School and James E. Gallaher, author of "Representative Deaf Persons" (1898) taught at the Chicago schools. Critics called the Emery schools "The Emery Family Trust."

Emery wrote and printed a number of books and pamphlets, many of them religious works. "Paddle Your Own Canoe" was an autobiography, and "Who Killed Cock Robin" was a pamphlet criticizing pure oral teaching. He made a comfortable living from the books. Emery died in 1907.

Rhode Island School for the Deaf
Providence

Opened: 1876

Founder: Mrs. Henry Lippitt

When four-year-old Jeanie Lippitt became deaf from scarlet fever in Providence, Rhode Island, the governor was the first to know about it—he was her father. He also learned that there was no school for deaf children in the state. Through the efforts of his wife, a class for deaf children was started in 1876. The following year the state took over responsibility of the school.

After 15 years the school outgrew its private residence and an appeal was made to the legislature for funds to build a school. Jeanie Lippitt, who had been taught orally by her mother, was invited to speak in favor of the bill and so impressed the legislators that they voted $50,000 to purchase land and construct a building. The school which Mrs. Lippitt had started became the Rhode Island Institute for the Deaf and the new school was placed under the control of a special board of trustees which included the governor and lieutenant governor. A law stipulated that all deaf children be taught by the oral method. Jeanie Lippitt was appointed to the board and remained a member until 1906. She died in 1940.

Henry Brenner is a graduate of the school. He attended the University of Rhode Island and earned a starting place on the football squad as guard. He was elected to the University's Hall of Fame. Brenner is a teacher, coach, and athletic director at the North Dakota School for the Deaf.

John Spellman was a 1944 graduate of the school. He received his B.A. degree from Gallaudet College and earned two master's degrees, one from Rhode Island College and one from California State University, Northridge. He returned to teach in 1958 and became director of the school's adult service program. He was active in the New England Gallaudet Association of the Deaf, adult education, and other

Governor Baxter State School for the Deaf, Mackworth Island, Maine.

organizations of the deaf. In 1976 he moved to Washington, D.C. to become program supervisor at the Kendall Demonstration Elementary School. He died of cancer in 1979. A tribute at the school memorializes him as the school's "most distinguished son."

Governor Baxter School for the Deaf
Portland, Maine

Opened: 1876

Founder: Portland School Board and Mary True

The Gov. Baxter School calls itself the "Easternmost School for the Deaf" in the United States. It is also the only school located on an island. The school began as the Portland School for the Deaf in 1897. Miss Mary True, who had taught Mabel Hubbard (who later married Alexander Graham Bell), was the first teacher.

In 1957 a new school was built on Mackworth Island in Casco Bay near Portland. This island was the former summer home of the Baxter Family. The school is named for Percival P. Baxter, who gave the island to the school.

The school added a high school department in 1967. Until that year Maine students continued their education beyond the ninth grade at the American School in West Hartford or at a public high school. In 1968 a work study program and vocational program were added.

In the summer of 1965 a workshop for interpreting for deaf people was held on the island. This workshop resulted in the publication of one of the earliest manuals on interpreting for deaf persons. In 1966 the school sponsored the New England Deaf Scouts Jamboree. In 1971 the school was host to the Eastern Junior National Association of the Deaf Youth Conference.

The school's literary and drama association is named for Melville Ballard, a native of Maine. He was the first deaf person to earn a degree at Gallaudet College.

Gallaudet School for the Deaf
St. Louis, Missouri

Opened: 1878

Founder: Delos A. Simpson*
and others

Samuel Brant, the father of a deaf child; Delos A. Simpson, a deaf man; and other spirited citizens have been credited with founding the St. Louis School for the Deaf.

Delos A. Simpson was one of at least three deaf brothers who gradually lost their hearing. Born in 1852, he was educated at the Michigan School for the Deaf and at Gallaudet College. In the fall of 1878 he went to St. Louis, Missouri, with a letter of introduction from Dr. Edward Miner Gallaudet, president of Gallaudet College. There he became involved with Brant and other concerned citizens and they founded this school. There were eight pupils in the first class. Simpson was appointed principal. He lived with the Brant family and was paid a salary of $50.00 a month. He held the position until ill health forced him to resign in 1889. He died not long afterwards at the age of 40.

Simpson was succeeded as principal by Robert P. McGregor who held the post only one year. In 1891 James H. Cloud became principal. Cloud was very active in the community, and his leadership brought much attention to the school. Cloud was deafened as a youth, but retained some hearing; his sons communicated with him by talking very loudly. Three years after becoming principal of the St. Louis School he was ordained a Protestant Episcopal priest as a "hearing" man at the insistence of his bishop. He orga-

45

New England Industrial School for Deaf-Mutes in Massachusetts in the 1890s. The name was later changed to the Beverly School for the Deaf.

nized the St. Thomas Mission for the Deaf in St. Louis which eventually grew into the third largest mission of its kind in the country. He ministered to deaf people in Missouri, Kentucky, Colorado, and Nebraska and to blacks in the St. Louis area while continuing his responsibilities at the school. He served two terms as president of the National Association of the Deaf. Cloud was principal for 32 years. (Cloud's son, Daniel, became a noted and influential educator of the deaf. He was superintendent of the Arkansas, Kansas, Illinois, and New York (Fanwood) schools.)

The school moved to its present location in 1925.

Beverly School for the Deaf
Beverly, Massachusetts

Opened: 1879

Founder: William B. Swett*

William B. Swett, a deaf man and the father of a deaf daughter, was con-

cerned over the lack of educational opportunities for deaf children in the area where he lived. So with a small legacy and the backing of friends, including the Rev. Thomas Gallaudet, he purchased a 57-acre farm overlooking the Bass River near Beverly, Massachusetts. There he opened the New England Industrial School for Deaf-Mutes. Swett became the first superintendent, his wife Margaret, the first matron, and Ralph H. Atwood, a deaf man, the principal. Swett's daughter, Nellie was an instructor.

Although organized in 1876 the school did not open until 1879 when ten deaf adults enrolled in the industrial arts program. The following year an academic program was added and young deaf children enrolled.

On Swett's untimely death in 1884 and the resignation of Atwood, Nellie Swett became the principal. She died in 1904.

The industrial program was eventually phased out, and in 1922 the name of the school was changed to Beverly after the city in which it is

located.

Richard Thompson, a deaf psychologist, was elected to the school's Board of Trustees in 1975.

Pennsylvania School for the Deaf
Scranton

Opened: 1883

Founder: Jacob M. Koehler*

Jacob M. Koehler left Gallaudet College in his sophomore year intent on starting a day school in his hometown, Scranton, Pennsylvania. The school was formed under a local board, and Koehler became principal. In its third year the board decided to make the school a state school and, unfortunately for Koehler, the pure oral method of instruction was adopted. Koehler lost his job. The school was known as the Scranton Oral School for many years.

Koehler entered the ministry and was ordained in 1887 as a Protestant Episcopal priest. Upon the death of the

Rev. Henry Syle, Koehler became pastor of the All Soul's Church for the Deaf in Philadelphia, where he stayed until his 1920 retirement. Koehler was noted for his "brilliant mind and great scholastic ability." He was fluent in German, French, and Dutch. Koehler was the fifth president of the National Association of the Deaf. He died in 1922.

Today the Scranton School is once again under the administration of a deaf man, Dr. Victor H. Galloway. Galloway is a graduate of the South Carolina School for the Deaf and Spartanburg High School. He holds undergraduate and master's degrees from Gallaudet College and San Fernando Valley State College and an Ed.D. from the University of Arizona.

South Dakota School for the Deaf
Sioux Falls

Opened: 1880

Founder: Rev. Thomas B. Berry

Deaf children attended the Iowa School for the Deaf at Council Bluffs before a school was built for them in the Dakota Territory. The Territory paid Iowa $5.00 a week for each pupil. In December, 1880, the Rev. Thomas B. Berry, an Episcopal minister, opened the first school in the Dakota Territory in a private home. He had taught at the New York and Maryland Schools and he was married to a deaf woman. Berry became the first superintendent and Miss Jennie Wright, a teacher from the Nebraska School, became the first teacher. Initially, the school was supported by donations. When Berry's wife died, he left to return East with his three children. Miss Wright became the teacher and superintendent. However, she gave up those positions after only a few days when she married Daniel Mingus. She was succeeded by James Simpson, her deaf brother-in-law. Simpson remained superintendent from 1881-1903. Miss Dora Donald succeeded him and served from 1903 to 1908 as one of the earliest women superintendents of a school for the deaf in the country.

Simpson's son, Howard W., was also superintendent of the school. E. S. Tillinghast later headed the school. Tillinghast's father, his father-in-law, his brother, and his wife were all connected with education of the deaf. Tillinghast's son and daughter continued the family's long tradition. The son, Edward W., was superintendent of the Arizona State School for the Deaf. Tillinghast's daughter, Hilda, was a teacher of the deaf and the wife of Boyce R. Williams, a deaf man.

When the Dakota Territory was divided into two states, a second school for the deaf was established at Devils Lake, North Dakota.

Nellie Zabel Willhite, who attended the SDSD, was the first woman pilot in South Dakota to earn a pilot's license in 1928.

Roy Holcomb, "the father of Total Communication," taught at the SDSD for several years.

Marie H. Katzenbach School for Deaf
West Trenton, New Jersey

Opened: 1883

Founder: State Legislature

The Marie H. Katzenbach School for the Deaf is the New Jersey School for the Deaf, by which name it was known until 1965, when the legislature renamed it in honor of Mrs. Katzenbach. She had served on the State Board of Education for 43 years, during 18 of which she was president of the Board. The school was always one of her special interests.

The original site of the New Jersey School was amid a number of state buildings in Trenton, in a building which had been a soldiers' home. In 1917 the Board appointed Dr. Alvin E. Pope as superintendent, a position he

The New Jersey School for the Deaf before its move to West Trenton.

Ronald Douglas

47

The Evansville, Indiana School for the Deaf.

accepted on the condition that a new school be built on a new site. As a result, the school began moving to a suburban site in West Trenton in 1923. The move was completed three years later. The first Eastern Schools for the Deaf basketball tournament was held at this school in 1927.

The attention of most of the adult deaf of the United States was focused upon persons and events at the New Jersey School from before the beginning of the century until around 1930. *The Silent Worker* was published at the school through most of these years, edited by George S. Porter, nationally known and highly respected printing instructor at the school. It was the leading publication of the deaf world.

The school has maintained one of the finest vocational training departments in a school for the deaf. Its printing department was one of the first to introduce photoengraving.

The teaching staff included some of the most capable deaf teachers in the country.

As a national publication, *The Silent Worker* became too large and compli-

cated to serve effectively as a school project. It was discontinued in 1929 when Editor Porter retired.

Dr. Pope retired in 1939 and was succeeded by Charles M. Jochem, who granted the NAD permission to resume publication of *The Silent Worker* in 1949. Under Dr. Jochem's direction the school program was highly developed and new buildings were constructed. The academic and vocational departments became state certified.

Utah Schools for the Deaf and the Blind
Ogden

Opened: 1884

Founder: Henry C. White*

The Utah School for the Deaf was established 12 years before Utah became a state. It was begun as a class at the University of Deseret in Salt Lake City. Henry C. White, a deaf man from Boston and a Gallaudet graduate was hired as teacher and principal. The school opened with one pupil, Elizabeth Wood, and within a month four students were attending the class. In 1886 White began to board the students in his home. Two years later the State Legislature passed a law making the school part of the public school system and a branch of the University, to be known as the Institute of Deaf-Mutes. The legislation provided funds for the construction of a building on the University campus. White remained as principal for five years. He was replaced by a hearing teacher from Kansas. White returned to Boston where he became a printer and published the *National Gazette*. In 1911 he moved west again and founded the Arizona State School for the Deaf and the Blind in Tucson.

In 1896 the school was moved to a 57-acre tract in Ogden, the second larg-

est city in the state. In 1959 the school started an Extension Department for deaf children in different parts of the state. In 1962 the school initiated a dual track educational program offering an oral/aural program in one department and a total communication program in another.

Robert G. Sanderson, a former president of the National Association of the Deaf, Ned C. Wheeler and the Wenger Twins, Ray and Arthur, are graduates of the Utah School.

Kenneth C. Burdett retired in 1974 after spending 53 years as a student and later a teacher at the school. The last 12 years he was the curriculum co-ordinator of the Total Communication Department.

Northern New York School for the Deaf
Malone

Opened: 1884

Founder: Henry C. Rider*

Concerned about the lack of educational opportunities for deaf children in the northern New York area, Henry C. Rider, a graduate of the New York School for the Deaf (Fanwood) set about starting one in 1883. There were six schools for the deaf then in existence, the nearest being the school at Rome, but with an enrollment of 170 it had no room for more students. Rider was aided in his efforts by the Rev. Thomas Gallaudet, eldest son of the founder of the Hartford School.

Rider met with many difficulties and frustrations. There was opposition to another school for the deaf in the state and opponents managed to limit the enrollment to twelve students before that restriction was rescinded. In searching for deaf children not in school, Rider met with mixed responses. As he described it: "The re-

The Utah School for the Deaf, Ogden.

sponses were varied. In some there existed a true sense of gratefulness and an eager desire to embrace the proffered opportunities. Others seemed indifferent and were most exasperating; while some refused to delegate to others the care of their dear ones."

The school finally opened its doors on September 10, 1884 with an enrollment of twelve students. Enrollment grew quickly and steadily and by December there were twice as many students and by the end of the year there were thirty-four. Two additional teachers had to be hired. One of them was Alphonso Johnson who had earlier been active in the establishment of the Central New York School for the Deaf in Rome. In 1887 the New York legislature appropriated $40,000 to purchase land and erect buildings for the school.

Rider resigned as superintendent in 1902 passing on the reins of the school to his son, Edward C. Rider. The elder Rider died on May 16, 1913 in Syracuse, New York.

The school is no longer in existence.

Florida School for the Deaf and the Blind
St. Augustine

Opened: 1885

Founder: Thomas H. Coleman*

While studying at Gallaudet College, Thomas Coleman began a correspondence with Governor W. D. Bloxham of Florida in 1882, calling the governor's attention to the fact that Florida was the only state in the Union at that time that did not have a school for the deaf. Bloxham was interested in filling that void and recommended that the State Legislature fund a school for the deaf and the blind which the legislature did. Bids were opened for the location

of the school and the City of St. Augustine offered the state $1,000 in cash and three acres of land and was selected as the site of the new school. Today the school is located on a 70-acre campus of which about half is reclaimed marshland.

When the school opened in February, 1885, Coleman was offered the post of administrator, but he declined because of poor health, asking instead to be head teacher. He taught at the school for a few years then accepted a teaching position at the South Carolina School, his alma mater. Coleman's daughter, Grace Coleman Park, was dean of women at Gallaudet College. She was a member of the Florida School Board of Trustees from 1963 to 1979.

The first graduates of the school were Artemus W. Pope and Cora Carlton, who married shortly after graduation. Their son, Verle, served many years as a state senator and as president of the senate. (A three building complex for intermediate deaf students was dedicated the Verle A. Pope Complex in 1980).

Artemus W. Pope returned to his alma mater as head of the printing department and taught at the school for many years. In the late 1940s the school's Industrial Arts Building was named for him. He was present at the dedication and snipped the ceremonial ribbon using the same scissors he had used as a student more than half a century before.

Governor Bloxham's interest in the school was permanent. When he died, he included the school in his will, bequeathing money to assist those graduates who were interested in continuing their studies.

In 1976 and 1979 the school's football team was chosen National Football Champions by Art Kruger, sports editor of *The Deaf American*. In 1978 the

school's track team won the State Class A Track Championship.

Mrs. Alva Dean Pritchard, an alumna, is a member of the school's Board of Trustees.

New Mexico School for the Deaf
Santa Fe

Opened: 1887

Founder: Lars M. Larson*

With a small legacy left him by his mother, Lars M. Larson moved to Santa Fe, New Mexico, where he operated a private school for deaf children from 1885 to 1887. In February, 1887, the Territorial Legislature passed an Act creating a Territorial Asylum for the Deaf and Dumb. The Territory provided funds to purchase a farm tract on Carrillos Road and the school opened in a two-story adobe farm house. It was the first publicly owned educational institution in the Territory. But the Act did not guarantee financial support, and the school had no regular means of support until tax-paying railroads were built in New Mexico near the end of that century. During those lean years Larson was forced to seek donations, dip into his own pocket, and sometimes operate the school as a private institution in order to keep it open. In the 1890s, the Territorial Legislature appropriated funds for a new brick school building. The appropriation was not enough to complete the building and being unable to secure funds Larson used $5,000 of his own money to finish most of the building. The building was used for classrooms, dormitories, and office space until it was razed in 1936.

Congress deeded New Mexico land in 1898 and again when the Territory became a state in 1912. This land was

Utah School for the Deaf

divided among various educational institutions and the Miners Hospital at Raton. Much of the land held by the New Mexico School for the Deaf is held jointly with the New Mexico School for the Visually Handicapped. Much of this land is barren, but in the 1920s oil was discovered on some of it. Royalties from the sale of the oil are placed into a permanent state fund under the management of a state land commissioner and the income is used to support the school. In recording this incident, Dr. Thomas J. Dillon wrote: "Little did Congress realize how bountifully it was providing for New Mexico's deaf children."

Since its founding the school has had only four superintendents. Dr. Thomas J. Dillon, a New Mexican, was the first principal employed at the school. He held the position for 32 years. He was hired as principal in 1943 at a time "when deaf administrators were practically non-existent." At one time in the 1940s Dillon was the only deaf principal of a school for the deaf in the United States. Marvin Wolach, the school's supervising teacher before his retirement, called Dillon "Mr. NMSD." Dillon attained national prominence as an educator and for 20 years was an officer of the Convention of American Instructors of the Deaf. Gallaudet College awarded him a Doctor of Humane Letters in 1966. He and his wife, Florence, who began her teaching career in 1943 and who was the school's first librarian, retired at the close of the school year in 1975. In 1979 Dillon was appointed by the governor to a six-year term on the school's Board of Regents. Shortly afterwards he was elected secretary-treasurer of the Board.

The school's gymnasium is named for Lars M. Larson, the founder. The school has a large oil painting of him, a gift to the school from the Santa Fe Chapter of the Gallaudet College Alumni Association.

Washington State School for the Deaf
Vancouver

Opened: 1886

Founder: Territorial Legislature

The Washington School opened in 1886 as the Washington School for De-

fective Youth. At that time the school enrolled deaf, blind and mentally ill students. George Layton, a graduate of the Virginia School for the Deaf and the Blind and Gallaudet College, was hired as the first teacher. For many years since the school has maintained a consistently high percentage of deaf teachers. The school's current superintendent, Archie Stack, is hearing impaired.

A year before the school opened, the Rev. W. D. McFarland had started a private class for deaf children in Tacoma. Prior to that some students were sent to the Oregon School which had opened in 1870. McFarland later moved his class to Vancouver and they stayed in a hotel until the school opened.

The school's 17-acre campus is located on the original site of Fort Vancouver, high above the Columbia River. Fort Vancouver was once the headquarters of Hudson's Bay Company.

Watson Hall, the school's main building was designed by Olof Hanson, the deaf architect. Hunter Gymnasium, Divine Hall, Deer Hall, MacDonald Hall and Northrop Hall are named for deaf people. William S. Hunter, a graduate of the Michigan School for the Deaf, was the school's first coach. He taught at the school for 49 years. The gymnasium was named for him in 1938. Divine School, which houses the junior and senior high school departments, was named in honor of Louis and Belle Divine, a deaf couple who taught at the school for many years. Deer Hall honors Dewey H. Deer, an alumnus, an outstanding athlete, community leader, teacher and coach. Another residential hall is named for Della MacDonald, a houseparent and an employee of the school for nearly 40 years. Northrop Hall was named for Dr. Helen Northrop, a teacher for many years and the first principal of the school. Northrop Hall houses the elementary school department.

Emil Rath, who was a statistician with the U.S. Air Force and Alan B. Crammatte, author of *Deaf Persons in Professional Employment* and a former faculty member at Gallaudet College, are alumni of the Washington State School for the Deaf.

Eastern Iowa School for the Deaf
Dubuque

Opened: 1888

Founder: William M. DeCoursey French*

French was connected with the Nebraska School for the Deaf in Omaha, where he was principal from 1869 to 1871. He moved to Wyoming, where he persuaded the State Legislature to pass legislation founding a school for the deaf in 1885. A building was erected the following year, but no provisions were made for the continuing support of the school, which never opened. French moved to Iowa where he started a day school in Dubuque named the Eastern Iowa School for the Deaf, which was supported by contributions and other means. French was principal. The school folded some years later.

Born, raised, and educated in Indiana, French taught for six years (1860-1868) at the Indiana School for the Deaf before his move west to Omaha. He claimed credit for starting the Nebraska School for the Deaf, but school records give the credit to the State Legislature. Little else is known about him.

North Dakota School for the Deaf
Devils Lake

Opened: 1890

Founder: Anson R. Spear*

The enabling act which divided the Dakota Territory into two states, North and South Dakota, and admitted them into the Union in 1889 included provisions for the education of deaf and other handicapped children. Since the southern part of the Territory which became South Dakota already had a school in Sioux Falls, it remained for North Dakota to start one. To encourage this, the federal government granted 40,000 acres to the state. The land was sold, the money placed in a trust, and the income used for the school.

A bill drawn up by Anson R. Spear, a graduate of the Minnesota School for the Deaf, to establish the North Dakota School for the Deaf passed the State Legislature, but was vetoed by the governor. Supporters of the bill persisted and on the last day of the legislative

Memorial honoring Thomas H. Gallaudet at the Missouri School. The original statue stands in Hartford, Connecticut, near the site of the first school.

session, March 18, 1890, both houses passed the bill, making it law, "objections of the governor to the contrary notwithstanding." Spear became superintendent, and his wife, matron. Deaf architect Olof Hanson was hired to design the new school building. One of the first teachers hired was Alto M. Lowman, the first deaf woman to earn a degree from Gallaudet College.

Attendance for those deaf children between the ages of 11 and 21 was compulsory at the new school, under penalty of a $10 to $50 fine.

Spear resigned in 1895 and returned to Minneapolis where he started the Minneapolis Day School for the Deaf with an enrollment of 50 students on the first day. The school closed two years later.

Spear had earlier spent seven years working in the Minneapolis post office, working his way to head clerk, and had invented an envelope. He turned his attention to manufacturing the "Spear Safety Envelope" first under the Spear-Heywood Envelope Company and later under the Spear Safety Envelope Company in Minneapolis. The

business flourished, and Spear hired several deaf employees.

In 1913 Spear helped in the establishment of the Minnesota "Division for the Deaf of the State Bureau of Labor and Industries"—the first of its kind. At the time of his death, he had introduced bills in the U.S. House of Representatives and the U.S. Senate to establish a Department of the Deaf in the Federal Bureau of Labor.

Spear was stricken with apoplexy while riding on a trolley car on his way to a "Gallaudet Day" celebration. He died in December, 1917.

Cleveland Day School for the Deaf

Cleveland, Ohio

Opened: 1892

Founder: John H. Geary*

Geary was a post-lingual deaf person, a graduate of the New York School for the deaf and a teacher at the Arkansas School for the Deaf. Little else is known about him or his school.

Montana School for the Deaf and the Blind
Great Falls

Opened: 1893

Founder: State Legislature

The Montana School for the Deaf, Dumb, Blind, and Feebleminded opened in 1893, four years after Montana became a state. The institution received a grant from the state consisting of 50,000 acres of public lands to be used, sold, or leased for revenue. The school was started in Boulder.

The opening day of school found four deaf, four blind, and two mentally deficient children present.

In 1894, J. A. Tillinghast was chosen superintendent and two years later his brother, E. S. Tillinghast succeeded him, so the school got its start under this famous family, whose name appears in connection with other schools discussed in these pages. In 1895 the school was placed under the supervision of the State Board of Education.

In 1901 a separate building was constructed for the mentally deficient, but all students were still on the same grounds and often mixed together. The name was changed to the Montana

School for the Deaf and the Blind, but the mentally retarded soon outnumbered both the deaf and the blind, a fact which aroused resentment among the deaf citizenry of the state. They began agitating for separation of the deaf students from the retarded.

By 1935, the number of mentally deficient students at the institution had risen to 435, while there were only 91 deaf and 21 blind students. The adult deaf decided it was time to push forward with renewed vigor. Led by Archie R. Randles of Missoula, the Montana Association of the Deaf finally succeeded in having legislation passed providing for a separate school for the deaf and the blind, leaving the feebleminded at the Boulder institution. It was decided to establish the new school at Great Falls. The deaf and the blind were relocated there in 1937, with Edwin G. Peterson as president. He was the son of Peter N. Peterson, a teacher in the Minnesota School.

The entire school at Great Falls was housed in a single building until 1944 when Glenn I. Harris, principal in the Colorado School, became superintendent. During his administration some buildings were added and a neighboring farmer willed the school two handsome cottages on land adjacent to the school. These cottages are rented to teachers and the income is given to the students for their needs and enjoyment.

Mervin D. Garretson, a former NAD president, was principal of this school.

Minneapolis Day School for the Deaf
Minneapolis, Minnesota

Opened: 1895

Founder: Anson R. Spear*

Wesley Lauritsen calls Anson R. Spear "one of the most phenomenally successful deaf men who ever attended the Minnesota School for the Deaf." Born in the Province of Quebec, Canada in 1860, Spear moved to Iowa when he was nine years old and the following year to Minnesota. Spear became deaf when he was eleven years old from spinal meningitis. He attended the Minnesota School for the Deaf briefly, graduating in 1878. After a brief stint as a clerk at the Bureau of Census in Washington, D.C., Spear returned to Minneapolis where he found employment in the post office.

After about seven years working in the post office Spear moved to Devils Lake, North Dakota where he was successful in establishing the North Dakota School for the Deaf. He was superintendent of the school for five years. He resigned and returned to Minnesota where he was involved with a second school, the Minneapolis Day School for the Deaf. The school opened in October, 1895 with an enrollment of 50 students. For some reason the school was not a success and it closed its doors two years later. Spear became a successful businessman.

Oklahoma School for the Deaf
Sulphur

Opened: 1898

Founder: Mr. and Mrs. Ellsworth Long*

The first known effort to teach deaf children in Oklahoma was at a school for deaf and blind children at Fort Gibson, Indian Territory, around 1880. A couple named Lowery were the teachers. This school was originally founded for blind children of the Five Civilized Tribes, but deaf children were also admitted.

In 1898 a deaf couple named Mr. and Mrs. Ellsworth Long started the Terri-

An early class at the Oklahoma School, Grover C. Farquhar is the teacher.

torial School for the Education of the Deaf at Guthrie, and deaf children were transferred to this school from Fort Gibson. Long was a graduate of the Kansas School and Gallaudet College. His wife had been educated at the Indiana School. The Longs had difficulty administering the school, and they turned the management over to a man named H. C. Beamer, who be-

came the first superintendent. Beamer retained Long as principal and Mrs. Long as a teacher. About two years after Oklahoma achieved statehood in 1907 the legislature created a permanent school in Sulphur.

W. T. Griffing is the school's best-known alumnus. His association with the school spans more than three-quarters of a century, first as a student then as a teacher. In 1958 Griffing was selected by the Conference of Executives of American Schools for the Deaf to represent the deaf teachers of America at the International Congress on Modern Education Treatment of Deafness in Manchester, England. In 1961 he was chosen Murray County Teacher of the Year; he holds an honorary degree from Gallaudet College, his alma mater. His wife, Wendell, who retired in 1965, was also a teacher at the school. When Griffing retired as editor of the *Deaf Oklahoman* the paper lost its most popular column, "The Melting Pot." The school has a bust of Griffing. On the base is inscribed: "A giant who walked in our land and loved our children, giving us all laughter and wisdom."

Arlie Gray, a vocational principal at the Louisiana School, and Ray Butler, a vocational principal at the Florida School, are graduates of the Oklahoma School. Other graduates include Ray Kolander who is on the Gallaudet College faculty, Herschel Johnson, an artist specializing in Indian pictures, and Mabel McDaniel Morgan, for many

Administration building, Oklahoma School for the Deaf, Sulphur.

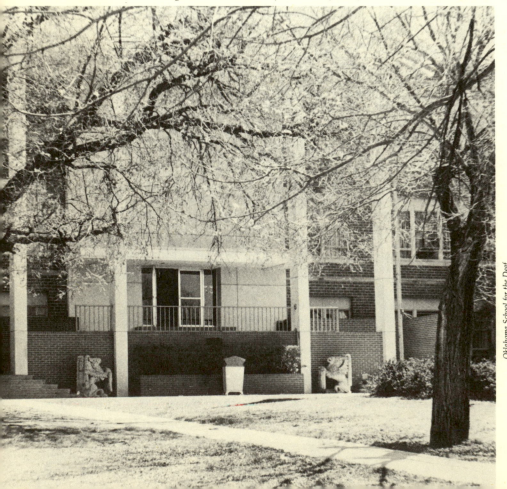

Richard Reed/The Missouri Record

Oklahoma School for the Deaf

years dean of girls at the Florida School. Melvin and Tince Brown are prominent cattlemen and dairy farmers, and Harold Moeller operates one of the state's largest and best farms.

Diamond Head School, Hawaii

Honolulu

Opened: 1902

Founder: Mission Helpers of the Sacred Heart

The state school for the deaf in Hawaii is known as the Diamond Head School, since it is but a short distance from Diamond Head the extinct volcano that is recognized around the world as the landmark of Honolulu.

The Mission Helpers of the Sacred Heart started educational facilities for the deaf in 1902 but the permanent school was not established until 1914,

when it was approved by an act of the Territorial Legislature.

Originally the school provided instruction for deaf, blind and mentally defective children, but in 1920 the mentally defective children were removed to other facilities.

The school was conducted for many years as an oral school, but, as in most schools, more flexible means of communication have been adopted. Classes are small and a considerable amount of individual attention is possible, employing the methods of instruction best suited to individual needs.

The school has had one or more deaf teachers on its staff for several decades. Alden Ravn, a Gallaudet graduate, went from the United States to teach there before World War II. He returned after Pearl Harbor to teach in the Illinois School for the Deaf for many years. He was followed to Hawaii by Hershel Mouton, a product of the Texas School and Gallaudet College.

Idaho School for the Deaf and the Blind
Gooding

Opened: 1906

Founder: State Board of Education

The Board of Education of the State of Idaho opened the first school for deaf children in 1906 in an old school building in Boise, on land now occupied by the state capitol. The enrollment included 23 deaf and a few blind pupils.

In December, 1908, the building was destroyed by fire and the school continued in 1910 in a hotel building.

In 1909, Frank R. Gooding, a former governor and later a United States senator, was busy with numerous efforts to establish a town named Gooding. He was a wealthy cattle and sheepraiser, interested in education and especially education of the deaf, since he had a deaf nephew. He knew that the school in Boise was not firmly estab-

A primary class at the New York School for the Deaf, ca. 1930.

53

lished, so in 1909 he offered land in Gooding as a site for the State School for the Deaf and the Blind.

After the fire in Boise, the Board accepted Mr. Gooding's offer and construction of a new school was started in Gooding. It helped Mr. Gooding realize his dream of seeing a city named Gooding. An administration building was first erected and other buildings followed.

The first superintendent of the Idaho School was James Watson, the father-in-law of E. S. Tillinghast, member of a noted family of educators of the deaf.

The school had only two buildings and by 1915 they had become overcrowded, so construction of other buildings was begun and continued through 1920.

Miss Ethel M. Hilliard, a graduate of the University of Chicago, was appointed superintendent in 1920, one of the first women superintendents of a school for the deaf. (Mrs. H. T. Poore of Tennessee and Mrs. Bess M. Riggs of Arkansas became superintendents at about the same time.)

Burton W. Driggs became superintendent in 1937. He inaugurated a program of improvements and new buildings which continued for 14 years and resulted in a practically new plant, completed in 1951.

Don G. Pettingill and Jack Downey are two of the school's most successful alumni. Pettingill operated a printing establishment and is a former president of the National Association of the Deaf. Downey is a successful Boise, Idaho, businessman.

Virginia State School for the Deaf at Hampton
Hampton, Virginia

Opened: 1909

Founder: William C. Ritter*

William C. Ritter had been deafened as a youth when ill with scarlet fever. He was educated at the Virginia School for the Deaf and Blind in Staunton.

Ritter, a printer, was approached one day by a black woman who offered to do his family's laundry if he would teach her deaf son. There was no school available for the boy.

After two futile attempts, Ritter persuaded the State Legislature to appropriate funds to establish a school for black deaf and blind children. The legislature voted to give Ritter $5,000 in 1906 to begin the school, but a careless clerical oversight delayed the funds until 1908. The school opened a year later in September with 23 children. Ritter was superintendent and teacher. The first deaf teachers he hired were R. Aumon Bass and Miss Mary Agnew Scott. The school was originally located in Newport News; later it was moved to Hampton.

Ritter was a competent adminsitrator praised by two governors for the businesslike manner in which he ran the school. Governor Pollard called the school "One of the outstanding institutions of its kind." When Ritter resigned in 1938, the school's enrollment was 74, and it was receiving $34,000 in annual appropriations. He died February 10, 1952 after a long illness. Ritter is buried in Greenlawn Cemetery, not far from the school he founded and loved.

Arizona School for the Deaf and the Blind
Tucson

Opened: 1911

Founded: Henry C. White*

Henry C. White, a Boston printer who graduated from Gallaudet College and then founded the Utah School for the Deaf and the Blind, went to Tucson, Arizona, in 1911 to start a school. He formed a class as a department at the University of Arizona—an arrangement similar to the one in Utah. White was appointed principal, and his daughter, Harriet T. White (Mrs. W. J. Bray), was hired as matron and teacher. That was a period when there was a bitter struggle going on between pure oralists and those who supported the combined system as White did. After only three years as head of the school he resigned in 1914.

In 1967 The Phoenix Day School for the Deaf was opened as a branch of the Arizona School.

In 1976 ASSDB's eight-man football team won the State Class C football championship. The team was coached by John Milford.

In the 1930s the superintendent of the school was Dr. Robert D. Morrow, who had graduated from the Normal Department of Gallaudet College and had taught in the Iowa School for the Deaf. He was one of the long list of superintendents who came from Westminster College, Fulton, Missouri. Morrow made such an impression as head of the Arizona School that he was induced by the city of Tucson to accept the superintendency of the city school system in 1941.

Edward W. Tillinghast succeeded Morrow and remained for more than 30 years. He was the last of that famous family of educators.

One of the graduates of the Arizona School was Angel Acuna, one of the finest deaf basketball players of all time. He played on the championship teams in the United States and, since he was of Mexican ancestry, he found his way onto the basketball team which represented Mexico in the Olympic Games.

Central Institute for the Deaf
St. Louis

Opened: 1914

Founder: Dr. Max A. Goldstein

The Central Institute for the Deaf is one of the leading pure oral schools in this country. It was founded by Dr. Max A. Goldstein, a St. Louis otologist who became interested in teaching the deaf. He opened the school in two rooms over his medical offices, but it developed into a research center, as well as a school, and a center for the training of teachers. It draws its support from donations, endowments, tuition fees, and other such means.

The guiding policy of the school is indicated by the following statement which appeared in a brochure: "The normal child needs only to be taught how to give meaning to the sounds he hears and produces through imitation. The deaf child, however, must be taught how to make sound and then how to lip read in order to communicate with those around him. The ultimate goal of the oral method employed at Central Institute is to eliminate any barrier between the handicapped child and normal persons in order that he may fit successfully into a normal social, economic, and educational environment."

The Central Institute is across the street from world-famous Forest Park in St. Louis, giving the children a rare opportunity for recreational activities and trips to museums, exhibits, and

The John Tracy Clinic, Los Angeles, California

botanical gardens.

Many of the graduates of the school have been highly successful in numerous lines of employment. Some have gone to Gallaudet College, and others have attended other colleges and universities.

The John Tracy Clinic
Los Angeles

Opened: 1942

Founder: Mrs. John Tracy

In the educational system of this country there are schools and classes, and clinics for parents of deaf children which admit pre-school deaf children and instruct their parents in means of communicating with and assisting them.

The most noted of these pre-school clinics is the John Tracy Clinic in Los Angeles, California. It was founded in 1942 by Mrs. Spencer Tracy, wife of the famous actor, and named in honor of their deaf son.

The primary purpose of the John Tracy Clinic is to train the parents, many of whom are at a loss as to how to work with their deaf children. Parents are taught to communicate with the deaf child and to include him in family activities. The method of communication stressed is speech and lipreading. Through the Tracy Clinic many parents have learned to make their deaf child feel that he is a member of the family.

The Clinic is well known for its correspondence course. The course was developed for parents who lived too far away to visit the Clinic. This is probably the most important of the Clinic's activities, for it has given assurance to thousands and thousands of parents that their deaf children can be educated and that they can lead a happy, full and useful life.

California School for the Deaf
Riverside

Opened: 1953

Founder: State Legislature

With the rapid expansion in population in California following World War II it was becoming evident that the state school for the deaf in Berkeley could not meet the needs of all the deaf children of the state. A second school was needed. Action to seek establishment of a new school in the southern part of the state was begun mostly by the members of the deaf community of the Los Angeles area. They held a meeting in 1945 and established a committee with one of their members, Perry E. Seely, as chairman.

Subsequent activity by the committee attracted the interest of other citizens and of members of the legislature. The California Association of the Deaf assisted with the effort. The legislature passed a bill to establish the new school in 1949 and the city of Riverside, some 60 miles east of Los Angeles, was chosen as the site.

In 1950, before construction had begun, Dr. Richard G. Brill was named superintendent. The first unit of the school was completed in 1953, and 56 children entered the school in February. By the beginning of the 1953-1954 year there was room for 225 students. The school was formally dedicated on November 1, 1953. By 1958 the enrollment had exceeded 500 and the school had become one of the largest residential schools for the deaf in the world, ranking close to the top in the numbers of students it sends to college each year.

Model Secondary School for the Deaf
Washington, D.C.

Opened: 1969

Founder: U.S. Congress

The Model Secondary School for the deaf is one of two schools founded by the U.S. Congress, the other being the National Technical Institute for the Deaf in Rochester, New York.

This school was founded to serve as a living laboratory school, to conduct research, and to develop and disseminate materials—to provide an exemplary comprehensive secondary program for deaf students.

It is part Gallaudet College's Pre-College Programs which is headed by Dr. Robert R. Davila. The Pre-College Programs (Kendall Demonstration Elementary School and MSSD) occupy approximately 25 of the college's 94 acres. In 1976 the school moved into its new academic building. In 1977 the dormitories were completed. The school was built to serve a minimum of 500 students and has one of the most modern school plants in the country.

This federally-funded school derives its primary population from the District of Columbia and five surrounding states: Pennsylvania, Maryland, Virginia, West Virginia, and Delaware. As space permits the school accepts students from the other U.S. states and territories. Approximately 75 percent of the students are in the residence program.

The Pre-College Programs serve students from the age of onset of deafness through age 19. The MSSD annual report states: "These two schools seek to develop, test, evaluate, and disseminate nationally top-quality models of education for deaf youngsters."

California State University at Northridge (CSUN)
Northridge, California

In 1962, a leadership training program was established at California State University, Northridge, California, (then called San Fernando Valley State College.) Participants were admitted from all parts of the United States; they completed a year of intensive training, leading to a master's degree in educational administration and supervision. The members of the first two classes were all hearing persons, but since 1964 nearly 100 deaf students have completed the program.

The program was highly successful from the beginning; its graduates assuming responsible positions in educational channels and rehabilitation agencies throughout the country. It was especially helpful to its deaf participants, enabling them to qualify for promotions and administrative positions in the schools where they were employed, or in other schools. A number of them have become supervisors and principals, and at least three have become superintendents.

With the program in deafness and the emergence of deaf leaders on its campus, the university soon opened its doors to deaf students in its undergraduate and graduate departments, as well as in the leadership training program. They have attended regular classes and, when necessary, are provided with interpreters and with

The entrance of the Model Secondary School in Washington, D.C.

Rochester Institute of Technology Bulletin

National Technical Institute for the Deaf in Rochester.

counseling, tutoring, and notetaking services.

All these services comprise the National Center on Deafness, which has a two-fold mission. Its primary mission is to make classes at the university available to qualified deaf students, enabling them to pursue their higher education objectives. Its secondary mission is to coordinate university programs which train personnel, both hearing and deaf, for professional careers in areas serving deaf persons.

The Center is under the direction of Dr. Ray L. Jones.

National Technical Institute for the Deaf
Rochester, New York

Opened: 1968

Founder: U.S. Congress

The need for a technical school for deaf persons was recognized before the turn of the century but it was not until 1965 when Congress passed Public Law 89-36 that the National Technical Institute for the Deaf (NTID) became a reality.

Rochester Institute of Technology

(RIT) won the nod for the location of the new school, and NTID was located on the expansive RIT campus. Dr. D. Robert Frisina, dean of the Gallaudet College Graduate School, was appointed the first director of NTID.

After a series of orientation programs and numerous preparatory activities had been carried out, a pilot group of 71 students was admitted to NTID at RIT in September, 1968. Construction of its own facilities were completed on the campus of RIT in 1974 and dedication ceremonies took place on October 5, 1974. The occasion featured the planting of a tree on the campus by Mrs. Lyndon B. Johnson. Her husband had been the president who signed the bill establishing the Institute.

Today NTID provides technical and professional training to nearly 1000 deaf students. Students have the option of attending classes through other colleges of RIT, classes at NTID or a mixture of both. Interpreters and notetakers, tutors, communications aid and other support services are provided. Degrees offered by NTID include certificates, diplomas and associate arts degrees. Students completing studies at RIT through NTID earn bachelor's and master's degrees. NTID's placement program helps graduates find employment and students participate in co-operative work programs.

Clarke School for the Deaf

This medallion was cast in observance of Clarke's centennial in 1967.

Robert F. Panara was the first deaf professional to join the faculty in 1967. He helped establish NTID's English department and organized the NTID Drama Club, now called the Experimental Educational Theatre (EET). Loy E. Golladay is another long-term employee of the Institute. He retired in 1980 and was honored with the title of NTID's first Professor Emeritus.

In 1977 Dr. William E. Castle was chosen to succeed Dr. D. Robert Frisina as Director/Dean of the Institute after Dr. Frisina had been promoted to Senior Vice President of Rochester Institute of Technology.

In 1979, Dr. Castle was promoted to RIT Vice President and Director of NTID, with Dr. Milo E. Bishop becoming the Dean of NTID.

The law that created NTID included research as one of the requirements. Today, NTID has one of the largest research programs on deafness in the country. The research program is involved in many different areas of inquiry, some of which are aimed specifically at improving the education of deaf students at RIT. Research of special interest to deaf people nationally includes work on the language of signs, captioning and studies of the employment of deaf people.

As part of RIT's 150th Anniversary celebration, NTID named its five buildings on October 19, 1979. Dormitory "B" was named for Peter N. Peterson. As a deaf teacher in the 1930s, Peterson was one of the early proponents of a National Technical Institute for the Deaf. Buildings were also named for Alexander Graham Bell and Lyndon B. Johnson. It was Johnson who, as president of the United States, signed the legislation creating NTID on June 8, 1965.

NTID at RIT established the National Center on Employment of the Deaf (NCED) in January 1979—the first effort of its kind anywhere—to help advance the employment of qualified deaf persons nationwide. NCED is a national service agency and authority on the employment of deaf people in the U.S. It provides information related to employing deaf persons; conducts active programs with employers on job analysis and job modification; and trains job placement professionals and employers who work with deaf persons. NCED offers placement assistance by establishing a job bank for deaf persons nationwide.

Community Colleges

Beginning during the last decade, or shortly before, a number of post-secondary and junior college educational programs for the deaf have appeared on the scene, most of them provided in conjunction with community colleges.

Notable among these centers are St. Paul Technical Institute, St. Paul, Minnesota; Delgado Junior College, New Orleans, Louisiana; and Seattle Community College, Seattle, Washington. There are at least two such programs in Canada. The three in the United States named above are regional centers, accepting students from surrounding states. Vocational or technical training is stressed.

In all these schools, students attend regular classes with hearing students. They are provided with interpreters and tutoring and note taking services.

There are at least 40 community colleges in 20 different states that provide special services for the deaf or hearing impaired. The State of California maintains ten such programs. These services have increased the educational opportunities of deaf persons throughout the land.

*An asterisk following person's name indicates founder was deaf.

Taking a time-out

Robert de Gast/Model Secondary School for the Deaf

58

Chapter 2

The 1880s

A Beginning

N EIGHTEEN HUNDRED AND EIGHTY, Helen Keller and Douglas MacArthur were born. Will Rogers was a one-year-old toddler. Lewis Wallace wrote *Ben Hur*—many of Wallace's novels include deaf characters who use sign language. Before the decade was out, Mark Twain produced *The Adventures of Huckleberry Finn*. Rutherford B. Hayes, a Republican from Ohio, was in the White House. The Industrial Revolution was underway. The transcontinental railroad linked the nation. Passengers could take the Central and Union Pacific Railroad from San Francisco to New York City—the world's longest trip by rail—for $110. First class cost $30 extra. The trip took six days and 20 hours.

In 1876 Alexander Graham Bell had patented a device for sending the spoken word over a wire. He called it a telephone. In 1880 Bell was awarded the Volta Prize and 50,000 francs (about $10,000) by the French Government in recognition of this gift to mankind.

The population of the United States was slightly over 50 million in 1880. The census that year, the country's tenth, listed 33,878 "deaf-mutes," a considerable increase over the previous census which had recorded 16,205.

More than half a century had passed since the founding of the first permanent public school for the deaf in Hartford. Some 38 schools dotted the countryside from Hartford to Berkeley, California. Eight of these schools were started by deaf persons.

The New England Gallaudet Association of the Deaf was 26 years old. There were state associations of the deaf in New York, Wisconsin and Indiana. Iowa and Pennsylvania organizations soon followed, and by 1890 there were state associations in Virginia, Minnesota, Texas, Michigan, Arkansas and Kentucky. The Gallaudet College Alumni Association was formed in 1889, following the unveiling of the Thomas Hopkins Gallaudet statue on the Gallaudet College campus.

In that year, 1880, a young deaf man named George M. McClure accepted a teaching position at the Kentucky School for the Deaf in Danville, beginning an association that would span eighty years. And, Mrs. Clerc, widow of Laurent Clerc, passed away.

Birth of the National Association of the Deaf

The idea of a national association of the deaf dates back to 1850. A group of deaf people had gathered in Hartford, Connecticut to pay tribute to Thomas Gallaudet and Laurent Clerc. They discussed the need for a national association, but agreed that the idea was impractical. No newspaper linked the deaf community, and what deaf leaders there were were scattered. Travel was slow and difficult. However, the suggestion of an organization persisted and resulted in the formation of the New England Gallaudet Association of the Deaf in 1853. It was named in honor of Thomas Hopkins Gallaudet. The Association has membership

William	Lars M	Thomas F	Edwin A	George B	Henry	Holmes	Robert	Henry C
Hoagland	Larson	Fox	Hodgson	Dougherty	White	(Mass)	McGregor	Rider
(Ky)		(N Y)	(N Y)	(Mo)	(Mass)		(Ohio)	(N Y)

The first convention of the National Association of the Deaf in Cincinnati, Ohio, 1880.

H Samual M Webster Englehart Theodore Philip
Freeman   George   Froelich Emery
(Ga)   (Ill)   (N Y)   (Ill)

lists and minutes dating back to 1910. Earlier records were destroyed by fire.

Why a national organization? Deaf Americans were beginning to realize that if anyone was going to resolve their problems it would have to be themselves. They were concerned about the educational conditions in schools for the deaf and about the method of instruction. Pure oralism was threatening the learning freedom of deaf children and the employment of deaf teachers. Deaf people needed better training for industrial work. Discrimination hampered the independence and well-being of the deaf. Perhaps worst of all was this lack of public understanding of deaf people, their handicap and their capabilities. At the first Convention of the National Association of the Deaf in Cincinnati the delegates resolved " . . . to bring the Deaf of the different sections of the United States in close contact and to deliberate on the needs of the deaf as a class. We have interests peculiar to ourselves which can be taken care of by ourselves."

Three leading men were involved in the inception of the National Association of the Deaf, and each was credited at one time or another with its founding. The three were Edmund Booth, Robert P. McGregor and Edwin A. Hodgson.

Robert P. McGregor
(1849-1926)

Robert P. McGregor was educated at the Ohio School for the Deaf and at Gallaudet College. He was a classmate of Amos Draper, another well-known educator, and of Wells L. Hill, who was called "that deaf Massachusetts publisher." With the exception of Booth, who was 71 at the time, and one or two others, McGregor, at 30, was among the oldest attendees at the first convention in Cincinnati.

McGregor was a skilled orator who "could sway a deaf audience at will." He was described as a forceful writer who always championed the cause of the deaf. He held the distinction of being elected the first president of the National Association of the Deaf. A year after the National Convention, he became principal of the Colorado School for the Deaf and the Blind, and he stayed there one year. He returned to Ohio and accepted the principalship of his alma mater in 1883. In 1920 he was retired on pension. McGregor was killed on the rainy evening of December 21, 1926, when he was struck by an automobile.

Booth was owner and editor of the *Anamosa Eureka*, a successful weekly and an official county newspaper in Iowa. (The newspaper is still in existence today.) He chaired the first business session of NAD and was therefore incorrectly singled out as the initiator of the movement to get the organization started. Booth was nominated for the presidency, but he declined in favor of a younger man.

Robert P. McGregor was the founder and principal of the Cincinnati Day School for the Deaf. When Cincinnati was chosen as the site of the first convention, McGregor, as a resident, was the logical choice for chairman of the local committee. He became the first president of the Association.

Most historians credit Edwin A. Hodgson with being the main driving force behind the founding of the National Association of the Deaf. George W. Veditz, seventh president of the NAD, called Hodgson "the father and founder of the National Association of the Deaf." Leon Auerbach, another researcher and a historical buff, agrees. Hodgson had nourished the idea of a national association with his New York newspaper.

The use of the term "Deaf-Mutes" in the title of the National Association occurred at a time when the teaching of speech to the deaf was spreading across the country. Educators were trying to eliminate the use of the term "mute," in schools for the deaf and particularly in the title of the National Convention of Deaf-Mutes. George Veditz, a vocal dyed-in-the-wool combinist observed: "If oral magicians who yank educational rabbits out of silk hats and pearls of speech out of the mouths of those who have never heard, choke over it, why bless 'em!" By the third convention, the Association had dropped the offensive term from its name.

Many others were involved in the first convention. There was Philip A. Emery, Lars M. Larson, Dudley W. George, Samuel M. Freeman, Charles W. Carraway; all but Emery were 21-year-old college students. Thomas F. Fox, at 20, was the youngest. Harry White, 23, had just graduated from Gallaudet College. George T. Dougherty, who was elected recording secretary, was still a college student. Later he became one of the leading analytical chemists in this country. Gallaudet College awarded him two honorary degrees.

Twenty-one states were represented at the first convention. Ohio, the host state, led with the most registrants—23. Illinois sent 14 and New York, 7. Nebraska and Kansas were the western-most states that sent delegates and Louisiana and Mississippi were the most southern. Massachusetts was the only New Eng-

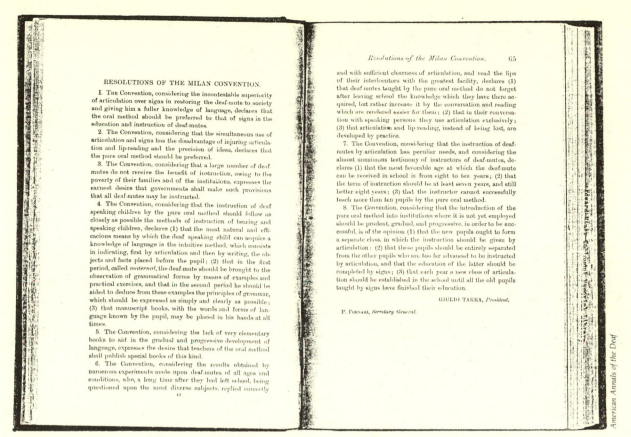

Resolutions adopted at the Milan, Italy convention in 1880.

land state with representatives in attendance.

There were three future school founders in attendence: Henry C. Rider, the Northern New York School for the Deaf in Malone; Lars M. Larson, the New Mexico School in Santa Fe; and Henry C. White, who founded two schools—the Utah School (1884) and the Arizona School (1911).

The convention had its headquarters at the Gibson Hotel, one of the city's most expensive. A room cost $2.50 per night. Cheaper rooms were available at other hotels for as little as 75¢. The convention meetings were held in Bellevue House, a beautiful structure high on a bluff overlooking the city.

Meeting at Milan: An Infamous Resolution

Strange things were happening that summer. While deaf Americans were organizing a national association in Cincinnati in August, hearing educators of the deaf would meet in Milan, Italy in September and pass a resolution that would have a profound impact on the lives of deaf people throughout the world for generations to come.

The Cincinnati attendees were the products of an American school system which was a little over 60 years old. Included in the lot were teachers, school founders, principals, business men and other leaders holding various positions. They were determined to improve the lot of deaf people by opposing laws that would restrict their rights, determined to discourage impostors and deaf peddlers, to create a better understanding of deafness by the public at large, to push for better vocational training in the schools and better educational methods, and to fight employment discrimination.

At the second International Convention in Milan there were 164 participants: 87 Italians, 56 Frenchmen, 8 Englishmen, 5 Americans, and 8 others. Thus the Convention was more international in name than in fact. The Americans were the only duly elected representative group. They spoke for the Conference of Principals of American Instructors for the Deaf and Dumb and had been chosen at the Conference's meeting in Northampton, Massachusetts, the previous May. These five represented 51 schools with a total enrollment of over 6,000 students, more than the number of students represented by the other 159 par-

63

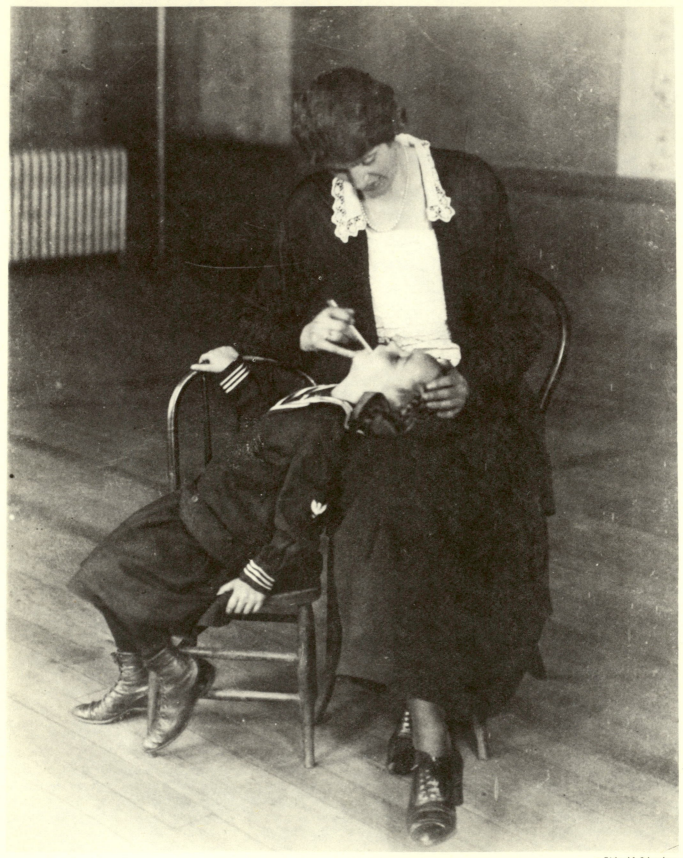

Richard J. Schoenberg

64

Edwin A. Hodgson
(1854-1933)

Edwin Allan Hodgson was born in Manchester, England in 1854. His family moved to America when Hodgson was a youth, and here he attended private school and excelled as a student. He studied for two years at Collegiate Institute and, with his father's encouragement, set his sights on becoming a lawyer. Hodgson was fairly proficient in French, Greek and Latin. However, his father died and then, in 1872, a case of spinal meningitis deprived him of his hearing. He was 18. He turned instead to learning printing, a trade he considered more of an art than a mechanical skill. In 1876 the New York Institution for the Deaf (Fanwood) hired him to establish a printing department at the school. That same year the school bought *The Deaf-Mute's Journal*, a weekly newspaper, from Henry C. Rider of Mexico, New York and Hodgson became editor. It was in this position that Hodgson continually publicized the idea of a national organization for the deaf. When nothing seemed to happen, he prodded. Veditz wrote of Hodgson: "The velvet gauntlet hid a fist of steel." Under Hodgson's guidance, the *DMJ* became one of the most popular, influential and widely-read newspapers of its day.

Hodgson's skills were not limited to editing. In 1883 he succeeded McGregor as president of the National Convention of Deaf-Mutes. He was a positive person. His walrus moustache and ruddy complexion linked him to a British heritage. Hodgson was active in the Gallaudet Home for the Aged and Infirm Deaf, the Empire State Association of the Deaf and the Fanwood Quad Club, a printers' organization. In 1880 he became a delegate to the World Congress of the Deaf in Paris. When the Thomas Hopkins Gallaudet and Alice memorial was unveiled on the Gallaudet College campus, Hodgson was "orator of the day." Of Hodgson it was said: "He is decided in his opinions and fearless in the utterance of them but always mindful of courtesy and fair play. . . ."

Hodgson compiled and published *The Deaf and Dumb, Facts, Anecdotes and Poetry* in 1891 and wrote the *Manual for the Printer's Apprentice.*

LEFT: An early speech lesson.

ticipants combined. The American delegates were: Edward Miner Gallaudet, president of the National Deaf-Mute College; the Rev. Thomas Gallaudet, an Episcopalian minister to the deaf and rector of St. Ann's Church in New York City; Isaac Lewis Peet, principal of the New York Institution; James Denison, principal of the Columbia Institution in Washington, D.C.; and Charles A. Stoddard, a member of the Board of Directors of the New York Institution. Denison was the lone deaf participant.

At the meeting, the members voted overwhelmingly to outlaw the use of sign language as a method for educating deaf children, in favor of the pure oral method. The group opposed a compromise motion to include sign language along with speech. The Americans opposed the decision, along with Richard Elliott, headmaster of the London Institution. The Americans favored the combined system, which employed both speech and sign language depending on the needs of the child.

"If You Seek His Monument. . . ."

In 1883 in New York, Charles K. W. Strong submitted a resolution at the second convention of the National Association of the Deaf calling for a bronze statue to be erected in memory of Thomas Hopkins Gallaudet on the campus of the National Deaf-Mute College in Washington. The location was chosen because Gallaudet's work was national in scope and the college, which attracted students from every state, represented his goal.

The NAD selected a young American sculptor named Daniel Chester French to do the work. Some felt that a deaf sculptor should have been chosen, but none as qualified as French seemed to exist. Also, French's work was familiar to them. A few years before, French had completed a marble bust of President James A. Garfield. Since his days as a member of the House of Representatives, Garfield had been a good friend to deaf people and a staunch supporter of the college. When he was assassinated, his friends on Kendall Green and elsewhere felt the loss keenly. French's bust of Garfield rests atop a high pedestal in Chapel Hall at Gallaudet, where Garfield had delivered his last public address.

I apprehend [sic] *that we shall take away from our pupils one of the most encouraging incentives to excel when we remove from them the influence of deaf teachers. . . .*
—DR. PHILIP G. GILLETT
1884

The Silent Worker

This engraving was one of the first to appear in The Silent Worker. *It appeared in the September 1889 issue and was made by a deaf engraver.*

French was in Paris at work on a portrait statue of General Cass when he received the commission to do the Gallaudet memorial. He came back to New York and began working on small clay models. The Gallaudet memorial was his first attempt at a human interest group sculpture. The memorial depicts the 30-year-old Thomas Hopkins Gallaudet showing his first pupil, the young Alice Cogswell, the letter "A" of the manual alphabet. He was introducing her to a language that would open her mind to knowledge. Elva Loe, the college's art teacher, observed of French's work: "The motive of the group is the teaching of the sign letters; but the real bond that holds the two figures together is the interchange of thought and feeling through the gaze, since the usual avenue of speech is closed."

The unveiling had been planned for 1888, the centenary of Gallaudet's birth, but it was delayed a year. French postponed his wedding to make some corrections on the model before sending it to the foundry to be cast. Finally, the June 26, 1889 program began. It was a tribute to Gallaudet. Laura Searing had written a lengthy poem to mark the event. All the speakers were deaf except Edward Miner Gallaudet, who ac-

I am ready to say, from my own observation and experience and knowledge, that some of the very best teachers of deaf-mutes are themselves deaf.

—DR. PHILIP G. GILLETT
1884

cepted the statue. A reporter who stood among the 300 well-dressed, intelligent men and women who represented the arts and professions noted: "as we followed the inspiring thoughts and admired the graceful gestures of the orator of the day, reflecting that but for Gallaudet and such as he, all this intelligence and character would have lain undeveloped, we felt like uttering again the hackneyed sentiment: 'If you seek his monument, look around you.'"

Outgoing NAD President Edwin A. Hodgson summed up the feelings of the group when he said: "This statue does not pay a debt; it simply acknowledges an obligation so great that it can never be cancelled. It forms but the outward expression of a widespread reverence and love. . . ."

Edmund Booth
(1810-1905)

Edmund Booth was a big man and a kind and generous person. When he was four years old he had been stricken by meningitis which left him blind in one eye and partially deaf. By the age of eight, his deafness was total. At seventeen, he enrolled in the American School where he studied, remaining afterwards as a teacher. One of his teachers was Laurent Clerc. Booth taught until 1839 when a lung affliction forced him to resign. He went west to Iowa, where he built the first frame house in Jones County. As the county grew, Booth prospered. He bought half an interest in the *Eureka* and later became sole owner. He married a former student, Mary Ann Walworth. At one time, he was county recorder of deeds and enrolling clerk in the Iowa House of Representatives. Booth was "noted for his mental qualities." Had he not been so isolated in the Midwest at the time when railroad transportation was in its infancy, Booth would probably have been much more active in the national affairs of the deaf community. Booth died in 1905 at the age of 95.

The Raindrop

That year *The Raindrop* appeared. James H. Logan, the deaf principal of the Pittsburgh School for the Deaf, and his staff had been writing stories and adapting Aesop's Fables and old literary masterpieces into simple stories for their deaf students. The students loved the stories. When the school got a printing press, the stories were printed in a 32-page monthly magazine called *The Raindrop*. Logan and his head teacher, George M. Teegarden, wrote most of the stories. Guilbert C. Braddock thinks that the name was selected because "like the gentle dew, it refreshed the parched minds of all the deaf children and allowed the imagination to blossom forth." Soon these delightful stories caught on. Teachers in other schools for the deaf began using them in their classes. The publication appealed to deaf and hearing children alike. *The Raindrop* ran out of funds in a year and folded. It had, however, been so popular that Logan decided to take a risk and publish all the stories in book form. The risk paid off; the book sold. It became one book that would be read by generation after generation of deaf children.

In 1910 *Raindrop* was reprinted by the Volta Bureau and illustrations were added. It has gone through four

The Reverend Job Turner

reprintings and is seen in almost every school for the deaf library in this country. (Unfortunately, little information about Logan and Teegarden appears in the current edition, and no mention is made that they were deaf.)

The Decade

During the decade of the 1880s a house in Indianapolis rented for $15 a month. A maid worked for $1.50 a week. A large beef steak sold for a quarter regardless of weight, calf's liver was free, and for another quarter you could pick out a chicken. The butcher would wring the neck, pluck the feathers, and prepare the dressing at no extra charge. Butter sold for 15¢ a pound, and eggs were delivered to your door for 10¢ a dozen. Milk went for five cents a quart.

Silver-haired John Carlin, one of the most prominent deaf men of his day, resided at West Twenty-fifth Street in New York City. A successful portrait painter, Carlin had been one of the first to persuade young Edward Miner Gallaudet to found a college for deaf persons, and he had received the first honorary degree awarded by the college.

In Newark, New Jersey, Alexander L. Pach, the

Job Turner
(1820-1903)

Job Turner, the first deaf teacher at the Virginia School for the Deaf and the Blind, had just passed middle age in 1880. Civil War trenches were still visible on the hillside of the school where he taught. Looking out one of the school building windows, one could see two messages scratched on a window pane. The first, no doubt written by a Confederate soldier, read: "The Yankees are expected." The second read: "They came."

Turner was born deaf. During his youth his parents searched for a miracle to restore his hearing. They found none. They even tried an Indian medicine man, who took a look at the youth and said: "Paleface papoose deaf. No can do. All same, deaf papoose make-um good chief someday." The medicine man proved a good prophet. Turner's family moved to Staunton when his father died. Turner was ten. Since there was no school for deaf children in Virginia, he went to the American Asylum in Hartford where Laurent Clerc was one of his teachers. Upon completion of his studies in Hartford, he was offered a teaching position at the new Virginia School by the Rev. Joseph D. Tyler, who, incidentally, is believed to be the first deaf superintendent of a school for the deaf. Tyler had become deaf at the age of 29 from a severe fever.

After his wife died, Turner decided to begin a second career; he entered the ministry. In 1877 he was confirmed in the Protestant Episcopal Church and the next day given a license to preach to deaf people. He was ordained a deacon in 1880 and in 1891 he became the fourth deaf man to be ordained an Episcopalian priest. Eventually, his missionary extended from Maine to Texas and he became a legend. Guilbert Braddock described Turner thus: "In the Solid South, from 1880 to 1900, the established institutions were, in the order of importance: sunshine, the cotton and tobacco crops, the Bible, the Democratic Party, chicken dinners, the poll tax, and the Rev. Job Turner, Missionary to the Deaf." Aside from being considered an "institution," Turner was well-liked and highly respected. He died in 1903 and was buried in the Thornrose Cemetery in Staunton. In 1909 a monument was erected at his grave.

James H. Logan
(1843-1917)

James H. Logan, publisher of *The Raindrop*, resigned the principalship of the Pittsburgh School for the Deaf and lived on the income from the collected *Raindrop* stories. He experienced a few years of ups and downs before taking a position as instructor in microscopy at Western University of Pennsylvania—a deaf man teaching a class of hearing students. He held other jobs as a microscopist and was one of the founders of the Iron City Microscopical Society. Gallaudet College, his alma mater, awarded him an honorary Doctor of Science degree in 1914. He died of pneumonia on December 9, 1917 in Pittsburgh, but the classic he created for deaf children lives on.

Sight can the signs of thought supply,
And with a look I hear.

—GEORGE M. TEEGARDEN

short, moustached, deaf Jewish photographer was being married to Miss Joanna S. Stewart by his good friend, the Rev. Austin A. Mann. After a short honeymoon, Pach and his wife hurried back to his thriving photography business in Easton, Pennsylvania. Such industry was the reason the Pach signature appeared on so many convention and group photographs in those days. The National Association of the Deaf and the Convention of American Instructors of the Deaf were among his better customers. Friends called Pach the "Photographer of Presidents" because he made a portrait of Teddy Roosevelt.

John M. Stout, the deaf trick bicycle rider, was thrilling audiences at the International Fair in Buffalo, New York. The Smithville, New Jersey bicyclist amazed throngs with his ability to stand on his head, do balancing acts, ride the bicycle forwards and backwards, up and down stairways, and "perform a hundred and one seemingly impossible feats."

George M. Teegarden
(1852-1936)

George M. Teegarden, James Logan's collaborator on *The Raindrop*, joined the Pittsburgh School upon graduation from Gallaudet College in 1876. He taught for 48 years. At that time, the Pittsburgh School was being reorganized into a residential school. It was renamed the Western Pennsylvania School and moved to Edgewood, Pennsylvania. Teegarden loved to write poetry and wrote many poems under the pen name of T. G. Arden. Elizabeth Peet, dean of women at Gallaudet College, called him one of the foremost deaf poets in America. His work appeared in the *Silent Muse*, an anthology of prose and poetry by the deaf.

H. Humphrey Moore, the Philadelphia-born artist, had just opened a studio in Paris. He had recently returned from an 18 month sojourn in Japan, where he found many buyers. Moore had exhibited his painting "Almeh" at the United States Centennial Exhibition in 1876. The New York *Nation* called it the finest piece of color work in the American collection. The painting was valued at $10,000. Unfortunately, it was destroyed in a fire some years later. While studying in Spain, Moore met and married a member of one of Spain's oldest families of nobility. His bride was given away by Don Carlos, a wealthy Spanish landowner.

President Grover Cleveland had been invited to attend the commencement exercises, called presentation day, of the National Deaf-Mute College in May, 1886. Also in attendance were several diplomats and the British Ambassador. The president, who weighed about 300 pounds, was invited to sit in one of the arm chairs on the small platform behind the rostrum. Albert Berg, a 22-year-senior from Indiana, was giving a presentation about labor and capital. During his talk, he turned to the President to make a point and found Cleveland asleep, his hands clasped over his expansive front, his chin on his chest.

The next year, Berg was teaching in Indiana at his alma mater. While at Gallaudet, Berg had been involved with the college football team, one of the first to be organized in the District of Columbia, and he knew the game well. When Purdue University in Lafayette, Indiana, decided to inaugurate football, Berg was offered the position of coach. His appointment was the first instance in which a deaf man coached a hearing college team and Berg earned a measure of fame. Berg also coached at Franklin College and Butler University.

John W. Michaels was a young instructor at the Virginia School. He began a baseball team called the "Silent Baseball Club." One observer commented: "Whilst the game is usually attended by a few broken fingers, the exercise is fine, and is a very fitting intiation for the hard knocks of life."

In New York Henry Haight won a gold medal at the National Poultry Exhibition for a hen coop he had invented. He also invented an improved incubator capable of hatching 20,000 eggs and a thermostat control that maintained an even room temperature.

In 1881 the National Deaf-Mute College completed construction of a $14,400 new gymnasium. It was the second gymnasium to have an indoor swimming pool. Physical education was catching on and it was reported that ". . . among adult deaf-mutes we can almost always recognize a graduate of the National College by his well-built frame and erect, alert bearing—the result of the admirable physical training which is compulsory upon that institution." Schools for the deaf throughout the country soon began adding physical education to their programs and opening gymnasiums in attics, empty shop rooms, and wherever they could find the space.

In 1885 the New York Home for the Aged and Infirm Deaf-Mutes was moved to a 156-acre farm with a large mansion at Wappinger's Falls, New York. The home's name was changed to the Gallaudet Home for Aged and Infirm Deaf-Mutes in honor of the Rev. Thomas Gallaudet. By 1891 the Home was valued at $30,000 to $40,000 and had 24 inmates. Efforts were underway to establish similar homes in Ohio and Pennsylvania.

A fire destroyed some buildings at the Missouri School for the Deaf. A roof was blown off the Alabama School and a cyclone did $16,000 damage to the Louisiana School. Students at the Illinois School tried out military uniforms for the first time. A number of the schools introduced courses in photography. The Minnesota and Illinois Schools installed electric lights on their campuses.

Superintendents of the Indiana, Pennsylvania and Kansas Schools had decided not to allow their students to go home for the Christmas holiday in 1888. Indiana School Superintendent Baker gave his reason: "The frequent injury to health by the change from warm to cold sleeping rooms, the discontent among the pupils who remain and the distraction of the vacation caused by the return of the absentees."

Some pupils at the Kansas School were raising funds to buy artificial legs for one student who had lost both feet in a train accident. In 1889 Monroe Ingram became the first deaf black person to graduate from the Kansas School. He was hired to teach in the Colored Department of the Missouri School for the Deaf. Faculty, staff and students at the New Jersey School were delighted to learn that the Horse Railroad Company had decided to extend its line along Hamilton Avenue near the school grounds. The excitement was shortlived for some. One teacher remarked: "We wish the cars would go so fast that we were not obliged to walk when we want to save time."

An outbreak of yellow fever prevented the Florida School from opening during the 1888-89 school term. The *Kansas Star*, the publication of the Kansas State School for the Deaf, was appealing to the state for funds for new buildings and necessary equipment, and this threat was added: "And may the Lord have mercy on your soul if you vote no."

70

The Deaf-Mute Times, a small four-page newspaper, began publication at the New Jersey School for the Deaf in Trenton in February, 1888. The name was changed to The Silent Worker a few months later. This paper was the forerunner of The Deaf American, the "National Magazine for All the Deaf," which became familiar to thousands and thousands of deaf readers and their friends.

Train Deaths

Train deaths became increasingly common in those years. When it rained, the muddy roads were impassable, and since there were few sidewalks many people took to walking on the railroad tracks. Many deaf persons did this, failed to hear an approaching train, and were killed. Repeated warnings in the press failed to stop these incidents. In one four-year period, 164 deaths were recorded, and news accounts such as the following two which appeared in the Deaf-Mute's Journal, reported:

Victim No. 47. Concord, N.H., Nov. 21. Curtis Pierce, a laborer, was instantly killed this afternoon, near that place, by a special train containing the Railroad commissioners, who were making their annual inspection of the Nashawa and Rochester line. Pierce was quite deaf and failed to hear the cars as they approached. He was 40 years old and leaves a widow and four children.—Boston Journal.

Victim No. 48. A deaf-mute named W. V. Tooton, a peddler, from New Orleans, was run over by a train on the Illinois Central RR, near Oxford, Miss.,

Gymnasiasts drill in front of the new Gallaudet College Gymnasium.

An early rhythm class at the Maryland School for the Deaf.

John J. Flournoy
(1800?-1879)

John J. Flournoy is best remembered as an advocate of a "deaf-mute" colony. He proposed that deaf people get a government land grant and form a self-existing community where all citizens would be deaf and the chief means of communication would be sign language. He also supported the idea of the colony having its own representative in Congress, and he was willing to be considered one of the candidates. His idea did not gain much support and many leaders of the day (including Edmund Booth) opposed it, arguing that after a few generations the colony would become non-existent because a very small percentage of the off-spring of deaf parents are deaf.

The date of Flournoy's birth is uncertain. It was sometime between 1800-1810. He grew up on an estate near Athens, Georgia. He was a descendant of Jean Jacques Flournoy, a Huguenot who had come to this country in 1720. He was educated at the American School in Hartford.

Flournoy was instrumental in the founding of the Georgia School for the Deaf and was one of the proponents of a national college for the deaf.

He died on January 18, 1879.

---

last week. His remains were taken to Abbeville, Miss., the next station above Oxford, and decently buried. He leaves a daughter and a host of friends in New Orleans to mourn his untimley death. He was educated at the Ohio Institution.

The Silent World suggested: "In the states that provide punishment for attempts at suicide, every deaf man found walking on the railroad should be arrested and given the full extent of the law." Regardless, warnings to stay off the tracks continued to fall on deaf ears until the advent of the automobile and better roads.

Intermarriages

Near the end of the decade, the question of the wisdom of permitting deaf persons to marry each other was getting considerable attention. In Minnesota a state senator named Chapman introduced a bill that prohibited deaf persons from marrying each other. The editor of *The Silent Worker* called him "by no means a level-headed man" and asked if Chapman next planned to introduce bills to prevent "the intermarriage of blind persons, the lame, the one-legged and people who talk and laugh at the opera; also men

who keep their seats in elevated trains with women who take a man's seat without acknowledging the courtesy."

Milestones

William Albert Bolling died in 1884. A relative of Pocahontas, he is thought to be the first deaf American to be formally educated in America. He attended the school at Cobbs that his father had founded on the family plantation near Petersburg, Virginia.

Laura Bridgman (1829-1889) was born in Hanover, New Hampshire. She was deafened and blinded at the age of two years when ill with scarlet fever. Her sickness also impaired her sense of smell and sense of taste. Bridgman was the first deaf-blind person to be formally educated in this country. When she was eight years old, she was placed in the Perkins Institution, where she studied under Dr. Samuel G. Howe. Bridgman learned the alphabet in less than three days and could fingerspell in two months. At 23, she returned to her Hanover home, but loneliness soon encompassed her and caused her to stay in bed. She returned to the Perkins Institution and stayed for the rest of her life. In 1842, Charles Dickens came to vist her and recorded his impressions. These recollections found their way into his "Notes on America."

Gallaudet College Archives

LEFT: *Laura Bridgman*
BELOW: *Colonel William Bolling and his two deaf children, Mary (left) and William Albert.*

Richmond Times Dispatch

Annual Staff and Teachers' Salaries
Washington State School for the Deaf

First assistant female teacher, without
    maintenance $720.00
Second assistant female teacher, without
    maintenance 600.00
Teacher of articulation, without maintenance 800.00
Teacher of drawing 450.00
Instructress of sewing and fancy work 360.00
Trade instructor and supervisor of boys 600.00
Assistant supervisor of boys 360.00
Housekeeper and nurse 400.00
Engineer and electrician 1,000.00
Night watchman 480.00
Cook and baker 600.00
Assistant cook 360.00
Laundryman and assistant 750.00

—THIRD BIENNIAL REPORT, 1882

First reunion of the Gallaudet College alumni. Picture taken in front of Chapel Hall, 1889.

Gallaudet College Archives

Chapter 3

The 1890s

Dr. Bell's 'Deaf Variety of the Human Race'

HOULD DEAF PERSONS be allowed to marry each other? That was a question that had been raised in the preceding decade and one that was being asked repeatedly during the 1890s. One of the persons who had grave doubts about the wisdom of such intermarriages was Dr. Alexander Graham Bell.

Dr. Bell studied former students of the American and Illinois Schools for the Deaf and concluded that intermarriages among deaf people increased the number of deaf children. By noting the recurrence of surnames he became suspicious of blood relation. He deducted that it was "highly probable" that "a considerable proportion" of deaf persons in the country belonged to families which had more than one deaf member, and suspected that the reasons for this were hereditary. If such intermarriages were permitted to continue, Bell believed, eventually there would be a "deaf variety" of the human race. This concerned him greatly, and the subject of such marriages became a great debate both among educators of the deaf and deaf persons.

Bell was not the first to wonder about the results of intermarriages among deaf persons. In 1868 William A. Turner warned in an article in the *American Annals of the Deaf* about the dangers of such marriages between congenitally deaf persons. Dr. James Kerr Love, also writing in the *Annals*, went a step further and proposed banning marriages between cousins and between individuals who had each had deafness within their families.

In 1883 Bell presented a paper, "Upon the Formation of a Deaf Variety of the Human Race," before the National Academy of Science in New Haven, Connecticut. In his presentation Bell noted that man was able to modify breeds of animals by careful selection, and he reasoned that it should be possible similarly to modify the varieties of the human race. He admitted that his statistics were incomplete and hoped that the publication of such information would lead to their completion. He also acknowledged that one could not dictate to a man or woman whom they could marry. Wrote Bell, "Those who believe as I do, that the production of a defective race of human beings would be a great calamity to the world, will examine carefully the causes that lead to the intermarriages of the deaf with the object of applying a remedy."

Bell blamed the educational system of the day for intermarriages among deaf persons. He would have razed all residential and day schools for the deaf. Bell believed that "herding" deaf children under one roof was a cruel thing to do, and he saw such action as creating life-time bonds and encouraging intermarriages. Bell quoted the Rev. W. W. Turner who had said, ". . . before the deaf and dumb were educated, comparatively few of them married" and that ". . . intermarriage (if it existed at all) was so rare as to be practically unknown. This suggests the thought that the intermarriages of the deaf and dumb have in some way been promoted by our methods of education."

There were other things that disturbed Bell. He saw deaf people's tendencies to socialize among them-

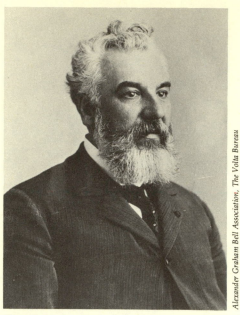

Dr. Alexander Graham Bell.

selves—to hold reunions, have social gatherings, form their own clubs and associations, publish their own newspapers, hold religious worship, and state and national conventions—as further encouraging social intercourse among them. Such association, Bell believed, restricted deaf persons' selection of partners and friends, thus encouraging deaf people to marry each other.

Bell broached the possibility of forbidding such marriages by law. He saw forbidding congenitally deaf persons from marrying each other as one way to check the "evil" although he admitted that "proving that a person had been born deaf" would probably make the law inoperative. He reasoned that legislation forbidding persons who belonged to families that had more than one deaf person to marry would probably be more practical although perhaps unwise. As an alternative he saw the possibility of friends discouraging such intermarriages.

Bell supported the establishment of small schools,

The segregation of deaf-mutes, the use of the sign language, and the employment of deaf teachers produce an environment that is unfavorable to the cultivation of articulation and speech-reading, and that sometimes causes the disuse of speech by speaking pupils who are only deaf.

—DR. ALEXANDER GRAHAM BELL
1890s

---

believing the smaller the better. To Bell the ideal condition would have been to place only one deaf child in a school with hearing children. Bell believed that integrating deaf children with hearing children would be advisable, although he realized that it was not practical on a large scale. With such an arrangement, Bell believed it would be possible to achieve what he saw as the main object of exposing deaf children to "the normal conditions of life."

Bell opposed the employment of deaf teachers and considered them "another element favorable to the formation of a deaf race, therefore to be avoided." He said that nearly one-third of the teachers in schools for the deaf were deaf themselves.

Bell's stand on intermarriage among deaf persons and his opposition to separate education for the deaf won him few deaf friends. Dr. Phillip G. Gillett, superintendent of the Illinois School for the Deaf, then the largest residential school for the deaf, studied 1,886 students and alumni of the school and found no justification for Dr. Bell's position. Gillett argued that if it became illegal for congenitally deaf persons to wed, then such a ban would have to apply to their hearing relatives as well, for they too could transmit hereditary deafness. Gillett said:

There are other inconveniences that descend by heredity that we might quite as well combat through matrimony as deafness. Baldness is a physical defect that is often (in fly-time and in cold weather, or when sitting in a draught, for instance) a great inconvenience; but who ever thought of classing the bald-headed among the defective classes, or of regarding baldness as a crime or a disgrace? Near-sightedness is a physical defect that is often very inconvenient; but who ever thought to trace the pedigree of bald or near-sighted people, to see if they might enter into wedlock?

Gillett maintained that deafness was rarely caused by heredity. He estimated that fewer than two percent of his students were the children of deaf parents. He encouraged deaf couples to marry "if their hearts so dictated."

One person who agreed with Alexander Graham Bell's position was quoted as saying, "Those who oppose Dr. Bell's views are teachers of the deaf who are actuated by selfish motives, and who wish the supply of deaf-mutes kept up to make the teaching of them a 'steady job'." To this Gillett responded, "Either the man does not know what he is talking about, or if he knows, he wilfully misrepresents [the facts]."

An administrator at one school disputed Bell's theories by pointing out that if heredity were a primary cause of deafness his school would be lacking pupils. Of 119 students attending the school, only two were the children of deaf parents.

The Volta Bureau Building in Washington, D.C.

At the third convention of the National Association of the Deaf, a concerned President Hodgson cited the urgent need for statistical information about the deaf to either refute or confirm Alexander Graham Bell's theories. Edward Allen Fay, editor of the *American Annals of the Deaf*, eventually undertook a survey on intermarriage and produced a 528-page report entitled "Marriages of the Deaf."

George W. Veditz, a deaf teacher, called Alexander Graham Bell the American most feared by deaf people, saying, ". . . he comes in the guise of a friend, and [is], therefore, the most to be feared enemy of the American deaf, past and present."

The Volta Bureau

In 1880 Dr. Alexander Graham Bell was awarded the Volta Prize for his invention of the telephone. The Volta Prize was begun by Napoleon and named for Alessandro Volta, the Italian who invented the electric battery. This award was given by the French Government to a person who discovered or invented something of exceptional value to mankind. Bell set the money aside in his "Volta Fund." His father and other people contributed to the fund.

Bell decided to use the funds to establish a center to house information on deafness. He named this building the Volta Bureau. He chose a site at the corner of 35th and Q Streets in northwest Washington, D.C. Ground was broken on May 8, 1894. The building was an impressive structure built in the classical style of the Renaissance. Long, broad steps led to the entrance of the three-story building. It contained a large museum in which portraits of leading benefactors of the deaf and a library with a capacity of 50,000 volumes were housed. By 1895 the library contained over 50,000 reference cards. It was one of the largest collections of material on deafness found anywhere. Its list of publications included 39 titles, one of which was the *Histories of American Schools for the Deaf*, edited by Edward Allen Fay.

The Bureau was dedicated to the "increase and diffusion of knowledge relating to the deaf." An 1895 report stated: "Although Dr. Bell is known as a strong advocate of the oral system of instruction, it is noteworthy that the Bureau has published, with entire impartiality, the ablest of the papers of the other side, and in like manner has published and circulated the arguments against Dr. Bell's theory as to the probable results of intermarriage among the deaf. The Bureau is not committed to the advocacy of a theory—its sole aim is to gather knowledge and to diffuse it."

Albert Ballin
(b.1861)

Deafened at the age of three, New Yorker Albert Ballin became a painter, writer, and actor. His father, David Ballin, who was born in Germany, had been deaf since infancy. At the age of 15, David Ballin was apprenticed to a lithographer. He became a skilled craftsman and emigrated to this country at the age of 22. The elder Ballin became a popular deaf businessman in New York, operating an engraving business in partnership with his sons until his death.

Albert Ballin attended the New York School for the Deaf. Encouraged by his father, Ballin became a painter, studying in France and Italy. In Italy he won a silver medal for a painting of a Venetian scene. His portrait of Isaac Lewis Peet was presented to the New York School for the Deaf by the Peet family. His painting of the Reverend Thomas Gallaudet was exhibited in a leading New York art gallery.

While studying in France, Ballin met Alexander Graham Bell whom he visited frequently thereafter. Their friendship is described in Ballin's book, *The Deaf Mute Howls*, published in 1930. Ballin was also an actor; he appeared in the motion picture, *His Busy Hour*.

Albert Ballin was a witty, interesting and skillful speaker of sign language. He taught sign language and was a strong proponent of making it a universal language—a recurring theme in *The Deaf Mute Howls*. He severely criticized residential schools for the deaf, although he had attended one himself.

The deaf in this country have risen from the lowest social levels to positions of honor in society. . . . They are independent and happy, the envy of their class of other nations. Is it any wonder then that the deaf rear monuments in marble and bronze to their benefactors? Is it strange that they are ready to fight valiantly for the system of education which has made their elevation possible? Is it remarkable that they look askance at those presenting different theories or advocating methods already tried and found wanting in essential qualities? Is it strange if they cry out in alarm at those who would wantonly throw down the ladder by which others of their class may ascend to their level and even climb higher?

—GEORGE M. TEEGARDEN
1890s

Albert Ballin Describes Bell

Albert Ballin described Alexander Graham Bell in his book *The Deaf Mute Howls*. Ballin characterized Dr. Bell as gracious, affable, and sincerely interested in deaf people. Yet, Ballin called Bell's interest in deafness a hobby.

Ballin, who was deafened at the age of three, was studying in Paris when he happened to meet Bell. They became good friends. Ballin frequently visited Bell and his wife in their Washington, D.C., home.

Albert Ballin said that Mrs. Bell, who was deaf, was a "comparatively fine lipreader." She did not know or use sign language. Ballin spoke to her without using his voice and she responded in writing.

Ballin found Bell a true friend. "His character," Ballin said, "was without blemish." But he did not agree with all of Dr. Bell's views on educating the deaf. Both opposed residential schools for deaf children. Bell maintained that they perpetuated deafness and Ballin felt residential schools encouraged "deaf characteristics." While Bell believed that the pure oral method was the best approach to teaching deaf children, Ballin felt that the answer to the communication problems of the deaf was to teach signs and fingerspelling to everyone. If the public would learn this language, he argued, then deaf children could attend public schools and there would be no communication problem.

Ballin felt that Bell's energy and a considerable amount of his wealth were "sadly misspent." Had it not been for Dr. Bell's fame and wealth, Ballin said, "his views on the subject [of deafness] would have had no more force and weight than a goose feather in a tornado. . . ."

Bell on Speech and Sign Language

Alexander Graham Bell knew sign language well. Albert Ballin described him as "a fluent talker on his fingers—as good as any deaf-mute—and [he] could use his fingers and arms with bewitching grace and ease."

But Bell insisted on speech. He blamed the lack of articulate speech among deaf adults for the separation of the deaf and the hearing. He therefore urged that all deaf students be taught solely through speech and speechreading. He was not successful, however, in proving that the pure oral method of teaching produced students whose English was better than those who studied sign language. A majority of educators of the deaf doubted that it did.

Edward Miner Gallaudet, president of the National Deaf-Mute College, believed that sign language was an important part of the education of the deaf. Gallaudet, whose mother was deaf, had grown up closely associated with the Hartford School and deaf people. He recognized that not all pupils could be taught successfully by the pure oral method and that alternatives to this approach were necessary. Gallaudet was a strong advocate of the combined system, the use of both speech and sign language. The battle lines were drawn: the two opposing sides in the education of the deaf in this country closed their ranks at the expense of many a deaf child.

The Debate over Technical Education for the Deaf

During the 1890s many people advocated opening a national technical school for the deaf. Others pushed for the expansion of technical programs in existing schools. Many educators and deaf persons felt that a national technical school could provide better facilities and more trades for deaf students to learn than could technical departments of academic schools. The National Association of the Deaf repeatedly called upon the schools for the deaf to install or upgrade their industrial training programs.

Warren Robinson, a graduate of the Wisconsin

> *Then again people do not understand the mental condition of a person who cannot speak and who thinks in gestures. He is sometimes looked upon as a sort of monstrosity, to be stared at and avoided.*
> —DR. ALEXANDER GRAHAM BELL
> 1890s

School and Gallaudet College was considered the first real specialist in training deaf students for manual trades. Robinson taught at the Wisconsin School and actively promoted industrial training as chairman of the National Association for the Deaf Committee on Industrial Status. Robinson was an early advocate of incorporating manual training programs into the regular school curricula.

In 1892 he wrote an article on technical training, published in the *American Annals of the Deaf*, in which he suggested the establishment of a technical department at the National Deaf-Mute College. His article

> *. . . deafness is neither a crime nor a disgrace; nor does it inflict any suffering on its subject. There was a time when the deaf were considered but brutes and classed as idiots, and treated accordingly. This time, all are thankful, is past; and in our time deaf persons are often in society the peers of any other, in all that makes true nobility of character and manhood.*
> —DR. PHILIP G. GILLETT
> 1890s

aroused much discussion. The following year a resolution was adopted at the Conference of Principals and Superintendents of American Schools for the Deaf urging the college to add a technical department. The National Association of the Deaf adopted a similar resolution. In September 1896, President Edward Miner Gallaudet announced that the college would add a course of technical study, offering architecture, practical chemistry, electrical and mechanical engineering and other courses to increase employment opportunities for graduates. This laid to rest, except for an occasional inquiry, the repeated call for a national technical school for the deaf.

The Fifer Cadets of Illinois

In the early 1890s, George H. Scurlock, the storekeeper at the Illinois School for the Deaf decided to form a military company at the school. Scurlock had been drilled in military tactics at a normal school and he saw no reason why deaf students could not excel in military drills. He realized that he would have to invent a special code in order to give quick commands.

His plans were greeted with enthusiasm. A company of about thirty students was formed. They began to drill regularly, marching in close formation, using sticks as rifles. When Superintendent Gillett learned of their efforts to form a company, he encouraged

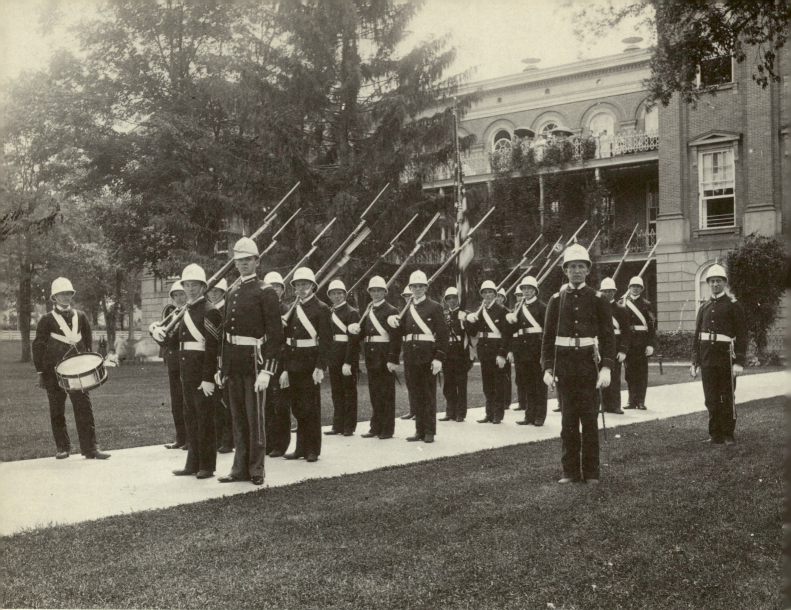

The Fifer Cadets of the Illinois School for the Deaf.

them. Gillett went to Springfield, Illinois and appealed to the adjutant general for rifles and uniforms. The adjutant, who had undergone military training himself, refused Gillett's request. He could not visualize a group of deaf students following march orders. Undaunted, the superintendent appealed to Illinois Governor Fifer, who had also borne arms. The Governor expressed some doubts about the venture but promised to look into it. In due course the boys received complete outfits and Springfield breech-loading rifles. In appreciation of the Governor's assistance, they decided to call themselves "Fifer's Cadets."

Strict military discipline was maintained. The cadets kept their rifles polished and their uniforms clean. They saluted their officers and underwent regular drill. Any misconduct meant suspension from drill practice, a punishment the students thought harsh. The cadets participated in many public ceremonies and attracted much attention to their school.

The Silent Wheelmen of the '90s

Bicycling became popular in the United States in the 1890s. Air-filled rubber tires, thin wooden wheel rims, and other improvements had made the bicycle safer and easier to ride. Before the decade was out, some four million Americans were riding those two-wheelers regularly. The bicycle was credited with revolutionizing modern life. It encouraged people to get fresh air and exercise, which prompted "body vigor and longevity."

CYCLING

About 85 different makes of bicycles were on the market. They were named after cities, individuals, birds and so forth. The manufacturers of the "Eclipse" boasted that their bicycle was so strong that it could carry a ton of weight. Their advertisement showed 20 men standing on a plank placed on top of one of their bicycles. The bicycles cost from $50 up.

There were so many bicyclists that they became a political force with which lawmakers had to reckon. A number of laws were enacted through the efforts of bicyclists. Their persistent demands for better roads resulted in a benefit to the whole country. Railroads were eventually persuaded that a bicycle should be treated as baggage.

The bicycle fever hit the deaf community, too. Alumni and teachers of the New Jersey, Kentucky, New York City and Rome, New York Schools formed bicycle clubs and held regular meetings. These clubs planned and promoted racing, century runs, and tours. The Mercer County, New Jersey Wheelmen met in an old mansion with a gymnasium. The club boasted a membership four times larger than the state association!

Articles such as "Some Truths About a Bicycle," "The Care of a Bicycle," "All About the Gears," and even poetry and fillers about bicycles found their way into publications of the day. Detailed cycling routes, lists of bicycle makers, and diagrams of bicycles appeared. *The Silent Worker* added a regular column on the subject and devoted its entire May, 1897 issue to it.

Charles LeClercq, an accomplished artist and an excellent engraver, and his wife were leading bicycle enthusiasts in the East. They made many trips on their "Niagara" and "Erie," and they wrote accounts of their travels. LeClercq illustrated the articles. In one of his write-ups, LeClercq observed that "The craze for the bicycle has resulted in a more intimate knowledge of the surrounding country than anyone dreamed of half a dozen years ago, and the old road houses, which went out when everyone except the rich gave up keeping horses, seem to be coming back again, and bid fair to be more plentiful than the rustic taverns ever were."

Valentine's Day, 1890

I'd like to praise your wavy hair,
Your dimpled cheeks, complexion fair,
Your sparkling eyes, your dress so neat,
Your shapely hand, your dainty feet,
Your graceful air, your tapering arms,
And all your thousand other charms,
But all, alas! would be in vain,
You'd never hear your lover's strain.

You're deaf to Cupid's tender lute,
And when he begs an answer, mute.
But still I act the suitor's part,
I clasp my hands across my heart,
I gently heave a melting sigh,
And cast on you a tender eye.
You'll surely understand my sign,
And take me for your Valentine.

New Jersey School for the Deaf
Daily Bulletin, 1890

Occupations

J. L. Smith reported at the sixth convention of the National Association of the Deaf in 1899 that deaf people were engaged in as many as 300 different occupations.

Early employment records kept by the New York School for the Deaf showed that of 232 graduates, 37 were teachers and 3 had become principals. Other occupations listed were: 10 clerks for the U.S. Government, 5 editors and newspaper proprietors, 6 merchants, 4 missionaries to the deaf and 11 artists, photographers and engravers. There were 27 farmers, 7 poultry farmers, 10 farm hands, 5 foremen and assistant foremen, 23 type compositors, 5 carpenters, 14

The Silent Worker

81

shoemakers, 9 tailors, among others. One was an undertaker, one a boilermaker, and two were cigarmakers.

In 1893 the Ohio School for the Deaf reported that 62 of its graduates were type compositors, 152 were farmers, 31 were shoemakers, 29 laborers, 27 shoe factory workers, 25 teachers, 3 principals, and 17 bookbinders. The list also include 5 professional baseball players, a card writer, a coal dealer, a deputy recorder, 3 editors, 2 grocers, and a horse dealer. Five were listed as peddlers, probably salesmen. One was a postmaster, 2 were portrait painters, 1 was a railroad foreman, 1 a saloon-keeper, and another was a ship builder.

Four were known to be teachers of hearing students. George C. Williams, who attended the American School and Gallaudet College, was employed as Director of Penmanship and as a teacher of art at the Hogarth Business University in New Haven, Connecticut. Sara T. Adams, a graduate of the Western New York Institution taught art at St. Margaret's School in Waterbury, Connecticut. Douglas Tilden, a graduate of the California School in Berkeley, taught at the Hopkins Art Institute in San Francisco.

In St. Paul, Minnesota, totally deaf Mrs. Philip Racha not only played the piano, but earned an income from giving lessons to hearing pupils. She had learned to play at seven and continued after she became deaf at the age of fourteen.

Cleveland, Ohio, in the 1890s had a deaf policeman who walked a regular beat. This man, whose name was not recorded, was deafened by a stroke after joining the police force. He persuaded his superiors to let him remain on the force on a trial basis. He did such a good job that he was able to retain his position. He communicated in writing and wore a badge with "Deaf and Dumb Policeman" printed on it.

Myron L. Crane, of Chicago, "deaf as a post," was a railroad flagman for the Chicago and Eastern Illinois Railroad Line. He tended the crossing at 60th and Wallace Street in a densely populated area of the city.

F. McGray was a grocer in Searcy, Arkansas. Thomas S. Marr worked as a draughtsman in Nashville, Tennessee. He later became a successful architect. A Cleveland printer named John E. Dwyer was such a fast hand compositor that he earned the nickname of "Lightning Printer" while employed at the Cleveland Printing, Company. Gust Geyer, an Ohio School alumnus, ran the largest harness business in the city of Galesburg, Illinois. Two other successful photographers of the day (in addition to the better known Alexander Pach) were Ranald Douglas of Liv-ingston, New Jersey, and Theophilus d'Estrella of Berkeley, California.

Reubin C. Stephenson played baseball for the Camden, New Jersey baseball club. He was paid $90 for the first three months and $125 for the remainder of the season. David Jones of Mahanoy City, Pennsylvania had a miner's certificate and worked in mines for years. Frederick Stickles, a graduate of the class of 1885 of the National Deaf-Mute College, was a telegraphic editor on the Duluth, Minnesota *News-Tribune.*

A schooner, the *Mary and Belle,* was known as "probably the only vessel in the world with a crew that are deaf and dumb." George W. Bennett, the captain, and his hand, Charlie Malone, were products of the American School for the Deaf. Bennett had worked for W. J. Brightman, owner of the ship, for 20 years.

Martin Gill was the deaf fireman on the steamship *Lucania,* when it set a record on its run between Queenstown and Sandy Hook, covering the distance in a little over five days.

"Endless Parade on The Boulevard." A drawing by Charles LeClercq, a deaf artist.

In August 1897, Theodore Grady, a deaf teacher at the California School for the Deaf in Berkeley, was licensed to practice law in the state of California.

The Arrival of the Linotype

In the 1890s, deaf printers who made their living by composing type by hand became concerned about a machine which was rumored to set more type than several hand compositors put together. If such talk were true, many of the printers would lose their jobs. Old timers tried to calm the fears of the young printers by assuring them that no machine was going to replace them.

The machine in question was the Linotype, a typecasting machine with a keyboard and approximately 3,000 moving parts. When the keyboard was operated, single brass matrixes, each with an alphabet mold, fell into a slot and composed a line of type which was then molded into a slug. It was this 'line o' type' from which the machine derived its name.

The Silent Worker

The Linotype was invented and patented by Ottmar Mergenthaler and was first used commercially by the New York *Tribune* in 1886. Fast operators could set three or four long galleys of type in an hour. While the advent of the Linotype caused the loss of many hand composing jobs, it created, for many others, an excellent, well-paying job. With the arrival of this typesetting machine, the *National Exponent*, an early publication of the deaf, pessimistically forecast the end of the printing trade for deaf printers. It also predicted that many publications of the deaf would fold because of the increased cost the new machine would surely create. George S. Porter, printing instructor at the New Jersey School for the Deaf and publisher of *The Silent Worker* took exception to this gloomy outlook. He said that the typesetting process was only one of several steps that were necessary to produce a newspaper. Proofreading, make-up, press work, and the press run were tasks that had to be performed before a newspaper could be completed. Porter also doubted whether hand composing would be entirely replaced by typesetting. Even with the machine, he realized that there would be "plenty of work for the hands to do." *The Michigan Mirror* predicted that "The 'tramp printer' who can only do straight work must go; the boy who leaves the (printing) office with his trade half learned will fail; but the perfect printer who knows his work from one end to the other need fear no machine competition."

In fact, the Linotype proved to be a boon to the deaf printer. Many schools added them to their printing departments, turning out excellent operators and giving deaf students an advantage over students attending public schools where vocational programs were not offered. Linotyping remained a popular trade for deaf printers until the 1970s when photocomposition began to replace the Linotype. By the late 1970s through photocomposition an entire newspaper page could be composed, made-up and proofread all in a single step. With the increasing popularity of this new process the Linotype operator realized that his days were numbered. Unless he learned the new process the Linotype operator was destined to go the way the hand compositor had gone decades before.

The Silent Worker

TOP LEFT: *Mrs. Charles LeClercq and her bicycle, "Niagara."*

LEFT: *A group of cyclists at the Kentucky School for the Deaf, May 1897.*

ABOVE: *Frank Wurdemann*

RIGHT: *Gallaudet College cyclists roll down faculty row.*

85

Silent Worker.

CYCLE NUMBER.

VOL. IX. NO. 9   TRENTON, N. J., MAY, 1897.   5 CENTS A COPY.

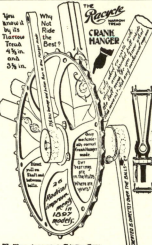

The Decade

The decade of the 1890s opened with the following deaf principals or superintendents administering schools: Henry C. Rider in Malone, New York; Robert Patterson in Ohio; Anson R. Spear in North Dakota; James Simpson in South Dakota; Paul Lange in Evansville, Indiana; the Rev. James H. Cloud in St. Louis; Lars M. Larson in New Mexico, and J. H. Geary in Cincinnati, Ohio. Anson Spear's school had just opened in Devils Lake, with 15 pupils. Within three years, the students moved into a new school building designed by Olof Hanson, a deaf architect.

People petitioned Congress for better roads. Some claimed that this country had the poorest roads in the civilized world. The petitioners argued that one horse could pull more over a hard surfaced road than two could pull over sandy or muddy roads. Good roads were also needed for farmers to bring their produce to market, for trotters to show their pace, and for bicyclists.

In New York City, a doctor named Leech was advertising a "recent discovery" that would restore hearing after a few months of treatment. His advertisement read: "There are thousands who will not believe this, but there are ten thousand who will. This is offered to the majority."

In his Paris studio, deaf American Douglas Tilden was at work on a piece of sculpture which he planned to enter in the World's Fair. The piece of art depicted a struggle between two Indians and a female grizzly bear whose cubs the Indians were trying to steal. Tilden had worked in Paris for four years and had won an honorable mention for an entry at the Paris Salon. Tilden exhibited four pieces of his work at the World's Fair in Chicago: *The Baseball Player*, *The Tired Boxer*, *The Young Acrobat*, and *The Indian Bear Hunter*. The last was valued at $15,000.

R. C. Stephenson was playing baseball for the Camden, New Jersey, semi-professional baseball team. In the summer of 1892, he batted in 36 homeruns and substituted for the centerfielder of the Philadelphia Phillies. He played so well that the Phillies retained him for the rest of the season. William Hoy, the Cincinnati Reds outfielder, was spending the off seasons running a shoe shop in Findlay, Ohio.

Seymour Redmond gave his painting "The Winter Evening," which had also been exhibited at the French Salon, to his alma mater, the California School in Berkeley.

In New York City, 70 printers formed the Fanwood Quad club—so named after the quad, a four sided piece of metal that printers use for spacing or filling

The Silent Worker

lines of hand-set type. The "Quadites" had socials, dinners, sponsored a baseball team, and held other events. At first, membership in the group was open only to printers and by invitation, but gradually the club broadened its aims, and the membership was opened to any deaf person who had "attained the age

Voices, Voices
(1883-1897)

Voices, voices of long ago,
Captive from that fated year,
Fill the halls to which is no
Outlet, since I ceased to hear,
O Memory!

Like the whispering which dwell
(I was once presumed to know)
In the windings of a shell
Nevermore to hear thy flow,
O far-off sea!

J. H. Hogan
The Deaf-Mutes' Journal

Linotype machines in operation in an 1890s printing plant.

An early printing press.

of discretion." Edwin A. Hodgson was the first president of the club.

George M. Weed, a deaf teacher at the Pennsylvania Institution, published a book of religious instruction, *Great Truths Simply Told*. Edwin A. Hodgson published his collection of *Facts, Anecdotes and Poetry*.

Philip Englehardt, a deaf businessman, lost five houses in the great Milwaukee fire.

Early in the decade George S. Porter joined the New Jersey School for the Deaf as instructor of printing. He inherited a four-page newsprint monthly called *The Silent Worker* and set about transforming it into a first-class, glossy magazine. When he retired in 1929, *The Silent Worker* was one of the most widely-read publications of the deaf in the country.

The Rev. Thomas Gallaudet, eldest son of Thomas Hopkins Gallaudet, resigned as rector of the first church for the deaf in the world, St. Ann's Church in New York City. He was 70 years old.

Dr. Isaac L. Peet, the second of the two Peets to head the New York School for the Deaf, retired. The school board conferred on him the title of Principal Emeritus and a salary pension of $3,000, retaining him as an advisor.

During the decade, the New Jersey School was moved from the control of a special Board of Trustees to the State Board of Education. Soon afterwards budget cuts forced all teachers to live off campus. The cutbacks also cost the school coachman his job. The responsibility of taking care of the school's livery stable was passed on to the older boys. The North Carolina Institution outgrew its facilities in Raleigh, and the legislature voted to separate the deaf and blind pupils. The deaf pupils were moved to Morganton, where the school purchased 113 acres. Another 100 acres were donated by the city. Two million bricks were ordered for the $20,000 building which was scheduled for completion in September 1893. The Pennsylvania Institution moved to a 16-acre campus in Mt. Airy. The new plant cost $450,000. Students at the Indiana and Illinois Schools were enjoying their new gymnasiums. The Illinois School had constructed

An early engraving department were cuts were made.

a gym at a cost of $10,000. The New York School added a gym in an upper room of the building, and the New Jersey School added one in the basement of the school's new industrial building. These new gyms were called places where the boys and girls "on alternated days received instruction in building up their health and learned to overcome the shuffling step and stoop shoulder posture which was prevalent especially among the deaf."

Officials at the Rome, New York, school suggested an athletic league among the schools for the deaf.

Kansas, Iowa, Alabama, Mt. Airy, and Fanwood schools reported that they had added barbering to their vocational training programs. The Departments of Agriculture at the Universities of Missouri and Minnesota began to admit graduates of the state schools for the deaf.

The Utah School moved from Salt Lake City to Ogden, Utah. The Arkansas School was occupying its new industrial arts building, new hospital, and the newly remodeled girls' dormitory. The St. Joseph's Institution moved into new buildings in Westchester, New York. A bill was passed in Ohio providing for the education of blind deaf students.

During two days' competition in 1899, the Georgia School for the Deaf Volunteer Fire Department team was the winner. Teams of fire fighters, in the contest pulled their carts with hose a given distance, hooked them up to a fire plug, and turned the water on. The team that accomplished this in the least time was declared the winner. The GSD boys were the quickest and received an engraved trophy.

Fanwood School had its own fire engine.

On Presentation Day, May 1898, Edward Miner Gallaudet presented to the college the bust of de L'Epée he had received from deaf people in France.

Tragedy struck one December evening in the early 1890s when L. W. Saunders, a teacher at the Mississippi School for the Deaf, decided to dress as Santa Claus and surprise his young nephew. He stopped at the boy's house on his way to a Christmas program and knocked on the door. His nephew, who was at home alone, became frightened after repeatedly asking who was there. Thinking it was a burglar he got the family gun and shot through the door killing his deaf uncle who had not heard his questions.

"ON THE ROAD FOR HEALTH."

Early "cures."

Artists

"Self-Portrait with Sound of Flowers," watercolor, 1969, by Morris Broderson, the Joan Ankrum Collection.

Hillis Arnold

Hillis Arnold, Sculptor

Hillis Arnold was born in North Dakota; he became deaf from spinal meningitis when he was six months old. When he was 12 his family moved to Minneapolis where he attended a class for deaf students in a public school. He graduated *cum laude* from the University of Minnesota in 1933 and studied at the Minneapolis School of Art and at the Cranbrook Academy of Art.

In 1938 Arnold became professor of sculpture at Monticello College in Illinois.

Arnold was the first noted sculptor to use the new medium of plastic aluminum. His major works have religious themes, and he has executed many pieces for churches. His sculpture of "Abraham and Isaac", two and a half feet tall, carved in mahogany and covered with polychrome, was selected to be one of 16 examples of American art exhibited in the International Biennial of Contemporary Christian Art in Salisbury, Austria in 1948. It was then displayed at the Religious Art Center of America in Pennsylvania where it was purchased by Cardinal Joseph Ritter for his private chapel in St. Louis.

Felix Kowalewski recognizes Arnold as one of the finest living American sculptors. He was elected to membership as a Live Fellow in the International Institute of Arts and Letters, a world-wide organization with a very restricted membership. The honor was a high point in his career.

Hillis' "Crucifix of Christ," a five and one-half foot wooden cross, adorns the Epiphany Lutheran Church in St. Louis, Missouri.

94

LEFT: "The Lord is My Shepherd," is seven feet tall and made of Georgia marble. It is located in Cardinal Ritter's garden in LaDue, Missouri.

BOTTOM: "Mother Ann and Child Mary," a 16-foot tall limestone sculpture at St. Ann's Catholic Church in Normandy, Missouri.

David Bloch, Porcelain Artist and Woodcut Printmaker

David Bloch was born in Bavaria, in South Germany, in 1910. He was enrolled in a school for the deaf in Munich when he was five years old. He attended the Technical School of the Porcelain Industry in Selb and was then apprenticed as a china decorator at a porcelain factory. He continued his studies in art at the Academy of Applied Art.

In 1938 Bloch was arrested by the Nazis and interned at the Dachau Concentration Camp. Two years later, following his release from prison, he fled Germany traveling eastward and arriving in Shanghai, China. For nine years he lived in that city. There he met and married a Chinese woman. In 1949 they emigrated to the United States.

Bloch is noted for his woodcuts and designs on china. He designed a service set of china for the White House during Lyndon B. Johnson's presidency. He had a one-man show at Gallaudet College in 1975, and his work has been exhibited in the Print Room at the National Gallery of Art. Several pieces of his work are on permanent display there. *Gallaudet Today*, the college's quarterly printed a story about him and his work in the Fall, 1975 issue.

A David Bloch playing card.

David Bloch

"Accident," a woodcut by David Bloch.

"Bringing Wreaths for the Mourning Family." Woodcut by David Bloch.

"Contrast," a Bloch woodcut, shows the contrast between a privileged few and the multitudes.

98

"A Long Beam Holds Up Traffic."
Woodcut by David Bloch.

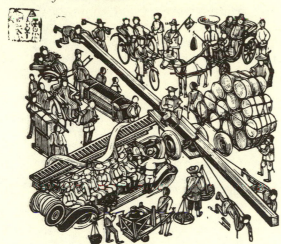

"Carrying Wares." Woodcut by David Bloch.

"Progress." Woodcut by David Bloch.

Morris Broderson and Joan Ankrum in Ankrum Gallery.

Arizona, the Corcoran Gallery of Art in Washington, D.C., Carnegie Institute in Pittsburgh, the Hirshhorn Museum and Sculpture Gardens in Washington, D.C., and at the 1964 World's Fair in New York. Joseph H. Hirshhorn is a major collector of his work. Broderson's painting "Angel and Holy Mary" was included in the inaugural exhibition of the Hirshorn Museum when it opened in November 1975.

The University of Arizona published a book about Broderson and his work in 1975.

RIGHT: "Tribute to Winslow Homer," watercolor and pastel, 1968, by Morris Broderson, the William Challee Collection.

"Lizzie's Dream," mixed, 1966, by Morris Broderson. The Agnes De Mille Collection.

Morris Broderson, Painter

In 1963 Morris Broderson's work was shown in Edith Halpert's Downtown Gallery in New York City. She described him with these words: "He is among the few artists of this generation who created his own vocabulary early and sustained his identity with a remarkable evolution of constant growth in concept and technical proficiency."

Born deaf in Los Angeles, California, November 4, 1928, Broderson attended the California School for the Deaf, Berkeley and schools in Los Angeles. He studied at the Pasadena Art Museum, California, Jessen Art Institute in Los Angeles, and at the University of Southern California.

Broderson was one of the first deaf artists to incorporate the manual alphabet into some of his paintings. He has had more than 20 one-man shows and his works are included in more than 35 public collections. He has exhibited his paintings at Dixie Hall Studios, Stanford University Museum of Art, and the University of California, all in California; at the Downtown Gallery, in New York, the Phoenix Art Museum in

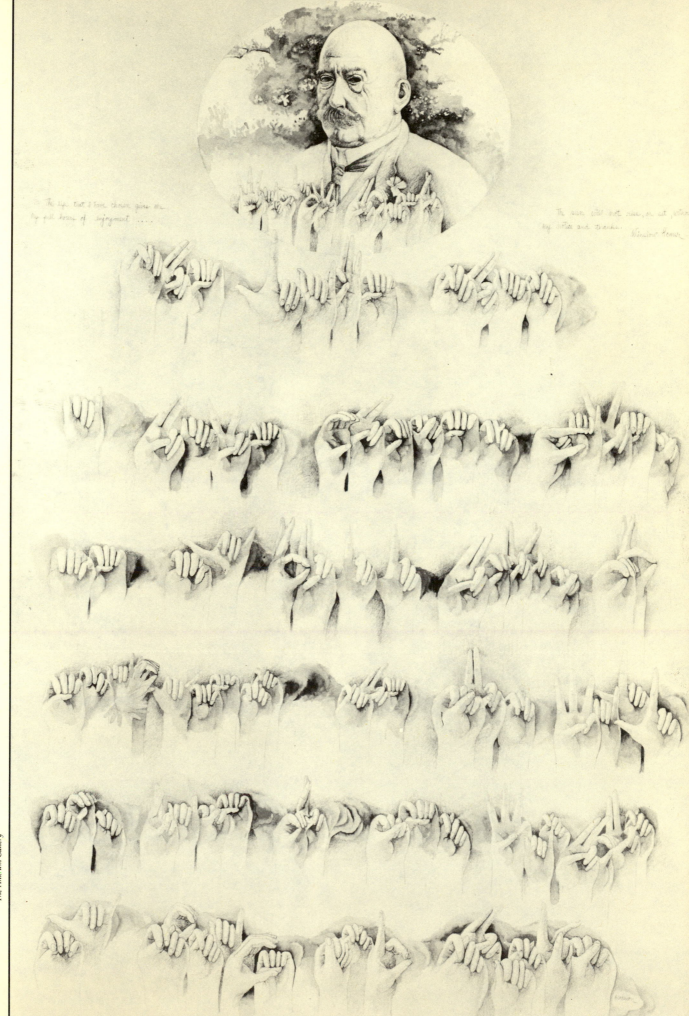

"Lament for Ignacio Sanchez II," pastel, watercolor and pencil, 1966, by Morris Broderson.

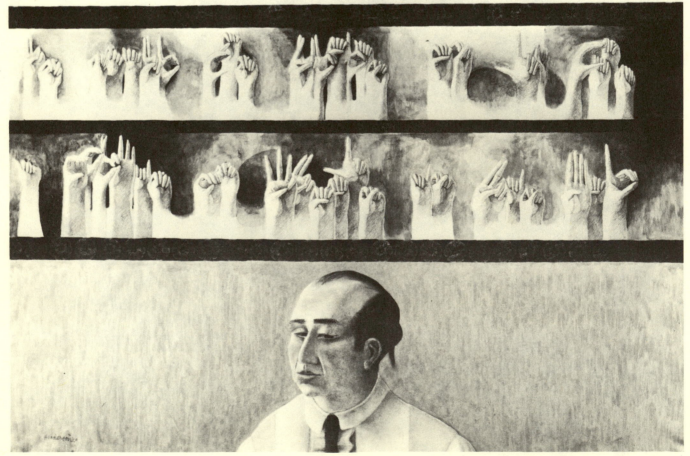

"Home of Sanchez Mejias," oil, 1966, by Morris Broderson, The Mr. and Mrs. J. Carney Collection.

"Thoreau," watercolor, 1968, by Morris Broderson, The Ankrum Gallery.

John Brewster, Portraitist

John Brewster was the sixth pupil to enroll in the newly opened Connecticut Asylum for the Education and Instruction of Deaf and Dumb Persons (now the American School for the Deaf) when it was opened in 1817. He was 51 years old, self-supporting, and already a successful artist at that time.

Brewster specialized in oil portraits. He traveled up and down New England painting pictures of members of well-to-do families. He advertised his work in the local newspapers, charged $15 for his oil portraits and $10 for miniatures, and evidently made a comfortable living. There are indications that he fared better than his father and brother who were doctors.

Unfortunately Brewster did not sign all of his paintings. Sometimes he just penciled in his name on the canvas wooden stretcher frame where it soon faded away. As a result many of his works have been lost, are unverified, or remain unrecognized in private hands. Other pieces of his work are in the Museum of Fine Arts, Boston; the Abby Aldrich Rockefeller

"Girl in Green," oil,
by John Brewster
Abby Aldrich Rockefeller
Folk Art Center,
Williamsburg, Virginia.

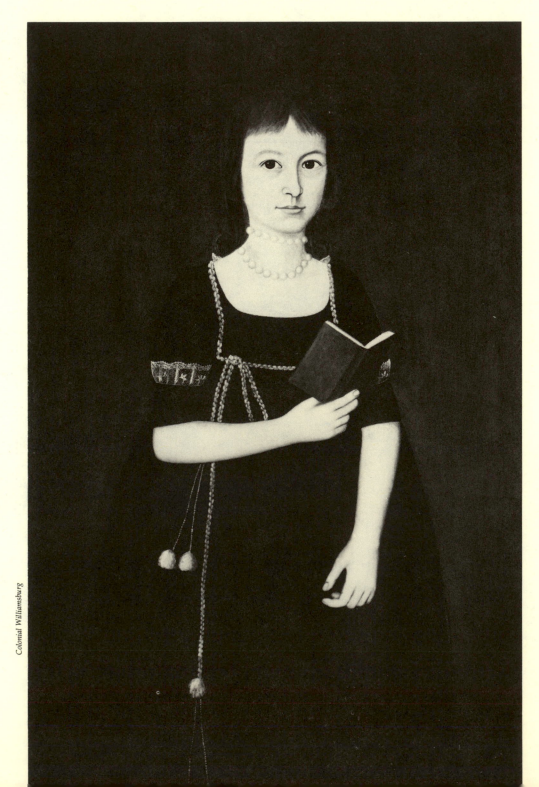

Colonial Williamsburg

Collection, Williamsburg, Virginia; and Old Sturbridge Village, Massachusetts.

Art in America called Brewster "perhaps the most appealing of Connecticut artists in the age of American Folk painting."

John Brewster was born May, 1766 and reared in a cultured eighteenth century environment together with his seven brothers and sisters. He died at the age of 88 in 1854 and is buried beside one of his brothers in Tory Hill Cemetery in Buxton Tower Corners, Maine.

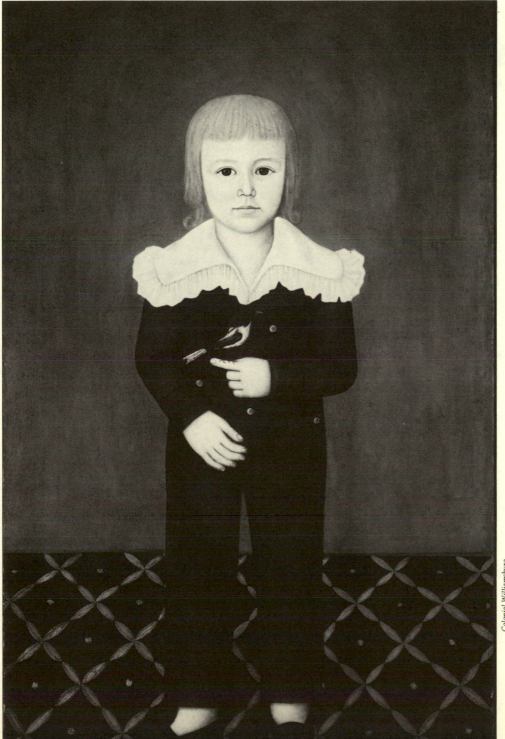

"Boy With Finch," oil,
by John Brewster,
Abby Aldrich Rockefeller
Folk Art Center,
Williamsburg, Virginia.

Colonial Williamsburg

105

John Carlin

John Carlin, Painter

"After a Long Cruise," one of John Carlin's masterpieces, was included in the collection of the exhibition at the Detroit Institute of Arts between 1820 and the Civil War. His charcoal drawing of Laurent Clerc is in the Gallaudet College collection. An oil painting of Laurent Clerc is at the Kentucky School for the Deaf.

John Carlin was born in Philadelphia in 1813. He graduated from the Philadelphia Institution for the Deaf in 1825. He studied in London and was a pupil of Paul Delaroche in Paris. He returned to this country in 1841 and became a painter of miniatures in New York City.

Carlin was also a poet. "The Deaf-Mute's Lament" was one of his better known poems. His ability to write poetry amazed many because he was born deaf.

With the increased popularity of photography he gave up painting miniatures and turned to painting oil portraits, landscapes, and general subjects.

John Carlin married Miss Seward of the family of Lincoln's famous Secretary Seward. Carlin died on April 23, 1891.

Oil painting of Laurent Clerc by John Carlin. American School for the Deaf Collection.

Charcoal drawing of Laurent Clerc by John Carlin. Gallaudet College Collection.

The Montana Historical Society, Helena

John Clarke working on a wood carving panel for the Montana Historical Society Museum in 1956.

John L. Clarke, Wood Carver

John L. Clarke was a successful wood carver. As a youth he became deaf from scarlet fever. He grew up in Glacier National Park in the Rocky Mountins of Montana where he loved the wild animals and studied them intently. He made figures of them out of clay and later began carving them from wood.

Clarke was born on January 20, 1881, of Indian parentage, in Highwood, near Great Falls, Montana. He attended the Montana and North Dakota Schools for the Deaf. He studied woodcarving at the St. Francis Academy in Milwaukee.

Clarke's Indian friends called him Cutapuis, meaning "man-who-talks-not." Clarke opened a studio in Montana where he sold his carvings to tourists. One of his customers was John D. Rockefeller.

Clarke's work is on display at the Montana Historical Society Museum in Helena, Montana, at the University of Montana, in Missoula.

John Clarke died on November 20, 1970; he was 89 years old.

John Clarke and one of his carved panels.

Theophilus Hope d'Estrella. Circa 1890.

Theophilus d'Estrella, Art Instructor and Photographer

Theophilus Hope d'Estrella was born deaf on February 6, 1851. He was orphaned at the age of five. He was the first student to enroll at the California Institution for the Education and Care of the Indigent Deaf and Dumb and the Blind (now the California School for the Deaf, Berkeley) when it opened May 1, 1860. He graduated in 1873 and became the first deaf student to enroll at the University of California in Berkeley. In 1879 he was admitted to the San Francisco Art Association's School of Design where he studied drawing and painting for five years. He became an art teacher at his alma mater, the California School for

"The Opening Gate,"
c. 1895,
by Theophilus Hope
d'Estrella

110

the Deaf, and taught at that school the rest of his life. He started Douglas Tilden and Granville Redmond on their careers as artists.

D'Estrella enjoyed hiking in the West, sketching, and photographing what he saw. He became a vivid photographer, and in 1901 he won first prize in the Photographic Salon at the Mark Hopkins Art Institute in San Francisco. His writings and photographs appeared in the *Overland Monthly Magazine* of March, 1887.

D'Estrella died on October 8, 1929. The auditorium at the California School for the Deaf is named for him.

A book about him, *The Magic Lantern Man: Theophilus Hope d'Estrella*, by Mildred Albronda was published in 1980 by TJ Publishers, Inc.

"A Rebuke,"
1892,
by Theophilus Hope
d'Estrella

LEFT: "A Mischievous Knowing Glance," circa 1888, by Theophilus Hope d'Estrella.

BELOW: "Wisteria Garden," circa 1898, by Theophilus Hope d'Estrella.

Robert J. Freiman, Painter

Robert J. Freiman was born deaf in New York City on March 19, 1917. At the age of three he began attending the Wright Oral School in that city. When he was six years old he transferred to the Lexington School. He spent the last two years of his elementary education at the New York (Fanwood) School.

He began showing an interest in drawing when he was four years of age. This interest continued as he grew older. He attended the National Academy of Design and spent most of his summers in Nantucket and France studying and painting. He has used many different media to express himself but his favorite form is mixed media using water color, acrylic, and pen and ink. He has been noted for his "color communication."

In 1950 Freiman won a prize for his work from the French Republic.

Freiman's work is on permanent display in the Boston Museum of Fine Arts, the Connecticut Museum at New Britain, the Kenneth Taylor Galleries at Nantucket, and the Musée Municipal de St. Paul de Vence in France, and in many private collections in this country and abroad.

He had a one-man show at Gallaudet College October 24-November 21, 1973.

Freiman is a member of the American Water Color Society.

Robert Freiman, Self-portrait, pencil.

The Deaf American

Robert Freiman

Gallaudet College Archives

113

LEFT: "Rosemarie Louit," portrait, by Robert Freiman.

BOTTOM LEFT: "Garconnet de St. Paul de Vence," crayon and wash, by Robert Freiman.

BOTTOM RIGHT: "Prince Doan Thai of Laos," crayon and wash, by Robert Freiman.

114

Louis Frisino

Louis Frisino, Wildlife Artist

Louis Frisino was born in January, 1934. Deaf at birth, he attended the St. Xavier School for the Deaf and the Maryland School for the Deaf, graduating from the latter in 1953. His love for dogs, in particular, and wildlife, in general, influenced his drawings and paintings beginning in his early years.

Frisino studied at the Maryland Institute, College of Art, graduating with honors in 1959. He was one of the recipients of the coveted Peabody Award. For 25 years he was an artist for the Baltimore *News American*, during which time he also pursued a private artistic career, establishing himself as a prominent Maryland wildlife artist. Frisino works predominantly with water colors, occasionally adding opaque tempera for the desired effect. His paintings are characterized by realism and fine detail; they highlight outdoor scenes or wildlife against a white background.

Frisino's work has been exhibited in numerous shows in Maryland, Delaware, and New Jersey. In 1976, his design "Canvasbacks" was selected for the Maryland Duck Stamp. In 1977, 1978 and 1979 (the first three years of the Fish Stamp Contest sponsored by the Maryland Department of Natural Resources and open to all Maryland Artists) Frisino's trout drawings were selected for the fishing permit stamps for those years. Forty-five of Frisino's fish drawings were featured in the 1970 edition of the magazine, *Fishing in Maryland.* His work has also appeared in the Spring 1972 issue of *North American Decoy* and Tom Cofield's *The Fisherman's Guide to North America.* In 1976 and 1977 the National Wildlife Federation used two of his paintings, "A Pair of Cardinals" and "Holiday Feast" on its Christmas cards.

This drawing ("Canvasbacks") by Louis Frisino was chosen for the 1976-77 Maryland Duck Stamp.

"Red Fox," by Louis Frisino.

"Chesapeake Bay Retriever with Goose," by Louis Frisino.

"Rainbow Trout," by Louis Frisino, appeared on the 1978 Maryland Trout Stamp.

"Brown Trout," by Louis Frisino. This drawing was chosen for the 1977 Maryland Trout Stamp.

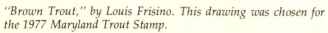

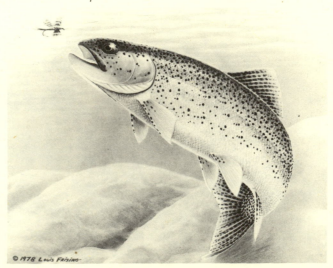

116

LEFT: "Pintails," by Louis Frisino.

BOTTOM LEFT: "Labrador Retriever with Pintail," by Louis Frisino.

BOTTOM RIGHT: "Golden Retriever with Hen Mallard," by Louis Frisino.

117

Eugene E. Hannan, Sculptor

Eugene Elmer Hannan is best remembered for his sculpture of the Abbé Charles Michel de L'Epée in Buffalo, New York. This piece of work memorializes de L'Epée, the founder in Paris, France, of the first free school for the deaf in the world. The statue was a gift of the National Association of the Deaf, which commissioned the work to mark the organization's golden anniversary in August, 1930.

Hannan was born July 26, 1875, in Washington, D.C. He became deaf from scarlet fever when he was three years old. His education began at the Kendall School for the Deaf in the District of Columbia, which he attended for six years. He then studied for one year at the Le Couteulx Institution for the Deaf (now St.

Mary's School) in Buffalo, New York, before transferring to St. John's Institute in Milwaukee. It was at St. John's that he began to display artistic talent and wood carving skill. Hannan attended Gallaudet College for one year and studied at the Corcoran School of Art in Washington, D.C. for three years. He attended the Art Institute in Chicago where he studied under the famous American sculptor, Lorado Taft. Later he joined the Art Student's League in New York City.

Hannan studied in Europe and worked in Spain with the two famous deaf Spanish brother-artists, De Zubiaurres. In France he became acquainted with Paul Chopin, another deaf sculptor.

In 1880 Hannan assisted Gutzon Borglum, one of his famous teachers, with the bronze equestrian statue of General Philip H. Sheridan, the brilliant Union

Hannan's statue of de l'Epée in Buffalo, New York.

St. Mary's School for the Deaf

general of the Civil War, which is located on Sheridan Circle in Washington, D.C.

Hannan did a plaster bust of Edward Miner Gallaudet. It was presented to the college by the class of 1926 and is located in Chapel Hall.

Hannan and his wife, Helen Constance, lived their later years in Westport, Connecticut, where he died on February 7, 1945 at the age of 69. He is buried there in the Willowbrook Cemetery.

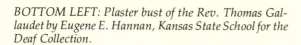

BOTTOM LEFT: Plaster bust of the Rev. Thomas Gallaudet by Eugene E. Hannan, Kansas State School for the Deaf Collection.

RIGHT: Plaster bust of the Rev. Thomas Hopkins Gallaudet by Eugene E. Hannan, Maryland School for the Deaf Collection.

BOTTOM RIGHT: Plaster bust of Edward M. Gallaudet by Eugene E. Hannan, Gallaudet College Collection.

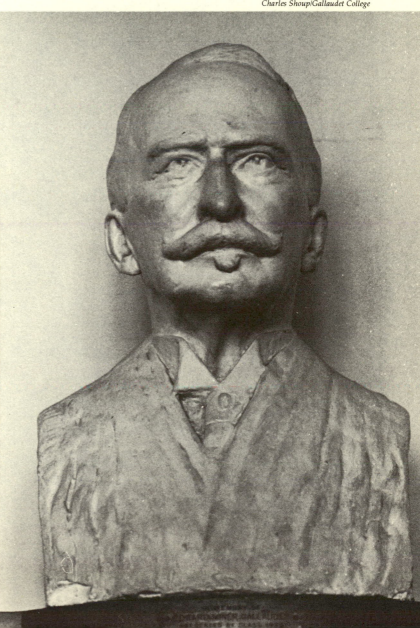

Charles Shoup/Gallaudet College

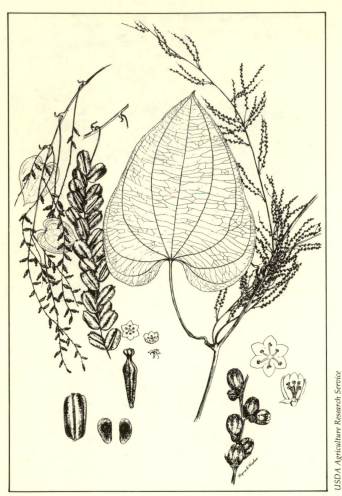

USDA Agriculture Research Service

"Tributo a una Planto, Dioscorea composita," by Regina O. Hughes.

Regina Olson Hughes, Scientific Illustrator

Regina Olson was born in February, 1895 in Herman, Nebraska. She lost her hearing gradually between the age of 10 and 14 due to a bout with measles and then complications. She was enrolled at Gallaudet College and graduated in 1918. In 1923 she married Frederick H. Hughes, a popular Gallaudet College professor and coach. She has done post-graduate work at a number of universities.

Regina Hughes began drawing before she could write. She studied with private art teachers as a teenager and taught drawing and painting during her summer vacations from college.

She attained stature as an artist and scholar during years of government service. She used her fluency in four languages—French, Spanish, Portugese and Ital-

ian—to work as a translator in the State Department during World War I. Following her marriage, she joined the U.S. Department of Agriculture as an artist—a position which was to provide challenges, interest, and the opportunity to use her extraordinary talents. In 1936 she became the scientific illustrator in botany for the Agricultural Research Service. Her pen and ink drawings meticulously and painstakingly reproduced many species. Much of her work is so detailed that it has been done with the aid of a microscope.

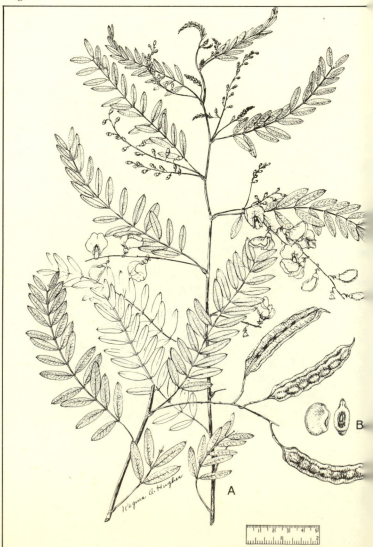

Daubentonia puncicea (cav.) D.C. Coffeeweed by Regina O. Hughes.
USDA Handbook 366

USDA Agriculture Research Service.

Brucea antidysenterica *Mill by Regina O. Hughes.*

Regina O. Hughes

Charles Shoup/Gallaudet College

Since her retirement in 1969 from the Department of Agriculture Dr. Hughes has been a resident scientific illustrator at the Smithsonian Institution in the Department of Botany. Her paintings and drawings have been exhibited in numerous shows including one-woman exhibits at the National Arboretum, the National Agricultural Library, and Gallaudet College. Her work has also been exhibited with the National League of American Pen Women, the Guild of Natural Science Illustrators, and the Hunt Institute for Botanical Documentation at Carnegie-Mellon University. Her drawings are included in the permanent collections of the Hunt Institute for Botanical Documentation, the Smithsonian Institution, and in many private collections.

The list of books and scientific publications Hughes has illustrated is long. Foremost among these are the Agricultural Research Service Handbook 366, which contains 224 full-page plates of her work and has been published under the title *Common Weeds of the U.S.* by Dover Press. The USDA Handbook No. 498, *Economically Important Foreign Weeds. Potential Problems in the United States,* contains over 6,000 of her drawings of seeds and plants.

In 1962 the Department of Agriculture presented her with the Superior Service Award for her illustrations and technical translations. In 1967 Gallaudet College granted her the honorary degree of Doctor of Humane Letters. In 1970 she was named "Woman of the Year" by the Gallaudet College Phi Kappa Zeta Sorority, and in 1979 the Smithsonian Institution honored her by naming a new species of Bromeliad, *Billbergia regina,* for Regina Olson Hughes.

Regina O. Hughes

Felix Kowalewski

Felix Kowalewski, Artist and Teacher

Felix Kowalewski was born in Brooklyn, New York, November 20, 1913. He became deaf from spinal meningitis when he was six years old. He attended the New York (Fanwood) School for the Deaf, graduating in 1932. During his last year at Fanwood he attended the New York School of Fine and Applied Arts where he studied anatomy and life drawing.

He was admitted to Gallaudet College and graduated in 1937. He studied art under Donald Kline. Later, he studied on his own and at the Washington Art League. During his sophomore year at Gallaudet, the students purchased his oil painting of Chapel Hall, which now hangs in the Edward Miner Gallaudet Memorial Library.

Felix Kowalewski is a well known artist, poet, and writer, although he prefers to be remembered as an art teacher of the deaf rather than as a professional artist. He has taught at four schools for the deaf—California School for the Deaf, Berkeley, Michigan School for the Deaf, West Virginia School for the Deaf and the Blind, and California School for the Deaf at Riverside.

Art lovers and critics have praised Kowalewski's fine paints in water color, pastels, and oils. He is interested in people, character, and costume portraits.

He had a one man show at Gallaudet College in December, 1974. He has exhibited at the National Gallery, the Corcoran Gallery, and the Washington Art League in Washington, D.C., the Roerich Museum, the American-Anderson Galleries, and Parsons in New York; the San Francisco Palace of Fine Arts, the Riverside Art Center and Museum, Flint Institute of Arts in Michigan, the Walt Disney Studios in Burbank and many other places.

He has written numerous articles about other artists in *The Silent Worker* and *The Deaf American*.

He and his wife, the former Laura Eiler of Minnesota, reside on the outskirts of Riverside. They have three grown children.

OVERLEAF: *"Apres le Bal," by Felix Kowalewski.*

"Chapel Hall," oil, by Felix Kowalewski. The Gallaudet College Collection.

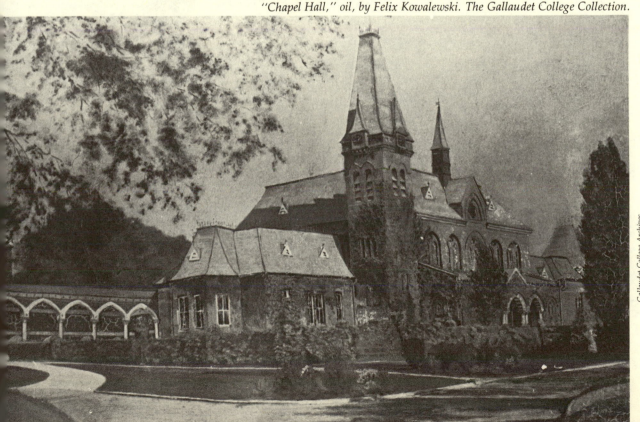

124

Frederick LaMonto, Artist and Sculptor

A very successful artist and sculptor, Frederick LaMonto, was born in Buffalo, New York, in 1921. He attended St. Mary's School in that city and also the Buffalo Art Center School. After a long dormant period he became acquainted with the internationally famous deaf artist, Morris Broderson, and his interest in painting was renewed.

His introduction into sculpture was by accident. One day while watching a deaf carpenter apply plaster to a wall in a house-remodeling project, he decided to experiment and began to create sculpture out of plaster. His break came when he had a one-man show at the famed Bognar Galleries in Los Angeles. His second piece of sculpture, "The Ten Commandments" sold for $1,000 at this first one-man show.

LaMonto works with wood and wire mesh which he covers with his own plaster formula. His work has been described as "explosive" and "a rare experience to view." It shows the influence of Giacometti, Henry Moore, and Rodin.

LaMonto's work has appeared at many art exhibits including the Laguna Beach Art Festival, the San Diego Fine Arts Gallery, and the Long Beach Museum of Modern Art. He has had more than seven one-man shows.

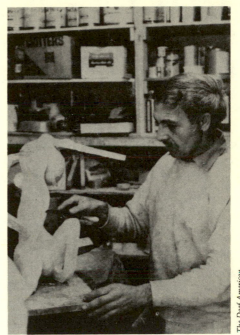

Frederick LaMonto

"Death in the Afternoon," by Frederick LaMonto.

LEFT: *"Helen Keller's Breakthrough," by Frederick LaMonto.*

BOTTOM LEFT: *Frederick LaMonto and his sculpture, "Lady Godiva."*

BOTTOM RIGHT: *"Leda and the Swan" by Frederick LaMonto.*

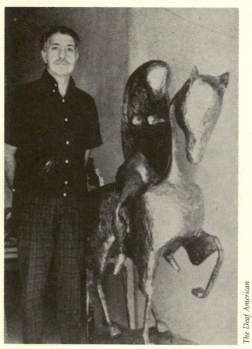

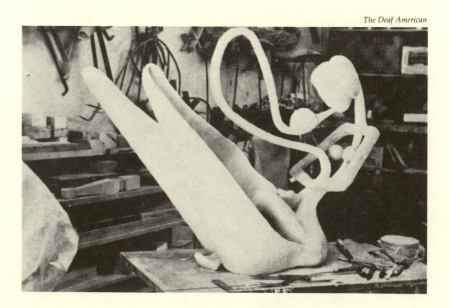

"Recycling," by Charles LeClercq.

The Silent Worker

Charles J. LeClercq

Charles J. LeClercq, Illustrator

Charles Joseph Lalon LeClercq was born in New Orleans. His family moved to St. Louis and later settled in New York City. LeClercq became deaf during a spinal meningitis epidemic (1871-72). After attending a public school for a few years he enrolled in the New York School for the Deaf. He began taking evening drawing lessons and made rapid progress. Eventually he enrolled in an art class at Cooper Union and

there he won recognition for his clay modeling and drawing from casts. After graduation he became apprenticed to a lithographer, and studied letter design, water color sketching, oil painting and drawing.

On his own LeClercq moved away from reproduction and adopted a more creative medium, doing pen and ink illustrations for newspapers and wash drawings for magazines. He designed posters and drew advertisement illustrations, and held jobs with advertising and other companies.

His achievements as a photo engraver made him a successful contributor to *The Silent Worker* in the 1880s. He authored and illustrated several pieces about his favorite sport, bicycling. In "Wheeling to Nyack" and "Bicycling to Oyster Bay," LeClercq describes bicycle day trips of up to forty-five miles undertaken by him, his wife, and other ardent "wheelers." His descriptive prose is enhanced by pen and ink drawings sketched enroute. LeClercq's sense of humor and joie de vivre

Scenes along the route to Rye Beach, pen and ink by Charles LeClercq.

The Silent Worker

Scenes along the bicycle trail, by Charles LeClercq.

The Silent Worker

RIVER-SCENE.   COURT HOUSE, TRENTON.   CHURCH, EWING.

Scenes from the Trenton area. *The Silent Worker*

are apparent as he muses, ''I'd like to see a semi-mute holding a long talk on wheels with a hearing person,'' (he goes on to explain that they dismount to discuss directions!), or when he describes 1880 roads to Rye Beach: ''The conditions of Union Avenue would make it difficult even for an elephant.'' Despite hazardous conditions, the cyclers made it to their destination and safely returned to New York by train.

LeClercq drew upon his bicycle trips around New York for material for his engravings and ink drawings. He was a successful illustrator during his lifetime.

Scenes from the pen of Charles LeClercq. *The Silent Worker*

Betty Miller, Artist

Betty Miller

Betty Miller is one of the first—if not the very first—deaf artists to introduce the methodological war into her art work. She has done collages and paintings depicting deaf chidren wearing hearing gadgets, and showing the emphasis placed on speech and lipreading and the restricting of the use of hands in communicating. In her art, hands are often shown tied together or chopped up. Her work has brought to the fore the deep-seated resentment held by many deaf individuals toward the rigid, pure oral method. Miller won first prize for her painting in an art exhibit sponsored by the Gallaudet College Alumni Association.

Betty Miller has been hard of hearing since birth. She attended Northbrook High School in Illinois and then Gallaudet College, graduating in 1957. She earned her master's degree from Maryland Art Institute in Baltimore in 1963. She was a professor of art

Richard J. Schoenberg

''Bell School, 1944,'' 1971, by Betty G. Miller

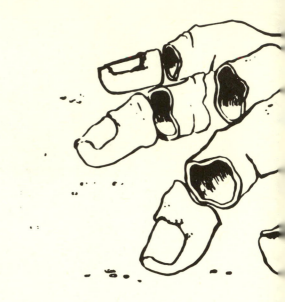

"Education for the Deaf," 1971, by Betty G. Miller, The Mary Beth Miller Collection.

"Education for the Deaf," 1971, by Betty G. Miller, The D. Buyas Collection.

130

"Ameslan Prohibited," 1972, By Betty G. Miller,
The Sandi Inches-Norris Collection

at Gallaudet College for several years. Miller holds the distinction of being the first female undergraduate alumna of Gallaudet College to earn a doctorate. She received her doctoral degree in art education from Pennsylvania State University in 1976.

Miller is currently executive director of Deafness Counseling Advocacy and Referral Agency in California.

OVERLEAF: *"Lipreading,"* 1972, by Betty G. Miller, The Sandi Inches-Norris Collection.

Ralph R. Miller, Commercial Artist

Ralph R. Miller was born deaf in Jonesboro, Illinois, in 1905. He attended the Illinois School for the Deaf, graduating in 1925. He studied at the American Academy of Art in Chicago and afterwards became a commercial artist, doing work for many nationally-known accounts. He has been an artist for nearly half a century.

Since 1972 Miller has been illustrating classic children's stories for the Gallaudet College Signed English project. All characters in the book, whether animal or human, are shown conversing in Signed English. The series includes such old favorites as ''The Three Little Pigs,'' ''Little Red Riding Hood,'' ''Goldilocks and the Three Bears,'' and many others. He has also served as a consultant to the Art Department at Gallaudet.

Miller and his wife, Gladys, have three children. One of them, Betty, who is also deaf, is an accomplished artist. She was the first undergraduate alumna of Gallaudet to earn a doctoral degree.

Ralph Miller

H. Humphrey Moore, Painter

Henry Humphrey Moore was born in New York in 1844. He died in Paris in 1926. A descendant of a noted miniature painter, Ozias Humphrey, Moore became deaf when he was three years old. Throughout his life he used a pad and pencil to communicate with a wide circle of influential friends and used his art as his vehicle of expression. "My brush is my voice," he once said.

Moore attended schools for the deaf in Philadelphia and Hartford and went to David Bartlett's private school for the deaf and hearing when it was located in Poughkeepsie, New York. He began studying art as a young man, concentrating on perspective and oil painting technique, and later continued his work at the Ecole des Beaux Arts, studying under Gerome, Boulanger, and Yvon.

Moore traveled widely. His 1870-74 visit to Spain brought him some notoriety through contacts with socially and politically influential people. He married a Spanish noblewoman, Isabella de Cistue, in 1872,

Henry Humphrey Moore.

The Silent Worker

"Mother and Daughter," by H. Humphrey Moore.

The Silent Worker

"Portrait of a Titled Lady," by H. Humphrey Moore.

The Silent Worker

and they traveled to Morocco, where the seeds of Moore's Moorish genre works were sown. These compositions depicted the life of the harems, bazaars, and mosques of the East, and earned him the title of Knight of the Order of King Charles the Third, conferred upon him by Queen Christina of Spain.

On his return to the United States Moore settled in New York City but soon left for Japan in the early 1880s. After two years there he became known as the "Painter of Japan." His exquisite miniatures, done in oil on wood, demonstrated his penchant for detail and meticulous realism, qualities illustrated by his miniatures "The Acrobats," and "In a Japanese Garden." His Japanese collection won a medal at the Paris Universal Exhibit in 1898.

In the late 1880s Moore settled in Paris, where he lived and worked for over 40 years. Wealthy most of his life, he did not try to sell or publicize his work until after World War I, when his personal fortune ebbed. During his years in Paris he exhibited his work solely within his studio to a select group of people. He did earn renown, however, as a portrait artist. His subjects included many women aristocrats and some English and French children of high birth, including Don Jaimie, the deaf son of King Alphonso.

After World War I, Moore lived both in the United States (at one point working with fellow artist Thomas Eakins in Philadelphia) and in Paris. He died in January, 1926 leaving a legacy of artistic treasures—a testimony to the artist's endless patience, attention to detail, and creativity.

H. Humphrey Moore in his New York studio.

Granville S. Redmond

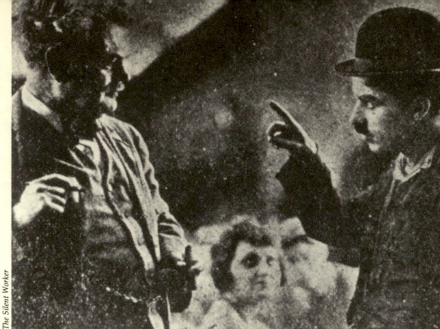

Charlie Chaplin fingerspelling to his friend, Granville Redmond.

Granville S. Redmond, Landscape Artist

Granville Seymour Redmond, who became a successful landscape artist was born on March 9, 1871 in Philadelphia. Guilbert Braddock states that Redmond was totally deaf from infancy. Other sources list him as becoming deaf at the age of two and a half years from scarlet fever. Regardless of the age of deafness, he never learned to speak. Redmond attended the California School for the Deaf at Berkeley where he was a pupil of deaf art instructor Theophilus d'Estrella. Following his schooling, he studied at the San Francisco School of Design and in Paris at the expense of the State of California, at the Julien Academy where he came under the tutelage of Benjamin Constan and Jean Paul Laurens.

In 1894, when he was 23 and studying in Paris, his painting, "A Winter Scene on the Seine," was one of 500 paintings selected for admission to the Paris Salon. The painting was his first masterpiece.

"A Winter Scene on the Seine" is now in the California School for the Deaf collection. He presented the painting to the school to repay the school for his study in Paris. Another of his paintings hangs in the Washington State Capitol at Olympia.

Redmond's work was exhibited at the Louisiana Purchase Exposition in St. Louis, at the San Francisco Art Association, at the Panama-Pacific Exposition, and at the Seattle Exposition. Together with William Keith, he was one of California's best landscape painters. He is listed in *Who's Who in America* and is one of the few deaf artists mentioned in Fielding's *Directory of American Artists*.

Tall, sturdily built, with a shock of thick wavy hair, and round-rimmed wire glasses, Redmond was a good friend of Charlie Chaplin, the star of silent films. His studio was located on Chaplin's lot in Hollywood. Chaplin was a collector of Redmond's work and once said of his friend's work, ". . . something puzzles me about Redmond's pictures. There's such a wonderful joyousness about them all. Look at the gladness in the sky, the riot of color in those flowers." Chaplin's favorite Redmond painting was "Low Tide" of which he said: "Isn't it beautiful! That moonlight—it makes you feel you ought to whisper!"

Albert Ballin gives Redmond credit for influencing Chaplin's acting. Chaplin did not move his lips in his silent films. He used gestures and expressions resembling those used by deaf persons. As a youth Redmond excelled in the art of pantomime. He took some minor roles in a few of Chaplin's films, according to Ballin. "The Gold Rush" was one of these.

Redmond's wife, Carrie Ann Jean, was a graduate of the Illinois School. They had three children. He died in Los Angeles in July, 1935, a few weeks before his friend and former roommate in Paris, Douglas Tilden, died.

136

William B. Sparks in front of one of the many portraits he has painted.

William B. Sparks, Portrait Painter

William B. Sparks was born in 1937 in Carbon Hill, Alabama. Known throughout the southeast today for his life-like portraiture, Sparks became deaf when he was three years old. His interest in art developed in childhood, "When I lost my hearing, maybe the visual arts were all I had, and in the beginning, that led me to drawing." Sparks attended the Alabama School for the Deaf in Talladega, seriously devoting himself to portrait painting after receiving a five year scholarship from the school to study under Lemuel McDaniel, a portrait artist in Birmingham.

Sparks initially painted as a sideline. He worked full-time as a technical illustrator for Western Electric in Winston-Salem, North Carolina, for over 15 years and then as an air brush retoucher for a few years with Pictorial Corporation of America. During the last few years he had devoted himself completely to portrait painting.

Sparks skillfully captures his subject's personality and individuality in his oil portraits. Lifelike and almost photographic, his works show careful attention to detail and faithful reproduction of character. Sparks works from photographs he takes of his subject and has the client pose for accurate complexion colors. In this process his deafness has enhanced his ability to concentrate; often his subjects watch television in his basement studio while the artist works uninterrupted.

Sparks' works have been exhibited widely and are in collections in the Eastern United States, Brazil, and Mexico. Some have been reproduced as lithographs by Bernard Picture Co. of New York. In 1979 Sparks was selected by the Gallaudet College Alumni Association to paint a portrait of Dr. Edward C. Merrill, Jr., the fourth president of Gallaudet College. His work has become so popular that at times he is booked up to three years ahead.

Sparks lives with his wife, the former Betty Sue Gibbs, and their four children in Winston-Salem, North Carolina.

137

Portraits In Oil
By

William Sparks

138

Artist William Sparks with his oil portrait of Dr. Edward C. Merrill, Jr.

RIGHT: Portrait of a young boy by William Sparks.

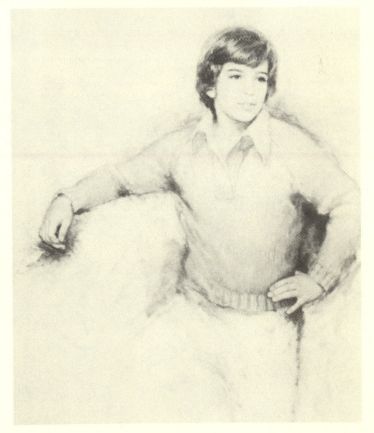

Kelly H. Stevens

Kelly H. Stevens, Painter

Kelly Stevens gives his sister credit for starting him on his art career. She recognized very early his ability to draw and sketch and gave him his first paint set. Kelly Haygood Stevens was born in 1896 in Mexia, Texas; he became deaf when he was five years old

from a bout with scarlet fever. A 1914 graduate of the Texas School for the Deaf, he went on to study at Gallaudet College. While a student at Gallaudet he continued his interest in art by studying at the Corcoran School of Art. After graduation from college he embarked on an art teaching career which spanned 18 years at two schools for the deaf, New Jersey and Louisiana.

Stevens also continued his study of art. He studied at the Trenton School of Industrial Art, the New York School of Fine and Applied Arts, Paris; Ateliex Louis Bilocal and Academee Colorossi, Paris; and Circulo Belles Artes, Madrid. In Paris he studied with Jean Hanau, a deaf French artist, and in Madrid he became a good friend of Valentin de Zubiaurres, one of the famous deaf Spanish painters. He studied portrait painting with Wayman Adams in Mexico and landscape painting also in Mexico. In 1938 he earned his Masters of Fine Arts at Louisiana State University.

Stevens also traveled widely; wherever he went his brush and palette captured local scenes. In Mexico it was the vivid, colorful landscapes. In Louisiana he recorded on canvas the life of the southern Negro, the moss-hung trees, and the floods of the Mississippi River. In the southwest he depicted the tribal costumes and dances of the Indians of New Mexico and

"Oaks, Levee Road," oil by Kelly H. Stevens.

The Mr. and Mrs. Alan B. Crammatte Collection.

Arizona. One such painting, "Before the Mass, in New Mexico," was widely lauded. In Spain he was inspired by the remote sections of the Iberian peninsula and the quaint villages of the Pyrenees.

In 1934 Kelly Stevens' work was exhibited at the Roerich Museum with the first International Exhibition of Deaf Artists in New York City. His work has been shown by the Southern States Art League, Texas Fine Arts Association, and in one-man shows in Shreveport and Baton Rouge, Louisiana, and in Abilene and Dallas, Texas. It has been exhibited with other internationally known deaf artists in Madrid, Paris, and Brussels.

As an artist, Stevens has been described as one "who paints with vivid coloring and is decidedly an adherent of the modern school." The Dallas *Times-Herald* called him "a master in his sureness of line and his flair for pleasing composition." His work is scattered throughout the world and can be found in such diverse locations as China, the Netherlands, France, and Spain.

Stevens is a member of the Salon International des Artistes Silencieux and is listed in *Who's Who in American Art*. In 1971 Gallaudet College awarded him a Doctor of Humane Letters. He resides in Austin in a house that was once a German Free School. It has been designated a Texas historical site.

Kelly Stevens has donated many objects of art to Gallaudet College including a bronze copy of the original model of the Thomas Hopkins Gallaudet and Alice Cogswell statue. Other contributions have been rare books, pictures, and paintings.

"I looked over Jordan," oil by Kelly H. Stevens.

Gallaudet College Archives

"Zinnia in White Pitcher," oil by Kelly H. Stevens. The Mr. and Mrs. Alan B. Crammatte Collection.

"Basque Boy in Red Cap," oil by Kelly H. Stevens. The Gallaudet College Collection.

"Enchantment," oil by Kelly H. Stevens.

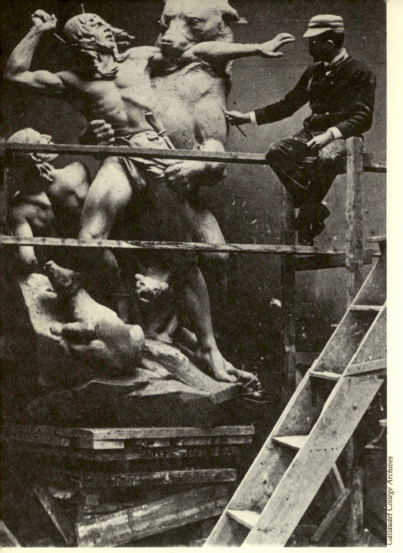

Douglas Tilden at work on "The Bear Hunt."

Douglas Tilden, Sculptor

Douglas Tilden has been called "the father of sculpture on the West Coast." He is one of California's most famous sculptors and the best-known deaf sculptor in this country.

Born May 1, 1860 in Chico, California, Tilden became deaf at the age of four from scarlet fever. He entered the California School for the Deaf in Berkeley in 1866, graduating in 1879. At the California School he came under the tutelage of Theophilus d'Estrella, the deaf artist, photographer and teacher.

Tilden attended the University of California for a few years then accepted a teaching position there. In 1887 he left that position to attend the Academy of Design in New York. He later studied in Paris. It was in Paris that he gained attention when he exhibited his work, "The National Game," a sculpture of a baseball pitcher all wound up and ready to throw the ball. This piece was admitted to the Paris Salon and was one of 19 to capture a medal among 1,115 competing pieces of art. His "The Tired Boxer" received honorable mention at the same Salon, the highest honor paid an American.

Tilden's work won international acclaim. He was considered a genius in sculpture. His work can be found along the west coast. "The Bear Hunt" also called "Combat With Grizzly Bear" is located on the campus of the California School. "The Mechanics" stands at Market and Battery Streets in San Francisco. Other works are in Los Angeles and in Tilden Park (no relation).

OVERLEAF: "The Bear Hunt," by Douglas Tilden. It is located on the campus of the California School for the Deaf in Berkeley.

RIGHT: Close-up of "The Bear Hunt."

144

Douglas Tilden died in his studio in Berkeley in August 1935. He was 75 years old.

Mildred Albronda has written a book about Tilden, *Douglas Tilden: Portrait of a Deaf Sculptor*. It was published by TJ Publishers, Inc. in 1980.

"The Mechanics," by Douglas Tilden.

"Admission Day," by Douglas Tilden, 1897. It is located at Market, Post, and Montgomery Streets in San Francisco.

145

"The Tired Boxer," by Douglas Tilden.

"The Football Players," by Douglas Tilden.

Cadwallader L. Washburn

Cadwallader L. Washburn, Drypoint Etcher

Cadwallader Lincoln Washburn was born in Minneapolis, Minnesota, on October 31, 1866 and lived 99 productive years until his death on December 21, 1965 in Farmington, Maine. His family abounded with successful businessmen, inventors, and politicians (his father and three of his uncles served in the U.S. Congress, representing Maine and Minnesota). Washburn

continued the family tradition of excellence despite his deafness, which occurred at the age of five from scarlet fever and spinal meningitis. He regarded his deafness less a handicap than an obstacle to be overcome, and at one point noted, "the lack of hearing undoubtedly sharpened my sense of sight and awareness of color, form, and line."

Washburn ultimately became one of the foremost drypoint etchers in the world, but the path he took was hardly one dimensional. He attended the Minnesota School for the Deaf, where he developed an interest in printing which he continued to study as an undergraduate at Gallaudet College. He graduated from college in 1890, valedictorian of his class, and, deciding to combine his printer's training and his love of art, he enrolled in the school of architecture at Massachusetts Institute of Technology. While at MIT he won a first place award in design, but despite this success, he decided after one year to become an artist. He studied art in Boston, and was then admitted to the Art Student's League in New York City, a privilege obtained only through severe competition. Washburn then traveled abroad, studying in Spain under Joaquin Sorolla and moving north to study the work of the Flemish masters. Inspired by an exhibit of etchings by James Whistler, Washburn at this point made

"Where Boats Beach," an etching by Cadwallader L. Washburn.

"Berber Khalife," an etching by Cadwallader L. Washburn, The Gallaudet College Collection.

"The Matriarch," an etching by Cadwallader L. Washburn, The Gallaudet College Collection.

the key decision to switch from oils to drypoint etching, combining, thereby, both his printing and artistic skills.

His life's work included over 970 etched plates and numerous paintings, all drawn from his wide range of experience as a world traveler, war correspondent, scientist (Washburn was both an oologist—collector of rare birds eggs and nests—and an authority on insects), author, teacher, and "speaker" of English, French and Spanish. For example, in 1904-05, Washburn worked as a war correspondent for the New York *Daily News* covering the Russo-Japanese War. Working with his brother, the two filed a scoop by locating two Russian cruisers which had violated the neutrality of French Indochinese waters. In 1910-11, Washburn was head correspondent for the *News* assigned to cover the Mexican revolution. He obtained a 500-word statement from President Madero, interviewing the soon-to-be assassinated president with pad and pencil! Another of Washburn's adventures took him to the Marguesas Islands on a research expedition for an oology museum. While there he was stranded on a remote island with cannibals. In the ensuing months

he not only taught them some sign language, but also persuaded the chief to build a canoe for his escape.

Washburn's etchings reflect his adventures. They depict people of all kinds, from cannibals to American Indians, as well as building facades and shoreline scenes. Washburn "captured the very soul of face after living face in such a wonderful cavalcade of humanity." His work gained wide recognition as early as 1910. He retained value by limiting quantity, making 30-40 copies of each print and then destroying the plates. Known throughout the world, his etchings have found their way into collections at Gallaudet College, the Library of Congress (more than 100), the Metropolitan Museum of Art in New York City, and in museums in England, France, and the Netherlands.

By 1937 poor eyesight forced Washburn to give up etching, but he continued to study and paint with oils into his later years. He received many awards in his lifetime—an honorary doctorate from Gallaudet in 1924 and a Doctor of Humane Letters from Bowdoin College in Brunswick, Maine, in 1947. The last honor placed him among a handful of deaf persons who have received an honorary degree from a college other

148

than Gallaudet. In May, 1969 the Arts Building at Gallaudet College was named after him in recognition of his many achievements. For Washburn, "everything in the world was something to know, to understand—and to record in ink and oil."

"Antonio Viale," an etching by Cadwallader L. Washburn, The Gallaudet College Collection.

"A Bedouin Girl," an etching by Cadwallader L. Washburn. The Gallaudet College Collection.

"Hopi Indian Tribesman" (Tuba, Arizona), an etching by Cadwallader L. Washburn. The Gallaudet College Collection.

"Bronze Dragon in Front of Temple," (Kiyoto, Japan), an etching by Cadwaller L. Washburn. The Gallaudet College Collection.

"Sacred Wall," (Guadalupe, Hidaljo, Mexico), an etching by Cadwallader L. Washburn. The Gallaudet College Collection.

James H. Whitcomb, Silhouettist

For a long time the work of silhouettist James H. Whitcomb, a New England artist, remained a mystery, and his identity was unknown because much of his work was not signed. When the artist's self-portrait was discovered, it led to the identity of James H. Whitcomb, one of several Whitcombs alive during that time.

James Hosley Whitcomb was born on October 7, 1806 in Hancock, New Hampshire. Scarlet fever deprived him of his hearing when he was two or three years old. He was admitted to the American Asylum for the Deaf in 1822, one of nine children in New Hampshire to be selected out of a group of 40 for admission to the American School. As a student he learned shoemaking and finished his schooling in 1827. On December 18, 1839 he married Sarah Ann Enos, a graduate of the New York Institution for the Education of Deaf Mutes. They had three sons and

Elizabeth (Whitcomb) Gates silhouette, probably by James H. Whitcomb c. 1830.

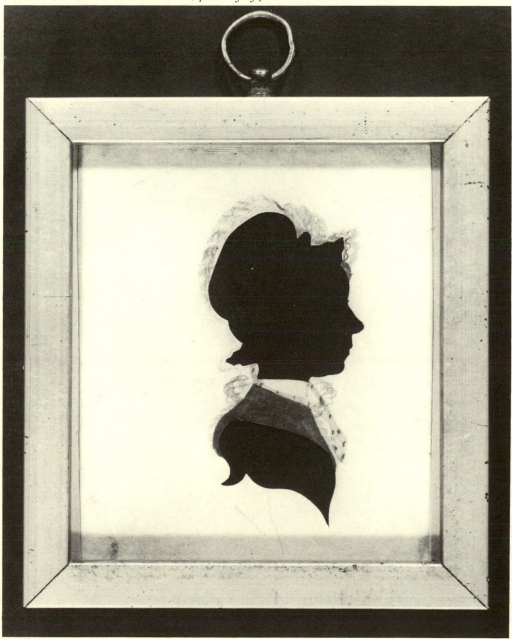

lived in Afton, New York, where he worked as a shoe maker.

Whitcomb specialized in producing silhouettes, both of the cut-and-paste variety and the hollow-cut type. With pen and brush he added color and details. Donna-Belle Garvin described him as "a courageous individual as well as a sensitive artist."

Whitcomb's silhouette of his sister, Elizabeth W. Gates, is in the New Hampshire Historical Society Collection. The self-portrait silhouette is in a private collection. This collector has another 14 silhouettes which he attributes to Whitcomb though none of them is signed. Another of Whitcomb's signed works is in the M. and M. Karolik Collection in the Boston Museum of Fine Arts. It is a silhouette of President Andrew Jackson mounted on a horse. It was cut with scissors, and color was then added with a brush.

Whitcomb died May 9, 1849 at the age of 43.

James Hosley Whitcomb, self-portrait by the artist.
Private Collection.

New Hampshire Historical Society

152

Tom Wood, Primitive Folk Artist

Tom Wood said "I love wood, to assemble it, carve it, and sometimes to decorate it. It is my whole life."

Wood was born in England in 1902. He became deaf at 18 months as a result of an attack of scarlet fever and whooping cough. He moved to Canada and attended a school for the deaf in Winnipeg, Manitoba. He attended Gallaudet College for one year. Then he worked in the U.S. Government Printing Office for 25 years.

Tom Wood had no formal art training. He has his own conceptions of art. His works uniquely display the craftsmanship of wood carving, wood tesserae, and sculpture. They were done in different kinds of wood from all over the world. Most of his works are in the forms of water birds, turtles, llamas, camels, and other animals. He does art symbols from his own imagination.

He had his first one-man show at the Art Gallery, Riverside City College in California.

Tom Wood and many of his wooden projects.

All photos by Robert Rosefield

153

Hilbert Duning at his drawing board.

Hilbert C. Duning, Architect

Hilbert C. Duning of Ohio was one of the few very successful deaf architects in this country. One of his former employers described him as "a credit to the profession as he was to the deaf community of Cincinnati and the nation."

Born in Richmond, Indiana, on August 16, 1906, he entered the Indiana School for the Deaf when he was six years old. When his family moved he transferred to the Ohio School for the Deaf. Another family move took him to the Cincinnati Oral School from which he graduated. He then studied at the Cincinnati Building Trades School for a year before enrolling in the Ohio Mechanics Institute from which he graduated with the highest honors, leading his class in architecture

Upham Hall, Miami University, Oxford, Ohio designed by Hilbert Duning.

Indian Hill Church, Cincinnati, Ohio, designed by Hilbert Duning.

and allied subjects. He continued his studies and completed a four-year night course in three years at the University of Cincinnati becoming the first deaf person to receive a certificate there. In 1941 Duning received his architect's certificate to practice in Ohio. He later acquired the right to practice in Kentucky, Illinois, and California.

Duning's work included private residences, hotels, and office buildings. He received first prize for the best design for a branch library. Herbert F. Hilmer, one of the partners in the architectural firm where Duning was employed for many years, called Duning's contributions phenomenal. Said Hilmer, "Herbert's deafness was never much of a handicap to his effectiveness as an architect. He communicated easily with clients, builders, and his fellow employees; they all respected him highly and marvelled at his ability to read lips and understand as readily as a hearing person. His production was phenomenal. I think he had it all over the rest of us in not having to waste as much time as we did on the telephone."

Hilbert Duning was married to the former Harriet Wilson of Delaware, Ohio, on February 20, 1937. He has a brother, LeRoy, who was also in the architectural field.

Women's Dormitory, Miami University, Oxford, Ohio designed by Hilbert Duning.

Olof Hanson

Gallaudet College Archives

Olof Hanson, Architect

Olof Hanson was born in Sweden on September 10, 1862. He became deaf in one ear when his ears were frostbitten and he tried to "thaw" his ears at the stove without telling anyone about it. When he was thirteen years old, his family moved to Minnesota. He lost his hearing entirely a few days after arriving in Minnesota by sleeping near an open window in a cold draft. He became deaf on his way to the doctor.

In 1878 he entered the Minnesota School for the Deaf, and he graduated in 1886. Then he entered Gallaudet College and graduated in 1881.

After graduation, Hanson worked for Hodgson and Son, architects in Minneapolis, until 1889. He studied in Europe for ten months and on his return he worked for a firm in Philadelphia. At that time he helped work on the plans for the new Pennsylvania School for the Deaf at Mt. Airy.

In 1891 Hanson returned to Minnesota, where he taught at the Minnesota School for two years. He opened an office in architecture in Faribault, where he conducted business on his own account for three years. He designed the North Dakota School for the Deaf, a boys' dormitory building at the Kendall School, Washington, D.C., a building for the Washington State School for the Deaf, a building for the State School for Feeble Minded at Faribault, Minnesota, a residence for Dr. J. L. Noyes, Faribault, and half a dozen other projects in Faribault and elsewhere.

Olof Hanson died in 1933.

A building at the Washington State School for the Deaf designed by Olof Hanson.

Washington State School for the Deaf

Thomas S. Marr

Thomas S. Marr, Architect

Thomas Scott Marr was born in Tennessee in 1866, and became partially deaf as a result of scarlet fever in infancy. Marr's parents feared the stigma of deafness, but young Marr was obviously bright. He could read and write before he entered school. His parents enrolled him in a public school where he was placed in the second grade. Unfortunately, those were wasted years. He was not promoted for three years. He seemed introverted, lonely, and unwilling to learn. When he was 11 his parents reluctantly sent him to the school for the deaf in Knoxville. When he entered Marr was unable to do simple arithmetic. But the principal, Thomas L. Moses, and a teacher, Kate Ogden, took a special interest in him. Young Marr learned quickly, and by the time he took the entrance examinations to Gallaudet College he got his choice of bedrooms, an honor reserved for top entering freshmen.

Marr graduated from Gallaudet with the class of 1889, and began working in an architect's office. To improve his position he attended the Massachusetts Institute of Technology for a year. He worked and saved for five years, accumulating $500 to start out on his own as an architect. The turning point in his career came several years later, when he hired Joe Holman, then a news boy, and taught him architecture. A talented protegé, Holman became Marr's "ears," and by 1909 the two secured many prestigious contracts.

Marr and Holman designed many buildings—schools, theatres, apartments, etc. Some noteworthy designs were those of the Methodist Publishing House in Nashville, Tennessee, the baseball grandstand in Toledo, Ohio, and the Tennessee School for the Deaf. Most famous in Tennessee, Marr gained nationwide recognition as an architect.

In 1924 Marr received an honorary Master of Science degree from Gallaudet College.

Marr was a generous philanthropist for many deaf-related concerns. He was an avid reader and traveler. He died March 2, 1936.

Thomas S. Marr (far right) and his co-workers in 1929.

Chapter 5

The 1900s

Birth of a Fraternal Insurance Society

 URING the alumni reunion held on the campus of the Michigan School for the Deaf late in 1898, a group of 13 young men met to explore the possibility of providing some form of insurance protection for themselves and other deaf men. As youths they had been members of the McKinley Lodge No. 922 of the Coming Men of America located in Honor Cottage on the campus. This organization was a national (hearing) secret society for young men in their teens. It had come into existence during the last decade of the 19th century. It sought to inspire lofty principles of patriotism, honor, and manhood. Coming Men of America had over 4,500 small lodges scattered over the country and eventually reached a membership of over 100,000 before it folded in 1907.

These 13 young men meeting on the MSD campus that summer were concerned about the difficulty they and other deaf persons had in purchasing life insurance. Insurance companies in those days considered deaf people high risks and accident-prone, and they believed, mistakenly, that the deaf had shorter-than-average lifespans. It was here that the groundwork was laid for the organization of the Fraternal Society of the Deaf, the forerunner of the National Fraternal Society of the Deaf. Peter N. Hellers, Jr., of Detroit, was elected president of the organizing group. Hellers and the other officers were instructed to look into the possibility of forming a fraternal insurance group and to report back to the members at the next MSD reunion. On June 14, 1901 the Fraternal Society of the Deaf was formally organized and, two months later, incorporated. Hellers was elected the first grand president and issued Certificate No. One.

In 1903 FSD held its first convention in Chicago. Two years later it met in Detroit, and in 1907, its third convention was held in Cincinnati. The Society has since held conventions in major cities throughout the United States and Canada and now meets every four years.

Those early years were difficult for the officers. They worked out of their homes. They were earnest and hardworking men, but they had little or no experience in running a fraternal insurance business. That the Society managed to survive those crucial early years is a credit to the faith, determination, and hard work of these pioneers.

The Society was founded initially to provide burial benefits. Membership was limited to deaf male adults. There were no reserve funds so when a member died others were assessed one dollar to cover the funeral expenses. This system was rather hard on the member who lived the longest, but it was a common practice among fraternal insurance groups in those days. The survivors of George Tate, a member of the Chicago #1 Division, were the first to claim the death benefits. Tate died at the age of 26.

Later life, sickness, and accident coverage were added. Membership opened to children of the members, and at the 1955 convention in Buffalo, New York, the members voted to admit women. Gertrude Elkins of Danville, Kentucky, became the first female mem-

Pioneer members of the National Fraternal Society of the Deaf.

ber. Women's divisions began to spring up around the country. Other divisions became co-ed. Billie Moehle of Chicago was the first female to serve as a national officer when she was appointed to fill the unexpired term of Grant Trustee Solomon Deitch, who died in 1976.

By 1905 the Society had grown to 200 members and eight divisions. That year the Society rented its first office space on South Clark Street in Chicago. The rent was $13.00 a month, but it was still a struggle to keep the Society alive. In 1907 the Society was reorganized, renamed, and incorporated under the laws of the State of Illinois as the National Fraternal Society of the Deaf. This move proved to be the right one because it made the Society a bonafide fraternal insurance organization. Within another two years membership jumped to 800, assets reached $6,000, and the Society hired its first full-time salaried officer, Francis P. Gibson, as grand secretary, at a salary of $800 a year, which was more than many deaf teachers of the deaf were making. When the Society celebrated its Diamond Jubilee in 1976 there were 14 employees.

Gibson gave the Society stability and integrity. Of him, Alexander Pach said: "No deaf man ever worked harder or made more liberal sacrifices for his fellow deaf than Francis P. Gibson, and no man ever surmounted more difficult and more persistent obstacles." By 1914 the Society was averaging 27 new members a month.

Gibson was elected to his second term as president in 1927. When he died in 1929, Frederick J. Neesam, vice president, succeeded him. In 1931 Arthur L. Roberts, the grand secretary, was elected to the presidency. Roberts' tenure as president spanned the Great Depression. David Mudgett defined Roberts as a person who "stared adversity in the face." That may explain, in part, why the Society emerged from the Depression stronger than ever. Another reason was the Society's practice of investing the bulk of its funds in mortgages. As a result, during and after the Depression, the Society had to foreclose on a number of properties, and it was through one such foreclosure that the Society acquired its first Home Office, a well-

"Divisions are the stepping stone from which leaders of the Deaf spring to prominence."
—DAVID MUDGETT, THE DEAF AMERICAN

158

NFSD's Home Office from 1936 to 1955.

The Society's home from 1955 to 1975.

The Society moved to this modern structure in 1975.

National Fraternal Society of the Deaf

located, two-story brick structure in Oak Park, a Chicago suburb. The Society remained in this building from 1936 until 1955 when it constructed larger quarters. In 1975 the Society moved to its newly-constructed and specifically designed $500,000 office building in Mt. Prospect, Illinois.

Ladislaw Cherry succeeded Roberts as president following the latter's death in 1957. During Cherry's administration the Society began paying cash dividends to policy holders, eliminated race discrimination, and began insuring members' children.

Cherry retired in 1967 and Frank B. Sullivan became the tenth NFSD president. Sullivan initiated a new sales and recruitment program, removed the limit on the amount of insurance a person could purchase, and recruited and trained a corps of deaf insurance agents. As a result, the annual enrollment figures doubled.

As the membership grew the number of divisions increased. These divisions—very similar to lodges—have been organized in most major cities and many smaller ones. They are community-based and provide the members with the opportunity for social interaction, self improvement, assumption of leadership and involvement in community service. Members are rewarded for their service by a point system, with the

This memorial marks the birthplace of the National Fraternal Society of the Deaf at the Michigan School.

National Fraternal Society of the Deaf

34th degree being the highest and most coveted award. Divisions elect delegates to the national convention and participate in a variety of community service and school projects. After the 1906 San Francisco earthquake, members of local divisions in the area contributed funds to deaf victims. In Alabama the Mobile Division gives a volunteer award to a local hearing citizen in recognition for his or her contribution to the city. In 1976 the division was one of the co-sponsors which brought the 1976 Freedom Train to the city. Efforts of the members of the Toronto Division resulted in the donation of a cottage to the Ontario Camp for the Deaf. The Jacksonville, Illinois Division provided packets of information on deafness to parents and others. The Home Office encourages such efforts and matches Division donations to charitable causes. Today there are 120 divisions in the United States and Canada.

In February 1904 Gibson started publishing a bi-monthly newsmagazine, *The Frat*, for the members. It sold for five cents a copy or sixty cents a year. Between 1907 and 1911 the publication was suspended and information which normally appeared in *The Frat* was printed in other publications of the deaf such as *The Silent Worker* (1907-08), the *Silent Success* (1909), and the *Silent Optimist* (1910-11). In 1911 *The Frat* resumed publication and has been published regularly since.

In 1930 J. Frederick Meagher, better known as Jimmy Meagher, began the "Spotlight" column in *The Frat*. It was a newsy, interesting, catch-all column about anything and everything. Leonard B. Warshawsky took over the column in 1951 on Meagher's death and has been writing it for more than a quarter of a century. The "Spotlight" remains today one of the most popular columns appearing in a publication of the deaf in the United States.

In 1964 NFSD began awarding U.S. Savings Bonds to outstanding young achievers in schools for the deaf. Within a decade 64 schools were participating in the program annually. In 1970 the Society began giving $500 scholarships to promising young deaf scholars.

NFSD Hall of Fame was established in 1973 to recognize those members who had made exceptional contributions to their divisons and to the community in general. The first year, 56 individuals were admitted to the Hall. The names of those admitted to the Hall of Fame are placed on an honor roll which hangs in

"Get accustomed to the automobile and learn to dodge it; it is a permanent institution."
—THE FRAT, 1908

Grand Presidents of the National Fraternal Society of the Deaf

P. N. Hellers, Jr.   F. P. Gibson   J. J. Kleinhans   E. M. Bristol

H. C. Anderson   F. J. Neesam   A. L. Roberts   L. S. Cherry   F. B. Sullivan

the Arthur L. Roberts Memorial Library in the Society's Home Offices.

The Society established a Frater of the Year award in 1973 and the first award was given in 1974. This award recognizes the outstanding contributions of a member to his Division, the community, or to the Society. The award consists of a $100 U.S. Savings Bond and a plaque. The Society also recognizes an outstanding Division with its Division of the Year award. Winners of this award receive a handmade banner with the NFSD logo and the year the Division won the award.

Grand Presidents of the National Fraternal Society of the Deaf and their Terms in Office

Peter N. Hellers, Jr. 1901-1903
Francis P. Gibson 1903-1905
Jacob J. Kleinhans 1905-1909
E. M. Bristol 1909-1912
Harry C. Anderson 1912-1927
Francis P. Gibson 1927-1929
Frederick J. Neesam 1929-1931
Arthur L. Roberts 1931-1957
Ladislaw S. Cherry 1957-1967
Frank B. Sullivan 1967-

National Fraternal Society of the Deaf
Hall of Fame

1973

Harry Anderson
Kreigh B. Ayers
Joe Balasa
Clarence Baldwin
Washington Barrow
Silas Baskerville
William Battersby
Rev. Guilbert C. Braddock
Daniel McG. Cameron
Harry Carlisle
Joseph Carter
L. S. Cherry
Estelle Davies
George F. Flick
Francis P. Gibson
Foster Gilbert
Fred Gustafson
Raymond Hale
Peter N. Hellers
Charles Hummer
Aaron Hurwit
Ray Kauffman
Charles P. Kemp
Jacob J. Kleinhaus
Herman Koelle
Albert Krohn
John Langford
Wesley Lauritsen
Albert Lazar
Harrison Leiter
Rush Letson
Paul Mark
Alfred Marshall
J. Frederick Meagher
Brooks Monaghan
B. W. Moore
Richard Myers
Frederick J. Neesam
Art Norris
James H. O'Leary
Thomas Osborne
David Peikoff
Nick Pleskatcheck
Sam Rittenberg
A. L. Roberts
Joseph N. Rosnick
Edward Rowse
B. M. Schowe
William J. Scott
John Shilton
H. J. Soland
Clifton Talbot
Noah Teitlebaum
Herman Von Hippel

Edgar Winchell
Styles Woodworth

1974

E. Conley Akin
Myrtle Allen
Mary Balasa
Charles Billings
S. Robey Burns
Abram Cohen
Leroy Duning
Charles Falk
Lucille Garrison
Rev. Homer Grace
George Hanson
Claude Hoffmeyer
Homer Humphrey
Uel K. Hurd
C. Ross Koons
James McDonald
Lera C. Moore
William F. Newell
William T. Peterson
Einer Rosenkjar
Oscar Sanders
Ned C. Wheeler

1975

Gordon B. Allen
Gordon L. Allen
Joseph Augustine
Kenneth Burdett
John B. Davis
Ruth G. Ludovico
S. Rozelle McCall
Colin McCord
Tom Northern
Thomas Peterson
James F. Royster
J. Horace Taylor
Theodore W. Tucker

1976

Doris Berman
Ernest Bush
David E. Early
Francis Keating
Saverio Minicucci
Hans A. Neujhar
Sylvan J. Riley
Eugene C. Turk

1977

Elmer Beuerle
Antonio Danti

Frank P. Galluzzo
William M. Gulley
Chester W. Heeger
James T. Hester
Konrad A. Hokanson
Ralph A. Hunter, Jr.
Lonnie Irvin, Sr.
William H. Isaacks
Franklin B. Jackson
Bertil Jennisch
John J. Kaufman
E. B. Kolp
Norman Larson, Jr.
Clifford Leach
Charline H. Lynch
Margaret Marshall
Roger McAuley
Samuel Parker
John Rewolinski
Margaret Royster
John F. Sciacco
Winford P. Simmons
Stella Stangarone
Rodney W. Walker
Kenneth F. Welch
Isadore Zisman

1978

Peter F. Amico
James B. Beauchamp
Herman R. Butler
John E. Crutchfield
Robert G. Davies, Sr.
Solomon Deitch
James A. Fry
Gabriel S. Gryszak
Rev. Silas J. Hirte
John A. Horrigan
Howard A. Johnson
George L. Laramie
Leo L. Latz
Stanley B. Main
Frank Malaguti
Arvin W. Massey
John P. Matthews
Edwin A. Roberts
Carlton B. Strail
Edward Szopa
Ernest Tilton
Adolphus E. Yoder
Nellie Yoder
Joseph Zocco

1979

Barbara Augustine
Harry Baynes

James Bresee
Waldo Cordano
Francis Fitzgerald
Percy Goff
Morton Hadlock
James Jones
Mario Leonardi
Clyde Morton
Charles Moskowitz
Henry Oaks
Jerry Strom
Frank B. Sullivan
Leonard B. Warshawsky
Norman Wesdcy
August Wriede

Frater of the Year

1973—Ernest E. Hoffman
    Denver #64

1974—Elsie McDaniel
    Nashville #12

1975—Elsie Martin
    Olathe, Kansas #14

1976—Charles D. Billings
    Denver #64

    Martin Maier
    Mobile, Alabama #159

1977—Celia May Baldwin
    Salt Lake City #56

1978—John E. Howell
    Durham, North Carolina #95

1979—Wesley Lauritsen
    Faribault, Minnesota #101

Division of the Year

1973—Danville, Kentucky #125

1974—Toronto, Canada #98

1975—No winner

1976—Mobile, Alabama #159

1977—Frederick, Maryland #163

1978—Morganton, North Carolina
    #161

1979—Salt Lake City, Utah #56

162

The Society is governed by a nine-member Board of Directors—which includes five regional vice presidents—and four executive officers. All are deaf. The executive officers manage the day-to-day operations of the Home Office.

Four NFSD presidents, Francis P. Gibson, Arthur L. Roberts, Ladislaw Cherry, and Frank B. Sullivan, have been awarded honorary degrees by Gallaudet College for their leadership and contributions to deaf America.

Many deaf individuals today are proud members of the National Fraternal Society of the Deaf. Except for automobile insurance coverage deaf people no longer encounter the kind of difficulty in purchasing insurance coverage which the NFSD founders experienced until 1901. The NFSD has built a financially successful international insurance business and proven that deaf people are good insurance risks. The Society has contributed to the elimination of such discrimination and invited some stiff competition. The Society remains, today, a popular company and continues to grow steadily. It stands as a fine example of the successful achievement of a determined group of deaf people, who over the decade have built onto a heritage of honest labor, wise, dedicated, and daring leadership. The National Fraternal Society of the Deaf has also proven that deafness need not be a barrier to one's success in the business world.

The Decade

Around 1900 many schools began to adopt the sloyd system of manual training but it did not catch on rapidly and was generally restricted to use by the younger students. Agriculture was a subject given high priority by many schools because prices were high for farm products and the trade was considered a promising one for deaf boys. Gallaudet College

Francis P. Gibson
(1870-1929)

Francis P. Gibson is remembered as a man who "stretched a shoestring into a million dollars" and who "left behind a healthy heritage of honest achievement"—an example for others to follow.

Born in Chicago on August 6, 1870, Gibson was deafened at the age of eight years. He attended the Chicago Public Schools. His father was an English sea captain.

Gibson became involved with the Fraternal Society of the Deaf in 1903 when he joined the organization and was elected president all in the same day. Wholesale graft was reported within the Society and threatened its existence, so, in no time at all, Gibson had a fight on his hands. He managed to oust those accused of cheating the members, but ironically, it cost him the presidency. But, he made it back to the top and, in 1909, he became the first full-time and salaried officer of the newly-reorganized National Fraternal Society of the Deaf. He served the organization as grand secretary from 1909 to 1927 when he was again elected president. When he joined the Society there were 73 members, three divisions and a treasury of $270.94. On his death the Society had gone international with the formation of a division in Toronto; grown to 6,849 members, 111 divisions with assets exceeding one million dollars; an achievement which earned him the shoestring-to-a-million-dollars label.

Gibson was "Gib" to his friends. He had a sad facial expression and he was a quiet person by nature. J. Frederick Meagher compared him to Abraham Lincoln and called him the "Lincoln of the Deaf." In Gibson, Meagher saw a man with a "Lincoln-face who suffered Lincoln-sorrow with a Lincoln-grace." Meagher believed that it was overwork and worry that killed his friend—not the blood clot which was officially listed as the cause.

As he departed the NFSD office at five o'clock that Saturday afternoon in November 1929, Gibson turned to Arthur L. Roberts, the grand secretary-treasurer, and said: "Bobs, if anything happens to me, carry on." Insiders knew that Gibson had been in failing health for some time and that he had put off a needed but dreaded operation, but all expected to see him back shortly. The operation was performed on the following Tuesday and although he rallied he did not make it. Those last two words—"carry on"—became a pledge and a commitment to those who followed in his footsteps in serving the Society. The motto can still be found in the masthead of *The Frat*, the Society's official publication, which Gibson had started.

The Rev. Philip J. Hasenstab, Chicago's popular deaf Methodist minister, officiated at Gibson's funeral. One hundred and fifty mourners crowded into the little chapel while another 250 shivered in the cold outside. Three hearses were needed to transport all the flowers to Rosehill Cemetery where he was buried. Of his departure, Meagher wrote:

A wreath of wizardy we wove around him—
 Quick on the quip and tender on the tear;
The Shadowland of Silence stoutly bound him—
 Our Muted Master of the Empty Ear.
In mellow melody of mystic motion
 He'd dedicate his deafness to our lot. . . .
Life's ebb-tide takes him to Time's endless ocean—
 Gib; unforgettable and unforgot!

started an agriculture department.

Congress was asked for a $100,000 grant "to aid in establishing homes in the states and territories for teaching articulate speech and vocal language to deaf children." The National Association of the Deaf opposed the request because "every state was already doing its utmost to develop and train deaf children and none neglected teaching articulation and lipreading." The editor of *The Deaf-Mutes' Journal* viewed the request as "a slur upon all of the schools to insinuate that a special grant from the Government, to be placed in alien hands, is either proper or necessary."

A William L. Skinner, a resident of St. Louis, claimed he had patented an electrical device which would make the deaf hear clearly. It had been "thoroughly tested," according to Skinner, and he had three persons who would testify to its efficacy. He announced that he was ready and willing to permit "the government" to say whether or not his claim was right. Apparently, the government did not think so because nothing more was heard of him or his "invisible miracle."

Tragedy struck the New Jersey School when a 17-year-old student arose early one morning and started to close the window of her third floor dormitory room. She lost her balance and fell to the ground. She was killed in the fall.

Ripley's — **Believe It or Not!** ®

WILLIE
BOULAR
of
Atchison, Kan.
DEAF, DUMB and
LEGLESS —
LAID 46,000
PAVING BRICKS
IN LESS THAN 8 HOURS. –1900

© RIPLEY INTERNATIONAL LIMITED 1933

Crowded conditions forced the Mississippi School to stop admitting new pupils. The school became so crowded that the printshop was converted into a dormitory for the boys, and the school publication was suspended. Classes were moved into the chapel, and some classrooms were changed to dormitory rooms for the girls.

Gallaudet College President Edward Miner Gallaudet was trying to persuade Congress to increase the number of scholarships at the college from 60 to 100.

In New York City the Deaf-Mutes' Union planned a "Tenth Year Vaudeville." The event was advertised as a program that would please the eye and delight the ear. For fifty cents a person could attend the grand reception and see professional talent perform. If a person wanted to sit in the balcony or in one of the first five rows the cost was 75¢. There was no charge for hat checks.

Orson Archibald
(1852-1927)

Orson Archibald was called "The Great Hoosier Benefactor." He is remembered in particular as the benefactor of the Archibald Memorial Home for the Aged and Infirm Deaf in Indiana.

Archibald was born on March 24, 1852, in a small frame house near Brookston, Indiana. When he was four years old his family moved to the farm which is now the location of the Archibald Home.

Archibald was deafened as a youth by spinal meningitis and entered the Indiana School for the Deaf from which he was graduated in 1872. He was the third student from Indiana to enroll at Gallaudet College, the other two being an uncle of his, Volantine Holloway, and Edward Stretch. (Stretch died while a student at Gallaudet and a memorial tablet to him, a gift of the residents of Indiana, is located in the college's Chapel Hall.)

Following graduation Archibald returned to the family farm and in 1878 he was offered a teaching position at the Indiana School. He taught there three years when he was discharged to make way for a political friend, and once again he returned to the farm. He was later rehired under a different administration and returned to teaching. He remained at the school until his retirement.

Archibald's mother, who was a very religious person—it was reported that she had read the Bible seven times—had frequently expressed interest in establishing a home for homeless women. When Archibald inherited the property from his parents and three sisters, he decided to deed the property to the deaf people of Indiana for the establishment of a Home for Aged and Infirm Deaf. He was very interested in that project but died in 1927 before it became a reality. The Home opened a decade later.

The National Association of the Deaf met in St. Louis, Missouri during the summer of 1904 during the Louisiana Purchase Exposition. It was the NAD's twenty-fifth anniversary.

The International Congress of the Deaf and the Conference of Superintendents and Principals of Schools for the Deaf met in St. Louis the same summer. Helen Keller was an invited guest and her appearance coincided with the opening of the International Congress which was held on "Gallaudet Day." The World's Fair had designated a day in Helen Keller's honor. She was the only living person to receive such recognition.

Miss Keller was invited to speak to the assemblage. The meeting place was so packed—one account stated that there were over 1,000 persons—that it was difficult to hear her voice, so another person repeated what she said. That evening the local committee of the NAD and the officers of the St. Louis Gallaudet Union planned a reception in Miss Keller's honor. The Rev. James Cloud presented her with a pearl brooch with the Exposition's emblem engraved on it, on behalf of the deaf.

The Gallaudet Day School won a gold medal for its exhibit at the World's Fair. Its entry consisted of written works of the students, photography, and class demonstrations.

On February 5, 1907, the 70th birthday of Edward Miner Gallaudet and the 50th year of his work on Kendall Green, the Gallaudet College Alumni Association established the Edward Miner Gallaudet Memorial Fund. A scroll was presented to him announcing the establishment of the fund and its purpose—which would benefit the college. This pleased Gallaudet. Eventually, it was decided to use the money to construct a memorial building on the campus in his honor. By 1917 the sum of $2,000 had been raised. That year a goal of $50,000 was set and every graduate of the college was urged to contribute at least $50 and every former student, $25. The fund raising committee also planned to ask every deaf person in the country to contribute one dollar. By 1929 the fund had reached $35,000.

During the decade fires destroyed the main buildings at the Arkansas and Western Pennsylvania Schools for the Deaf. Gallaudet Home, the New York Home for the Aged and Infirm Deaf was another casualty of fire.

---

*How to pronounce some common words: Off-of, not **awf**. Ostrich-**os-trich**, not **os**-tridge. Parent—**pa**-rent, not par-ent. Patent—**pat**-ent, not pa-tent. Quay—key, not as spelled. Radish as spelled, not **red-ish**. Resort—rezort.*
—THE SILENT WORKER

Homes for the Aged and Infirm Deaf

Around the turn of the century there was a growing amount of interest in homes for aged deaf persons.

Four years earlier, in 1886, the Gallaudet Home for the Aged and Infirm Deaf had opened on a 156-acre farm six miles from Poughkeepsie, New York. This Home was founded through the efforts of the Rev. Thomas Gallaudet, the eldest son of the Rev. Thomas Hopkins Gallaudet. The founder hoped that this home would become a national home for aged deaf persons, but most of the help for constructing the home had come from New York residents. Residents of that state were given first choice and the home never reached the point where it served the nation. It was the first home of its kind in the USA.

In 1900 a fire destroyed the main building and one wing of another. A new and larger structure was built at Wappinger's Falls and completed in 1902. The new structure was built to accommodate about 50 persons. The new home was managed by the Church Mission to Deaf-Mutes of the Episcopal Church.

In 1901 the New England Home was organized in Everett, Massachusetts by the Rev. Stanley Searing, an Episcopal priest. This home was supported by the New England Gallaudet Association and six neighboring New England States. In 1929 the home was moved to a new site in Salem, Massachusetts.

In Indiana a few enterprising deaf people recognized the need for a home for the elderly deaf residents and set out to raise funds with which to construct one. The fund-raising campaign was not too successful until 1901 when Orson Archibald, a teacher at the Indiana School for the Deaf, became interested in the project. As a challenge to the fund-raising effort

---

In opening a way to deaf people for broader and higher education, and for equal standing in the community with their hearing brothers and sisters, in setting an example of courage, character, and leadership, Edward Miner Gallaudet has performed a work for which his name should be kept forever in the hearts of the deaf people of this country.
—THE EDWARD MINER GALLAUDET MEMORIAL FUND BOOKLET
1902

he offered to deed his large White County farm as a location for the home if the deaf Indianans would raise the sum of $10,000 within a given period of time. This challenge worked and the deaf community not only met the goal but exceeded it. Archibald was so pleased with the outcome that he deeded the home an additional large tract of land making the total some 347 acres.

Archibald continued his interest in the home, but unfortunately, passed away in 1927 before it became a reality. Construction was started on the home under the supervision of Arthur H. Norris, another teacher at the Indiana School, and completed and opened in 1937. John S. Miller was appointed the first superintendent. It was a large 17-room, one-story concrete building and was completely fireproof.

Initially the home was open only to those deaf persons who had attended the Indiana School or who were residents of the state. The restriction was later relaxed and today elderly deaf persons from other states are admitted.

The residents pay what they can from social security benefits and other means, but this is not sufficient to maintain the home and it is subsidized with income from the rented part of the farm. The home is operated by a superintendent who reports to a nine-member board of directors.

There was a Home for the Aged Deaf in Moultrie, Florida. It was maintained by the Dixie Association of the Deaf. The home was started around 1932 and admitted those aged and infirm deaf persons who could not pay free of charge. The Home was supported by the Dixie Association. The Home and the Dixie Association went out of existence early in the 1940s.

The Deaf Driver

J. L. Smith described the arrival of the automobile in our society with these words: ". . . a queer looking affair, with a stove-pipe sticking up behind. When it rattled through the streets, human beings turned to stare, sedate farm horses tried to climb telephone poles, and dogs and cats sought cover."

As the automobile gained popularity shortly after the turn of the century, hundreds of deaf persons bought their own cars and learned to drive them. Noted Smith proudly in 1923: "Quite a number of deaf people in the state are the owners and drivers of autos today. I can check off as many as 35 on my fingers, and it is likely that there are anywhere between 50 and 100 deaf owners, drivers of cars in Minnesota."

Early Deaf Drivers

BELOW: *Frank Wurdemann was one of the earliest, if not the first, deaf persons to drive an automobile in the District of Columbia. Circa 1900.*

RIGHT: *Reuben S. Weaver and his first automobile. He was the first automobile owner in Virginia. Circa 1900.*

FAR RIGHT: *J. B. A. Benoit and his home-made automobile in 1902. He is in the driver's seat and his son, Alex, is seated next to him. In the rear seat are daughters Leontine and Rosalie and Mrs. Benoit.*

166

Ralph Weaver at the wheel of a Ford in 1911.

Ernest O. Shipman and his new Model A Ford. It cost him $600.

Ralph and Ben Weaver drove this Overland for a doctor in Iuka, Illinois. Ben is in the driver's seat. Circa 1910.

As more and more automobiles appeared on the roads, however, the number of auto accidents and fatalities increased. To stem this flow many states began in the 1920s to enact motor vehicle codes. Among those drivers to attract close scrutiny were those with physical handicaps. In at least four states deaf persons were refused driving licenses and other states considered such a ban. There was even some talk of a federal law to require hearing tests for all drivers.

So shortly after the automobile arrived, deaf persons had a battle on their hands to protect their right to drive. In Pennsylvania they raised $4,000 to repeal a code that denied a license to any person with less than two percent hearing. The National Association of the Deaf formed an Automobile Bureau (actually a committee) to compile statistics on deaf drivers and to keep an eye on discriminating legislation; in Southern California deaf motorists formed an auto club to protect their driving rights. Besides the infringement of their rights which these laws caused, deaf persons resented being barred from the highways which their tax money helped build and maintain.

But deaf people, because of their safe driving records along with assistance from their friends and support from the superintendents of state schools for the deaf, gradually won the right to drive in all states. Some restrictions were imposed. In Maryland, for example, a law required that the deaf drivers be accompanied in the front seat by a person with normal hearing. That was during the days before stop signs and traffic lights when it was the practice of motorists approaching an intersection to honk as they neared the crossroads. In theory, at least, the driver who honked first went first. In Pennsylvania a deaf person applying for a license had to pass all required tests and then appear before a three member committee consisting of deaf persons who refused to recommend any deaf person they did not consider qualified to drive.

As deaf people's safe driving records became better known, however, there was less hostility towards permitting them to drive. In 1929 *The Philadelphia Record* printed statistics which showed that none of the 177 licensed deaf drivers in the city had been involved in an accident. Other areas began reporting similar results. A 1937 survey of 1,011 deaf drivers turned up only one driver who had been in an accident involving damage costing $200 or more.

In 1948 *Ford Times* printed Arthur H. Lewis' article, "World's Safest Drivers" which gave deaf drivers a considerable boost. That article was frequently quoted or referred to years afterwards whenever well-meaning but poorly-informed legislators began toying with the idea of introducing legislation to ban deaf drivers.

In the 1960s a Colorado judge named Sherman G. Finesilver brought national attention to the safe driving records of deaf drivers. He published articles about their driving records, compiled statistics, and conducted defensive driving workshops for them around the country. This publicity was a benefit to deaf people and helped focus increased attention on their safe driving records.

Inventors

John R. Gregg, the inventor of Gregg Shorthand, had a severe hearing impairment. As a youth, growing up in Great Britain, he was caught one day in school whispering to his classmate. As punishment the headmaster knocked their heads together. The impact broke Gregg's ear drum and resulted in a life-long hearing impairment.

In his teens Gregg became interested in speedwriting or shorthand. He studied the different systems in use at that time and soon mastered several methods. He invented a system of his own using curves, slashes and other lines natural to the hand's movement. When he was about 20 years old he published 500 copies of his system in a 28-page pamphlet called "Light-Line Phonography!" He later revised his first system, renamed it the Gregg Shorthand and published another edition in 1893. He moved to Chicago where he started the Gregg School, later renamed Gregg College, and organized the Gregg Publishing Co. He wrote a number of textbooks on shorthand and commercial education. Gregg's Shorthand system spread rapidly and by the late 1930s it was being taught in more than 95 percent of the schools which offered shorthand courses. His system was adapted to French, Spanish, Italian, Polish, Irish, Gaelic, and Esperanto and was used widely in Canada, Great Britian, and the Latin-American countries.

President Hoover appointed Gregg a member of the American delegation to the International Congress on Commercial Education at Amsterdam, Holland where he was elected vice president of the Congress. Boston University awarded him an honorary Doctor of Commercial Science degree. A portrait of him was painted by Sidney E. Dickinson, and was exhibited at the National Arts Club in New York City. Twice married, Gregg was the father of two children. He died February 23, 1948.

Deaf inventors who have received mention in the press at different times during the century:

Thomas J. Brown of St. Louis, Missouri patented a

device for holding an ironing table.

Robert C. Wall, a Philadelphia manufacturer, built the first "safe" bicycle and gasoline-powered automobile seen in the city. He also invented and patented a bicycle luggage carrier rack.

Anton Schroeder, a graduate of the Minnesota School for the Deaf, invented a candle lighter, hangers for storm windows and several other things. He sold some of his patents to Stanley Co.

George Wing, a graduate of the American School for the Deaf and a teacher at the Minnesota and Illinois Schools, invented Wing's Symbols, a system to help deaf students acquire better written language. His system helped students construct correct sentences. It placed less emphasis on memorization. Wing also invented a convenient gauge pin for printers. It became a money maker, earning him $300 a year.

Edith Fitzgerald attended public schools and the Illinois School for the Deaf. She became a teacher of the deaf and created "Straight Language System" for deaf students, better known as the "Fitzgerald Key." Her system provided guidelines for the proper placement of words in sentence construction. At one time her system was reportedly used in three quarters of the schools for the deaf.

Roscoe Augustin, a sheep shearer by trade, invented a back reliever to ease the strain on the sheep shearer's back. It was a simple contraption that involved a chest vest, rope and a sling. It was very popular in sheep-shearing circles.

J. B. A. Benoit was an automobile pioneer. He owned a shop that specialized in repairing and selling bicycles. In 1902 he built a horseless carriage.

George T. Dougherty, a chemist, developed a method that was used for years in the manufacture of steel.

As a youth, Philip A. Emery, the founder of the Kansas State School for the Deaf and the Chicago Day Schools for the Deaf, designed a number of gadgets which were already in existence but which he had never seen. When he was nine years old he "invented" a case knife handle and when he was ten a sun dial and sextant.

Henry Haight invented an improved incubator for hatching baby chicks. His coop could hold 20,000 eggs. He also invented a thermostat which maintained a uniform temperature. He won a gold medal at the National Poultry Exhibition for his inventions in the 1890s.

Ben Oppenheimer invented a rubber cape with a parachute attachment. It opened (claimed the inventor) when a person jumped into the air. A pair of thick elastic soled shoes accompanied the contraption to ease the shock on striking the ground. With this device, the inventor stated, a person need not be afraid of jumping off great heights in an emergency. There is no record of his offer to personally demonstrate his invention.

Pollard Paxton, a deaf Norfolk, Virginia printer, invented and patented a toy cart with two figures on top. When pulled, a wire attached to the axle moved the figures. The toy also made a whistling noise. The *Scientific American* predicted that this toy would become more popular than the "jack-in-the-box."

In the 1890s, at the age of 10, Willie Masher invented what he called a "Mute's Telephone." It was an instrument with tiny keys on both ends. Each key had an alphabet letter. When one key was activated by the sender, it moved the same key on the receiver's end making it possible to send a message. His model was made from a crackerbox and twine. It so impressed officials at a large school for the deaf that they agreed to have a larger and more accurate model built to determine its practical value. It is not known what became of young Willie's invention.

George Shanklin was an electric cable and insulation expert. He held 17 patents in his field and was credited with the discovery of ionization of high voltage cables.

Daniel Tellier, Jr. invented a door alarm.

W. F. Pope, who had a trucking business in Florida, invented an irrigating system which a newspaper account called the first in the state.

Dale Paden of Omaha, Nebraska invented a special type of vise-grip pliers, a pipe wrench, and other items.

Wesley Lauritsen, who was athletic director at the Minnesota School for the Deaf for 40 years, designed an athletic schedule book in 1946. It became very popular and was in great demand at schools and colleges. He later added an Athletic Memory Book, a New Century Basketball Scorebook, and a New Century Football Diagram Scorebook.

R. Aumon Bass of Virginia created an alarm clock which turned on a light at a pre-set time. He called his device "The Big Boss."

Emerson Romero manufactured wake-up alarms for deaf people. His line included clocks with built-in lamps, baby cry signals, doorbell lights, vibrators, and buzzers. He got into the business quite by accident when he built a wooden replacement clock case for a friend. In 1959 he formed the Vibralarm Service.

In 1980 Francis Jancik of Maryland received a patent for his lifter which permits one man to carry a mattress or a large sheet of glass or plywood. When not in use it doubles as a storage hanger.

David O. Watson

El Mudo

El Mudo stood there in the darkened room, tall, lean, and alone. His hands were clasped behind his back and his head was slightly bowed. His eyes were on the three customs agents gathered around the table near the back of the room. Along one side of the room, next to the wall, stood eight-year-old Angelia and her younger sister, Edna. Light from the kerosene lantern flickered and danced on the walls. Angelia could see the worried look on her father's face. She realized he was in serious trouble.

Angelia Watson, whose family had moved to Mexico around the turn of the century, would recall the scene many times in later years—the sunset on the western horizon that afternoon. It was but one of their many adventures.

El Mudo (The Mute) was David Otis Watson, an alumnus of the Tennessee School for the Deaf. His wife, Alice Blansit, had attended the Alabama School. Watson had moved his young family to Cananea, a small village in the state of Sonora, Mexico, in search of fame and fortune. Cananea was a gold mining town. There he set up a saddle and hardware business and built a 12-room attached home and shop. Of the family of seven only young David and the family dog, "Jip," could hear.

Watson's saddlery was the only business of its kind in the area. He attracted ranchers and peons from miles around. Since he could not talk and knew little Spanish he communicated with his customers in gestures. He was fair and honest and soon won their friendship and respect. Because of the way he communicated he was known as "El Mudo."

During their stay in Mexico, a bandit named Francisco "Pancho" Villa was fighting with other factions for control of the country. Villa's men frequently came to Cananea. The Watsons suffered at the hands of the bandits, who broke into their store and stole merchandise, tools, and equipment and personal belongings. Once Mrs. Watson was forced, with a pistol pointed at her, to open the family safe. They lost what savings they had. As conditions worsened the family and other Americans were forced to take refuge in nearby Naco, Arizona. During their absence from Cananea Villa's men occupied Watson's home and shop, leaving it in a shambles.

Following their return the Watsons started their business again on credit and capital borrowed from relatives. About this time the United States turned against Villa because of his brutality and threw its support to his opposition. In retaliation, an enraged Villa began shooting Americans. He led his men on a rampage into Colum-

171

David Watson was known as "El Mudo."

TOP: *David Watson and his bride, Alice Blansit Watson. They were married by the Rev. Philip J. Hasenstab.*

BOTTOM: *The Watson children (from left): Angelia, Prince, David and Edna.*

bus, New Mexico, leaving 16 persons dead. The U.S. retaliated by sending General John Pershing and his soldiers into Mexico in pursuit of Villa. This unauthorized expedition into their country angered the Mexicans and created bitter resentment against Americans residing there. The Watsons were among the Americans who suffered the consequences. Anti-American mobs broke into their store, damaging it, and stealing many of their things.

And now this. The three customs agents had been huddling around the pile of rifle ammunition on the table talking. One of the agents now approached El Mudo and using homemade signs gestured to him: "You know you jail?" he signed pointing to the bullets on the table. El Mudo knew the penalty. He nodded. The agent returned to the other two beside the table. They talked some more.

El Mudo knew the seriousness of his crime. With Mexico in the middle of civil strife and roving bandits raiding the ranches and villages, the citizens were desperate for guns and ammunition to protect themselves. As a businessman El Mudo had received special permission from the Mexican and United States government to import and sell rifles and ammunition under a strict quota system. The demand was so great and the citizens so desperate, however, that he had risked smuggling across the border more ammunition than his quota allowed and he had been caught.

The agent returned and stood to one side of El Mudo so that his body would not block the light from the lantern. Using gestures again he pointed to the ammunition on the table and signed, "That you jail." El Mudo nodded solemnly. The agent continued, now pointing to El Mudo, and putting his index finger to his lips, "You shhhhh! You no jail. We keep (pointing to ammunition). You go." El Mudo nodded that he understood. He knew that the agents would sell the ammunition and

keep the money, but he was happy to let them have it in exchange for his freedom. He bowed slightly and went out the door. Angelia and Edna followed.

Chapter 6

The 1910s

Preserving Sign Language

N 1914 Roy J. "R. J." Stewart succeeded Oscar H. Regensburg as chairman of the National Association of the Deaf Motion Picture Committee upon the latter's death. When oralism took a strong hold on education of the deaf during the early part of this century, concern was expressed that the beauty of sign language might be lost. The NAD established a Motion Picture Committee to record on film some of the better signers of the day for preservation. The committee developed quite a collection of films which included the following titles:

"The Lorna Doone Country of Devonshire, England" by Dr. Edward Miner Gallaudet; "Memories of Old Hartford," by Dr. John B. Hotchkiss; "Lincoln's Gettysburg Address," by Dr. Thomas F. Fox; "Preservation of the Sign Language," by George W. Veditz; and many others. These films were rented to schools, clubs and other groups, and they were quite popular. The committee's coffers were filled by the rental fees.

Unfortunately, for the committee, the members voted at the Hartford Convention to transfer $1,000 from the Motion Picture Fund to the NAD Endowment Fund. The Picture Fund never recouped from this large withdrawl, and many of the old 35-mm films deteriorated so much that they could not be transferred to 16mm film. Many of the old films were lost. Nevertheless, Stewart remained the guardian angel of these old films through the many years they were in his care. His biennial request for funds to restore old films and enlarge the collection became as common an item on the NAD convention agenda as the regular resolution supporting sign language which was inevitably adopted at each convention. Although RJ was not very successful in getting the financial support he needed, he took care of the films as best he could and arranged for their preservation in the Library of Congress and at the Edward Miner Gallaudet Memorial Library. He faithfully reported on their condition at each convention. It is due largely to RJ that today's students of sign language can see on video-tape the rare old sign language presentations made from those early films.

The Deaf Nurses of Mercy Hospital

One hot summer day in 1897 two doctors who were sisters—Dr. Katharine B. Richardson and Dr. Alice A. Graham—found a homeless crippled child in Kansas City, Missouri. Unable to find the child's parents or relatives, they decided to take care of her and their experience with this little waif led to the founding of Mercy Hospital. Both doctors were widows and, having no children of their own, they felt called upon to care for children of all kinds.

One day, some years later, Dr. Richardson was approached by May Paxton, a graduate of the Missouri School for the Deaf, who wanted to become a nurse. Such an idea—a deaf nurse—was unheard of, but then, Dr. Richardson realized, so had been the idea

Student nurses May Paxton and Marion Finch at Mercy Hospital in Kansas City, Missouri.

of female doctors! An ardent feminist who had experienced rebuke and ridicule, Dr. Richardson tried unsuccessfully to dissuade Miss Paxton, explaining that the work was long and hard and the pay was small. May Paxton was unswerving so the doctor decided to give her a chance. Dr. Richardson was so pleased with Paxton's performance that she admitted three other deaf girls—Marion Finch from South Dakota, Lillie Speaker from Kansas, and Emma Brewington. Miss Brewington was in charge of the linen and worked in the nursery. The others worked in the operation room when tonsillectomies were performed, in the post-operation rooms and in the nursery.

Finch was the first to leave. She returned home to South Dakota to tend to family business, and she later became a girls' supervisor at the Oregon School for the Deaf. Speaker left on account of illness, later married and raised four children.

After three years May Paxton left to get married. On the occasion of her departure, one doctor wrote: "Your quick feet and clever hands and cheerful smiles have been an inspiration to all of us." Dr. Graham also wrote Miss Paxton a letter in which she said: "I try to be thankful and rejoice with you that you are to have a good husband and a dear home of your own,

The Gallaudet Auxiliary making bandages during World War I.

The Gallaudet airplane built by Edson F. Gallaudet. Note propeller in center of fuselage. It was called the "Gallaudet Drive."

---

but when you leave The Mercy it will be such a loss to us. . . . "

None of the girls completed the nursing course, but Dr. Richardson expressed faith in their ability to do so.

The Gallaudet Airplane

Edson F. Gallaudet, a hearing man and the second son of Edward Miner Gallaudet, was an aviation pioneer. He was born on Kendall Green where his father was president of Gallaudet College. He was a graduate of Yale and earned his engineering degree at Johns Hopkins University. He was rowing coach and physics instructor at Yale where he became interested in the warping wing principle. In 1897 he constructed a model kite which resembled the airplane which the Wright Brothers flew a few years later at Kitty Hawk. His "fooling around with gimcracks," however, was frowned upon by Yale authorities and he was told to quit "making an ass of himself and a laughing stock of the faculty." He was given the alternative of discontinuing his experiments or resigning.

Gallaudet resigned and his model was stored in a barn in Connecticut, unpatented. (It is now at the Smithsonian Institution in Washington, D.C.)

Gallaudet's interest in aviation continued. He possessed pilot's license #32 in this country, in addition to a French license. He built Gallaudet Aircraft Corporation in Rhode Island, one of the first aircraft manufacturing concerns in the country. He designed and built a number of seaplanes and bombers. His monoplane, which had an estimated speed of 130 mph,

THE WASHINGTONIAN

Vol. XXIV   Vancouver, Wash., February 17, 1916   No. 10

Fifty Deaf Marksmen Dead

Defending Chicago's finest hotel against rioting German spies, 50 out of 70 deaf sharpshooters die while frustrating attempts to rescue the captive Crown Prince of Germany, Frederick William, according to part of the "Diary of James E. Langston, war correspondent of the London *Times*, 1922."

That is the idea spread over two columns on page 18 of the February number of *McClure's* magazine, in the concluding installment of the big serial of 1915, "Saving the Nation" by Cleveland Moffett, a famous metropolitan newspaper editor.

Fighting side-by-side with 50 big game hunters against odds of ten to one, and using their own rifles against machine guns, the deaf lose five out of every seven men, as against five out of ten lost by the militant millionaires—but foil the one consumate masterstroke of the wily enemy in the German-American War of 1921.

Harry Whittemore, Otto Egger, Fred Bengry, Clark Miller, Arthur Hanson and David Brettauer are mentioned by name, with the publisher of the WASHINGTONIAN as Lieutenant in command.

This characterization of the deaf as military heroes is not a Jules Verne artifice designed to entertain the public. The present European war shows the deaf are doing their share in defence of wives and hearthstones. A Dutch newspaper, *De Courant*, says two companies of deaf infantry sent to reinforce the German lines in Flanders, took part in the battle of Ypres. Although educated in German pure oral schools commands were issued by signs, observers report. The Russians claim to have taken prisoners deaf Germans in full uniform of the invading corps. In England the deaf are working in munition plants.

Sharpshooters are by no means as common in America as in the days of Indian forays, and notwithstanding the fact big guns and high explosives are the whole thing in modern warfare, 150 deaf patriots able to shoot the left eye out of a gnat at fifty yards would be invaluable in trench fighting, or in holding some strategic defile—picking off the officers and artillerymen.

President Howard of the N. A. D. is seriously considering preparations to line up a company of deaf marksmen such as Cleveland Moffett writes of, realizing what a chance it is to answer for all time the query of the uninformed, "Does the education of the deaf PAY?"

There are a number of rifle experts in the Pacific Northwest now being sounded, such as the crack of the Spokane Rifle and Revolver club, Erve Chambers, who once went to school here, and big game hunters like Roy Harris, of Seattle, John Cookman, of Bellingham, and the deaf Indian whose wonderful wood-carvings Portland newspapers have been raving over, John Clarke. He was one of the best grizzly killers in the Blackfoot tribe.

Among our own pupils Sanders, Scipp, Martin, Coic, Gillis, Kelly and Kotula are all good shots. They don't hunger for war, but say they would fight like furies did some foreign foe presume to offer their mothers and sisters the indignities Germans offered to Belgian, Serbian and Polish womankind.

The deaf are not adaptable to war on the same footing as the hearing. The deaf are almost helpless at night, either in answering the challenge of sentries or in night alarms. They could hold some strategic point and, picking off the vanguard with deadly precission, hold back the enemy till the last succumbed. "Since the best blood of the nation would be sent to slaughter, why should not we afflicted die likewise," one expressed it.

"Our country educates and protects us" he continued. "There isn't a man but would deem it a privilege to return to America in distress the life she has made worth living lifting us from the depths of ignorance and eternal silence to an enlightened understanding and fuller enjoyment. If for no other reason than to show our gratitude by one glorious example, I believe President Wilson would accept our voluntary services."

Melvin Davidson and Deidterich Kaiser, enthusiastic young deer hunters of San Francisco, are getting a line on deaf marksmen further down the Pacific Coast. It is planned to so perfect arrangements that forty-eight hours after war is declared fifty deaf sharpshooters, each fully armed with his own high-power rifle and equipped with a day's ammunition, will be assembled at a prearranged point ready for dispatch to the front. There they will lay down their lives holding back the PREPARED invaders while America slowly gathers her tremendous resources to hurl them into the sea.

revolutionized aircraft design. One of his planes had the propeller in the center of the fuselage behind the pilot's cockpit. The four blades revolved around the fuselage. The design was called the Gallaudet Drive.

The manufacturing business was not a financial success and was sold. It became part of Consolidated Aircraft which became Convair and, later, a division of General Dynamics.

Reuben Fleet called Gallaudet an innovative engineer. Gallaudet played a part in the development of the turbine engine and the three-dimensional camera. He invented the silk gut used in tennis rackets before Nylon became popular.

Had Gallaudet continued his experiments uninterrupted and had his models been successful it is possible that Yale would have received credit for the invention of the airplane and the name Gallaudet would have gone down in aviation history along with its prominence in education of the deaf.

The Decade

The Ku Klux Klan was organized in 1915. By the 1920s it had grown into a powerful organization. The Armistice was signed on November 11, 1918 ending World War I, "the war to end all wars." A year later in July, 1919 the Prohibition Act took effect and the "Roaring Twenties" followed.

The *New York Daily News,* the first successful tabloid, made its debut and within a decade had a circulation of over one million. Women's skirts were six inches from the floor. Automobiles with such names as the Maxwell, Briscoe, Lexington, Templar, Dodge, Buick, Cadillac, and Hudson passed in the streets. Before the end of the decade there were seven million registered passenger cars in this country.

There were disputes involving the Jews, the Negroes, and the Roman Catholics. Race riots occurred in Chicago and Tulsa, Oklahoma.

That was the era that saw Jack Dempsey flatten Georges Carpentier in the decade's first million-dollar bout. Babe Ruth hit 59 homers and the "Praying Colonels" of Centre College in Danville, Kentucky, made sports history by upsetting Harvard in a football contest, 6 to 0.

The dance was frowned upon and seen as offensive to "woman's purity" and it was proposed to start an organization to discourage "excess nudity."

You could stay at Hotel Elmer in Cincinnati, Ohio, which claimed to be "strictly modern," on the European Plan for $1.00 and up. Or, dine at Hoffman's Cafe on Vine Street which immodestly called itself the "Finest Cafe in America." And, your savings account brought three to four percent on time deposits at the

Deaf women employees at Goodyear plant in Akron, Ohio.

Burdick Album

Children at St. Rita's School for the Deaf in Cincinnati, Ohio, sign the "Star Spangled Banner." Ca. 1918.

local bank.

The decade found C. W. Charles of the Ohio School for the Deaf, in Columbus, Ohio, selling a 16-page booklet of the single and doublehanded manual alphabets and the *Most Common Signs of the Deaf* for five cents. You could subscribe to *The Ohio Chronicle* or *The Kentucky Standard* for 75¢ a year or purchase a copy of J. Schuyler Long's *A Sign Directory*, "The first and only book of its kind issued in America." The book included 500 illustrations by the author and sold for $2.00 postpaid.

The Silent Worker, an illustrated monthly magazine,

There is no danger of sign language disappearing. It will live long after you and I are dead. If we were all to die tonight, a hundred years from now it would still be alive and serving the deaf.

—JOHN W. JONES
1913

---

was "acknowledged everywhere [as] the finest and best monthly magazine for the Deaf in the World," to quote the publisher, and sold for 50¢ a year—in advance.

In Lead, South Dakota, C. G. Herbert, a deaf landlord, was mistakenly shot to death by one of his renters. Herbert, who had returned from the East, knocked on the door of the house he owned. The woman's husband was away at work and she did not know that Herbert was deaf. When Herbert failed to respond to repeated inquiries, the frightened woman fired through the door, killing him instantly.

On Sunday, February 6, 1910, fire destroyed the roof and top floor of College Hall, the men's dormitory at Gallaudet College, and did $25,000 damage. That same year *The Volta Review* appeared. It replaced *The Association Review*, which had been published since 1899 by the American Association to Promote the Teaching of Speech to the Deaf.

In Filbert, South Carolina, Mrs. Ollie S. Lynn, the deaf daughter of deaf parents, was the postmistress. She was married to a hearing man who tended the

178

family farm while she ran the post office. Her performance was rated highly and several times she was commended for catching discrepancies in the mail.

In 1911 the Nebraska State Legislature passed a bill requiring all children at the Nebraska School for the Deaf to be educated by the oral, aural, and lipreading method. Fingerspelling and sign language were forbidden. The National Association of the Deaf sent a petition signed by 1,700 persons and a lobbyist, who worked two months, to fight the bill, but it was to no avail.

The Rev. James H. Cloud of St. Louis, Missouri and the Rev. Philip J. Hasenstab of Chicago, Illinois, along with Arthur Norris, who represented the Indiana Association of the Deaf, participated in the dedication program of the new Indiana State School for the Deaf at its new location on East 42nd Street in 1912.

The flood which hit Indianapolis a year later was so bad that many teachers and school employees were unable to get to work for a week.

In 1913 Edmund Price, a graduate of the Washington School for the Deaf was awarded a Carnegie Medal and $1,000 in cash for heroism. On May 26, 1907 in Seal Gardens, California, Price had saved a young girl from being hit by a trolley car and escaped within inches of being killed himself.

John D. Rockefeller attended a Baptist church service conducted by a deaf preacher during the 1913 National Association of the Deaf convention in Cleveland. Afterwards, he invited the members to visit his home at Forest Hill. Many accepted and a picture was taken of the assemblage with Rockefeller. There was hope among some members of the NAD Endowment Fund Committee that Rockefeller "might see reason to suitably endow the organization" but no such contributions were forthcoming.

In 1914 a bill was brought before the Connecticut legislature which would exempt deaf people from taxation. A group of deaf people appeared before the Finance Committee to oppose the measure. The committee was so surprised by the action that they had the bill framed.

Friends of Sophia Fowler Gallaudet erected a monument at Mrs. Gallaudet's birthplace near Guilford, Connecticut. The bronze tablet with her likeness was designed by deaf sculptor, Eugene E. Hannan. On the tablet was inscribed: "At this place was born on March 20, 1798, Sophia Fowler wife of Thomas Hopkins Gallaudet founder of the first public school for the deaf in America at Hartford A.D. 1817." Funds for the memorial were raised by deaf women and their friends through popular subscription and the monument was unveiled during the National Association of the Deaf

convention at Hartford in the summer of 1917.

In the fall of 1918 an influenza epidemic hit the West Virginia School in Romney leaving about 200 pupils and employees stricken. Four nurses were hired but they too became sick. Teachers, officers, and volunteers from the town who escaped the illness and two Red Cross nurses from Parkersburg worked together to take care of the sick. Four deaths resulted.

Milestones

Sister Patricia (Bridget Hughes) (d. 1910) was one of the first deaf women to become a nun in the United States. Stricken with black fever when she was seven years old, she was educated at the Pennsylvania School for the Deaf. Although she retained the use of her speech she preferred to use sign language when communicating with her schoolmates. She was a leader among her peers and showed an early leaning towards religion. Hughes entered the novitiate of the Sisters of St. Joseph at Chester Hill in Philadelphia and received the habit on August 16, 1880, becoming Sister Patricia. As Sister Patricia she was appointed a sacristan of the convent chapel, a duty she performed until her death. She worked with deaf Catholic children at her alma mater and was influential in persuading Archbishop Ryan to establish a Catholic institution for deaf children in Pennsylvania, a school that became a reality and was named the Archbishop Ryan Memorial Institute for the Deaf. Sister Patricia was stricken with pneumonia in December, 1910 and died on Christmas eve.

A physical education class at the Missouri School for the Deaf. Ca. 1915.

Regulations.

Excerpts from a Gallaudet College regulations handbook, published in the early 1900s:

College Exercises.

Students are required to attend Chapel exercises, to be present at all recitations of their respective classes, and to attend such other exercises as may be announced by the Faculty from time to time.

Chapel exercises are held every day except Saturday at 9:00 a.m. On Sunday they are held at 9:00 a.m. and at 5:00 p.m.

Special Prohibitions.

Students are not allowed to walk upon the railroad track; nor to use tobacco; nor to use intoxicating liquors, except by permission of the President on the prescription of the attending physician; nor to have or use fire-arms or gun-powder in the buildings or on the grounds of the College; nor to engage in "hazing," by which is meant harassing or annoying a student by abusive or ridiculous tricks; nor to require of another student the performance of any menial service.

Conduct Record.

A conduct record is kept of each student.

The effect of thirty demerits during the year, or twenty demerits during the term, is to suspend the student.

Fifteen demerits are equivalent to a reprimand, strict probation, and a letter to the parents or guardians.

Ten demerits are equivalent to a censure and a letter to the parents or guardians.

Five demerits are equivalent to an admonition, and students having five demerits will be notified by the office.

The word "term," as used above, not only includes the period during which recitations and examinations take place but the vacation following.

Chaperonage.

9. All calls and gatherings and excursions in which the men and women mingle, shall be supervised by chaperons approved by the Faculty.

Calls.

5. The men may make social calls upon the women students on Sunday evenings between 8 and 9 o'clock.

6. Emergency calls (i.e. calls for purposes that can not wait) may be made on week-days from 1:15 p.m. to 2 p.m.; and from 7 p.m. to 7:30 p.m. Men making such calls must enter by the front door, as in making formal calls, state their errand to the person in charge, and abide by her decision as to its urgency.

7. No young man shall make calls upon one young woman exclusively. Persistence in doing so debars one from the privilege of calling.

Escorting.

8. When permission has been given the women to attend gatherings outside the College precincts, the men may escort them. The men may also escort the women home from such social gatherings and athletic contests on the College grounds as the latter may be permitted to attend.

Association.

10. The men and women may sit intermingled only at their dramatic and other social entertainments. No tickets for particular reserved seats at dramatic performances shall be sold.

11. The men and women may associate in the presentation of dramas and other stage-entertainments only when such presentation is originated and supervised by members of the Faculty.

12. The men and women may join in the editorial and business management of *The Buff and Blue*.

Grounds.

13. That part of the College Grounds east of the line of the west face of the Chapel-terrace wall extended to Florida Avenue, and between this Avenue and the College Buildings, is reserved for the use of the women students.

Athletic Contests.

14. The women students may without special permission attend only such athletic contests within the College precincts as occur on Wednesday and Saturdays.

15. The women may not attend wrestling contests.

Conduct Marks.

Dirty or disorderly room	1 demerit
Student under supervision absent from his room at any time during the evening study hours	1 demerit
Student visiting room under supervision at any time during the evening study hours	1 or more demerits
Unexcused absences from recitation, gymnastic or athletic work, or from chapel	1 demerit
Disorderly or improper conduct	1 or more demerits
Trespassing upon the premises of the young women	1 or more demerits
Improper dress	1 demerit
Tardiness at meals	1 demerit
Use of tobacco.......................	5 demerits

Chapter 7

The 1920s

The Decade

HE 1920s saw the arrival of the washing machine, electric irons, and vacuum cleaners. The radio appeared, linked Americans, and changed their lives. The automobile became popular, and travel increased. The 1920s was the decade of Prohibition, America's move from the farm to the city, the "Roaring Twenties," the stockmarket collapse, and the St. Valentine's Day Massacre in Chicago.

Charlie Chaplin, Douglas Fairbanks, Gloria Swanson, Rudolph Valentino, and Clara Bow were top box office draws at the movies. Emily Post's *Book of Etiquette* became a best seller. Sinclair Lewis wrote *Main Street* and became America's first author to win the Nobel Prize in literature. Tall, youthful Charles A. Lindberg and his *Spirit of St. Louis* flew to Paris and fame, ushering in the air age. The John Scopes trial took place in Dayton, Tennessee.

Red Grange, the "Galloping Ghost," was setting records on the gridiron at the University of Illinois that would make him an all-time football great. Man O'War was the race horse of the time and Gertrude Ederle became the first woman to successfully swim the English Channel.

Deaf Clergy
Episcopal

It was the Episcopal Church which took the lead in meeting the religious needs of the deaf community in America. Thomas Gallaudet, eldest son of Thomas Hopkins Gallaudet, began a Sunday School class for deaf people at St. Stephens Church in New York City in 1850. Gallaudet was then an instructor at the New York Institute for the Deaf (now the New York School for the Deaf-Fanwood). Concerned about the lack of religious services for deaf people, he later resigned his teaching position and entered the ministry full time, becoming an ordained priest of the Episcopal Church in 1851. He founded St. Ann's Church for the Deaf in New York City, "the first church exclusively for deaf people in this country." Gallaudet is also considered the originator of the use of sign language in religious services for the deaf.

One day Gallaudet received a letter from a young schoolboy named Henry Syle. Syle wanted to know what the chances were for a deaf boy to become a clergyman. Gallaudet knew of no deaf clergymen then. He responded that he saw possibilities. He was encouraging. Of course, neither knew at that time that one day they would meet again and that Syle would become the first deaf man ordained as a priest in this country.

Except for poor health, Syle was the perfect choice. The son of the Rev. E.H. Syle, a missionary in China, young Henry was born in Shanghai in November, 1846. His mother was the sister of Senator H.W. Davis of Maryland. Young Syle's poor health prompted his parents to send him to America to live with his mother's sister in Alexandria, Virginia. When he was six years old he contracted scarlet fever which left him

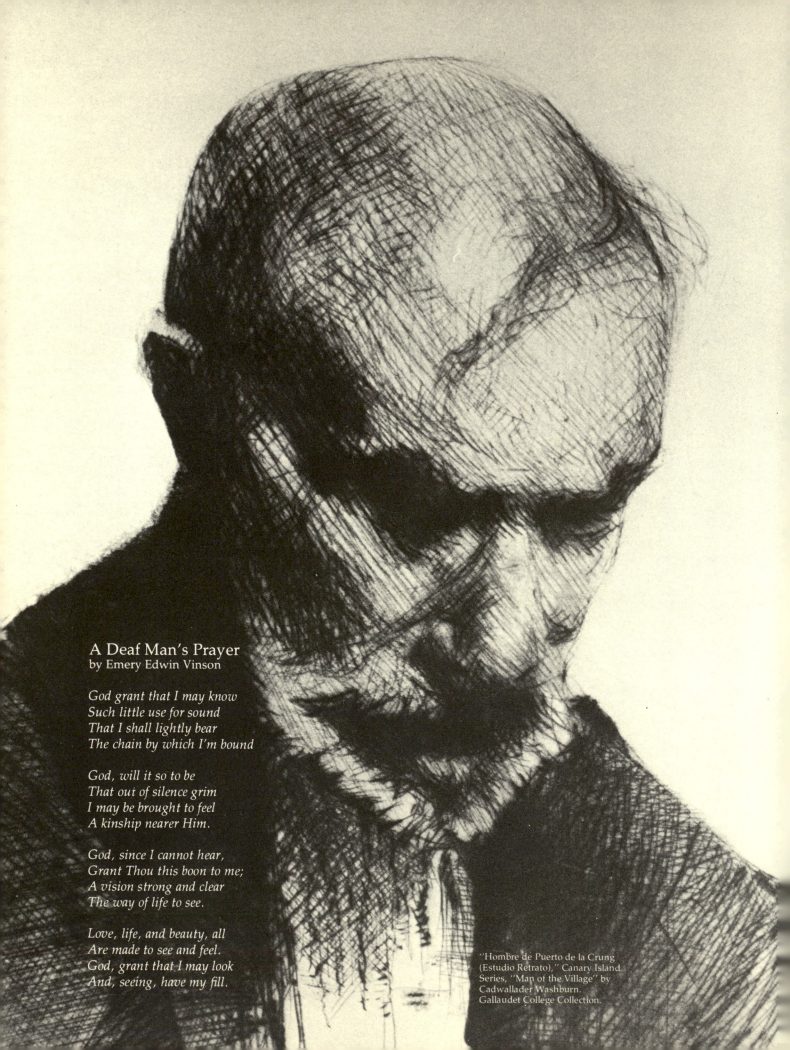

A Deaf Man's Prayer
by Emery Edwin Vinson

God grant that I may know
Such little use for sound
That I shall lightly bear
The chain by which I'm bound

God, will it so to be
That out of silence grim
I may be brought to feel
A kinship nearer Him.

God, since I cannot hear,
Grant Thou this boon to me;
A vision strong and clear
The way of life to see.

Love, life, and beauty, all
Are made to see and feel.
God, grant that I may look
And, seeing, have my fill.

"Hombre de Puerto de la Crung
(Estudio Retrato)," Canary Island
Series, "Man of the Village" by
Cadwallader Washburn.
Gallaudet College Collection.

totally deaf. He was sent to Mr. Bartlett's Family School for Young Deaf-Mute Children, a private school, located in Fishkill Landing, New York. Syle had learned to read the Bible when he was three years old, and he was intellectually ahead of the other children at the school. When the Bartletts moved their school to Hartford, where they later joined the teaching staff of the American School for the Deaf, Syle enrolled at ASD. Next he entered Trinity College in Hartford, then studied at St. John's College in Cambridge, England, but both times he was forced to suspend his college studies because of poor eyesight. When he returned to this country, he accepted a teaching position at the New York School where he taught from 1867 to 1874. It was while teaching that he managed to complete work for his Bachelor of Arts degree by correspondence at Yale College. He completed a four-year course in one year. He continued his studies and earned two Master of Arts degrees, one from Yale in 1872 and one from Trinity College in 1875.

When he moved to Philadelphia to accept an assayer's position at the U.S. Mint, he became involved with the deaf congregation at St. Stephen's Church, and his earlier ambition to become a clergyman was once again whetted. He was already a licensed lay-reader, and he began studying for the ministry while conducting services for the deaf members.

To qualify for priesthood Syle not only had to pass an arduous examination which included Latin, Greek, Hebrew, philosophy, history, and church doctrine, but he also had to overcome the strong opposition of those who objected to the ordination of a deaf priest. Guilbert C. Braddock, in writing about Syle and the obstacles he overcame, said, "Only a deaf man of the highest type of intelligence and scholarship could have succeeded at this crucial moment." Syle's success opened the door for others.

Much of the credit goes to Bishop William Bacon Stevens of the Diocese of Pennsylvania. He was willing to break with tradition and ordain a deaf man in spite of much opposition. The prevailing notion was that only a man in possession of all five senses was qualified to become a priest. Also, Bishop Stevens thought sign language "as much a language as Chinese" and believed that it was "as fully acceptable to ordain a deaf man to preach in signs, as to ordain an Indian to preach in the Cherokee dialect." Bishop Stevens realized that the sacraments had to be administered in a language that would be understood by the congregation. Following his ordination, Syle established the All Soul's Church for the Deaf at St. Stephen's and remained there until his premature death

from pneumonia in 1890.

Austin W. Mann (1883), Jacob M. Koehler (1887), Job Turner (1891) and James H. Cloud (1893) followed Syle to the priesthood. Opposition to ordaining deaf men continued and when Charles O. Dantzer, the seventh deaf man to be ordained, approached his bishop for the Holy Orders, his bishop responded, "My son, I dare not lay hands on you, but will ask Bishop Huntingdon to do it for me." Nevertheless, by 1900 there were seven ordained deaf Episcopalian priests and by 1930 the number had grown to 22. The early popularity of the Episcopal Church in the deaf community can be credited to these deaf priests. Not

The Silent Worker

The Rev. Henry W. Syle

Members of the Conference of Church Workers Among the Deaf which met in Philadelphia in 1926 (left to right, first row): Franklin C. Smielau, Oliver J. Whildin, Warren M. Smaltz, and Clarence E. Webb. Second row, same order: Homer E. Grace, Olof Hanson, Hobart L. Tracy and George F. Flick. Third row, J. Stanley Light, Jacob M. Koehler, Collins S. Sawhill, Clarence W. Charles, Herbert C. Merrill, Roma C. Fortune, Henry J. Pulver and Guilbert C. Braddock.

only did these men provide spiritual leadership for the deaf community but many of them filled prominent leadership roles on the national level.

As principal of the Gallaudet Day School for the Deaf in St. Louis, Missouri, Cloud was a leading educator of the deaf. He was teacher and principal at the school from 1890 to 1923 and minister to the St. Thomas Mission for the Deaf. He served two terms as president of the National Association of the Deaf.

The Rev. Herbert C. Merrill was president of the Gallaudet College Alumni Association at a crucial period in the college's history, when the college was searching for its third president. Merrill preached at missionaries in Washington, D.C. and surrounding areas. He was later transferred to Northern New York. The Merrill Guild for the Deaf in Johnson City, New Jersey is named for him.

The Rev. Robert C. Fletcher of the Birmingham,

Alabama Church opened a session of the U.S. Senate with a prayer in sign language in 1952. Dr. Irving S. Fusfeld, vice president at Gallaudet College, interpreted for him. Fletcher and his wife, Estelle, gained the national limelight in 1976 when their daughter, Louise, won an Oscar as "Best Actress of the Year," for her performance in "One Flew Over the Cuckoo's Nest." Upon receiving the award, Louise signed her acknowledgment over national television and thanked her parents for teaching her to have a dream.

Fletcher was deafened at the age of four years. His was a most unusual cause of deafness; while standing on the family porch he was struck by a bolt of lightning! For days he lay in a coma and when he woke up he was deaf. At the age of twelve the accidental thrust of a pair of scissors left him blind in one eye. The remarkable thing about Fletcher is that neither of these misfortunes left him bitter or remorseful. Instead, he seemed to gain strength in overcoming them. He maintained a pleasant, cheerful personality throughout his life. Returning to Alabama after earning his divinity degree at the Philadelphia Divinity School, he became minister of the Church of the Advent in Birmingham, inheriting a congregation of three persons but no church. That year a little white clapboard church was given to Fletcher; soon his congregation reached 97. The church had been built as a Methodist Church many years before. It was purchased by the Episcopal Church, dismantled, and moved 40 miles to Elyton Village. It was the first Episcopal Church in Jefferson County. When Fletcher and his flock acquired it, the building was older than the city of Birmingham.

The Rev. Guilbert C. Braddock, ordained to the priesthood in 1926, served the Church some 46 years. He had been vicar of St. Ann's Church in New York City, missionary to the deaf in the District of Columbia and neighboring states, vicar of All Soul's Church in Philadelphia, and vicar of All Angels' Mission to the Deaf in Baltimore. His most important legacy, however, is the information he left us on the early lives of successful deaf persons in this country. A knowledgable person, careful and thorough researcher, and clear writer, he left us a rare treasury with his collection of "Notable Deaf Persons" which was originally serialized in *The Frat* and printed in book form by the Gallaudet College Alumni Association in 1975.

The Episcopal Missions for the Deaf in Connecticut began when the Rev. George H. Hefflon started worship services in 1909. He was succeeded in 1925 by the Rev. J. Stanley Light, who had a very active ministry

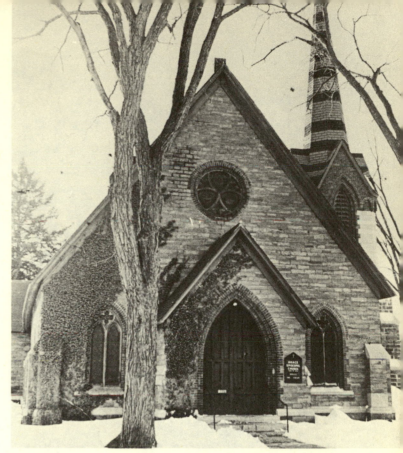

Grace Episcopal Church in Mexico, New York William F. Harter/Harold H. Roach

throughout New England. In 1966 the Diocese established its own full-time ministry to the deaf and the Rev. Camille Desmarais succeeded Light.

While a freshman at Gallaudet College, Desmarais won the 121-pound Mason-Dixon Conference wrestling championship. He defeated all four of his opponents by falls, wrestling a total of less than nine minutes in the tournament! A week later he retained his 121-pound crown in the District of Columbia American Athletic Union tournament. If he could pin the devil with the same skill, his congregation was in good hands.

The Rev George F. Flick was an Episcopal minister to the deaf in Chicago in the near north side. Because so many of his congregation lived in the area, it became known as "Flicksville." Flick, who died in 1951, was an active member of the National Fraternal Society of the Deaf and a life member of the National Association of the Deaf.

To illustrate the influence some deaf Episcopal priests had on deaf people, an article appearing in *The Silent Worker* mentioned a gathering on a Wisconsin farm to witness the Rev. A.G. Leisman's interpretation of the Twenty-Third Psalm. Of the 23 persons present only three were Episcopalians.

Leisman was called "The Flying Parson." He regularly flew across Lake Michigan to minister to the

Stained glass window in Grace Episcopal Church in memory of John W. Chandler. William F. Harter/Harold H. Roach

Rev. Steve L. Mathis, III

Rev. Camille Desmarais

Rev. Robert Fletcher

Rev. Homer E. Grace

Rev. Otto Berg

deaf in Grand Rapids, and Kalamazoo, Michigan, in the early 1950s. He edited and published *Mission Lane*, a little church publication described as "fraught with pithy news items and comments." Leisman wrote the poem (page 187) describing his experience as a minister. It appeared in the February, 1949, issue of *The Silent Worker*.

On a bitterly cold winter day in 1859 the Rev. Thomas Gallaudet arrived in Baltimore, Maryland, and managed to round up 19 persons for a service at Grace Church. That evening the All Angels' Mission to the Deaf was born, although it would go through some trying times before it was firmly established. Samuel A. Adams, a teacher at the school for the colored deaf and blind in the city, became the first deaf lay-reader. Adams was described as a "brilliant, wise and successful leader of the deaf" and when he died in 1873 his death was called "a loss to the entire deaf community." Louis Tuck and James Sullivan, two deaf teachers, followed Adams as lay-readers; then the Rev. Oliver J. Whildin took over, eventually becoming the rector.

In addition to the Rev. Dr. Gallaudet, the Reverends Henry Syle, Jacob Koehler, Oliver Whildin, Otto Berg, Guilbert C. Braddock, and Steve L. Mathis III served

tenures as ministers at All Angels'.

In 1916 Whildin formed "The Society for the Promotion of Church Work Among the Deaf" and in 1924 he started *The Silent News-Letter*, a mimeographed newsletter which became *The Silent Missionary* in 1927. In 1926 the publication was adopted as the official organ of the Conference of Church Workers Among the Deaf and in 1938, the Conference bought the publication and became its publisher. It is the forerunner of today's *Deaf Churchman*.

The Rev. Homer E. Grace was responsible for one of the largest regularly visited territories of any deaf clergyman during his time. Operating out of Denver, Colorado, his area stretched south to Pueblo, Colorado, east to Des Moines, Iowa, and north to St. Paul, Minneapolis, Minnesota. It included services in Colorado Springs; Omaha, Nebraska; Faribault, Minnesota, and Sioux Falls, South Dakota. He covered this area some forty years.

Grace, who was deafened at the age of seven, is one of a handful of deaf persons who have received honorary degrees from colleges other than their alma mater, Gallaudet College. In 1958 Seabury-Western Seminary awarded him a Doctor of Divinity degree in recognition of his contributions to the ministry of deaf

186

Rev. Jacob M. Koehler

and face Him, He won't ask me how many times I stood before how many people and preached. He won't ask how many miles I drove, or how many people I visited. He won't care how much the offerings were or how much I spent to travel. My Big Boss, the Lord Jesus Christ, won't care about all that. He will ask me other things. He will want to know how many persons heard about Him through me, and received His love and peace. . . ."

Lutheran

There are three major Lutheran synods in the United States, each operating independently of the others. The three are: The American Lutheran

people. In 1965 Gallaudet College recognized him and his classmate and fellow priest, Edwin W. Nies, both of the class of 1911, with honorary Doctor of Humane Letters degrees.

The Rev. Canon William M. Lange inherited the diocese which had been started in 1894 by Harry Van Allen, a deaf printer and lay reader. Van Allen was ordained a deacon in 1898 and a priest in 1902. His territory included four dioceses stretching from Albany to Buffalo, New York. It included the Eastern, Central, and Western part of the state. One week while Van Allen was preaching at St. Paul's Church in Albany, a nine-year old boy named William Lange lay ill with spinal meningitis in the same city. This illness deprived Lange of his hearing one month short of his tenth birthday.

The Rev. Herbert C. Merrill of Washington, D.C. succeeded Van Allen on the latter's death in April, 1919. When Merrill retired in 1943, Lange, then a newly-ordained priest, stepped into his mentor's shoes. It had been Merrill who had urged him to consider the ministry. Lange began to cover the large diocese which then included 20 towns. When he retired in 1978 at the age of 69 he had conducted 8,250 services before 126,000 persons; baptised 211 persons; presented 192 for confirmation; married 57 couples; visited 18,800 individuals and buried 139 persons. He had travelled a total of over one million miles. "But really," he reminded his congregation as a good preacher would, "when I finish my work here on earth

The Deaf Minister
by A.G. Leisman

I feel alone, the silence growing strong
  Where lips and ears unite to pray,
And lost am I when voices lift in song—
  So near and yet so far away.

But when, imbued with love of common ties,
  Before my silent clan I stand
And voicelessly convey to hearing eyes—
  In symbols they can understand—

The meaning of the inner spark divine,
  I feel as one returning home
To find at last beneath his humble vine
  The bliss he sought across the foam.

Sometimes to fill the void imposed by chance,
  I play the console in my heart,
And sense, away from world dissonance,
  My music Master's kindly part.

The course is richer far than it appears,
  Though stillness reigns from dawn to dark;
Grown mellow with the hush of two score years,
  My life, I trust, has found its mark.

So when the bells in cross-crowned belfries ring,
  And silent are the forms I face,
I thank the Lord for what the signs do bring:
  The blessings from His love and grace.

The Silent Worker,
1949

Edward Kaercher

Church, the Lutheran Church in America and the Lutheran Church-Missouri Synod.

The Lutheran Church-Missouri Synod (LCMS) was the next to take an interest in the spiritual needs of the deaf community. In 1873 the LCMS opened an orphanage in Detroit, Michigan, but a year later it became the Evangelical Institute for the Deaf. Out of this venture grew the church's interest in working with deaf persons.

In 1894 the Rev. August P. Reinke, the hearing pastor of Bethlehem Lutheran Church in Chicago, was asked to combine work with the deaf with his regular ministerial duties. Reinke obliged and on March 4, 1894 he conducted the first Lutheran services in sign language for 16 deaf persons near Detroit. Reinke, however, found the work too strenuous for one man and recommended that a mission to the deaf be established. In 1896 Our Saviour Lutheran Church for the Deaf was organized in Chicago. Emmanuel Lutheran Church for the Deaf was started in Milwaukee in 1898.

Around 1903 the Lutheran Church—Missouri Synod formed the Ephphatha Conference of Workers Among the Deaf. This organization was similar to the Episcopal Church's Conference of Church Workers Among the Deaf, which had been established in 1881. Members of these organizations met to exchange ideas, explore ways of improving the teaching of religion to the deaf, to discuss ways of making its social and religious work more effective and strengthening local congregations, and so forth.

In 1908 the Lutherans began publishing *The Deaf Lutheran,* and in 1910 a mission to the deaf opened in Cleveland. Within three years, another opened in New York City. The New York City mission was unique in that it included a Sunday School. About this time missions were reaching the West coast and on the 25th anniversary of the LCMS's work with the deaf there were 10 missions with pastors serving deaf congregations in 65 cities, coast to coast.

The number of persons working with the deaf had begun to grow around the turn of the century and by 1924 there were 14 Lutheran missions reaching 86 cities. By 1946, the 50th anniversary of work with the deaf, there were 20 pastors conducting services in approximately 275 cities, and thirteen chapels had been constructed. In the 1940s the Lutheran Church began to move south, establishing nine missions in southern cities. Simultaneously, the missions were reaching an increasing number of deaf children in schools for the deaf. It is somewhat of an irony, however, that with so many Lutheran pastors working with the deaf, not one at that time was deaf. The Lutheran Church—Missouri Synod did not get a deaf pastor until William A. Ludwig was ordained in 1959.

Pastor Ludwig was born in Winner, South Dakota, in the home of his aunt, who was a registered nurse. He contracted measles and pneumonia soon after birth and the illness caused his loss of hearing. Ludwig attended the Lutheran School in Detroit and the Colorado School for the Deaf, graduating from the latter in 1949. He earned his bachelor of arts degree at Gallaudet College where he became interested in the ministry. He enrolled in the Concordia Seminary and earned a Bachelor of Divinity degree in 1959. He was ordained into the ministry the same year. In 1977 Kjell Omahr Mork, a native of Oslo, Norway, was ordained and became pastor of Bethlehem Lutheran Church in Omaha, Nebraska. Robert Case became the third deaf person to be ordained. He accepted a pastorate in Houston, Texas.

The Lutheran Church in America, formerly called the United Lutheran Church, unlike the Missouri Synod, did not serve the deaf on such a large scale,

---

. . . as teachers, preachers, missionaries, artists, artisans, scientists, businessmen, sculptors, architects, laborers and citizens they (deaf people) take their place in proportion to their numbers by the side of their hearing brothers, reflecting credit upon the schools which have trained and educated them.

—JOHN W. JONES
1929

---

but they ordained a deaf pastor first. He was Edward Kaercher, a graduate of the Pennsylvania School for the Deaf. He graduated from Gallaudet College and the Lutheran Theological Seminary which, incidentally, is across the street from the Pennsylvania School for the Deaf in Philadelphia. It was at this seminary that work had begun with the deaf before the formation of the United Lutheran Church. Kaercher was ordained in June, 1929, following his graduation from the seminary. He was called by the Board of Inner Missions of the Ministerium of Pennsylvania, which provided financial support for his work until he was forced to cease his duties in 1942 due to illness. By then he had established "preaching points" in eight towns in Pennsylvania, and in Trenton, New Jersey, New York City, Baltimore, and the District of Columbia.

Methodist

Chicago was the focal point for the Methodists' work with the deaf. The Methodist Church was the third Protestant denomination to enter work with the deaf. The work had originated in Jacksonville, Illinois. The Chicago deaf community had petitioned Dr. Philip G. Gillett, superintendent of the Illinois School for the Deaf in Jacksonville, to send an ISD teacher to the Windy City every Sunday to preach to them. Gillett was himself the son of a minister and he had organized a non-demoninational Sunday School at the school. He was receptive to the request and approached Philip J. Hasenstab, one of his deaf teachers, with the request. Hasenstab began going to Chicago regularly and became so interested in the spiritual welfare of the deaf Chicagoans that he eventually left teaching to enter the field of ministry full-time. He was licensed to preach in 1890, became pastor of the Chicago Mission for the Deaf in 1893 and was ordained a local deacon in 1894, becoming the first deaf man so ordained in the history of Methodism. Hasenstab was a product of the Indiana School for the Deaf, having been deafened at the age of two and one-half years. He received his Bachelor of Arts degree from Gallaudet College in 1885 and ten years later, his Masters. He taught at the Illinois School for seven years before resigning to enter the ministry. While a teacher at ISD, he introduced football at the school and carried on religious work with the students at the Grace Methodist Church in Jacksonville. After his death in 1941 his daughter, the Rev. Constance Hasenstab Elms, carried on the work her father had begun in the Chicago area.

The Rev. Henry Rutherford, who was also active in Methodist work, was a graduate of the Illinois School.

The Methodists' efforts to work with the deaf centered around Chicago, Baltimore, Cincinnati, and Florida.

In Baltimore the Christ Methodist Church for the Deaf was founded in 1896 by Daniel W. Moylan, a graduate of the Maryland School for the Deaf. Moylan had been a lay reader at All Angels' Episcopal Mission to the Deaf in that city for five years. When his application for Holy Orders was rejected ("because he did not possess a college background") he resigned and started the Christ Methodist Church. There is no indication that he was ever ordained.

In 1932 the congregation of the Cameron Methodist Church in Cincinnati purchased an old church building on East Pearl Street. The work with this congregation had been organized by the Rev. Philip J. Hasenstab, who began conducting once-a-month services in the city in 1910. The mission is named for Virginia Cameron, a deaconess and active leader of Methodist work among the deaf in that city.

When the neighborhood began to deteriorate and the Great Ohio River flood hit in 1937 the congregation was forced to relocate. They acquired the Asbury Methodist Church on Sycamore Street.

The Crusselle-Freeman Mission at St. Mark's Methodist Episcopal Church in Atlanta, Georgia, owes its origin to the editor of *The Atlanta Constitution Tri-Weekly*. One day W.F. Crusselle, the editor, hired a deaf typist. She performed so well that he began hiring other deaf employees. Eventually he learned that his deaf employees had no place to worship so he started a class for them. As the attendance grew Crusselle called upon his friend, the Rev. Samuel Freeman, a teacher at the Georgia School for the Deaf in Cave Spring. The mission is named after this team. Freeman's daughter, Mrs. M.M. Simmons, carried on the work following her father's death in 1940. She was fondly called "the little pastor."

Latter Day Saints

In 1891 a Sunday School class was organized in Salt Lake City to serve the needs of members of the Latter Day Saints. When the School for the Deaf was moved to Ogden, Utah, in 1896 another class was organized in that city. In 1917 the "general authorities" of the Latter Day Saints Church approved a building for deaf members. Max W. Woodbury, a teacher and principal at the School for the Deaf, was chosen presiding elder of the Ogden Branch for the Deaf, Church of Jesus

Christ of the Latter Day Saints. The new building had three units, a chapel, recreation hall, and rooms for classes.

Baptist

While the Episcopalians were building strength in the major cities in the East, and the Lutherans were moving West, the Baptists emerged and began heading South. In 1906 the Baptists entered the foray between the devil and the deaf with its one-man army in the person of John W. Michaels. Small in stature, sporting a thick moustache and a balding top, Michaels had as much energy as a stick of dynamite. He became a legend in Baptist circles and it's doubtful if the devil has forgotten him either.

That year Michaels called Southern Baptist Convention's attention to an estimated 45,000 deaf persons who had no access to religious services in the states covered by the Convention. The SBC Board of Missions responded by appointing him the first missionary to the deaf, a task Michaels tackled with enthusiasm and determination. Of Michaels, who travelled extensively throughout the South performing his work, it was said, jokingly, that whenever the train stopped for a few minutes layover he would rush off and organize a Sunday School class. That was exaggerating things a bit, of course, but it is a tribute to the man who organized the Southern Baptist Ministry to the Deaf.(He travelled widely but at little cost to the SBC. He was given a complimentary pass by the railroads. One month his travel expenses amounted to less than two dollars!) He organized classes at Baptist churches wherever he could get sufficient attendance. Classes met in balconies, on stairway landings, in the back of regular classes or, when there was no space, at different times on Sunday. Or, if there was no Baptist church available, he met at a church of a different denomination. By 1914, 11 states reported 19 Baptist classes with three of them meeting in Methodist churches and one at a Presbyterian church. By the 1960s there were over 240 classes in existence.

Michaels realized early that the success of his work depended on voluntary support and leadership. He recruited and trained many deaf and hearing leaders. To them fell the mantle of responsibility to keep the classes going. In 1923 he completed a *Handbook of Sign Language of the Deaf* to assist ministers, laymen, seminary students, and others interested in working with deaf people. It was one of the earliest books on sign language published in this country and for Michaels, it was largely a labor of love. He was assisted in the

---

John W. Michaels
(1850-1942)

Prior to joining the Southern Baptist Convention, Michaels was a businessman and educator. He was a partner in Michaels, Dunscombe, & Company, a harness and collar manufacturing firm in Knoxville. Later he opened his own harness business and added a tannery in Goshen, Virginia. Next, he dabbled unsuccessfully in real estate, ran a livery stable, and was elected to a four-year term as a town councilman. When he was offered his old position as head teacher at the Arkansas School he was ready for another change and accepted. He was principal when he received the call to enter the ministry full-time. The Michaels had four daughters, all of whom became teachers of the deaf. All four became involved in religious work with the deaf also. One, Mrs. Bess Michaels Riggs, was superintendent of the Arkansas School from 1927 until her death in 1935.

Born in Virginia on December 18, 1850, Michaels was seven years old when a combination of a malady called erysipelas, inadequate medical attention, a bad cold, and the roar of Civil War cannons near his Petersburg home rendered him deaf. He attended the Virginia School and Gallaudet College. When ordained a Baptist minister in Little Rock in 1905 he was issued the charge by James P. Eagle, the governor of Arkansas, who was also a Baptist minister. Michaels organized the Virginia and Arkansas Associations of the Deaf. Gallaudet College awarded him two honorary degrees, a Bachelor of Pedagogy in 1902 and a Doctor of Divinity in 1939. He died September 29, 1942.

---

preparation of the book by L.B. Dickerson, a deaf Atlanta linotypist.

To assist him in his work Michaels recruited Adolph O. Wilson, a good friend and a fellow teacher at the Arkansas School for the Deaf. Of Swedish birth, Wilson was deafened at the age of 10 by scarlet fever. He came to this country in his late teens. In 1926 Wilson became the second deaf man to be ordained a Baptist minister.

In 1955 a young deaf Texan named Carter E. Bearden followed in John Michael's footsteps at the SBC Mission Board. Carter was appointed superintendent of the Deaf Missions and field consultant to the deaf in the Language Mission Department.

Carter was born in 1928 in Dallas, Texas and lost his hearing at the age of three years. He attended the Texas School for the Deaf and Gallaudet College for two years, transferring to Baylor University in Waco, Texas. In 1951 he earned his bachelors degree at Baylor and four years later a Bachelor of Divinity degree from New Orleans Baptist Seminary. In 1966 he received his Th.M. from the Columbia Theological Seminary in Decatur, Georgia. He was ordained a Baptist minister April 24, 1949. Bearden is the author of *A Handbook for the Religious Interpreters for the Deaf* (1975) and co-author of *A Manual of Religious Signs* and *Sing Praise, A Hymnal for the Deaf*. He also wrote *The History of Southern Baptist Convention's Ministry to the Deaf.*

Deaf men who have been ordained Baptist ministers are: Philip W. Packard, John W. Michaels, Arthur D. Bryant, Adolph O. Wilson, W. L. Ashbridge, Clifford P. Bruffey, Carter E. Bearden, J. W. Gardner, Gary Shoemaker, Jerry Jamison, Robert H. Boltz and Phillip Goldberg.

Although never ordained, it would be an injustice not to mention the contributions of Francis C. Higgins as lay pastor of the Calvary Baptist Church in Washington, D.C. The Calvary Baptist Church is the oldest mission for the deaf in the nation's Capital. It was established in 1885. Amos Kendall, that generous philanthropist to deaf people, (he started Kendall School) gave $100,000 towards the construction of the church. The mission began by providing interpreters for the deaf worshippers, among them: Edward Miner Gallaudet, Professor J.E. Gordon, Miss Mary T.G. Gordon, and Charles Grow. In 1909 the mission was reorganized and placed under the leadership of Gallaudet Professor Arthur D. Bryant. Two years later Byant was ordained a Baptist minister and continued in his role until his death in 1939. (A room at the church is named Bryant Hall in his memory.) Bryant was succeeded by Harley D. Drake. Drake continued the work until his retirement from Gallaudet College and his removal to his farm in Ohio in 1949. When Drake retired, Francis Higgins became the leader and has continued the work since.

Judaism

The Jewish deaf community has the same problem as any other deaf congregation—communication—and that unifies them more than the different tenets within the religion. In 1956 Jewish deaf people organized the National Congress of Jewish Deaf (NCJD) to "advocate religious and cultural ideals, and fellowship for Jewish deaf." This organization encourages rabbis to work with the deaf, learn to communicate with them, and become familiar with their needs. In 1960, the organization established an endowment fund to further the work of their religion. Some funds from this endowment were used to assist Alton Silver, a graduate of Gallaudet College, to enter Hebrew Union College to study for the rabbinate. Had he

succeeded he would have become the first deaf rabbi in the country. Unfortunately, his untimely death cut short those plans and the deaf community still mourns his passing.

With the founding of the NCJD, the Jewish deaf became better organized through a system of affiliates. The oldest organizations to join the NCJD were the Hebrew Association of the Deaf of Philadelphia and the Hebrew Association of the Deaf of New York which were formed in 1907. There are similar Hebrew Associations in Brooklyn, Baltimore, Cleveland, Chicago, Los Angeles, Boston, Van Nuys, California, and Washington, D.C. Most of these groups meet regularly and observe Jewish holidays. Three have access to rabbis who know sign language and the others rely on interpreters.

The NCJD serves as a clearing house for information about the Jewish faith and its culture. It promotes religious services at schools for the deaf, maintains a directory of interpreters of the Jewish faith, publishes the NCJD Quarterly and holds biennial conventions. The organization has a national headquarters and a non-salaried executive director, Alexander Fleischman. NCJD was one of the founders of the World Organization of Jewish Deaf.

Catholic

In October 1912 an editorial appeared in *Ephpheta*, a monthly published in the interests of the Catholic deaf community stating: "It is always interesting to note the activity of other churches in behalf of deaf members of their persuasions. Thus the Episcopalians have 18 ordained deaf ministers; the Lutherans, six; the Methodists, four; and the Baptists, one." It would be 65 years before the Catholic Church ordained its first deaf American priest when Thomas Coughlin took his vows in 1977.

Born deaf and the son of deaf parents, as a young student at St. Mary's School for the Deaf in Buffalo, New York, Coughlin keenly felt the need for priests with whom he could communicate freely when death claimed his favorite priest. He was determined to fill that vacuum. Following graduation from Gallaudet College Coughlin studied theology at the Catholic University of America and began his novitiate with the Trinitarian Fathers the same year.

After five years of study, Coughlin was ordained at the Basilica of the Assumption in Baltimore, the oldest Cathedral Church in the United States. The 90-minute ceremony was conducted by Cardinal Lawrence Sheehan in May, 1977.

While visiting elderly Catholic deaf persons in the

Father Thomas Coughlin, O.SS.T.

Boston area Joseph Bruce, a member of the Society of Jesus, heard many stories about their experiences, about the church and about priests who worked with deaf people. His interest was stimulated and encouraged by these elderly persons and others. He began to collect and preserve information about deaf Catholics in the United States. He continued this interest as a student at the Weston Jesuit School in Cambridge and began organizing all the newspapers, magazines, photographs and newsclippings he could get his hands on. Within two years he had a well-organized and impressive collection which included issues of some publications of the Catholic deaf periodicals not found elsewhere. It was during a visit with Bruce at his Jesuit Community house that much information and many leads for this section of *Deaf Heritage* were acquired. (See Appendix B for list of known deaf clergymen.)

Oralism and the Teaching of Religion

As oralism was the leading method used in teaching deaf children during the early decades of this century, clergymen who visited schools for the deaf to teach religion used that method. While educators were claiming that the oral method was the best approach for educating the deaf, the clergy were finding it an ineffective tool for imparting religious training to deaf children and adults, and they were becoming increasingly frustrated.

After an unsuccessful attempt at using the oral method in the 1890s, the Rev. Reinke gave up and started learning sign language. Religious groups began to go on record supporting the use of sign language and a recommendation was made to study its use and to include other visual aids in the teaching of religion. Some oral schools refused to permit the clergy to use sign language. Others compromised. The New Jersey School, which was oral at that time, required teachers to use the oral method but permitted the clergy to use sign language. By the 1940s members of the different denominations realized that if they were to reach and serve the deaf community, a knowledge of sign language was necessary. An increasing number of seminaries began adding sign language to their curricula to better prepare those who chose to work with the deaf community.

Interpreters

Interpreters have played a very important role in making it possible for God's word to reach deaf peo-

ple. Hundreds of them are the offspring of deaf parents. Many other excellent interpreters began learning their skills in churches. So many, in fact, that the clergy have often complained that they train interpreters then government agencies and private industry steal them. That is an understandable complaint because churches must depend heavily on volunteers and often cannot compete with the lure of the dollar.

When the Rev. George Kraus of St. Mathews Lutheran Church in Long Island was invited to deliver a sermon on the "Television Chapel" in the fall of 1950 he asked Mina Burt to interpret for him. This was one of the earliest religious programs interpreted over television. Burt handled the chore with ease. She had started interpreting sermons in 1916 and had been at it for 35 years.

Mrs. O.A. Schneider, the interpreter at the Silent Berean Congregation of the Union Avenue Christian Church in St. Louis, was the daughter of deaf parents. Mrs. S.H. Youngblood was called to interpret at a Bible Class in Shreveport, Louisiana, when she was 13 years old. Carter Bearden, Jr. was ten years old when he first reverse-interpreted for his pastor dad. When a class for the deaf was organized at the Twelfth Street Baptist Church in Paducah, Kentucky, there was no interpreter so Mrs. Kathy Roberts, knowing not a single sign, stepped forward and bravely announced she would try. Within six weeks she had mastered the manual alphabet and 600 signs!

In Sulphur, Oklahoma, services at the First Baptist Church were interpreted for deaf children from the nearby Oklahoma School for the Deaf by Mrs. Tommy G. Hall, wife of the school superintendent. To be sure the children arrived regularly, her husband was assigned the bus driving chores.

Unable to locate a local interpreter, one church in Tennessee regularly brought one in by plane from another city. In the early 1960s Ed Davis, minister of music at the Oak Ridge, Tennessee Central Baptist Church, took an interest in working the the deaf congregation and was elected director of that work, although he had little knowledge of the language of signs. Today Davis is the superintendent of the Tennessee School for the Deaf in Knoxville.

When a minister in the Pacific Northwest learned that he would be working with a deaf congregation he was determined to be able to communicate with the members. After studying J. Schuyler Long's sign language book for two days, he pronounced the blessing and sang the Doxology on the first Sunday. On the second Sunday he signed all of the liturgy. Within a month he was preaching his own sermons.

While a student at Baylor U. Carter Bearden taught

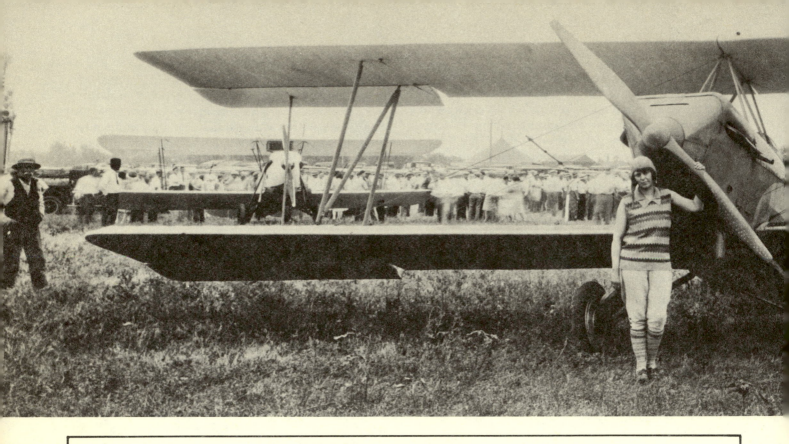

Laura C. R. Searing
(Howard Glyndon)
(1840-1923)

Laura Catherine Redden Searing was a successful journalist and poet. Her work appeared under the pseudonym Howard Glyndon.

Searing was a strong pro-Unionist and her writing reflected it. During the Civil War she was a Washington correspondent for the *St. Louis Republican*. While in the nation's capital, she became friends with President Lincoln, General Grant, General Garfield, and other statesmen of the day. During this period she published two books, *Notable Men in the House of Representatives* (1862) and *Idyls of Battle* (1864). Her patriotism and her writings brought her fame. Her poem, "Belle Missouri", was adopted by the Missouri Unionists as their war song. It was written in response to "Maryland, My Maryland." Hurd and Houghton, Boston publishers, printed a collection of her articles and poems in *Lyrics of Battle*.

After the Civil War, Searing spent nearly four years in Europe where she learned French, German, Italian, and Spanish, and continued as a correspondent for the *Republican*. She also wrote for *The New York Times* and the *New York Sun*. On her return to America she secured a position on the staff of the *New York Evening Mail* and her work appeared in *Galaxy*, *Harper's*, *Putman's Magazine*, *Arena* and the *Alaska-Yukon Magazine*. She also contributed to *The Silent Worker* and wrote the dedication poem for the Thomas Hopkins Gallaudet Memorial.

Laura Searing lost her hearing when she was 11 years old from a severe illness. Quinine, used in the treatment of her illness, was considered the cause of her deafness. It also affected her voice and speech. She attended the Missouri School for the Deaf, graduating in 1858. Later she took a two-year course at Clarke School and was one of Alexander Graham Bell's pupils in Boston. From Bell she learned modulation and inflection and at the Whipple Home School in Mystic, Connecticut, she learned to control the tone and pitch of her speech. She also studied lipreading but never became proficient.

In 1873 she published a volume of her verse in *Sounds from Secret Chambers*.

In 1876 she married Edward W. Searing, a well-known New York lawyer. They had one daughter. In 1886 she moved to California and settled in Santa Cruz in hope that the climate would restore her declining health. There she wrote, "The Hills of Santa Cruz," among her last pieces of work. Her friend John G. Whittier, the poet, described the poem as one that would "cling to the Santa Cruz mountain range forever." He predicted that it would do for the little city beside the sea what Bret Harte did for San Francisco.

In 1921 Searing's daughter published a collection of her mother's work in *Echoes of Other Days*. Searing is one of a very few deaf persons listed in the *Dictionary of American Biography*. She was a semi-invalid during the last years of her life. She died in 1923 and is buried in the Holy Cross Cemetery in San Mateo, California.

Rise Studio

Nellie Zabel Willhite and her airplane, "Pard."

a Sunday School Class in Waco, Texas. On his graduation he was succeeded by another Baylor U. student, the son of deaf parents, who led the class as an undergraduate. The young man's name was Louie J. Fant.

Milestone

Juliette Gordon Low, (1860-1927), the founder of Girl Scouts, died during the decade. On her wedding day a grain of rice lodged in her ear and after its removal she was deaf in that ear. She had married a wealthy Englishman and they moved to Scotland where she organized a group of girls called Girl Guides. On her return to the United States she organized another group in 1912. A year later the name was changed to Girl Scouts. In 1917 the Girl Scouts began to include handicapped girls in the program. In 1919 a Girl Scout troop was organized at the Illinois School for the Deaf.

Deaf Pilots

When Charles A. Lindberg flew *The Spirit of St. Louis* alone across the Atlantic Ocean in 1927 he stimulated great interest in flying. Among those to catch the "flying bug" was a young deaf woman in Yankton, South Dakota, named Nellie Zabel Willhite. She had been deaf since the age of four due to a bout with measles.

Willhite realized that she had to overcome two barriers in order to pursue her interest in flying. First, she was a woman and second, she was deaf. Female pilots were almost unheard of in those days, much less a *deaf female* pilot. Nevertheless, she enrolled in a class and after thirteen hours of instruction she soloed on January 13, 1928. She became the first woman in South Dakota and most likely the first deaf person in the world to become a pilot.

Her father gave her a plane as a gift and she became a barnstormer, flying in air shows and participating in air races throughout the Midwest. She took passengers aloft at country fairs charging children fifty cents and adults a dollar. Willhite was a charter member of the Ninety Nines, a women's pilot organization of which Amelia Earhart was one of the founding members.

Willhite's feats in the air earned her a folk heroine status in her home state. The original propeller of her plane, an Eagle Rock, which she named the "Pard" after her father, is on permanent display in the Taylor Museum at Hill City, South Dakota.

In May, 1929 Edward T. Payne, a resident of Ontario, Canada, earned his pilot's license. Many per-

195

James Stirling, Jr. of Vermont

sons believe he is the first licensed deaf male pilot in the world.

As the years passed, others joined the ranks of deaf pilots. In 1937 James Stirling, Jr. of Barre, Vermont qualified for his student license. He flew for pleasure until 1941 when World War II broke out. He and many other pilots were grounded. After the war he resumed flying briefly.

Around 1942 Almon Miner Lippincott of Madison, Connecticut earned his license. Lippincott, a graduate of the American School for the Deaf, has owned two Piper Cubs. He built a hangar and a 125-foot runway in Madison.

In 1947 Rhulin A. Thomas, a 38-year-old *Washington Evening Star* Linotype operator, earned a modest measure of fame when he became the first deaf pilot to fly solo across the United States. He made the flight to greet two globe-circling hearing pilots, George W. Truman and Clifford U. Evans, when they arrived in California on the last leg of their around-the-world flight. Truman and Evans had taught Rhulin to fly.

Rhulin's relatives and friends thought he was crazy to make the attempt, but, with the spirit of daring possessed by all such adventurers, he set out on October 26, 1947 from Rehoboth Beach, Delaware, in his 65-horsepower Piper Cub. He flew through storms and against strong headwinds. Between Indianapolis and St. Louis he became lost in a storm, ran out of gas, and made a forced landing on a farm with a dead engine. The greatest hazard he encountered was crossing the Banning Pass in the Rocky Mountains at 9,500 feet. This area is known as the "graveyard of pilots." He arrived in Van Nuys, California on November 7.

A year later on September 30, 1948 Rhulin was presented with a medal at the White House for his achievement by Major General Harry Vaughan, on behalf of President Truman. The medal had been sponsored by the National Association of the Deaf and the Missouri Association of the Deaf through the efforts of Max Mossel, a teacher of the Missouri School for the Deaf. Rhulin was a graduate of that school.

Bill Wilkins

Karen J. Imhoff

Rhulin accepted the medal on behalf of deaf people and expressed the hope that his feat would focus attention on the capabilities of deaf people and interest other deaf persons in flying.

Walter Wettschreck became deaf at the age of 18 years. He attended the Minnesota School for the Deaf for one year, graduating in 1935. He landed a position as a photographer with the Minnesota State Conservation Department; the work required taking many aerial photographs. These assignments stimulated his interest in flying and in 1954 he decided to learn to fly. After eight hours of instruction he soloed and forty flying hours later he applied for his license. Because of his deafness (like many other prospective deaf pilots) he had to undergo a medical flight examination. He passed his flight tests with a score of 100 percent and on his written tests he scored 98 percent. He also qualified for a seaplane rating.

In 1956 Wettschreck joined the Civil Air Patrol as a private. So skillful and knowledgable was he as a pilot that he rose to the rank of captain, a most unusual achievement for a deaf pilot. During his career with

continued on page 202

Bill Wilkins aloft in his restored Stearman Biplane

Raymond P. Barton

George Culberton (right) and his son-in-law with Culbertson's Piper Tri-Pacer in 1968.

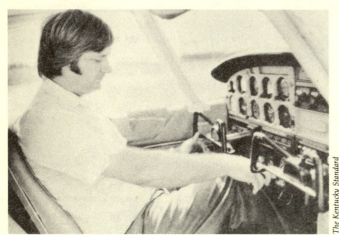

Don Belcher

Robert Weitbrecht

Harold Rehn

Gilbert Evans

Almon Miner Lippincott

Bernard Gross flying his home-built amphibian over Lake Erie in 1977.

199

Firsts Among Deaf Pilots

1928   Nellie Zabel Willhite licensed to fly in South Dakota.

1929   Edward T. Payne of Ontario, Canada earns license in May.

1937   James Stirling, Jr. of Barre, Vermont receives student pilot's license.

1947   Rhulin Thomas of Alexandria, Virginia flies solo across the continent.

1959   Walter Wettschreck promoted to captain of a Civil Air Patrol squadron in Minnesota.

Jean C. Hauser and her instructor, Ed Emanuel

ABOVE: *Harold Wright*
BELOW: *Merlin Tice and his wife, Sandra, and their airplane.*

Deaf Persons in the United States
Who Have Earned a Pilot's License

(Date and State Licensed)
(Compiled by George Culbertson and Jack R. Gannon)

Adams, Roger
Michigan

Aviles, Francisco J. 1970s
Maryland

Barton, Raymond P. 1959
California

Belcher, Don 1977
Kentucky

Berg, Martin 1950
Colorado

Bradford, Donald
New Mexico

Brant, Willie
South Carolina

Calveard, Jack 1950
Kentucky

Campbell, Claude
Montana

Cassetti, Edmund
Connecticut

Culbertson, George 1952
Virginia

Dick, Robert 1960s
Alaska

Evans, Gilbert H. 1951
Michigan

Fahr, Morris*
California

Flanders, Kennith
California

Floyd, Carl
Virginia

Gallaway, David W.
Maine

Goodson, James 1965
Arizona

Gordon, George 1965
California

Grisselbrecht, Charles 1978
Arizona

Gross, Bernard
New York

Hauser, Jean 1965
Wisconsin

Himmelspach, Charles 1965
California

Hinnant, Leslie 1950s
Virginia

Hykes, John
Washington

Joiner, Allie
Colorado

Jordan, Jerald 1950s
Maryland

Kelsey, Jack T.
Michigan

Lardinelli, Argo
California

Leitch, Margaret
California

Lippincott, Almon Miner 1940s
Connecticut

Marsters, James C. 1939
California

Moore, Roland Jr.
Michigan

Norville, Thomas 1950s
California

O'Kefe, Jack
New York

Petrides, Peter
Ohio

Rehn, Harold 1940s
California

Roper, David
Missouri

Saks, Andrew
California

Schwartzman, Barry
New York

Stephenson, Kirk 1970s
California

Stirling, James Jr. 1937
Vermont

Thomas, Rhulin 1947
Virginia

Tice, Merlin

Truglio, Peter
New York

Vleck, Charles

Weitbrecht, Robert 1967
California

Wettschreck, Walter 1954**
Minnesota

Wheeler, John T.**
Alabama

Wilkins, William D. 1940s
Ohio

Willhite, Nellie 1928
South Dakota

Williams, Stephen T.
Virginia

Woodward, William
California

Wooten, Art
Indiana

Wright, Harold 1950s
Texas

Zellerbach, Richard C.
California

**Member of Civil Air Patrol
* Killed in crash in 1964

the CAP he has been involved in four successful search missions.

In 1967 George R. Culbertson of Colorado Springs, Colorado tried to locate and organize deaf pilots. He found the names of 45 deaf pilots in the country. He verified approximately half that number as license holders. He was convinced that the number of deaf pilots was closer to 100, but he was unable to reach them all.

Culbertson, who became deaf at fifteen years, earned his license in 1951. He soloed after less than four and a half hours of instruction—something of a record in itself.

Most deaf pilots hold licenses which do not allow them to land at radio-controlled airports except in an emergency. As more and more airports add radios the number of airports with no radio control towers de-creases, placing additional restrictions on deaf pilots. These limitations and the expense associated with flying have discouraged many would-be deaf pilots and grounded others.

One deaf pilot, Morris Fahr, lost his life in a plane crash. Fahr had over 900 flying hours when he crashed in September 1964. He was flying a sports plane he and a friend had built and was taking it through maneuvers when the engine stalled and the plane took a nose dive; Fahr was killed.

When Gilbert Evans applied for his license in 1951 he was informed by the Federal Aviation Administration that there were 51 licensed deaf pilots. By 1980 the number of active pilots had shrunk to 25, but included one deaf commercial pilot, according to an FAA report.

Chapter 8

Our Deaf World

Two deaf friends meet. They had attended residential schools where it was the practice to label all the children's clothes so that it would not get lost in the laundry.

These two friends have not seen each other for awhile and although they know each other's name they pretend they don't.

"Your name?" asks the first one.

The second one lifts the collar of his shirt and glances backwards to the area where name labels used to be attached and responds: "Arrow, Yours?"

The first one goes through the same motions and responds, "Sears."

◇

Two deaf men, one tall and thin and the other short and fat, round the hallway corner coming from their rooms on the third floor of the hotel and stop at the elevator area. They are attending a National Association of the Deaf convention and have not seen each other for several years. They are busily engaged in a conversation and pay rapt attention to each other. They stop at the first of a long row of elevators, one pushes the "down" button and they resume their lively conversation.

The doors of the elevator on the same side, but at the far end, open, stand open briefly, then close and the elevator moves on to another floor.

After awhile, the two men stop talking and look around at each shut elevator door. One signs to the other: "Long!"

"Yes," the other agrees and signs, "Maybe this now," and the two move

down the hall towards the elevator on the far end that had just opened and shut. As they walk, the doors of an elevator behind them open, stand open briefly, then close. The two friends reach the far end, stand facing the elevator and resume their busy conversation. As they do so, the elevator doors directly behind them open and close.

After a reasonable wait they again pause, look around them and examine the doors of all elevators.

"Long!" repeats the short man. "Broke?"

"Lousy h-o-t-e-l" signs and fingerspells the tall one.

"I protest manager!" signs the short man, getting red in the face.

"Yes!" vigorously agrees the tall man, and both head for the stairs.

By the time they reach the lobby area they are again busily engaged in another conversation and have forgotten all about the incident with the elevators on the third floor and the reason for their hike down the stairs.

◇

A barber called the local priest who worked with deaf people and asked his assistance in locating a deaf manicurist. Puzzled, the priest wanted to know why the barber specifically wanted a deaf one.

"Because," said the barber, "the girl I have working for me now talks too much!"

The Sign, 1951

A deaf woman, Rae Johnson, took her poodle to the veterinarian's office. While waiting in the lobby, her dog became very nervous and started walking around. Johnson signed to her dog to sit down.

A man in the lobby saw her signing to the dog and told her that his friend's dog was deaf. Johnson asked how they talked to their dog and the man responded: "There's no problem. The dog lipreads."

◇

While working for the Mott Program in Flint, Michigan, Tom Mayes had a small office in a large building. Each day many members of the staff passed his office as they went about their business. They would glance in while passing and see Mayes sitting there and probably think to themselves: "That poor deaf guy! He never hears anything. He never overhears incidental office gossip. He doesn't know what is happening here." Out of sympathy they began to stop in Mayes' office, one by one, and share with him the latest news.

After awhile the situation reversed itself and word began to get around that Mayes was the best informed person in the building. His colleagues then began to stop by and ask him what was new.

◇

Four deaf travelers, weary of a long day's travel, pulled over and registered at an old lodging house. On their departure to the town for a snack they asked the owner if there were any movie houses or other entertainment where they might spend the evening, carefully writing their request on a pad so that there would be no misunderstanding.

"Why sure!" she said, "Be glad to oblige."

After digging around for awhile she fished out a program of a local Piano and Violin Concert.

—Marcus Kenner
The Silent Worker, 1950

◇

Irene Leavitt, a deaf resident of Lincoln, Nebraska, was stopped by a police car while driving one day. As the officer approached her she pointed to her ears and shook her head negatively to inform him that she was deaf.

"I know, I know," he said with a resigned look on his face. "Your horn is stuck!"

◇

A young deaf man got a job washing police cars. When he finished one he would drive it to a distant parking lot and pick up another.

One day while returning a clean car he was puzzled to see all the cars in front of him pull over to the curb and quickly looked in his rearview mirror to see if there was an ambulance or firetruck behind him. There was none and his puzzlement remained until he reached his destination and realized that he had accidentally switched on the siren and flashing lights on top of the car.

◇

"Were you born deaf?" asked a man of one whose hearing was poor.

"No, I was born in Ohio," was the unexpected answer.

—*The Silent Worker, 1891*

◇

A deaf man meets a stranger, takes out his pad and pencil and writes a note. The stranger reads the note, looks the deaf man up and down slowly, then writes on the pad: "Can you read?"

The disgusted deaf man reads the note, takes the pencil and pad and responds, "No, can you write?"

Byron B. Burnes stops by the neighborhood tavern after work one day for a drink. He walks to the long bar and seats himself next to a stranger. Being in the conversation mood, Burnes takes out his pad and pencil and strikes up a conversation with the hearing fellow. Shortly, another hearing man joins them at the bar and sits on Burnes's left. So Burnes includes him in the three-way conversation. After awhile Burnes looks at his watch and

205

realizes that it is time for him to go. He excuses himself, pays his bill and heads for the door. As he is about to exit he looks back at the two hearing fellows and notices that they are still writing back and forth to each other. Burnes shrugs his shoulders, arches his eyebrows and leaves.

◇

Deaf people often wonder why it always happens that a stranger who wants directions always asks the lone deaf person in the crowd.

◇

A deaf man has to catch an early flight the next morning. Worried that he might miss his plane he approaches the hotel desk clerk, takes out his pad and pencil and explains that he is deaf and asks if there is some way he can be awakened at a specified hour.

The clerk is most reassuring, and tells him not to worry. Relieved the man heads for the elevators to go to his room. On his way he stops, realizing something is wrong and returns to the desk.

"How," he asks the clerk, "do you plan to wake me?"

The clerk cheerfully points to the telephone and responds, "I'll call you."

"But I just told you I am deaf," he scribbles.

"Oooh!" responds a startled clerk. He rubs his chin and thinks. Then his face lights up; he smiles and writes on the pad: "Don't worry! Don't worry! I'll write you a note and slip it under your door."

A deaf man was invited to a party at a hotel. On his arrival he realized that he had forgotten the room number, but he remembered the floor. So he knocked on all the doors on that floor. The door that didn't open, he knew was where the party was. He opened it and walked in.

◇

Out of the night crept the raiding Scouts. Stealthily they surrounded our tents. The raid was on—they began yelling and screaming, trying to awaken our sleeping Scouts. They did succeed in arousing our Scoutmaster, who looked outside, smiled then went back to sleep. No one else stirred. The puzzled "raiders" left scratching their heads. The Scoutmaster's smile remained as he thought of the "raiders" trying to awaken our boys. You see, every boy in our troop is deaf.

—The Illinois Advance

Wilbur J. Ruge, who drew the cartoons appearing on this and the preceding pages, has been a technical editor/writer with Boeing Aircraft Manufacturing Company in Wichita, Kansas for more than 30 years. He is a graduate of the Nebraska School for the Deaf and Gallaudet College. His wife, Dorothy, who is also deaf, is director of the Deaf and Hard of Hearing Counseling Service in the same city. Cartooning is but one of Ruge's many hobbies.

207

Classroom Humor

The Child's Been Sick Before But Nothing Fatal

While browsing through old school records, George Propp, editor of The Nebraska Journal, *the publication of the Nebraska School for the Deaf, came across an unintentionally funny answer on a school admissions form. On this form parents had been asked to list any past illnesses the child had experienced and explain what the effects were. To that question, one mother had written that her child had been sick with some specific illness but that it had been nothing fatal. Propp's editorial eye quickly caught the humorous quirk and the title to the school humor column—"The Child's Been Sick Before, But Nothing Fatal"—was born.*

Some sampling of classroom humor which has appeared in the *Journal* and elsewhere:

The high school student informed his teacher that he would have to go to a funeral that afternoon.

Teacher: "Oh, I am sorry. Who died?"

Student: "My hearing aid battery."

◇

Teacher: "What's your next class?"

Student: "Sentence class."

◇

From an excited youngster: "I outed a tooth."

◇

The Intermediate boy found a picture of his teacher in her college yearbook. His remark: "pretty—before."

◇

We were amazed at the look of sheer terror and dismay on the face of a sixth grader when he saw his picture on the front of the November *Journal* cover. Seems his mother is very strict about his wearing his hearing aid glasses, and there he was as big as life in the picture, with naked eyes and ears.

◇

A teacher observed two little girls arguing about the date of one's birthday. "But you told me it was in March," said one.

"I know; that's what my mother said. But my teacher said it's in May, so I guess my mother didn't know."

◇

"Do you like liver?" asked the teacher.

"Yes," responded the student. "I would like best to liver in California."

◇

An English teacher received a gift from her class at the close of the school year. A note was attached and on it was written: "We appreciate you teaching us how to English."

◇

A story dating back to 1889 deals with the prefix *dis*. The teacher attempted to explain the meaning by giving examples: disabled—not able; dishonest—not honest; disobey—not obey; etc. The teacher thought he had made the meaning clear until the following day when one of the football players had written about football practice being cancelled. "Yesterday," he wrote, "we *dis*played football."

◇

Albert Berg of the Indiana School for the Deaf recalls this story in his "From my Reliquary of Memories," A young lad had returned to school very sad. He had received a letter from home and the teacher knew, from the look on his face, that it contained bad news.

"Is there something wrong?" the teacher asked.

"Yes," said the little fellow, "My sister died."

"Oh, I am so sorry," said the shaken teacher.

The young lad then handed his teacher the letter and she read it. Suddenly she exclaimed: "NO! No! Your sister is fine. When your mother wrote that your sister was *tickled to death* over the present you sent her she meant that your sister was very, very happy or thrilled to get it."

◇

Mel Carter, while teaching in North Carolina, noticed that one youth was frequently remorseful. Talking with the young lad he learned the cause. The lad did not look forward to going home because he could not communicate well with his parents. So, during a teacher-parent conference, Carter brought the matter to the attention of the boy's mother and urged her to learn sign language.

The mother agreed and secretly began taking sign language classes to surprise her son when he came home for the holidays.

Following the school holiday the beaming youth paraded into Mel Carter's class and proudly proclaimed: "My mother is now *a little deaf.*"

Hazards of Deafness

by Roy Holcomb

In the early 1970s Roy Holcomb, area supervisor of the Program for the Deaf in the Santa Ana (California) Unified School District, began compiling a list of "hazards" of deafness. This collection represented some of the funny, embarrassing and absurd incidents which deaf people have become accustomed to in their daily lives. It was published under the title 95 Hazards of Deafness. It was a hit and was quoted in publications, and used in classes of hearing students interested in working with deaf people. Deaf readers read the short paragraphs and chuckled as they saw themselves portrayed throughout the little book. It was like doing a re-run of their lives. As a result, Holcomb became a collection center for many more such incidents and, in 1977, he printed a second and larger edition of Hazards of Deafness through Joyce Media, Inc., in Northridge, California, from which the following have been selected with permission.

Holcomb is working on a third edition.

3. Your car dies at a stop light. You don't know it until the light changes green and you attempt to go. By the time you get your car started the light is red again and there is a long line of impatient drivers behind you. You thank God that you are the only one who knows that you are deaf.

4. Your car knocks and knocks and nearly falls apart before you realize it has a problem that will set you back a few hundred dollars.

5. You only half-close your car door and don't notice it until you are on the freeway doing 80.

9. A pebble gets into your hub cap and you go 800 miles before someone brings it to your attention.

12. While eating at a restaurant the waitress asks you if you care for more coffee. You reply in the negative since your cup is still half full. Later the waitress comes back and says something again. You catch only the word "coffee" at the end of her question and reply "yes" assuming that she is repeating her previous question—only this time she has said, "are you through with your coffee?"

13. You smack your lips while eating and then wonder why all at once you seem to be a very popular guy, with everyone looking in your direction.

14. You go into a cafe and order a ham and cheese sandwich and they bring you a hamburger. The sad part is your speech teacher in school led you to believe that you had the world's best speech.

18. You go to the dentist and everyone in the waiting room except you has a scared look because they heard a kid crying his head off in the dentist's chair.

20. While cleaning your house your vacuum sweeper's cord is unintentionally pulled out. You continue to use the vacuum for several minutes before you realize that it is off. Boy, do you feel dumb.

21. You go to bed one beautiful night and wake up the next morning to find that your house was nearly blown away by a storm during the night and that you slept like a log through all of it.

26. The toilet bowl flusher lodges and water runs for hours before you discover it. Then you wish you had bought some utility stock.

36. You put silver or dishes away and make enough noise to compare with the battle of Gettysburg.

38. Burglars come near your house during the night, and your dog nearly barks its head off trying to warn you, but you sleep through everything as if your place was guarded by the entire U.S. Army.

39. A stranger asks you for a match, directions, or something behind your back or when he does not have your attention. You, of course, do not know it and say nothing. The stranger then gives you a "dirty" look when you do see his face and you wonder why.

40. You are introduced to a stranger. You do not "catch" the name after several repetitions. You try to alibi your way out of the embarrassing situation by saying that people's names are often difficult to speech read unless they are easy ones like Smith, Brown, Reed or Jones. Then the stranger's name turns out to be Smith, Brown, Reed or Jones.

41. You are waiting for an elevator and one opens in back of or to the side of you and you fail to notice it. Do you feel funny when you do see it! Then it is just your luck to have the door close on you as you get halfway to the elevator.

44. You ask a friend to make a call for you, never knowing that the message that you wanted to give and what he actually said were as different as day and night.

---

45. You are stopped by a policeman. When you reach for your pad, he reaches for his gun—he can't take a chance. If you talk, your deaf speech may make him think you are a dangerous character. So you could be in real trouble either way. The best thing to do, it seems, is to act both deaf and dumb and not to say or do anything.

---

55. Your spouse snores and snores and snores, but you sleep like a log through it all, never knowing what snoring sounds like.

---

59. You are at a store purchasing something. The clerks says $3.30 when you think she says $3.13; $3.40 when you think she says $3.14; $3.50 when you think she says $3.15; $3.60 when you think she says $3.16 and any of the numbers vice versa as well as a thousand and one more confusing look alike speechreading words.

---

60. You pay full admission to movies, night clubs, or other places where sound of one kind or another is an important part of the price. Then you sit back and "watch" what your money has bought.

---

61. A news flash caption crosses your T.V. screen. Dialogue which you cannot hear, follows. You can imagine all kinds of things happening from Martha Raye winning a beauty contest to Martians invading New York. You must wait until you read the next day's paper to find out what really happened.

---

64. You watch a football game for ages wondering what the score is before it is finally flashed on the screen.

---

69. At the movies you laugh aloud when others cry and cry when others laugh, because you don't see things the same as other people hear them in the movies.

---

72. You drag your feet because it gives you a comfortable, secure feeling, not knowing that it does not sound very romantic to others.

73. You are sitting in a room all by your lonesome self watching a T.V. program or reading with your mind a thousand and one miles away. Then someone comes into the room without your hearing him and half scares the living daylights out of you by merely tapping you on the shoulder.

---

74. You take something out of your pocket. Other things come out, too, and fall on the floor without you knowing it. Later, much later, you will find yourself missing keys, loose change, or something which should be in your pockets.

---

78. You go on vacation trips, visiting many interesting places and pay for guides who tell you practically nothing since you can't understand them. Worse still are the sites that have pre-prepared tapes to explain interesting facts about the beautiful places you are paying to visit.

---

80. You get dizzy at a meeting trying to locate who is talking and when you finally locate the speaker, he has finished and someone else has started and you must begin your game of "hide and seek" all over again.

---

81. At socials and meetings you whisper when you should talk and speak loudly when you should whisper and are forever putting your foot in your big mouth.

---

83. You are in a crowd of a thousand people and feel more alone than if you were standing in the middle of the Sahara Desert.

---

84. You are driving along with a hearing friend. Talk about captive audience! You have one who has to listen to you explain all about the education of the deaf and he can't say a word, as you don't dare take your eyes off the road to look at him to give him a chance to "talk."

---

86. You start to go outdoors and are very much surprised to find it has been raining "cats and dogs" for hours.

---

88. You nearly get your hand bitten off by petting a dog that was growling to let you know that it didn't like people, much less you.

Chapter 9

The 1930s

Labor Bureaus

S THE NATION was coming out of the Depression there was clamor in the deaf community for the establishment of state labor bureaus for the deaf. The Depression had created so much unemployment that it was very difficult for many deaf people to find jobs. It was easy for an employer to find all the help he needed and a disabled worker was not likely to be his first choice. Work Progress Administration officials were also accused of discrimination against deaf workmen. Many deaf people felt that the answer to the labor problem was the establishment of labor bureaus. These bureaus, they believed, could help overcome discrimination and help "sell" the capabilities of deaf workers.

Another reason the deaf worker found the job market increasingly competitive was because public schools had begun adding vocational training programs to their curriculums. This had once been an area where schools for the deaf had a monopoly. Schools for the deaf were among the earliest—if not the first—to offer vocational training to their students. As a result, most graduates left school with skills in a trade which stood them in good stead and helped them get work. As the years passed, however, many of these schools did not keep pace with changing industries. Their equipment became outdated or obsolete, and they began losing ground to those public schools with more modern machinery and equipment.

Jay Cooke Howard was an advocate of the labor bureaus. He believed that each state should have a Division for the Deaf within the State Labor Departments. He saw them as one way to overcome weak vocational programs. He believed that such Divisions could "force" schools for the deaf to "discard obsolete methods and equipment and assist the schools in securing appropriations for modern equipment and competent instructors."

Only four states were reported to have labor bureaus. Minnesota, the first, established a bureau in 1915. North Carolina followed in 1923. Michigan and Wisconsin had bureaus. Attempts were made to establish a labor bureau for the deaf on the federal level but it never got through Congress.

The law establishing the North Carolina bureau stipulated that the Commissioner of Labor "appoint a competent deaf man to devote his time assuring the deaf citizens a chance to support themselves." James M. Vestal, a Tennessee School for the Deaf and Gallaudet College graduate, was hired to fill the position in 1933. He built it into a nationally known bureau.

In Minnesota Petra F. Howard became chief of the newly established Bureau of the Deaf in 1915. She later left the position, but returned as a counselor in the Bureau in 1929, a position she held until 1956 when she was appointed specialist for the deaf in the Vocational Rehabilitation Department. She held that position until her retirement in 1959. (On her retirement she received letters of commendation from President Eisenhower and Governor Orville Freeman and a resolution from the Minnesota Association of the Deaf. Gallaudet College awarded her an honorary degree in 1960.)

The labor bureau idea never really caught on. In the 1940s Indiana hired Boyce R. Williams as a Specialist for the Deaf and Hard of Hearing in the State Office of Vocational Rehabilitation. This was a statewide program and it was in the direction of the future. In 1945 Williams was appointed Consultant for the Deaf, the Hard of Hearing, and the Speech Impaired, Rehabilitation Services Administration in the Department of Health, Education, and Welfare, and moved to Washington. Richard M. Phillips succeeded Williams in Indiana. Other states eventually followed Indiana's lead and began adding specialists to serve deaf people within their vocational rehabilitation programs.

A Tall Story

Each year, as George Washington's birthday approaches, Felix Kowalewski recalls the time he touched the tip of the Washington Monument in Washington, D.C. When he mentions this fact to someone the response is almost always, "Oh, yeah, another one of your tall tales."

But, the truth of the matter is Felix Kowalewski has touched the tip of the Washington Monument and he has pictures to prove it.

In the early 1930s the monument was so dirty that a decision was made to clean it. It was encased in a steel framework and sandblasted. Kowalewski was then a student at Gallaudet College. The father of his friend, Alex Ewan, was one of the supervisors on the

job. One cold Sunday Ewan's father agreed to take a small group of his son's friends to the top. In the group were Professor Powrie V. Doctor, Stan Patrie, a student photographer, Kowalewski, Ewan, and Ewan's father. They gathered at the foot of the monument where they crowded into a small cage elevator and slowly went up through the framework outside the shaft. The cage stopped at the 500 foot level and the group got out and gingerly made their way to the top by ladder. The ladders were enclosed in wire cages. Some of the ladder rungs were icy. At the top there was only a flimsy waist-high railing around the platform—but there was the very tip of the Washington Monument.

After a picture-taking session the group returned to the ground, completing an adventure few can boast of.

Hearing Aids

The use of hearing aids began to increase during the 1930s. It took a while for them to gain acceptance by the hard of hearing as well as by the public. At first people were reluctant to use them because they "advertised" a defect.

Dr. Edmund P. Fowler, president of the American Society of the Hard of Hearing, who encouraged the use of hearing aids, argued that deaf and hard of hearing persons should not be any more sensitive about wearing hearing aids than people who wore eyeglasses. An article appearing in *The Volta Review* noted that it took nearly 500 years for eyeglasses to find acceptance. There was even resentment towards

LEFT: *The Washington Monument encased in scaffolding in preparation for sandblasting. ABOVE, left to right: Alexander Ewan, Felix Kowalewski, Alexander Ewan, Jr., and Dr. Powrie V. Doctor and the monument's tip.*

Lars M. Larson
(1856-1931)

Founder, teacher, and first superintendent of the New Mexico School for the Deaf, Lars M. Larson was born in Wisconsin in 1856. He became deaf when he was two years old. He could neither speak nor lipread, and he had a very lonely childhood. He could not understand his hearing brothers and sisters, and they largely ignored him. He communicated with his father by homemade family signs and through this means of communication his father taught him how to raise livestock and poultry. It was not until he was 13 years old that the family learned about the existence of the Wisconsin School for the Deaf in Delavan. Larson would recall years later that "life began for him when they opened the school door in Delavan."

From Delavan, Larson went to Gallaudet College and then landed a teaching position in the Chicago Day Schools for the Deaf where he taught for three years.

He founded the Wisconsin Association of the Deaf and was active in the formation of the National Association of the Deaf.

His desire to help other unfortunate deaf children led him to Santa Fe, New Mexico, where he started a small school that became the New Mexico School for the Deaf. In Santa Fe he experienced many hardships and frustrations. Financial support for the school was difficult to get during those early years and although it was a "public" school there were times when he had to run it as a private school in order to keep it open. Besides academic subjects he taught his students woodworking, how to take care of fruit trees and raise horses, cows, and chickens as his father had taught him.

His second wife died in December, 1905 and shortly afterwards he was informed by the school trustees that his services would no longer be needed.

The following summer Larson boarded a train north for Minnesota, leaving behind as a legacy the school he had started and loved.

He died of heart failure on June 30, 1931 and is buried in Dundas, Minnesota.

early users of eyeglasses and sometimes a wearer's intelligence was questioned.

D. H. Lawrence, an author, did not give hearing aids much of a boost when he was quoted making the following statement: "I cannot think of anything to say to a black box." But as time passed and hearing aids became more compact and more efficient, their use spread.

Carnegie Medal Winners

By 1930 there were two known deaf Carnegie medal winners. The first was Edmund M. Price and the second was George H. Eversaul.

Ripley's ——— Believe It or Not!®

MRS. KATHERINE KRUEGER
Detroit
BORN TOTALLY DEAF
CAN UNDERSTAND PHONE CONVERSATIONS
PERFECTLY BY HOLDING THE RECEIVER TO HER CHEST

© RIPLEY INTERNATIONAL LIMITED 1939

One May afternoon in 1907, 37-year-old Edmund M. Price, a legging maker in a harness shop, was walking in Seal Garden, California, when he saw a small girl walking on the railroad tracks. He dashed

Pests to Exterminate
by Guie C. Cooke

—1—

*With mouthings that would frighten one
She tries to make us read her lips.
She swears that only harm is done
With graceful signs and finger-tips!*

—2—

*He says that everyone who hears
Finds the all-talking shows are best.
Well, let the fools wear out their ears!
Like ours, some day, they may have rest.*

—3—

*There is a pest we can't endure:
He is the one who has a cure,
And comes around with this or that.
Politely, we pass him his hat.
(If there's a cure we'd like to try
It's socking him upon the eye!)*

—4—

*This one of us exterminate!
The pest who mourns his own sad fate,
And, doing naught, tells all he'd do
If he could hear. Thank God, there's few!*

*The Washington Deaf Record
1938*

213

Douglas Craig
Angelia Watson Album

land Y.M.C.A. Eversaul attended the Oregon State School for the Deaf.

Milestones

Douglas Craig (d. 1936) was a homeless waif found wandering the streets of the District of Columbia in 1871. He was placed in Dr. Edward M. Gallaudet's care. Gallaudet gave him a name and enrolled him in the Kendall School. Afterwards, Craig secured employment on Kendall Green, where he spent the rest of his life. He became a legend, known and loved by generations of Gallaudet students. A street on the college campus is named for him.

George T. Dougherty (1896-1938) was one of the first to make his mark as a chemist and assayer. Educated at the Missouri School for the Deaf, Gallaudet College, and Washington University, Dougherty held positions in large industrial establishments and during his later years was head chemist and metallurgist of the American Steel Founders Co. His writings appeared in professional journals and established him as an authority in analytical chemistry and assaying. One of his contributions on steel analysis became part of a textbook. While still a student at Gallaudet College he was elected the first secretary of the National Association of the Deaf. He later served the organization as vice president. He was active in the deaf community, serving as president of the Chicago Pas-a-Pas Club and chairman of the World Congress of the Deaf

across the tracks in front of an on-coming electric car, grabbed the child and jumped to safety just in the nick of time. For this heroic deed he was awarded a Carnegie medal and $1,000 cash. He is the first deaf person known to win the award. Price was educated at the California and Washington State Schools for the Deaf.

On August 20, 1930, George H. Eversaul, then 19, saved a friend from drowning in the Columbia River near Deer Island, Oregon. He and some friends decided to swim to a small island in the middle of the river. When they reached it Eversaul looked back and saw one of his friends in trouble. Although not an expert swimmer himself, Eversaul decided to try to save his friend. His friend became panicky and fought him, causing them both to go under several times and at one time Eversaul lost his grip on his friend. He was swimming in circles looking for the boy when he accidentally kicked him and managed to grab his hair and finally pull him ashore. For this act of bravery Eversaul was awarded the Carnegie medal and $500. He also received a Life Saving Medal from the Port-

What Experience Taught Them

Years ago there was established in one of our large cities a club composed of graduates of an oral school, with the intention that all communications in the club life of its members should be strictly oral. The members were bright and enterprising young men, and sought honestly to live up to the advice and warnings that had been inculcated by their teachers as to the debilitating effects on their speech of the use of signs in any manner as a means of communication. After a fair trial they were obliged to own that it was impracticable to get along together by and through lip-reading alone, and had the good sense to acknowledge their failure. They amended their rules so as to permit the free and unlimited use of any method of communication among the members. Today this organization is one of the largest of the deaf in the country, and its membership embraces graduates of schools employing different systems, while the general mode of communication is the sign language so abhorred by those who do not fully understand its value.

—The New York Journal of the Deaf
ca. 1939

214

J. Schuyler Long
(1869-1933)

J. (Joseph) Schuyler Long was born on January 1, 1869 in Marshalltown, Iowa. He began losing his hearing at the age of 11 years from a childhood accident and spinal meningitis and became totally deaf at 16. He graduated from the Iowa School for the Deaf in 1883 with the school's first regular graduating class and was the first Iowan to enroll at Gallaudet College. He was 15 years old. At Gallaudet he was quarterback of the football team that beat the Naval Academy, 16-0.

Following graduation, he moved to Wisconsin where he taught gymnastics. In 1901 he accepted the head teacher position at his alma mater, ISD, and was made acting principal the following year. In 1908 he was appointed to the position permanently. Long edited *The Iowa Hawkeye*, the school's publication, from 1901 to 1923 and made it a widely-respected magazine. He was also a contributor to the *American Annals of the Deaf*. For a decade he worked for the Council Bluffs *Nonpareil* as a proofreader and telegraph editor and wrote editorials and special features. One of his contributions, "A History of the Army of Tennessee," resulted in a personal letter of congratulations from General Greenville Dodge.

Long also wrote poetry and in 1908 he published a collection of his work in *Out of the Silence*. The following year he published *The Sign Language, A Manual of Signs* which included some 500 illustrations.

Gallaudet College awarded him an honorary degree in 1914.

Long died of pneumonia on October 31, 1933, ending a long, distinguished, and productive career. He was 64 years old. Forty-four of those years had been devoted to education of the deaf.

It is a great handicap to be deaf, but the educated deaf do not look upon deafness as a misfortune. They do not want it to provoke pity nor to serve as a cloak for charity. They ask only for an equal opportunity for an education.
—JOHN W. JONES
1929

Thomas A. Edison (1847-1931), one of the world's greatest inventors, had a hearing impairment. When asked what he thought was the best remedy for deafness he is credited with responding: "A cupped hand behind the ear." Edison blamed his deafness on an accident during his youth. He was trying to board a moving train when a conductor trying to help him grabbed him by the ears and pulled him aboard. Edison patented over 1,000 inventions during his life.

The Rev. Adolph O. Wilson (1867-1939) died at his home in Dallas, Texas. Born in Sweden, he moved to this country as a youth and became a teacher at the Arkansas and Texas Schools for the Deaf. He was a good friend of the Rev. John W. Michaels and became an ordained Baptist minister in 1926.

Edmund M. Price (1870-1907) the first deaf person known to win a Carnegie Medal for heroism, was the subject of a chapter in the book, *The Biography of Spring Street in Los Angeles*, by William R. Swigart. Price resided on Spring Street, known also as Banker's Row, during the later years of his life. As a youth he excelled in athletics and his love for sports earned him the nickname "The Champ." *The Biography* is a collection of biographies and stories about the residents who lived, worked, and played on that famous thoroughfare. One chapter is devoted to "The Champ."

when it met in Chicago in 1893. He died on December 2, 1938.

Robert Carr Wall (1858-1939) was a successful manufacturer. He built the first "safe" bicycle and the first gasoline driven automobile in Philadelphia. The "safe" bicycle had two wheels of the same size and was an improvement on the English version. He produced stationary engines and in 1900 built an automobile which he sold for $1,800. In 1904 he began manufacturing rattle-proof windshields for Packard automobile builders. His business slogan was: "We manufacture what others can't or won't." Born deaf, Wall attended the Western Pennsylvania School for the Deaf when it was located at Turtle Creek. He started working in the steel mills of Pittsburgh, where he learned about metals. He moved to Philadelphia and became a manufacturer. He was noted for his innovative engineering. He died on November 26, 1939, at the age of 81.

IMA WOODRUM of AKRON, Ohio
TOTALLY DEAF
CAN ACTUALLY *SING* ON HER FINGERS!
SHE USES THE MUTE SIGN LANGUAGE
AND KEEPS PERFECT TIME WITH THE MUSIC
BY MEANS OF VIBRATIONS
© RIPLEY INTERNATIONAL LIMITED 1935

A Tragedy of Deafness
by James Beauchamp

In 1934, a handsome fifteen-year-old boy was brought to school in Kentucky for the first time. His parents explained that they had been unable to part with him when he became old enough for school and thus he had grown up entirely uneducated and had never learned to obey, or live under restrictions of a regular school.

The school administration had to admit this boy, but foresaw the difficulty of training him, also teaching him.

They got an older boy to be his "big brother" and help keep him in line. This proved quite difficult, since the new boy was powerfully built and showed great distaste for the life at school.

Despite the difficulties encountered, most of the school population were of the opinion that the new pupil would gradually adjust to the new life and surroundings.

One Saturday afternoon, the older boys were allowed to attend the movies in town and took this boy with them in hopes he would have a good afternoon. By some unexplained ruse, the boy gave his big brother and the other boys the slip and disappeared in the darkened theatre.

It was later discovered that he had left the theatre, unobserved, and gone to the bus station. Since he couldn't read or write, he in some unexplained way, had bought a ticket to a town far into the eastern part of the State to the line's end at West Liberty, where they had recently had a bank robbery, arriving at midnight.

The boy got off the bus and, being in a strange darkened town, made for a lighted window. This happened to be the bank, where an armed guard was stationed overnight.

The boy banged on the bank door seeking to gain admittance. This alarmed the guard, who drew his gun and walked to the door.

Seeing the guard with his gun pointed at him, the boy took flight and was shot to death when he failed to halt when ordered to do so.

Identification was easily established because in his coat pocket was a letter written to him at the school by his mother, in which she told him to be a good boy and do as he was told.

This is only one of the many tragedies attributed to deafness which could be recounted in our long history, but it is a true story and explains why our educators are so determined in getting young deaf children into school.

Hazards of Deafness
by Roy Holcomb

97. You put dishes and silverware away as if there was an earthquake, never realizing that you are making so much noise.

———◆◆———

98. Your cooking on the stove boils over and over and is not brought to your attention until you smell something burning, you see smoke, or your husband tells you; in the latter case, pray that you have a sweet husband.

———◆◆———

105. You are trapped all alone in an elevator and can't talk with anyone on the emergency phone or on the outside. You just hope people are trying to get to you even if you can't hear them.

———◆◆———

117. You are a Ph.D. and know just about every word in the Webster's Dictionary, but just try finding words to tell your paper boy that you are missing papers and he'll make you feel you are both deaf and dumb.

———◆◆———

121. You are on the freeway or the tollway. You have car trouble. You go to an emergency phone booth and give your location. You wait awhile but no help shows up. Thinking that your deaf speech may not have been understood, you call twice more. Soon three detour trucks and a police car come to your rescue.

122. After brushing your teeth, you gargle with some mouthwash. Your mother comes running as she thinks you are strangling to death from all the noise you are making unconsciously.

———◆◆———

128. Your hearing aid leaks and makes a beeping noise. People look at you as if you were a doctor and your beeper is going off and you should call in to your office immediately.

———◆◆———

138. You type away and don't hear the bell at the end of the carriage and many of your words end up beyond your right margin stop.

———◆◆———

146. You drink Manhattans instead of other drinks and you smoke certain brands of cigarettes because your favorites are often difficult to pronounce correctly.

———◆◆———

148. People think that you are rich because your pockets always jingle with change from small purchases for which you paid with bills to be on the safe side of not underpaying. You didn't wish to be embarrassed by being asked for more money. And again, you don't trust lipreading strange people.

216

160. You are involved in an accident with a hearing person. The police are called. Each of you has a different version of what happened. The policeman listens to the story of the hearing person. He cannot understand you, and you cannot understand the policeman. The policeman does not want to wait until you write down a long description of the accident. The policeman tells both of you to report the accident to your insurance companies. You are given a ticket, but the hearing person is not.

---

161. Your car is hit by the car of a hearing person. You want to call the police, as you feel you were entirely in the right. The hearing person refuses to call the police and leaves. There were no witnesses. You drive into the police station to report the accident. Since a policeman was not at the scene of the accident, your report is inconclusive. This makes it difficult for you to collect from the other party's insurance company.

---

165. You have an argument with a deaf friend. He closes his eyes and will not "listen" to you. Then you have to decide whether to punch him in the nose, walk away, or literally open his eyes so you can finish your argument.

---

166. Your stomach growls. You reason that since it occurs in your stomach, it can't be heard outside, never knowing that the growling is louder than that of a mad dog.

---

172. You apply for a job at a place where a deaf person was fired for being a slow worker. You don't get the job because the employer considers all deaf people alike even though you have a reputation for being a fast and effective worker.

---

173. You put some water in the kettle and turn on the stove. You fail to hear the kettle whistle. Soon you have lost your water and your kettle.

---

174. You are a star football quarterback. You take the ball through the middle, throwing opponents right and left as you go seventy yards for a touchdown, only to find that the whistle was blown twenty yards back where a clipping penalty occurred.

---

175. You have a neighbor, who loves to talk, call your doctor for you. Soon your entire neighborhood knows your medical history and then some. John R. Seidel, Phoenix, Arizona.

---

188. You let a friend out of your car. Your car door slams on her coat. You start up; your friend runs for dear life, hollering all the time. You finally glance to

the right and wonder what in the world a sixty-year-old lady is doing racing your car on foot before you realize what has happened.

---

194. Grace is said. You bow your head, but look up from time to time to know when grace is over. It is a long prayer and your neck gets a lot of exercise before it ends. In order not to be embarrassed by lifting your head so much, you become an expert at looking out of the corner of your eyes.

---

211. You have a lot of gossip you wish to share with your best friend. You take her out to lunch. You start telling her about Mrs. Jones, Mr. Jones, Mrs. West, Tom Franks, Mr. and Mrs. Smith, Dr. Peterson, etc., etc. Two hours later, while you are not out of gossip, you happen to look up at a balcony above you and are most surprised to find a dear friend there who has been watching your every word.

---

212. You live in a two-story house. You wear out your downstairs light switch flashing it to call people upstairs to come downstairs and your downstairs light switch flashing it for people downstairs to come upstairs. (Deaf people often get others' attention by flashing lights.)

---

217. You are talking with a hearing person. You are getting along fine with your conversation until another hearing person comes along. Then you are dropped cold, so cold that you couldn't be colder if you were at the North Pole.

---

226. You give your newborn daughter a beautiful name and then find for the next fifty years you never pronounce it correctly.

---

284. You are engrossed in a torrid love scene presented in a movie by the Captioned Films of the Deaf. After breathing a hefty sigh, you found that the spring governing the take-up reel had snapped and hundreds of feet of the film was on the floor.

---

294. You always get up early on Saturday mornings to cut your lawn. You never know how happy your neighbors are when your lawnmower breaks down.

---

296. You are eight years old and playing a game of hide and seek. When you finally get brave enough to return to the base, you find that the game was over a half hour ago, and everyone went home.

---

303. You visit your wife and your precious newborn baby in the hospital. Several nurses from another floor pass by and express their congratulations on the ar-

rival of your young Adonis while you gape in awe and marvel at how he is going to be even more handsome than yourself. Unfortunately, you and your wife don't see the nurses and, therefore, give no acknowledgement. Even more unfortunate are the rumors that spread among the hospital staff of two snobby parents of a beautiful baby.

---

307. One night you go out to dinner. You arrive at your destination. You turn off your car lights and get out of the car. You notice the brake lights still on. You check your car lights again. You check all doors but your brake light remains on. Then you discover that your car motor is still running and you forgot to turn off the ignition.

---

310. You talk on the phone for yourself. An interpreter listens and interprets for you from another phone. Later you meet the person who you talked with and he won't believe that you are deaf because you talked so well and replied so quickly.

---

312. There is laughter in the room, laughter in the air, laughter all around you and you hear it not but you see some of it and this makes your heart glad.

---

321. You go to a mountain resort for your vacation. The birds sing, the squirrels eat their nuts. A brook twists and runs with its clear blue water. Children run and laugh. All these things have their sounds. For once you don't mind being deaf since there is great beauty even without sound.

---

324. You became deaf from spinal meningitis and have poor balance. You walk in a zig-zag manner, especially at night. One morning your landlady notes your footsteps in the snow and concludes you have been drinking. She won't have drunks in her house so she asks you to move out. It takes a little explaining to convince her of your problem and that it is not drinking.

---

327. You are going to California. The plane runs into trouble and is detoured to Las Vegas. The plane lands and the passengers are let out for a two-hour or more wait. Boy, are you surprised to see how much "California" has changed with all its slot machines, gambling tables, and the like.

---

330. You are on the plane and in the air. The stewardess comes down the aisle asking everyone something. You guess it must be cocktail time. When she gets to you, she asks something. You say "Manhattan." She shakes her head and repeats her question— Chicago or California?

---

334. You are on vacation. You leave loved ones at home. You worry about them. You cannot call them so you worry more about them. Your vacation is half spoiled by not being able to be reassured that all is well at home.

---

339. You visit a class in a school for the deaf. You try to communicate with the children. The teacher scolds you and says, "We are oral. We are oral. We don't use sign language." You try again to communicate with the children and ask them something orally other than how old are they or what is their name. You get little or no response. You leave the room knowing the teacher is oral but having grave doubts about the children in more ways than one.

---

352. You work in a factory. You have a break. You sit alone. At lunch you sit alone. For fifty years you are pretty much alone at work. When you retire and they give you a gold watch, you go out and celebrate alone.

---

372. Some people avoid you like deafness is contagious. These people go out of their way in order not to come in contact with you, no kidding. (You may have to be deaf to believe this.)

---

379. You give a talk at a convention. One thousand people hear you. You talk under strain because of your hearing handicap. Your deaf voice is intelligible for awhile, but soon gives way to hoarseness and it is next to impossible to understand you. You do not know this and continue "preaching" away. Finally, some kind soul gives you a glass of water and you wonder how he knew that you were thirsty.

---

388. You never hear your father's farewell as he goes to work; his talking to mother; his telling of stories to your brother and sisters; his discussion of the day; his plans and hopes for the future or his greetings as he walks into the house from a day at work.

---

489. You call your sick wife at home. She has a TTY phone, but has to get out of the bed with a temperature of one hundred five to answer it.

Chapter 10

The 1940s

The Decade

N THE EARLY 1940s there were an estimated 60,000 deaf persons in this country; one deaf person for every 2,150. Deaf persons were classified as congenitally (born) deaf and adventitiously deaf (deafened later). The term "deaf-mute" was used liberally in the press and the term "partly deaf" was used to define hard of hearing persons. Scarlet fever, spinal meningitis, brain fever, colds, malarial fever, and influenza were still leading causes of deafness. There were 20,367 pupils enrolled in 312 schools for the deaf. Of that number 65 were public residential schools which had a collective enrollment of 4,800; and 20 were denominational or private schools with an enrollment of 1,000.

"Superior facilities" was given as the reason for the popularity of the public residential schools. Economics, no doubt, also played an important role in attendance at these tax-supported schools because this country was just emerging from the worst depression in its history and money was tight.

A bill was introduced in the House of Representatives to establish a Bureau of the Deaf within the Department of Labor. The bill called for the establishment of a department under the direction of a chief who would report to the Secretary of Labor. This Bureau, it was proposed, would be responsible for maintaining records on deaf people; studying fields of employment available to them and creating new areas of employment; promoting the capabilities of deaf workers among prospective employers; expanding employment opportunities in the public service area and cooperating with vocational rehabilitation agencies. Unfortunately, the bill did not pass.

In the pre-war days of April, 1941, you could purchase a Cadillac coupe in Detroit for $1345 or, if you preferred, buy a Hudson, Studebaker, Nash or DeSoto for less than $900. "Holeproof" nylon socks were advertised for fifty cents a pair; white shirts were $2.95 and women's three-piece suits sold for $39.75. You could fly from New York City to Washington, D.C. on Eastern for $12.20 or take the train from New York City to St. Louis for $21.15, and if you had the urge to get away from it all—and $70—you could take a four-day cruise to Bermuda.

Winston Churchill's book, *Blood, Sweat and Tears*, was being advertised as a bestseller and sold for $3.00 hardbound. General Motors stock was going for $38.12 a share, and Camel cigarettes claimed 28 percent less nicotine than the other four leading brands.

And, then the war came and many things changed.

Pearl Harbor

Eight-year-old Bill Sugiyama and his schoolmates at the Diamond Head School for the Deaf on Oahu in the Hawaii Islands had just finished breakfast that bright, sunny Sunday morning of December 7, 1941. While most of the students went outside to play Bill decided to stay in the dormitory and read *Life* maga-

219

zine. Suddenly, he started feeling vibrations and thought his schoolmates, elsewhere in the dorm, were making a racket and really roughing it up. In reality, the "racket" was being made by members of the Japanese Imperial Air Force who, at that very moment, were bombing Pearl Harbor some ten miles from the school. Few of the students and their supervisors believed what was happening until a stray shell whistled overhead and exploded in a shed two blocks away.

Alden C. Ravn, a deaf teacher, was working in the school's woodwork shop early that morning when he was informed of the Japanese attack. He had not been aware of the bombing in the distance, but he had heard the shell that had whined over the school and struck the shed. About mid-morning the school's principal came to tell Ravn that he had heard over the radio that the United States had declared war against Japan.

That afternoon the school's principal instructed the older boys to take heavy tables from the dormitories and put them around the porches and cover them with mattresses. These areas became the school's bomb shelters until underground shelters could be dug on the campus. That night the students and teachers could see the fires glow from Pearl Harbor and the first of many nightly blackouts began. All windows were covered completely and lights were turned out before outside doors were opened. Food was rationed, drinking water was boiled and everyone was required to carry a gas mask wherever they went. Children slept with their clothes on and one little boy would not go to bed without an iron bar at his side. Everyone feared that the Japanese army was planning an invasion of the islands.

School remained unofficially closed until February. Children who lived in Honolulu or elsewhere on Oahu stayed home. Those children who lived on other islands stayed at the school. They did yard work, helped in the kitchen, and performed miscellaneous jobs. When the yardman quit, Ravn assumed those duties in addition to his other responsibilities.

In early 1942 the military began urging all pregnant women from the mainland to return home. Ravn's wife signed up and was called in early April, but Ravn had to remain to fulfill his contract. He left for the mainland in June aboard a military transport in a convoy of five freighters escorted by four destroyers. The ships were required to zig-zag the first two days out to avoid possible enemy submarine attacks. On board the ship the passengers and crew slept in canvas bunks. The first night Ravn was frightened awake suddenly by a loud grinding noise. He later realized that he had inadvertently selected a bunk right next to the rudder gear housing. Every time the ship zigged or zagged he could feel a terrible noise.

Joining Up

On that fateful day, December 7, 1941, some 5,000 miles east of Hawaii at Gallaudet College, stunned deaf students gathered around a radio—as did millions of other Americans—to learn through an interpreter's hands that our country was at war.

As thousands of Americans marched off to army recruitment offices deaf people wondered glumly what they could do to aid the country's war effort. A number of them even attempted to enlist, four of them from Gallaudet. One of them was Eric Malzkuhn, who was classified 1-A by his hometown doctor. Malzkuhn had been deafened at the age of ten and when he returned home for his registration, which was required of every 18-year-old American male during the war, his doctor was unaware that Malzkuhn had become deaf. Malzkuhn assumed his doctor knew of his deafness and, being a good lipreader, the physical went off without a hitch. When he received his papers later, a surprised 1-A deaf Malzkuhn headed for the local induction center at nearby Fort Mead, Maryland as instructed, with visions of glory in the offing. At the induction center the waiting lines were so long that many of the men were put on paper-picking detail to keep them occupied. Malzkuhn was one. While he was leaning on a pole to rest, a sergeant came up behind him and started giving orders, which, of course, Malzkuhn ignored. Finally, the sergeant tapped Malzkuhn on the shoulder and demanded, "What's the matter with you—you deaf or something?" A startled Malzkuhn turned around and nodded sheepishly, "Yes."

Of the four Gallaudet students receiving call-up papers, two were drafted. Archie Stack spent the war as an intelligence clerk in the United States and Wayne Schlieff was with the Mortar Division stationed at Camp Breckenridge, Kentucky.

Prior to the war, life on Kendall Green was the same as on any other college campus. The girls wore knee-length dresses or skirts and white and brown or black saddle shoes. Wide-lapel, pin-striped suits, black pointed toe Florsheim shoes and round, metal-rimmed or frameless glasses were popular with the boys. In College Hall, the men's residence, poker

---

No special consideration need be given to the deaf; they do their work one hundred per cent.
—HENRY FORD
1940s

The clubmobile on the right was donated to the American Armed Services by the National Association of the Deaf.

chips went five for a penny and a student had to play all night, and be very lucky, to win enough money to take his date to the movies. Before the war ended those same poker chips were going for a quarter apiece. Another favorite pastime of the students was to get together and sign-sing "My Bonnie Lies Over the Ocean," "Clementine," and other popular songs of the times. Someone adapted "The Marine's Hymn" into this version of a college song:

From the halls of Gallaudet College
To the shores of Chesapeake Bay
We will fight our college battle
From September into May.
First for right and reason
And to keep our honor clean,
We are proud to be the guys and gals
Of Kendall Green.

When the students sang their voices rang out through the confines of College Hall and mingled with the occasional loud "thump!", "thump!" coming from the "doorbells." This particular doorbell which some genius had conceived was made by placing a heavy lead window weight inside a pipe. One end was attached to a chain and the other end of the chain had a knob. The pipe and weight part were located inside the room and the knob on the outside wall. When the knob was pulled and dropped it made a loud, thud which vibrated through the floor. Many a sleepy deaf resident swore that such contraption had been made to wake the dead not the deaf. It's amazing that Gallaudet's "normals" (hearing graduate students studying to become teachers of the deaf) survived all this din. Perhaps, it was one of the reasons a number of them enlisted.

SILENT NUPTIALS

LAWRENCE MOODY AND EVA HALL
- BOTH BLIND AND DEAF MUTES
WERE MARRIED BY REV. W<u>m</u> LANGE - A DEAF MUTE!
(All Saints Episcopal Church, Johnson City, N.Y. June 27, 1947)

© RIPLEY INTERNATIONAL LIMITED 1947

Soldiers on the Assembly Line

During World War I patriotic deaf men tried to enlist in the armed services. Some managed to lipread their way past the recruiting officer, but in most known cases, their hearing impairment eventually surfaced and they were released. With the outbreak of WWII, that old patriotic spirit arose once again and for many the temptation to serve their country in uniform was strong.

One deaf man who had read about deaf men serving in the Canadian Home Guard wrote the Adjutant General at the War Department and asked what plans had been made for deaf persons to participate in the defense set-up. The Adjutant General responded: "It goes without saying that people with loss of hearing are just as patriotic as any other group," but, in essence, he offered no hope or encouragement for deaf people's involvement.

Manpower shortage eventually attracted many deaf persons to war work. They flocked to shipyards, aircraft manufacturing plants, tire and rubber factories and other war production plants across the country. They filled badly-needed jobs, built enviable personal work records, set production records and helped this country win the war. And, in doing so, they became a special kind of soldier . . . soldiers on the assembly line.

Although war is hell, ironically it did deaf people a good turn. It brought this group of invisibly-handicapped Americans out in the open, gave them an opportunity to perform an important role and a large variety of jobs and to prove to government agencies and private businesses that when given the opportunity and proper training, deaf people can make valuable contributions to any work force.

Doing One's Share

As the war progressed everyone wanted to help. School children collected grease, scrap iron and rubber and saved their coins to purchase Victory Stamps. In Staunton, Virginia, deaf children at the Virginia School for the Deaf and the Blind sold over $3,200 worth of stamps and bonds, collected 4,500 pounds of scrap iron and 5,000 pounds of paper. Boy Scout troops everywhere had paper drives. Girls at the Maryland School made approximately 18,000 surgical dressings for the Red Cross. Deaf ladies in Washington, D.C. organized "The Silent Service Unit of the American Red Cross" to sew and knit for the armed forces. Forty deaf persons in Atlanta, Georgia enrolled in first aid classes.

The National Association of the Deaf purchased $5,300 worth of Defense Bonds, the Louisiana Athletic Association of the Deaf bought $1,500 worth and the Boys' Athletic Association at the California School invested $1,000 as did the Minnesota Association of the Deaf. The Washington State Association of the Deaf purchased $4,500 worth of bonds. Individuals everywhere withdrew their savings and placed the money in Defense Bonds.

Learning of the copper shortage, one deaf couple in Virginia decided to turn in their four cigar boxes full of pennies. After the weary bank teller had finished counting the 6,192 pennies, weighing approximately 44 pounds, they put the money in war bonds. Students and teachers at the Rochester (NY) School sent contributions to schools for the deaf in China enabling them to remain open during the war.

But there was also a black side of deaf America during that period. In Oregon deaf Japanese students were denied admission to the school for the deaf.

The National Association of the Deaf in the 1940s bore little resemblance to a national organization as

222

we know it today. There were no paid employees or officers. President Tom L. Anderson was, at that time, principal at the Iowa School for the Deaf in Council Bluffs. The two vice presidents were Winfield S. Runde of California and T. Y. Northern of Colorado. Byron B. Burnes, a teacher at the Minnesota School for the Deaf in Faribault, was the secretary-treasurer. Such persons as Marcus L. Kenner (New York), Thomas F. Fox (New Jersey), the Rev. R. C. Fletcher (Alabama), James N. Orman (Illinois), George G. Kannapell (Kentucky), Kenneth Murphy (New Jersey), Robert M. Greenmun (Ohio), Lawrence Yolles (Wisconsin), Reuben Alitzer (District of Columbia), Arnold Daulton (Ohio), Leonard Warshawsky (Illinois), and others were active in NAD affairs in those days.

Membership stood at around 2,500. The Association derived its support from dues of $1.00 a year or $10.00 for life. The main issues facing the Association in those days were public ignorance of deafness, a strong oral philosophy in the education of the deaf, deaf peddling, unemployment of deaf Americans, and the American Federation of the Physically Handicapped (AFPH). With no home office, weak financial backing, no official publication of its own, a poorly organized network of state associations, and the need to handle Association business through the mail or at conventions every three years or so, it is amazing that the NAD managed to survive and accomplish what it did.

The NAD was successful in getting the Civil Service Commission to revoke a ruling that discriminated against deaf printers. The ruling stated that a Government Printing Office (GPO) printer "had to be able to hear an ordinary conversation at a distance of at least fifteen feet from the ear." The elimination of this barrier opened the door to well-paying positions for many deaf printers.

In 1942 the NAD launched a national "Victory Fund" drive. Working with state associations, the NAD raised $7,771.68. The money was used to purchase three Red Cross clubmobiles which saw service overseas. They were: "A gift from the American Deaf to their Fighting Forces."

Gallaudet's "Five Iron Men"

The year, 1943, was the year the sports world, especially in the environs of the Mason-Dixon Conference, heard from Gallaudet College. In the fall of 1942, the college's undefeated cross country team won six consecutive meets and beat Bridgewater, American University, Loyola College, Johns Hopkins University, and Catholic University to capture the M-D Conference cross country championship. Then, the following winter the college's basketball team accomplished the unbelievable.

The male enrollment at the college that year was 55. The Bisons entered the M-D Basketball Tournament in Baltimore with just five players and a dismal 4-11 win-loss record. Two standout players had left earlier to enter war work and a third had been drafted leaving Don Padden (Minnesota), Earl Roberts (Missouri), Paul Baldridge (Utah), Roy Holcomb (Texas), and an All-American from Wisconsin, Hal Weingold. Baldridge was the team's captain and English Sullivan, a graduate of Centre College in Kentucky, was the coach.

Considering their season's record, the Bisons were appropriately seeded eighth in a field of eight teams. They opened against Randolph-Macon, a team with a 7-0 regular season record and one of the tournament favorites. Everyone expected the Bisons to make a quick return trip to Kendall Green except, of course, the players. Then the unexpected began happening in what one sports writer later called the "Tournament of Upsets." The Bison five upset Randolph-Macon, 48-37, and went on to beat American University, 45-40, to meet seventh-seeded University of Delaware in the semi-finals. The Bisons beat Delaware by two points, 42-40, and the Gallaudet players who had played every minute of the three games were immediately dubbed "The Five Iron Men" and became immortalized in the college's sports history.

Gallaudet's "Five Iron Men," left to right: Hal Weingold, Earl Roberts, Paul Baldridge, Roy Holcomb, and Don Padden.

Our Heritage

DEAF MUTE CHURCH, Norfolk, Va.
ALL PREACHING AND SINGING IS DONE IN THE *SIGN LANGUAGE*

© RIPLEY INTERNATIONAL LIMITED 1940

Jim Henneman of the *Baltimore News-Post* called that tournament "one of the most stunning reversals of form in the history of sports."

Wrote Lewis F. Atkinson in the *Washington Star:* "The Associated Press recognized their skill and courage, by picking the whole shebang, kit and kaboodle for its all-conference team. That was no hollow honor."

The advancement of the entire Gallaudet squad to the Mason-Dixon Conference All-Star team was an accomplishment that has never been repeated.

In March of that year spunky Marvin Marshall, a 126-pound cowboy from Utah, went all the way to the finals of the featherweight boxing contest in the Amateur Athletic Union boxing tournament in the District of Columbia. Although Marshall did not win the championship that year more would be heard from him.

And, that was the year the sports world heard from Gallaudet.

The 'Most Misunderstood Sons of Men'

In December, 1943, Dr. Harry Best's book, *Deafness and the Deaf in the United States*, was published by MacMillan. This book was an expansion of an earlier book written by Best entitled: *The Deaf: Their Position in Society and the Provision for Their Education in the U.S.* which appeared in 1914. Best was Professor of Sociology at the University of Kentucky. A graduate of Centre College, Best held a masters degree from Gallaudet College, an M.A. from George Washington University, and a doctorate from Columbia University. During his career he wrote about twelve books on such subjects as crime and criminal justice, the handicapped person, the Soviet Union and labor. In 1954 Helen Keller awarded him the Migel Medal of the American Federation for the Blind for his book, *Blindness and the Blind in the United States*. Centre Col-

lege (1937), Gallaudet College (1944), and the University of Kentucky (1965) awarded him honorary degrees.

His book about deaf people was considered by many as an authoritative text on social and educational aspects of deafness. It was dedicated to "those bearing a grievous burden and the most misunderstood among the sons of men but the 'gamest' of them all."

The National Fraternal Society of the Deaf hopes that the NAD will continue to guard its long tradition of unselfish service to the cause of the deaf; that it will continue to entrust the direction of its activities to the best available minds among the deaf; that it will continue to be a force for good in our beloved American democracy, a force we deaf can ill afford to do without.

—ARTHUR L. ROBERTS
1940

The U.S.S. *Thomas Hopkins Gallaudet*

On October 21, 1943, California Shipbuilding Corporation in Los Angeles, launched Liberty Ship #1898. It was one of 2,571 Liberty Ships built for the U.S. Maritime Commission during the war. This ship had a capacity of 10,626 deadweight tons of cargo and a sea speed of 12.5 knots.

The following month, on November 13, 1943, the ship was completed and named the *Thomas Hopkins Gallaudet*. The ship was christened by author Pearl S. Buck who said, "This is a lucky ship built by great hands and named for a great soul. I am sure that this ship, too, has a great soul and that it will ride all storms as Gallaudet did."

At 4:15 p.m. that same day the *Gallaudet* was delivered to the Soviet Union under the Lend-Lease Program. The Soviets renamed the ship the *Maikop* and used it throughout the war. The *Maikop* was returned to the United States Government five years later on March 19, 1948, at Yokohama, Japan and renamed the *Thomas Hopkins Gallaudet*. The American Pacific Steamship Co. sailed the *Gallaudet* under an agreement with the U.S. Government for six months. Then the *Gallaudet* was placed in the National Defense Reserve Fleet which is maintained by the Maritime Administration for national emergencies.

On March 9, 1951 the *Gallaudet* was sold to Traders Steamship Corporation and renamed the *Amberstar*. Afterwards it changed hands a number of times and

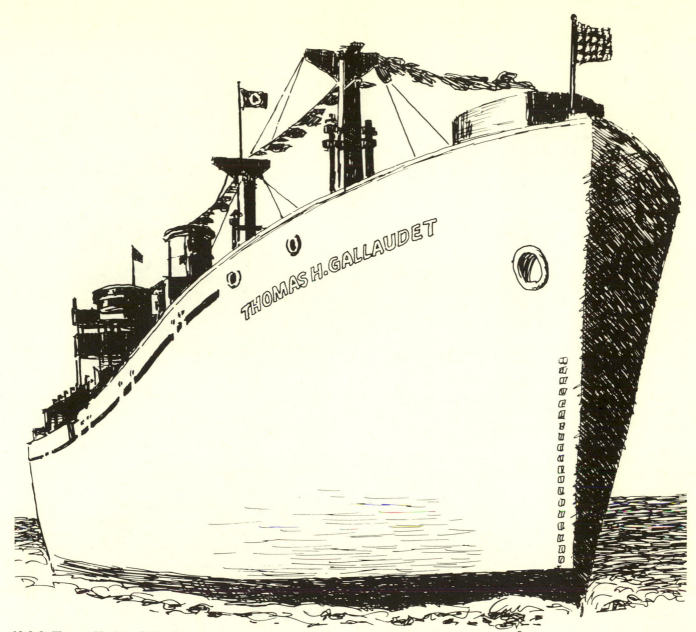

U.S.S. Thomas Hopkins Gallaudet

sailed under the names of *Elmira*, *Pontos* and *Samuel S.* In 1955 it was converted to a standard cargo ship at a shipyard in Scotland. In addition to Russia, it operated under the Liberian and Greek flags.

The final chapter of the *Thomas Hopkins Gallaudet* began in 1965 when it was sailing under the Liberian flag and bore the name of *Samuel S.* In the spring of 1969, the *Samuel S.* was en route from Guam to Pusan, South Korea with a cargo of scrap iron when it ran aground on Kuchinoerabu Island, off the southern coast of Japan. It broke in two and later sank. The ship was over 35 years old. It had served throughout the world.

Another ship of interest to deaf people was the *U.S.S. Rhodes*. In June, 1943 a destroyer escort vessel, the *U.S.S. Rhodes* was christened in sign language by Mrs. G. E. Rhodes of South Carolina. The ship was named for the Rhodes' son, Lt. (j.g.) Allison Phidel Rhodes, who was killed near the Solomon Islands in the Pacific. Mr. and Mrs. Rhodes were graduates of the South Carolina School for the Deaf.

Butch, the Little Lady Dog

The little fox terrier went through the familiar routine. As his master commanded the little dog sat,

Charles Moskowitz fingerspelling instructions to Butch.

stood, walked on its hind legs, turned around, fetched something, played dead or performed some of the many other tricks it knew.

There is nothing unusual about dogs performing such tricks, of course, except that the little dog's master had not uttered one vocal command. Butch's master, Charles Moskowitz, was deaf and did not speak. So, Moskowitz had taught his little dog to respond to commands in fingerspelling. Fingerspelling, yes; signs, no. So amazing was this feat that many people would not believe it could be done until they had seen

the little dog perform themselves. One of the non-believers, according to Moskowitz, was Robert Ripley, creator of *Ripley's Believe It or Not!* cartoons.

The Moskowitz family had received the lttle mixed spitz and fox female terrier for Christmas in 1941 and the children had named her Butch. Moskowitz began teaching her to do tricks when she was two months old. Butch learned the tricks easily but it took three years to teach her to respond to fingerspelled commands.

Moskowitz and Butch performed before many audiences and at the National Association of the Deaf convention in Cleveland. They were popular attractions wherever they went. They were featured on the covers of *The American Weekly*, *The Greenville* (S.C.) *News* and *The Silent Worker*.

The Post-War Years

The American Federation of the Physically Handicapped, mentioned earlier, was a coalition-type organization of other physically handicapped Americans. It had the support of some deaf persons but the NAD officers, instead of cooperating and working with it, saw it as a threat to the NAD and refused to join the federation. To a degree the NAD officers' stand could be justified. They feared a drain on its already small membership and financial structure. They believed that only an organization of the deaf could speak for deaf people and best serve their interests. They feared a "take-over" by hearing persons, something all deaf people had experienced at one time or another during their lives.

In retrospect, it was probably unfortunate, however, that there was not, at least, a cooperative effort between those two organizations. Deaf people could have benefited had there been a better relationship.

Male students at the Fanwood (New York), Missouri, Maryland, Minnesota, and Florida Schools for the Deaf wore military uniforms. The Texas School football team went undefeated. The Iowa School won the sixth annual Midwest Basketball Tournament in

In each earnest face I see a trace
Of the boy I used to be:
May yet he vision in my place
The man he hopes to be!
—GROVER C. FARQUHAR

South Dakota and the American School captured the 14th annual Eastern States Schools for the Deaf Basketball Tournament at Philadelphia.

In West Hartford, Connecticut, Superintendent Edmund Boatner was making news with his ability to find employment for deaf persons. In Northampton, Massachusetts, a wealthy widow willed to the Clarke School for the Deaf a 17-room mansion valued at $58,000 and a $50,000 endowment to maintain it. The Mississippi Association of the Deaf led by President Bilbo Monaghan was successful in getting the legislature to approve three laws concerning education of the deaf in that state. One of those laws provided that

Edith Fitzgerald
(1877-1940)

Edith Fitzgerald was the originator of *Straight Language for the Deaf*, more widely known as the Fitzgerald Key. Straight Language is a system used to teach deaf children the correct placement of words in a sentence. At one time the Fitzgerald Key was used by approximately three-fourths of the schools for the deaf in teaching language to deaf children.

Edith Mansford Fitzgerald was born on August 29, 1877 in Memphis, Tennessee. She was born either deaf or hard of hearing and educated in a regular school until her transfer to the Illinois School for the Deaf where she studied four months. She graduated from Gallaudet College in 1903 as class valedictorian.

Her teaching career included 17 years at the Wisconsin School where she began to formulate many of her ideas of a better way to teach language to deaf children. Fitzgerald believed that it was possible for a deaf child to acquire good English and that every deaf child should have the opportunity to do so. Teaching positions with the Louisiana, Arkansas, and Virginia Schools for the Deaf followed. It was at the Virginia School, in 1926, where she was principal, that the first edition of her *Straight Language for the Deaf* came off the press. By 1963 it had gone through six editions.

The system made her well-known, and she was invited to lecture on it at schools for the deaf, Columbia University, Michigan State Normal College, and Gallaudet College. In 1939 she collaborated with Marie Kennard of the Georgia School in the preparation of two booklets, "Suggestions for Mental Development" and "Straight Language Discusses Arithmetic."

She died June 26, 1940 in Oak Park, Illinois.

227

those pupils who were unable to progress satisfactorily under the oral method be taught by manual instruction and every teacher was required to master the manual alphabet "in order to communicate with those who could not read lips."

A bandit lost his aplomb when he entered a drug store on Florida Avenue in Northeast Washington near Gallaudet College, and, with drawn revolver, ordered everyone to the rear of the store. Everyone immediately obeyed except eight deaf students who were busily eating banana splits. They sat there unaware of the thief's vocal orders. The bandit lost his nerve at such defiance and fled empty handed.

The Better Vision Institute cited figures to show that deaf drivers were the safest drivers in the state of Pennsylvania and argued that sight is the most important safety factor in driving. A lady in Chicago won a $24,000 lawsuit against a doctor who was charged with destroying her hearing through an unsuccessful operation.

In the late 1940s trained teachers of the deaf were scarce. Teacher training programs were not turning out enough teachers to meet the needs of the schools and their increasing post-war enrollments.

In 1947 the Ohio School led with the most deaf teachers. It had 18 deaf teachers on its faculty. The Arkansas School and the North Carolina School at Raleigh were second with 16 each. The Indiana School and Kentucky School had 15 each and the South Dakota, Iowa, and Tennessee schools each employed 14 deaf teachers. Thirteen public residential schools reported in the *American Annals* that they did not employ

G. Dewey Coats
(1899-1965)

G. Dewey Coats was born in Coal Hill, Arkansas. Measles caused his deafness at the age of five and he enrolled in the Arkansas School for the Deaf in Little Rock, graduating in 1917. He matriculated at Gallaudet but remained only one year, leaving to enter World War I work and and never returned. He taught woodworking at the Washington and Missouri Schools before becoming vocational principal at the latter in 1949.

Coats loved cigars. A visitor to Baker Building, the vocational building on the MSD campus, could immediately tell on setting foot in the entrance whether or not he was present by the smell of his cigar.

Coats was a warm, friendly, and helpful person. He was articulate, well-read and a past master of storytelling. He was a person who enjoyed working with his hands as well as his head and, as a jack-of-all trades, he was creative and industrious. He could turn a piece of walnut wood into a beautiful piece of furniture as skillfully and with as much ease as he could sort out a jumble of words and present them in a clear, meaningful statement.

Coats invented the phrase "Manual English." Writing in the March 1948 issue of the *American Annals of the Deaf* he noted "a valid difference between ideographic signs and a combination of signs and fingerspelling which followed the pattern of grammatical English." He proposed to call this combination "Manual English" arguing that it was "subject to the same rules of grammar and syntax no less than written or spoken English."

Coats was a staunch supporter of the National Association of the Deaf. A committee he chaired at the Diamond Jubilee convention in Cincinnati in 1955 came up with a "Dollar-A-Month" plan which probably saved the NAD from financial disaster. Under this plan persons who retained their membership in the Association a minimum of three consecutive years became members of the "Order of the Georges," a phrase Coats coined. Those who could not pay the membership dues at one time were encouraged to send in a dollar a month. This honorary Order was organized on the thesis that all of us tend to "let George do it." "Because most of us 'let George do it,'" Coats wrote, "it falls upon the few mature and responsible persons in many organizations to do the unexciting but necessary duties of many. . . ." The Order of the Georges under Coats' leadership grew and eventually became the backbone of the NAD.

The Knights of the Flying Fingers award was another of Coats' creative innovations. This award was established to recognize those individuals who made extra-ordinary contributions to the Association. This award was designed by Hubert Green, a deaf Canadian artist. It consists of a certificate enclosed in a plastic cover imprinted with a gauntlet fingerspelling the letters "KFF." Only three of these highly-prized certificates are given by the NAD president at each convention.

Coats was elected third vice president of the NAD at Cincinnati in 1955 and moved up to second vice president at the St. Louis convention in 1957. He was reelected in 1960 in Dallas and again in 1964 in Washington.

Following the Dallas convention Coats noticed a small persistent sore on his lip and had it checked. It was diagnosed as cancer. He began making regular trips to St. Louis for treatment. The disease spread to his throat and he gradually began losing the battle. When G. Dewey Coats died on September 4, 1965 the NAD lost a tireless worker and the founder and driving force behind the Order of the Georges. He was acclaimed "the noblest George of them all." It was no small coincidence that G. Dewey Coats' first name was George.

Lawrence Yolles
(1912-1953)

Lawrence Yolles' parents emigrated to the United States from Vienna, Austria. His father, Philip, became a factory worker and rose to the presidency of the firm. He invented a new padlock and established the Master Lock Co. in 1925, and he was president until his death in 1944. Young Lawrence Yolles began working at this factory when he was 12 years old. In 1940 he became secretary of the company, a position he held at the time of his death.

Born November 19, 1912, in Milwaukee, Wisconsin, Yolles was deafened when he was four years old. His schooling included stints at the Paul Binner School (a public oral day school in Milwaukee), the Wisconsin School for the Deaf in Delavan and the Wright Oral School in New York, from which he was graduated. He earned a bachelor's degree in business administration from Ripon College in Wisconsin and did additional studies at the University of Pennsylvania and Drexel Technical College.

Yolles was described as a top-notch golfer. After college he became actively involved in sports in the deaf community and began learning sign language. He was generous with his time and talents and at one time listed membership in 14 clubs and organizations. He was general chairman of the 1953 American Athletic Association of the Deaf basketball tournament held in Milwaukee, but he died on January 19, 1953.

Yolles was elected first vice president at the National Association of the Deaf convention in Cleveland and was appointed chairman of the NAD Endowment Fund, an assignment he assumed with energy and enthusiasm. He died of a heart attack in his sleep.

any deaf teachers in their academic departments. Of the 119 public day schools which employed a total of 549 teachers not one had a deaf teacher. Of 22 denominational and private schools which hired a total of 233 teachers on their teaching staffs, there were a total of ten deaf teachers.

In 1948 four of the superintendents of residential schools for the deaf had earned doctorates and four had no college degrees at all. Ten of the schools offered courses in poultry culture and seven in dairying.

That year the Maryland legislature granted a liberal salary increase to teachers at the Maryland School. College graduates with an "A" certificate could start at $2,200 and earn up to a maximum of $3,200.

The Dallas Pilot Institute for the Deaf, dedicated to teaching speech and lipreading to the pre-school deaf child, was the recipient of a 20-room mansion situated on eight acres. The estate, valued at $300,000 was a gift of Mr. and Mrs. T. Leonard Bradfoot, Jr. and their two daughters.

About this time Washington, D.C. had a new resident. His name was Boyce R. Williams and he had moved to the city to accept a new position with the federal government. The position was specialist for deaf and hard of hearing in the Advisement, Training and Placement Section in the Office of Vocational Rehabilitation, within the Federal Security Agency.

In June, 1948, members of the Christian Deaf Fellowship approached officials of the Central Bible Institute and Seminary in Springfield, Missouri and discussed the possibility of establishing a program for deaf students interested in studying for the ministry. The Christian Deaf Fellowship had been organized a few years earlier under the leadership of Rev. John W. Stallings, the son of deaf parents. The CDF was "an undenominational union for fellowship among those with faith found in the Gospel." This meeting in Springfield led to the establishment of a department of the deaf at CBIS and the hiring of Miss Lottie Riekehof to head it. The following September two deaf students enrolled in the program and in January, a third. In addition to interpreting for those deaf students Riekehof organized and taught sign language classes to hearing students.

In June, 1949, deaf Lutherans and their friends gathered in Cleveland, Ohio to dedicate a $64,000 modern structure, the Christ Lutheran Church for the Deaf. The following September, the First Lutheran Church for the Deaf in Washington, D.C. was dedicated to serving the deaf. In December, a third one, the Trinity Lutheran Church for the Deaf, was dedicated to bringing God's word to the deaf. This church was built on 9th and Maple Avenue across the street from the South Dakota School for the Deaf.

Welcoming participants to the fifth annual American Athletic Association of the Deaf in Oakland, California, Harry Jacobs, the general chairman told them,

Ripley's — Believe It or Not!®

ALBERT BERG A DEAF MUTE — WAS FOOTBALL COACH AT PURDUE

© RIPLEY INTERNATIONAL LIMITED 1943

229

TOP: *Front and back of medallion presented to Rhulin Thomas at the White House for his solo flight across the U.S.*

BELOW: *Thomas and his plane.*

"We are proud that we are better able to provide for your entertainment than those who greeted the '49ers of the past century." The Des Moines, Iowa Club defeated Oakland, Little Rock and Los Angeles to win the fifth tournament. Helen Coffey was named Queen of the Tournament and Florita Tellez and Lucy Beare were chosen ladies-in-waiting.

Just before the decade came to a close the Dallas Club purchased a $27,500, two story brick building at Ervay and Beaumont Streets and an additional lot. Tired of being booted from one location to the next, the members under the leadership of Troy E. Hill, got together and came up with the necessary $5,000 down payment. Members were charged 50¢ a month dues. Elderly persons, those too ill to work, and those who were unemployed were excused from paying dues.

The Silent Worker Revived

In September, 1948, Byron B. Burnes, who had been elected to the National Association of the Deaf presidency two years previously in Louisville, Kentucky, revived *The Silent Worker*.

Young George S. Porter had inherited a four-page newsprint tabloid named *The Deaf-Mute Times* in 1892 when he became printing instructor at the New Jersey School for the Deaf. Porter, whom John H. McFarlane called "the maker of silent workers," changed the name of that small school paper to *The Silent Worker* and built it into a slick national magazine. On Porter's retirement in 1929, *The Silent Worker* was the most popular publication of the deaf in the country. When Porter retired, however, the *Worker* also ceased publication. It was succeeded by *The Jersey School News*, a strictly school-related publication.

During its absence other publications came and went. There were *The American Deaf Citizen*, *Modern Silents*, *The Broadcaster*, and *The Cavalier*. *The Cavalier*, a highly influential and popular newspaper, continued to publish into the 1950s.

B. R. White of California assumed the editorship of the revived *Worker*. He was assisted by Loel F. Schreiber as news editor. (She would eventually succeed White as editor.) John H. McFarlane and J. Frederick Meagher, who had written for the old *Worker*, joined the staff of the new magazine. New contributors in that first issue included Gordon (Bud) Allen, Lillian Hahn, Richard G. Brill, and Mervin D. Garretson. Proclaimed volume one, number one: "*The Silent Worker* lives again!"

Toward a Greater Gallaudet

In the early 1940s Gallaudet College was a small liberal arts college existing quietly on an expansive tract of land in northeast Washington, D.C. As the second president of the college, Dr. Percival Hall, neared retirement a rumor was circulated among the alumni that Hall was planning for one of his sons to succeed him to the presidency. Hall was off-campus at that time and before he had the opportunity to respond to the rumor it had reached quite a number of alumni, some of whom did not take kindly to the idea. Without bothering to check on the truth, they wrote to the White House complaining about such a move. These complaints brought the Bureau of the Budget into the picture, and the Bureau began asking questions. Hall denied he ever had such plans.

The first public expression of discontent with the college occurred in a hearing before the Austine Kelley Congressional Committee in 1944. Paul Strachan, president of the American Federation of the Physically Handicapped and Alan B. Crammatte, editor of *The*

Cavalier, were invited to appear before the committee. They gave detailed testimony in which they identified many of the services needed by deaf people and how these services could be met and the role they saw for Gallaudet College, as a national college for the deaf. From that time on, Crammatte kept pushing in the pages of *The Cavalier* for expansion and for an alumnus on the college board.

After the war the Federal Security Agency (which had been assigned jurisdiction over Gallaudet College in a 1939 Congressional reorganization of the federal government) received an appropriation of $7,500 for a study of Gallaudet College. The Agency hired Dr. Harry Best, a professor of Sociology at the University of Kentucky to do the study. Best had graduated with the 1902 Gallaudet normal class and had been a teacher of the deaf. A few years earlier, MacMillian & Co. had published Best's book, *Deafness and the Deaf in the United States*. This contribution was considered monumental and Best was recognized as an authority on deafness.

In 1945, 46-year-old Leonard M. Elstad, superintendent of the Minnesota School for the Deaf was selected to suceed Dr. Percival Hall as president of Gallaudet College. Gallaudet then had an enrollment of 157 stu-

> *In my forty-eight years of teaching, it was my good fortune to be associated with far more people whom I admired and loved than time-servers or self-seekers. My lines have indeed been "cast in pleasant places," with superintendents, principals, teachers and counselors who have tried to understand their deaf charges and truly help them along the road to an education.*
>
> —GROVER C. FARQUHAR

dents and a faculty of 24. Some critics called the college nothing more than a glorified high school. When the Best Survey got underway, talk of expansion began to drift around the campus. There was even mention of moving the college elsewhere.

Change was inevitable. Harry N. Rosenfield predicted on March 11, 1946: "The future of the Columbia Institution for the Deaf (of which Gallaudet College was part) is a bright one. We in the Federal Security Agency are anxious to do all in our power to lend lustre to that future."

Addressing the alumni at the 20th Reunion in 1947 for the first time as the college's president, Leonard M. Elstad told those in attendance: "We want every young man and woman who can profit from a college education to have an opportunity here. If that means 100 new students each year that is fine."

Three years later with the alumni again meeting in reunion on Kendall Green, Elstad was in Holland. He had been invited to address the International Congress on Education of the Deaf. He told the group that expansion plans were in the making at Gallaudet and predicted that: "Expanded to its proposed size, the college will be large enough to accept all qualified deaf candidates in the years to come. A student body of 350 to 500," Elstad predicted, "will satisfy these needs." Those figures were a bit modest because within a decade the college's enrollment had doubled and by 1970 it had grown to over 1,000.

What had happened? Where had all the deaf students come from? Why the sudden surge in attendance? Had the rate of deafness suddenly taken an upward swing? Not really. Several factors were involved.

It was about this time during the presidency of Ben M. Schowe, Sr., that the Gallaudet College Alumni Association began publishing the *Gallaudet Alumni Bulletin*. Elstad, Schowe and officers of the Alumni Association realized that if changes were to take place it was important that the alumni be kept well in-

231

formed. The GCAA was a more or less dormant national organization which had confined most of its activities to Kendall Green. Prominent alumni including Schowe, Boyce R. Williams, James N. Orman, David Peikoff, Alan B. Crammatte, Leon Auerbach, and some others realized that if the college was to grow and fulfill its obligations to deaf America it was necessary that there be a vigorous Alumni Association. They saw the changes taking place as an opportunity for the alumni to assume a more influential role in policy making in the months and years ahead. The establishment of the *GAB* would, it was hoped, create a better informed alumni membership and help unify the alumni. The *GAB* became an important vehicle for dialogue between the college and the alumni. Important issues were discussed in its pages and it soon became a popular publication. Years later, when the news magazine format was changed to a four-page newsletter and the publication was renamed the *Gallaudet Alumni Newsletter,* old timers continued to refer to the newsletter as the "GAB."

But, the *GAB* cost money and the GCAA treasury was a pitiful sight. Here was a national organization trying to survive on a shoestring. Annual dues in the Association were then fifty cents, largely voluntary. Life membership dues were $10.00. The GCAA then had about 200 life members. It's a wonder that the *GAB* managed to survive and it most likely would not have were it not for David Peikoff and his Canadian friends who volunteered to do much of the printing gratis. Chapters and classes also helped. They sponsored individual editions and assumed the printing costs thus easing the burden on the national treasury.

The subject of accreditation—or perhaps it was really the subject of change—was a sensitive issue. It split the campus into two groups, became a topic discussed on and off campus and in the pages of the *GAB.* The "cons" generally revealed a pessimistic view. "Where would Gallaudet get the students for an accredited program?" The gap between the residential schools (which fed Gallaudet the majority of its students) and Gallaudet, they contended, was too great to overcome. Some expressed doubts about the ability of the average deaf college student to make it through an accredited program. Then, there was the concern over the admission of hard of hearing students.

The war had created a decline in the enrollments in many schools for the deaf. If Gallaudet College were to increase its enrollment there was fear that the college would have to admit more hard of hearing students. This was pointed out by one faculty member who concluded his argument with: " . . . and as we understand it Gallaudet College is a college *for the deaf. . . ."*

Hard of hearing persons had long been the orphans of the deaf and hearing worlds. With their partial hearing, which, naturally, varied in degree from individual to individual, most did not fit comfortably into the hearing world. They felt neither welcomed nor that they belonged in the deaf world. Many relied heavily on what limited hearing they had and lipreading and did not bother to master the language of signs. Most, also, had a better command of the English language than the average deaf person. This and the ability to use their speech and the telephone set them apart from deaf persons. It is important to remember, also, that up to this time admission to Gallaudet College had been strictly limited. Deaf students and the alumni were sensitive to admitting large numbers of hard of hearing students to the college. They believed that hard of hearing students could make it at a college for the hearing. They saw the admission of these students as an invasion of their college. They believed that for each hard of hearing student admitted, a more deserving and equally qualified deaf student would be turned away.

Elstad argued: "An audiometer test determines the degree of loss of hearing, but it does not tell everything," which was true. But he also assured the alumni that: "Gallaudet will never be a college for the hard of hearing although there will always be a few in attendance."

Admission to the college during the Edward Miner Gallaudet and Percival Hall eras was largely dependent on the number of scholarships granted by Congress. In the old days to seek admission to Gallaudet College, a student had to first contact his congressman and apply for a scholarship. This put a limit on the number of students the college could admit. Students who were known to be holding good jobs were discouraged from applying for admission. Those students who were already enrolled and who were offered employment were encouraged to accept it and forsake their college studies. A few deaf students were able to pay their own way.

On the other side of the accreditation argument were those who saw it as a more positive development. They saw accreditation as a necessary step if the college was to grow. They questioned the wisdom of the financial outlay required to maintain a college for such a small student body.

College officials realized that if the college was to provide a sound academic program with a wide range of fields of concentration (which were necessary to qualify for accreditation) a larger enrollment was

Dr. Leonard M. Elstad (left) and Dr. Percival Hall looking north on Kendall Green in the direction of the college's growth.

needed. They felt that not all potential student sources were being tapped. Between 1936 and 1945, for example, most of the college's enrollment came from some 45 public residential schools for the deaf in the United States. There was occasionally a student from a private, denominational or day school, but these programs were largely untapped. There were no black students. A few foreign students enrolled from time to time but they were there more by chance than by design, and most of them were "normals" or hearing members of the graduate class.

The college administration also realized that many schools for the deaf were not providing the preparation needed for college-level studies. Many oral schools discouraged their students from considering Gallaudet; some were even hostile to the idea of their students attending the college.

This was the situation Best found when he began his survey in 1946. He had been asked by FSA to analyze and evaluate the trends and future needs of the Columbia Institution. He was asked to evaluate the role of the Institution in the educational area it served; to study the special schools for the deaf; and to examine the legal and administrative relationship of the Institution and the federal government. It can be assumed that this was the beginning of what would much later lead to the federal government's broader involvement in the education of the deaf.

According to Best, only one-fifth of one percent of the deaf population was attending college. Best saw accreditation of Gallaudet College as the ultimate goal and he believed that it would affect not only the college but education of the deaf in general.

In his report to FSA Best criticized the college for not being more aggressive in presenting its needs to Congress. He believed that the purpose and aims of the college were not well understood nor appreciated off campus and he felt that the college had not kept abreast of the changing times. There was, he found, too much of a conception of an institution and not enough of a conception of a college.

Best saw the college remaining fundamentally a liberal arts college. He suggested the addition of vocational guidance, placement and rehabilitation programs. He recommended a second preparatory year for those students from schools which provided only the equivalent of a tenth grade education. Regional high schools were considered as an alternative but the idea was dropped when it was realized that they would cost much more than a second preparatory year.

Best made many recommendations. He recommended higher salaries and better retirement benefits. (It was noted that some school for the deaf superintendents were earning more than the president of Gallaudet College.) He favored the addition of an alumni representative to the college Board of Directors and pointed out a need for new facilities. He recommended abandoning the free scholarship concept,

Some educators are glad to hide away in obscure nooks and corners the products of their labor. It is best for their theories. It is best for the unfortunate recipients of their methods that the public see them not. The intelligent deaf, however, have no reason to hide or lose themselves in the press of the hearing world. They need not fear to come forth in the full glare of the public gaze, and express their opinions and support their ideas in educational matters or whatever else that pertains to their welfare.

—GEORGE M. TEEGARDEN
1890s

suggesting instead that the college be appropriated a lump sum. He argued that states should share part of the costs. Best recommended that the college remain at its present site and suggested that half of the campus could be sold. He felt that the faculty should be encouraged to participate in more professional activities off campus and that the students should be encouraged to attend certain classes at other local programs. He recommended that the college provide a summer school "at least every few years if not on alternate years."

Best encouraged the establishment of a research department to serve as a national clearinghouse and an information bureau to respond to queries about deafness. He saw a need for a department to train deaf teachers of the deaf since only hearing students were admitted to the existing teacher training program.

He urged for an extension department offering non-credit courses and he urged expanding visual education through the use of motion pictures, slides, charts, exhibits, etc. He proposed a better organized sports program, the construction of a gymnasium and the hiring of a full-time athletic staff. Best also suggested making Kendall School a national model school. He advised against admitting hard of hearing students to the college.

Some saw the Best Survey as the "Gallaudet renaissance." The alumni applauded it. Some believed that if the recommendations were implemented they would make Gallaudet the "Educational Mecca of the Deaf World."

Others were disappointed with the Best Survey. One called it wishy-washy. Government officials felt that the study failed to respond to more important and more specific questions. They wanted to know what methods of instruction should be employed in teaching the deaf. They wanted to know whether

Gallaudet College in the 1920s.
Gallaudet College Archives.

higher educational opportunities for deaf persons should be provided in a separate institution such as Gallaudet or in a regular college program for hearing students. What bearing did audiology training and the use of hearing aids have on the education of the deaf? What type of curricular program was best? What were some of the problems encountered by deaf students and what special instructional facilities or methods were needed to meet those needs?

The officials at the Federal Security Agency did not feel they could go before Congress and ask for increased support for Gallaudet College on the basis of the Best Survey. In search of a solution they turned to Dr. Buell G. Gallagher, a consultant to the Federal Security Administrator and a former college president.

On a shelf in the Deaf Collection of the Edward Miner Gallaudet Memorial Library is a bound, fading copy of a report entitled: "The Federal Government

The aim of the education of the deaf should be to make him a well-balanced, happy individual and not a pale imitation of a hearing person. Let us aim to produce happy, well-adjusted deaf individuals, each different from the other, each with his own personality.

—DR. RUDOLPH PINTNER

and the Higher Education of the Deaf." The check-out card bears only two dates. Few people know who Gallagher was or know the importance of this document, which played such an important role in expanding higher educational opportunities for deaf people and changing the face of Gallaudet College.

Gallagher's study was more extensive than Best's and involved a broad selection of interested individuals including alumni, professional people, people

Gallaudet College in the 1970s.
Gallaudet College Archives.

interested in the education of the deaf and others. It was divided into two parts. The first part identified the educational needs of deaf students and the second part made recommendations for responding to those needs.

In his report, Gallagher noted that in an earlier National Health Survey five stages of deafness had been identified. These five stages ranged from partial deafness to a person born totally deaf who had no speech. For his study he chose the term "educationally deaf." This group included the student with "acoustical handicaps" who could not "be satisfactorily taught in the regular classes for hearing students" without special instruction to meet and master his handicap."

Gallagher identified the educational needs of deaf students, noted the prevalence of deafness according to family income, age and sex; estimated the number of "educationally deaf" persons in the United States of school age and included information on the number of them enrolled in different programs. Based on these figures Gallagher observed: " . . . there is a disquietingly wide discrepancy in opportunity for higher education between deaf and hearing youth in the United States . . . the discrepancy between the numbers needing instruction and the numbers receiving it is so great as to constitute a major challenge to the conscience of American citizens. At the college level, the discrepancy is shocking." He compared, for example, the 210 deaf students then in college (at Gallaudet and elsewhere) to the estimated 5,586 who would have been attending college if the percentage of deaf high school students who enrolled in post secondary programs equalled that of hearing students.

To provide a "first-rank National college for the deaf" Gallagher prescribed "an imaginative and bold reconstruction of prevailing patterns and programs at Gallaudet College." He suggested that the federal government either provide adequate support for the college or abandon it completely. He proposed that the corporate name of the Columbia Institution for the Deaf be changed to Gallaudet College and that the charter be revised clarifying the relationship between the college and the federal government.

Best's Study received much publicity and space in the *Gallaudet Alumni Bulletin* and *The Cavalier*. There was little mention of Gallagher's report. Those familiar with the Gallagher report and its significance are somewhat irritated that Best received so much of the credit for what eventually transpired when the work of Gallagher contributed so greatly to the success of the growth of Gallaudet College.

To many, Gallagher's report was a challenging and exciting document. James N. Orman, then secretary of the Gallaudet College Alumni Association, recalls: "The impact of this [Gallagher] study was without question much greater than the previous [Best's] one." Boyce R. Williams remembers Gallagher as "the most persuasive and effective person I have ever met, a joy to work with." In Williams' opinion Gallagher was the most important individual in bringing about the changes.

In September 1950 approximately 70 new students were admitted to Gallaudet College, an all-time high. Among the newcomers were six foreign students. They came from Israel, Sweden, China, Trans-Jordan, Canada and Denmark. A year later Boyce R. Williams, president of the GCAA, was named the first alumni representative to the college Board of Directors. The following year the college applied for but failed to qualify for accreditation.

In 1954 Congress approved H.R. 6655. This Act of Congress changed the corporate name of the Columbia Institution for the Deaf to Gallaudet College and clearly defined the college's corporate powers. The college retained its private character, and this bill recognized and confirmed the financial responsibility of Congress to Gallaudet College.

On June 4, 1955 ground was broken for the $350,000 Edward Miner Gallaudet Memorial Library. Funds for the construction of this building included $100,000 from the alumni's Edward Miner Gallaudet Memorial fund, $240,000 from Congress and $10,000 from the Eugene Meyer Foundation. That first spadeful of dirt marked a very significant transformation process that would in time change the small, sleepy liberal arts college into a Greater Gallaudet. A federally funded multi-million dollar construction program had just begun.

Chapter 11

Publications of the Deaf

T H E R A D I I

VOLUME 1. CANAJOHARIE, N. Y. FRIDAY, AUGUST 11, 1837. NUMBER 28.

THE RADII
IS PUBLISHED EVERY FRIDAY AT CANAJOHARIE, MONTGOMERY COUNTY, NEW YORK, BY
LEVI S. BACKUS,
(Formerly an instructer in the Central Asylum, and professor of the sign language.)
Terms of Publication.
To village subscribers, $2.
Those who take their papers at the Office, or receive them by mail, $1.50, payable in advance, or two dollars, if not paid within the current year.
No paper will be discontinued until all arrearages are paid, unless at the option of [illegible]

POETRY.

TO SUSAN.

Fair sunny girl, bright as the flowers
O'er which young Eve's sparkling showers
Her mantle throws.
Pure as the lily's op'ning bell,
That loveliest blooms, in loneliest dell,
My sweet bewitching Su.

Well might the star of summer night,
Pale 'neath the bright and sunny light
Those eyes disclose.
And coral cells, and pearly caves,
Rest not alone beneath the waves,
My sweet enchanting Su.

But there's a charm far richer dye
Than coral tip, or laughing eye,
[illegible]
A flower whose bright and lasting bloom,
Outlives the darkest, dreariest tomb,
My fond and faithful SU.

Love is the stream's perpetual flow—
Truth is the flower's enduring glow,
That every fragrance throws.
Mine own sweet friend, around that heart,
So guileless in this world of art,
My fond and faithful SU.

The Blue Laws of Connecticut.

The following is a transcript of the primitive judicial code which existed in the state of Connecticut during the time of its first settlers and their immediate descendants [illegible] of Connecticut.

The Assembly of the people shall not be dismissed by the Governor, but shall dismiss itself.

Conspiracy against the dominion shall be punished with DEATH.

Whoever says "there is a power holding jurisdiction over and above this dominion," shall be punished with DEATH and loss of property.

Whoever attempts to change or overturn this dominion shall suffer DEATH.

The Judges shall determine controversies without a jury.

No one shall be a freeman or give a vote unless he be *converted or a member in full communion of one of the churches allowed in this dominion.*

No one shall hold any office who is not *sound in the faith*, and faithful to this dominion; and whoever gives a vote to such a person shall pay a fine of a pound. For the second offence he shall be disfranchised.

No Quaker, or Dissenter from the established worshipper of this dominion, shall be allowed to give a vote for the election of magistrate or any officer.

No food and lodgings shall be allowed to a *Quaker, Adamite, or other heretic.*

If any person shall turn Quaker, he shall be banished, and not suffered to return on pain of DEATH.

No Priest shall abide in this dominion. He shall be banished and suffer DEATH on his return. Priests may be seized by *any one without a warrant.*

No one shall cross a river but with an authorized ferryman.

No man shall run of a Sabbath day or walk in his garden or elsewhere, except reverently to and from church.

No one shall travel, cook victuals, make beds, sweep houses, cut hair, or shave on the Sabbath day.

No woman shall *kiss her child on* Sabbath or fasting day.

A person accused of trespass in the night, shall be adjudged guilty, unless he clear himself by his oath.

When it appears that an accomplice has confederates, and he refuses to discover them, he may be RACKED.

No one shall buy or sell lands without the permission of the select men.

A drunkard shall have a master appointed by the select men, who is to debar him the privilege of buying or selling.

Whoever publishes a lie to the prejudice of his neighbor shall sit in the stocks or be whipped [illegible]

No minister shall keep a school.

Man-stealers shall suffer DEATH.

Whoever wears clothes trimmed with silver or bone lace above two shillings a yard shall be presented by the grand jurors; and the select men shall tax the offender at the rate of three hundred pounds estate.

A *debtor in prison*, swearing he has no estate, shall be let out and *sold to make satisfaction.*

Whoever sets fire to the woods, and it burns a house, shall suffer DEATH, and persons *suspected* of the crime shall be imprisoned without the benefit of bail.

Whoever brings cards or dice into this dominion shall pay a fine of five pounds.

No one shall read common prayer, keep Christmas or saint's day, make mince pies, dance, play on any instrument of music, except the drum, the trumpet, and Jew's harp.

When parents refuse their children suitable marriages, the magistrate shall determine the point.

The select men, on finding children ignorant, may take them away from their parents and put them in to better hands, at the expense of the parents.

[illegible] that strikes her husband shall be punished as the court directs.

A wife shall be deemed good evidence against her husband.

No one shall court a maid without first obtaining the consent of her parents—five pounds penalty for the first offence—ten pounds for the second; and for the third, imprisonment during the pleasure of the court.

Married persons shall live together or be imprisoned.

Every male shall have his hair cut round according to a cap.

She would be a Sailor.—It will be recollected, that about two years ago an individual was arrested in this city upon a charge of stealing a horse, and was tried and found guilty of the offence, and sentenced to two years' imprisonment in the State Prison, under the name of *Charles Stewart*. It was soon afterwards discovered by the prisoners, that Charley belonged to the feminine gender, and information having been given to the keepers of the fact, she was divested of her roundabout and trowsers, and sent over to the female department of Bellevue prison. Yesterday the term of imprisonment having expired, she was told that she was at liberty to depart, offering her at the same time a decent dress of female attire to begin the world anew with. This proposition, however, she indignantly rejected, demanding as her right the same clothing that was taken away from her. Finding she could not obtain them, she came down in the forenoon, in her prison dress, and solicited aid of the Almshouse, and was told to wait till one of the commissioners arrived. In the mean time she paraded herself up on the grass plots of the Park, and excited so much interest, after the spectators found out who she was, as to attract a considerable mob, when she was persuaded to submit to a temporary commitment until a hearing of her case could be had. It appears that this singular young woman, who is not over 19 or 20 years of age, had for six years followed the sea in the capacity of a common sailor, doing all sorts of hard duty, and subject to all the privations and toils of a sea life, without her sex ever having been discovered. The reason for assuming the character of a sailor she would never disclose.— She is a Scotch girl, and is represented by the officers as the most decent being they ever had under their charge. Sometimes she has been known to maintain a good conduct with two of her keepers at [illegible] She never wor[illegible] a day in prison, although she has been beaten, starved, and chained to effect the object; she has been chained to the floor 15 months of her imprisonment. Scarcely any one dared to approach her cell to give her food, as she would knock them down with a [illegible] as soon as they entered. Her moral character, with the exceptions above alluded to, is good. Her object is to get a suit of sailor's clothes, and go to sea again.—*N. Y. Express.*

From the Saturday Morning Transcript.

RECENT OCCURRENCES.—We are indebted to the New York Sunday Morning News for the following interesting items:

Gentleman advertises for a wife. Member of Deaf and Dumb Asylum offers. Gentleman doesn't think she'll answer.

Man at Weehawken kills seventeen black snakes. Walks in that neighborho[od] [illegible] and *serpentine.*

Western paper describes a duel, and says, "one of the parties was shot through the *fleshy* part of the thigh *bone.*"

[illegible] in dirty linen. [illegible] to no sole [illegible] scarcity of shirts, and not to any philosophical negligence in the wearer of them.

Short man in green spectacles and pale young lady in lilac colored bonnet, display their oratory in Broadway. Short man, it seemed, had jilted pale young lady. Lady says she's "A LONE WOMAN." Man replies, she "may be so and be—."

Judge in Connecticut decides that all roads are *passable*—if you pay the turnpike.

Actress at a party, rather thinly clad. Not exactly an evening dress, but a dress suitable for *Eve.*

Scene opposite Niblo's, between a hack driver and a journeyman tailor. Tailor *sheers* off, *clips* it, and stops on the *skirts* of the town.

Mrs. Cent, of Wisconsin, presents her husband with three little ones. Husband poor; children *copper-colored.*

Woman sick up town. Wants food; physician substitutes physic; woman dies.

Sailor on Peck's slip falls down in an apoplexy. Lookers on think him dead, but recommend bleeding. Man jabs a jack-knife into him. Sailor under the impression that he is still alive.

Surgeon Hazlehurst buys a subject. Subject, child two years old. Price agreed on shilling an inch.— Resurrectionist dislocates child's neck in trying to make it an inch longer. Doctor considers goods damaged, and refuses to pay.

Two JOINT EXECUTORS at the Globe hotel, in Broadway, commence carving each other. Recorder orders them to "FORK-UP,"—in default of which, cooks removed from the kitchen to the BAR ROOM.

Gentleman in Greenwich street witnesses the ceremony of lowering a porter hogshead from a dray into a beer cellar. Drayman gives him a certificate of attendance, by throwing a greasy rope over his white pantaloons.

Big ship at Philadelphia. End of her flying jibboom knocks over a city steeple; tail of her pennant sweeps a flock of sheep off the Jersey shore.

Rich widow at the Astor house goes on a sailing excursion down the bay. "Great speculation afloat."

Fishing excursion to the banks. Passengers all sick. "A-vast heaving!"

[illegible] [From the New Orleans Picayune of the 19th.] This notorious black scoundrel was yesterday killed by a Spaniard in the swamp near the Bayou road. It will be remembered by all our citizens that Squire was the negro who has so long prowled about the marshes in the rear of the city, a terror to the community, and for whose head a reward of two thousand dollars was offered some years ago. The life of this negro has been one of crime and total depravity. The annals of the city furnish records of his cruelty, crime and [illegible] He had killed several white men in this place before he fled to the swamp, and has, up to the time of his death, eluded with a dexterity worthy of a more educated villain, all the searching efforts of justice to capture him. He has lived for the last three years an outlaw in the marshes in the rear of the city. Many years since he had his right arm shot off; he is said, notwithstanding this deprivation, to have been an excellent marksman, with but the use of his left arm. Inured by hardships and exposure to the climate, he has subsisted in the [illegible] murder with the most perfect impunity—the marshes surrounding the city being almost impenetrable to our citizens. This demi-devil has for a long time ruled as the "Brigand of the Swamp." A supposition has always found believers that there was an encampment of outlaw negroes near the city, and that Squire was their leader. He has done much mischief in the way of decoying slaves to his camp, and in committing depredations upon the premises of those who live on the outskirts of the city. His destruction is hailed by old and young, as a benefit to society. A Spaniard was yesterday morning in the swamp and proved the successfully enemy of this foe to society. Squire raised his gun to shoot him, but failed, the gun having snapped. Immediately the Spaniard rushed upon him with a big stick—he gave him a blow which brought him to the ground, when his brains were literally beat out by the infuriated man. Proud of his victory, the conqueror came into the city, and reported what he has done. On hearing that Squire was dead, the authorities determined to have his body hauled to the city, and forthwith appointed a guard of men to repair to the swamp and bring it in. About two o'clock yesterday his body was exhibited on the public square of the First Municipality. It is to be hoped that the death of this leader of the outlaw negroes supposed to be in the swamp, will lead to the scouring of the swamp round about the city. This nest of desperadoes should be broken up.

AWFUL DISTRESS.—A correspondent relates the following circumstances illustrative of the terrible hard times. About a week ago, at the request of his wife, he advertised for a maid servant. Applications for the place commenced the day after the advertisement appeared. The first one who applied inquired what wages would be paid her. The answer was six dollars a month. "I'll not work for any body for less than seven; and she went off. The next made no objection to the pay, but inquired how many there were in the family. Being informed, she said it was too mighty a concern for her to manage, folded her arms and bade the lady of the house good morrow. The third refused the place because there was no carpet on the kitchen floor. The fourth because she could not be allowed to go to mass every Sunday morning while the mistress prepared the breakfast, [illegible] the privilege of two afternoons in the week for recreation. The fifth on account of the unwillingness of employer to allow the nightly visits of her dear cousin St. Patrick Shelaly. The seventh could not wash—she did not like the looks of par boiled hands. The eighth made pretty fair promises to do all the prescribed requisites but the last. "If you wish your front steps scoured so often as that, you may do that [illegible]

[illegible] Snyder Rumajum, a Dutch sugar and gin merchant in London, many [illegible] creditors so uncompromising, that to save his merchandise from their greedy clutches, and his body from immurement in the Fleet Prison, he transferred the nominal ownership of his property to a friend, dismissed his clerks, provided himself with sufficient provender, and locking up and barricading his store with himself in it, resolved to abide there until he could dodge the bailiffs and beat a nocturnal retreat to Holland. His enraged creditors placed their bailiffs and catchpoles about the store for a long while to [illegible] smoked his pipe in security and bade them all go to the teufel!"— The bailiffs in grand consultation, at last hit upon a scheme. It was, for all to retire from the premises apparently, and then one of the Dutchman's discharged clerks, whom they had bribed, was to persuade his master to hoist up by the windlass a hogshead of materials to assist his escape. In this hogshead one of their number was to be privately secreted, and when safely hoisted into the store might arrest the Dutchman without farther trouble. The bailiff headed up in the hogshead with a writ in his pocket, was hoisted up by the unsuspecting trader to the scuttle door, when imagining himself housed, he knocked off the top of his narrow hiding-place, and poking out his long head and gaunt shoulders, with writ extended at arms length in left hand, and staff of office in his right, exclaimed with triumphant chuckle, "Snyder Rumajum, I arrest you in the King's name!" Unfortunate bailiff—ill-timed chuckle! In pretended amazement the phlegmatic Dutchman seized his hands into his pockets, of course quitting hold of the rope which supported the hogshead and officer! and down they tumbled four or five stories "coming the circumrotary" in fine style, and eventually precipitating the astounded bailiff into a hogshead of molasses which stood in the yard below—from which he was extricated with some difficulty, but no further damage than a tremendous sweetening! The Dutchman finally escaped to Holland.

In the town of T——, N. Y. a young man had concluded to be wedded to a Miss of 'sweet eighteen.' The day was set—friends invited, and the clergyman called. After the nuptial vows were made and the usual ceremonies performed, the bridegroom, with much dignity and solemnity, stepped up to the Rev. Sir, and in a respectful tone, said—"*Sir, will you wait till fall and take your pay in corn?*"—Obs'r.

Library of Congress

The 'Silent' Press

Evi S. Backus (b. 1803) is credited with being the originator of what eventually became known as the silent press. The word "silent" was a popular term used to describe newspapers and magazines published in the interests of deaf people in the early part of the century but it has since lost its popularity.

Backus was a product of the American School for the Deaf, where he studied for five years and was a pupil of Laurent Clerc. Backus became editor and proprietor of the *Canajoharie* (N.Y.) *Radii*, a weekly newspaper printed in that city which was once the location of the Central New York Asylum for the Deaf and Dumb. Backus had taught at that school. When it closed he acquired the *Radii* in 1837, becoming the first deaf editor of a newspaper on record in the country. The *Radii's* banner was in fingerspelling. Backus added a column consisting of news of interest to deaf persons in the community addressing, at least partially, some of the needs of his deaf readers while continuing to serve the interests of the hearing population. In 1844 he was successful in persuading the New York State Legislature to appropriate some funds so that he could mail the *Radii* to "educated deaf people" throughout the state.

Horace Greeley, writing in *The New Yorker*, described Backus' editorials as being "sententious and sensible, his selections judicious," and his newspaper, "every way respectable."

When Backus' printing office burned down in 1846 he moved his printing plant to Fort Plain, New York and the *Radii* was renamed the *Montgomery County Phoenix.* This name did not catch on, however, and it was later changed to the *Radii and Phoenix.*

On February 19, 1847, nine members of the faculty of the American Asylum for the Deaf wrote a letter to the school administration and the Board of Directors proposing the establishment of a quarterly periodical which would be "devoted to the discussion of topics relating to the Deaf and Dumb . . ." The group had investigated the costs of printing such a periodical and found that 1,000 copies of an average of 80 pages each could be printed four times a year at a cost of $488. The Board was receptive to the suggestion and shortly afterwards the *American Annals of the Deaf* was born. The *Annals* became the organ of the Conference of American Instructors of the Deaf and the Conference of Executives of American Schools for the Deaf. Today the *Annals* is the oldest journal devoted to the education of the deaf in the world and the oldest American educational journal in continuous publication since its inception, according to the Library of Congress. The *Annals* was initially printed at the American School. (It suspended publication in June 1861 on account of the Civil War and resumed publication in 1868 at the North Carolina Institution then located in Raleigh.)

In 1860 *The Gallaudet Guide and Deaf-Mutes' Companion,* the first periodical printed exclusively for deaf persons, began appearing monthly. It was edited by William M. Chamberlain and printed in Boston from 1860 to 1865. The banner of the *Guide* included pictures of Thomas Hopkins Gallaudet and Laurent Clerc. The newspaper proclaimed itself "An Independent

This letter led to the creation of the American Annals of the Deaf

American School for the Deaf

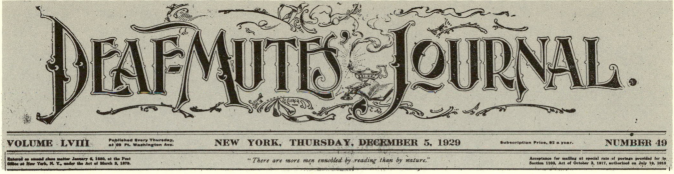

VOLUME LVIII   Published Every Thursday, at 95 Ft. Washington Ave.   NEW YORK, THURSDAY, DECEMBER 5, 1929   Subscription Price, $2 a year.   NUMBER 49

Entered as second class matter January 6, 1885, at the Post Office at New York, N. Y., under the Act of March 3, 1879.

"There are more men ennobled by reading than by nature."

Acceptance for mailing at special rate of postage provided for in Section 1103, Act of October 3, 1917, authorized on July 19, 1918.

Mast head of the old Deaf-Mutes' Journal.

Monthly Journal Devoted to the Interests of Deaf Mutes." It was the official organ of the New England Gallaudet Association of the Deaf.

Sometime around 1870 Henry C. Rider acquired possession of Backus' *Radii*. A year later Rider began a column for deaf readers in the *Mexico* (N.Y.) *Independent*. This column grew into a full page and Rider named it the *Deaf-Mutes' Journal*. With the state subsidy which he had also acquired from Backus, Rider began sending the newspaper to deaf persons throughout the state. In 1875 Rider started his own printing business and began printing the *Deaf-Mutes' Journal* independently. The *Journal* became the first weekly newspaper of the deaf. Later the New York School for the Deaf took over publication of the newspaper with Edwin A. Hodgson, the school's printing instructor, as editor. Hodgson was editor from 1878 to 1931 for a total of 53 years. Under his leadership the *Journal* became one of the most popular newspapers of its day. Hodgson was succeeded as editor by Thomas F. Fox. The name of the *Deaf-Mutes' Journal* was changed to *New York Journal of the Deaf*. It ceased publication in 1951.

In 1871 Melville Ballard, John B. Hotchkiss, Joseph B. Parkinson and James Denison teamed up and started the first literary magazine for the deaf, *The Silent World*. The *World* was published in Washington, D.C. Unfortunately, the publication lasted only five years. Its demise was blamed on the fact that the average deaf reader did not appreciate its highly literary nature. In 1887 the name was adopted by the Mt. Airy School, which began publishing *The Mt. Airy World*.

In 1894 O. H. Regensburg of Chicago formed a stock company and began publishing *The National Exponent*, which was described as "a bright, lively and fearless weekly paper published in the interests of the deaf." Regensburg owned a printing business in partnership

Ten Oldest Educational Publications of the Deaf Still Being Published

Compiled by Steven A. Frank

(Edward Miner Gallaudet Memorial Library)

Year	Current Name (Original Name)	Publisher
1847	*American Annals of the Deaf* (same)	Convention of American Instructors of the Deaf and Conference of Executives of American Schools for the Deaf
1849	*The North Carolinian (Deaf Mute)*	North Carolina School for the Deaf
1868	*The Ohio Chronicle (The Mute)*	Ohio School for the Deaf
1870	*The Illinois Advance (Deaf-Mute Advance)*	Illinois School for the Deaf
1874	*The Kentucky Standard (Kentucky Deaf-Mute)*	Kentucky School for the Deaf
1874	*The Michigan Mirror (Deaf-Mute Mirror)*	Michigan School for the Deaf
1874	*The Nebraska Journal (Mute Journal of Nebraska Deaf)*	Nebraska School for the Deaf
1874	*The Virginia Guide (The Goodson Gazette)*	Virginia School for the Deaf and the Blind
1875	*The Colorado Index* (same)	Colorado School for the Deaf and the Blind
1875	*The Kansas Star* (same)	Kansas School for the Deaf

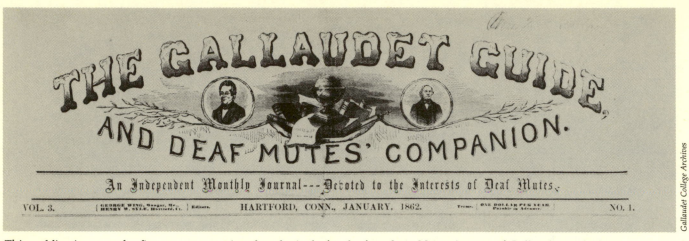

THE GALLAUDET GUIDE, AND DEAF MUTES' COMPANION.

An Independent Monthly Journal---Devoted to the Interests of Deaf Mutes.

VOL. 3. { GEORGE WING, Manager, &c., HENRY W. SYLE, Hartford, Ct. } Editors. HARTFORD, CONN., JANUARY, 1862. Terms. { ONE DOLLAR PER YEAR, Payable in Advance. } NO. 1.

Gallaudet College Archives

This publication was the first to appear printed exclusively for deaf readers. Note pictures of Gallaudet and Clerc.

with a hearing man. The firm was called Regensburg & Seckbach, Printers. On the *Exponent* staff were some of the best deaf journalists of the day. Robert P. McGregor was editor-in-chief; James H. Cloud and J. Schuyler Long were associate editors; George W. Veditz was foreign editor and James E. Gallaher was managing editor. Regensburg retained the title as manager. The paper reached a peak circulation of over 1,200. It folded in August, 1896.

Among the editors of publications of the deaf, short, portly George S. Porter was one of the giants. As a youth growing up in Liberty, New York, Porter delighted in spending his leisure moments at the town print shop watching the presses run. It is probably here that he got his first whiff of printer's ink and the type lice bit. He was educated at the New York School (Fanwood) where he came under the tutelage of Edwin A. Hodgson, editor of the well-known *Deaf-Mutes Journal*. Upon graduation from NYSD in 1884, Porter was offered the position of assistant foreman. Six years later he moved to Little Rock to become printing instructor at the Arkansas School for the Deaf. From Little Rock he moved to Trenton, New Jersey where he accepted the position of printing instructor and

associate editor at the New Jersey School. In Trenton, Porter inherited a small tabloid-size, four-page newspaper named *The Deaf-Mute Times*. After a few issues, the *Times* was renamed *The Silent Worker* and, as if using a magic wand, Porter and Editor Weston Jenkins began transforming that flimsy four-pager into the best magazine deaf readers in the country had ever seen.

For seven years *The Silent Worker* was printed on a small Gordon job press, one page at a time. The increase in circulation and the growth in the number of ads made this press inadequate. When the print shop was moved to new quarters in the school's new industrial building a new press was purchased. Porter was one of the first to add photoengraving equipment to his shop. This new printing plant had separate composing rooms, one for the boys and one for the girls.

Porter changed the tabloid to a magazine format and filled the pages with features about outstanding deaf and hearing leaders of the day, histories of schools for the deaf, travelogues, and news on major events. There was an industrial column and news written by correspondents from other parts of the country. For a while the *Worker* even printed a garden column written by the editor's wife. *The Silent Worker's* pages were filled with pictures and attractive works of art, most of it done by deaf photographers and artists. On the covers of many issues were pictures of deaf persons of note. Porter admitted at one time that *The Silent Worker* was paying more for paper and cuts (pictures) than it was receiving from subscriptions. With this attractive, news-packed magazine, he gave his former mentor, Hodgson, and the *Deaf-Mutes' Journal* some stiff competition. Porter was a man who was obviously in love with his work and each issue of the *Worker* reflected that. He always placed emphasis

---

There is some complaint with Uncle Sam's mail, or some misunderstanding about mailable packages. One father wrote making application for his son [for admission to the North Carolina School] and said: "I have a deaf and dumb son, as you will find enclosed." But the boy was not found. Whether the package was rifled, remains to be seen.

—THE KELLY MESSENGER
1895

The SILENT WORKER

OCTOBER 1928

Dactylology

An early cover of the old Silent Worker.

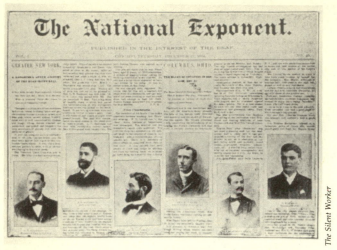

The National Exponent *was written and published by some of the best writers a publication of the deaf ever had.*

on quality, and in his writings he steered clear of personal controversy, a practice not all editors adhered to in those days.

An ad promoting The Silent Worker.

HONEYMOONING

When your honeymoon is over read THE SILENT WORKER every month and be always happy.

When Porter announced his retirement in 1928 after 36 years—it was later postponed a year—friends, fellow editors and former students got together and produced a special 46-page issue of *The Silent Worker* which was dedicated to him. With his retirement the new school administration decided not to continue publication of *The Silent Worker* in the school's print shop. The administration felt that the magazine had become more than a school paper and that it no longer fulfilled the school's objective. On June, 1929 the last issue of the magazine was put to bed; the great *Silent Worker* was no more.

Other publications came and went.

The American Deaf Citizen appeared in March 1929 the same year *The Silent Worker* ceased publication. It was printed at Versailles, Ohio and edited by Roy B. Conkling. It ceased publication in 1942.

In June 1937 *The Modern Silents* began publication in

A Cavalier *promotion.*

Dallas, Texas. It appeared in a large magazine format and was printed on glossy stock similar to the old *Silent Worker*. It was edited and published by Leo Lewis, a printer and president of the Texas Association of the Deaf. *The Modern Silents* was the official organ of the Texas Association of the Deaf. The magazine was dedicated ". . . to the interests of the deaf and with the purpose of showing the accomplish-ments of deaf citizens." The first few issues were filled with advertisements. It printed a religion column, poetry, general news and many pictures. The magazine's most notable achievement was the changes in the administration at the Texas School for the Deaf that it helped bring about through persistent and hard-hitting editorials. *The Modern Silents* ceased publication in 1939.

Miscellaneous publications of the deaf that have appeared through the years.

The Sports Parade

The Sports Parade *sought to appeal to the deaf sportsman. It folded after a few years.*

In October 1938 the *Digest of the Deaf* rolled off the press. The *Digest* was a monthly magazine printed in Springfield, Massachusetts. In format it was slightly larger than *The Reader's Digest.* It was supported by subscriptions, contributions, and a few ads, and was sent gratis to hearing persons in important positions, agencies and corporations to acquaint them with the accomplishments of deaf people in such fields as art, science and industry. Willard H. Woods and Eleanor E. Sherman were editors. Woods was the publisher. Charles Moscovitz was managing editor and Florence B. Crammatte was associate editor. Such names as Guilbert C. Braddock, Petra F. Howard, Wesley Lauritsen, Margaret E. Jackson and Howard L. Terry appeared among the list of contributing editors. The *Digest of the Deaf* was printed from October, 1938 until March 1940. It contained art work by deaf artists, poetry, biographies of deaf persons, and other related material of interest to or about deaf persons.

In the 1940's Reuben S. Altizer, a deaf Virginian, started *The Silent Cavalier,* a monthly newspaper named for the state in which he resided. It started as an organ of the Virginia Association of the Deaf but gradually grew into a national newspaper. In 1943

Altizer moved the paper to Washington, D.C. and enlarged the staff to include Alan B. Crammatte, Henry Holter, Wallace Edington and Gunnar Rath. Altizer was publisher and Crammatte was the editor. The paper began to grow in prominence and circulation and soon dropped the word "silent" from its banner because it did not jell with its increasingly vocal editorial stand on issues affecting deaf people. The *Cavalier* bought *The Silent Broadcaster,* then being published in California by Toivo Lindholm and acquired the mailing list of the *Deaf-Mutes' Journal.*

The *Cavalier* became a very vocal newspaper. It criticized the National Association of the Deaf for not being more active, attacked the peddling issue and supported an enlarged Gallaudet College and more and better federally sponsored services to deaf people. At its peak the *Cavalier* had over 4,000 paid subscribers.

The *Cavalier* was sold to Edgar M. Winecoff and Luther Bunn and moved to Winston-Salem, North Carolina where it was merged in October 1952 with *The Southerner* and Troy Hill's *American Deaf News* to become *The National Observer.* The *Observer* was printed in a print shop owned by the publishers. The

Silent News is a more recent newspaper.

Silent News

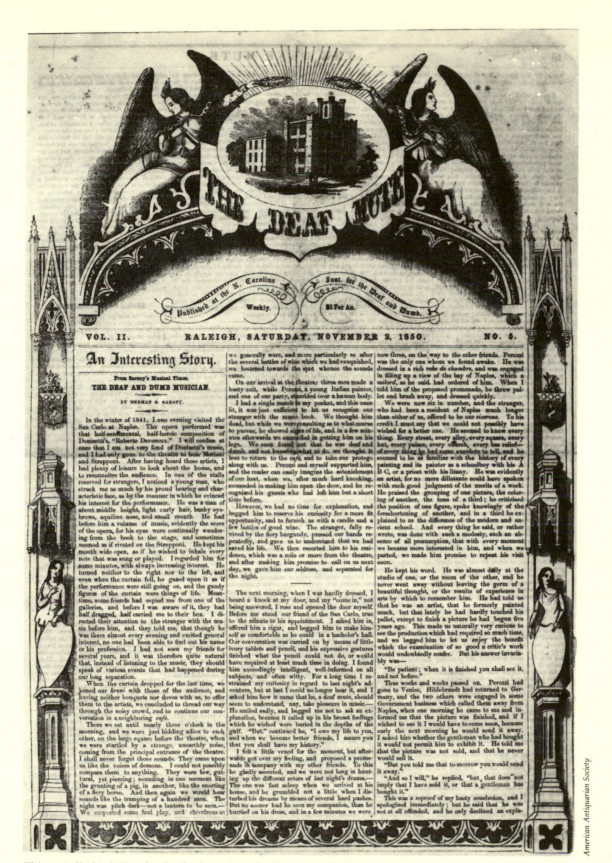

This periodical is believed to be the first school for the deaf publication in this country.

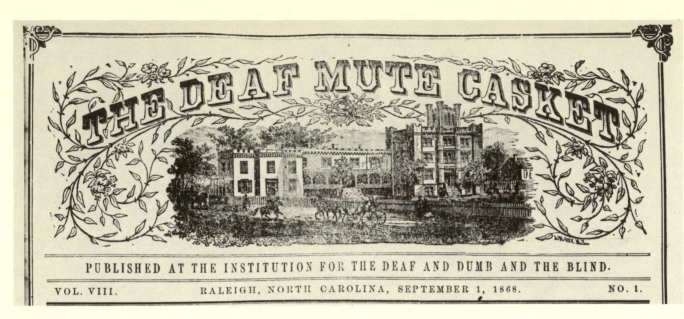

The Deaf Mute Casket succeeded *The Deaf Mute* (preceding page).

publishers were on the verge of publishing it bi-weekly but were unable to generate enough income from subscriptions to keep the publication going. It folded in 1956.

In September 1948 *The Silent Worker* was revived as the official organ of the National Association of the Deaf with Bill R. White as editor and Harry M. Jacobs as business manager. Leo M. Jacobs and Catherine A. Marshall were associate editors. Others on the staff included Mrs. Loel F. Schreiber, Gordon B. Allen, Richard G. Brill, Mervin D. Garretson, John H. Mc-Farlane, Lillian Hahn and J. Frederick Meagher. McFarlane had contributed to the old *Silent Worker* and Meagher had been one of its regular columnists. Loel Schreiber replaced White as editor when he resigned about a year later and when she had to give up the responsibilities in 1951, Byron B. Burnes assumed the task on a temporary basis. That "temporary basis" lasted until January 1959 when Jim M. Smith, first vice president of the NAD and a teacher at the Tennessee School for the Deaf, was appointed editor.

Smith was a graduate of the University of Tennessee. During his undergraduate days he was sports editor and editor-in-chief of the university's student newspaper. He later did a stint at the copy desk of a Knoxville daily while teaching English at TSD. Under Smith's tenure *The Silent Worker* went through some very lean years and for a time was printed at the Tennessee School for the Deaf and at Pettingill's Printcraft in Lewiston, Idaho. The shop was owned by Don G. Pettingill. Gradually the magazine gained in circulation and in 1964 the name was changed to *The Deaf American*. (Another publication by that name had

been published from 1888 to 1929.) In 1980 the magazine was moved to the National Association of the Deaf headquarters in Silver Spring, Maryland, and Muriel Horton-Strassler was hired on a full-time basis to edit it and a companion newspaper, *The NAD Broadcaster* which had been started in 1979.

The Silent News, a monthly newspaper, began appearing in January 1969. Julius Wiggins and his wife publish the newspaper in their print shop in Lincoln Park, New Jersey. It is edited by Walter M. Schulman. A year after its appearance, the newspaper had over 1,000 subscribers and within a few years it had exceeded the 3,000 mark.

The Deaf Spectrum made its appearance in January 1970. It was an eight and one-half inches by 11 inches newsletter, mostly typewritten, and with the pages stapled together. The *Spectrum* was probably the closest thing the deaf community has ever seen to a muckraking newspaper. The *Spectrum* was pro-total communication and attacked oralism with a rabid fervor. It attracted quite an audience. It was published by Clarence Supalla in Beaverton, Oregon.

There have been close to 500 publications—ranging from mimeographed newsletters to slick magazines—printed in the interest of deaf persons in this country. Most have been religious and school publications. Others have included club, state association and national publications. Around 63 have used the word "silent" in their banner.

The Ranch Hand, published by the Bill Rice Ranch in Murfreesboro, Tennessee, with its 100,000 circulation, is probably the most widely disseminated religious publication.

246

The *NTID Focus* (17,000), the *Gallaudet Alumni News-letter* (16,200), *The Frat* (12,000), *The Volta Review* (7,100), *The Deaf American* (7,000) are leading national publications.

The *Dee Cee Eyes,* a monthly, started in Washington, D.C. by Frederick C. Schreiber and the *Lincoln Silent Club News* started by John Reed are two club publications which have maintained long continuous publication. The *LSC News* is no longer published.

Ye Silent Crier of the New England Gallaudet Association of the Deaf, the *Empire State News,* and the *W.A.D. Pilot* are among the oldest state and regional publications.

The Little Paper Family

In 1849 *The Deaf Mute,* a monthly and the first school for the deaf newspaper made its appearance at the North Carolina Institution for the Deaf, Dumb, and the Blind. It was first called *The Deaf Mute* and later *The Deaf Mute Casket,* the last word being added for reasons known only to those individuals involved with the publication during those bygone years. Three copies of original issues of this publication are known to exist. Two copies are in the North Carolina Collection at the University of North Carolina, Chapel Hill, and one copy, dated November 2, 1850, is in the American Antiquarian Society in Worcester, Massachusetts.

In 1868 *The Ohio Chronicle* appeared, followed two years later by *The Illinois Advance.* In 1873 *The Kentucky Standard* made its debut. In 1874 the Virginia School received a bequest from John H. Goodson and used the money to purchase some type and a printing press. In December the Goodson Printing Office began issuing the *Goodson Gazette,* which later was renamed the *Virginia Guide* for better identity with the Virginia School. That same year *The Michigan Mirror* and *The Nebraska Journal* appeared.

In those early days print shops were generally called "printing offices" and the teacher referred to as the

foreman. Vocational training was not then considered part of the academic curriculum. In many cases the foreman owned the newspaper printed in the shop by the students and earned revenue from the subscriptions and ads. All newspapers were handset in those early days and printed first on presses operated by foot power, then steam power, and finally by electricity.

The rationale given for these papers was explained by one: "Constant employment will be guaranteed; an opportunity will be afforded the pupils of seeing their own ideas and their own compositions in print; they will have an addition to the stock of reading matter suited to their comprehension and wants; the friends of the pupils will receive in their distant homes a souvenir fresh from the busy little world of which their loved ones are for a time residents." There were other reasons. These school publications served other important purposes. They kept the school's constituencies—the parents, legislators, alumni, and interested persons—informed of the progress of the school, and they served to educate an uninformed public about deaf people.

Many of the papers originally appeared monthly, but as the students mastered the art of typesetting the papers came out more frequently. By the 1890s three schools—the New Jersey, Mt. Airy and Western New York schools—were publishing daily papers during the school year. More than 30 schools were printing weeklies, and the rest of the school papers appeared either semi-monthly, monthly, or less frequently.

Sometime during the 1890s a writer coined the phrase, "Little Paper Family" to describe the newspapers and magazines coming out of the schools for the deaf. The name quickly caught on and was often referred to simply as "lpf." These school publications were exchanged freely and they also became known as "The Exchange." Many of the school papers carried interesting columns of items lifted from "The Exchange." Others quoted lengthy articles, editorials and stories from sister publications, and through this regular exchange the editors formed a fraternity, sometimes referred to as "the brethren of the quill." Thus was formed, and grew, a common bond, a

These publications reflect the changes in printing formats that have taken place over the years.

friendly camaraderie and some tough competition as each editor attempted to put out a neater, newsier, and better publication. They complimented one another for work well done and criticized poor workmanship. When one publication appeared poorly printed it drew this dour comment: ". . . the forms were inked with a mop, and the printing was done on a cider press." When the opportunity presented itself they delighted in taking digs at one another. Once a *Colorado Index* editor, who had the reputation for being a perfectionist, announced that his next issue would be error free. He read the proofs over and over again carefully and then issued the challenge to his fellow lpf brethren to find an error in it. Quickly came a response from another editor who had spotted a typo on the very front page in the first few lines. "Thereafter," recalls Dr. George M. McClure, Sr., "it required a search warrant to find a typographical error in the *Index* as long as he was editor."

Out of this informal group grew the Little Paper Family Editorial Association. It was organized in Chicago in 1893, adopted a By-Laws and Constitution and elected officers. James L. Smith, editor of the Minnesota *Companion,* was elected the first president. The lpf Editorial Association held its first regular meeting at the Convention of American Instructors of the Deaf held in Staunton, Virginia. There were banquets thereafter during the meetings of the CAID until the 1970s when dwindling interest and increased activities crowded it off the program.

From the 1920s through the 1950s most of the school papers were models of printing craftsmanship equal to commercially produced publications. A stranger unfamiliar with them would find it hard to believe that they were the products of students' work. These publications were neatly typeset. They used ornamental cuts and line drawings liberally. Large letters were indented at the beginning of stories and Bodoni dashes or other ornaments were used to separate the news items and stories. Extra spacing was used at the end of each sentence and paragraphs were evenly leaded out. The name of the publication, when used in the text, was set in capital and small letters to

And finally, a doctor in London, according to the **Nashville** *(Tenn.)* **Banner,** *has discovered that radio is sometimes beneficial in cases of deafness. On the other hand, deafness (we'll assume) is sometimes beneficial in the cases of radio.*

—THE NEBRASKA JOURNAL

The Silent Worker

An ad in The Silent Worker.

distinguish it from the names of other publications which were set in italics. Most of these papers were printed on a good grade of paper, usually an enamel stock, and some appeared with two-color covers.

After the typesetting and proofreading were done the pages were made up. Then the heavy metal forms were carried to the press and "put to bed" on a large cylinder press which was handfed. Collating, stitching and trimming followed. Then the publication was prepared for mailing and distribution—how familiar those steps were to so many former deaf students. Like their printing teachers, the students took pride in their work, and it is no surprise that so many of them became successful printers.

The decades following the Second World War, however, began to witness a decline in the quality of many of these school publications. One by one, the old editors and their printing instructors retired from the scene. The new lithography process arrived. It was a much quicker and easier way than the old process and it gave the printer much more freedom with the layout. With this modern technique, it is an irony that the quality of so many of the school publications began to decline. While a few improved as a result of the new method, some became quite sloppy. Attention was no longer given to careful typesetting, even spacing or layout. Along with the slip in the mechanical quality was a decline, in many cases, in the editorial content. Many of the retiring editors' replacements did not view the responsibility as the same "labor of love" as their predecessors. Instead they saw the responsibility as another unpaid extracurricular activity. This attitude was reflected in the content. Gone was the sparkle and creativeness and the balanced content of earlier journals. In its place was the appearance of a labored effort, a duty performed because it had to be done. It was a sad commentary of the changing times.

LPF Editors

In 1892 the students at Gallaudet College started a monthly magazine, *The Buff and Blue,* named after the college colors. James E. Stewart of Michigan was the first editor and Charles D. Seaton of Illinois was the first business manager. *The Buff and Blue* was written, edited and printed by the students. As those students associated with this publication left college and landed teaching jobs in schools for the deaf many of them were appointed editors of those school publications. The list of former *Buff and Blue* editors who made a name for themselves as editors of school publications reads like a *Who's Who* listing. Some of them were: John H. McFarlane (*The Alabama Messenger*), Odie Underhill (*The North Carolinian*), Tom L. Anderson (*The Iowa Hawkeye*), Grover C. Farquhar (*The Missouri Record*), Wesley Lauritsen (*The Companion*), James N. Orman (*The Illinois Advance*), Uriel Jones (*The Tennessee Observer*), W. Ted Griffing (*Deaf Oklahoman*), James B. Beauchamp (*The Kentucky Standard*), Byron B. Burnes (*The Companion* and *The California News*), Norman G. Scarvie (*The Iowa Hawkeye*), Loy Golladay (*The West Virginia Tablet* and *The American Era*) Anthony Papalia

This Powell publication attempts to serve the needs of the black deaf community.

A PUBLICATION OF NEWS MAGAZINE OF INTER-COUNCIL COMMUNICATIONS OF THE DEAF COMMUNITY

Vol. 5 No. 8 March-April, 1979

Black Deaf News ©

NEWS & FEATURES

Powell Ltd.

(*The Washingtonian*) and Jack R. Gannon (*The Nebraska Journal*).

Others were involved with other publications. Ladislaw Cherry edited *The Frat*. Ben M. Schowe and David Peikoff started the *Gallaudet Alumni Bulletin*. Peikoff also started the *OAD* (Ontario Association of the Deaf) *News* and edited the *Gallaudet Alumni Newsletter*. Byron B. Burnes was instrumental in reviving *The Silent Worker*. Alan B. Crammatte became the sparkplug behind *The Cavalier* and later edited the *Gallaudet Record*. The Rev. Otto Berg edited *The Deaf Churchman*. Harold J. Domich edited a Maryland weekly. Richard M. Phillips and Eugene Schick edited *The Silent Hoosier*. Jack R. Gannon was co-founder of *The Deaf Nebraskan* and edited the *Gallaudet Alumni Newsletter* and *Gallaudet Today*. John Schroedel edited the *Gallaudet Alumni Newsletter*.

Other former *Buff and Blue* editors continued their editorial pursuits in different ways. James W. Sowell published privately a collection of his poetry entitled, *To Her I Love*. Thomas A. Ulmer published some of his poems and an autobiographical sketch in *The Badge of Honor*. In his job as chief of the Family and Fertility Statistics Branch of the Population Division of the Census, Wilson H. Grabill has contributed to reports and government publications too numerous to mention and he has co-authored several books. Terrence J. O'Rourke authored the National Association of the Deaf bestseller, *A Basic Course in Manual Communication* and started his own publishing firm, the T.J. Publishers, Inc. Robert F. Panara, John H. McFarlane and Taras Denis teamed up to produce *The Silent Muse: An Anthology of Poetry and Prose by the Deaf* which was published by the Gallaudet Alumni Association in 1960.

Rex Lowman, Mervin D. Garretson, Willard J. Madsen, Linwood Smith, and Dorothy Miles each edited *The Buff and Blue* literary number during their undergraduate days. They all have continued to have their poetry published. Lowman published a collection of his work in *Bitterweed* in 1964. Garretson's work has appeared in many publications. Madsen's poem, "You Have to be Deaf to Understand," has appeared in scores of periodicals and has been translated into seven different languages. International Books printed Linwood Smith's work under the title of "Silence, Love, And Kids I Know" in 1973 and Dorothy Miles' poetry appears in *Gestures*.

George M. McClure, Sr. of *The Kentucky Standard* was dean of the lpf editors. He was associated with that publication some 70 years, first as editor then, after he retired, as a regular contributor. (For more on McClure, see the 1960s.) James B. Beauchamp succeeded McClure in 1942 and was editor of *The Standard* when it reached volume 100.

James L. Smith became the third editor of *The Minnesota Companion* when he joined the staff in 1885. He held the post until his retirement in 1935, accumulating a total of 50 years with the magazine. In 1941 Wesley Lauritsen assumed the editorship of *The Companion* and added a senior number. His 21 years was the second longest tenure as editor of *The Companion*.

Grover C. Farquhar was associated with *The Missouri Record* for 47 years. At least two of his students became lpf editors.

Byron B. Burnes was editor of *The Companion* for four years, and *The California News* for 27, for a total of 31 years as an lpf editor.

Others who were associated with school publications for long durations were W. Ted Griffing who edited the *Deaf Oklahoman*. Griffing conducted a folksy column in his newspaper called the "Melting Pot" and referred to himself as "the stoker." J. Schuyler Long edited *The Iowa Hawkeye* for 22 years. Loy E. Golladay (*The American Era*), Marvin S. Rood (*The West Virginia Tablet*) and Dwight L. Rafferty (*The North Dakota Banner*) were associated with those school publications for many years.

Most lpf editors and printing instructors took their tasks very seriously. In at least one instance, a bit too seriously. It was reported in the press that Charles Lashbrook, printer of the Rome (N.Y.) *Register* braved a howling blizzard while suffering from pneumonia to get his paper "to bed." He succeeded in getting the paper out but the effort sent him to bed with a relapse from which he never recovered.

Lashbrook was succeeded as printing instructor at the Rome School by his wife, Annie, who shortly afterwards was struck by a trolley car and nearly killed. Fortunately, she recovered from the episode and an lpf colleague commented: "It takes more than a plebeian streetcar to kill an l.p.f. aristocrat."

For four years Arthur L. Roberts was editor of the *Kansas Star*. When appointed to the position he was one of the youngest editors in the lpf. He was described by a fellow editor as "a fearless fighter of oralmalochism (who) knows how to call a spade 57 different names—each worse than the previous one."

Running for sheriff's office, a deaf man in Mississippi had this on his campign card: "You have elected many dumb sheriffs in the past. Why not a deaf one for a change?"

—THE NEBRASKA JOURNAL

"That," concluded the writer, "is probably the reason he was removed as editor, last week. . . ."

Deaf Newspapermen

A number of deaf men who learned the printing trade in schools for the deaf went on to run their own newspapers. Edmund Booth (1810-1905) was one of the earliest and most successful. Totally deaf by the age of eight, he was educated at the American School for the Deaf where he taught for seven years following his graduation. In 1856 he purchased half interest in the *Anamosa* (Ia.) *Eureka* in the settlement he helped start. Six years later he bought out his partner. His paper was the leading and official journal in Jones County. He installed a Hoe press becoming the first country newspaper publisher in that part of Iowa to have a power driven printing press. His eldest son joined him as a partner in the business. His youngest son, Frank, was a teacher of the deaf and superintendent of the Nebraska School for the Deaf.

Edmund Booth's name is mentioned in the Jones County history. The *Eureka* is still being published. (For more on Booth see the 1880s.)

James G. George (1825-1876) owned and edited the *Richmond* (Ky.) *Messenger* which he acquired in 1861. He was an outspoken editor and openly supported the Union cause, a stand that got him in trouble with supporters of the Confederacy. Southern sympathizers ransacked his printing office and forced George to flee for his life. He moved to Louisville and enlisted as a private in the Unionist Home Guard. During the war he recorded the names of some 50,000 Confederate soldiers at the military prison in Louisville.

In 1871 George joined the faculty of his alma mater, the Kentucky School for the Deaf, where he organized the school's printing department and began publishing the *Kentucky Deaf-Mute* in 1874.

George was the father of Dudley Webster George, whom Guilbert Braddock called "one of the rarest of deaf scholars." Dudley George was the first student from Kentucky to enter Gallaudet College.

Joseph Mount (b. 1827) was deafened as an infant. He entered the Pennsylvania School for the Deaf when he was ten years old.

As a writer Mount contributed articles to *The Christian, The Ladies Repository,* the *National Deaf-Mute Gazette,* the *Gallaudet Guide Advocate, Scott's Dollar Weekly* and other periodicals. He wrote extensively under such pseudonyms as "The Merry Mute," "Joe, A Jersey Mute," "Deaf-Mute Typo," "Manual Alphabet," and probably other pen names. He also wrote poetry,

Proppaganda
by George

George Propp in *The Nebraska Journal.*

The best friend of the deaf is not the fellow who gives them advice and assistance. It is the man who asks them for it.

* * *

Fractured Bromides—Every silver lining has a dark cloud: We read somewhere not long ago that Navy research has shown that subjects with a certain type of nerve deafness can't get seasick. They can't, on a dark night, pass a standard sobriety test either.

* * *

A recent publication warns us that the telephone is about to become a reality for deaf people. By George, there goes another of our advantages.

* * *

They're having a workshop for interpreters in the near future. Shouldn't they have one for the speakers first? Then, in logical sequence, have one for interpreters and finally another for people like us who can't stay awake during speeches?

* * *

Horrible thought! Suppose Hoffa slips an organizer into this assemblage of interpreters, and henceforth we'd have to pay them what they are worth!

* * *

A $14,000 research project at the University of Pittsburgh reveals that children who learn the sign language early have better educational achievement. By George, Ed Scouten told us nearly the same thing about fifteen years ago and he didn't charge us a dime.

* * *

On the other hand, our hearing friends also possess some advantages. At least we've never heard of a hearing worker who had to stick his "vocal organs" into the maw of a 75-ton press.

* * *

An eighth-grade boy with an ear ache was sent to the infirmary. He came back cured and told his teacher, "Boy, I was really worried. I thought I was becoming deaf!"

and his work was considered refreshing for the times because instead of lamenting about his deafness, as did many poets of the day, he looked on his handicap as a "lovely silence." That unabashed attitude towards his deafness is also reflected in his choice of the pen names he used.

Mount moved to Kansas in the early 1860s where, in partnership with Philip Emery, the founder of the Kansas School for the Deaf, he started a newspaper called the *Home Circle*. It was not a successful venture, and in 1864 he purchased the Baldwin, Kansas, *City Observer*. He had what appeared to be a going concern when he was appointed the third superintendent of the Kansas School in February 1865.

Mount was briefly associated with the Arkansas School; then in 1871 he became publisher of *The Prairie Banner* in Lee's Summit, Missouri and still later he edited *The Sunny Clime* in Dallas, Texas.

Mount was an early advocate for a national college for the deaf.

Guilbert Braddock defined William M. Chamberlain (1832-1895) as "one of the earliest and most versatile leaders of the American deaf." If one reads his biography it is easy to understand why he earned such description. He was a sailor, fisherman, carpenter, shoemaker, printer, editor, soldier and instructor. Yet, the same biographer says of him: "Although a man of varied accomplishments, William Martin Chamberlain made no niche for himself in the hearing world."

Chamberlain was involved with a number of publications and worked briefly as editor of the weekly newspaper, the *Marblehead* (Mass.) *Messenger*. Although his tenure as editor was short, he was credited with many reforms. He served briefly as managing editor of a comic paper, the *Boston Owl*, but as Braddock observed, ". . . after a few hoots the new enterprise folded its wings and died."

Chamberlain was editor of the first magazine of the deaf, the *Gallaudet Guide and Deaf Mute's Companion*. He was also involved with two other publications, both short-lived, the *National Deaf-Mute's Gazette* and the *Deaf-Mute's Friend*. In 1875 he became an instructor at the Central New York School for the Deaf. He started the school's print shop, carpenter shop, and shoe shop. He also started the school's publication, *The Register*, which he edited.

Wells L. Hill (1850-1929) was editor and publisher of the successful *Athol* (Mass.) *Transcript*. During the early years Hill had several partners, but as one of his biographers explained the situation, it was *they* not he, who were silent. By 1898 Hill had bought out the last of his partners and become sole owner of the

newspaper. One account described the *Transcript* as one of the best newspapers in the country, and it was given credit for Athol's steady growth. Hill had a modern plant and hired as many as a dozen employees. Many of his editorials were reprinted in other newspapers.

Hill lost his hearing at the age of 12. He was educated at the American School for the Deaf and entered Gallaudet College as a freshman, skipping the preparatory year. As a college student he was correspondent for the *Worcester* (Mass.) *West Chronicle* and the *Athol Transcript*. He graduated with the class of 1872, which included Amos G. Draper and Robert P. McGregor.

An account of Hill's life is included in the local history of Athol, "Athol, Past and Present," written by L.B. Caswell. Hill's son took over the management of the newspaper when he retired.

Michael J. Smith (1855-1896) and Alfred J. Lamoreaux (b. 1864) teamed up to start *The Merry World* in Pueblo, Colorado in 1887. They advertised their paper as one "devoted to everything in general and to the city of Pueblo in particular." The paper was an instant success. In only 11 weeks it had 1,000 subscribers and was selling many more copies on the street. It received praise from other Colorado newspapers. One described it as "the first and only real live newspaper Pueblo has ever had." Another called it "the best, spiciest, and brightest weekly in Colorado."

Smith was a transplanted Philadelphian. He had become deaf at the age of four years and was educated at the Pennsylvania School. After moving to Colorado, he became a popular figure in Pueblo and was a humorous writer. Sometimes his barbs or articles with apparent hidden meanings brought lawsuits down on his neck. In 1890 a grand jury refused to indict him for libel because of his popularity and because "such a conviction would have been against public opinion."

After several years *The Merry World*'s novelty began to wear off and Smith moved to Denver and entered a different line of work. He later wrote for the *Globeville News*, the *Denver Dispatch* and the *East End Echo*. He also wrote for the *Deaf-Mute's Journal* under the pen name of "Solid Muldoon." He died in his early forties leaving a young family to be cared for by charity.

Alfred J. Lamoreaux, Smith's partner, had been educated at the Colorado School where he taught for awhile. He was a reporter for the *Kansas City Daily Times* then a foreman at *King's Life*, a widely-read humorous weekly. In 1887 he joined Smith to put out *The Merry World* but sold his share within a year and moved to La Junta, Colorado, where he started *The*

Derrick. While publishing *The Derrick* he was correspondent for United Press in the southeastern region of Colorado. In 1891 he sold *The Derrick* and accepted employment with the Denver *Daily News*. Two years later he returned to Pueblo where he became foreman of the *Evening Star*, an afternoon daily.

F. H. Flint, who was deafened at the age of three and educated at the Michigan School, was connected with four newspapers. He started the newspaper in Hickory Corners, Michigan, later moving it to Hastings. He also started the *Barry County Democrat*, Published the *Sunfield News*, and bought the *Augusta Times* with a partner. They were all Michigan newspapers.

Joe G. Bradley (b. 1861) was born in Bienville Parish, Louisiana. An attack of scarlet fever at the age of one year deprived him of his hearing. He was educated at the Texas School for the Deaf. He taught printing at the Mississippi School, then with his brother-in-law, A. M. Martin, started the *Sulphur Rock* (Ark.) *Wheel*. They later moved to Batesville, Arkansas where they published the *Batesville Journal*. Five years later fire destroyed their plant and in 1892 Bradley opened a job printing plant in Hillsboro, Texas. He was one of the first in the area to have a printing press run by electricity.

George H. Allen (b. 1865) began as a printer's "devil" and rose to become an editor. He was editor of the Sioux City, Iowa, *Daily Tribune* for nearly a decade and worked on the editorial staffs of the *Bisbee* (Ariz.) *Review* and the *Arizona Gazette*. He was appointed by the governor as Secretary of the Sheep Sanitation Commission and served so well that on his death, offices in the state capitol were closed and the flag was flown at half staff in his honor.

Allen was six years old when he became deaf. He attended the Minnesota School for the Deaf and Gallaudet College. He withdrew from college after a brief period on account of poor health.

Albert W. Brunson (b. 1866) and his younger brother started the *Quitman* (Mo.) *Record*. Brunson was publisher and business manager. After a year or so he sold his interest in that paper and purchased half interest in the Maitland, Missouri *Herald*, a leading Holt County newspaper. He sold his share in the Herald and became editor of the Forest City, Missouri, *Independent*. In 1896 he was one of the three candidates nominated for assessor for Green Township, losing a close race. He later became publisher and business manager of the *Lake Como Argus* in Mississippi.

Albert Brunson became deaf at the age of nine years. He was a product of the Missouri School.

John H. Howlett (b. ca. 1896) was city editor of the *Chicago Sunday Hero* in 1890. The *Hero* was a publication for the black community and had about 1,000 subscribers. Howlett started a publication for deaf blacks in Minnesota called *The Afro-American World* in 1891. The name was not well received and after a few issues the paper was renamed *The Topic*. Apparently *The Topic* was not a success, and Howlett moved to Kansas where, at the age of 24, he became editor of the *Atchison Blade*, a weekly newspaper for the area. Howlett also edited a 4,000-circulation populist newspaper in Texas named *The Protest* and the Oskaloosa, Kansas, *Gazette*.

Howlett was deafened at the age of six years. He attended the Iowa and Minnesota schools. *The Silent Worker* called him the "only colored deaf and dumb newspaperman on earth."

Alvis L. Hurt (b. 1869) was part owner and associate editor of the *Greeley County Republican*. He was born in Kentucky and educated at the Kansas and Colorado schools for the deaf. He was an assistant sheriff for four years in Greeley County.

In the fall of 1924 Enoch L. Schetnan started *The West River Progress*, a weekly newspaper in Redelm, South Dakota. He later moved the paper to the county seat in Dupree. He had published the *Progress* about 15 years when he acquired a second weekly, *The Eagle Butte News*. He continued publishing both each week.

Newspaper accounts called Schetnan a "forceful writer." His editorials were reprinted widely and many appeared in large dailies in Minnesota and the Dakotas. Schetnan did his own news collecting and interviewing, preferring to use a pad and pencil.

Schetnan became deaf at 18 years when he emigrated to this country from his native Norway. When the ship reached the New World, a suspected case of smallpox placed the whole shipload of immigrants in quarantine on a small island in the St. Lawrence River, near Quebec. There Schetnan contacted spinal meningitis which left him deaf. He attended the Washington State School for the Deaf, graduating in 1880, and St. Olaf College in Minnesota.

Owen G. Carrell (1878-1960) is probably our most recent editor and publisher of a community newspaper. Deafened when he was 11 years old, he attended the Iowa School for the Deaf and Gallaudet College, where he earned both a bachelor's and a master's degree. He taught and coached at the Texas School in Austin where he officiated at the University of Texas basketball games. He was head teacher at the Oklahoma School and taught at the Kansas School.

In 1923 Carrell purchased an interest in the *Duplin Record* in Warsaw, North Carolina. When his partner died he moved to Burgaw, North Carolina, and purchased the *Pender Chronicle*, which he published for 17 years. At one time he was publishing three other newspapers in his plant. In 1935 he moved his plant to Wilmington, North Carolina, where he continued to publish those newspapers and where he started the *Wilmington Post*, a daily newspaper. The *Post* competed with two other established dailies. Carrell sold out to a newspaper chain when he retired in 1946 and moved to Washington, D.C.

And, of course, there were others.

Literary Efforts of Deaf Persons

James Nack (1809-1879), deafened at the age of eight years from a fall down a stairway, was the first deaf man to publish a book in this country. It was a collection of 68 of his poems written when he was between 14 and 17 years old. Nack entitled this work "Legend of the Rock and Other Pieces." It appeared in 1827. In all, Nack published four volumes of poetry.

Since Nack, many other deaf authors have seen their work appear in print. In 1974 *The Gallaudet Almanac* published a list of over 100 books authored by deaf writers. These books include such subjects as autobiographies, biographies, histories, poetry, sports records, curriculum material, novels, science fiction, anthologies and sign language texts. Strange as it may seen to some persons, much of the work coming from the pens of deaf writers has been poetry.

Howard L. Terry (1877-1964) has been called the best known deaf writer and "Our Venerable Dean of Letters." Terry wasted no time setting out to make his mark in the world of literature. When he was 12 years old he produced "Half-a-Penny Tales" on a toy typewriter and sewed the pages together. Two years later he completed a manuscript for another story which his father had published in pamphlet form. By the time Terry was 21, he had written three books. He tried his hand at writing poetry, prose, feature-stories, drama, novels, short stories and even verses for greeting cards and enjoyed the pleasure of seeing much of it published. His poem, "The Hollow of the Moon," was printed on the front page of the Los Angeles *Times* Sunday Magazine in 1917. An article, "The Deaf, Their Education and Place in Society," was published in *Social Science* in 1931. His other writings have appeared in *The Mentor, Out West, The Hesperian, Poetry World,* and *Wee Wisdom*. He has published five volumes of his poetry.

Terry became hard of hearing as a result of illness, later becoming totally deaf when he was around 12 years old. He also suffered poor eyesight. He attended public school, the Rugby Academy in St. Louis, and Gallaudet College. Trouble with his eyes interrupted his studies at Gallaudet, and he never completed the course. Gallaudet awarded him an honorary Master of Letters in 1938 in recognition of his contributions to the field of literature. He was listed in *Who's Who Among North American Writers*.

Laura C. Searing's contributions earned her inclusion in the *Dictionary of American Biography* published in 1928. She wrote under the pseudonym Howard Glyndon. (For more on Searing, see Chapter Seven.)

Abbie M. Watson's writings have appeared in *McCall's* and *The Saturday Evening Post*. Her name was listed in *Who's Who Among Texas Writers Today* in 1935.

The Rev. Warren M. Smaltz, an Episcopalian priest, has had his work published in *The Reader's Digest, The American Mercury, The Expositor,* and *The Living Church*.

In addition to those already mentioned, scores of other deaf authors have appeared in print. A partial list: *Verses* by Mary Toles Peet (1903); *A Deaf Mute Howls* by Albert Ballin (1930); *Along With Me* by Earl Sollenberger (1937); *Green Pavilions* by Helen E. Muse (1961); *Valley Forge* by James A. Sullivan (1964); *The Law and The Deaf* by Lowell J. Myers (1967); *Deaf Persons in Professional Employment* by Alan B. Crammatte (1968); *Deafness* by David Wright (1969); *Sound of the Stars* by Frances M. Parsons (1971); *No Sound* by Julius Wiggins (1972); *The Forgotten People* by Willard H. Wood (1973); *I'm Deaf Too* by Frank G. Bowe and Martin L. A. Sternberg (1973); *Road Girl* by Hester Parson Bennett (1973); *A Deaf Adult Speaks Out* by Leo Jacobs (1977); and *Handicapping America* (1980) and *Rehabilitating America* (1980) by Frank G. Bowe.

In 1972 Eugene Bergman and a hearing colleague, Trenton Batson, published *The Deaf in Literature: An Anthology* and a year later, *The Deaf Experience*. In these books the authors identified books in which deaf characters have appeared.

Chapter 12

The 1950s

"The Deaf Do Not Beg"

S A LADY carrying a grocery bag in each arm emerged from the supermarket she was approached by a peddler. She nodded her head, "yes," when he showed her a card and the peddler followed her to her car where she unloaded her groceries. She looked into her purse. Realizing that she had only a twenty-dollar bill, she held up her index finger to the peddler motioning him to wait. She returned to the supermarket for some one-dollar bills and then gave the peddler one and with a satisfied look on her face, drove off.

A housewife beamed when her deaf cousin arrived for a visit. She could hardly wait to share her excitement with him. "Joe," she said excitedly, as soon as they had sat down, "the other day *one of your kind* came to the door selling needles. Because of you I gave him an extra dollar!" Joe silently groaned and smiled sickly.

Following the second World War and throughout the fifties, an increasing number of deaf Americans found reason to groan. Peddling by deaf persons was on the increase.

From the earliest times it was assumed that deaf persons did not beg. It was thought that the real culprits were imposters—hearing persons posing as deaf persons—and indeed many were. For some time, the National Association of the Deaf had a slogan which proudly boasted: "The deaf do not beg." The public was assured that: ". . . the genuine deaf were too proud, too self-respecting, to use the fact of their handicap as a means of arousing pity or of extracting

charity." Unfortunately, after the war, the NAD and the public were to find that not every deaf person was concerned only about self-respect. Peddling was becoming a racket so widespread that the NAD was forced to chuck the slogan. It was not true. But that fact did not completely clear deaf persons of such acts. A letter appearing in an 1874 issue of the *Deaf-Mute* (Ill.) *Advance* noted: "It is a shame that a number of deaf-mutes live by begging." The letter concluded: "Every deaf-mute owes a debt to the State for its beneficence, which can only be liquidated by making himself useful."

"Just why the sudden resurgence of peddling?" asked a journalist in a 1946 issue of *The Frat*. "It seems strange that so many should turn to seeking charity, rather than honest work." It was not all that strange. One reason was the end of the war. Factories that had hired thousands of deaf workers to turn out war materials and equipment were shutting down or cutting back on their production. The layoffs were inevitable. Returning soldiers, anxious to resume the lives they had left behind, came home in search of jobs. The job market became a highly competitive one, and many a deaf person suddenly found himself without a job. For some, the only way to subsist was peddling.

Furthermore, peddlers found many Americans happy the war was over and in generous moods. When a panhandler plunked down a manual alphabet card and asked for a donation, most of them reached for their loose change or a dollar and placed it in the outstretched hand. In return, they received the good feeling of thinking that they had given to a good cause

255

and helped a less fortunate American.

The Missouri Record warned in 1949: "If we do not find some very effective formula for combating this evil influence now so widely prevalent all over the country, the deaf will in large measure become a mendicant class of human beings, an unworthy people through lack of proper guidance, and wholly unworthy of the large sums spent annually by the various State and Federal Government for their education."

Peddling continued to flourish. It was becoming such a problem that the National Association of the Deaf, the National Fraternal Society of the Deaf, schools for the deaf, and local organizations of the deaf all launched efforts to stem peddling. School publication after school publication carried articles on its evils. School children were given lectures about the disgrace of peddling.

The NAD published and distributed thousands of leaflets attacking the peddling racket. Articles with titles such as "The Deaf Do Not Need To Peddle or Beg" and scores of the others appeared in the press. Matchbooks were printed with messages warning people against patronizing peddlers and hundreds of letters were written to editors of newspapers throughout the country. What effect all this had on the racket is hard to say but NAD officers believed it was considerable, although they conceded that such effect had to be continued endlessly.

Deaf citizens—knowing how long it took to build a good reputation and how quickly that reputation could be tarnished by one visit of a gang of deaf peddlers—began to fight back also. Feelings ran strong.

The Mascia Club of the Deaf in Mason City, Iowa inserted advertisements with the manual alphabet in the local newspaper and informed readers that such cards were not for sale. "Do not donate a cent to such a panhandler!" the message urged.

The Binghamton Civic Association of the Deaf and the Empire State Association of the Deaf, Inc., countered the peddling of alphabet cards by printing their own with this message: "THIS CARD IS FREE! Respectable deaf citizens do not beg nor peddle. They have good jobs and neither need nor want charity." The cards were distributed widely.

We have the responsibility of molding a future deaf citizen. Are we going to add another handicap or are we going to be able to say: "Here, world, is an asset to your society, give him a chance and he will not fail you"?

—BEN E. HOFFMEYER
1958

A 1948 Cavalier *cartoon.*

The Cavalier

In Kansas City, Missouri a delegation of 25 persons led by Fred R. Murphy, president of the Missouri Association of the Deaf, appeared before the city council to express concern about their city becoming a "soft spot" for deaf peddlers. The city invited the group to help develop an ordinance to control such activity.

In Springfield, Massachusetts police were tipped off about a group of peddlers about to start soliciting. Police accosted the group and asked them to leave the city. The group was selling band-aids worth five to ten cents for 25 to 30 cents.

Letters appeared in the *Ogden* (Ut.) *Standard-Examiner,* the *Scranton* (Pa.) *Times,* The *Deseret News* of Salt Lake City, Utah, and the *Sioux Falls* (S.D.) *Argus Leader* and elsewhere calling local citizens' attention to the racket and asking that they assist by not patronizing peddlers.

In some localities and states efforts were made to pass legislation which would outlaw peddling. The success of such laws, however, depended heavily on enforcement. Enforcement varied from locality to locality and unless law enforcement officers got complaints, many did not give a deaf peddler a second look. Clever peddlers knew this and took advantage of it. All was not roses for the peddlers, however. In San Francisco, one ring leader was arrested and sentenced to two years in prison for forging a government bond. During the trial his peddling activities surfaced.

Profile of a Deaf Peddler

He entered the restaurant door, paused briefly to give his eyes time to adjust to the darkness, saw me and came to the table where I sat. He was still very lean with gaunt cheeks and square jaws. I noticed that he still wore an over-sized shirt and it hung over his shoulders as on a hangar. His blue eyes were deep-set behind a pointed nose. In spite of these rugged, bony features, he was still quite a handsome fellow. And, as always, his hands were clean, with well-trimmed fingernails. Those were the highly-skilled hands that I knew when as a youth I watched them expertly turn pieces of lumber into beautiful pieces of furniture in the school's woodworking shop.

I remembered the first day I had met him. He was much older than I and he had come forward and introduced himself. "My last name Gisser," he had signed. "My first name Johnnie." (not his real name.) And, then he had shown me his personal sign, "J-on-the-wrist." He was a likeable person and I discovered he lived not far from my home in southern Missouri. We became good friends.

The only thing that made Johnnie different from my other deaf friends is that he became a peddler.

To some the deaf peddler was the lowest form of the deaf human animal. Educators resented the peddler because he represented a failure of school and society to cope with him. To the college educated deaf person the peddler is generally loathsome. To the average deaf American he is resented, feared, hated or ignored. The deaf community leader sees the peddler portraying a harmful and mistaken image of the average hard-working, honest deaf American. These leaders believe that no self-respecting deaf person would peddle.

It has been years since I had last seen Johnnie. He had gone his way and I had gone mine. His once thick wavy hair which he had taken so much pride in combing was thinning now. We sat there and re-lived events of bygone years and brought each other up-to-date on our lives.

Deaf peddlers are not a new or recent phenomenon. Accounts of deaf persons begging appeared in early publications. No statistics exist on deaf peddlers, however, so other than personal accounts, little is known about them. It is generally believed that a majority are young deaf adults, who did poorly in school and dropped out. These low-achievers generally see themselves as failures at home and at school and have developed an apathetic attitude. They are generally the victims of no communication at home and are not understood or liked at school. They are considered "trouble makers." The self-respect deaf leaders talk about does not bother them. They either never developed any or soon lost whatever self-respect they had through repeated failure and frustration. Peddling gave them independence. It brought in money which they had never had access to before. It provided them with the opportunity to break free, to travel, to seek adventure, to be "somebody" even if that somebody was the peddler's label they wore. They had been on the "other side" too long to care.

Johnnie had been "voc" which means that he was majoring in vocational subjects and if he completed the course he would graduate with a vocational certificate. Johnnie had come to school when he was about 12 years old—his family had not known that there was a school for deaf children—too late and too far behind to fit into the regular academic program. He was much older than many of the other children in his class. But there was no question about his skill in the woodworking shop. Unfortunately he was unable to get along with the dormitory supervisors and he grew disillusioned with school. When he was 19 years old he quit and got a job in Kansas City.

Like Johnnie, most of the peddlers seem to have acquired good vocational training or at least have a marketable skill, but they are unable to hold a job for a variety of reasons. The inability to communicate—to understand and be understood—is one. This lack of communication makes it difficult for them to become a member of their families, to get along with their employers or co-workers.

They mistake friendly teasing as abuse. They become suspicious and think they are being cheated with low salaries—sometimes true—and they feel that they are always being given the undesirable tasks, the ones that the other workers shun. They become loners, disillusioned, bitter and frustrated at work and their absences begin to increase or they start coming to work late until it reaches a point where they either quit or get fired.

After quitting his job in Kansas City Johnnie joined the company of two veteran deaf peddlers. They travelled throughout the United States and Johnnie learned the "tricks of the trade." He enjoyed the travel. He learned where to buy the items they peddled at the best discount prices. He learned which cities or areas gave the biggest return for their efforts. From his take he managed to save enough to buy his own car. After he felt he had learned enough he left the other two and struck out on his own, and it was in the summer of that year that he visited me to show me the new Dodge he had just purchased with cash. Evidently he was doing quite well. He also told me of his adventures, bragged of his sexual conquests and told of embarrassing encounters he had when he ran into other deaf persons and about the threats he had received from some of them.

Not all peddlers, of course, are as independent-minded as Johnnie. Many of them work for ring leaders who provide the items to peddle and transportation and who scrape off a large percentage of the intake as "expenses." Peddlers' "merchandise" varies and includes such items as packages of needles, shoe laces, razor blades, pencils, band-aids, trinkets, combs, the manual alphabet and other cheap items.

The income also varies. In the late forties and early fifties there were reports of some peddlers making $75 a day. Another claimed he made $40 in three hours and still another reported grossing $4,600 over a 16-week period. One crew leader bragged of making $1,300 in 14 days. It is doubtful *if any of them pay taxes on this income. It is generally believed that most peddlers want their listeners to believe that their peddling is a highly-rewarding undertaking. Such intake only creates more resentment among the honest deaf wage-earners.*

It was on one of his trips that he visited a local club of the deaf and met Yvonne. She had been making the rounds with another peddler. They hit it off well and he invited her to join him. She accepted. Together they spent long hours and weeks at a stretch peddling. They made the rounds of bars, restaurants and resort areas which they knew were the most responsive. They slept in the car to save motel expenses and ate meagrely. They managed to save money and decided to get married. They purchased a small house in a little town near Yvonne's parents' home. With what was left Johnnie purchased a used dump truck and went into the trash removal business. "People liked me," he said. "I picked up around the cans. The hearing man (his competitor) didn't." Whenever they found themselves short on cash they peddled in other localities during weekends.

Deaf leaders, educators of the deaf, public officials and the taxpayer have a justifiable reason for opposing deaf peddlers. Deaf persons have been laboring under a mistaken public image for years. They have been trying to steer that prevalent image of deaf persons away from one of charity. Deaf people realize that if they are to ever reach full citizenship they cannot continue to be considered "objects of charity."

Peddling also gives education of the deaf a black eye. Educators tell the public that they teach deaf youth to become independent-thinking, hardworking, tax-paying citizens then the listener bumps into a peddler.

Most peddlers pay no taxes and unless they find employment before old age they have no social security benefits and have to be placed on welfare.

Peddling or begging goes against the grain of the American dream. This country was built on hard work. Yet, many of these hard working Americans are generous and sympathetic to those they consider less fortunate than themselves. When it comes to deaf peddlers deaf Americans believe that such sympathy is misplaced.

Today, because of increased vocational training programs for the deaf with a growing number of community service programs staffed by well trained deaf and hearing personnel which provide assistance to those who need it, with more persons learning sign language, and with a growing awareness of deafness, it is likely that peddling is on the wane.

Problems began surfacing in his and Yvonne's lives, problems they were not able to cope with. There were no community services where they could get assistance or counseling. Friction developed and their marriage went on the rocks and divorce followed. Johnnie lost his family, the trash removal business and the house and had returned to peddling.

It was getting dark outside the restaurant. We had chatted for over two hours. I was saddened to learn of the bad news, still it had been good to see him again. I could not help notice how much he had changed. His once cheerful personality had been dulled. His zest for adventure had gone out. What was once exciting to him was now a chore.

Johnnie got up from the table and took some cards from his pocket. With a wry grin he tossed one in front of me. On one side the American manual alphabet was printed and on the other, this message: "I am a deaf-mute. I have a family to support. I have no job. Please pay what you wish. God bless you." He walked to the front of the restaurant and began placing a card before each patron. When he had completed the round of the room he returned to the beginning again and began picking up coins and those few cards which the patron did not wish to pay for.

He returned to the table where I sat and signed, "I go." At the door he turned and looked at me momentarily. His eyes had no message and his face was expressionless. He opened the door and stepped outside and vanished into the night.

Newspaper men called him a "Fagin" and reported that some 50 deaf peddlers attended his trial and were happy to learn he received a prison sentence. It meant that they no longer needed to kick back a heavy commission to him.

In Florida, two peddlers went up to a bank teller and handed her a note asking for a coin bag. Suspecting a hold-up the teller triggered the bank alarm and kept stalling while the peddlers waited patiently. Finally, tired of waiting the two picked up their note and left. Federal Bureau of Investigation agents were able to trace them to the home of one's grandmother. They were taken to police headquarters where it was learned that they had only wanted a bag to deposit 2,500 coins they had collected from peddling alphabet cards. They were released and no charges were filed.

The Decade

The fifties gave us Joe McCarthy, Communists and loyalty oaths. Alger Hiss, and a young Congressman named Richard M. Nixon. Marilyn Monroe reigned as sex symbol of the decade, and Roger Bannister broke the four-minute mile. A young black preacher named Martin Luther King, Jr. was just beginning his ministry in Montgomery, Alabama.

Crew cuts and duck tails, narrow ties and belts, and Bermuda shorts were in. Drive-in theatres were new,

Arthur L. Roberts
(1881-1957)

Arthur Laurence Roberts was born on a Kansas farm on August 9, 1881. He was an only child and when he was 12 years old he lost his hearing. His parents enrolled him in the Kansas State School for the Deaf in Olathe from which he graduated just before the turn of the century. From Olathe he went to Washington, D.C. where he enrolled in Gallaudet College. He earned his bachelor's and, not long afterwards, a master's degree from the college. After a stint as a printer he was offered a position as a teacher at his alma mater in Kansas. His tenure as editor of the school's publication, *The Kansas Star*, brought him national attention and in 1918 he was appointed principal of the Kendall School for the Deaf on the Gallaudet College campus.

While in Washington Roberts became active in the Washington Division of the National Fraternal Society of the Deaf. In 1921 he was elected delegate to the Frat's convention in Atlanta. That summer he was working as a carpenter and had just helped complete a sheet metal faculty garage on the campus before he left for Georgia. He did not know it then, of course, but he was setting out on a different building career. At the convention he was elected assistant secretary and that put an end to his teaching career. In 1923 he became treasurer and four years later secretary-treasurer. In 1931 he was elected president.

Roberts was influential in persuading insurance companies to insure deaf drivers. He was a leader in protecting the rights of deaf people to drive automobiles and the information he compiled on the records of deaf drivers was used to convince legislators who were thinking about outlawing deaf drivers that such laws were unrealistic, arbitrary and unnecessary. Of Roberts, Joseph S. Grant, the Frat's legal counsel said:

"No person can expose himself to the rare, the unique personality, without being affected thereby."

Roberts was a man of small stature. He was described as a person who possessed much tolerance, understanding and an unerring perception. He was a modest and courageous individual, a wise business executive and a strong, vigorous leader. He was looked upon as the "true fraternal gentleman." Under his leadership the Society quadrupled its assets and became one of the strongest fraternal insurance organizations in America. The membership doubled from 5,000 to 10,000, an auxiliary for deaf women was started and the Society built a new $175,000 modern office building in Oak Park, a Chicago suburb. This growth is remarkable when it is remembered that Roberts' tenure as president spanned the period which included the Great Depression and one World War. And, if his involvement in the NFSD were not enough, Roberts found the time and energy to serve two terms as president of the National Association of the Deaf from 1923 to 1930. With this background in education, civic service and the business world it is not difficult to understand Roberts' strong dislike for deaf peddling and the poor image it presented of law-abiding deaf citizens.

To friends Roberts was known affectionately as "Bobs." Somewhere along the way he picked up the rather unusual personal sign of "Rooster." Some old timers believe it could be traced back to his college days. They think that his diminutive stature or jaunty stride earned him that sign. Regardless of where he got it, for a man as dignified as Roberts it was indeed an eye-catching personal sign and one that stayed with him throughout his life.

THE LUCKY PUNCH! DANNY LONDON BORN DEAF AND DUMB WAS HIT IN THE HEAD IN THE BOXING RING AND SUDDENLY FOUND HE COULD BOTH SPEAK AND HEAR! Brooklyn, N.Y. 1929

that he had been named winner of the Virginia Association of the Deaf safest deaf driver in the state award. Harper had averaged 38,571 miles a year over a fourteen year period and maintained a clean slate. He had had no accident and received no traffic violation tickets during that period.

In Los Angeles a group of municipal and superior court judges doffed their judical robes and donned work clothes and set about scrubbing Douglas Tilden's statue of Senator Stephen M. White. The statue of the senator who had been called "the father of Los Angeles Harbor" stands on a pedestal on the Los Angeles Courthouse lawn. For years flying creatures had been using it as an object of their painting parties.

Luther Taylor, who had been a pitcher for the New York Giants at the turn of the century at a spry 74 years old was spending his summers officiating softball and baseball games in the Chicago area.

A well-meaning, but poorly-informed North Dakota senator decided to propose legislation which would grant deaf persons a special tax exemption. During this decade the officers of the National Association of the Deaf and, presumably, a majority of deaf Americans were a proud lot and wanted no corners cut for them. All they asked was a fair deal and nothing more. Evidently the senator had not done his homework and much to his embarrassment his good intentions were met with a loud outcry and strong opposition. The bill was withdrawn.

Meanwhile, in South Dakota a misinformed newspaper editor started a campaign to ban all deaf drivers in the state when he learned of an accident involving a deaf driver. Once again the National Association of the Deaf and deaf drivers had another right-to-drive battle on their hands. A letter-writing campaign finally brought the effort to a halt.

While visiting her mother-in-law one day Mrs. Eulalia Burdick of Akron, Ohio saw some very old buttons she liked and began collecting them. Before she knew it her collection had grown to over 10,000 buttons. Her collection included buttons decorated with characters from Aesop's Fables, political campaign buttons, and what-nots. She has in her collection some buttons from the military uniforms worn by students at the New York School for the Deaf (Fanwood). These buttons have the manual alphabet letter "A" enscribed on them.

By the end of the fifties, military uniforms in schools for the deaf had gone out of style.

One day Mrs. Marie McCarthy was thrilled to learn from her hearing neighbor that her home address had been chosen by the local radio station as the lucky winner that day. To claim her $100.00 prize she had

as were 3-D movies and hula hoops. Sputniks and the Korean conflict dominated much of the world news. The fifties was also the decade of the A-bomb scare and bomb shelter craze. If many deaf people built bomb shelters, they did not publicize it. It is likely that most did not since no system for forewarning them existed.

The events of the decade included the landmark 1954 Supreme Court decision striking down segregation in the public schools, Khrushchev's visit to America, and the admission of Alaska and Hawaii to the Union as the 49th and 50th states. Television made its commercial debut, and Ford Motor Co. tried to tell everyone who would listen that "There's a Ford in Your Future."

In Virginia Robert S. Harper was delighted to learn

to phone in immediately. Since she was deaf McCarthy asked her neighbor to place the call for her and was stunned to learn that she was ineligible for the prize money because she did not place the call herself. On learning of the incident McCarthy's husband, his co-workers and friends deluged the station with protests. After reconsidering the matter the station managers agreed that McCarthy had been treated unfairly and sent her a check for $100.00.

The Chicago Club of the Deaf donated $200.00 to deaf friends in Japan. The money was used to purchase playground equipment for the children at the Osaka School for the Deaf. As an expression of appreciation the school named the area the "CCD Playground." Sufficient funds were left over to purchase sewing machines for the girls and athletic equipment for the boys. The purchases were made by Caroline M. Leiter, hearing daughter of deaf parents, who was stationed in the area as recreational director for the U.S. Armed Services.

Jane Wyman, an American actress, won Britian's Picturegoer Annual Film Award for 1950 for her performance in "Johnny Belinda," the story about a young deaf woman who was raped and whose baby authorities had threatened to take away from her because she was deaf. *The Silent Worker* called the film "a major contribution to the cause of the deaf."

Under the leadership of President Louis B. Orrill, the Texas Association of the Deaf defeated a bill in the State Legislature which would have required parents of deaf children attending the Texas School for the Deaf to pay $60 per month tuition. The TAD, parents, and educators with the assistance of others were successful in removing control of the Texas School from the Board of Hospitals and Special Schools to the State Board of Education.

In Missouri, deaf drycleaning businessman Oscar Sanders and his wife discovered a 27-year-old deaf woman who had never been to school. They contacted Superintendent Truman L. Ingle at the Missouri School for the Deaf who made special arrangements for her to work at the school, and Max N. Mossel, a deaf mathematics teacher, volunteered to teach her. A similar situation occurred at the Maryland School for the Deaf. It accepted a 25-year-old illiterate deaf man.

A $500,000-dollar, 128-bed boys' dormitory at the Oregon State School for the Deaf was dedicated to Thure A. Lindstrom. Born in Sweden, he had taught at the school and for a short time was acting superintendent. He was the founder of the Oregon Association of the Deaf.

The vocational building at the American School for the Deaf was named in honor of Walter G. Durian, who had taught printing at the school for 40 years. The gymnasium and auditorium building were named for Walter C. Rockwell. Rockwell was an outstanding athlete and teacher at the school.

Some 3,000 persons attended the dedication of the Mill Neck Manor School, a new Lutheran School for the Deaf, when it opened in 1951 in Mill Neck, New York.

A Miss Jean Walter living in Holton, Michigan, was reported to have lost her hearing as a result of shock when she saw her father fall to his death.

In Oakland, California the Catholic Church acquired the residence of former California Governor Earl Warren and converted it to a center for the deaf.

On January 14, 1950, the Volta Bureau, headquarters of the Alexander Graham Bell Association, which had just undergone remodeling, was re-dedicated. The two women who as young girls had turned the first spadefuls of dirt at the groundbreaking ceremony for the building in 1893, were present for the re-dedication program. They were Helen Keller and Mrs. Gilbert Grosvenor, daughter of Dr. and Mrs. Alexander Graham Bell. During the program, Mrs. Grosvenor told a story about her deaf mother. A big party was being planned and as people were busy making arrangements someone asked Mrs. Bell where she thought the orchestra should be placed. Mrs. Bell is

Jim Hurburt and John Tubergen on Zenith-sponsored television program.

said to have looked at her questioner and responded: "What a strange question to ask a deaf woman!"

Advent of Television

Owning a television set in the fifties was sufficient news to rate an item in "Swinging 'round the Nation" column in *The Silent Worker* and there was some truth to that popular joke of the times that you did not realize you had so many friends until you purchased a television set. But, deaf people were soon to find to their disappointment that television was little more than a radio with pictures and much like the "talkies," the movie films with sound tracks which had replaced the old silent films and their captioned scripts. It was not long before deaf viewers were appealing to the television networks to include more meaningful visuals on the TV screen. In sporting events they suggested flashing the names of the players who made touchdowns or hit homeruns. They encouraged program directors of cooking demonstration programs to label the ingredients being used, show the dimensions of measuring cups so that deaf housewives watching those programs could follow them. Most suggestions were ignored.

While reading the newspaper one day John M. Tubergen, Jr. learned about a tornado warning which had been broadcast over the television the day before. Fortunately, the tornado had decided to go elsewhere, but Tubergen was upset because he realized that he and other deaf persons could not afford to take such chances or wait to read about such warnings in the newspaper. He called his concern to the attention of the network directors and pointed out that there were an estimated 100,000 deaf persons within the station's broadcasting area who received no benefit from the news because they were deaf. William B. Ray, news director of NBC's central division, became interested in the project and before Tubergen realized it he was sitting on a high stool before a television camera interpreting the weekly news. While Jim Hurlbut read the program's five-minute newscast Tubergen interpreted the script for deaf television viewers. This program which started in May, 1959, was one of the first efforts by a television station to reach deaf audiences through a regularly scheduled program. The first interpreted program was sponsored by Zenith, then NBC took over the sponsorship. The program was cancelled along with other live broadcasts when there was an electricians' strike. The program was on the air about 39 weeks.

"Operation Lipread"

In the October 28, 1957 issue of *Life* magazine there appeared a story entitled: "How the Queen Saw an Odd New Game—And What She Said." It was a news story about Queen Elizabeth's reaction to the great American sport—football—during her first official visit to the United States. The story quoted the Queen's observations and the questions she asked her hosts. To reporters and editors of other publications this story was intriguing. It was definitely a scoop because all reporters had been banned from within earshot of the Queen and her party. How then had *Life* managed to quote her conversation verbatim?

Just before the Queen's visit a *Life* magazine editor had approached Robert F. Panara, an associate professor at Gallaudet College, a highly skilled lipreader. He was asked if it were possible to lipread a person at a great distance, say, at a football stadium. Panara thought it was possible if the lips could be seen. He was taken to Byrd Stadium at the University of Maryland in nearby College Park and given a tryout. The experiment proved a success and *Life* staffers offered him a job to lipread the Queen of England! Panara enlisted the assistance of Alton Silver, a college freshman, and another skilled lipreader, for "insurance."

On the appointed day, while the Queen sat on the 50-yard line between Maryland Governor Theodore McKeldin and University of Maryland President Wilson H. Elkins, 200 yards across the stadium on specially built scaffolding stood Panara and Silver, their eyes glued to high powered binoculars. They could see the Queen as big as life and, unknown to her or anyone else, they relayed her conversation to *Life* correspondents standing next to them who then dictated the information into a tape recording machine.

Following the game Panara, Silver and the other members of the group were rushed to a nearby airport under police escort and flown in a waiting charter plane to New York City. They had a deadline to meet. There they helped match the conversation with pictures taken by *Life* photographers.

Panara had one question. He hadn't dared to take his eyes off the Queen for the duration of the game and he wanted to know who had won the game.

When word got out about how *Life* had accomplished the feat a story appeared in *The Washington Post* headlined: "Royal Scoop by Gallaudet." *The Reporter*, a trade magazine, called it "A Scoop, A Palpable Scoop!" and suggested that a special citation be awarded *Life* for "aggressiveness far beyond the call of duty."

The publicity attracted some criticism and about a

month after the incident Gallaudet's president let it be known that lipreading with binoculars was considered an invasion of privacy and that faculty members were no longer to engage in such "eavesdropping."

The NAD Endowment Fund

When tall, bespectacled Byron B. Burnes, a California School for the Deaf teacher was elected 16th president of the National Association of the Deaf at Louisville, Kentucky in 1946, he pledged to give top priority to increasing the Association's Endowment Fund. The Endowment Fund had been started during the Veditz Administration, the objective being to raise an endowment large enough to support a national headquarters with the income.

In 1950 the NAD retained a Chicago public relations firm to help publicize its work and solicit contributions for the NAD Endowment Fund, and opened an office—the NAD's first—in that city. The public relations firm had led officials to believe that they could raise about a million dollars. This did not happen and one of the reasons was because the firm knew nothing about deaf people in the beginning and had planned to appeal to thousands of persons, as one NAD official described their approach, ". . . for help for the poor benighted helpless deaf mutes." The NAD, of course, refused such strategy, and knocked the props out from under their fund-raising plans. As a result, deaf people themselves—notably Lawrence Yolles and David Peikoff—ended up raising most of the money.

But, the firm did excellent work at disseminating information, most of which Robert M. Greenmun, the NAD secretary-treasurer, and President Burnes, had prepared. The publicity attracted national attention and many a night the NAD officers burned the midnight oil responding to inquiries, appeals for assistance and requests for information.

One of the first acts the firm did was to undertake a two-month study of the NAD and the plight of deaf people. Their study reported ". . . an obvious need for establishing the fact that oralism, alone, is not the solution of the need for equipping the deaf to 'hear' what may go on around them—apparently a combination of oralism and dexterity in the use of the manual alphabet is the real answer. The general public is not aware of this. Many mistaken people assume that for a deaf person to use the manual alphabet is for him to advertise his deficiencies. That belief is no more true than it might be to assume that all people who wear glasses are blind—and that by wearing glasses they confess their incompetence." The firm ap-

plauded the NAD's refusal to seek an extra income tax exemption for deaf people and predicted that such action would be an advantage in a fund raising campaign.

Under the leadership of Vice President Larry Yolles the Endowment Fund began to grow slowly. By July 1950 it had $34,048.55. A Century Club was started for those who contributed or pledged $100.00 or more and the list soon reached 54 entries. An Iowa mother of two young deaf sons pledged $100.00 each explaining that she wanted her sons to be involved in such an important project. Rallies were held throughout the country. Clubs and organizations, members and friends contributed. State associations gave. The Michigan Association contributed $1,924.00 and the Empire State Association sent in $1,040.00. The Gallaudet alumni contributed $1,380.00. A group of Canadian thespians, led by a spirited David Peikoff, put on a play in Toronto and raised $800.00. Within a year the dollar mark in cash and pledges had gone over the $50,000.00 mark.

With the Endowment Fund project, the revived *Silent Worker,* the peddling issue and an increasing volume of mail created by a national publicity effort the NAD had its hands full.

Battling Misleading Claims

Another problem the National Association of the Deaf confronted during the fifties was exaggerated advertising claims of some hearing aid dealers and the confusion resulting from the public's failure to understand the difference between a hard of hearing person and a totally deaf person. Read one hearing aid ad: "If you act today you may stop being deaf . . . for only $69.50." The NAD expressed concern that hearing aid advertisements used the term "deaf" instead of "hard of hearing." Such ads were misleading and gave false hope to deaf persons and parents of deaf children. One hearing aid manufacturer candidly admitted knowledge of the difference between deaf and hard of hearing individuals and stated that the company had found that the use of the term "deaf" resulted in a greater response to their ad campaign. And, if misleading hearing aid claims were not enough, this ad found its way into the press: "Amazing New Medical Discovery Checks Deafness" it read. "One tablet daily at meal time helps restore hearing to normal usefulness."

The NAD appealed to the *Chicago Tribune,* then the largest standard-size newspaper in the country, about the untruthful hearing aid advertisements. The *Tri-*

Representatives and observers attending the Fulton Conference clockwise, starting at top left: Oliver Childress, James Smith, Grover C. Farquhar, George Propp, Glenn Hawkins, Jess Smith, (unidentified), Gordon G. Kannapell, (unidentified), Curtis Rodgers, Max Mossel, (unidentified), Robert M. Greenmun, G. Dewey Coats, B.B. Burnes, Ray Stallo, Dewey Deer, Palmer Lee, Peter Graves, (unidentified), Leslie Massey, Gordon Allen, Robert Heacock, Mervin D. Garretson, (unidentified) and LeRoy Duning.

bune agreed with the NAD stand and a *Tribune* official wrote a letter to the manufacturers supporting the NAD.

In Syracuse, New York totally deaf Rev. William Lange, read one of the misleading ads and decided to call the company's bluff. He made an appointment with a salesman and asked for a hearing aid that would restore his hearing. The salesman tried one aid after another then a bone conductor before finally admitting that the mechanical devices were of no help. Regardless of such facts and the experiences of salesmen, some manufacturers were reluctant to change their sales approach because the term "deaf" had greater appeal.

NAD Reorganization Plans

Soon after the founding of the National Association of the Deaf the leaders realized that the organization did not have the nationwide base a national organization should have. Officers were elected and business was transacted by those members who happened to be attending the convention, natives of the host city outnumbered outsiders. This meant that only those who were willing and able to attend the convention controlled the destiny of the organization. Little input came from the membership, and there was no organized representation. The NAD was not truly a national organization representing deaf people of America.

Edwin A. Hodgson, the second president of the NAD, noticed this problem and suggested that a system of representation be developed. Obviously, his suggestion fell on deaf ears because nothing happened.

Thomas F. Fox, a teacher at the New York School for the Deaf (Fanwood) and the fourth NAD president, was also concerned about representation. He proposed organizing the NAD along the lines of a federation. The federation, in Fox's view, would consist of state and local associations with each state sending an official representative to the national convention. This, he argued, would strengthen the organization and make it more representative. Fox was way ahead of his time. It would be more than half a century before the NAD was reorganized, basically along the lines Fox had proposed in 1889.

Other reorganization proposals followed Fox's. George W. Veditz, Anson R. Spear, James W. Howson, Warren M. Smaltz and James N. Orman all tried their hand at wrestling with the unwieldy reorganization question. These plans were either discarded or ignored.

Orman proposed "A New National Association of the Deaf." Orman was more concerned about the existing gap between the state associations and the National Association than with reorganizing the NAD. He suggested stronger unity between the two. He believed that what was needed was a well-planned educational campaign among the states stressing the need for better unity. Chosen chairman of the Committee on Reorganization at the 1937 convention he and his committee worked hard on their plan and publicized it widely. The Orman Plan, as it was known, like Fox's, was similar to the present organization set-up with one clear distinction. It proposed that membership in the NAD be through state associations only. In other words, a person could not join the NAD directly.

When the Orman Plan was presented to the membership at the 1940 convention in Los Angeles, few of those attending the convention seemed familiar with it. They had not done their homework. Orman, himself, was unable to attend and support the plan due to a death in the family. It was proposed that the plan not be considered by the membership until it had been ratified by 36 state associations. Thirty-six state associations did not even exist at that time. Orman and his committee were chagrined. They felt that their work had been for naught.

At the following convention held in Louisville, Kentucky in 1946, Orman reported that nine states had considered the plan; six had ratified it, two had postponed action on it and only one had opposed it. Those present at the convention did not think the plan was the answer to the needs of the organization and voted to discharge the committee. While official action did not exactly discard the Orman Plan, it was as good as dead. Another attempt to oil the creaky machine had failed.

Nine years later at the 23rd convention held in Cincinnati, Ohio, Peter Graves of Pennsylvania called for a reorganization committee. It was the NAD's Diamond Jubilee. Graves was president of the Pennsylvania Society for the Advancement of the Deaf, one of the strongest state associations of the times. Graves was a "real politician" and carried considerable weight. The members approved the committee and it was instructed to prepare a report for the next convention. That would mean St. Louis, Missouri in 1957. Charles Kepp was selected to chair the committee. Like Graves, he was an official of the Pennsylvania Society. Others on the committee included G. Dewey Coats of Missouri, Ray Stallo of California and President Burnes and Secretary-Treasurer Greenmun. Edwin Hazel, of Chicago, a parliamentary expert, served as special adviser to the group. Kepp resigned from the committee soon after the convention and Coats was appointed chairman. Ray Grayson of Ohio was added to the committee. Coats arranged for a meeting of state representatives at the Missouri School for the Deaf in Fulton. That meeting would be remembered long afterwards as the "Fulton Tontine."

Turning Point at Fulton

The meeting at Fulton took place a year later on June 12-14, 1956 at the Missouri School for the Deaf. The meeting was held in the school's multi-purpose building which had been designed by Coats and built largely by the students in Arthur Merklin's woodworking classes. If students could undertake such a huge building project, could not adults?

The presidents of all state associations had been repeatedly urged to send a representative to this important meeting. Most heeded the call and 19 states were represented. Of those attending this meeting whom we would hear more from in later years were: Gordon L. Allen (Minnesota), Leslie Massey (Indiana), Mervin D. Garretson (Montana), LeRoy and Hilbert Duning and Lilly G. Andrewjeski (Ohio), Dewey Deer (Washington), George Propp (Nebraska), Jess Smith (Tennessee), George G. Kannapell (Kentucky), Peter Graves (Pennsylvania) and W. Ted Griffing and Ed S. Foltz (Oklahoma). Garretson and Smith were destined to lead the NAD in later years. Allen would later become a vice president and Propp, secretary-treasurer. There were others attending the meeting in addition to NAD officers, Byron B. Burnes and Robert Greenmun. Most were Fulton residents.

From this meeting emerged a bicameral legislative system which would give all members of the NAD a voice, either through their state association or in attendance at a national convention. Official business transactions would be handled by elected delegates from member states, called the Council of Representatives. The new system further proposed a quota system to improve the shaky financial condition of the Association.

The two-day meeting in Fulton wasn't all work and no play, of course. It is said that Graves received permission to transform the student canteen into a bar and that he practically bought out a small neighboring liquor store by week's end, forcing the owners to make hasty plans to replenish their depleted stock. Before the group departed that weekend a bottle of wine was purchased and it was agreed that it would be retained and passed along until there remains only one survivor. That person will then open it and duly extinguish its contents as one last final drink to the Fulton Tontine! At each NAD convention the surviving members of the Fulton conference get together for a Fulton Tontine breakfast, pass around the unopened wine bottle and reminisce.

The reorganization plan was presented at the 1957 convention held July 21-27 in St. Louis. The issue came before the members by midweek. Except for the proposed $2.00 per member annual fee, the plan was acceptable. The fee, called a tax, met with strong opposition. A compromise was finally worked out to refer the question on fees to the Council of Representatives which was provided for under the new system. After more than four hours' debate, Gordon Allen moved that the new by-laws be approved as amended. His motion was seconded by Ray Stallo. The vote was unanimous.

One final hurdle remained. It was necessary to get 15 state associations to ratify the plan, but that was not quite as stiff as the 36 required for the Orman Plan.

These new by-laws gave the president sweeping powers in addition to his regular duties of presiding at a meeting. He served as ex-officio member of the local convention committee, appointed all committees and the editor of the Association's publication, was in charge of the Home Office and was responsible for all activities and transactions of the Association between conventions. Some of these responsibilities were later rescinded. The Council of Representatives decided that henceforth no convention would be held in a state which was not a cooperating member.

Following the convention President Burnes stopped over in Oklahoma City, on his way home to California, to speak to the Oklahoma Association of the Deaf and to urge OAD members to ratify the new plan. While he was on the platform he was handed a telegram from Gorden Allen in Minnesota. Following the St. Louis convention Allen, too, had hurried home to tell his fellow Minnesotans about the new NAD plan. Allen had wired Burnes to inform him that Minnesota had voted to ratify the new plan, becoming the first state association to do so. Oklahoma followed suit

within the hour, leaving 13 states to go. By August 1958 after most states had had their conventions a total of 16 had ratified the plan. By year's end the total had reached 27 of the existing 34 state associations. Not a single state which had considered the matter had opposed it. The new National Association of the Deaf was on its way.

Byron B. Burnes gives much credit for the success of the reorganization plan to Gordon Allen and G. Dewey Coats. Of the two, he said: "Allen fashioned laws that could be acceptable and Coats wrote lucid interpretations that helped put them across."

Captioned Films for the Deaf

Sometime around 1947 Emerson Romero, a deaf Cuban-born New Yorker bought some feature, documentary and short subject films and began adding subtitles to them. He spliced in captions between the scenes similar to the method used with the old silent films. He rented these captioned films to schools for the deaf, clubs, and churches for the deaf and they became popular. Romero began to envision a library of captioned films for the deaf. His method of captioning the films, however, had one serious drawback. Inserting captions between the scenes often broke up

Emerson Romero
(1900-1972)

Deafened at the age of six years by whooping cough, Romero was educated at the Wright Oral School in New York City, Stuyvesant High School, Blair Academy, and Lafayette College. At Blair he captained and coached the school's wrestling team, lettered in basketball and dabbled in dramatics although he was the only deaf student in the school. After a year with the Federal Reserve Bank in New York City, he decided to join his brother in Havana, Cuba. His brother had a contract to make some tourist films. Those were the days of the silent films and Romero acted in "A Yankee in Havana." This provided a chance encounter with a director from Hollywood and Romero was invited to the West Coast for an audition. In Hollywood he acted in 24 two-reel black and white silent comedies under the stage name of Tommy Albert. "Tillie's Punctured Romance," "The Cat's Meow" and "Sappy Days" were some of the films in which he performed. With the advent of the "talkies" Romero gave up acting and returned East but he never lost his attachment to the old silent films. (Romero's cousin, Caesar, became a movie star.)

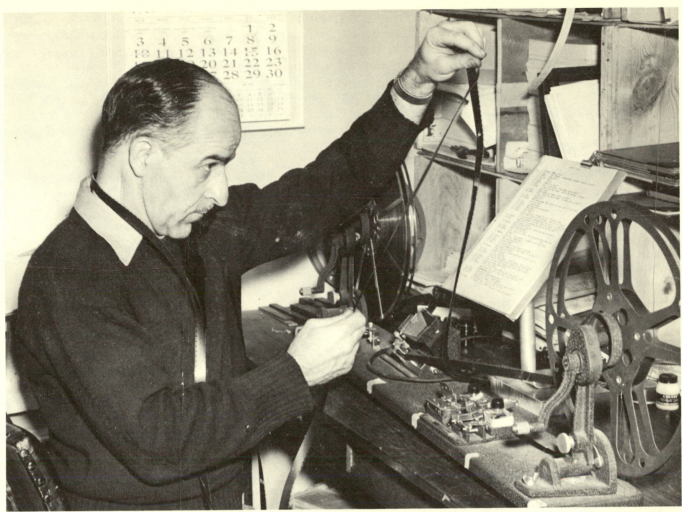

Emerson Romero working on a captioned film in his workshop.

the dialogue in mid-sentence and tended to make the films too long for the average audience. Also, the cost involved in acquiring and producing captioned films was difficult for one man to handle. Although Emerson had no direct contact with the Captioned Films for the Deaf which eventually evolved, he is considered a pioneer of the idea of a captioned films library for the deaf.

While visiting Dr. Clarence O'Connor at the Lexington School for the Deaf one day in 1950, Dr. Edmund B. Boatner, headmaster of the American School for the Deaf, observed the attempts of a young teacher to provide captions to a movie on a transparency for his deaf students. Boatner and O'Connor were struck by the attempt. There were talking books for the blind, they reasoned, why not captioned films for the deaf? They discussed their idea with colleagues in the field and with the encouragement of the Convention of

American Instructors of the Deaf Boatner began looking into the possibility of acquiring captioned films for deaf persons. With a grant of $5,000 from the Junior League of Hartford, he established Captioned Films for the Deaf, a non-profit corporation. Next, he approached J. Pierre Rakow, the supervising teacher in the vocational department at his school and discussed the project. Rakow was interested and volunteered to study the different methods used in captioning films. He found the superimposed method used to caption foreign films the most suitable. Eventually, Captioned Films for the Deaf was able to acquire, caption and rent 30 feature films. These superimposed captioned films quickly caught on and became popular, but Boatner soon realized, as Emerson had, that it was not economically feasible to maintain a captioned film library on a private basis. Purchasing the rights to films, adding subtitles, making repairs, cleaning the films

267

and distributing them proved too costly. So, Boatner set about seeking a solution. He believed that the only answer was a government-sponsored program. He approached Connecticut Senator William Purtell who agreed to introduce a bill in Congress to establish a free-loan service of subtitled motion pictures for the deaf. On September 2, 1958, P.L. 85-905 establishing Captioned Films for the Deaf was enacted into law.

The project was assigned by the Secretary of Health, Education and Welfare to the U.S. Office of Education to be administered. John A. Gough, principal of the Kendall School and chairman of the Department of Education at Gallaudet College was hired to administer the program. With passage of the law the original Captioned Films of the Deaf, Inc., group in Hartford disbanded and transferred its collection of films to the government program.

Gough, a hearing man, had a rich background in education of the deaf. As principal at the Missouri School for the Deaf, in 1938, he had experimented with the telautograph which provided a visual display of written classroom work projected on a screen, possibly one of the earliest versions of the overhead projector so widely in use today.

At the Kendall School he added closed circuit television to the classroom observation and teacher training program. His experience as an administrator at schools in the southern states convinced him that some federal aid to education was necessary to equalize learning opportunities. As director of Captioned Films for the Deaf he was now in a position to distribute large amounts of needed visual aid equipment and materials. (Years later Gough would express concern about the federal government's role in special education. He saw this aid used to dominate state educational programs to a degree that was disproportionate to the federal aid given. Out of this situation, he observed, had grown a monster known as mainstreaming which threatened to bring disaster to the special schools for the deaf if pursued to the extent favored by many well intentioned but misguided zealots.)

In 1960 Gough hired Malcolm J. Norwood as program specialist and research assistant. Norwood was the first deaf professional to join the Office of Education. As director of curriculum and supervising teacher at the West Virginia School for the Deaf in Romney, he had built up a large collection of filmstrips and was an early advocate of their use. He had also made it a regular practice to order captioned foreign films for the students.

When the Captioned Films for the Deaf program was enacted into law only $78,000 was appropriated.

During the fall and winter months of 1959-60 the program operated in low gear, receiving those films already captioned at the American School and setting up procedures for their circulation. The new law made provisions for the receipts of gifts but none was in sight. The Office of Education was so absorbed in carrying out the National Defense Education Act that Captioned Films was scarcely even a forgotten stepchild.

In May, 1960, as the federal fiscal year drew to a close, $3,000 was made available to the program. It was not sufficient for new films so Gough decided to use the money to fund a meeting in New York City to explore some of the needs of this new program and to examine what potentialities existed.

Under contract with the Lexington School for the Deaf in New York City, a committee was called together under the direction of the school librarian, Patricia Corey. Dr. Byron B. Burnes, president of the National Association of the Deaf and Dr. Boyce R. Williams of the Office of Vocational Rehabilitation were there representing the deaf community. Among the participants were film makers, film distributors and members of the Captioned Films staff. Maurice Mitchell, head of Encyclopedia Britannica Films based

They Say I'm Deaf

They say I'm deaf,
These folks who call me friend.
They do not comprehend.

They say I'm deaf,
And look on me as queer,
Because I cannot hear.

They say I'm deaf,
I, who hear all day
My throbbing heart at play,
The song the sunset sings,
The joy of pretty things,
The smiles that greet my eye,
Two lovers passing by,
A brook, a tree, a bird;
Who says I have not heard?
Aye, tho' it must seem odd,
At night I oft hear God.
So many kinds I get,
Of happy songs, and yet

They say I'm deaf!

—SAUL N. KESSLER
The Silent Muse

268

in Chicago, had been invited but sent in his stead his administrative assistant, Elliott Newcomb.

Demonstrations had been set up for the participants. One included an oral interpreter sitting next to a screen on which a sound film was being shown. The interpreter tried to explain orally to a group of deaf children what was being seen and heard on the screen. Totally unfamiliar with deaf students and deafness, Newcomb was shocked and amazed at the absolute futility of trying to communicate in this manner.

The following August, Elliott Newcomb was transferred from Chicago to head Encyclopedia Britannica Films' new Washington office. Shortly after his arrival Newcomb contacted John Gough and asked what was really needed to get the Captioned Films program moving. In the beginning Gough and other educators of the deaf had quickly realized the importance and vast potentialities of media in the classroom, but the law as it had been written limited the program to entertainment films. So, the answer to Newcomb's question was simple: sufficient funding and authorization to include educational materials as well as recreational films. The wheels began to turn.

A native of the state of Maine, Newcomb was a personal friend of Senator Edmund Muskie. Newcomb had directed Muskie's successful campaign for governor some years previously. Within weeks of Newcomb's arrival in the capital, the director of Captioned Films got a call from Senator Muskie's office and was invited to lay out a comprehensive design for expansion. Joining Muskie as the original sponsors of an amended bill were Senator Clariborne Pell and Representative John Fogarty, both of Rhode Island. The bill to expand the program was supported by teachers and professionals working with the deaf, industralists and, of course, deaf people themselves. It passed with no dissenting vote in either the House or Senate. President John F. Kennedy signed the bill into law in 1962.

The expanded program now embraced both educational and recreational films. Public Law 87-715 increased the scope and responsibilities of the program to include acquisition and adaption, research and development, production, distribution and training.

The establishment of four regional media centers and 60 educational film depositories followed. Annual workshops and institutes to introduce and train teachers in the use of media and other instructional materials were held around the country. In 1962 only one of the 300 schools registered with the program reported a person knowledgeable in the use of media. By 1969 over 700 schools had at least one person on their staff who was familiar with instructional media.

By 1974 more than 15,000 teachers of the deaf had received some kind of training in its use. Captioned

---

On His Deafness

My ears are deaf, and yet I seem to hear
Sweet nature's music and the songs of man,
For I have learned from Fancy's artisan
How written words can thrill the inner ear
Just as they move the heart, and so for me
They also seem to ring out loud and free.
In silent study, I have learned to tell
Each secret shade of meaning, and to hear
A magic harmony, at once sincere,
That somehow notes the tinkle of a bell,
The cooing of a dove, the swish of leaves,
The raindrop's pitter-patter on the eaves,
The lover's sigh, and thrumming of guitar—
And if I choose, the rustle of a star!

—ROBERT F. PANARA

Films for the Deaf was in business.

Gough assigned the responsibility of acquiring films to be captioned to Norwood. Initially, Norwood found many film producers reluctant to lease their better films fearing that the captioned versions would find their way to the public at large and cut into their profits. Norwood was able to assure them that it would not happen and they began leasing an increasing number of their more popular films. Then the rights to each film had to be negotiated individually. Twelve copies of an average length entertainment film with a five year lease cost at least $20,000. (The shorter 11-minute educational films averaged $12,000 for 65 prints.) Over the years Norwood was able to get many excellent films. One of his "scoops" was "Gone With the Wind" which he managed to lease (for $30,000) and caption before it appeared on national television. By 1970 Captioned Films for the Deaf was spending over $3 million on films and media material for the deaf. Approximately $600,000 was being spent for entertainment films which permitted the program to lease an average of 40 to 50 new titles a year.

When John Gough retired to Pittwillow Farm in Pennsylvania after ten years with the program, he was succeeded by Dr. Gilbert Delgado. Within two years, however, Delgado left to become dean of the Graduate School at Gallaudet College and Malcolm J. Norwood was named chief of the $19 million federal program.

The Fifties

The nineteen fifties were the decade which gave us Captioned Films, our first glimpse at a regularly interpreted television news program, a revitalized Gallaudet College and a reorganized National Association of the Deaf. More changes lay in store in the coming years.

Who were some of the persons who would appear on the national scene and help mold the coming decade?

Frederick C. Schreiber was pounding a Linotype keyboard at the Government Printing Office in Washington, D.C. Robert G. Sanderson was a soils analyst in Utah. Mervin D. Garretson was principal of the Montana School for the Deaf at Great Falls, and Edward C. Carney was working in a factory in St. Louis, Missouri. Terrence J. O'Rourke was teaching in North Carolina, and Roy Holcomb was teaching in South Dakota. James N. Orman was principal of the Manual Department at the Illinois School and Thomas J. Dillon was principal of the New Mexico School in Santa Fe. Jess M. Smith, and Ralph White were teachers. Alan B. Crammatte was on the Gallaudet College faculty, and Boyce R. Williams was with the Social Rehabilitation Services. Malcolm J. Norwood was a supervising teacher at the West Virginia School in Romney. Robert Lankenau was a chemist in Akron, Ohio. Don G. Pettingill was running a printing business in Lewiston, Idaho. Gertrude Galloway and Albert T. Pimentel were Gallaudet College students. And, of course, there were many others.

In the 1950s, for deaf America, things had finally begun to happen. An even more exciting decade awaited deaf Americans around the corner.

Milestones

Frederic G. Fancher (1890-1953) was educated at the New York School for the Deaf (Fanwood). As a student he learned to play various instruments in the school's military band (the first such band in a school for the deaf). He became a bandmaster at the Texas, Tennessee, and Illinois Schools for the Deaf. At ISD he organized and directed a band that attracted considerable attention and played before the Illinois Association of the Deaf, the National Fraternal Society of the Deaf, Rotary Clubs and other groups. One summer the band toured the eastern United States. Those who heard the band play rated it highly according to David Mudgett, one of the members. He recalled that students considered being a member of "Fancher's Band" as "the greatest thing in our lives." Fancher was also a houseparent at ISD.

Born December 14, 1890 in Staten Island, New York, Fancher died on November 27, 1953 in Jacksonville, Illinois.

Monroe Jacobs (1887-1950) was one of California's best known and highly respected deaf citizens. He was the father of Harry and Leo Jacobs. At one time he owned a print shop and published *The Deaf*, a small, state-wide newspaper. Jacobs died in August, 1950.

Chapter 13

Sports

Luther Taylor and his New York Giants teammates. Taylor is kneeling at far left.

Deaf Athletes' Contributions to the World of Sports

Deaf people claim two important contributions to the world of sports, both difficult to authenticate: the baseball umpire's hand count and the football huddle.

William E. Hoy, the deaf baseball outfielder for the Cincinnati Reds and Washington Senators claims that he was the reason for the hand count. He could not hear the call so umpires began raising their arm to indicate a strike and it soon caught on.

The evolution of the football huddle is difficult to trace but Paul D. Hubbard claims credit for its invention and many persons think he deserves the credit. The huddle was a necessary and natural evolution for a deaf football team because it was necessary for the deaf players to hide their signals from the scrub team they practiced against and from the deaf opponents they played. Hubbard was a quarterback on the 1892, 1893, 1894, and 1895 Gallaudet football teams. He captained the 1893 and 1895 teams and was nicknamed the "Eel" by other coaches. Gallaudet had begun playing the sport earlier but did not officially field a team until 1883.

Dr. I. H. Baker's encyclopedic *Football: Facts and Figures* states that the first football huddle was used by the University of Georgia in a game with Auburn in 1896. Baker bases the statement on information from Fuzzy Woodruff's account of the game in his *History of Southern Football*, written 32 years after the event. Hubbard was playing football before then.

Logic for the invention of the huddle is on the side of deaf players, unfortunately there is no printed documentation. William J. Marra and Stanley Ferguson of Kansas knew Hubbard personally and both recall Hubbard telling them that he had invented the huddle. He claimed that he had invented the huddle while playing at Gallaudet College.

Paul D. Hubbard

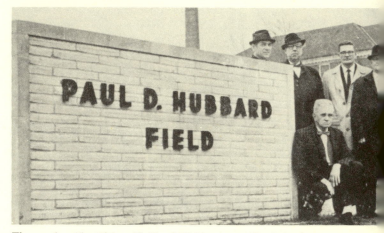

The marker identifying Hubbard Field was a gift of the Kansas Association of the Deaf.

Hubbard was a member of the Gallaudet College class of 1896 but he did not graduate. In a letter to him from his college classmate Herbert C. Merrill written March 6, 1942 is reference to the huddle. It reads: "The item ascribes the origin of the football "huddle" to you. It must have been during the time that the College had that "scrub" team that made all the teams around Washington, including the Naval Academy, look silly." The letter is in the William J. Marra Museum at the Kansas School for the Deaf, in Olathe.

On learning that the athletic field at the Kansas School had been officially named the Paul D. Hubbard Field, J. Frederick Meagher, the columnist wrote: "Congrats, Eel; am using your dope [in his column] with pride and joy. Hope to huddle on Hubbard Field with you someday."

In his September 1946 column in *The Frat* Meagher noted: "But Zuppke [an Illinois College coach] admits he took it from an un-named deaf football team he saw somewhere."

One final point. As many Gallaudet graduates left

continued on page 276

Any deaf athlete individually or a number of deaf athletes welded together as a team have through the years built up a tradition based upon the excellent competitive principles so well followed by all true sportsmen. Whether on the football gridiron, the baseball diamond, the basketball court, the track, the bowling alley, or in the natatorium, these hard driving competitors, whether in victory or defeat, have shown always the stuff of true manliness and the spirit of unfailing sportsmanship.

**—HADLEY W. SMITH, EDITOR
THE OHIO CHRONICLE (1950)**

Milestones in Sports

1870s—Ohio School became the first school for the deaf to play baseball.

1886—William E. Hoy began a 15-year baseball career in the majors.

1887—Albert Berg accepted an offer to coach football at Purdue University.

1897—William Geiluss, a place kicker on the Gallaudet College football team, sent the ball over the bar 27 times out of 31 tries between 1897 and 1901.

1898—The Gallaudet College football team beat Georgetown University, 18-6.

—The Gallaudet College football team beat the University of Virginia, 11-5.

1904—Frederick J. Neesam organized a basketball team at Gallaudet College.

1905—Luther H. Taylor played on the 1905 New York Giants team which won the World Series.

1915—The Colorado School for the Deaf and the Blind basketball team became the first school for the deaf team to go undefeated in regular season play. The team won 22 games.

—The Arkansas School for the Deaf baseball team won the state high school championship.

1918—J. Frederick Meagher won the 108-pound Amateur Athletic Union (AAU) wrestling championship and repeated in 1919.

1919—Glenn Smith won the 145-pound National AAU wrestling title.

1920s—Joe Allen quarterbacked an Ohio professional football team.

—Joe Worzel, a product of the Lexington School, captained the Silent Separates, a professional basketball team.

1922—Rolf Harmsen became the first deaf athlete to run the 100-yard dash in 9.8 seconds.

1929—The Arkansas School for the Deaf wrestling team coached by Nathan Zimble won the first of 13 consecutive state wrestling championships spanning a period from 1929 to 1941.

—In a game against Shenandoah College Gallaudet College fullback John Ringle made nine touchdowns and scored 59 points though playing in only half the game.

1930—Bilbo Monaghan became the first Gallaudet College athlete to become a professional foot-

ball player when he signed to play for the Memphis Tigers.

1931—The Nebraska School for the Deaf basketball team coached by Nick Petersen, won the state championship. The team won 29 games without a loss that year.

1933-34—Everett "Silent" Rattan won 109 straight wrestling matches as a professional wrestler.

1935—The Indiana School for the Deaf won the first official National Basketball Tournament held at the Western Pennsylvania School for the Deaf.

—The first bowling association of deaf bowlers, the Great Lakes Deaf Bowling Association, was organized.

—S. Robey Burns entered the first deaf American athletes in the International Games for the Deaf (World Games for the Deaf). John Chudzikewicz won America's first gold medal with a record javelin toss.

1936—Morris Davis won the National AAU 15-kilometer walking championship.

—The Missouri School for the Deaf won the state championship in track and field.

1940—Akron beat Toledo in the first softball tournament for the deaf held at Columbus, Ohio.

1941—The Arkansas School for the Deaf basketball team became the third school for the deaf to post an undefeated basketball record, 26-0.

1943—Gallaudet's "Iron Men" (Hal Weingold, Paul Baldridge, Earl Roberts, Don Padden and Roy Holcomb) won the Mason-Dixon basketball tournament. All five players were named to the All-Tournament Team.

1944—The American Deaf Women Bowling Association was organized.

1945—The American Athletic Association of the Deaf was organized; Buffalo (NY) Club won the first national AAAD basketball tournament.

1946—The Michigan School for the Deaf track team, coached by Earl Roberts, won the Class D State title. The school repeated the feat in 1947, 1950 and won three straight titles from 1961 to 1963.

—Eugene "Silent" Hairston won National AAU and Golden Gloves boxing titles.

1948—Chicago's Southtown Club of the Deaf won the

Central Athletic Association of the Deaf Fast-Pitch Softball Tournament six years in a row, 1948 to 1953.

—Angel Acuna, a graduate of the Arizona State School for the Deaf and the Blind, played on the Mexican Olympic basketball team and was the second highest scorer in the Olympics.

1949—The Nebraska School for the Deaf track team coached by George Propp, won the State Class D crown.

—The Arkansas School for the Deaf won the State Class B basketball championship.

1950—Camille Desmarais, a Gallaudet College wrestler from the American School for the Deaf, won the Mason-Dixon and the District of Columbia AAU 121-pound titles and was named Outstanding Wrestler in the country.

1950s—William Schyman played on the Boston Whirlwinds professional basketball team.

—The Gallaudet College wrestlers won a string of 36 consecutive Mason-Dixon Conference matches.

1951—The Gallaudet College wrestlers won the Mason-Dixon Conference tournament.

1952—The American Athletic Association of the Deaf Hall of Fame was organized. William E. Hoy and Luther H. Taylor, professional baseball players, were the first to be admitted to the Hall.

1953—Gertrude Ederle was admitted to the Helms Foundation Hall of Fame.

1954—Henry Brenner, a guard on the University of Rhode Island football team was named National Alpha Epsilon Pi's ''Jewish Athlete of the Year'' and was selected to the Little All-America team.

1955—Fifteen-year-old Helen Thomas became the youngest woman in history to win the Woman's Clay Target Championship of North America and the second to win the Women's Doubles Championship in the same year. She was the first Athlete of the Year to be selected by the AAAD Hall of Fame Committee.

—Gallaudet College won its third Mason-Dixon wrestling tournament.

—The Louisiana School for the Deaf won the State Class C Track and Field Championship. The school repeated in 1956, 1958, 1959, and 1962.

1957—The United States entered its first large team under AAAD sponsorship in the World Games for the Deaf at Milan, Italy.

1958—The Arizona State School for the Deaf and the Blind won the State Class C title in track and repeated in 1961 and 1962.

1960—The North Carolina School for the Deaf Negroes won its first of three straight National Schools for the Deaf Negroes basketball championships.

1961—Mary Ann Silagi, ranked the third best tennis player in the state by the Wisconsin Tennis Association, won a gold medal in the Women's Singles competition at the World Games for the Deaf in Helsinki, Finland.

1964—The National Deaf Bowling Association was organized.

1965—The United States hosted the Tenth World Games for the Deaf in Washington, D.C.

—Kevin Milligan became the first Gallaudet College cager to score 1,000 points during a four-year career. His basketball jersey, No. 24, was retired.

1966—Thirty-seven-year old Clyde Nutt, then with the Houston Club, scored his 1,000th point in AAAD tournament play against the Los Angeles Club.

1967—The United States sent its first team to the World Winter Games for the Deaf at Berchtesgaden, West Germany.

1968—The National Deaf Skiers Association was organized.

1969—Martin Willigan, wrestling for Hofstra University, won the 137-pound Middle Atlantic Wrestling title and was chosen Most Valuable Wrestler of the tournament.

1970—The Los Angeles Club of the Deaf became the first team to win five consecutive AAAD basketball tournaments.

1971—Ann Reifel won the Indiana state hurdles events.

1972—The Mississippi School for the Deaf girls track team won the first of its four State Class B titles.

—Washington State School for the Deaf won the Class A-B Track and Field title.

—Leon Grant became the first player in AAAD history to be named to the All-Tournament team nine times (out of nine appearances). He was selected the Most Valuable Player a record five times.

1973—Bonnie Sloan was drafted by the St. Louis Cardinals in the National Football League.

—Tom Berg and Art Kruger were inducted into the Helms Foundation Hall of Fame.

—Steve Blehm of the North Dakota School for the

Deaf, ended his high school basketball career with an average of 41.1 points per game over a four year period, the highest recorded career scoring average in high school competition in the nation according to *Letterman* magazine. The year before the national high scoring average was set by Bennie Fuller of the Arkansas School for the Deaf. He averaged 39.4 points.

1974—The Gallaudet men's volleyball team won the Potomac Intercollegiate Conference title and represented the conference at the National Association of Intercollegiate Athletics National Volleyball Tournament. The team won four consecutive PIC titles.

1975—The United States hosted the Eighth World Winter Games for the Deaf at Lake Placid, New York.

—The United States earned the most medals in Pan American Games for the Deaf competition held in Maracaibo, Venezuela.

1976—The Arizona State School for the Deaf and the Blind won the state eight-man football championship.

—Marvin Tuttle, one of Iowa School for the Deaf's outstanding basketball players, was inducted into the Iowa High School Athletic Association's Basketball Hall of Fame.

—Westchester (NY) Silent Club won the first AAAD National Slo-Pitch Softball tournament by beating Metropolitan Washington Association of the Deaf, 3-2.

—Mike Paulone of the Mt. Airy (Pa.) School for the Deaf became the first All-America Schools for the Deaf Player of the Year to win recognition for his performance in both basketball and football. He won the award again in 1977. Pau-

lone quarterbacked a hearing team in an All-Star city league.

—Renonia Greer bettered the Tennessee State High School (all classes) Girls' record with a long jump of 19 feet, 3¼ inches (5.87 meters) in the state indoor track and field meet at Murfreesboro.

—Lawson Pair, a Gallaudet College pitcher, led the nation in the National Collegiate Athletic Association Division III with the most strikeouts (101) and the best strikeout average (13.5). He was voted the Most Valuable Player in the Potomac Intercollegiate Conference twice.

—Kitty O'Neil set a land speed record in a rocket-powered racer in Oregon.

1977—The Colorado School for the Deaf and the Blind won the eight-man football State Class A Championship.

—The Americans won the most medals (103) at the World Games for the Deaf held at Bucharest, Romania for the highest total by any country since the Games began. The U.S. team overtook the Soviet Union with the most medals won since 1924.

—Fourteen-year-old Laura Barber and 17-year-old Jeff Float each won ten gold medals in swimming events at the World Games for the Deaf in Bucharest, Romania.

1978—Jeff Float became the first deaf swimmer to win a national AAU swimming title.

—The Florida School for the Deaf and the Blind won the State Class A track championship.

1979—The Washington Diplomats outlasted Chicago Lincoln, 115-103, in three overtimes to win the 1979 AAAD basketball title.

Gallaudet College football team, 1885.

Washington to accept teaching positions around the country, many of them started football teams at these schools and it was only natural that they adopted the Gallaudet "system," which other teams were quick to copy. Today millions of people watch football on television but few realize that the huddle they see forming regularly through the game is most likely a contribution to America's most popular sport by deaf football players.

Football

Football became a major sport in many schools for the deaf around the turn of the century. Gallaudet College was playing the sport in the 1880s and many of the college's graduates are credited with initiating the sport at these schools.

Gallaudet College was one of the first colleges in the Washington, D.C. area to begin playing football and during the 1890s the Gallaudetians were the undisputed city champs. Five members of the college's first officially-organized football team in 1883 later became presidents of the National Association of the Deaf. They were: Thomas Francis Fox, George W. Veditz, Olof Hanson, James L. Smith, and James Cloud.

Philip J. Hasenstab, who later became a minister, introduced the sport at the Illinois School in 1885. The California School in Berkeley was playing the game in 1889 with nearby University of California. The Tennessee School introduced the sport in 1892 and dropped an 18-8 contest with the University of Tennessee that year. But, by 1907, the Tennessee School had won the first City Prep School Championship.

Football became a major sport at the Minnesota School in 1895 and Paul Hubbard organized the first football team at the Kansas School in 1899. By 1902 the Missouri School, American School and many other schools were playing the sport.

In 1928 the Kansas School football team scored a total of 239 points against two Missouri teams. The KSD Jackrabbits beat St. Paul's College in Concordia, Missouri, 128 to 0; and the American Legion team of

276

Independence, Missouri, 111 to 0.

John Ringle was an all-around athlete at the Kansas School and Gallaudet College. He made the KSD football team when he was only 13 years old. At Gallaudet he earned the nickname "Jackrabbit" for his running ability. In one game against Shenandoah College, Ringle made nine touchdowns and five place kicks to beat them almost single-handedly in an 80-0 rout. And, he did that in only half the game. In his second year at Gallaudet Ringle was one of the leading college scorers in the country.

Inter-School Football Competition

Art Kruger, sports editor of *The Deaf American*, estimates that there have been over a thousand inter-school for the deaf football contests since 1903 when the North Carolina and Tennessee Schools for the Deaf first met on the gridiron. Tennessee won that match, 51-0. The second inter-school contest took place in 1920 between the Kansas and Missouri Schools with KDS winning, 26-0.

The Kansas-Missouri competition is the longest series among schools for the deaf. It has been interrupted three times during the 1920s, 1930s and 1940s. Missouri holds the edge with 23 wins to Kansas' 21. Three of the games have ended in ties.

Kansas has been credited with pioneering inter-school competition and has played more inter-school games than any other team. Over a period of 60 years Kansas has played 136 games against Missouri, Nebraska, Oklahoma, Texas, Iowa, Wisconsin, Minnesota and Illinois, winning 77 games, losing 53 and tying 6.

In 1976 the first international football game between two schools for the deaf was played when the Michigan School for the Deaf and Ontario (Canada) School for the Deaf met. Michigan won the contest, 74 to 12.

Percentage-wise the Illinois School has the best record. In 105 contests with other schools for the deaf the Illinois Tigers have won 78 games while dropping 20 with 7 games ending in a tie for a .791 percentage, according to Art Kruger. North Carolina has the second best percentage-wise record and Alabama is third.

Waldo Cordano, coach at the Wisconsin School has built one of the best percentage-wise won-lost records in modern times. From 1974 to 1977, his football teams have won 33 games, losing only 3.

The longest inter-school series in the East has been between the American School and Fanwood. That series began in 1935. ASD leads the series with 19 victories to Fanwood's 13. Two of the games ended in ties.

In the South, the Alabama-Tennessee series, which began in 1927, is the longest. Alabama leads with 18 victories to Tennessee's 8. Three games were ties.

The Mississippi-Louisiana annual contest is the longest in the Southwest. It began in 1945 and Louisiana has beaten Mississippi 18 times while dropping only 7 games.

State Football Champions

In 1976 the Arizona State School for the Deaf and the Blind won the State Class C eight-man football title. The following year, 1977, the Colorado School for the Deaf and the Blind won the Class A eight-man championship.

Undefeated Teams

Art Kruger has compiled a list of 64 football teams dating back to 1909 which have gone undefeated (page 278). Kruger has singled out the 1947 team of the Texas School for the Deaf as the best prep team of all time. The Texas Rangers, led by Lee Montez, went through the season undefeated and untied. They racked up 516 points in nine games to their opponents' 13 and accumulated 3,320 yards while surrendering only 748. Their total points were 12 points more than the all-time college team record in a single season set by Army in 1944. Lee Montez, the team's five-foot, seven-inch, 150-pound, 19-year old quarterback scored 30 touchdowns and made 59 extra points (out of a possible 66) for a total of 239 points in 9 games, a record that has never been surpassed.

Too many deaf people seek a soft way to circumvent a tough situation. Football does not teach short cuts.

—FRANK R. TURK
GALLAUDET COLLEGE FOOTBALL COACH

Winningest Seasons

The North Carolina School probably has the most winning seasons among schools for the deaf according to Art Kruger. The NCSD Bears have had 17 consecutive winning seasons from 1952 to 1968. During that period the school won 122 games, lost 33 and tied 4. The Pennsylvania School is second with 15 winning seasons in a row running from 1918 to 1933. The Mt. Airy Panthers won 97 games, lost 24 and tied 9.

All-Americans

Three deaf football players have made the National High School All-American Football Team. They are: Joe Russell of the Mississippi School in 1955, Robert Poncar of the Illinois School in 1961, and Jeff Lambrecht of the Louisiana School in 1962.

Professional Football

In the 1920s Joe Allen joined the Sandusky Maroons, a tough Ohio professional football team. Allen was an all-around athlete. He had played at the Col-

orado School for the Deaf and the Blind, with the Goodyear Silents, and he was the lone deaf cager on the Goodyear Wing's basketball team. Although he could not speak, he became the signal-calling quarterback on the Sandusky Maroon team and called signals by pointing to numbers written on his pants leg!

A few deaf football players have made it to the pros. In the 1930s, Bilbo Monaghan, fresh out of college, hitchhiked to Memphis, Tennessee to try out for Ernie Nevers' professional football team. Having little money, Monaghan slept on park benches until he made the team. Monaghan, who had picked up the

---

Undefeated Schools for the Deaf Football Teams
(Compiled by Art Kruger)

11-Man Football

Year	School and Coach	W-L-T	Pts.	Opp.
1909	Kansas (Luther Taylor)	9-0-0	127	6
1920	Oklahoma (Edward S. Foltz)	5-0-0	233	0
1920	Colorado (Alfred L. Brown)	5-0-0	198	21
1920	Washington (William Hunter)	5-0-0	185	53
1922	Washington (William Hunter)	6-0-1	211	12
1923	Michigan (unknown)	6-0-1	77	3
1924	Mt. Airy (George W. Harlow)	8-0-1	179	22
1925	Kansas (Edward S. Foltz)	6-0-1	73	3
1925	Colorado (Alfred L. Brown)	5-0-1	127	33
1929	Illinois (S. Robey Burns)	7-0-1	186	38
1930	North Carolina (Odie W. Underhill)	5-0-1	164	0
1930	New Jersey (Dwight Reeder)	6-0-0	108	7
1931	Illinois (S. Robey Burns)	6-0-2	214	18
1931	Wisconsin (Frederick Neesam)	7-0-2	114	32
1932	New Jersey (Fred Burbank)	7-0-0	131	0
1932	Ohio (Charles Miller)	5-0-2	107	12
1936	Tennessee (Jesse Warren)	6-0-1	172	44
1936	Mt. Airy (George W. Harlow)	7-0-2	159	18
1937	American (Walter C. Rockwell)	7-0-0	138	6
1938	Arkansas (Clyde Van Cleve)	9-0-0	250	46
1938	West Virginia (Kenneth Huff)	4-0-2	69	32
1939	American (Walter C. Rockwell)	5-0-1	113	6
1939	Virginia (T. Carlton Lewellyn)	8-0-0	201	33
1940	American (Walter C. Rockwell)	3-0-4	98	6
1940	Fanwood (Max Friedman)	4-0-2	102	0
1941	Colorado (Alfred L. Brown)	7-0-0	302	18
1941	Kansas (Edward S. Foltz)	6-0-0	136	12
1943	Louisiana (Edward Rodman)	7-0-1	—	—
1943	Texas (Rudolph Gamblin)	7-0-0	230	26
1944	Kansas (Charles Bilger)	8-0-0	198	75
1944	Iowa (Nathan Lahn)	4-0-2	156	20
1947	Texas (Jessee Hawthorne)	9-0-0	516	13
1947	Tennessee (E. Conley Akin)	8-0-0	381	33
1947	Washington (Harvey C. Haynes)	8-0-0	224	54
1949	North Carolina (Carroll Gainer)	9-0-1	351	46
1952	Oklahoma (Kenneth Norton)	9-0-1	280	32
1952	North Carolina (John Kubis)	8-0-1	192	40
1953	Kansas (Charles Bilger)	8-0-0	324	33
1953	Mississippi (Cecil B. Davis)	8-0-1	213	41
1954	Virginia (T. Carlton Lewellyn)	9-0-0	340	12
1954	North Carolina (John Kubis)	8-0-0	248	63
1954	Fanwood (Paul Kennedy)	5-0-0	153	0
1955	North Carolina (John Kubis)	8-0-0	309	38
1955	Alabama (Moran Colburn)	7-0-0	122	19
1955	Fanwood (Paul Kennedy)	6-0-0	249	33
1956	Fanwood (Paul Kennedy)	6-0-1	224	113
1958	West Virginia (Donald Bullock)	8-0-0	261	48
1958	Kansas (Charles Bilger)	7-0-0	236	27
1959	West Virginia (Donald Bullock)	6-0-2	225	59
1960	American (Oscar Shirley)	8-0-0	322	32
1960	North Carolina (Willard Hord)	8-0-1	271	32
1960	Texas (Raymond Butler)	8-0-0	258	51
1961	Louisiana (John Shipman)	8-0-0	180	27
1962	Washington (Harvey C. Haynes)	6-0-1	228	79
1962	Michigan (Earl Roberts)	8-0-0	236	38
1962	Kentucky (James D. Morrison)	6-0-0	133	0
1966	Fanwood (Paul Kennedy)	6-0-0	154	64
1969	Illinois (Jim Bonds)	9-0-0	361	44
1969	Virginia (Rocco De Vito)	10-0-0	400	46
1974	Wisconsin (Waldo Cordano)	9-0-0	234	120
1976	Florida (Mike Slater)	10-0-0	302	57
1976	Wisconsin (Waldo Cordano)	9-0-0	316	132
1978	Washington (Bob Devereaux)	8-0-0	238	57
1979	Model (Bob Westerman)	9-0-0	362	16

8-Man Football

Year	School and Coach	W-L-T	Pts.	Opp.
1967	Nebraska (Jack R. Gannon)	8-0-0	305	169
1971	Colorado (Joe Sisneros)	8-0-0	314	126
1972	Colorado (Joe Sisneros)	8-0-0	292	44
1977	Colorado (Joe Sisneros) (State Class A Champions)	11-0-0	444	128

6-Man Football

Year	School and Coach	W-L-T	Pts.	Opp.
1957	North Dakota (Henry Brenner)	6-0-0	193	38

278

Illinois School for the Deaf

Illinois School for the Deaf football team in 1894. (DD probably stands for Deaf and Dumb.)

nickname, "Mule" while in college, was the first Gallaudet College athlete to make it to the pro football ranks. He was a drawing card at home games and in a game against the Chicago Cardinals he made two interceptions and ran 82 and 75 yards for touchdowns. His coach, Frosty Peters, learned sign language so the two could communicate with each other. Afterwards, Monaghan was a successful coach at his alma mater, the Mississippi School for the Deaf.

In the late 1960s Ray Parks, a Virginia School alumnus and Edward Gobble, a standout performer at the North Carolina School, and William Zachariasen of the Illinois School played for the Frederick Falcons, a semi-pro team.

In 1973 Bonnie Sloan, a six-foot, four-inch, 270-pound player from Austin Peay State College became the first deaf player to be drafted by the National Football League. He was the tenth round draft choice of the St. Louis Cardinals, who signed him to a contract. Sloan earned a starting defensive tackle position

in his first season with the Cards. Unfortunately, he damaged a ligament in his right knee early in the season and had to sit out the remaining seven games. When he returned to the Cardinals camp the following year he again re-injured his knee during the preseason and was dropped from the squad. The following spring he signed to play for the New Orleans Saints but once again his knee buckled under him and he was out for the season. In 1976 he signed up with the New York Giants only to re-injure his knee forcing him to abandon his dream of a pro football career.

Competing thus in a hearing world, it is then only natural that the athletic field of endeavor will again find the deaf maneuvering with serious effort and challenging power to meet once more the test of making good, no matter what odds may loom to deter them.

HADLEY W. SMITH, EDITOR
THE OHIO CHRONICLE

279

The undefeated 6-man football team coached by Henry Brenner in 1957. This North Dakota School team won six games.

Sloan attended Austin Peay State College in Clarksville, Tennessee where he was a B-minus student majoring in health education. The head coach there was the father of a deaf boy. In college Sloan was a two-time all-conference selection and twice made honorable mention on Little All-America. He was his team's most valuable player during his senior year.

The Goodyear Silents

No sports story about deaf athletes would be complete without mention of the Akron, Ohio, Goodyear Silents. The team was composed of graduates of schools for the deaf and Gallaudet College attracted to the rubber plants of Akron during World War I. Organized in 1916, the team played amateur and semi-pro football teams in Ohio and nearby states. In its brief history the team produced a record of 65 victories, six defeats and three ties.

The 1917 Silents won eight of ten games and laid claim to the Central Ohio Championship. The team was undefeated in 1918 and the following year ran its string of victories to 16 before dropping a roughly fought but well-played game with the Goodyear Reg-

KRAMP   CHRISTNER   COOMB   HICKMAN   STOTTLER   PAYNE   FITZGERALD   ROLLER   DYER   DAVIS   MOOI   GOC

CLASS A 8-MAN
STATE CHAMPIONS
1977

This 1977 8-man Colorado School for the Deaf and the Blind team compiled an 11-0 record. The team was coached by Joe Sisneros and won the state championship.

ulars, 14-0, in the season's final game. That year, 1919, word of their prowess reached into Canada where a team named the Windsor Blue Jackets heard about them and challenged them to a contest. The Blue Jackets had not lost a game in two years. Following the game the Blue Jackets wished they had never heard of the Akron Silents. The Silents steamrolled over them, 115-0!

In 1920 the Silents were 9-1 and in 1921 the team won nine games, lost two and tied one. They won 12 consecutive games in 1922 before dropping a 20-7 contest to the Akron Professionals. From 1919 to 1922

the Silents built a record of 39 wins, three losses and three ties and scored 1,100 points to their opponents' 161.

Then post-war depression struck and layoffs and better opportunities elsewhere began to drain the team of its top players. To keep the team going, hearing co-workers were invited to join and fill the gaps. By 1925 there were not enough players to maintain the team, and one of the greatest chapters in Rubber City and in deaf sports came to a close.

The Goodyear Silents football team of 1921.
AAAD Hall of Fame Collection

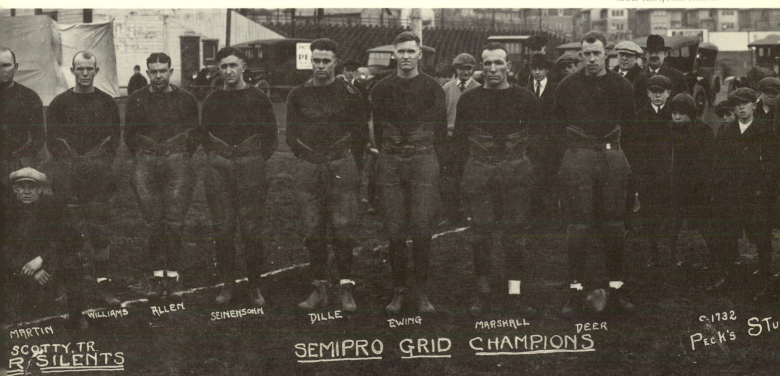

MARTIN
SCOTTY, TR.
R/SILENTS

WILLIAMS   ALLEN   SEINENSOHN   DILLE   EWING   MARSHALL   DEER

SEMIPRO GRID CHAMPIONS

S.1732
PECK'S STUO

Bowling

No other sport attracts as much participation among deaf men and women as bowling. There are the local leagues, state, regional, and national competitions.

Many clubs of the deaf have their own leagues or sponsor teams which participate in hearing leagues. The Chicago Club has a bowling league dating back to the mid-thirties. The Greater Los Angeles Deaf Women's Bowling Association has been in existence for over a decade. The Southern California Associated Mixed Bowlers of the Deaf has ten mixed leagues and sponsors an annual tournament of champions from each league in the Los Angeles area, men and women All-Star competition, and doubles competition.

The Great Lakes Deaf Bowling Association, which calls itself the "American Bowling Congress of the Deaf," is the oldest and largest bowling tournament in the country. GLDBA which, as its names applies, covers the Great Lakes region, is ideally located and annually attracts 130 or more teams of 650 men who compete for the $10,000-plus prize money. The American Deaf Women's Bowling Association, the female counterpart, is also the oldest and largest deaf women's bowling organization. It holds its tournaments concurrently with GLDBA, attracts over 50 teams and more than 900 bowlers. It was organized in the mid-forties.

There are other bowling associations: The Eastern Deaf Bowling Association, the Atlantic Coast Deaf Women's Bowling Association, the Pacific Coast Deaf Bowling Association, which has a special attraction—the Pacific Coast Deaf Masters. The Pacific Coast Deaf Women's Bowling Association also has a version of the Masters called the Deaf Queens tournament. Other bowling associations include the Southwest Deaf Bowling Association, the Dixie Bowling Association of the Deaf, the Northwest Bowling Association of the Deaf, and the Midwest Deaf Bowling Association.

The National Deaf Bowling Association was organized in 1963. This organization holds a special World's Deaf Bowling Championship. It is trying to get all seven regional bowling associations to affiliate with it. NDBA publishes a quarterly newsletter named *The Deaf Bowler*, with news and information geared to the interests of deaf bowlers.

Michigan and New York have their own state bowling associations and hold annual bowling tournaments.

Art Kruger has recorded a list of eight deaf bowlers who have bowled a sanctioned perfect game of 300:

1941—Andy McGrath, Detroit, Michigan
1952—Byron McDaniels, Madison, Wisconsin
1963—Ralph Reese, Peoria, Illinois
1967—Lowell Kumler, Minneapolis, Minnesota
1973—Bob Brame, Arlington, Texas
1974—Robert Coker, Tolono, Illinois
1974—Frank Gallo, Jr., Deer Park, New York
1979—Ron Smith, Rochester, New York

Basketball

In 1904 Frederick J. Neesam organized a basketball team at Gallaudet College. When he returned to his alma mater, the Wisconsin School for the Deaf, in 1906, he introduced the game there. Before long other schools for the deaf were playing the sport.

In 1914-15 the Colorado School for the Deaf and the Blind basketball team was undefeated. Alfred L. Brown coached the team to a 22-0 record. One of his stars was Joe Allen.

In 1931 Nick Petersen's Nebraska School for the Deaf team made history when it became the first school for the deaf to win a state basketball tournament. A total of 850 Nebraska high school teams started the all-class state playoffs. The Nebraska School was the only one to emerge unbeaten. NSD beat three other undefeated teams along the way and closed the season with a 29-0 record.

In 1940-41 the Arkansas School for the Deaf basketball team went through its regular 23-game season undefeated. The team beat six other schools for the deaf and won the southern and national championships, becoming the third school for the deaf to finish a season undefeated.

In the 1949 the Arkansas School became the second school to win a state championship. Coached by Edward S. Foltz, the ASD Leopards won the state Class B title that year.

In 1937 the Mississippi School was invited to participate in the third national basketball tournament at the Illinois School in Jacksonville, Illinois. The Mississippi team coached by a youthful Bilbo Monaghan made the 700-mile trip in a truck. The Wisconsin School coached by Frederick J. Neesam won the tourney.

Nate Echols, a five-foot, seven-inch tall 170-pounds star from the St. Mary's School was the first black player to participate in the Eastern State Schools for the Deaf Basketball Tournament. Echols was also the first of his race to compete in the American Athletic

This 1931 Nebraska School for the Deaf basketball team was the first school for the deaf team to win a state basketball championship. Nick Petersen was the coach.

Association of the Deaf Basketball Tournament. He made the all-tournament team four times and led his Buffalo, New York club to two national titles.

Regional Basketball Tournaments

Today there are six annual regional basketball tournaments for schools for the deaf. They are Central, Eastern I, Eastern II, Mason-Dixon, New England, and the California Classic.

The first regional tournament was held at the Nebraska School in 1924 with the Kansas, South Dakota, Iowa, and Nebraska schools competing. The Kansas School won that tournament. The competition resumed in 1936 and continued until 1941. The tournament was abandoned in 1942 when the National Federation of State High School Athletic Associations ruled against unsanctioned meets.

School for the Deaf Basketball Teams Which Have Won 20 or More Games In a Season

(Compiled by Art Kruger)

Year	School	Coach	W-L
1915	Colorado	Alfred L. Brown	22-0
1926	Ohio	Philip Holdren	21-2
1927	Indiana	Arthur Norris	21-9
1928	Arkansas	Earl Bell	24-6
1930	Mt. Airy	George W. Harlow	21-12
1931	Nebraska	Nick Petersen	29-0
	Mt. Airy	George W. Harlow	26-2
	Texas	Unknown	20-3
	Illinois	S. Robey Burns	24-10
1933	Mt. Airy	George W. Harlow	22-10
1936	New Jersey	Fred Burbank	24-3
1938	New Jersey	Fred Burbank	26-4
	Mississippi	Bilbo Monaghan	26-10
1939	Arkansas	Clyde Van Cleve	27-6
	Mississippi	Bilbo Monaghan	28-4
	Maryland	James McVernon	21-3
1940	Texas	C. R. Brace	27-7
	Arkansas	Clyde Van Cleve	23-8
	Illinois	Spike Wilson	22-10
1941	Arkansas	Clyde Van Cleve	26-0
	Iowa	Nathan Lahn	22-3
1945	Utah	Kenneth Burdett	21-2
1948	Arkansas	Edward S. Foltz	25-2
1949	Arkansas	Edward S. Foltz	24-1
1951	St. Mary's	John Rybak	20-4
	New York	Paul Kennedy	20-5
	Arkansas	Perl Dunn	25-3
1952	Arizona	Frank Sladek	21-5
	Illinois	Art Yates	21-8
	Arkansas	Perl Dunn	20-7
1953	Virginia	T. Carlton Lewellyn	23-3
1955	St. Mary's	John Rybak	22-2
	North Carolina	George K. Brown	20-5
1956	Illinois	Jim Spink	22-7
	Iowa	Nathan Lahn	20-6
	Missouri	Paul Baldridge	20-10
1957	West Virginia	Malcolm Norwood	21-3
1960	North Carolina Negro	Bill Nelson	24-5
1961	North Carolina Negro	Bill Nelson	26-1
	Florida Negro	James Magness	22-4
1962	North Carolina Negro	Bill Nelson	26-2
1964	Mississippi Negro	Eugene Dorsey	23-7
	Alabama Negro	Harlteen Stamps	21-4
1965	St. Rita	Pat Sweeney	20-2
	Texas Negro	Matthew Caldwell	30-6
	Mississippi Negro	Eugene Dorsey	25-6
	Alabama Negro	Harlteen Stamps	26-12
1966	Alabama Negro	Harlteen Stamps	27-6
1966	North Carolina Negro	Bill Nelson	20-8
1967	Boston	John Muir	21-2
	Florida	Frank Slater	20-3
	Alabama Negro	Harlteen Stamps	21-5
1968	Arkansas	Houston Nutt	24-9
	Texas	Billy Snowden	25-2
	Alabama Negro	Harlteen Stamps	27-6
	Mississippi Negro	Eugene Dorsey	20-4
1969	Texas	Billy Snowden	26-2
	Arkansas	Houston Nutt	23-4
1970	Rhode Island	Jim Cooney	24-2
	Arkansas	Houston Nutt	26-4
1971	Rhode Island	Jim Cooney	20-6
	North Dakota	Henry Brenner	20-4
	Arkansas	Houston Nutt	20-13
1972	Rhode Island	Jim Cooney	23-6
	North Dakota	Henry Brenner	20-6
	Texas	Prentis Ming	21-7
1973	Rhode Island	Jim Cooney	21-5
1975	Texas	Richard Black	24-9
1976	Rhode Island	Jim Cooney	21-6
	Georgia	Ezekiel McDaniel	23-3
	Illinois	Mike Moore	20-6
	Texas	Richard Black	20-9
1978	Georgia	Ezekiel McDaniel	20-6
1979	Kansas	Larry Beaver	21-3

Art Kruger's National Deaf Prep Basketball Coach of the Year

Year	School	Coach	W-L
1949	Arkansas	Edward S. Foltz	27-1
1950	Nebraska	George Propp	18-1
1951	St. Mary's (NY)	John Rybak	20-4
1952	Arizona	Frank Sladek	21-5
1953	Virginia	T. Carlton Lewellyn	23-3
1954	St. Mary's (NY)	John Rybak	19-5
1955	Missouri	Paul Baldridge	14-11
1956	Illinois	Jim Spink	22-7
1957	West Virginia	Malcolm Norwood	21-3
1958	Alabama	Harry L. Baynes	18-4
1959	Pennsylvania	Erv Antoni	12-9
1960	American (CT)	Oscar Shirley	19-1
1961	Oklahoma	Kenneth Norton	17-5
1962	Tennessee	Ron Bromley	15-7
1963	Tennessee	Ron Bromley	18-9
1964	Washington	Robert Devereaux	16-6
1965	St. Rita	Pat Sweeney	20-2
1966	Alabama Negro	Harlteen Stamps	27-6
1967	Boston	John Muir	21-2
1968	Texas	Billy Snowden	25-2
1969	Arkansas	Houston Nutt	23-4
1970	Rhode Island	Jim Cooney	24-2
1971	North Dakota	Henry Brenner	20-4
1972	Tennessee	Dave Bailey	18-9
1973	Wisconsin	Alexander Rubiano	16-5
1974	Georgia	Zeke McDaniel	18-5
1975	Kentucky	Don Hackney	14-10
1976	Riverside	Seymour Bernstein	11-9
1977	South Carolina	Bob Morrow	12-10
1978	Illinois	Mike Moore	18-7
1979	Washington	Frank Karben	14-10

Indiana School for the Deaf girls basketball team, 1921-22.

The first Central States tournament was held at the Indiana School in 1925 through the efforts of Arthur Norris, Sr. Teams from the Central states competed in the tournament until 1941 when it was suspended because of the war. The competition was resumed in 1971 through the efforts of Mike Moore, the Illinois School coach. The Illinois School has won the tournament eleven times.

In 1927 schools in the southern part of the United States began competing against each other in tournament play. The Rev. J. W. Michaels offered a traveling trophy to the school which won three consecutive tournaments. His own Arkansas School wasted no time in winning it by capturing the first three tournament championships from 1927 to 1929. This tournament offered competition to the participants on and off until 1948 when the high school athletic association ruled against unsanctioned meets.

The Eastern Schools for the Deaf Basketball Tournament was conceived by Frederick A. Moore, a teacher and coach at the New Jersey School for the Deaf in 1927. The Jersey School had moved to its new plant in West Trenton in the Fall of 1926. The tournament was held in the school's new gymnasium that winter. Host NJSD beat Maryland for the first title. Except for 1928 and during the second World War, the tournament has been held consistently since. In 1960 the tournament was divided into two divisions, one for the smaller schools and one for the larger schools.

T. Carlton Lewellyn, coach and athletic director of the Virginia School for the Deaf and the Blind, was the originator of the Mason-Dixon Basketball Tournament. It was first played at the Virginia School in Staunton in March 1953, and it has been held annually

since. The North Carolina and Tennessee Schools have won the tournament six times each.

The New England Schools for the Deaf Basketball Tournament began at the Mystic Oral School in Connecticut in 1964 with six schools participating. In 1973 the tournament was split into two divisions to provide more evenly-matched competition among schools with comparable enrollments. The Rhode Island School has won the tournament five times.

In 1976 the California Classic Basketball Tournament was organized and played at the California School in Berkeley. The New Mexico School for the Deaf captured that first tournament and the Washington School won the following two.

National Basketball Tournament

In 1935, through the leadership of J. Frederick Meagher, a National Basketball Tournament was organized. It continued until 1941 and the outbreak of World War II. During those brief years, with the exception of 1940, four regional school for the deaf teams competed for the national crown. The winners were:

1935—Indiana at the Western Pennsylvania School
1936—New Jersey at the Western Pennsylvania School
1937—Wisconsin at the Illinois School
1938—New Jersey in New York City
1939—New Jersey at the Illinois School
1940—Indiana at the Indiana School
1941—Arkansas at the Illinois School.

This Model Secondary School for the Deaf girls' basketball team won the Eastern Schools for the Deaf Basketball Tournament.
MSSD Preview

LeRoy Colombo   Nathan Zimble

All-American Selections

During the 1930s J. Frederick Meagher initiated selection of mythical national champions among schools for the deaf. He was aided in making these selections by an All American Deaf Schools Basketball Board, now defunct, consisting of Everett H. Davies of the Western Pennsylvania School, Edward S. Foltz of Kansas, S. Robey Burns of Illinois, Harry L. Baynes of Alabama, George W. Harlow of Mt. Airy, and John Wilkerson of the New York Fanwood School.

Art Kruger began naming All-America teams for *The New York Journal of the Deaf* in 1935, and Leonard Warshawsky of *The Frat* started his selections in 1949. These All America team selections have brought recognition to hundreds of deserving deaf athletes throughout the country.

Swimming

LeRoy Colombo, who is listed in the *Guinness Book of World Records* for the number of lives he saved, an

incredible 907 over a 40-year period, was a deaf lifeguard on the beaches of Galveston, Texas. Deafened at seven years, he started swimming in his teens. Colombo won his first race in 1924 when he beat Herbert Brenan, the AAU National Endurance Champion in a one-mile race. The following year he beat Brenan again in a ten-mile swim, finishing a mile ahead of him and setting a new record by covering the distance in 6 hours and 55 minutes.

A reporter once asked Colombo if he had ever received an award for saving a life. "Yes," Colombo had responded. A grateful owner gave him $25.00 when he saved a dog from drowning. What about people, were they appreciative? No, responded Colombo. They were embarrassed and they even crossed the street to avoid passing him face to face.

Colombo was born in 1905. He attended the Texas School for the Deaf. He died July 2, 1974. On the occasion of his death the members of the Texas Senate stood for a moment's silence in his honor. There is a plaque in his memory in Galveston.

Another swimmer, Gillian Hall, won the Connecticut State Championship in synchronized swimming three years in a row in the late 1950s. A graduate of the American School for the Deaf, she was chosen Athlete of the Year by the American Athletic Association of the Deaf in 1959.

Frederick Savinsky of Warren, Michigan, became the first swimmer to win five gold medals in the World Games for the Deaf. At the Belgrade, Yugoslavia Games in 1969 he set world records in the 100-meter freestyle, 200-meter butterfly, and 400-meter freestyle events, and he was a member of two relay teams.

Another swimmer from Warren, Michigan, Ronald P. Rice, 17, won the 100-meter, 400-meter and 1,500-meter freestyle races and was a member of the 400-meter medley and 800-meter relay teams at the seventh World Games for the Deaf held at Malmo, Sweden, in 1973. Seven world records were established in all those events. Rice became the second swimmer

Led by such coaches and mentors, the deaf athletes have graven an enviable record, which forever will stand as another indelible proof that the deaf can and do lead normal lives, oftentimes more "normally" than some of our hearing opponents actually enjoyed upon comparing final scores.

—HADLEY W. SMITH, EDITOR
THE OHIO CHRONICLE

and the second USA athlete to win five gold medals in WGD competition.

In 1977 Jeffrey Float of Sacramento, California and Laura Barber of Allison, Pennsylvania won 10 gold medals each in swimming events at the World Games for the Deaf in Bucharest, Romania. Float set nine individual world records and Barber set ten. The following year, Float became the first deaf swimmer to win a national AAU swimming title when he won the 400-meter freestyle event at Houston, Texas.

Wrestling

The Arkansas School was the most successful school for the deaf in wrestling. The sport was organized at the school in 1926, and in the years that followed the school's teams won a total of some 20 state AAU championships. Teams coached by Nathan Zimble won 13 straight state titles from 1929 to 1941.

Zimble himself was a successful deaf wrestler. He entered Gallaudet College in 1919 as a 95-pound preparatory student. He wore glasses, was slightly stooped from a childhood illness, was pale and thin and the smallest boy in the college. He became the butt of campus jokes. Every time he stuck his head in the gym the bigger boys grabbed him and tossed him around like a medicine ball. As a practical joke the Class of 1920 presented him with a pair of dumb-bells, so heavy that he could not lift them and had to ask two of his friends to carry them to his dormitory room. The teasing, which he took good-naturedly, only increased his determination, however, to develop his physique. By his junior year he made the wrestling team, and as a senior he was elected the team's captain, to everyone's surprise. That year he and seven teammates entered the South Atlantic Division of the

This Gallaudet College wrestling team won the 1951 Mason-Dixon Conference championship. Front row, from left: Don Bullock, Dean Swaim, Sanford Diamond and Camille Desmarais. Second row: Coach Thompson Clayton, David Carlson, Clyde Ketchum, Frank Turk and Harry Schaffner.

AAU wrestling tournament. He alone emerged a winner. He won the 112-pound championship and a new campus identity: "The Mighty Atom."

Zimble accepted a teaching position at the Arkansas School and eventually became principal. He left the school in 1945 and returned to his native Philadelphia where he became a watch repairman. ASD dropped wrestling as a sport a few years later.

In the 1970s a number of schools for the deaf began adding wrestling to their athletic programs. By 1979 there were at least 24 schools offering the sport.

Alonzo Whitt, an alumnus of the Kentucky School and a coach at the Colorado School, has been the most successful wrestling coach in recent years. During his ten years at Colorado he has produced six wrestlers who have won state Class A titles. One of them, Jesus Contreras, won the state title three times. During his

four-year high school wrestling career he won 107 matches and lost only three. Contreras was selected outstanding wrestler in the state in his final year, named the *Gazette Telegraph* Athlete of the Year, chosen *The Deaf American* Wrestler of the Year, and selected a member of the USA World Games for the Deaf wrestling team, which competed in Bucharest, Bulgaria in 1979 where he won the silver medal in freestyle wrestling and a bronze in Greco-Roman wrestling.

Contreras' teammate, Bernie Atencio, also made it to the World Games where he won a bronze in freestyle wrestling. As a sophomore Atencio won the 112-pound Class A state championship and was honored as the state's outstanding Class A wrestler. He compiled a 105-win, four loss and one tie record as a high school athlete.

Harold Deuel, a Missouri School product, coached the North Carolina School for the Deaf wrestling team to a 103-61-1 record over eleven years.

Harold Koch is another successful deaf wrestling coach. An alumnus of the Minnesota School, Koch became head wrestling coach at the Pennsylvania School at Mt. Airy in 1977. His teams have won four straight Eastern Schools for the Deaf wrestling tournaments. Five of his wrestlers—Tom Buckingham, Frank Imparo, Eugene Miller, Alfred Estrada and Mike Estrada—have had 20 or more wins per season. Miller was *The Deaf American* Wrestler of the Year in 1978 and 1979 and had a record of 42 consecutive wins.

Gallaudet College Wrestling

Roy J. Stewart credits Tom Jenkins, a champion heavyweight wrestler of the world, with introducing wrestling at Gallaudet College. In the fall of 1904 a strong and well-built lad from Kansas named Thomas S. Williams entered Gallaudet College and immediately tried out for the football team. He earned a starting position as right guard on the first team. He was playing his second game in his second year when it was discovered that he was blind in one eye. He was immediately dropped from the squad rather than risk injury to his remaining good eye.

Everett "Silent" Rattan

The Silent Worker

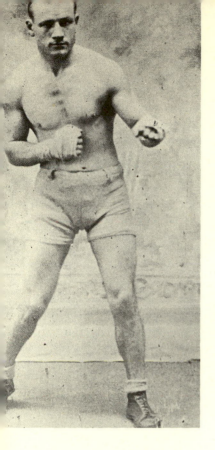

A heartbroken Williams was looking for another sport to participate in when he learned that Tom Jenkins, the champion wrestler, was also blind in one eye. That ended Williams' search. He decided to take up wrestling. He read every book he could find on the sport. Jimmie Virstein, the college football trainer, who was a 135-pound Navy wrestling champ, volunteered his services as coach. Gilbert O. Erickson, '03, became William's wrestling partner and Roy J. Stewart became all-around handyman. It was Stewart's responsibility to raise money to purchase equipment, serve as timekeeper and the sport's reporter. From that beginning grew Gallaudet's involvement in wrestling. Stewart recalled that during those early years the wrestlers were not recognized by the Gallaudet College Athletic Association (which sanctioned and financed all college athletic teams) until the wrestlers started bringing home gold medals, then "they were eagerly taken in and wrestling became part of the GCAA program," said Stewart.

In the early 1930s Thompson Clayton appeared on the campus to referee a wrestling meet between Gallaudet and Johns Hopkins University. Clayton had started a wrestling team at St. Alban's High School. In 1935 he was coaching the Gallaudet team, the Central YMCA, the Washington Boys Club, the Racquet Club, and other teams. "It was not that I was such a great coach," Clayton reminisces, "there were few people around Washington who knew anything about the sport." The Gallaudet matmen that year won the District of Columbia AAU championship.

Clayton returned to Gallaudet College in 1947. The team placed second at the conference meet. In 1949 they again won the local AAU title. From February 1950 to February 1956 Clayton's teams were undefeated in Mason-Dixon Conference competition and ran up a string of 36 consecutive victories. What makes this even more remarkable is the fact that Clayton seldom had more than two men on his squad who had ever been on a wrestling mat before coming to college. In 1955 Gallaudet won its third Mason-Dixon Conference championship and *Body Builder* magazine named Clayton All American Wrestling Coach of the Year.

National AAU Wrestling Champions

J. Frederick Meagher won the 108-pound Amateur Athletic Union National wrestling championship in 1918 and 1919. Art Kruger, sports editor of *The Deaf American*, believes Meagher was the first deaf person to win a national title. Glenn Smith, another wrestler, won the 145-pound AAU title in 1919. Meagher and Smith were members of the same Gary, Indiana YMCA wrestling team. It won the national team title

Thomas Martin

come a wrestler like "Silent" Olson. He did. He became "Silent" Rattan, a very successful deaf professional wrestler and a better-known wrestler than Suttka, the man who inspired him.

In 1926 Rattan won the Missouri AAU 118-pound title. He turned professional in 1930 and toured Texas and the Southwest, winning 109-straight matches. He took on Jack Reynolds, who was the undisputed welterweight champion of the world for 18 years, and three times wrestled Reynolds to a draw. He won the National Junior Heavyweight title, and held the Great South and Southwestern States Welterweight crown from 1930 to 1933 and the World Junior Middleweight crown from 1933 to 1934. He retired from the ring in 1949.

After World War II, Rattan coached a hearing wrestling team in Oregon. Five of his wrestlers made it to the national AAU meet. Rattan was an intelligent, likeable, outgoing person. After he quit the ring he worked in a Los Angeles bakery.

Professional Boxers

William O. Dilsworth, a deaf Marylander known also as "Dummy Decker," won a draw in 1910 with

Edward Dundon

in 1919. As a collegiate athlete, Smith was a center on the 1912-13 Notre Dame football team. One of his teammates was the immortal Knute Rockne.

Deaf Professional Wrestlers

One day in the 1920s a deaf professional wrestler named William Suttka, who wrestled under the name of "Silent" Olson, visited the Missouri School for the Deaf and spoke to the students. He was a big, mean, muscular looking man. The young students were awed at his appearance. One of them wanted to know if Suttka had always been as big and muscular as he was. "No," said Suttka, and looking around the group he pointed to one small, skinny lad and said, "I used to be skinny like *him*." The lad he pointed to was a young boy named Everett Rattan, who did not like to be picked out for such a comparison. He decided right there that he would develop a strong body and be-

290

Deaf Professional Baseball Players

Edward J. Dundon

Isaac H. Sawhill

William L. Sawhill

William E. Hoy

William Funkhouser

Reuben C. Stephenson

George P. Kihm

Luther H. Taylor

Dalton H. Fuller

George M. Leitner

Lester G. Rosson

Paul S. Curtis

Harry F. Dix

Richard F. Sipek

NOTE: William J. Deegan, Pitcher, 1901 — 1 Year, New York (No Photo)

Ralph E. LinWeber Sports Bureau

Jack Britton, who later became a welterweight champion.

Thomas "Silent" Martin of New York City fought 256 fights over a 13-year period. He also fought Britton to a draw, in 1916.

Hilton "Fitzy" Fitzpatrick, who was a 1940 All-America selection on the West Virginia School for the Deaf football team, chalked up nearly 100 fights as an amateur, losing only six of them. In 1941 he won the West Virginia AAU Middleweight championship and became a professional boxer. As a pro he knocked out Jimmy Reeves in five rounds. In 1947 he met Ezzard Charles, the reigning light heavyweight champion, twice, but Fitzy was knocked out both times. Fitzpatrick retired from the ring in 1951 when he was 30 years old. During his years as a pro he fought 94 fights and won 77 of them. Twenty-two of these victories were first-round knockouts. At one time he was rated the nation's number one light heavyweight and number three heavyweight challenger.

In 1946 Eugene "Silent" Hairston won the National AAU Championship and the National Golden Gloves Championship. This was a 60-win, one-loss record. The following year he became a professional boxer when he was only 17 years old. As a pro, he won 45 matches and lost 13 with five ending in draws. His record included 24 knockouts. At one time Hairston was the number two ranking middleweight behind World Champion Sugar Ray Robinson. Hairston fought and knocked out Paul Pender in the third round. Pender later became the World Welterweight and Middleweight champion. Hairston fought a number of other contenders such as Robert Villemain, Paddy Young, Lee Sala, Lester Felton, Kid Gavilan, Jake LaMotta, Joe Rindone, and Charley Humez. Hairston was a hard puncher and a crowd pleaser.

Thirteen of his fights were telecast. A severe cut over his right eye forced him to retire from the ring when he was 22 years old.

Baseball

The Ohio School was the first school for the deaf to begin playing baseball. It introduced the sport around 1870. The school team played against Ohio University, Capitol University, and the U.S. Barracks, a military school located in Columbus.

In 1879 many of the former players of the Ohio School organized the Ohio Independent Baseball team, a semi-professional deaf club, and barnstormed the Eastern states playing town teams and National League clubs. With Edward Dundon on the mound, this team won 44 games and lost 7. Dundon's feats caught the attention of others. On June 1, 1883 he signed a contract to play for the Columbus American Association Baseball Club, becoming the first re-

corded deaf professional baseball player.

Dundon played for Atlanta in the Southern League and Syracuse in the International Association. He was on two pennant-winning Atlanta teams. He won 21 games and lost 12 while pitching Atlanta to one pennant and in the process struck out 188 batters in 36 games. He played outfield when not pitching and had a high batting average. His highest was with Syracuse in 1887 when he made 65 hits in 200 times at bat for an average of .325. Dundon also umpired baseball games and is probably the first deaf person to officiate at a professional baseball game.

William E. Hoy, Reuben C. Stephenson, Luther H. Taylor, George M. Leitner, William J. Deegan, and Richard F. Sipek also made it to the major leagues.

Hoy played in 1,668 games in 15 seasons in the majors and 398 games during three seasons in the minors for a professional career of 18 years. During his last year, at the age of 42, he played in a total of 211 games for Los Angeles in the Pacific Coast League.

Illinois School for the Deaf baseball team, 1890.

Illinois School for the Deaf

"Hoy Baseball Team" of the Ohio School for the Deaf, 1895.

In all, he played for four clubs in four leagues. Hoy was a small man, only five feet, five inches tall and weighing under 150 pounds. As an outfielder he threw out three runners at home plate in a game in Washington, D.C. in 1889 setting a record. He was a good base stealer, stole 82 bases during his career, and is listed among the top 20-all time base stealers. He has been credited with asking umpires to raise their right arms to signify a strike, since he could not

Maurice Potter was a popular baseball umpire.

hear the call, and that practice started the strike and ball hand count. Hoy played on four pennant-winning teams, the Oshkosh, Wisconsin team in the Northwestern League; Chicago in the American League; Los Angeles in the Pacific Coast League; and for the Cincinnati Reds. In 1888 he played for the Washington Senators and was their leading hitter.

Born on May 23, 1862, Hoy was deafened when he was two years old and attended the Ohio School. He threw out the first ball to open the 1961 World Series between the Cincinnati Reds and the New York Yankees when he was 99 years old. He died on December 15, 1961.

William Funkhouser moved to Elkhart, Indiana in 1897 when Charles G. Conn, owner of the Conn Company, saw him playing second and third bases and offered him a job in his factory so that Funkhouser could play on the company team. Funkhouser appeared in Ripley's "Believe It or Not!" cartoon as a deaf man who made clarinets and saxophones at the Conn Company for 52 years but never heard one play.

George P. Kihm, a product of the Ohio School for the Deaf, began his playing career on the Findlay, Ohio team of the Interstate League in 1895 and ended it 19 years later with Akron in the same league. Kihm played on five pennant-winning teams and led the American Association in fielding for six straight years, setting an all-time record. In 1907 he made 1,725 putouts. Kihm was also an excellent boxer.

Luther H. Taylor, a graduate of the Kansas School, began his baseball career in Nevada, Missouri. He

Richard Sipek   Pap played a total of 19 seasons in major and minor league baseball. In 1900 he joined the New York Giants as a pitcher and was with them for nine seasons. The 1904 and 1905 teams were pennant winners. The 1905 team captured the World Series. With Taylor on the mound pitching for the Giants, no player succeeded in stealing third base. After his baseball career, Taylor returned to the Kansas School where he was a supervisor and the school's athletic director. He worked at the Iowa and Illinois schools and became a scout for the Giants after he retired from the Illinois School. He continued his attachment to the game by umpiring semi-pro, sandlot and college baseball games until 1956. He was elected to the American Athletic Association of the Deaf Hall of Fame in 1952 and in 1961 the gymnasium at the Kansas School was named for him. Born in Oskaloosa, Kansas, February 21, 1876, he died of a heart attack in Jacksonville, Illinois on August 22, 1958.

George M. Leitner and William J. Deegan had brief pitching careers with the New York Giants. They were teamed up with Luther Taylor, who was the best, and Manager George S. Davis decided to let them go. Leitner was a product of the Kansas School for the Deaf, and Deegan attended the St. Joseph School in New York.

According to J. Frederick Meagher, Thomas Lynch of Illinois was the first Gallaudet College athlete to break into the majors. Nicknamed "Jumbo" Lynch, he pitched briefly for "Pop" Anson's Chicago Nationals before William Hoy began his baseball career. Lynch died shortly afterwards.

Reuben C. Stephenson was born in New Jersey and attended the New Jersey School for the Deaf. He was signed to play for the Camden, New Jersey semi-professional team in 1890. His .380 batting average soon caught the attention of the manager of the nearby Philadelphia Phillies. When one of their outfielders, Ed Delehanty, was temporarily disabled, Stephenson was called up as a replacement. In 22 games with the Phillies Stephenson batted .420, a feat even the great Delehanty would have had difficulty matching, but Stephenson's lack of experience and game savvy hurt him and when the star outfielder recovered, Stephenson was released. Stephenson continued to play semi-pro ball for several more years. Afterwards, he secured employment with the New Jersey State Highway Department.

Paul S. Curtis was a southpaw from the Kansas School. He played professional ball for seven years, beginning in 1901. He played in the Missouri Valley League and helped Sedalia win the league title. In 1903 he appeared on the mound 38 times winning 22

Ruth Peterson

"Dummy" Taylor Communicates

It was raining when the baseball game between the New York Giants and their opponents started one day early in the 1900's. The players wanted to call the game on account of the rain, but the umpires refused. The players argued with them to no avail. The "umps" were determined to go on with the game.

The rain continued and the game proceeded and soon all the players were soaking wet, but the umpires were just as stubborn as ever.

When the seventh inning arrived, and it was the Giants' turn at bat, there strode to the third base coaching box a very strange looking figure. It was Luther "Dummy" Taylor, the Giants' deaf pitcher. He was wearing rubber galoshes and carrying an umbrella! The sight of him was so funny that all the players . . . and the umpires . . . broke into gales of laughter. And because of him the game was halted.

The word "dummy" was a label given to deaf persons who had little or no speech. It was a term widely used during the early part of this century. For one who could not talk, "Dummy" Taylor had *communicated* his message well.

294

and dropping 12 while striking out 177 batters and yielding only 7 bases on balls. While a student at the Kansas School, Curtis pitched the KSD team to a 2-1 upset victory over the highly touted University of Kansas nine. The University team had just returned from a successful tour of the Midwest and on their arrival in Olathe they expected the KSD boys to be a quick push-over but found out too late how mistaken they were.

Lester G. Rosson, a 1902 Gallaudet College graduate, pitched a Wheeling, West Virginia team to a 5-1 victory over Boston in an exhibition game in 1903. In another exhibition game the same year he held the Detroit Tigers to a 0 to 0 score for 11 innings. Rosson's brother was a coach at the Tennessee School for the Deaf.

Harry P. Dix played with the Vicksburg, Mississippi team in the Cotton States League in 1907. He was called a great southpaw, but he lasted only one season. He was a good friend of Denton T. "Cy" Young.

Richard F. Sipek is the most recent deaf athlete to make it to the pros. Sipek was an outstanding student and athlete at the Illinois School for the Deaf, where Luther Taylor was his housefather. Taylor was instrumental in getting Sipek a chance to play in the big league. Sipek was acquired by the Cincinnati Reds and shipped to their farm team, the Barons, in Birmingham, Alabama. The Barons farmed him out to a Class D team in Erwin, Tennessee, but Sipek hit .455 during the first month so the Barons recalled him and installed him in their right field. He batted .336 in 1943 and .319 in 1944 and was named the team's most popular player both seasons. After the first season the *Jacksonville* (Il.) *Journal* called him "one of the most outstanding first-year men in minor league baseball." Sipek joined the Cincinnati Reds in 1945 where he played 31 games in the outfield and hit .244. He was sent to Syracuse in 1946 and did not return to the majors.

American Deaf Softball Guide

In 1961 Ralph E. LinWeber, founder and director of

This Los Angeles Club of the Deaf won the 25th AAAD basketball tournament in Akron, Ohio. Front row, left to right: Jerry Moore, Leroy Bookman, Leon Grant, Maurice Mosley, James Renshaw. Second row: Reeca Cain, Billy Spears, Norman Green, Saul Brandt, Darby Burrell. Back row: Marvin Greenstone, Coach Lou Dyer, Saul Lukacs. The LACD has won ten AAAD tourneys, more times than any other club.

the Baseball Research Bureau in Toledo, Ohio, published the *American Deaf Softball Guide.* This 286-page book contains the records of official deaf softball tournaments, covering a span of 20 years. It took him five years to complete. The book includes the names of players, lists of all-stars, and the results of the Deaf Softball World Series. Included is information about the Eastern Athletic Association of the Deaf and the Mid-West Athletic Association of the Deaf.

LinWeber's Research Bureau, which is located in his home and is open to the public, contains pictures of deaf and hearing baseball stars and some 500 volumes of a highly-prized collection of Reach Baseball Guides dating back to 1882. Many sports editors have visited his Bureau which was opened in 1939 (during the centennial of the sport) to check out some player's record.

LinWeber was one of seven contributors to the *Official Encyclopedia of Baseball* which was written and compiled by Hy Turkin of New York City and S. C. Thompson of Long Beach, California. It was published by A. S. Barnes & Co., Inc. of New York, and Thomas Yoseloff, Ltd. of London and Toronto. This encyclopedia is the most comprehensive record book of our national pastime. It contains the names and records of some 10,000 players who have played in the major

Poster announcing the Games in the U.S.

leagues since 1871. LinWeber contributed information about seven deaf baseball players. They are: Dundon, Deegan, Hoy, Leitner, Sipek, Stephenson, and Taylor.

LinWeber also compiled and published two other books: *Toledo Baseball Guide of the Mud Hens* (1944) and *Graduation Classes of the Ohio School for the Deaf, 1869-1949* (1950).

LinWeber attended the Ohio School.

World Games for the Deaf

The International Games for the Deaf were organized in Paris, France in 1924. American participation began in 1935 when S. Robey Burns, a coach at the Illinois School for the Deaf, took two athletes to the Games in London. The name of the Games was later changed to World Games for the Deaf.

In 1957 the United States involvement reached an all-time high with 40 athletes participating. That year the American Athletic Association of the Deaf became involved in organizing the United States' team.

In 1965 the Games came to America under the sponsorship of the AAAD and were held in Washington, D.C. Unlike previous Games, these were completely planned, organized, and run by deaf persons.

In 1949 the first Winter Games for the Deaf were held at Seefeld, Austria. The Winter Games were held at Lake Placid, New York in 1975.

The American Athletic Association of the Deaf

During both World Wars, Akron, Ohio became the "crossroads of deaf America." The wars attracted large numbers of deaf workers to the sprawling Firestone and Goodyear rubber plants. As a result of these large congregations of deaf persons the Akron Club of the Deaf was born.

In 1945 the Akron Club of the Deaf sponsored the first annual National Basketball Tournament which attracted four teams in addition to the host. What followed was the birth of the American Athletic Union of the Deaf, later renamed the American Athletic Association of the Deaf. The AAAD was organized to foster competition among clubs and regulate uniform rules; provide social outlets for the members and their friends; serve as a parent organization for regional athletic associations; conduct an annual national basketball tournament; improve and maintain the standards of athletic competition; and assist the participation of United States teams in international competition.

The AAAD is composed of seven regions. It has grown from 58 participating clubs to over 150. It was the first national deaf organization to prohibit racial discrimination. Basketball tournaments are held annually in different parts of the country, and sites are selected on a competitive basis. A majority of the tournaments, which offer exciting and tough competition, are a financial success. The AAAD also promotes an annual softball tournament.

**American Athletic
Association of the Deaf Hall of Fame**

In 1952 the American Athletic Association of the Deaf established the AAAD Hall of Fame. This Hall recognizes outstanding deaf athletes, coaches and sports leaders who have excelled in the world of sports or made exceptional contributions to sports. A Hall of Fame Committee screens and nominates the candidates for whom a Selection Board votes.

Helms Foundation Hall of Fame

The Helms Foundation Hall of Fame was founded in 1936 to recognize those athletes and coaches and other individuals who have contributed to the promotion of amateur athletics. Three deaf persons are known to have been enshrined in this Hall, the first was a deaf woman: Gertrude Ederle, Tom Berg, and Art Kruger.

Ederle was the first woman to successfully swim the English Channel. She made the crossing in 1926 on her second attempt and broke several men's records in the attempt. She became deaf as a result of the swim when the pounding waves damaged her hearing. She was named to the Hall in 1953.

Tom Berg has been track coach at Gallaudet College since 1957. He was head coach of the USA track and field teams which competed in the World Games for the Deaf five times. In 1962 Berg was picked as "Small College Track Coach of the Year" by the Rockne Club of Kansas City, Missouri. The selection was made based on a poll conducted among sportswriters, radio and television sportscasters and coaches. He was Games Director of the 10th World Games for the Deaf held at Washington, D.C. in 1965. He was named to the Hall in 1973.

Art Kruger has been active in all levels of sports promotion for deaf athletes dating back to his college days in the 1930s. He has been a sportswriter; is one of the founders of the American Athletic Association of the Deaf and was its first president. He has been Team Director of the USA teams which have competed in the World Games three times and Chairman of the USA World Games Committee since 1966. Kruger was admitted to the Hall in 1973.

Kitty O'Neil, Fastest Woman On Earth

In Hollywood, California, Kitty O'Neil is known as "The Deaf Daredevil." She is a member of the prestigious Stunts Unlimited, a small group of people who earn their livelihood by risking their lives performing daredevil stunts. In her work O'Neil has jumped off a ten-story building, crashed cars, been set afire, plunged over a 100-foot waterfall, and jumped off a 105-foot cliff, the highest jump ever filmed of a woman. She has performed daredevil acts for such television shows as "Bionic Woman," "Gemini Man," "Quincy," and "The Family."

A combination of measles, mumps, smallpox, and high fever caused her deafness when she was five months old. Her mother taught her during her early years. She attended public school graduating from Anaheim High School in California in 1963.

As a teenager she took up diving seriously and won the 1961 Amateur Athletic Union (AAU) Southwest District Junior Olympics diving title in Texas. Her

Kitty O'Neil

Peter Moran/Model Secondary School for the Deaf

S. Robey Burns
(1894-1967)

S. (for Sanford) Robey Burns is best remembered as the "Father of American Participation in the World Games for the Deaf."

Born in Freeport, Illinois in April, 1894, he was deafened when he was three years old. After a year at an oral school in Chicago, he transferred to the Illinois School for the Deaf in Jacksonville where he graduated in 1914. He next enrolled in Gallaudet College, earning his Bachelor of Arts degree in 1919.

Burns returned to his alma mater as a printing instructor and immediately set about organizing athletic teams. The Illinois School had no football field in those days and the first games were played away. Burns was instrumental in getting the Illinois School admitted to the Illinois High School Athletic Association, and from 1922 until he retired from coaching in 1936, he produced powerful teams in all sports. His 1927 football team began a winning string which reached 19 games without a loss. Burns was also involved in the formation of the Central States Basketball Conference.

In 1936 Burns took two of his athletes to the fourth International Games for the Deaf (since renamed World Games for the Deaf) being held in London, England, thus beginning America's participation in the competition. One was John Chudzikiewicz, a weightman, and the other was Wayne Otten, a sprinter. Chudzikiewicz won America's first gold medal with a record toss of the javelin.

Burns was one of the best known persons in deaf sports. He was a coach of high school sports and a leader in adult sports through his involvement in the American Athletic Association of the Deaf and the World Games for the Deaf. He was president of the AAAD from 1947 to 1949 and the fourth coach to be enshrined in the AAAD Hall of Fame. In 1953 the Comite International des Sports Silencieux awarded him the CISS Diploma of Honor and the Bronze Medal of Gratitude for his contributions towards the promotion of international sports of the deaf. In 1955 he became the first deaf American to be elected to the Executive Committee of the CISS, and he was first vice president for six years. Over a 30-year span he never once missed the Games.

Burns lived to see his dream come true when the 10th World Games for the Deaf came to the United States in 1965. The Games, held in Washington, D.C., were dedicated to him. He died two years later on April 22, 1967 from heart failure. He is buried in his hometown.

picture appeared on the cover of the August 1961 *Times Feature Magazine.*

During her senior year she was selected "Young American of the Month" by the *American Youth Mag-*

azine, a General Motors publication. In 1964 she won the National AAU Women's 10-meter diving championship and accompanied the Olympic team to Tokyo where she placed eighth.

In 1970 O'Neil set a world speed record as the fastest woman water skier when she skimmed over the water at 104.85 mph. In December 1976 O'Neil set a number of land speed records in a rocket-powered car driven by a woman. She hit 512.083 mph and established a new record with an average speed of 322 mph. The following summer in July, 1977, she set a quarter-mile mark of 392.54 mph with an average speed run of 178.962 and a new acceleration record in the 500-meter run. In the record-breaking process she earned a new title: "Fastest Woman On Earth." O'Neil is listed in the Good Housekeeping *Woman's Almanac* as one of the world's outstanding sportswomen.

Deaf Coaches of Hearing Teams

Albert Berg made a mark for himself when he accepted an offer to coach football at Purdue University "for the novel experience that would accrue." Novel, did he say? The idea of a deaf man who had lost his sense of hearing and ability to talk as a youth coaching a team of hearing players was so unusual in the 1880s that it made Ripley's "Believe It Or Not" and many persons didn't. Years later, Albert Berg lamented that that one year he spent on the West Lafayette campus was blown way out of proportion and overshadowed more important achievements which he accomplished over a span of some forty years.

Berg was surprised to receive the offer to coach at Purdue and wondered how they knew about him. He thinks that his reputation as captain and fullback of the "Kendalls" at Gallaudet College may have preceded him when he returned to his hometown of Lafayette. At any rate, he accepted the challenge that fall of 1887 and spent much of the season teaching fundamentals. He adopted the system and signals used by the "Kendalls." The team played only one inter-collegiate game that season with Butler University and lost by the lop-sided score of 48-6, but football had been started at Purdue University, and Albert Berg would always be remembered as the first coach.

The next season Berg coached at Franklin College at a nominal salary. Afterwards he volunteered his services on and off at Butler University.

Berg taught at the Indiana School for the Deaf from 1888 to 1933. He was a teacher, coach, librarian, and an editor of *The Silent Hoosier* for approximately forty years; the last twenty-four as alumni editor. On the side, he sold insurance for the New England Mutual Life Insurance Company of Boston. Berg's son, Lloyd E. Berg, was superintendent of the Iowa School for the Deaf.

Paul D. Hubbard, who started football at the Kansas State School for the Deaf, also coached for a few years at the Olathe High School.

Rudolph Gamblin, a product of the Texas School for the Deaf, had a successful coaching career in the public school system. He coached the Nixson Junior High School football team and the Amarillo High School baseball team. His baseball team in 1948 had a 16-2 won-lost record, were district champions, and narrowly lost the state championship, losing 1-0. Gamblin's football squad won the city championship in 1945 and were undefeated the following year. In two seasons the team lost only one game.

Gamblin was deafened at the age of three from spinal meningitis. He attended Gallaudet College after graduating from the Texas School and made the Washington All Star team as a college football player. He coached at the New York School for the Deaf and at his alma mater in Texas. His 1941, 1942 and 1943 TSD football teams were selected national champions among schools for the deaf.

Deaf Athletes on Hearing Teams

Several deaf athletes played on hearing college teams. Glenn Smith, who won the 145-pound National Amateur Athletic Union wrestling title in 1919, was a center on the Notre Dame football team in 1912 and 1913.

Henry Brenner, a graduate of the Rhode Island School for the Deaf, was a guard for four years on the University of Rhode Island football team from 1951 to 1954. During that period the URI Rams had the best

---

It is a proud moment in the life of an American deaf athlete when, while wearing the uniform of the greatest nation on earth, he commits his brain, skill, strength and spirit to the noble ideals of world competition. But the proudest moment of all comes to those American deaf athletes who, with high honor, face our nation's flag on the victory stand, even though—in the perpetual silence surrounding them—they cannot hear "The Star Spangled Banner."

—ART KRUGER
USA-WGD COMMITTEE CHAIRMAN

J. Frederick Meagher
(1886-1951)

J. Frederick Meagher, better known to most deaf people as Jimmy Meagher, was an all-around handyman. In stature, he was a small thin man with a scowl on his face. As an achiever, he was a giant. He was an athlete, a writer, and a sports and community leader.

As a writer, he filled the columns of the old *Silent Worker, American Deaf Citizen, The Deaf-Mute's Journal,* and *The Washingtonian* with verse (and sometimes worse), astute observations, comments and "people news." He was editor and publisher of *The Washingtonian* and he originated "The Spotlight" column in *The Frat,* one of the most popular columns to ever appear in a publication of the deaf.

George Porter of the *Silent Worker* defined Meagher's writing style as "a style all his own." Others called it "ungrammatical, and at times even uncouth." But whatever it was, he never pulled a punch. It was said that "He made enemies and he held friends but he wrote what he thought." His vocabulary was compared to that of Winchell's, ". . . as prolific and just as original."

As an athlete, Meagher excelled in wrestling. In the early 1910s he won the national Amateur Athletic Union (AAU) 108-pound wrestling championship, wrestling out of the Gary, Indiana YMCA. He earned the nickname of "The Mighty Mite." He also excelled as an amateur boxer and played football for sixteen years.

As a sports leader he originated the National All American Schools for the Deaf Basketball selections in the early 1930s and began naming mythical national basketball champions among the schools. He was among the first to be admitted to the AAAD Hall of Fame in 1953.

Meagher was an active member of the National Fraternal Society of the Deaf and the National Association of the Deaf.

James Frederick Meagher was born in 1886 in Rochester, New York. He became deaf at the age of seven and attended the Cincinnati Oral School and the Rochester School for the Deaf in New York. He was foreman of a small weekly newspaper in Seattle, Washington. He taught and was athletic director at the Washington State School for the Deaf; worked at Goodyear in Akron, Ohio and for the *Gary Post* in Indiana. The last several years of his life he was an ad compositor for the *Chicago Herald & Examiner.*

Meagher and his wife, Frieda, had one son whom they fondly called "Naddie" because he was born during a National Association of the Deaf convention. "Naddie" died during his youth from football injuries. Meagher died of a heart attack in Chicago on February 22, 1951.

Art Kruger

In 1931 J. Frederick Meagher, the originator of the All-America basketball team selections among deaf prep schools, picked the first All-American Schools for the Deaf National Basketball team and printed his selections in *The Deaf-Mutes' Journal*. Meagher invited anyone who might disagree with his choice to come forward and say so. One who did so was a short, scrappy Gallaudet College sophomore from Pennsylvania named Art Kruger. Kruger, who had become a student of the American deaf sports scene agreed with some of Meagher's selection, but named some other players who he thought were more deserving. He argued knowledgeably and rationally for his selections. His submission attracted several letters of congratulation, one of them from Meagher, himself. Kruger did not know it then, of course, but he had just embarked on a voluntary sports-writing career which would span nearly half a century. In 1935 he began writing regularly for *The Deaf-Mutes' Journal* (later renamed the *New York Journal of the Deaf*). In 1945 he became sports editor of the *Silent Broadcaster* (now defunct) which was printed in Los Angeles, California. He was the first editor of *The AAAD Bulletin* and in 1949 he joined *The Silent Worker* (now *The Deaf American*) as sports editor and the following year he began selecting annual All-America school for the deaf teams in football and basketball. He has not missed a year since. But, sports reporting is only part of the Art Kruger Story.

Born in Philadelphia on March 6, 1911, Kruger became deaf when he was only three years old from shock caused when the family home caught fire and burned down. He attended an oral school in Baba, Pennsylvania, the McIntyre Grammar School in Philadelphia, Northeast High School and the Pennsylvania School at Mt. Airy before emigrating to Gallaudet College.

At Gallaudet College Kruger was too small and too light for most sports so he turned to managing sports events, record keeping, reporting and was athletic director of the college basketball team responsible for scheduling the team's competition—experiences which would stand him in good stead in later years.

Following graduation from college in 1933 Kruger worked for several years in New York City. When World War II broke out, he found himself along with many other deaf persons in Akron working in the war plants.

Kruger became a charter member in the founding of the Akron Club of the Deaf and the first chairman of the first national club of the deaf basketball tournament in the country. This tournament was sponsored by the Akron Club and was held on April 14, 1945. Despite war-time restrictions the tournament attracted basketball teams from Los Angeles, Buffalo, New York, Philadelphia, and Kansas City, Missouri which Buffalo won. This event led to the birth of the American Athletic Union of the Deaf and Kruger was elected the first president. The name was later changed, at the request of the American Athletic Union, to the American Athletic Association of the Deaf. He spent his first year getting the Association established and organizing member clubs into seven regions, an activity which years later earned him the title of "Father of the AAAD." The same year he organized the Central Athletic Association of the Deaf.

In the 1950s Kruger became involved with the United States participation in the World Games for the Deaf, very similar to the Olympics, except that all the participants must be deaf. The World Games had been organized in 1924 but it was not until 1935 that the United States sent two athletes to participate through the efforts of S. Robey Burns. The first serious effort took place in 1957 in Milan, Italy with Kruger as Team Director. That year the United States sent 40 athletes and reaped 23 medals, including seven gold. Kruger held the Team Director post of the United States Committee of the World Games for the Deaf until 1966 when he was elevated to the chairmanship of the Committee. He has been reelected three times since. He has also been active in this country's participation in Summer and Winter Games for the Deaf and in 1975 spearheaded this country's involvement in the Pan-American Games for the Deaf.

Like the U.S. Olympic Team, deaf athletes are not funded as are teams from many other countries. As a result, athletes chosen to participate in the Games must raise funds to cover their expenses. As a fund raiser Kruger has assisted these athletes meet their financial obligations and, with the assistance of others, he estimates he has raised over $1,300,000 in his life time for the benefit of athletes.

Kruger was the first sports leader to be recognized by the Selections Committee when he was elected to the AAAD Hall of Fame in 1954. He has since received many other honors, not all sports-related. Other honors include being one of two deaf persons chosen to the Helms Foundation Hall of Fame in 1973. Helms, the founder, was a nephew of William "Dummy" Hoy, the deaf professional baseball player. Other honors include: Honorary membership in the American Coaches of the Deaf Association, a medal of gratitude from the CISS (Comite International des Sports Silencieux), an award from the U.S. Skiers Association of the Deaf, the Block G, S. Robey Burns Sportsman of the Year award and many others. In 1976 Gallaudet College awarded him the Powrie V. Doctor Medallion for International Service and in 1980 the Gallaudet College Alumni Association awarded him the Edward Miner Gallaudet International award.

Kruger is married to the former Eva Segal, a graduate of the New York School for the Deaf. After the second world war, the Krugers moved to Los Angeles where he was employed with the Western Costume Corporation, a firm owned by the six major movie producers and the largest movie and television costume firm in Hollywood. He retired in 1975 after 30 years with the company, the last several years as department supervisor. The Krugers moved to Virginia where he continues his far-flung activities in the sports world.

The feats and achievements of deaf athletes would not exist or would be lost over the years were it not for dedicated people who faithfully and laboriously keep records and write about such events. Deaf Americans owe much to people like Art Kruger.

defensive and offensive record in their conference. In his sophomore year Brenner was selected for the All Conference Defensive Team. He was later elected to the University of Rhode Island Sports Hall of Fame.

Lou Mariano, who attended the Alexander Graham Bell School for the Deaf in Cleveland joined the All-State team as a halfback. He played for Kent State University. As a high school back he played for McKinley High School in one of the nation's strongest circuits. He scored 35 touchdowns and, according to one sports writer, "covered more territory than a Fuller Brush man." Mariano tried out for the Pittsburgh Steelers team but did not make it.

Sammy Oates was one of Texas School for the Deaf's greatest athletes. He was selected to the Deaf Prep All-American team for four years. After his graduation from TSD he enrolled at Hardin-Simmons University on a football scholarship and made the varsity his first year. His teammates learned sign language so that they could transmit signals to him in the huddle. As a freshman, Oates caught 31 passes and ran for 402 yards. He was named to the Border Conference first team and received honorable mention on the Associate Press and United Press International All-America teams. He was first in his conference and eighth in the nation in pass receiving. As a sophomore, he finished 19th nationally as a receiver and was named Sophomore of the Year. He played fullback his last two years at Hardin-Simons and after college he tried out with the Houston Oilers. He played briefly for the Indianapolis Warriors in the United Football League then was acquired by the Toronto Argonauts of the Canadian Football League but was released during training

William Schyman played for DePaul University.

camp. He was admitted to the AAAD Hall of Fame in 1979.

Gary Klingensmith, who was a star running back at Brownsville High School in Uniontown, Pennsylvania, was the leading ground gainer in ten games as a halfback for the Penn State University Nittany Lions in 1963. He coached football for three years at Gallaudet College.

Gary Washington, a Colorado School for the Deaf and the Blind football star, was selected for the All-State eight-man and 11-man team. One of the Colorado School's greatest all-around athletes, he played briefly on the University of Colorado football team as a tailback.

Yancey Sutton, who led his Leon High School team in Tallahassee, Florida to the state championship, played linebacker for the University of Florida. In a game with Georgia Tech he was selected Chevrolet Outstanding Defensive Player of the Game, which was telecast on ABC-TV.

Angel Acuna (of the Arizona State School for the Deaf and the Blind) played three years of basketball

Art Kruger, 1949.

Lenny Meyer

301

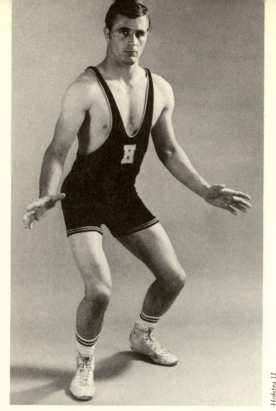

Martin Willigan starred as a wrestler at Hofstra University.

for Chihuahua State Teachers College in Mexico. He played for the Los Angeles Club of the Deaf when the club won the 1946 American Athletic Association of the Deaf championship. He was selected Most Valuable Player. He played for the 1948 Mexican Olympic team and toured one year with the Harlem Globetrotters.

From 1960 to 1962 Leon Grant, a six-foot, eight-inch center, led his school to three straight national Schools for Negroes basketball titles. During that period Grant averaged 28 points a game and his team won 76 games while dropping only 8. Grant played two years at North Carolina College in Durham.

Don Lyons played for the University of Nevada at Las Vegas where he led the team in field goals. During his two seasons with the team he averaged 20 points per game. He also excelled in track and field and in 1969 was picked Las Vegas Athlete of the Year. An article about him appeared in *Sporting News*. He tried out for a pro basketball team but did not make it because of his hearing impairment. He played two years on the Contra Costa Junior College in San Pablo,

Bonnie Sloan (79) played tackle for the St. Louis Cardinals.

302

California where he had a 17.1 point average, before transferring to Las Vegas. Lyons was a graduate of the California School for the Deaf in Berkeley. In 1963/64 season he was picked the nation's top deaf cager and his jersey, number 14, was retired. He broke three national deaf Prep records as a high school player, setting the most career points (2,072), the most points in a single season (918) and the most points in a single game (69). He averaged the most points (58) in Northern California for two consecutive years and made their All-Star first team.

As an athlete, a rugged 6-foot, five-inch William Schyman earned the nickname of "Moose." He starred in basketball at Lane Tech High School in Chicago where, as a senior, he led the City League in scoring with a 27.9 point average. He made both the All-City League and All-Chicago Area teams. Schyman made the varsity as a sophomore at DePaul University and led the Blue Demons to a successful 18-6 season and a slot in the National College Athletic Association tournament following the 1952-53 season. Schyman played for the United States basketball team in the World-famed Maccabiah Games in Israel during the summer of 1953. The U.S. basketball team beat 30 other teams for the championship. Schyman played briefly for the Baltimore Bullets in the National Basketball Association until the team folded, then he joined Abe Saperstein's outfit and played three years for the Boston Whirlwinds, the touring opponents of the Harlem Globetrotters. He later played for the Washington Generals; and was on three champion teams in the American Athletic Association of the Deaf; captained the 1965 USA basketball team that won the 1965 gold medal in the World Games for the Deaf and coached (1962-1969) at Gallaudet College. Art Kruger rates Schyman the best basketball coach Gallaudet College has ever had.

Noah Downes played basketball for the Maryland School and led the Gallaudet basketball team to a 11-5 record in 1918-19 and to the top of the District of Columbia Intercollegiate basketball conference.

Downes made it to the pros. He played for professional teams in St. Petersburg, Florida, Hazelton, Pennsylvania and for the Silent Separates, a professional team in New York City. He also played for the Akron Goodyear Silents.

Martin Willigan, a hearing impaired athlete, was an outstanding wrestler. Art Kruger called him "probably one of the greatest (deaf) grapplers of the century." Willigan wrestled for Hofstra University in Hempstead, Long Island, New York, where he compiled a 44-1-1 record with 38 of his victories by falls. He set four records at Hofstra: the most falls in a

---

One day an Arkansas School for the Deaf 90-pounder was having no end of difficulty with his hearing opponent. Finally the deaf boy was nearly pinned and his cause was apparently hopeless. Suddenly an inspiration came to him. He reached around his opponent's body and tapped him twice on the back. The hearing boy naturally thought it was the referee signalling him that the match was over and that he had won. He released his grip and was astounded when the deaf wrestler jumped up, executed a body slam and won by a fall.

—NATHAN ZIMBLE

---

season, the most falls in a career, the most individual points in a season, and the most wins in a career. Willigan won the 137-pound Middle Atlantic Wrestling Conference championship and was selected the most valuable wrestler. He placed second in the NCAA championships in 1969. He won a gold medal at the World Games for the Deaf in freestyle and a silver in Greco-Roman wrestling at the 1969 Belgrade Games and repeated the performance at the 1973 Malmo Games. Willigan is wrestling coach at Gallaudet College.

The Speed Demon

by Harold O. Berger

This is an old story of a boy, which grows more impressive as the years roll on.

In a southwestern section of Philadelphia a traffic jam was slowly being untangled. New and shiny limousines were crawling alongside battered flivvers, with taxicabs racing around overloaded buses and trolleys. The caravan was on its annual jaunt to the campus of the University of Pennsylvania.

The first such trip was made back in the spring of 1893 by a quartet of Princeton University athletes . . . to compete with Pennsylvania in the first one-mile relay race ever run in America. From this small gathering grew the gigantic University of Pennsylvania Relay Carnival, which annually attracts 3,400 athletes from 500 colleges and schools with an audience of 30,000.

To better acquaint the reader with this type of running—one-mile relay is based on team competition. Four men comprise a team. Each runner speeds around a quarter-mile track, carrying a lightweight wooden stick called a baton.

At the end of each run the baton is relayed to a waiting teammate. The last runner on the squad, usually the fastest, must beat out all the other challenging rivals in the race, to give his team a victory.

Many a thrilling chapter has been written into this baton-passing classic. And out of the record book comes a story of an unknown schoolboy who rocked the carnival with a dynamic performance back in 1918. The youngster was a pupil in the Mt. Airy School for the Deaf, which makes the story all the more interesting.

On that memorable Saturday the institution's relay team showed up at the stadium in good condition. Naturally the young athletes were amazed and a little nervous at the large spectacle emerging before them.

Came the race and the first Mt. Airy [Pennsylvania School for the Deaf] runner gave the team a nice start. He handed the baton to the second teammate who completed a well-timed run. The third man took the stick and was running close behind the pacesetters until half way around the track when he was suddenly stricken and slowed down.

The ailing boy's hands were clutching at his sides and his face had an expression of intense pain. As the runners rounded into the home stretch, the lad was staggering and ready to drop out. Somehow he managed to hang on to the finish.

The fourth man seized the baton from the faltering teammate who had suffered an attack of indigestion. The task looked hopeless with the leaders so far ahead in this fast field. But here was a competitor with a fiery and unmatched fighting spirit—Bernard McGinley, one of Mt. Airy's finest all around athletes. He tore down the track in a blind rage, setting a blistering pace.

Veteran observers watched the aroused McGinley and shook their heads. They had seen many schoolboys run such a killing pace and crack up. But the Mt. Airy sensation flashed past opposing rivals with blind speed until he was a few feet from the pacesetters. The overflowing crowd was quick to sense what was going on and put up a wild demonstration.

College athletes competing in the field of events stopped their work to watch the 17-year-old speed demon. Coaches and trainers keenly studied McGinley's running form—only a well-trained champion could maintain such a terrific clip.

The gruelling grind began to tell on the lad, who at the age of 16 had made the school's varsity football team. Straining at every muscle, McGinley was now only inches behind the leader in the race as they approached the home-stretch.

The curly haired 5-foot-8-inch 142-pound speedster, who was also a good baseball player and a fine guard on the basketball team, now was steadily pulling abreast with the opposing front runner. The crowd was leaning over the guard rails, shouting and frantically waving their arms at the struggling marvel.

With only a few feet more to go, Bernard McGinley's face gave a picture of a man being cruelly tortured. The muscles in his legs and arms were tightening up and his body was turning white. In a painful gesture McGinley stretched out an arm and lunged ahead of his rival. But his finger tips missed the tape and he fell to the ground, losing the race. The disappointed hero had run the quarter mile in 49 seconds flat—2-2/5 seconds behind the world's record.

—The P.S.A.D. News

The A.A.A.D. Hall of Fame

Players

Year	Athlete, Residence	Sport	Team and Position
1951	William E. Hoy, Cincinnati, Ohio	Baseball	Cincinnati Reds, Washington Senators—Outfielder
1952	Luther H. Taylor, Jacksonville, Illinois	Baseball	New York Giants—Pitcher
1953	Frederick A. Moore, Columbus, Ohio	Football	Kansas, Gallaudet, Akron Goodyear—Quarterback
1953	Noah Downes, Baltimore, Maryland	Basketball	Semi-Pro, Maryland, Gallaudet, Akron Goodyear—Forward
1953	J. F. Meagher, Chicago, Illinois	Wrestling	AAU, Flyweight
1954	John Ringle, Knoxville, Tennessee	Football	Kansas, Gallaudet—Fullback
1954	Dalton Fuller, Wichita, Kansas	Baseball	Professional—Catcher and Shortstop
1955	Walter Rockwell, Hartford, Connecticut	Baseball, Basketball, Football	Gallaudet—All Around
1956	Willie Riddle, Clinton, South Carolina	Basketball	Semi-Pro, South Carolina, Gallaudet—Center
1957	Everett Rattan, Venice, California	Wrestling	Professional, Middleweight
1958	Louis Massey, Chicago, Illinois	Football	Illinois, Gallaudet—Fullback
1959	Joseph Worzel, New York City	Basketball	Semi-Professional, Forward
1960	Thomas Martin, New York City	Boxing	Professional, Middleweight
1960	Louis Seinensohn, Akron, Ohio	Football	Akron Goodyear—Fullback
1960	William Dilworth, Baltimore, Maryland	Boxing	Professional, Welterweight
1960	William Suttka, Chicago, Illinois	Wrestling	Professional, Junior Heavyweight
1962	Louis A. Dyer, Los Angeles, California	Basketball	Colorado, Piggly-Wiggly, Gallaudet, Regis—Forward
1963	Thomas Cuscaden, Sr., Omaha, Nebraska	Football	Gallaudet, Akron Goodyear—Lineman
1963	Nat Echols, Buffalo, New York	Basketball	AAU & AAAD (Buffalo)—Forward
1964	Charles Ewing, Louisville, Kentucky	Football	Akron Goodyear—Center
1965	Morris Davis, New York City	Walking	International Competition
1966	Charles Marshall, Jacksonville, Illinois	Baseball, Football	Nebraska, Gallaudet, Goodyear Silents
1967	Rolf Harmsen, Bismarck, North Dakota	Track	North Dakota, AAU, Gallaudet
1968	Joseph Allen, Miami, Florida	Football	Semi-Pro Goodyear Silents, Akron, Ohio
1969	Maurice Potter, Windom, Minnesota	Football, Baseball	Semi-Professional—Outfield; Fullback
1969	Dewey Deer, Vancouver, Washington	Football	Gallaudet, Goodyear Silents—Fullback
1969	Louis Byouk, Berkeley, California	Football	Colorado & Gallaudet—Fullback
1969	Ben Shafranek, New York City	Basketball, Baseball, Track	New York
1969	Harley Stottler, La Crescenta, California	Football, Track	Goodyear Silents, Goodyear Track Team
1970	Angel Acuna, Houston, Texas	Basketball	Professional, AAAD Teams, Mexican Olympic Team
1971	Bilbo Monaghan, Knoxville, Tennessee	Football	Mississippi, Gallaudet College, Memphis Tigers (Pro)
1972	John L. Jackson, Little Rock, Arkansas	Basketball, Football	Arkansas, Little Rock, WGD
1972	James H. Brehens, Frederick, Maryland	Baseball, Basketball	Maryland
1973	Joseph F. Russell, Sardis, Mississippi	Football, Basketball, Track	Mississippi, 1957-61-65 WGD
1973	Leonard H. Downes, Washington, D.C.	Baseball, Basketball	Maryland, Frederick (Md.) "Hustlers" & Wash., D.C. Heurich Brewers
1974	Clyde Nutt, Pine Bluff, Arkansas	Basketball	Arkansas, Little Rock, WGD
1975	Eugene "Silent" Hairston, New York City	Boxing	AAU, Golden Gloves, Canadian Champion, Middleweight
1975	Edward Rodman, Burlington, New Jersey	Track, Basketball, Football, Baseball	New Jersey School for Deaf
1975	Richard Sipek, Chicago, Illinois	Baseball	Ill. School, Cincinnati Reds
1976	Carl Lorello, La Mirada, California	Basketball	Fanwood, GTAC (New York City)
1976	Edward Paul Loveland, Salt Lake City, Utah	Basketball	Utah, LACD (Calif.)
1977	Larry Marxer, Shreveport, Louisiana	Basketball	Iowa School, Des Moines
1978	Winfield Roller	Football	Moscow, Idaho
1978	Paul Curtis	Baseball	Kansas School
1978	Hilton Fitzpatrick	Professional Boxing	West Virginia
1978	William Schyman, Beltsville, Maryland	Basketball	DePaul Univ., AAAD clubs, Professional, Maccabiah, WGD
1979	Sammy Oates, Austin, Texas	Football	Texas, Hardin-Simmons U.
1979	John Wurdemann	Football, Baseball	Washington, D.C.
1979	Marvin Tuttle	Baseball, Track	Iowa School
1979	Reuben Stephenson	Baseball	New Jersey

RINGLE

WORZEL

ECHOLS

DAVIS

HARMSEN

ALLEN

SHAFRANEK

ACUNA

MONAGHAN

JACKSON

RUSSELL

L. DOWNES

NUTT

HAIRSTON

RODMAN

LORELLO

MARSHALL

MARXER

DEER

FRASER

CORDANO

BUCKMASTER

SEEGER

TUBB

NORTON

SHIBLEY

BROWN

JACOBS

CONNELL

RITTENBERG

SCHREIBER

CUSACK

BARRACK

LAURITSEN

CARNEY

JORDAN

FLEISCHMAN

WARSHAWSKY

The A.A.A.D. Hall of Fame

Coaches

Year	Elected	School or Term	Years	
1953	Frederick J. Neesam	Wisconsin	41	Football, Basketball
1953	Edward S. Foltz	Miss., Okla., Kans., Ark.	30	Football, Track, Basketball
1953	Paul D. Hubbard	Kansas	15	Football
1954	S. Robey Burns	Illinois	17	Football, Basketball, Track
1954	Thomas Lewellyn	Virginia	41	Football, Basketball, Baseball
1955	Frederick Hughes	Gallaudet	20	Football
1955	William Hunter	Oregon & Washington	36	Basketball, Football
1956	Harry Benson	Maryland	48	Basketball
1957	Charles Miller	Ohio	27	Football, Basketball
1962	Harry L. Baynes	Alabama	38	Basketball
1963	Rudolph Gamblin	N.Y., Tex., Amarillo H.S.	10	Football, Baseball
1964	Albert Berg	Indiana	40	Football
1965	Nathan Lahn	Iowa	39	Football, Basketball
1966	Nick Petersen	Nebraska	23	Basketball
1966	Anthony Panella	Milwaukee	15	Basketball
1967	Thomas Berg	Gallaudet, Idaho	21	Track
1968	Earl Roberts	Mich. School for Deaf	25	All Sports
1969	E. Conley Akin	Tennessee	31	All Sports
1969	Nathan Zimble	Arkansas	20	Wrestling
1970	Ken Norton	Okla. & Calif.	16	Track, Football, Basketball
1971	George K. Brown	North Carolina	33	Basketball
1972	Charles Bilger	Kansas	25	Football, Basketball, Track
1973	Early R. McVey	Houston	15	Basketball
1974	None			
1975	Ruth Seeger	Texas, World Games	20	Track
1976	Lonnie Tubb	Little Rock, World Games	8	Basketball
1977	Cecil B. Davis	Mississippi	28	Football, Basketball, Track
1978	Waldo Cordano	Wisconsin	28	Football, Basketball, Track, Baseball
1978	Hope Porter	Kentucky	NA	Softball
1978	James McVernon	Maryland	17	Basketball
1980	John Kubis	North Carolina, Gallaudet	13	Football, Track

NA—not available

Sports Leaders—Writers

1954	Art Kruger, California
1957	Leonard Warshawsky, Illinois
1962	Thomas W. Elliott, California
1963	Troy E. Hill, Texas
1964	Hugh J. Cusack, Pennsylvania
1965	Alexander Fleischman, Maryland
1966	Charley E. Whisman, Indiana
1967	Max Friedman, New York
1968	Edward.C. Carney, Maryland
1969	Harry M. Jacobs, California
1970	Jerald M. Jordan, Washington, D.C.
1971	James A. Barrack, Maryland
1972	William Fraser, Colorado
1973	Joseph D. Marino, Connecticut
1974	Gordon B. Allen, Texas
1974	Dr. Wesley Lauritsen, Minnesota
1975	Sam B. Rittenberg, Alabama
1975	Herb Schreiber, California
1976	Richard "Duke" Connell, Ohio
1976	Luther Shibley, Arkansas
1978	John Buckmaster, South Dakota
1978	Ross Koons, Des Moines, Iowa
1979	Richard Caswell, Maryland

Athlete of the Year

Fred Savinsky

1962 JOSEPH RUSSELL
Mississippi
Outstanding Athlete

1963 JEFF LAMBRECHT
New Orleans, Louisiana
Outstanding Trackman

1964 DONALD LYONS
Berkeley, California
Basketball and Track Star

1965 JAMES DAVIS
Oakland, California
and
VIACHESIAN SKOMAROKHOV
Kiev, Russia
Track

1966 CLYDE NUTT
Little Rock, Arkansas
Basketball

1967 TERRY SHISTAR
San Anselmo, California
Swimming

1968 LEON GRANT
Los Angeles, California
Basketball

1969 FRED SAVINSKY
Michigan
Outstanding Swimmer
Five Gold Medals Winner
at Belgrade Games

Helen Thomas

Donald Lyons

1955 HELEN THOMAS
Los Angeles, California
Women's North American
Skeet Shooting Champion

1956 MARIO D'AGATA
Florence, Italy
World's Bantamweight
Boxing Champion

1957 DENNIS WERNIMONT
Carroll, Iowa
Outstanding Track and
Basketball Player

1958 SAMMY MARVIN OATES
Austin, TEXAS
Outstanding Football Player

1959 GILLIAN HALL
Bristol, Connecticut
Outstanding Synchronized
Swimming Star

1961 JAMES MacFADDEN
Hollywood, California
Outstanding Track Star

Terry Shistar

James Davis

1970 BENNIE FULLER
Arkansas
Outstanding Basketball Player
for Arkansas School

1971 GARY WASHINGTON
Colorado
Outstanding Track & Football
Player for Colorado School

1972 STEVE BLEHM
North Dakota
Outstanding Basketball Player
for North Dakota School

1973 RONALD P. RICE
Michigan
Swimmer, won 5 gold medals
at WGD.

A.A.A.D. Hall of Fame photos

Craig Healey

1974 **BRIAN SHEEHEY**
Outstanding Football Player
Arizona School

1975 **CRAIG HEALY**
California (CSUN)
Javelin record holder
LACD Basketball

1976 **LYLE GRATE**
South Dakota
Track (Decathlon), Basketball
for S. Dak. School for Deaf

1977 **LAURIE BARBER**
Allison, Pennsylvania

JEFF FLOAT
Sacramento, California
Swimming

1978 **JEFF FLOAT**
Sacramento, California
Swimming

1979 **JOEY MANNING**
Florida School
All-around athlete

Bennie Fuller

Gary Washington

Lyle Grate

Leon Grant

Ronald Rice

Jeff Float

Brian Sheehey

Steve Blehem

Schools for the Deaf
Regional Basketball Tournament Champions

(Compiled by Art Kruger)

Eastern

Year	School	Coach
1927	New Jersey	Fred Moore
1929	American	Joe Bouchard
1930	Mt. Airy	George W. Harlow
1931	Mt. Airy	George W. Harlow
1932	Western Pa.	Everett Davies
1933	Mt. Airy	George W. Harlow
1934	Lexington	George Fairhead
1935	New Jersey	Fred Burbank
1936	New Jersey	Fred Burbank
1937	Western Pa.	John Egan
1938	New Jersey	Fred Burbank
1939	New Jersey	Fred Burbank
1940	New Jersey	Fred Burbank
1941	Mt. Airy	George W. Harlow
1942	New Jersey	Fred Burbank
1948	Western Pa.	James Mackin
1949	Fanwood	Paul Kennedy
1950	Fanwood	Paul Kennedy
1951	St. Mary's	John Rybak
1952	St. Mary's	John Rybak
1953	St. Mary's	John Rybak
1954	St. Mary's	John Rybak
1955	St. Mary's	John Rybak
1956	St. Mary's	John Rybak
1957	Fanwood	Paul Kennedy
1958	New Jersey	Jim Dey
1959	Mt. Airy	Erv Antoni
1960	American	Oscar Shirley
1961	American	Oscar Shirley
1962	Mt. Airy	Erv Antoni
1963	American	Oscar Shirley
1964	Fanwood	Paul Kennedy
1965	Kendall	Wilbert Stewart
1966	Mt. Airy	Erv Antoni
1967	St. Mary's	Lee Murphy
1968	St. Mary's	Lee Murphy
1969	New Jersey	Jim Dey
1970	New Jersey	Jim Dey
1971	St. Mary's	Lee Murphy
1972	New Jersey	Jim Dey
1973	St. Mary's	Frank Podsiadlo
1974	St. Mary's	Frank Podsiadlo
1975	New Jersey	John Fedorchak
1976	Mt. Airy	Erv Antoni
1977	Mt. Airy	Erv Antoni
1978	New Jersey	John Fedorchak
1979	American	Joe Giordano

Eastern, Division II

Year	School	Coach
1961	Kendall	Dominick Bonura
1962	Rome	John Comstock
1963	Maryland	Don Phelps
1964	Kendall	Wilbert Stewart
1965	Austine	Dominick Bonura
1966	Maryland	Don Phelps
1967	Rome	James Magness
1968	Rome	James Magness
1969	Rome	James Magness
1970	Rhode Island	Jim Cooney
1971	Rome	James Magness
1972	Rochester	Ed Niedzialek
1973	Rhode Island	Jim Cooney
1974	Lexington	William Byrd
1975	Lexington	William Byrd
1976	Lexington	William Byrd
1977	Mill Neck	Mike Rosenbaum
1978	Lexington	William Byrd
1979	Lexington	William Byrd

New England

Year	School	Coach
1964	Clarke	Henry Wilhelm
1965	Austine	Dominick Bonura
1966	Austine	Dominick Bonura
1967	Boston	John Muir
1968	Clarke	Henry Wilhelm
1969	Mystic	Don Norcross
1970	Mystic	Don Norcross
1971	Mystic	Don Norcross
1972	Rhode Island	Jim Cooney
1973	Rhode Island	Jim Cooney
1974	Rhode Island	Jim Cooney
1975	Rhode Island	Jim Cooney
1976	Rhode Island	Jim Cooney
1977	Mystic	Don Norcross
1978	Clarke	Greg DeLisle
1979	Austine	Steve Butterfield

Mason-Dixon

Year	School	Coach
1953	North Carolina	Carl Barber
1954	Mississippi	Cecil B. Davis
1955	North Carolina	George K. Brown
1956	North Carolina	George K. Brown
1957	Mississippi	Cecil B. Davis
1958	North Carolina	Bill G. Blevins
1959	Virginia	Jim Dilettoso
1960	Alabama	Harry L. Baynes
1961	Mississippi	Cecil B. Davis
1962	Tennessee	Ronald Bromley
1963	Tennessee	Ronald Bromley
1964	Virginia	Claude Crawford
1965	Tennessee	Jim Collins
1966	Texas	Billy Snowden
1967	Tennessee	Dave Bailey
1968	Florida	Frank Slater
1969	Tennessee	Dave Bailey
1970	Virginia	Rocco DeVito
1971	Alabama	Alfred Deuel
1972	Tennessee	Dave Bailey
1973	Mississippi	Thomas Kearns
1974	North Carolina	Elmer Dillingham
1975	North Carolina	Elmer Dillingham
1976	Georgia	Zeke McDaniel
1977	South Carolina	Bob Morrow
1978	Georgia	Zeke McDaniel
1979	Florida	Dennis Bennett

Southern

Year	School	Coach
1927	Arkansas	Earl Bell
1928	Arkansas	Earl Bell
1929	Arkansas	Earl Bell
1930	Kansas	Edward S. Foltz
1934	Texas	C. R. Brace
1937	Mississippi	Bilbo Monaghan
1938	Mississippi	Bilbo Monaghan
1939	Mississippi	Bilbo Monaghan
1940	Arkansas	Clyde Van Cleve
1941	Arkansas	Clyde Van Cleve
1947	North Carolina	Ray Butler
1948	Arkansas	Edward S. Foltz

Midwest

Year	School	Coach
1924	Kansas	Edward S. Foltz
1936	Minnesota	Lloyd Ambrosen
1937	Kansas	Edward S. Foltz
1938	Minnesota	Lloyd Ambrosen
1939	Minnesota	Lloyd Ambrosen
1940	Kansas	Edward S. Foltz
1941	Iowa	Nathan Lahn and Cecil Scott

Central

Year	School	Coach
1925	Illinois	S. Robey Burns
1926	Ohio	Bill Holdren
1927	Indiana	Arthur Norris
1928	Indiana	Arthur Norris
1929	Indiana	Arthur Norris
1930	Kentucky	Ashland Martin
1931	Illinois	S. Robey Burns
1932	Illinois	S. Robey Burns
1933	Illinois	S. Robey Burns
1934	Wisconsin	Fred Neesam
1935	Indiana	Jake Caskey
1936	Illinois	S. Robey Burns
1937	Wisconsin	Fred Neesam
1938	Wisconsin	Fred Neesam
1939	Illinois	S. Robey Burns
1940	Indiana	Jake Caskey
1941	Wisconsin	Fred Neesam
1971	Wisconsin	Alex Rubiano
1972	Wisconsin	Alex Rubiano
1973	Wisconsin	Alex Rubiano
1974	Illinois	Mike Moore
1975	Illinois	Mike Moore
1976	Illinois	Mike Moore
1977	Illinois	Mike Moore
1978	Kansas	Larry Beaver
1979	Illinois	Mike Moore

California Classic

Year	School	Coach
1977	New Mexico	William Stirling
1978	Washington	Frank Karban
1979	Washington	Frank Karban

National Deaf America Track and Field Records (Men)

(Compiled by Art Kruger)

Event	Record	Holder/Homestate	Year
		Prep	
100 Yards	9.6	Thomas L. Williams, Mississippi	1960
		Edward Wright, Florida	1964
		Charles Coward, Mississippi	1967
		Curtis Garner, Mississippi	1976
220 Yards	21.2	Thomas C. Williams, Florida	1962
		Lonnie Winston, North Carolina	1966
440 Yards	48.4	Leo Bond III, Minnesota	1972
		Drexel Lawson, North Dakota	1975
880 Yards	1:54.6	Ken Pedersen, California, Berkeley	1966
One Mile	4:25.3	Brian Armstrong, Oregon	1977
Two Miles	9:21.5	Steve McCalley, Indiana	1973
120 Yards High Hurdles	14.9	Ted McBride, North Carolina	1960
		Ken Landrus, Washington	1971
		Duwayne Davis, Arizona	1978
180 Yards Low Hurdles	19.3	Jeff Lambrecht, Louisiana	1963
330 Yards Int. Hurdles	39.3	Donald Scott, South Carolina	1978
High Jump	6' 7"	Willie Wooten, Georgia	1976
Long Jump	23' 1¼"	Robert Milton, South Carolina	1977
Triple Jump	47' 2½"	Robert Milton, South Carolina	1976
Pole Vault	14' 1"	Scott Stephens, California	1976
12 lb. Shot Put	59' 6"	Willie Poplar, Tennessee	1969
High School Discus	159' 10½"	Anthony Strakaluse, Rhode Island	1973
Javelin	188' 6"	John Och, Washington	1974
12 lb. Hammer	209' 10"	Anthony Strakaluse, Rhode Island	1972
440 Yard Relay	43.0	South Carolina School for the Deaf	1978
		Douglas Stephens	
		Mike Oxendine	
		Donald Scott	
		Robert Milton	
880 Yard Relay	1:31.1	South Carolina	1978
		Douglas Stephens	
		Mike Oxendine	
		Donald Scott	
		Robert Milton	
One Mile Relay	3:23.2	South Carolina	1978
		Mike Oxendine	
		Douglas Stephens	
		Lynwood Wilson	
		Robert Milton	
Two Mile Relay	8.43.8	South Carolina	1978
		Ronnie Harris	
		Le Lance Hall	
		David Platte	
		Lynwood Wilson	
One Mile Walk	7:00.3	Gregory Warren, New York	1976

Event	Record	Holder/Homestate	Year
		Men	
100 Yards	9.3	Edward Wright, Florida	1965
100 Meters	10.6	John Milford, Georgia	1977
220 Yards	21.2	Thomas C. Williams, Florida	1962
		Lonnie Winston, North Carolina	1966
200 Meters	21.3	Gary Washington, Colorado	1973
440 Yards	247.2	Leo Bond III, Minnesota	1977
400 Meters	47.0	Leo Bond III, Minnesota	1977
880 Yards	1:52.1	Leo Bond III, Minnesota	1977
800 Meters	1:49.7	Leo Bond III, Minnesota	1977
One Mile	4:11.6	Thomas Bachtel, Ohio	1977
1500 Meters	3:49.5	Steve McCalley, Idaho	1977
Two Miles	9:07.3	Steve McCalley, Idaho	1978
Three Miles	13:57.8	Steve McCalley, Idaho	1978
5000 Meters	14:36.6	Steve McCalley, Idaho	1978
Six Miles	30:25.0	Steve McCalley, Idaho	1974
10000 Meters	31:28.6	Steve McCalley, Idaho	1977
120 Yard High Hurdles	14.8	Donald Lyons, California	1967
110 Meter High Hurdles	14.9	Bernard Ruberry, Kansas	1977
330 Yard Int. Hurdles	39.5	Donald Lyons, California	1967
440 Yard Int. Hurdles	54.8	Michael Mitchell, Texas	1976
400 Meter Int. Hurdles	55.2	Jeff Lambrecht, Louisiana	1965
		Dean Dunlavey, New York	1973
3000 M Steeplechase	9:32.6	E. John Hunter, Jr., Idaho	1973
25 KM Mini Marathon	1H:27:17.0	Bob Backofen, Connecticut	1973
High Jump (2.01M)	6' 7"	Harold Foster, California	1973
Long Jump (7.04M)	23' 1¼"	Robert Milton, South Carolina	1977
Tri-Jump (14.39M)	47' 2½"	Robert Milton, South Carolina	1976
Pole Vault (4.33M)	14' 2½"	Joe Michiline, Pennsylvania	1969
16 Shot Put (15.14M)	49' 8"	Dan Fitzpatrick, Illinois	1977
Discus (46.90M)	153' 10"	Jeff Holcomb, Iowa	1977
Javelin (70.77M)	232' 2"	Craig Healy, California	1976
Hammer (51.13M)	167' 9"	Anthony Strakaluse, Rhode Island	1973
Pentathlon	2953 pts	Wallace Hughes, Jr., Tennessee	1969
Decathlon	6237 pts	Lyle Grate, South Dakota	1977
Mile Relay	3:19.7	Gallaudet College	1977
		John Milford, Georgia	
		Greg Rohlfing, Nebraska	
		Mike Farnady, California	
		Matthew Gallo, Florida	
1600 Meter Relay	3:17.1	USA National Team	1973
		Tony Spiecker, Florida	
		John Klaus, Washington	
		Leo Bond III, Minnesota	
		Gary Washington, Colorado	
880 Yard Relay	1:30.4	Gallaudet College	1977
		John Milford, Georgia	
		Greg Rohlfing, Nebraska	
		Mike Farnady, California	
		Matthew Gallo, Florida	

National Deaf America
Swimming Records (Men) Short Course (25 Yards)

Event	Record	Holder/Homestate	Year
50 Yard Free	22.8	Ronald Rice, Michigan	1975
100 Yard Free	47.7	Jeffery Float, California	1977
200 Yard Free	1:42.5	Jeffery Float, California	1977
500 Yard Free	4:27.9	Jeffery Float, California	1977
1650 Yard Free	15:28.08	Jeffery Float, California	1977
50 Yard Breast	29.2	Jimmy Cromwell, Tennessee	1978
100 Yard Breast	1:03.5	Jimmy Cromwell, Tennessee	1978
200 Yard Breast	2:23.0	David Ritchey, Missouri	1976
		Jimmy Cromwell, Tennessee	1977
50 Yard Back	25.2	Jeffery Float, California	1977
100 Yard Back	55.0	Jeffery Float, California	1977
200 Yard Back	1:56.3	Jeffery Float, California	1977
50 Yard Fly	23.9	Jeffery Float, California	1977
100 Yard Fly	53.2	Jeffery Float, California	1977
200 Yard Fly	1:55.8	Jeffery Float, California	1977
200 Yard I.M.	1:56.5	Jeffery Float, California	1977
400 Yard I.M.	3:54.04	Jeffery Float, California	1978

Event	Record	Holder/Homestate	Year
4×50 Medley Relay	1:47.09	Tennessee School for Deaf	1978
		Jimmy Davenport	
		Phil Huckaby	
		Howard Johnson	
		Jimmy Cromwell	
4×100 Yd. Medley Relay	4:01.4	USA/WGD Tune-Up Team	1973
		Jeffrey Lewis, New York	
		Neal Arsham, Ohio	
		Kenneth Dardick, Missouri	
		Ronald Rice, Michigan	
4×100 Yd. Free Relay	3:32.76	Tennessee School for Deaf	1978
		Howard Johnson	
		Phil Huckaby	
		Jimmy Davenport	
		Jimmy Cromwell	
4×200 Yd. Free Relay	Vacant		

National Deaf America
Swimming Records (Women) Short Course (25 Yards)

Event	Record	Holder/Homestate	Year
50 Yard Free	27.0	Laura Barber, Pennsylvania	1976
100 Yard Free	56.7	Laura Barber, Pennsylvania	1976
200 Yard Free	2:00.5	Laura Barber, Pennsylvania	1977
500 Yard Free	5:17.6	Laura Barber, Pennsylvania	1977
800 Yard Free	11:29.0	Pamela Scurlock, Texas	1976
1650 Yard Free	Vacant		
50 Yard Breast	34.4	Laura Barber, Pennsylvania	1977
100 Yard Breast	1:14.8	Josefa Muszynski, New Jersey	1968
200 Yard Breast	2:42.1	Josefa Muszynski, New Jersey	1968
50 Yard Back	28.9	Laura Barber, Pennsylvania	1977
100 Yard Back	1:01.1	Laura Barber, Pennsylvania	1977

Event	Record	Holder/Homestate	Year
200 Yard Back	2:16.5	Laura Barber, Pennsylvania	1977
50 Yard Fly	29.9	Laura Barber, Pennsylvania	1977
100 Yard Fly	1:05.5	Laura Barber, Pennsylvania	1976
200 Yard Fly	2:30.0	Laura Barber, Pennsylvania	1976
200 Yard I.M.	2:16.8	Laura Barber, Pennsylvania	1976
400 Yard I.M.	4:54.1	Laura Barber, Pennsylvania	1977
4×50 Yd. Medley Relay	2:18.61	Tennessee School for Deaf	1978
		Karen Dyer	
		Sherry Britt	
		Barbara Ogle	
		Kristi Dyer	
4×100 Yd. Medley Relay	Vacant		
4×100 Yd. Free Relay	4:18.2	USA/WGD Tune-Up Team	1973
		Carol Tufts, California	
		Lynn Ballard, New York	
		Lee Johns, California	
		Anna Tufts, North Carolina	

National Deaf America Track and Field Records (Women)

Event	Record	Holder/Homestate	Year
100 Yards	11.0	Donna Barker, Texas	1969
		Linda Shell, Mississippi	1975
100 Meters	12.7	Donna Barker, Texas	1969
220 Yards	25.7	Donna Barker, Texas	1969
200 Meters	25.6	Sherry Barnett, Florida	1977
440 Yards	60.01	Sharon Banks, Georgia	1976
400 Meters	57.1	Louise Hudson, Florida	1977
880 Yards	2:20.2	Glenna Stephens, California	1969
800 Meters	2:18.4	Betsy Bachtel, Ohio	1977
One Mile	5:26.0	Cheryl Pivorunas, New Hampshire	1973
Two Miles	14:13.0	Mary Ann Edwards, Texas	1978
1500 Meters	4:41.8	Betsy Bachtel, Ohio	1977
80 Yard Hurdles	10.2	Donna Barker, Texas	1971
80 Meter Hurdles	11.8	Donna Barker, Texas	1969
100 Meter Hurdles	14.7	Donna Barker, Texas	1972
High Jump (1.62M)	5' 3¾"	Annie Taylor, Tennessee	1977
Long Jump (5.70M)	18' 8¼"	Renonia Greer, Tennessee	1976
Shot Put (12.25M)	40' 2¼"	Gwendolyn Jones, Texas	1973
Discus (40.54M)	133' 0"	Dorothy Adamietz, Texas	1969
Javelin (43.30M)	142' 1"	Julie Olney, Michigan	1973
Pentathlon	3386 pts	Ann Reifel, Indiana	1977
440 Yard Relay	49.9	Mississippi School for Deaf	1975
		Bobbie Scurlock	
		Cecelia Clincy	
		Barbara Smith	
		Linda Shell	

Event	Record	Holder/Homestate	Year
400 Meter Relay	49.3	USA National Team	1977
		Barbara Smith, Mississippi	
		Gloria Moton, Tennessee	
		Sheery Barnett, Florida	
		Renonia Greer, Tennessee	
880 Yard Relay	1:50.7	Florida School for Deaf	1978
		Renee Fields	
		Sandra Maines	
		Gloria Swift	
		Joyce Houghton	
One Mile Relay	4:25.5	Texas School for Deaf	1977
		Debbie Bradshaw	
		Lucia Robles	
		Evon Boecker	
		Gretchen Forgey	
1600 Meter Relay	3:59.0	USA National Team	1977
		Betsy Bachtel, Ohio	
		Sandra Phillips, Maryland	
		Sharon Banks, Georgia	
		Louise Hudson, Florida	

World Deaf Swimming Records (Men) Long Course (50 Meters)

Event	Record	Holder/Country	Year	Site/Country
100 Meter Free	55.74	Jeff Float, USA	1977	Bucharest, Romania
200 Meter Free	2:02.46	Jeff Float, USA	1977	Bucharest, Romania
400 Meter Free	4:31.20	Ronald Rice, USA	1977	Bucharest, Romania
800 Meter Free	9:10.30	Jeff Float, USA	1977	Bucharest, Romania
1500 Meter Free	17:04.42	Jeff Float, USA	1977	Bucharest, Romania
100 Meter Breast	1:10.70	Dominique Filippi	1978	Saint-Louis, France
200 Meter Breast	2:34.30	Dominique Filippi	1978	Saint-Louis, France
100 Meter Back	1:04.19	Jeff Float, USA	1977	Bucharest, Romania
200 Meter Back	2:14.51	Jeff Float, USA	1976	Southfield, USA
100 Meter Fly	1:00.29	Jeff Float, USA	1977	Bucharest, Romania
200 Meter Fly	2:15.14	Jeff Float, USA	1977	Bucharest, Romania
400 Meter I.M.	4:55.76	Jeff Float, USA	1977	Bucharest, Romania
4×100 M Free Relay	4:06.01	USA National Team	1975	Maracaibo, Venezuela
		Phil Clarkson		
		Neal Arsham		
		Dave Ritchey		
		Ronald Rice		
4×200 M Free Relay	8:32.31	USA National Team	1977	Bucharest, Romania
		Ronald Rice		
		Eric Craven		
		Peter Stanford		
		Jeff Float		

Event	Record	Holder/Country	Year	Site/Country
4×100 M Medley Relay	4:16.89	USA National Team	1977	Bucharest, Romania
		Jeff Float		
		Jimmy Cromwell		
		Phil Clarkson		
		Ronald Rice		

American Deaf Swimming Records in Long Course (50 Meters) same as above except in the following events . . .

Event	Record	Holder/Country	Year	Site/Country
*400 Meter Free	3:53.42	Jeff Float, California	1978	Berlin, West Germany
**1500 Meter Free	16:19.53	Jeff FLoat, California	1977	Mission Viejo, USA
**400 Meter I.M.	4:40.29	Jeff Float, California	1977	Mission Viejo, USA
100 Meter Breast	1:11.86	Jimmy Cromwell, Tennessee	1977	Bucharest, Romania
200 Meter Breast	2:39.15	Greg Tompkins, USA	1977	Bucharest, Romania

*Made at World Swimming Championships at Berlin, West Germany, but too late to be accepted by C.I.S.S.

**These two marks were made at the 1977 National AAU Senior Long Course Swimming Championships at Mission Viejo, California, August 18-21, 1977 and these were global marks for the deaf, but were too late to be submitted for approval by the C.I.S.S.

World Deaf Swimming Records (Women) Long Course (50 Meters)

Event	Record	Holder/Country	Year	Site/Country
100 Meter Free	1:05.54	Laura Barber, USA	1977	Bucharest, Romania
200 Meter Free	2:18.73	Laura Barber, USA	1977	Bucharest, Romania
400 Meter Free	4:45.60	Laura Barber, USA	1977	Bucharest, Romania
800 Meter Free	10:20.30	Theresa Helm, Canada	1977	Bucharest, Romania
1500 Meter Free	19:53.68	Theresa Helm, Canada	1977	New Westminister, Canada
100 Meter Breast	1:21.87	Elena Shilipina, URS	1977	Bucharest, Romania
200 Meter Breast	2:56.00	Shannon Brophy, Canada	1977	Bucharest, Romania
100 Meter Back	1:11.03	Laura Barber, USA	1977	Bucharest, Romania
200 Meter Back	2:32.74	Laura Barber, USA	1977	Bucharest, Romania
100 Meter Fly	1:13.50	Cheryl Hayes, Canada	1977	Saskatoon, Canada
200 Meter Fly	2:41.10	Cheryl Hayes, Canada	1977	Saskatoon, Canada
400 Meter I.M.	5:31.19	Laura Barber, USA	1977	Bucharest, Romania
4 × 100 Meter Free Relay	4:26.96	USA National Team	1977	Bucharest, Romania
		Mary Cordano		
		Toni Oates		
		Barbara Ogle		
		Laura Barber		

Event	Record	Holder/Country	Year	Site/Country
4 × 100 M Medley Relay	5:00.90	USA National Team	1977	Bucharest, Romania
		Laura Barber		
		Sharon Getty		
		Toni Oates		
		Barbara Ogle		

America Deaf Records in Long Course (50 Meters) same as above except the following events . . .

Event	Record	Holder/Country	Year	Site/Country
800 Meter Free	10:59.50	Lori Manson, Maryland	1977	Bucharest, Romania
1500 Meter Free	Vacant			
100 Meter Breast	1:26.60	Josefa Muszynski, New Jersey	1969	Newark, USA
200 Meter Breast	3:06.20	Josefa Muszynski, New Jersey	1969	Belgrade, Yugoslavia
100 Meter Fly	1:14.04	Laura Barber, Pennsylvania	1977	Bucharest, Romania
200 Meter Fly	2:42.77	Laura Barber, Pennsylvania	1977	Bucharest, Romania

World Deaf Track and Field Records (Men)

Event	Record	Holder/Country	Year	Site/Country
100 Meters	10.6	Valery Lukash, URS	1973	Malmo, Sweden
200 Meters	21.3	Gary Washington, USA	1973	Malmo, Sweden
400 Meters	47.0	Leo Bond III, USA	1977	Bucharest, Romania
800 Meters	1:49.7	Leo Bond III, USA	1977	Bucharest, Romania
1500 Meters	3:49.5	Stephen McCalley, USA	1977	Walnut, California, USA
5000 Meters	14:42.2	Wilfred Zapfe, DDR	1973	Malmo, Sweden
10000 Meters	30:35.2	J. M. Rebry, Belgium	1976	Renaix, Belgium
20000 Meters	IH:05:24.4	Pauli Savolainen, Finland	1966	Jyvasklya, Finland
25000 Meters	IH:22:37.8	Pauli Savolainen, Finland	1966	Jyvasklya, Finland
110 Meter Hurdles	14.3	V. Skomorokhov, URS	1969	Belgrade, Yugoslavia
400 Meter Hurdles	51.4	V. Skomorokhov, URS	1969	Belgrade, Yugoslavia
3000 M Steeplechase	9.02.8	Wilfried Zapfa, DDR	1973	Leipzig, DDR
4 × 100 Meter Relay	41.1	USA National Team	1977	Bucharest, Romania
		Gary Namba		
		John Milford		
		Michael Farnady		
		Curtis Garner		

Event	Record	Holder/Country	Year	Site/Country
4 × 400 Meter Relay	3:16.6	Russian National Team	1969	Belgrade, Yugoslavia
		Igor Magnitsky		
		Nikolaj Stepchenko		
		Victor Skomorokhov		
		Vladimir Nikonov		
20000 Meter Walk	1:25:37.8	Gerhard Sperling, DDR	1972	Erfurt, DDC
High Jump (2.02M)	6' 7¼"	Nikolai Vassiliev, Bulgaria	1977	Bucharest, Romania
Long Jump (7.25M)	23' 9½"	Vesa Hannu, Finland	1971	Kuortane, Finland
Triple Jump (15.27M)	50' 1"	Viktor Judelevitch, URS	1969	Belgrade, Yugoslavia
Pole Vault (4.30M)	14' 1¼"	Vladimir Krejdnev, URS	1977	Bucharest, Romania
Shot Put (16.94M)	55' 7"	Bo Henriksson, Sweden	1973	Malmo, Sweden
Discus (46.60M)	153' 10"	Jeffery Holcomb, USA	1977	Bucharest, Romania
Javelin (70.77M)	232' 2"	Craig Healy, USA	1974	Charleston, Illinois, USA
Decathlon	6309 pts	Alexander Potoalski, URS	1977	Bucharest, Romania

World Deaf Track and Field Records (Women)

Event	Record	Holder/Country	Year	Site/Country
100 Meters	12.3	Rita Windbrake, Germany	1967	Opdalen, Germany
		Marina Mitschke, Germany	1977	Gaggenau, Germany
200 Meters	25.1	Rita Windbrake, Germany	1966	Opdalen, Germany
400 Meters	56.6	Rita Windbrake, Germany	1977	Bucharest, Romania
		Helina Zawadzka, Poland	1977	Bucharest, Romania
800 Meters	2:07.5	Rita Windbrake, Germany	1977	Bonn, Germany
1500 Meters	4:31.8	Rita Windbrake, Germany	1977	Recklinghaus, Germany
3000 Meters	9:59.9	Rita Windbrake, Germany	1978	Koln, Germany
100 Meter Hurdles	14.7	Donna Barker, USA	1972	Morganton, North Carolina, USA
4 × 100 Meter Relay	48.8	West Germany Team	1977	Bucharest, Romania
		Barbara Kruger		
		Marina Mitschke		
		Gabriele Lehmschloter		
		Rita Windbrake		

Event	Record	Holder/Country	Year	Site/Country
4 × 400 Meter Relay	3:59.0	USA National Team	1977	Bucharest, Romania
		Betsy Bachtel		
		Sandra Phillips		
		Sharon Banks		
		Louise Hudson		
High Jump (1.65M)	5' 5"	Tatiana Smirnova, URS	1977	Bucharest, Romania
Long Jump (5.68M)	18' 7½"	Nina Ivanova, URS	1969	Belgrade, Yugoslavia
Shot Put (14.49M)	47' 6½"	Olga Kalina, URS	1973	Malmo, Sweden
Discus (46.52M)	152' 8"	Olga Kalina, URS	1973	Malmo, Sweden
Javelin (43.30M)	142' 1"	Julie Olney, USA	1973	Washington, D.C., USA
Pentathlon	3592 pts	Nina Ivanova, URS	1977	Bucharest, Romania

316

Chapter 14

The 1960s

The Sizzling, Bountiful Sixties

REDERICK C. SCHREIBER called the decade the "Sizzling Sixties." To Hugo Schunoff, an educator and superintendent of the California School for the Deaf at Berkeley, it was the "Bountiful Sixties." Both were appropriate labels for that decade.

It was the decade that witnessed the founding of new national organizations such as the Council of Organizations Serving the Deaf, the Registry of Interpreters for the Deaf, the Professional Rehabilitation Workers Among the Deaf, and Teletypewriters for the Deaf, Inc.

The National Association of the Deaf moved its headquarters to Washington, D.C. and hired its first full-time executive secretary. And, the long Burnes era came to an end.

Higher education of the deaf reached a crossroads during the 1960s. Gallaudet College and the Gallaudet alumni experienced their first major disagreement over the direction the college should take. A special study was made of education of the deaf in the United States, and the federal government became more directly involved in the education of deaf Americans.

The Gallaudet alumni gave their alma mater half a million dollars as a centennial gift and established three permanent endowments. One, the Graduate Fellowship Fund, which provides financial assistance to deaf doctoral degree candidates, would begin to reap rich dividends in the decade ahead. A permanent alumni office was established on the college campus.

The Bureau of the Handicapped in the Department of Health, Education, and Welfare came into existence, and the role of Captioned Films for the Deaf, which had originally been charged with providing entertainment films for deaf adults, was greatly expanded to include the educational needs of deaf children.

Government-funded national and regional workshops brought educators, rehabilitation counselors, religious workers, and others together for the first time and began to create a better understanding of the needs of deaf people. Common problems were identified, better working relationships formed, and common goals agreed on. More and more deaf leaders began to emerge on the national scene, and deaf administrators began to arrive.

Congress founded the National Technical Institute for the Deaf at Rochester, New York, and the Model Secondary School for the Deaf in Washington, D.C. Post-secondary regional programs were begun at Delgado College in New Orleans, Louisiana, at Seattle Community College in Washington, and at the Technical Vocational Institute in St. Paul, Minnesota. A National Leadership Training Program in the Area of the Deaf was started at San Fernando Valley State College, now California State University at Northridge.

A Vocational Rehabilitation Service grant gave birth to the National Theatre of the Deaf at the Eugene O'Neil Theatre Center in Waterford, Connecticut.

317

Accessibility to the telephone was achieved late in the decade, and sign language began to come out of the closet.

The Conference of Executives of American Schools for the Deaf and the Convention of American Instructors of the Deaf opened an office on MacArthur Boulevard in Washington, D.C., and hired an executive manager, Howard M. Quigley, superintendent of the Minnesota School for the Deaf. The CEASD and CAID joined forces with the Alexander Graham Bell Association for the Deaf to form the Council on the Education of the Deaf.

Federal title funds made money available to schools for the deaf, provided educational programs for teachers of the deaf, helped schools acquire new equipment, and provided funds to improve academic and vocational programs. Public Law 86-276, passed by Congress in 1961, provided funds for training urgently-needed teachers of the deaf.

A Catholic college for deaf students opened as a division of Mount St. Joseph College in Buffalo, New York. It offered deaf students the opportunity to major in one of five fields—art, business, education, home economics, or physical education and study theology. Although a Catholic college, the program was open to all creeds and proclaimed its purpose to "develop well-informed, well-educated deaf leaders intellectually and spiritually." Classes began on September 17, 1962 with approximately a dozen students enrolled. The venture was not successful, however, and the program closed a few years later.

The United States hosted the 10th World Games for the Deaf in the summer of 1965. It was the first time, since 1924 when the Games were organized, that they were played on American soil. Six hundred eighty-one athletes representing 27 nations participated in the competition. They were housed at Gallaudet College and the Games were played at the nearby University of Maryland. Jerald M. Jordan of Maryland, a member of the International Committee of Silent Sports (CISS), was chairman of the event.

In Salt Lake City, Utah, in June, 1964, oral deaf adults formed the Oral Deaf Adult Section of the Alexander Graham Bell Association. The organization's announced purpose was "to encourage, help, and inspire all concerned with deafness so that deaf children and adults may improve their educational, vocational, and social opportunities in the hearing world through cultivation of their speech, speechreading, and residual hearing." Dr. H. Latham Breunig, a senior statistician at the Eli Lily Co. in Indianapolis was elected the first chairman of the new section.

Large, bold headlines in the March/April 1966 issue of *The ICDA News* proclaimed: "MASS IN LANGUAGE OF SIGNS." It was a historical event and good news for the nation's estimated 90,000 deaf Catholics as well as for deaf Catholics throughout the world. Pope Paul VI had granted permission to use sign language during Mass. It meant that the liturgy could be presented in a language that deaf worshippers could understand. It also meant that, for the first time, they could participate more meaningfully in worship services.

Lawrence Newman, a California School for the Deaf, Riverside teacher, was named 1968 California Teacher of the Year. He was selected in competition with teachers throughout the state and was recognized for his contributions to his students and to the profession. Newman's alma mater, the New York School for the Deaf (Fanwood), delighted at his selection, added another laurel. The school established the Lawrence E. Newman Award for Creative Writing in his honor.

During the decade *A Dictionary of Idioms for the Deaf* was advertised as the greatest book for deaf children since *Raindrop*. It was published by the American School for the Deaf. This dictionary was designed to supplement existing school dictionaries and to introduce the deaf student to English idioms. The descriptions were prepared in simple, illustrative sentences and accompanied by explanations. The book was made possible through a research grant from the Vocational Rehabilitation Administration of the Department of Health, Education, and Welfare. Dr. Maxine Tull Boatner, wife of the headmaster of the American School, was the project director.

It was, indeed, a busy decade.

Jr. National Association of the Deaf

Another national organization of the deaf started during the 1960s was the Jr. National Association of

President Lyndon B. Johnson speaking at the Gallaudet College Centennial Banquet in 1964. Elizabeth Benson is interpreting.

the Deaf. At the National Association of the Deaf convention in Dallas, Texas, during the summer of 1960, Mrs. Caroline H. Burnes, wife of NAD President Burnes, proposed that steps be taken to form a Jr. NAD organization with chapters in schools for the deaf. The purpose of the organization was simple: to develop new leadership among the young deaf people in the schools. Mervin D. Garretson, principal of the Montana School for the Deaf, was chosen director of the project. On his committee were Lawrence Newman of the California School for the Deaf, Riverside; Marvin S. Rood of the West Virginia School for the Deaf; G. Dewey Coats of the Missouri School for the Deaf; and Caroline Burnes of the California School for the Deaf, Berkeley. The first year saw the establishment of chapters at schools for the deaf in Missouri, Montana, South Dakota, Oklahoma, and Riverside and Berkeley, California. When Garretson moved to Washington, D.C., to join the Gallaudet Graduate Department faculty in 1962, Mrs. Viola McDowell, of Montana became the Jr. NAD director. She was succeeded in 1965 by Richard Tuma of the New Jersey School for the Deaf. In 1966 the Jr. NAD national headquarters were moved to the Gallaudet College campus, and Frank R. Turk was chosen director. Turk held the post for 12 years until 1980 when he was succeeded by Melinda Chapel Padden, a teacher at the Maryland School for the Deaf in Frederick.

Over the years, the Jr. NAD grew by leaps and bounds, and in the 1970s it reached a total of 94 chapters and a membership of over 3,000.

The organization began publication of *The Jr. NAD* (later renamed *The Junior Deaf American*), a quarterly magazine, in May 1962. The first issue was printed by Pettingill Printcraft, owned by Don G. Pettingill, in Lewiston, Idaho.

To encourage deaf youth to excell, the organization established several awards named for deaf leaders. These awards included the Robert M. Greenmun Creative Writing Award, the Lawrence Newman Award for Journalism, the Loy Golladay Award for Essay Writing, the Robert F. Panara Award for Poetry, the Helen Muse Award for Fiction, the Robert Welsh Award for Photography, the Byron B. Burnes Leadership Award, the David Peikoff Athletic-Scholar Award, and sports awards named for Art Kruger, S. Robey Burns, Thomas Lewellyn, Frederick Neesam and Anthony Panella. The organization also gives the Leonard M. Elstad Community Service Award and the G. Dewey Coats Service Award to an adult who has contributed the most toward the growth of the Jr. NAD.

In May, 1968 the Jr. NAD held its first national convention at Gallaudet College. One hundred twenty young deaf leaders and their school advisors attended the event. Since then, national conventions have been held at Gallaudet College (1970), the National Technical Institute for the Deaf (1972), Gallaudet College (1974), the North Carolina School for the Deaf (1976), Swan Lake Lodge, Pengilly, Minnesota (1978), and Cincinnati, Ohio (1980) in conjunction with the NAD Centennial.

The first national Youth Leadership Conference was held at the Indiana School for the Deaf in November, 1968, under the leadership of Gary Olsen. The conference was chaired by 17-year-old Melinda Chapel. Twenty-four schools sent representatives. A second national Youth Leadership Conference followed in 1969 at the Texas School for the Deaf in Austin and was coordinated by Gwendol Butler. These conferences led to the start of bi-annual Eastern and Western Deaf Youth Conferences. The first were held at the Governor Baxter School for the Deaf, Maine, and at the Washington State School for the Deaf. Other regional conferences have been held at the Maryland, Minnesota, South Carolina, Oregon, California (Berkeley), Indiana, New Jersey, and Montana Schools.

In 1969 the Jr. NAD held its first four-week Youth Leadership Development Camp at Pine Lake Lodge in Stroudsburg, Pennsylvania. The following year the camp program moved to Swan Lake Lodge in Pengilly, Minnesota, where it has since been held each summer.

Jr. NAD Chapters have become involved in their local communities by raising funds, planning deaf awareness programs, and collecting money, clothing, and toys for needy families. The chapter members have participated in work and clean-up projects, planned lecture series, and organized student-parent,

---

Walter J. Krug

(1905-1962)

Walter J. (John) Krug was dean of men and professor of biology at Gallaudet College for 35 years. He also taught Latin and mathematics at one time or another as the need arose. Born in San Francisco of German ancestry, he was deafened in an automobile accident on Christmas Day, 1918. The accident also left him blind in the right eye. He was educated in Oakland, California, public school and at the California School for the Deaf, Berkeley. He earned his bachelor's degree at Gallaudet in 1927 and a master's in 1932. For many years Krug and his family resided on the Gallaudet campus. In addition to teaching he also coached basketball, football, and baseball, and for almost two decades he was in charge of the college's health program. He died at his home on the campus on May 11, 1962, at the age of 57, following a long illness. Funeral services were held in the college's Chapel Hall.

Is it too much to say that Captioned Films for the Deaf has had the greatest impact on the education of deaf children in the United States of any program, method, equipment, or event since the advent of the Yale Charts and the Fitzgerald Key?

—Dr. HUGO F. SCHUNHOFF

---

leadership, and safety workshops. Their programs have brought them into more frequent contact with deaf and hearing adults, and they have benefitted from these experiences.

Melinda Chapel Padden, who, as a student, chaired the first Youth Leadership Conference at the Indiana School in 1968, was picked to succeed Frank Turk as director of the Jr. NAD in 1980. Other early participants in the Jr. NAD program have made marks of their own. They have continued their leadership roles by becoming officers of clubs for the deaf and active in organizations of the deaf. Some have been elected president of their state association, and some have become Jr. NAD advisors. Celia Laramie Baldwin and Deedra Blaylock have served on the Gallaudet College Board of Fellows. Baldwin's contributions to the deaf community won her the 1977 National Fraternal Society of the Deaf Frater of the Year Award. John Yeh is a successful businessman in the computer field. These are but a few examples of the influence of the Jr. NAD program on the lives of young deaf people. Hundreds of other young people are today better, more assertive, and more knowledgeable individuals because they participated in the Jr. NAD program and had the opportunity to become exposed to many different learning opportunities and to adults who were genuinely interested in them.

The Fort Monroe Workshop

A Workshop on Community Development Through Organizations of and for the Deaf was held at Fort Monroe, Virginia, in April, 1961. This workshop was sponsored by Gallaudet College and supported by a grant from the Office of Vocational Rehabilitation, Department of Health, Education, and Welfare, through the efforts of Boyce R. Williams. Alan B. Crammatte, associate professor at Gallaudet, was the coordinator and Jerald M. Jordan, instructor in the college's Preparatory Department, was assistant coordinator.

Two years earlier, an effort was made for the first time to involve deaf participants in a national work-

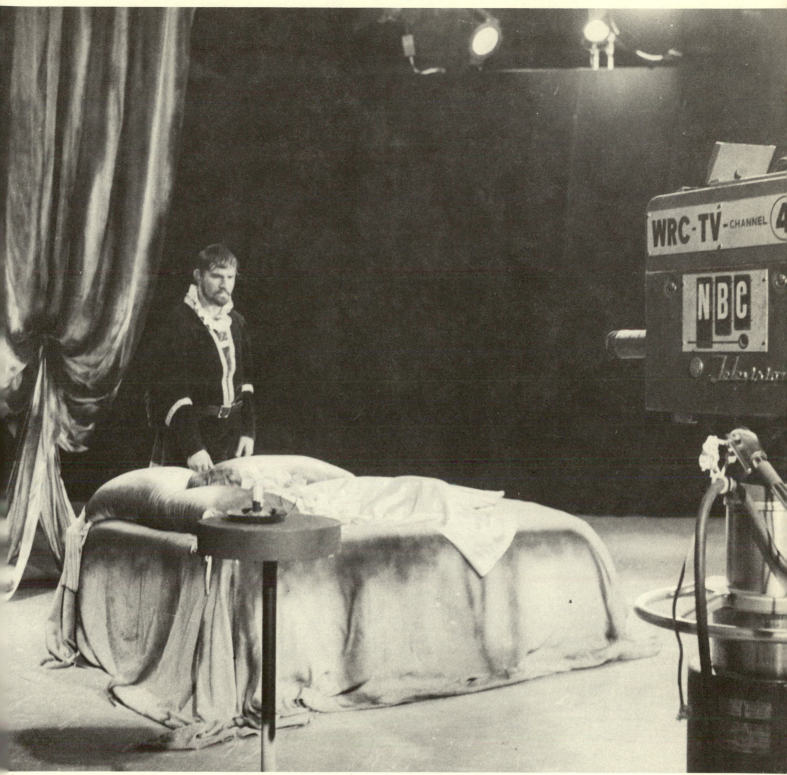

In the late 1950s drama became popular at Gallaudet College. Here Howard Palmer performs a scene from "Othello," in his role as Othello, on television. WRC-TV Photo

Harley D. Drake
(1882-1962)

Harley Drake (right) and his good friends, Roy and Ellen Stewart.

As a youth Harley D. Drake dreamed of becoming a jockey and a college professor. When deafness struck it changed the course of his dreams until he learned that there was a college for the deaf and that his chances of teaching at a college were still a possibility.

Harley Daniel Drake was a "son of the soil," a love he never lost. Born on a farm in Miami County, Ohio, he attended public school until he became totally deaf at the age of nine years. The cause of his deafness was unknown and mysterious. He suffered no illness, had no pain, and recalled no symptoms of disease. From public school he transferred to the Ohio School for the Deaf in Columbus and from there he entered Gallaudet College as a member of the freshman class.

Following college, Drake was boys' supervisor at the California School for the Deaf in Berkeley and taught at the Nebraska School for the Deaf before returning to Ohio to run his parents' farm. He married

Lillian Swift from Utah of the Gallaudet Class of 1905. They had four children. Drake was one of the earliest—if not the first—deaf persons in Ohio to own an automobile.

In 1911 Dr. Percival Hall, president of Gallaudet College, offered Drake the position of manager of the college farm together with a part-time agriculture teaching position. In this new position, Drake introduced new crops, built modern farm buildings, and improved the production of the college's Holstein herd. Roy J. Stewart remembers Drake's arrival. "Soon the farm began to prosper like a greenbay tree. More corn and more hay appeared. There was an increase in the supply of milk and a disappearance of the taste of garlic. Even the pigs and poultry cooperated. The pigs put on more weight and the poultry produced more eggs."

For many years the Drake family resided in House #8 on the campus, now named Drake House. In 1915 Drake was appointed professor of English while he continued to teach agriculture. In 1917 he completed his studies for a Master of Science degree at the University of Maryland.

For a decade Drake taught a Sunday School class at the Calvary Baptist Church in Washington, D.C. He was chairman of the alumni's Edward Miner Gallaudet Memorial Fund which culminated in the construction of the Edward Miner Gallaudet Memorial Library on the college campus. In 1958, he prepared and published at his own expense, a four-color manual alphabet card and gave the proceeds to the Gallaudet Fund.

Harley D. Drake retired to his Piqua, Ohio, farm in 1949, the same year the college awarded him an honorary degree. His portrait is part of the college's Hall of Fame collection. He died on December 15, 1962. He was 80 years old.

---

shop at Fort Monroe with educators, rehabilitation counselors and others who worked with deaf people. In a way, the involvement of these deaf participants was a trial and the results would determine the direction of the future. Chosen to participate in this workshop, which was managed by Dr. Powrie V. Doctor, were Mervin D. Garretson and Robert W. Horgen. Garretson was principal of the Montana School for the Deaf and Horgen was a printer and part-time director of the Wisconsin Association of the Deaf State Service Bureau. Both did well and Boyce Williams, pleased with the outcome, recalls: "Their splendid performance greased the way for Fort Monroe Number Two."

The second Fort Monroe Workshop was the first national workshop of its kind to bring together a large, representative number of deaf leaders from the deaf

community. And, it was the first to be coordinated by deaf persons. This meeting was, in Williams' opinion: "A sharp break in traditional paternalism; a benchmark in the evolution of the independence of deaf people." Williams also noted that it "demonstrated a budding awareness in government that consumer leadership and involvement are fundamental to proper program development."

The list of deaf participants included six printers, five Linotype operators, nine teachers, and persons

---

Deafness per se does not prevent a person from accomplishing what he sets out to do—if he really wants to do it.

—Dr. ROBERT G. SANDERSON

from a variety of other occupations, including a principal, a placement consultant, an aircraft sheetmetal mechanic, a carpenter, a pot tender in an aluminum plant, an architect, a tax attorney, and a rubber worker. Some of these participants would later rise to national prominence. Others would fade from the scene.

Although officially called the Workshop on Community Development Through Organizations of and for the Deaf, this workshop is better remembered as the Fort Monroe Workshop. Out of it came ideas that would have a positive impact on the lives of deaf people and the deaf community for years to come. At this workshop participants identified many needs and concerns of deaf people. They proposed local leadership workshops for deaf persons, the establishment of an information clearinghouse, an extension course for deaf leaders, and proposed that courses in social services for the deaf be offered to undergraduates at Gallaudet College. Schools were requested to include a course in civic responsibility. The cooperation of the Conference of Executives of American Schools for the Deaf, the Convention of American Instructors of the Deaf, and the Alexander Graham Bell Association for the Deaf was sought to develop better awareness and understanding of the needs and concerns of deaf people. It was proposed that a manual be developed to aid local organizations of the deaf to work with other local service agencies in defining and meeting the needs of deaf people on the local level. The need was identified for a sign language dictionary and instructional material to train interpreters and others who work with deaf people. The participants requested that serious consideration be given to the inclusion of deaf people in community activities of all kinds. Another need identified was to find ways to assist deaf persons to acquire professional training and to encourage them to enter professional work.

One other major recommendation of the Fort Monroe Workshop was the concept of formation of a council of organizations of the deaf. It became clear to the participants that if deaf people were to receive the kind of services they needed, they would have to speak with a united voice. This concern led to the founding of the Council of Organizations Serving the Deaf.

Honoring de l'Epée

During the summer of 1962 Leon and Hortense Auerbach were selected to represent Gallaudet College at the 250th anniversary of the birth of the Abbé Charles Michel de l'Epée in Paris, France. The event was planned by the French to honor the man they call the "liberator of deaf-mutes." It was de l'Epée who started the first free school for the deaf in the world in Paris and who incorporated sign language in the education of the deaf. Also attending the event from the United States were S. Robey Burns, Mario Santin,

The ceremony took place at the French Royal National Institute for the Deaf on Rue St. Jacques, the school which de l'Epée had started some 200 years previously. It was from this school that Laurent Clerc, America's first deaf teacher of the deaf, travelled to Hartford, Connecticut, with the Rev. Thomas Hopkins Gallaudet.

While in Paris, Leon Auerbach was presented with a medallion by the mayor of the city in recognition of his status as a teacher of the deaf.

The Auerbachs returned to the United States with a 400-year-old plank of wood from the church where the Abbe had preached before he became involved in teaching deaf children. This piece of wood was given to them by the vicar of the church. The church, reputedly built in the 15th century, is located in Feuges, a village about 50 miles northeast of Paris. The board was used along with pieces of wood from the American School for the Deaf and the Gallaudet College's Chapel Hall to construct the Gallaudet College mace.

The Telephone Arrives

With the invention of the acoustic coupler, by Robert Weitbrecht in 1964, and with the availability of a surplus of old teletypewriters, the telephone was finally made accessible to deaf people. Weitbrecht, a deaf electronic scientist residing in California, is the

Howard T. Hofsteater
(1909-1964)

Howard T. (Tracy) Hofsteater almost did not make it into this world. He was born "blue from head to foot," the result of nearly being strangled by the umbilical cord. Both of Hofsteater's parents were deaf, graduates of the Iowa School for the Deaf, and teachers. Thus, young Hofsteater grew up in an academic atmosphere and in a home filled with good literature.

Hofsteater's mother, Ollie Tracy, was a primary teacher. She had lost her hearing before she was two years old from a tumble down some stairs. Although she never attended college, his mother was "an expert with retarded children," Hofsteater recalled. She taught "children with mental deficiencies, children who arrived at school at embarrassingly late ages."

Hofsteater's father, Howard McPherson Hofsteater, had become deaf at the age of two when his father misread the label on some carbolic acid and squirted it into the boy's ears in an attempt to relieve an earache. Howard McPherson Hofsteater dropped out of college—a decision he would always regret later—to accept a teaching position at the South Dakota School for the Deaf. Both parents were always searching for new techniques for teaching their students.

Young Howard arrived when both his parents were in their forties. His parents began to suspect that he was deaf when he did not respond to sound following a bad cold when he was eight or nine months old; this suspicion doctors later confirmed. At this point Howard Hofsteater's life took a different turn from that experienced by other deaf babies. Realizing that their son was deaf, his teacher-parents decided that they would give him the same language background as that acquired by a child with normal hearing. They reasoned that if a hearing child could pick up spoken language by hearing it and imitating it, a deaf child could do the same by seeing it. They decided they would expose their son constantly to manual English through fingerspelling. This revolutionary approach to give a deaf child language alarmed friends and colleagues when word got out about what they were doing. Friends urged them to stop lest they cause their son to have a mental breakdown. Others feared that they were creating a "Frankensteinian horror." Some even went as far to accuse the parents of trying "to produce a mental prodigy to satisfy their vanity." This criticism hurt, but the Hofsteaters stubbornly persisted. They talked to their baby with their fingers at all times and always used fingerspelling in his presence. They fingerspelled to him whether or not he was paying attention, but they never forced him to look at their hands or to copy them. Eventually, and while still in his crib, Howard began responding. He began by spelling "m-k" for milk at the same age a

hearing baby would normally attempt to say the word orally. "W-t-r" became water, "p-d-y" became puddy, "s-g-r" became sugar, and other words followed. He learned the correct sequence of the alphabet after he had mastered many words. Also, his parents began reading to him when he was very young. They would fingerspell by placing their hands close to the page of the book. Whenever he requested a story they would drop what they were doing to oblige him. By the age of four and one-half years, he was reading on his own. His parents kept him out of school until he was nine years old. At that age he was enrolled in the fourth grade at the Alabama Institute for the Deaf, where his parents were teaching. The next year he was promoted to the seventh grade and the following year to the ninth. He spent a total of five and one-half years at the Alabama School and then at the age of 14, he enrolled at Gallaudet College.

Following graduation from college Hofsteater taught at the Michigan and Alabama Schools. While in Alabama he married Marie Parker and operated briefly the *Coosa Valley Press* in Talladega in partnership with Harry Baynes. In 1947 he joined the faculty of the Illinois School, where he continued to teach until his death.

Howard Hofsteater—friends called him Hoffy— was a popular storyteller. Once while telling a story he was sitting and rocking in an antique cane seat chair. As he signed "pull in your neck" he began to sink lower and lower in the chair, graphically illustrating the point. His audience began to feel that he was being especially dramatic when they realized that the legs of the chair had given way and he was sitting on the floor!

Hofsteater earned his master's degree at the University of Illinois. There Dr. Samuel Kirk urged him to write a term paper describing his parent's early experiment to develop his language. The paper was printed in *The Silent Worker* and Gallaudet Press picked it up and printed it in one of its bulletins under the title of "An Early Experiment in Preschool Education." This booklet is still widely used in college courses on education of the deaf.

Hofsteater coined the term, "Simultaneous Method" which Gallaudet College adopted to define the method used at the college. The term first appeared in an article he wrote for *The Illinois Advance*.

Howard T. Hofsteater died September 25, 1964 from severe burns caused from spilled lighter fluid. On his passing, his friend David Mudgett observed, "We have lost one of our finest language of signs raconteurs."

Ten Fingers Have I

Ten fingers have I, twining smooth and white
Wherewith I tell that which my tongue cannot.
No laggards they to set Love's eyes alight,
While my rude tongue sounds strange and polyglot.
Ten points of flame to tell the poet's fire
Or trace the lightning from a turbid sky;
To pluck soft music from a stringless lyre,
Or hurl toward heaven that great question: Why?
Ten tongues that bid the speaking tongue be still,
Ten rebel tongues that these my woes declare,
Though light these woes be (have it so I will),
That may infrequently be found in prayer.
If these be tongues, then ten-fold told my tale
Than one rude tongue in speaking could avail.

—LOY E. GOLLADAY

originator of world-wide radio time (known as WWV time). He has a number of other inventions to his credit.

It had been a long wait since Alexander Graham Bell had invented the telephone in 1876. Instead of benefiting deaf people as he had hoped it would, the telephone actually became a hindrance and a barrier. It had been used many times as an excuse to deny a deaf employee a job promotion ("I'd like to promote you, but you can't answer the telephone"). It was a nuisance and caused a loss of privacy because it required the assistance of a hearing person. Frequently the hearing person making the call knew as much about the deaf person's personal life as the deaf person did.

Teletypewriters are machines with a typewriter keyboard. When one key is struck it activates a similar key on the machine on the other end and a message is typed out. These machines are used to send news, stockmarket and weather reports, and telegrams. With the Weitbrecht invention, it was possible to link these machines and other telecommunication devices to the telephone and use the telephone to send a message.

Surprisingly, it took awhile for the teletypewriter to catch on. By 1978, Teletypewriters for the Deaf, Inc., listed only about 7,000 dues-paying members. (It was believed by TDI officers that the number of TTY users was twice that figure.)

The terms, GA (for "go ahead"), and SK (for "send kill" or end message) became new terms in our vocabulary. Blinking lights (signaling a ringing telephone) and "getting tied up on the telephone" were

new experiences for deaf people. They were beginning to understand better their fellow hearing Americans' gripe about the telephone. Anthony Papalia put that new experience into poetry when he wrote the following ditty:

Now the Deaf Are Doing it!

She ran to cook his pancakes, and the phone light flashed.
She rushed to start his coffee, and the phone light flashed.
Breakfast? He went without it.
"Goodbye!" No doubt about it.
She would have wept about it, but the phone light flashed.
She tried to dress the children, and the phone light flashed.
She went to wash the dishes, and the phone light flashed.
The furniture needed dusting,
The pots and pans were rusting,
And the silverware—disgusting!—but the phone light flashed.
All day the housework waited while the phone light flashed.
No time for rest or labor when the phone light flashed.
At last he came to fold her
In his arms, "Poor girl," he told her,
For a second he consoled her, then the phone light flashed!

That's not all. Deaf people were learning to type or were brushing up on their already acquired skills. (By the 1970s, it is doubtful if any other minority group had as many members with typing skills!) But, along with the good, came the bad. Deaf housewives in some localities experienced, to their shock and dismay, a rash of obscene TTY calls, and for awhile administrators at Gallaudet College had to cope with bomb threats phoned in over the TTY, usually just prior to an examination period. The TTY had, indeed, changed deaf people's lives.

With the TTY came other benefits. A TTY news service was started in St. Louis, Missouri. By ringing a certain number, the caller could receive the latest pre-taped local and national news on his TTY. Soon the idea spread to other cities. Answering services

Parents have the right to know just what is in store for their deaf children. They have the right to an honest assessment of their child's potential and his chances for success.
—FREDERICK C. SCHREIBER
1960s

TLA in the 1930s.

Tom L. Anderson
(1888-1966)

Tom Lewis Anderson was an educator, editor, national leader and pioneer in the field of vocational rehabilitation. He was best known to close associates as "TLA."

Born June 2, 1888, in Denison, Texas, he was left permanently lame and deaf by an attack of scarlet fever at the age of 12. He was so ill that it was six years before he regained mobility with the aid of a cane. He spent one year at the Colorado School for the Deaf and the Blind then embarked on a college education, graduating from Gallaudet College in 1912. That year he married Anna V. Johnson from Nebraska.

The Andersons settled down in Minden, Nebraska, where Anderson taught a manual training class in the local public high school. (He had good speech and usable hearing.) One of his students—and later a good friend—was Carl T. Curtis, who became the U.S. Senator from Nebraska. Next, Anderson became a journalist, purchasing an interest in the *Minden* (Neb.) *Courier*, and serving as editor for awhile. His wife died during the influenza epidemic of 1918, leaving him with two small children. In 1920, he married Effie Weseen, another Nebraskan, and they accepted teaching positions at the Iowa School for the Deaf. A year later Anderson became vocational principal, a position he held until 1940. As vocational principal, he was a strong advocate for modern vocational training. He was a key figure in the industrial section of the Convention of American Instructors of the Deaf. He founded and published *The Vocational Teacher* and edited *The Iowa Hawkeye*.

In 1940, Anderson moved to Texas to become placement officer at the Texas School for the Deaf. Shortly afterwards, he joined the state agency as a counselor. During the war he was credited with placing 400 deaf workers with the North American Aviation Company. In 1945, he accepted a similar position in California, where he remained until his retirement in 1952. He served as vice president of the National Rehabilitation Association and was a member of the National Advisory Council of the Federal Security Agency.

Anderson was an active member of the deaf community. He served two terms as president of the National Association of the Deaf (1940-46) and two terms (1936-43) as president of the Gallaudet College Alumni Association. In 1939 Gallaudet College awarded him an honorary doctoral degree in recognition of his service to his fellow men.

He retired to his home in Oakland, California, where he died on September 16, 1966. He was 78 years old.

came into existence. A deaf person could call a number and ask for information or ask that person to relay a message to a number that did not have a teletypewriter hook up. These answering services were usually manned by housebound or disabled individuals who had a teletypewriter installed in their home so that they could place calls for deaf persons. In some areas such answering services were handled by churches, AT&T Pioneers, or other voluntary service groups. Slowly hospitals, police departments, utility companies, libraries, airports, government agencies, legislators, and commercial establishments began installing TTYs so that they could respond to the needs of the deaf consumer. While providing an important service, the TTY was simultaneously creating a better awareness of the deaf population.

As the use of the TTY spread, deaf people began

calling their friends and relatives coast-to-coast, and the battle of the telephone bill began. Since typing is much slower than speaking over the telephone, deaf people began to feel that they were being charged unfair rates for the use of the telephone. Congress, state legislators, and telephone companies began getting the message. In September, 1979, California passed a bill requiring telephone companies in the state to provide deaf consumers with telecommunication devices. The companies were given four years to implement the program and the machines will be rented at the basic exchange rate charged hearing persons for their phone service. By 1980 there were 11 states—Connecticut, Delaware, Idaho, Maryland, New York, North Carolina, Pennsylvania, Tennessee, Utah, Wisconsin, and New Mexico—providing special rates for long distance calls placed by deaf customers.

With the emergence of the TTY, there came a demand for trained persons to recondition, sell, and service the machines. Workshops for training TTY technicians began springing up around the country, and a new line of employment—TTY agents—was soon added to the long list of occupations held by deaf workers. Soon, too, a variety of newer and better models—electronic and mechanical, portable and standard-size TTYs—began appearing on the market. This prompted Teletypewriters for the Deaf, Inc., to change its name to Telecommunications for the Deaf, Inc., to represent more correctly the many different modes of communications used by its members and the term, telecommunications device for the deaf (TDD) came into use. No longer did a deaf person have to drive across town to see a deaf friend and take

a chance on finding him at home. For deaf people, the luxury of the telephone had arri . . . excuse me, the TDD light is blinking.

Telecommunications for the Deaf, Inc.

Teletypewriters for the Deaf, Inc. was organized in 1968 in Indiana through the efforts of Latham Breunig and Jess Smith. It was an outgrowth of joint committees set up by the Oral Deaf Adult Section of the Alexander Graham Bell Association and the National Association of the Deaf. TDI was organized to coordinate the collection and distribution of used teletypewriters to deaf persons. The organization is supported by membership dues and donations. It annually publishes an international telephone directory of telecommunications users. When Dr. Breunig retired from his position with the Lily Co. in Indiana, the organization was moved to Washington, D.C. Breunig moved with it and became the first executive director. The organization is now located in Halex House in Silver Spring, Maryland, and Barry Strassler is the executive director. In 1979 the name of the organization was changed to Telecommunications for the Deaf, Inc.

Registry of Interpreters for the Deaf

Participants attending the Workshop on Interpreting for the Deaf at Muncie, Indiana, during the summer of 1964 agreed to form an interpreters' organization. Graciously chairing the first meeting was Dr. Edgar L. Lowell, administrator of the John Tracy Clinic

The Registry of Interpreters of the Deaf was formed at this workshop on interpreting at Ball State U. in 1965.

Gallaudet Archives

in Los Angeles. (Lowell was not eligible for membership in the organization because he was neither an interpreter nor a deaf participant, two criteria established for membership.) Originally the National Registry of Professional Interpreters and Translators for the Deaf (NRPITD), the organization's name was later shortened to the Registry of Interpreters for the Deaf (RID). Kenneth Huff, superintendent of the Wisconsin School for the Deaf, was elected first president. Forty-two interpreters and 22 sustaining members registered at the organizing meeting.

The Registry of Interpreters for the Deaf changed the scope of interpreting services for deaf America. What had once been a largely voluntary service was on its way to becoming a profession. The idea of *paid* interpreters caught some people unprepared. Some deaf people thought it absurd to have to pay an interpreter $7.50 an hour or more for services they used to get gratis. Some old-time interpreters, who had spent much of their lives habitually interpreting for relatives and friends without thought of recompense, could not with clear conscience bring themselves to charge for the service.

The Registry established criteria and classifications for interpreters, set up evaluation procedures, printed a national directory, opened a headquarters, offered workshops and training sessions, and gave interpreters a new respectability.

As deaf people became more involved in the community at large, the demand for skilled interpreters increased, and the freelance interpreter was born. More involvement of deaf people and their interpreters brought an increased awareness of the hearing handicapped American.

The Mantle of Leadership Is Passed On

In 1934 NAD President Marcus L. Kenner had appointed Byron B. Burnes to the Education and Membership committees. This tall, slim, bespectacled mathematics teacher, at that time from Minnesota, attended his first NAD convention in 1937, when the Association met in Chicago. At this convention, Burnes was elected secretary-treasurer, and when the NAD met in Louisville, Kentucky, six years later, he

The N.T.I.D. [National Technical Institute for the Deaf] adds a completely new spectrum of post-secondary opportunities for the deaf.
—Dr. HUGO F. SCHUNHOFF

Learning to speechread when a person has English as a base because he is postlingually deaf is not the same as having to learn English by speechreading when prelingually deaf.
—LAWRENCE NEWMAN, 1967

was elected to the presidency, beginning the longest presidential tenure ever served by an individual.

By the summer of 1964, when the convention opened at the Hotel Sheraton in Washington, D.C., Burnes had been president of the NAD for 18 years. After almost two decades at the helm of a struggling national association, he felt that the time had arrived to pass on the responsibilities to a younger person. During his administration the organization had opened its first home office in Chicago. *The Silent Worker* had been revived, the organization had observed its Diamond Jubilee, inaugurated a dollar-a-month membership program, increased the membership by 66 percent, started the Order of the Georges and the Knights of the Flying Fingers awards, founded the Junior National Association of the Deaf, and, co-sponsored with Gallaudet College, an occupational study of deaf workers. It had accumulated approximately $50,000 toward a fund for a permanent home office, and it had finally been reorganized into a federation of state associations.

At the Washington convention, for the first time Burnes had a serious challenger for the presidential office, and in Robert G. Sanderson, a supervisor of a plat office in Utah, he saw a capable leader. Unfortunately, what transpired during the business session prevented Burnes from bowing out the way he probably would have.

At the NAD convention in Miami two years previously, the Ways and Means Committee had set up a budget for the succeeding biennium. It provided for expenditures based on a predicted income of $38,566. Actual expenditures amounted to $39,856.06, an excess of $1,285.06 over the budget. Actual income had been $36,320.80, which was $2,245.20 below the income anticipated in the budget. The Miami committee had recommended that if reductions in budget allotments became necessary they should be proportionate for every item.

Burnes and his officers felt that they had cut costs as best they could, but after the treasurer's report had been read one member took the floor to question certain expenditures and other activities. His chief argument was that the president had not adhered strictly to the budget, and that reductions had not been proportionate all down the line, although it was

George M. McClure, Sr.
(1861-1966)

Death claimed George Morris McClure during his sleep, on his 105th birthday, ending a long, distinguished, and charmed life. This well-known educator of the deaf had spent a life-time in Kentucky, where was closely associated with the Kentucky School for the Deaf in Danville. He was a student, then a teacher and editor of the school's publication and, when he retired he was named editor emeritus, an association that spanned eight decades.

George McClure speaking to students at the Indiana School for the Deaf.

Indiana School

Born in Lawrence County, Kentucky, in 1861, McClure was deafened at the age of nine by a severe attack of typhoid fever. He attended public school and later enrolled in the Kentucky School. After two years of study, and while studying part-time at Centre College, he was hired as a teacher at KSD and placed in charge of a class which included a young lass named Carrie Jasper, who would later become his wife. They had three children.

Although a very successful teacher, McClure was best known as editor of the widely respected *Kentucky Standard*. During his later years he was frequently referred to as the "Dean of the Little Paper Family." (The Little Paper Family was the name given to the publications of schools for the deaf.) When he retired from teaching in 1937, he continued to write a regular column, "Among My Books," which was widely read. He continued the column until he was 100 years old. He was a delightfully descriptive writer. He co-authored an early history of the Kentucky School for the Deaf with Charles P. Fosdick, also an alumnus of the school.

In 1896 Gallaudet College awarded him an honorary Master of Arts degree. In 1934 Centre College conferred on him a Doctor of Literature, making him one of the few deaf persons so honored by a college for hearing students. In 1951, he was invited to give the commencement address at Gallaudet College and was awarded another honorary doctorate, a Doctor of Pedagogy degree. The degree was presented to him by his boyhood chum, Chief Justice Fred M. Vinson. (Vinson had taken the oath of office on a Bible given to him years before by the McClure family.)

McClure received many other awards. One which he cherished highly was the Edward Allen Fay Award, named for the esteemed editor of the *American Annals of the Deaf*. A building on the Kentucky School campus is jointly named for him and a former KSD superintendent.

One of McClure's sons, William D., and his grandson, William J., became educators of the deaf.

One favorite story told about the senior McClure involved a subscription to *Time* magazine. At that time he was past 100 years old and when his subscription ran out, he approached his son with the request that it be renewed. His son told his father that he would take care of it and order another year's subscription. The elder McClure informed his son that it would be cheaper to order a three years' subscription than one for just a year. Rather than argue, the son did as his father suggested. By strange coincidence, the subscription expired the same time the elder McClure died. When his son called his father's friends and informed them of his passing, it is said that he told them: "Dad's *Time* has run out."

Jerald M. Jordan in a moment of weightlessness. He was one of the participants in the space experiments.

pointed out that certain items, such as rent and withholding taxes, could not be reduced.

The officers made efforts to clarify all points, and they were supported by the Association's certified public accountant, but the discussion consumed so much time, it was decided to appoint a committee to investigate the matter.

The committee reported the next day that it could find no discrepancies. Its report stated that deficit spending was undesirable but justified under the circumstances.

Burnes believed that if any cloud of suspicion still lingered, he would be in a delicate position. For him to decline to run for re-election, he felt, would be mistakenly interpreted that he was trying to cover up. He saw no chance but to run again.

There was another issue involved. It was the question of whether or not the NAD home office should be moved to Washington, D.C. Boyce R. Williams wanted the NAD to move its headquarters to Washington. He saw an advantage in increased visibility,

better access to federal agencies, closer and more frequent contacts. Burnes was leery of such a move. He saw the move to Washington as taking the NAD away from the people. He did not believe that the NAD should become dependent upon government grants and handouts and placed in a situation where the government could tell the organization what it should or should not do. Burnes' beliefs had been molded in the old school of experience where you either do it yourself or it does not get done. It was difficult for him to believe then, after years of raising money for the NAD Home Office Fund, that you could get "something for nothing." He saw no reason for such a move and argued that the state of California was as much a part of the Union as was the District of Columbia—it just happened to be on the other side of the continent.

Sanderson supported the move of the NAD headquarters to Washington. He and his running mate for secretary-treasurer, Harold Ramger, had been the first to conduct a vigorous national campaign for office through flyers and through advertising in *The Silent Worker*. During the convention week, however, Ramger felt that he was becoming a liability to Sanderson, and withdrew his candidacy. (Ramger was later elected secretary-treasurer at the Las Vegas convention in June, 1968. The following September he and his two daughters died of carbon monoxide poisoning. One of the family cars parked in the basement had been accidentally left with its engine running.)

Sanderson defeated Burnes for the presidency. Robert M. Greenmun, Burnes' long-time teammate declined to run again as secretary-treasurer. They had worked together since Louisville.

Frederick C. Schreiber, a Government Printing Office employee, was nominated for the office of secretary-treasurer and ran unopposed. The mantle of leadership had been passed on to a new generation.

By vote of the convention, Burnes was named president emeritus.

Donald Peterson was another participant in the U.S. Navy experiments.

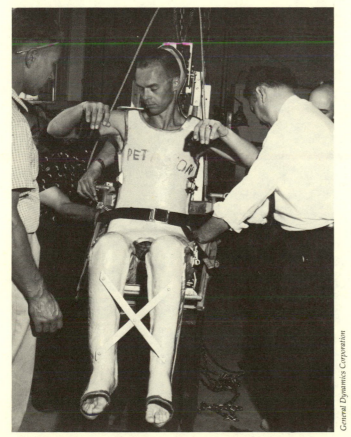

General Dynamics Corporation

U.S. Navy and Space Experiments

In the mid-1960s the U.S. Navy was interested in studying the effects of weightlessness on deaf persons whose deafness had affected their sense of balance. Medical personnel selected several deaf men to participate in these experiments. The group included Jerald Jordan, Harold Domich, Donald Peterson, David Meyers, and Robert M. Greenmun among others. Most tests were conducted during the summer months at the U.S. Naval School of Aviation Medicine in Pensacola, Florida.

One series of tests were conducted on board an ocean-going ferry off the coast of Newfoundland. The area where the experiments took place is known for some of the worst weather in the Northern Hemisphere. The ferry, with its French captain and crew, regularly plied these icy waters between Nova Scotia and the French island of St. Pierre, carrying food, fuel, and other essentials for the island residents. The Navy selected one of these trips during February, the worst winter month of the year, to conduct the studies. It was the best place they could find to see if deaf persons with poor balance become seasick.

The trip to St. Pierre was uneventful. The group stayed on the island for three or four days waiting for bad weather. Eventually, a storm came up with gale force winds, which had sunk two fishing schooners. That was the type of weather the Navy had been waiting for and orders were given to leave port.

Shortly after the ship left harbor, it began to roll and toss and wallow in the raging sea. One Navy medical man after another became seasick and had to go to his bunk. The ten Navy men who had accompanied the group also became sick. Eventually, there was not one medical tester left to conduct the tests. Meanwhile, the deaf participants busied themselves with a game of cards. At regular intervals, the French captain, an old salt with years of experience plying these seas, would come to the ship's galley where the deaf men were, go to the stove, unchain the big pot of coffee, and pour himself a cup. From the table where the deaf men sat and where they had no sense of direction (they could not see out the portholes), it looked as if the captain were pouring his coffee horizontally. The captain would fill his cup, riding the

OVERLEAF: The Gallaudet alumni donated a second statue to Gallaudet College in 1969. This one honors Edward M. Gallaudet, who along with Amos Kendall, founded the college. Photo by Chun Louie.

On The Edward Miner Gallaudet Statue

Behold this bronze, this tribute to our Guide,
Our Founder, Friend, and son of renowned sire,
On whom we gaze with reverence and pride!
He in our yearning bosoms lit the fire
To gain the meed we see there in his hand;
See how his eyes into the distance peer
On greater laurels for the silent band
Who thru his vision shed new lustre here!
Here shall his likeness stand thru coming years
Upon this hallowed Green of world-wide fame,
Where faith of his has wiped away our tears;
Here shall his spirit fan his altar flame
That may thru ages hence still brightly glow
While consecrated lives here toil and grow.

—STEPHEN W. KOZIAR

The new National Technical Institute for the Deaf under construction in Rochester, New York.

swaying deck with the ease of a youngster on a rocking horse, return the pot to the stove, chain it with one hand while holding the cup in the other, and not spill a drop. Then, he would walk over to the group, put one hand to his forehead and then to his stomach and inquire repeatedly in gestures: "Sick?" The participants would pause between hands, look up at him, nod their heads negatively, and resume their game. After each query, the deaf participants detected a look of disappointment on his face and thought it strange that he would look disappointed that they were not sick.

NTID . . . will become an important bridge for many deaf persons in their quest for successful economic, personal, and social growth.

—Dr. ROBERT FRISINA
1968

Later they learned that the ship's captain and the U.S. Navy captain in charge of the experiments had made a wager. The French captain bet that the deaf participants in the experiment would become seasick. The Navy captain said that they would not. The latter won the bet, a case of Scotch whiskey.

Cued Speech

During the decade another new term entered the vocabulary of education of the deaf—"Cued Speech." Developed in 1966 by Dr. R. Orin Cornett, vice president for long range planning at Gallaudet College, it was an effort to combine the advantages of the oral and manual methods. Cued Speech, as the name implies, consists of cues in which eight different handshapes are placed in four different locations around the lips on the face and throat. These cues, as ex-

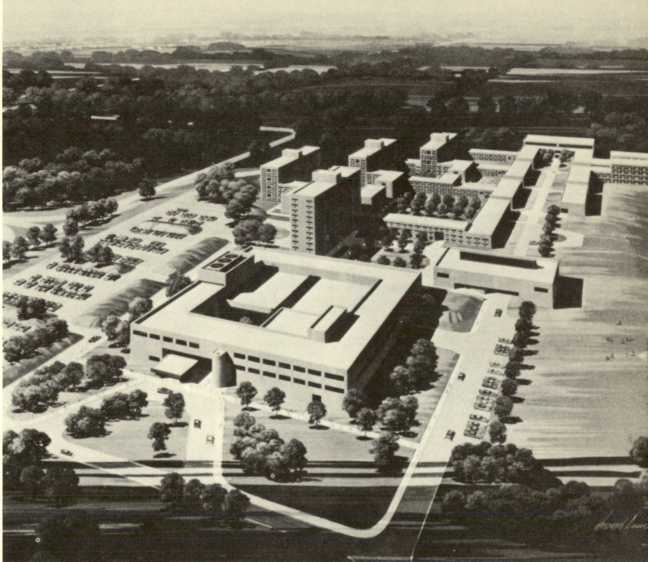

An architect's drawing showing how NTID will look when completed.

plained by its inventor, combine with what is seen on the mouth to provide a visible representation of syllables and phonemes of the spoken language and assist a deaf individual to learn spoken language through conversation and to speak and lipread better.

These hand signals or cues are easy to learn and make it possible for hearing parents to establish visible communication with their deaf child at an early age without having to learn a totally new language. The cues reduce the guesswork of lipreading and assist in the pronunciation of words. Cornett also states that Cued Speech provides a verbal foundation which assists a deaf child to learn to read.

Cued Speech created much interest when it was first introduced, but most schools which have adopted it have been small oral programs. It has experienced a slow, but steady growth except in Australia, England, and France where it is becoming very popular. The system appeals to many hearing parents of young deaf children, but it has not been accepted with the same enthusiasm by members of the deaf community. Some skeptics see it as a threat to sign language, although Cornett sees his invention more as a tool and never intended it to be a substitute for sign language. It is not intended to be a form of communication among deaf people, except for deaf children who have not yet learned sign language.

The N.T.I.D. [National Technical Institute for the Deaf] does not lessen the importance of the function of Gallaudet College any more than the Massachusetts Institute of Technology competes with the glories of Harvard, Princeton, or Yale.
—Dr. HUGO F. SCHUNHOFF

335

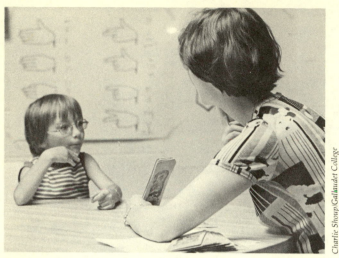

A youngster and teacher cuing. Note chart of cues in background.

The Council of Organizations Serving the Deaf

The Council of Organizations Serving the Deaf was incorporated in New York City in 1967. It was hoped that through this Council the various organizations serving deaf people would speak with a strong and united voice. The COSD was also intended to serve as a clearinghouse for information about deafness and deaf people; to strive to eliminate social and economic barriers; to coordinate and strengthen services of member organizations; to serve as a liaison between organizations of the deaf and other organizations; to support activities directed toward the prevention of deafness; and to enlist the support of individuals and

Glad Recompense

What though my ears be closed to vocal song
    That, stirring, cannot set my soul afire!
Shall I grieve o'er this loss my whole life long?
    Ah, nay! My glad heart is a silent lyre
On which all inward songs are grandly strung!
    Those would I miss through ear—glad recompense
Is mine to watch night's spangled garment hung,
    For then, within, the fire and rime commence!

And when my muted strings I fain would ply,
    I seem to hear the waves beat loud and strong,
And all the murmurs 'neath the forest sky—
    Oh, sweet the joy of heart attuned to song!
My silent chords respond with ecstasy
To music of the inner harmony.

—STEPHEN W. KOZIAR

Roy J. Stewart
(1878-1967)

If ever there was a man well-known and well-liked by the alumni of Gallaudet College, it was the gentle, friendly, and lovable Roy J. Stewart—better known as "RJ."

Born in Michigan in 1878, scarlet fever left him temporarily deaf at the age of five. He regained his hearing then several years later he became permanently deaf. He spent his youth roaming the northern forests where he hunted, fished and camped until his father accepted a position with the Post Office Department in Washington, D.C. and the family moved East.

After graduation from Gallaudet College—he was in the class of 1899—he secured a position first with the U.S. Census Bureau and later with the Public Health Department, and built a 50-year service record.

Roy J. Stewart was a regular visitor to Kendall Green where his wife, Ellen Pearson, a member of the Gallaudet Class of 1917, was a teacher at the Kendall School. These visits brought him into contact with generations of Gallaudetians. He served as president of the Gallaudet College Alumni Association (1932-36), was a member of the GCAA committee that raised funds for the Edward Miner Gallaudet Memorial Library and, for 30 years, recorded the activities of the alumni as alumni editor of *The Buff and Blue*. Stewart loved sports and was a regular visitor at athletic practices, particularly wrestling, a sport he had helped organize as a student. He was called an alumnus *semper fidelis* and a living legend.

RJ was seldom seen without a cigar stub in his mouth. When talking, he would clench the cigar between the first two fingers of his left hand, squint his left eye as smoke drifted upwards, then with both hands grasp the sides of his jacket and pull it over his well-rounded midriff (which, the moment he let go, fell right back where it was), and then he would raise his right hand and always start a conversation by fingerspelling, "S-a-y. . . ."

RJ served as the chairman of the NAD Motion Picture Committee for a record-setting 54 years. He submitted his resignation to NAD President Burnes before the Washington Convention in 1964. RJ felt that he had done all that he could, and with old age creeping up on him, he felt that he should step aside and let someone younger take over. Burnes not only refused to honor the request, but would not even recognize it. Burnes would later record his rationale. He "wanted beloved old Roy to shuffle off to glory the same way he usually appeared in Washington, with a tin film container in his hand and a day-old stub of a cigar in his teeth."

Roy J. Stewart died three years later in Washington at the age of 89. Burnes had described RJ as most of his friends will always remember him.

organizations to advance opportunities for deaf people.

The Council was funded by a five-year grant from Social and Rehabilitation Services, Department of Health, Education, and Welfare, with the hope that eventually the Council would become self-supporting. Mervin D. Garretson, a member of the Department of Education at Gallaudet College, was hired as the first executive director. Alfred Cranwill joined the staff as assistant director and Lee Katz as administrative assistant.

At its peak, the Council had 18 national organization members. The COSD sponsored several national forums in major cities throughout the United States with such themes as "New Horizons on Deafness," "The Deaf Man and the World," "Legal Rights of the Deaf," "Medical Aspects of Deafness," "Perspectives in Education of the Deaf," "The Deaf Child and His Family," "Organizations and Agencies Serving the Deaf." Proceedings of many of these forums were published and widely disseminated. They added much to the literature in the field.

When Garretson accepted the position of principal at the new Model Secondary School for the Deaf, he was succeeded at COSD by Edward C. Carney. Carney was able to get a three-year extension of the grant. However, about eight months into the first year of the renewed grant, the COSD was informed that federal support would be terminated at the end of that year. This occurred at the same time other programs for the deaf were suffering similar cut-backs. The Council was unable to generate the financial support it needed to maintain its operations and had to close the office. The organization existed on paper for a few more years before it folded.

The Christensen Case

Pangs of fear, anger, disgust swept the deaf community in 1966 when word spread that a California judge had refused a deaf couple permission to adopt a foster child they had been caring for. Because of their deafness, Judge A. A. Scott believed, Wayne and Madeline Christensen could not provide the boy with a "normal" home environment.

The Christensens and their attorney, Ivan Lawrence, appealed the decision. Meanwhile, two-year-old Scott James Richardson was taken from the Christensens, returned to them a few days later, and then taken away again.

Local and national organizations of the deaf set about raising funds for the Christensen's defense. There was fear that loss of this case could set a dangerous precedent and affect other deaf families. The California Association of the Deaf set up an Adoption Fund. The National Association of the Deaf entered the case as "a friend of the court" and started raising funds under the slogan: "The child you save may be your own." In the Maryland area deaf residents sponsored a dance with "May Day," the international distress signal, as the theme.

The case attracted national attention and Lawrence's office was flooded with offers of help. He had never seen anything like it and said: "I had never had a case where so many people came forth voluntarily to offer assistance."

Wayne and Madeline Christensen were a middle-aged couple residing in the southern part of Los Angeles. He was a clerk and she was a relief society president of the Mormon Deaf Branch in Los Angeles. They had successfully been raising another foster child, a fact that was crucial in their case.

The case ended favorably for the Christensens on September 19, 1967 when Superior Court Judge Bayard Rhone approved the adoption of Scott. Judge Rhone overturned Judge Scott's decision ruling that it was biased and prejudiced. His decision was upheld when the State Supreme Court refused by unanimous vote to grant Judge Scott a hearing on the decision.

Lawrence called the outcome a landmark decision for the rights of all handicapped people.

Mary E. Switzer

When God made Mary Switzer, He placed great beauty in her heart and soul. She was a sensitive, intelligent, straightforward, and sincere individual.

Mary Switzer started her federal career service as a junior economist in the Treasury Department and moved to the Federal Security Agency as assistant to the administrator when that agency was organized in 1939. In 1967 she became administrator of the Social and Rehabilitation Service in the Department of Health, Education, and Welfare. She once told an interviewer, "We feel an [handicapped] individual is entitled to his place in the sun somehow." And she spent all her efforts making that somehow happen.

The programs Mary Switzer administered had a

tremendous impact on the lives of deaf people. She worked closely with Boyce R. Williams who had joined the Rehabilitation Services Administration as a consultant for the deaf, the hard of hearing, and the speech impaired in 1945. He was the first deaf professional to be appointed to such a position, and he was responsible for the delivery of many of those services.

Mary Switzer helped design the legislation and later guidelines for the National Technical Institute for the Deaf. She was one of the first to support the National Theatre of the Deaf and funding from her program made the NTD possible. In 1969 she chaired the Committee on the Role and Function of Gallaudet College as an Institution of Higher Learning for the Deaf. The work of this important committee set the direction the college would follow in the years ahead, turned the college into a multi-purpose institution, and made it more responsive to a larger segment of the deaf population.

The admiration and respect people had for Mary Switzer were reflected in many ways. The walls of her office were covered with plaques, awards, scrolls, honorary degrees, and commendations. Her contributions earned her at least 16 honorary degrees; one of the first was from Gallaudet College. In 1970 the Gallaudet College Alumni Association gave her the organization's first Edward Miner Gallaudet International Award, and the National Association of the Deaf presented her its Distinguished Service Award. The NAD commended her for her "outstanding and singular achievement toward the advancement of deaf people of America." "She has," the NAD citation read, "given us the most precious gift that one can bestow upon man, the opportunity and the means to help ourselves."

Mary Switzer retired in 1970, ending a 48-year government career. She died of cancer on October 17, 1971. In Edward C. Merrill, Jr.'s words, the world had lost "a person who has given the concept of rehabilitation of human life its fullest and noblest meaning."

Deaf Administrators

Early in the 1960s there were few deaf administrators. Boyce R. Williams was with the Office of Vocational Rehabilitation and Malcolm J. Norwood was in the U.S. Office of Education. Richard M. Phillips and Walter J. Krug were deans at Gallaudet College. James N. Orman, Thomas J. Dillon, Mervin D. Garretson, G. Dewey Coats, Norman G. Scarvie and Uriel Jones were principals in schools for the deaf. L. Stephen Cherry was president of the National Fraternal Society

of the Deaf, Byron B. Burnes was president of the up and coming National Association of the Deaf , Robert W. Horgen was director of the Wisconsin Service Bureau, and Roger M. Falberg was executive secretary of Wichita Social Services for the Deaf.

As the decade progressed and new programs came into existence, more and more deaf persons moved into administrative roles. With the move of the National Association of the Deaf office to Washington, D.C., Frederick C. Schreiber was hired as executive secretary. Edna P. Adler, a supervising teacher and placement counselor in Michigan, joined Boyce R. Williams as a consultant of the Deaf and the Hard of Hearing, Deafness and Communicative Disorders Office. Mervin D. Garretson became executive director of the Council of Organizations Serving the Deaf, and Albert T. Pimentel became director of the Registry of Interpreters of the Deaf. Terrence J. O'Rourke was

---

Bitterweed

Beware the dark eyes on you in the street
And the impersonal glances
Of those who pass you by—
They have no love for you, though you be their brother;
Though you should cry for pity, there would be none.

Growing in alien soil, the strange plant dies
From rocks that press too hard, that block its root,
Sent underground for nourishment in earth
That holds no sustenance for such as come
Unbidden through the tunnel of the rain.
Wherever you may go, the word shall pass
That you are stranger there, and you shall know
The unreceptive ground and fierce sunlight
In the press of hostile faces: they will shout
In a bitter voice the wisdom of the old,
Who have no will to live nor strength to die
And speak the blind prejudice of the stone,
And close the shadowy door.

Only the bitterweed can sink its root
Into the powerful rancor of the soil
And blossom forth in strong integrity,
Undaunted by a hatred. You must send
Your anger forth to rend the strangling rock
And with your strength build shelter from the sun;
And send them also
A word as bitter as theirs, as filled with hatred:
Then only will they let you pass in peace.

—REX LOWMAN

hired to head the NAD's new Communicative Skills Program, and David Peikoff was appointed director of the Gallaudet College Development Office. Jack R. Gannon was hired as the first director of Alumni Relations, and executive secretary of the Gallaudet College Alumni.

When Garretson left COSD, he was succeeded by Edward C. Carney, and when Pimentel became director of the Gallaudet College Public Service Program, Emil Ladner replaced him at RID. Richard K. Johnson, one of the first recipients of a fellowship from the Gallaudet College Alumni Association Graduate Fellowship Fund, was appointed director of the Counseling and Placement Center at Gallaudet College.

The sixties were the beginning. The coming decades would witness the number of deaf administrators grow and move into important areas such as mental health, rehabilitation, education, social work and other fields.

"Greatest Cause on Earth"

As 1964 approached, Gallaudet College was nearing the end of its first century. The alumni wished to mark this milestone in a significant way. At their 24th Triennial Reunion in 1960, the members of the Gallaudet College Alumni Association voted unanimously to start a Centennial Fund drive with a goal of at least $100,000. This money was to be presented to the college as an expression of appreciation from deaf people of America.

The first move, following the reunion, was to find a chairman for this huge undertaking. The GCAA Board knew that for the fund to succeed, they would need a tireless and aggressive go-getter and a person who was deeply committed to the project. They did not have to look far because that person was right there in their midst—in fact, he was president of the Association—David Peikoff.

As a fund raiser few deaf men could hold a candle to Peikoff. And, as an organization of the deaf activist, he held a record few could equal. He was rightly described by a friend as a "many-sided character with his fingers in a hundred pies."

Peikoff, a Canadian at that time, was active in three of the most prominent organizations of the deaf in the United States—the National Association of the Deaf, the National Fraternal Society of the Deaf, and the Gallaudet College Alumni Association. He was also very active in the affairs of the deaf in Canada. He had

David Peikoff assuring an audience that deaf people can meet the Centennial Fund goal.

conceived the idea, and successfully spearheaded the effort, to raise $50,000 and establish the Canadian Deaf Scholarship Fund. At that time the Canadian government made no provisions to assist qualified deaf students further their education beyond the secondary level. This scholarship fund made it possible for many deaf students to enroll at Gallaudet College and other post-secondary programs. During the 1950s Peikoff had also been involved in raising funds for the National Association of the Deaf Endowment Fund.

As president of the Ontario Association of the Deaf he became a champion of the educational rights of deaf children. He led the fight in Canada against the pure oral method. Mel Williams, writing about Peikoff's contributions, defined him as an "uncompromising, unalterable foe of those who would stand in the way of deaf education and progress." So bitter did the struggle become over education of deaf children in Canada that when Peikoff visited his chief rival at the Ministry of Education, the Minister refused to

339

shake Peikoff's outstretched hand!

Born in Poltava, Russia, in 1900, the fifth child in a family of fifteen, David Peikoff's first brush with education, ironically, almost cost him his life. When he was five years old he decided he was ready to begin his formal education and, unknown to his parents or sisters, he followed the two girls when they left for school. On the way he became lost and stranded in a blizzard and was found hours later unconscious and nearly frozen to death. As a result of this ordeal he developed a high fever and lost his hearing, but other than that, fared no worse. Shortly afterwards, the family emigrated to Canada and settled on a farm called Bird's Hill near Winnipeg.

Schooled at the Winnipeg School for the Deaf, he dropped out at the age of 17 and entered the Mergenthaler Linotype School in Chicago. He found employment on a series of newspapers and while working on one he became acquainted with an older deaf printer who urged him to continue his education at Gallaudet College. Peikoff had never heard of the college but his appetite for more learning was whetted and he decided to give it a try. He was accepted for admission and, at the age of 24, became the oldest preparatory student enrolled.

When approached by the GCAA Board to become chairman of the Centennial Fund drive, Peikoff accepted the challenge with the zeal of a missionary and

As comptroller of the Centennial Fund, Alan B. Crammatte, played a significant role in the drive's success.

Our Heritage

set to work. He called it the "Greatest Cause on Earth," which he earnestly believed it was. As the end results would show later, he made believers out of many and they did not consider the statement much of an exaggeration. W. Ted Griffing, an alumnus and friend of Peikoff's, observed: "When Dave started on this project, you could have heard the snickers without a hearing aid." Peikoff could not have cared less. He had encountered many Doubting Thomases before.

It did not take Peikoff long to get the Centennial Fund drive airborne. Alan B. Crammatte, '32, joined him as comptroller and Hortense Auerbach, '40, became secretary in the Alumni Office. The first thing they did was to ask a group of close associates to become pacesetters and contribute $1,000 each to help begin the fund-raising efforts. The sum of $12,275 was quickly raised.

In February 1961 Peikoff was invited to address the Metropolitan Chapter in New York City to kick off the campaign among the GCAA Chapters. A snowstorm was forecast for that weekend, but in typical Peikoff fashion, he set out for New York City in his Oldsmobile with his usual optimism and no snow tires or chains. Meanwhile, one of the worst snowstorms in years was hitting the East. On his arrival in New York City he was a bit puzzled to see the streets devoid of moving traffic. Unknown to him, all traffic had been banned from the streets. Stopped by a policeman, Peikoff was warned to get off the streets. Learning that the banquet had been cancelled on account of the storm, he decided to proceed to Hartford. But how would he get out of New York City? Peikoff hand lettered a sign reading "Emergency" and proceeded towards the outskirts of the city. Twice along the way he was stopped by policemen but when they saw his sign they waved him on. To David Peikoff nothing could be more of an emergency than raising $100,000 for the benefit of deaf people.

In Hartford the Connecticut Chapter became the first chapter to kick off the Centennial Fund Drive. Appropriately enough, the Connecticut Chapter had been founded by Edward Miner Gallaudet, the first president of the college.

Peikoff's experience in New York was typical of the drive he displayed throughout the fund-raising campaign. He would encounter difficult obstacles along the way but he was unstoppable. The energetic zeal Peikoff and his team—the Auerbachs, the Crammattes, his wife Polly, the Ormans, Boyce R. Williams, and others—displayed soon became contagious. Members of the Ely Literary Society at the Maryland School for the Deaf pledged $500 and sent in half in cash, becoming the first students to give to the fund. College sophomore Suzanne Richardson spent most of her summer vacation handcrafting items which she sold at a college bazaar, donating the proceeds to the fund. Bernard Bragg, an alumnus and nationally-known pantomist, volunteered his services at fund-raising rallies.

The alumni chapters started raising funds. Classes began competing with each other to see which class could raise the most money or get the highest percentage of their classmates to give. Memorial contributions in honor of friends and loved ones began arriving at the alumni office. National Fraternal Society of the Deaf divisions began contributing. To encourage more such philanthropic gestures the national officers announced that the Society would match all such contributions. Gallaudet students and student organizations got into the act. The Phi Kappa Zeta Sorority, the oldest Greek-letter organization on the campus, set a group record with its gift of $4,000. The Parents Association of the New York School for the Deaf at White Plains contributed over $350.

Frederick W. Schoneman, a Gallaudet alumnus and a retired teacher of the Illinois School, and his wife topped all individual contributors and gave the fund a soaring boost with a pledge of $10,000 early in the campaign. The Bickerton Winston family of Minnesota and the William W. Duvalls of Arkansas contributed $5,000 each. Herman Cahen, his brother, Julius, and their mother gave $5,000. The British Deaf and Dumb Association surprised everyone with a voluntary contribution of $1,000. Tom Mayes, a deaf man employed at the Mott Foundation in Michigan and his wife, Julia, urged the trustees to contribute. The Mott Foundation had a policy restricting giving to local groups but the trustees voted to authorize a token contribution of $500 because "Mr. Mayes was one of our most valuable co-workers."

While on a fund-raising trip to New York City, Peikoff became acquainted with Henry C. Trundle, a Wall Street stockbroker and the son of deaf parents. Trundle offered Peikoff office space, volunteered to interpret for him and, most important, put him in contact with key persons of foundations, corporations, and businesses.

One of the biggest and most pleasant surprises for the Centennial Fund team was the generosity of some 800 deaf friends who contributed to the fund. At one point non-alumni pledges exceeded those of the alumni.

On their first barnstorming tour of the country, Peikoff and his wife, Polly, spent five months on the road. They visited 22 states, covered 14,000 miles, and raised $88,000.

A year later the records showed that 2,017 persons had pledged a total of $230,443.01 and given more than one third of the amount in cash.

As word of his success spread, Peikoff became the subject of some ribbing. Local deaf residents, it is said, were advised: "When David Peikoff arrives in town, hold on to your wallet!" W. Ted Griffing was somewhat more tactful: "There is no need to introduce Dr. David Peikoff," he said, "If you know him, you must have finished writing a check or signing a pledge card; if you don't, the chances are that your bank account is a whole lot healthier than it would be . . . ."

In the end, after a six-year effort, David Peikoff had travelled more than 56,880 miles, visited all states, and persuaded 5,687 persons and 121 civic and service organizations to contribute to the Centennial Fund. A total of $500,000 in cash and pledges was raised.

In June, 1967, the Centennial Fund was officially presented to the college and an agreement was signed designating its use. Three permanent endowments were established. One would be used to construct an alumni house. The second endowment fund would provide financial assistance to deaf persons interested in studying for doctoral degrees. The third fund would concentrate on promoting cultural activities for deaf people.

The 1970s would witness the results of the generosity of those individuals and organizations who believed in and gave to the "Greatest Cause on Earth."

Higher Education at the Crossroads

James Nestor Orman was cast in the genuine loyal-to-alma-mater mold. Elected secretary of the national Gallaudet College Alumni Association in 1947 during the Ben M. Schowe administration, he held the position until January 1961 when President David Peikoff resigned to accept the chairmanship of the GCAA Centennial Fund drive. Orman was picked to succeed Peikoff and head the less than 800-member strong alumni organization with 25 chapters, most of them inactive. Orman would lead the association through its stormiest period with a firm and steady hand. He "met his responsibilities with courage and resolve," wrote Bert Shaposka.

Orman was principal of the Manual Department at the Illinois School for the Deaf in Jacksonville, and editor of the school publication, *The Illinois Advance.* Short and thin, with thinning hair combed straight back, he found nothing new in being placed in the role of leader. As a seven-year-old growing up in Brooklyn, he was leading playmates in a game of "cops and robbers" one day when he fell from a fence and hit his head on concrete. The fall resulted in a cracked skull and permanent deafness. Orman enrolled in the New York School for the Deaf (Fanwood), where he came under the influence of Edwin A. Hodgson and Thomas Fox, two giants of their times. He matriculated at Gallaudet College and graduated with the class of 1923 at a time when the faculty openly discouraged the seniors from considering teaching careers. Oralism was then at its peak and there was little opportunity for deaf teachers. In spite of those odds, Orman landed a teaching job, working for Dan Cloud, and beginning a working relationship that spanned 16 years and involved three schools.

When Orman assumed the presidency of the Gallaudet College Alumni Association, higher education of the deaf was at a crossroads. There was disagreement between the alumni and the college administration over the direction Gallaudet College should take. The alumni were concerned over the "fantastic expansion" plans with no regard for quality or design. They believed that enrollment should be restricted, quality maintained, and additional opportunities for deaf students should be provided elsewhere. The college administration took the stand that Gallaudet College was not serving as many deaf students as it could. The chairman of the college Board of Directors held hearings on November 15-16, 1962, in an attempt to resolve the disagreement. Individuals and representatives of organizations were invited to share their concerns. Little was resolved, however, and the matter surfaced on Capitol Hill during the college's budget hearings. Orman and GCAA Vice President Loy E. Golladay, were invited to appear before the committee. (The national treasury, at that time, was in such bad shape that the Connecticut Chapter had to help finance the expenses of officers appearing before the committee!) It was before this committee that Orman called attention to the need for another program for deaf students to supplement the post-secondary program at Gallaudet. Orman suggested a junior technical institute. The committee liked the idea but expanded it to a national technical institute. Representative Hugh L. Carey (D-N.Y.) later introduced legislation establishing the National Technical Institute for the Deaf, which became a reality in 1965.

One off-shoot of these Congressional hearings was an appropriation of $100,000 to the Secretary of Health, Education, and Welfare, with a request that a thorough and special study be undertaken of Gallaudet College, the state schools for the deaf and the whole field of education of the deaf. Homer Babbidge was later selected to head this study and out of it came the statement that Americans did not have very much to brag about in education of the deaf. The report recommended the formation of a permanent National Advisory Committee on the Education of the Deaf. Legislation that followed would greatly expand and improve the learning opportunities of deaf students in America.

It is time that the deaf are studied as the human beings that they are as a living representation of the experience of Everyman in his journey through life.

—ROBERT F. PANARA

Gallaudet's Fourth President

In 1969 Gallaudet College gained a new president for the fourth time in its 105-year history. When Leonard M. Elstad announced his retirement, effective June 30, 1969, two search committees were formed to select his successor. Dr. Edward C. Merrill, Jr., dean of the College of Education at the University of Tennessee, was the unanimous choice of both committees. Merrill was not well known in the field of education of the deaf and had had limited contact with deaf people, but his credentials as an educator were impressive. He brought to the campus an attitude towards deaf people that they had seldom experienced before. Merrill knew no signs when he arrived on Kendall Green, yet within ten months, when he was officially inaugurated as the college's fourth president, he delivered his own message in the simultaneous method, quickly establishing a practice of declining the use of interpreters. He has followed that practice throughout his administration. The example he set influenced many others.

Merrill is a goal-oriented, decisive leader, yet a sensitive person and firm believer in an individual's rights. He aspired to see Gallaudet College ". . . serve all deaf citizens of America." He believed that the college should be both an educator and a partner of deaf people.

Merrill's wife, Frances, possesses a warm, friendly, down-to-earth personality and a knack for relating to all kinds of people.

ARE YOU DEAF OR HARD OF HEARING

(What's wrong inside your ears? Born deaf? Deaf after serious illness? Hearing just fade away?)

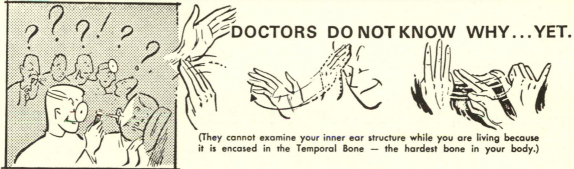

DOCTORS DO NOT KNOW WHY...YET.

(They cannot examine your inner ear structure while you are living because it is encased in the Temporal Bone — the hardest bone in your body.)

MAYBE MORE OF YOU AND YOUR FRIENDS COULD HEAR IF THE DOCTORS KNEW WHAT WAS WRONG

(Now it is squarely up to YOU, the deaf and hard of hearing people of America. Only YOU can provide the answers. The hearing world is watching to see what you do.)

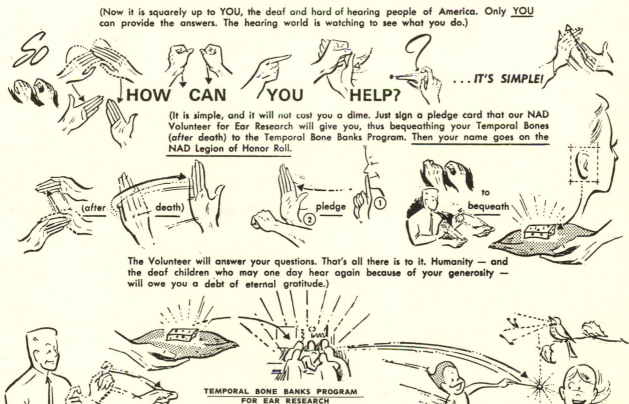

SO HOW CAN YOU HELP? *...IT'S SIMPLE!*

(It is simple, and it will not cost you a dime. Just sign a pledge card that our NAD Volunteer for Ear Research will give you, thus bequeathing your Temporal Bones (*after death*) to the Temporal Bone Banks Program. Then your name goes on the NAD Legion of Honor Roll.

(after death) pledge to bequeath

The Volunteer will answer your questions. That's all there is to it. Humanity — and the deaf children who may one day hear again because of your generosity — will owe you a debt of eternal gratitude.)

**TEMPORAL BONE BANKS PROGRAM
FOR EAR RESEARCH**

The Deafness Research Foundation is conducting a national Public Education Program (through a grant from the John A. Hartford Foundation) urging the deafened to bequeath their inner ear structures for research.
As part of a plan to aid this Program, this ad was prepared by the National Association of the Deaf and financed and sponsored by the DRF.

WATSON

The Temporal Bone Bank program began in the 1960s.

The Deaf American

343

The National Theatre of the Deaf

RIGHT: *The poster announcing a new form of theatre.*

The lone actor strutted proudly to the center of the stage, chest out, and head held high. He bowed slightly, then straightened and moved his head slowly sideways as his eyes scanned the audience. He raised his right, white-gloved hand and fingerspelled with machine-gun rapidity: "G-i-a-n-n-i S-c-h-i-c-c-i." He clapped his hands and suddenly the stage was overflowing with colorfully-costumed actors and movement . . . movement everywhere. Hands, fingers, faces, bodies, and voices began to communicate. No one had ever seen anything like it before.

The year was 1967. A new era in American theatre had begun. The National Theatre of the Deaf had arrived.

Samuel Hirsch described what he had seen as, "Pure art, drawn from a new medium of human expression." *The National Observer* called it, "Exciting, inventive, beautiful, and unusual."

And it was unique. While deaf persons in the audiences followed the performance in sign language, hearing actors signed and spoke their own roles and interpreted the spoken word for their deaf colleagues for the benefit of the hearing patrons. The result was, indeed, a performance where "you not only see everything that is said, you also hear everything that is shown."

The previous spring NTD had taped "Experiment in Television," for NBC, conducted its first three-week summer school, and gone on its first national tour. In addition to performing Giacamo Puccini's "Gianni Schicci," the NTD cast performed Saroyan's "The Man With His Heart in the Highlands," Tsuruya Namboku's "The Tale of Kasane," and "Tyger! Tyger! and Other Burnings."

When word got out of NBC's plans to show "Experiment in Television," which was the first major production using sign language on national television, the network received a telegram from the Alexander Graham Bell Association objecting to such plans and arguing that the exposure of sign language on television would undermine the efforts of "thousands of parents of deaf children and teachers of the deaf who are trying to teach deaf children to speak." The telegram also predicted that "This program will evoke

PRECEDING PAGE: *A scene from "Parade."*

NTD photo.

unfavorable reaction from educators and parents and the informed public."

Next, NBC received a letter from the director of the Bell Association which stated: ". . . we are opposed to any programming which indicates that the use of the language of signs is inevitable for deaf children or it is anything more than an artificial language, and a foreign one at that, for the deaf of this country."

This opposition to the program caught unsuspecting NBC executives by surprise. They turned to NTD Director David Hays for reaction. Hays responded to the Bell objections and pointed out that such programs would "bring enormous cultural benefit to the deaf who are deprived of theatre" and "show highly gifted deaf people working in a developed art form of great beauty . . ."

When word reached the deaf community of the Bell Association's objections, NBC began receiving letters in support of the program. NBC decided to proceed with the program, and it appeared on national television that year.

But how did the National Theatre of the Deaf come about? It had been started at the O'Neill Theatre Center in Waterford, Connecticut, in 1965. The O'Neill Memorial Theatre Foundation had come into existence only a year before. Named in memory of Eugene O'Neill, the O'Neill Theatre Center was formed to preserve and promote legitimate theatre in America. This Center presented an ideal place and an organization for the creation of a new theatrical medium.

The concept of a national theatre of deaf actors goes back to the 1950s when Anne Bancroft was learning sign language for her role in "The Miracle Worker." She became acquainted with Dr. Edna S. Levine, a well-known psychologist of the deaf, who told her of a dream she had of a professional theatre of the deaf. When she saw one of Bernard Bragg's performances in New York City she was convinced that a theatre of the deaf would appeal to all people. Levine's dream was shared by Mary Switzer and Boyce Williams, who saw in it an instrument which could positively influence social attitudes toward deaf people.

The widespread adoption and use of pure oralism in teaching deaf children in the late 19th century had relegated sign language to a villain-like role and blamed it as the obstacle to the satisfactory development of speech by deaf children. As a result, sign language became unpopular and a stigma was attached to it which made many persons uncomfortable

THE EUGENE O'NEILL MEMORIAL THEATRE FOUNDATION
presents

THE NATIONAL THEATRE OF THE DEAF

A SPECTACULAR EVENING —

FOUR PLAYS

Directed by

YOSHIO AOYAMA

JOHN HIRSCH

GENE LASKO

JOE LAYTON

FIRST NATIONAL TOUR

A scene from "Priscilla, Princess of Power."

and unwilling to use it in public. Some educators and parents openly forbade its use. Those who continued to use sign language were often led to feel that they did so only because they were oral failures. Consequently, with their own language under attack, deaf people felt guilty and very much like an unwanted minority. The attempt to make hearing persons out of deaf people led to their loss of identity. While their deafness and the daily problems it created persisted, there was,—except for an occasional newspaper article or within family circles—little awareness of the plight of deaf people. They were, as Mack Scism noted, "America's great unknown minority."

Could a national theatre of the deaf change attitudes towards deaf people and their language?

When David Hays, one of Broadway's outstanding scenic designers, saw Thornton Wilder's "Our Town," at Gallaudet College, he was struck by the beauty of sign language on the stage. Hays saw signs as "sculpture in the air." To him sign language was not the crude gesticulation it had been portrayed to be but "fluid, delicate, powerful, image-rich language."

Edna Levine, Anne Bancroft, and Arthur Penn had submitted a proposal to the federal government requesting funds to establish a national theatre of the deaf, but the proposal had been turned down. When the O'Neill Center began, David Hays helped George White start it. He remembered the Levine proposal and seeing "Our Town." He began to envision a new

348

theatre concept based on visual language and approached Levine about it. Levine introduced Hays to Bernard Bragg, who had studied mime under the famous French pantomimist, Marcel Marceau. Bragg was the first deaf professional actor-mime to gain national attention in the United States. He had performed many one-man shows throughout the country and in Europe. He had appeared on national television and, at one time, had his own weekly television show which featured him as "The Quiet Man."

Hays developed a proposal with input from Bragg, Levine, and others and submitted it to the Social and Rehabilitation Service of the Department of Health, Education, and Welfare. He was mainly interested in the artistic possibilities, but he was in essence proposing to use the theatre to address social ills affecting deaf people. Was such an approach possible? To some the idea was startling, but Hays argued that before social attitudes could be changed and better employment opportunities gained for deaf people there had to be a more truthful and accurate image of deaf people and their capabilities. More awareness had to be created. What would be a better way than to expose the public to a group of deaf people at their best—articulate, well-trained, highly skilled, professional deaf actors in a totally new setting? It was a bold idea in the late 1960s—some even thought it a bit radical. When many first heard of the proposal their first question was "A National Theatre of the *What*?" Fortu-

David Hays, NTD

Players' Guide *is published to promote the careers of deaf actors.*

Andy Vasnick is administrative director of NTD.

National Theatre of the Deaf

nately, a planning grant was approved and the National Theatre of the Deaf was on its way.

If the National Theatre of the Deaf were to be successful, it had to be different, Hays, Bragg, and their colleagues realized. They would have to attempt an approach never tried before by other professional theatre groups. They decided to make NTD a language theatre—a theatre that would concentrate on visual language. While pantomime was considered part of this theatre it was decided early to avoid excessive use of that medium (which was popular among deaf theatre groups in Europe) because it was a form which belonged to hearing theatre and because it emphasized muteness—an image deaf actors did not wish to convey.

And, did it work? In comparison to the first tour which took the company to major cities in the United States, the 23rd tour took the troupe on a 30,000-mile swing through nine states and to Japan, South Korea, and Singapore. During the past two decades of the company's existence, it has done almost 3,000 performances, and appeared in more than 400 theatres, the first company to perform in all 50 states. It has performed in 16 foreign countries making it the most traveled American theatre company. The company

(continued on page 356)

349

CAROLE LEE AQUILINE

BETTI BONNI

JANICE COLE

PAUL JOHNSTON

CHARLES COREY

RITA COREY

GILBERT EASTMAN

RALPH WHITE

SAMUEL E. EDWARDS

350

TIM SCANLON

JULIANNA FJELD

RAYMOND FLEMING

TIMOTHY JOHNSON

CHARLES JONES

RICHARD KENDALL

LEWIS MERKIN

LINDA BOVE

Jay Aarc, NTD

SHANNY MOW

FREDA C. NORMAN

PHYLLIS A. FRELICH

AUDREE L. NORTON

RAY S. PARKS, JR.

JOSEPH MARTIN SARPY

PATRICK GRAYBILL

352

MICHAEL A. SCHWARTZ

GARY THEILER

JIMMY TURNER

BERNARD BRAGG

EDMUND WATERSTREET

KEVIN VAN WIERINGEN

SHARON WOOD

353

A scene from "My Third Eye."

Jay Aarc, NTD

"My Third Eye"

In 1971 the National Theatre of the Deaf produced its first original work, a five-part piece entitled, "My Third Eye." Written by members of the cast, this production introduced the audience to the world of deafness and to sign language and included an amusing "side-show" where "strange" people *talked* instead of signed. The actors also shared their personal experiences of being deaf. Some excerpts from the biography segment:

Bernard Bragg: When I was four and a half years old, I was awakened one morning, bathed, dressed in fresh, new clothes, and given my breakfast. My mother and I left the apartment together, and I never went back there again.

As we walked to the subway, I asked, "Where are we going?" but my mother didn't reply. I felt a peculiar panic I'd never felt before. "Mother, where are you taking me," I asked again.

"Don't worry, I am with you. Everything is all right," she replied. For the first time in my life, this reassurance wasn't enough. I was frightened.

When the subway ride was over, we walked several blocks to an ominous building on Riverside Drive. Once inside, I smelled, for the first time, the institutional odor of cleanliness and disinfectant. I felt confined by the high ceilings, and dwarfed by the emptiness of the glistening corridors.

I was at the New York School for the Deaf where I would be a boarding student for the next thirteen years of my life. We were standing in the superin-

tendent's office. I was filled with the sickening panic of a washed-away world. My mother kissed me and said, "This is the place where you will get all your education . . . ," She kissed me and was gone.

Everything I loved and trusted had left me. I was bathed again, and given my uniform. My hair was combed and the supervisor took me into a playroom where other children were playing. It was the first time I had ever seen other deaf children. I knew they were deaf because they behaved differently from the hearing children I knew. "Is this what school is?" I wondered, "a place where children are taken, and left?" The children in my neighborhood went to school, but they came home every day. I wanted to live at home with my parents, like they did. A boy came to me and began to sign. He was the son of deaf parents like I was. I was overjoyed because I had someone to talk to. We talked excitedly, and the preoccupation with this new friendship eased my sorrow temporarily.

That night when I was put to bed in a large dormitory, I cried. I thought about my mother and father. I longed for the comforting darkness of my own room. I had watched the other children playing and talking after dinner. They seemed happy. They had each other, but I still had a mother and father.

Maybe they had mothers and fathers . . . Maybe someday I would be as happy as they were . . . Maybe some day . . . and I drifted off to sleep. My first day of school was over.

Freda Norman: A teacher said to me, "Teaching the deaf children through the means of oralism is the best method to adopt because: the majority is hearing and it is up to the minority like you to join them. Being able to speak is likely to help you people to be accepted into the world."

So I spent my life trying to be like the others and I can speak, and read lips. And I wonder, now, how valuable it is that we must always try to be like others. My deafness is . . . myself, it is

"The quick brown fox. . ." from "My Third Eye."

not something that I must fight against, or hide, or overcome.

Joe Sarpy: When I was small, my parents wanted me to attend oral school where children were not allowed to use the language of the hands—sign language or fingerspelling, but had to learn speech and lipreading. My parents are hearing. They wouldn't learn sign language. They hoped I would communicate with them in their way. The teacher said OK and started to teach me how to say different sounds. The teacher held my hand on my throat and nose to feel the vibrations. The teacher wanted me to feel the vibrations that happen when I said M . . . M . . . M . . . and N . . . N . . . N . . . . And the teacher put a stick to hold down my tongue and it touched my windpipe, the teacher wanted to hear me say Ah . . . Ah . . . Ah . . . , and I almost vomited.

Mary Beth Miller: My teacher would use the same stick for all of the children.

Bernard Bragg: It took me weeks and weeks before I was able to make my "K" sound right. At the end of my first school year, there was a demonstration for parents and visitors. I came up on

a platform and made just that one letter. The audience applauded, but my mother who is deaf just stared at me as if to ask, "Was that all I had learned during all that time?"

Mary Beth Miller: I would teach some of the kids who knew no sign language. The teacher would tie my hands together.

Ed Waterstreet: Same in my school, when I tried to sign with my friends the teacher caught me and made me sit on my hands.

Bernard Bragg: Spontaneous outbursts of laughter in the classroom were often stilled by scornful reprimands from our fifth-grade teacher not so much because they were impolite or erupted at inappropriate times as because he said they sounded disgustedly unpleasant or irritating—even animalistic. Young and uncomprehending as we were, we were given long lectures on the importance of being consistently aware of what our laughter sounded like to those who could hear. From that time on, we were forced to undergo various exercises like breathing through nose only—breathing through mouth only—either with sound or without—

Jay Aarc, NTD

doing these repeatedly with our hands on our stomachs or heads.

Compliments were often lavished upon those who came up with forced, but perfectly controlled laughter—and glares were given to those who failed to laugh "properly" or didn't sound like a "normal" person. Some of us have since then forgotten how to laugh the way we had been taught.

And there are two or three from our group, who have chosen to laugh silently for the rest of their lives.

Mary Beth Miller: When I was 15 or 16—Sam, my brother-in-law and I were talking in the front room about different kinds of fire crackers he bought in Tennessee. He had regular fire crackers,—cherry bombs, and TNT. I was fascinated by the TNT. My father was in the living room but he was busy reading. Then he got up and took the paper with him. I knew instantly that he was going to the bathroom. Because he was deaf he always left the door open a crack because the insurance man or paper boy or someone might come—and we might need to let him know. Then Sam and I started talking about the firecrackers again. I asked him all kinds of questions like, "What will happen if I threw a TNT in a garbage can?" He told me that TNT will make dents in the can. He also told me that if I throw a cherry bomb in the toilet it will split open. Sam said, "Father in bathroom?" I said, "Yes." All of a sudden we both got the same idea and smiled. Sam handed me a cherry bomb and said, "Go on." I took it and walked through the bed room—dining room and kitchen. I paused because I was a little bit nervous and jittery about it. Sam encouraged me and finally I gave in. I opened the bathroom door and could barely see my father—although the newspaper and his hands were visible. I lighted the cherry bomb—ran to the front room. As I ran I felt the shock of the explosion. Sam and I sat down and talked about something else. It was very hard to keep a poker face. Sam said that father was coming. His pants were half down and the torn newspaper in his hand. "What happened?" Then he looked at me and signed, "Don't you *ever* do that again!" Then he turned and went back to the bathroom. For three days after that he was constipated.

has done television specials—"A Child's Christmas in Wales," and "Who Knows One" for such networks as NBC, CBS, PBS and Dutch and Danish TV. NTD officials estimate over one hundred million television viewers have seen their performances. NTD has been credited with "sparking the establishment" of similar theatres of the deaf in Sweden, England, Australia, France, and Canada.

Three smaller companies have been formed, two Little Theatres of the Deaf and a Theatre of Sign. A Professional School for Deaf Theatre Personnel offers summer workshops for promising deaf playwrights, aspiring actors, and persons interested in developing community theatres.

NTD actors have appeared on national television productions, in soap operas, movies, and commercials. Audree Norton has performed in "Mannix," "Family Affair," "Man and the City," and "Streets of San Francisco." Bernard Bragg has appeared twice on the David Frost Show. Linda Bove is a regular on Public Broadcasting Service's "Sesame Street." She played the role of Melissa in the television serial, "Search for Tomorrow." Tim Scanlon has appeared on "Mister Rogers' Neighborhood," "Sesame Street," and "What's My Line." Edmund Waterstreet, who has appeared on "The Mike Douglas Show," was a Cleo Award finalist for his United Way television commercial in 1978. Phyllis Frelich starred in Mark Medoff's "Children of a Lesser God," which appeared on Broadway. The play was based on her and her hearing husband's lives.

Today sign language no longer carries a stigma. It is respected as a language and is used widely in the education of deaf children. On stage and on television it has been seen by millions at its best—the beautiful, artful, expressive means of communication that it is. Thousands and thousands of Americans have begun to learn sign language so that they can communicate more freely with their fellow deaf Americans. The increased popularity of sign language has given deaf people a new pride and a better self-image. Job opportunities have broadened because of increased awareness of deaf people and their capabilities. Deaf actors have become the heroes and models of deaf and hearing children alike. Bernard Bragg noted these changes when he observed: "People used to push my hands down in embarrassment and tell me not to sign in public. Now people pay to see me perform in sign language."

Let us display the deaf, who can be just as talented, intelligent, charming, and beautiful as hearing people, in a glamorous and exciting new setting. Let us send them forth as actors equal to the best hearing actors in the world.

—DAVID HAYS

Chapter 15

American Sign Language: Our Natural Language

"The Noblest Gift"

George W. Veditz, the seventh president of the National Association of the Deaf, called sign language "the noblest gift God has given to deaf people."

Sign language traces its recorded history back to some Benedictine monks in Italy around A.D. 530. These monks had taken vows of silence and, it is believed, created a form of sign language in order to communicate their daily needs. Sign language has been passed down through the centuries. Pedro Ponce de Leon, also a Benedictine monk, used sign language to teach his deaf pupils. When the Abbé de l'Epée started his school for the deaf in Paris, he learned French Sign Language from deaf people, modified it to approximate spoken French, and used this variety of sign language to instruct his students.

Thomas Hopkins Gallaudet was introduced to signs used in de l'Epée's school when he visited the Paris Institution at the invitation of Abbé Sicard, de l'Epée's successor. It was the French Sign Language which Laurent Clerc and Gallaudet brought back with them to America in 1816. Of course, signs already existed in America before Clerc's arrival; historical records support that fact. A family friend, observing John Brewster, the deaf portraitist, wrote on December 13, 1790, that Brewster could "write well and converse in signs." That statement was made 26 years before the arrival of Clerc. A recent article about predominantly deaf communities on Martha's Vineyard, off the coast of Massachusetts, traces the use of sign language on the island back to the mid-18th century. Dr. James Woodward, a linguist at Gallaudet College, who has studied both American Sign Language and French Sign Language, estimates that approximately 60 percent of American signs are of French origin.

Clerc, Gallaudet, and the teachers and students at the Hartford School most likely combined the French signs with American signs. From the Hartford School, American Sign Language spread to other schools for the deaf. Sign language then enjoyed widespread use in the education of the deaf until the 1860s.

The heavy emphasis early schools placed on manual communication was one of the reasons that led to the establishment of pure oral schools in this country. Some parents and educators felt that no effort was made, or little attention given, to teach articulation in these schools. The establishment of pure oral schools

PRECEDING PAGE: Logo of the National Symposium on Sign Language Research and Teaching.

in this country in the 1860s forced the manual schools to change, as did the Milan resolution 20 years later. At the second International Congress on Education of the Deaf meeting in Milan, Italy, in September 1880, those present voted to outlaw the use of sign language in the education of deaf children in favor of the pure oral method. The U.S. delegation and an educator from Great Britain opposed the move but were heavily outvoted. One writer described the meeting as having an atmosphere rivalling religious fervor. Prevailing conditions in the education of the deaf in Europe at this time had much influence on the action taken. Mismanagement of schools for the deaf, the flagrant practice of nepotism, lack of training programs, and little or no accountability had resulted in a drastic decline in the quality of many educational programs. As usual, sign language was blamed as the cause. As a result of the meeting at Milan, education of the deaf in America became more oral. Some schools became pure oral schools while others became "combined" schools. The latter system was born as a result of disagreement with the pure oral philosophy. Rather than surrender the use of sign language, these schools added speech and speechreading for the beginning pupils while retaining signs and fingerspelling in the more advanced and vocational classes. This approach became known as the combined system. These two different approaches, oral or combined, began a heated controversy in this country that was to rage for decades and become what was commonly called, "The War of Methods."

The War of Methods

No history of deaf America, unfortunately, would be complete without mention of this war.

Why the controversy? Why the division among educators in the field of deafness? Why did it have to happen to deaf children, who, with their communication handicap, need input so badly? Perhaps one of the reasons is because deaf individuals look so normal. A blind child, or a paraplegic, for example, has a visible handicap. There is no escaping the disability. But a deaf person's deafness is invisible. It is possible, to a point, to hide deafness. Deafness remains unseen until some act gives the deaf person away—the use of sign language, for example, or the failure to respond when spoken to from behind, or wearing a hearing aid. No parents want to admit that their child is handicapped or different from other healthy children. Usually, the parents' first instinct on learning that their child is deaf is to search for a cure, a miracle, or a remedy that would make their child normal. The word "normal" almost always enters into conversation with hearing parents of a deaf child. The oral philosophy holds out the hope and reassurance to parents that their child can learn to talk and lipread, and that with these tools he or she will fit into hearing society as a "normal" person would. How many deaf persons wish that this were true! They may wish also that it were that simple; but they know from personal experience, that it is not.

Oralism is not the easy way, parents are warned—and it certainly is not. They must stay away from signs, they are told. If they use signs or permit their deaf child to sign they will retard or ruin his speech development. The use of signs will become a "crutch"; the child will depend on them and neglect speech and speechreading, they are reminded. In other words, signing is bad for those who wish to develop speech.

This obsession against signing has scared parents of deaf children away from deaf adults who use sign language. Many parents have been told that those who use signs become clannish when they grow up and that many live in "deaf ghettos." Parents do not realize, often until it is too late, that such contacts with deaf adults could be beneficial and could help them make constructive contributions to their child's development. Frequently, the deaf adults they chance to see are the models for their children.

This attempt to make a "hearing" person out of a deaf child; to demand that the child talk, talk, talk and to forbid him or her the use of that natural means of communication, to refuse to permit him or her to relate to other members of the deaf community are seen by many deaf people as cruel, unrealistic and unfair. People who do this would never think of giving a blind child a pair of glasses and demanding that the child see, see, see. Nor would they be so hardhearted as to take away the crutches from a crippled child. Yet in their determination to make a deaf child "normal," these same people unconsciously deny the deaf child the right to be himself. They are, in effect, saying that it is wrong to be deaf.

Normal? What is a *normal* deaf person? Deaf people have often asked themselves that question. Is a poor imitation of a hearing person a normal deaf person? Is pretending to understand, smiling and nodding at what is being said when one does not really comprehend, normal? Is rejecting the use of sign language

---

In order to communicate effectively and fluently, people must feel at home in their language, and the deaf are no exception.

—ROBERT F. PANARA

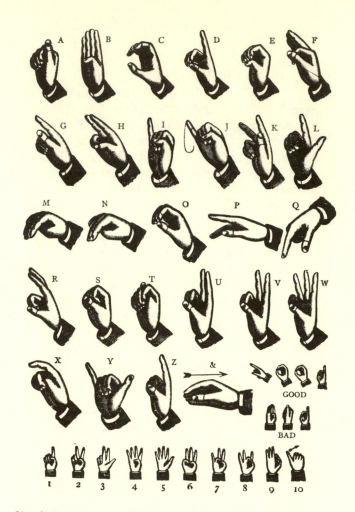

Sign language users will note how the letter "F" differs from its use today on this early manual alphabet.

because it is "the easy way out" and because hearing people do not use it and because it "classifies" you as deaf normal? Is not admitting one's disability and learning to cope with it the best you can normal? Why, then, do some people try to make an abnormal person out of a normal person who just happens to have a hearing disability? Why do they try to instill a sense of inferiority in a deaf person who initially sees life as a challenge? Why throw cruel, unnecessary stumbling blocks in the path of a deaf person or forbid him the right to use his natural means of communication? Is it not ironic that deaf people are rarely, if ever, asked what they believe is best for them? Wouldn't it be amusing if those who think they know what is best for deaf people could be deaf for a while, experience the frustration, and grope helplessly trying to understand what is being said? These are some of the questions deaf people have asked themselves. But, the overriding question remains: What is wrong with being deaf and trying to live with one's deafness?

The Controversy

The controversy over the best way to educate deaf children in this country raged from the 18th Century into the 20th. Hundreds of articles appeared in print, salvos of criticism were fired back and forth, and claims and counterclaims were made as each camp tried to win over parents and supporters. While the pure oralist proclaimed that speech was the way, the combinist argued that it was necessary to fit the method to the child, not the child to the method. Research findings, statistics, and statements, some lifted out of context, were used, further confusing parents who were neither familiar with the terms used in the studies nor with the persons conducting them. Personal testimonies of carefully selected deaf adults were held up as evidence of the "better way."

The controversy split families, broke up marriages, and led to divorces. It embittered deaf children and adults alike, leaving lifelong scars on the lives of many. It ran deep. In Nebraska, a mother of a deaf man made him promise on her deathbed that he would never use signs. Although he had attended a prestigious oral school his speech remained unintelligible throughout his life. As a result of that promise, neither hearing nor deaf people could understand him, and he had to resort to a pad and pencil to carry on a conversation with both groups.

Deaf children who did not succeed in oral schools were labelled "oral failures" and sent to residential schools where they were exposed to the more flexible combined system. Administrators in residential schools complained that their schools were becoming "dumping grounds" for oral failures and that the lateness at which they received these students, usually when the students were in their teens, made it impossible to make up for the lost years.

Contrary to widely held beliefs, most deaf adults did not oppose the teaching of speech and speechreading. National Association of the Deaf President James L. Smith stated in 1904: "We are friends and advocates of speech and speech-training, but not for all the deaf. In order that the deaf may get the highest measure of intellectual, social, and moral happiness in this world, an adaption and combination of methods is necessary." Smith's stand has been held by a majority of deaf leaders through the decades. Many of them who can talk and lipread, as well as those who cannot, stress the value of those skills. But, deaf adults also repeatedly express concern over the heavy emphasis placed on the teaching of articulation at the expense of an education. "What good is it to be able to talk if you have nothing to say?" is a popular refrain.

W. L. Hill, a deaf man who became a successful newspaper publisher, said: "My object in going to school was to obtain an education, not simply a means of communication with hearing people." Issac Goldberg said: ". . . what I am today I certainly do not owe to my ability to speak or read the lips." Goldberg was a product of an oral school, a chemist, and an inventor of perfumes.

Nevertheless, the oralist-dominated years that followed had a profound impact on the lives of deaf people, most of it negative. Parents who had been convinced that sign language was detrimental to the speech efforts of their deaf child would have nothing to do with deaf teachers. Many schools came under pressure to switch to the pure oral method. In some states, deaf teachers became extinct or an endangered species.

Attempts To Suppress Sign Language

As oralism took a strong grip on education of the deaf in the United States in the 1860s and onward, there were attempts to suppress the use of sign language. It came under a mounting barrage of criticism. In the eyes of oral advocates, sign language was the culprit for everything wrong in the education of the deaf. It was blamed for deaf children's lack of speech, for their poor grasp of the English language; it was accused of promoting clannishness among deaf persons. If anything were wrong with deaf people, sign language was rapped as the cause.

In order to concentrate on teaching speech and speechreading, oral educators tried to provide an uncontaminated pure oral atmosphere for their students. They solicited the cooperation of parents. They refused to hire deaf teachers, even their own products. Deaf children were told that using signs was bad and degrading. They were told that it would prevent them from growing up "normal" and that they would not be able to live in a hearing world if they relied on signs and did not learn to talk and lipread. Even in the purest oral atmosphere, nevertheless, deaf children continued to use signs. Suppression only succeeded in driving sign language out of sight, behind the desk or the teacher's back, under the table, into the bathroom. Those who were caught breaking the rules were scolded or punished. Rapping a child's hand with a ruler was one of the punishments; clapping a child's mouth with a chalky eraser was another. Children had their hands tied behind their back or placed in brown paper bags. Still others were made to sit on their hands to keep them from going astray and forming signs. Although this natural way of communicating by deaf people defied suppression, the attempt to suppress it created a stigma towards sign language and a negative, guilty attitude about its use.

As sign language became outlawed in an increasing number of schools, there was a growing concern among deaf leaders that the beauty of the American Sign Language as used by the masters of old would be lost. Those masters had a special delivery of their own, a poetic motion, a Victorian dignity, standing ramrod straight with their lips tightly shut as they graphically etched in the air spellbinding presentations of beauty. It was considered gross in those early days to mouth words; platform signers placed emphasis on signs. If fingerspelling could be avoided it was.

Except at the Ohio School for the Deaf, Gallaudet College, and possibly a few other places, sign language was never formally taught. Children picked it up from their peers. Teachers, new and veteran, learned it from their students or from other teachers. Under such circumstances there was little control over its originality, and signs underwent many changes. William H. Weeks of Connecticut, addressing the National Association of the Deaf convention in 1889 expressed concern about this: "The sign language is the grandest means yet devised for rapidity and clearness of communication with the deaf. We must hold fast to the original purity and strength of our signs. There is a tendency to invent new signs, some of which mean nothing. Many of the good old signs have been chopped and clipped so that they have lost much of their original force."

Dr. James L. Smith, a teacher at the Minnesota School for the Deaf, echoed Week's concerns at the

This old chart shows both the one-hand and two-hands alphabets. Laura Bridgeman (lower right corner) was reputedly the first deaf-blind person educated in this country.

A. J. Norris

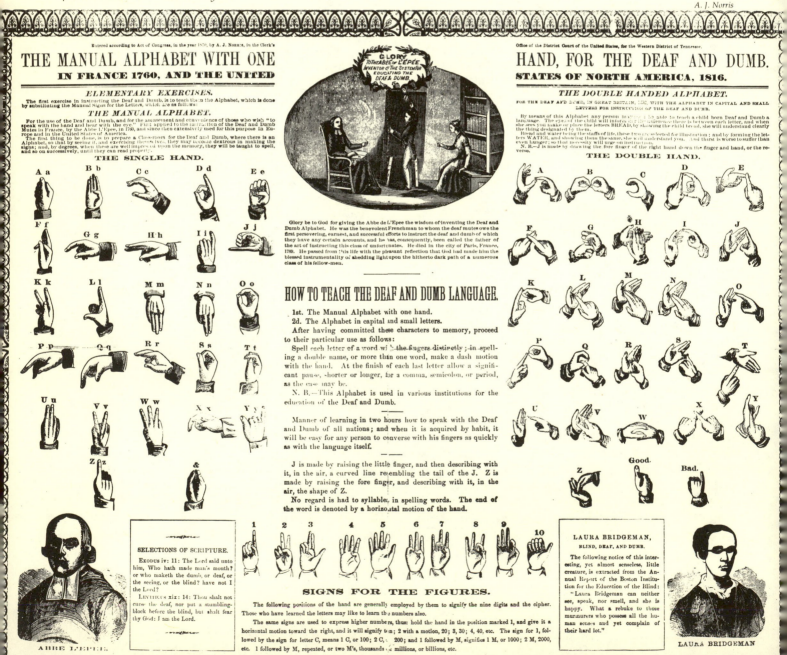

1904 National Association of the Deaf convention: "The enemies of sign language are not confined to those who decry it and call for its abolition entirely. Its most dangerous enemies are in the camp of its friends, in the persons of those who maltreat it and abuse it by misuse. The sign language, properly used, is a language of grace, beauty, power. But through careless or ignorant use it may become ungraceful, repulsive, difficult to comprehend."

In the early 1900s George W. Veditz expressed concern that "'A new race of pharaohs that knew not Joseph' are taking over the land and many of our

... the educator of the deaf must learn through the experience of the educated deaf wherein to modify and improve his methods.

—ENOCH CURRIER

American Schools. They do not understand signs for they cannot sign. They proclaim that signs are worthless and of no help to the deaf. Enemies of sign language—they are enemies of the true welfare of the deaf."

The Deaf: "By Their Fruits Ye Shall Know Them"

When the New York School for the Deaf came under pressure to abandon sign language in favor of the pure oral method in the instruction of deaf children, Principal Enoch H. Currier decided to solicit the opinions of deaf leaders of the day. Here are some excerpts from some of the letters he received. The letters were published in a booklet, **The Deaf: "By Their Fruits Ye Shall Know Them."**

"It is hard to conceive that there are minds and hearts so small and shriveled that they would say to the deaf, 'You are to acquire knowledge and understanding by watching the motion of the lips or not at all.' The deaf, as well as the hearing, are entitled to learn all they can by such methods as are most expeditious."—J.C. Howard

". . . I feel that it is my right to come by knowledge in whatever way God has given me, since it was His good will that I should not hear. I do not recognize the right of any human being to deprive me of the means of communication that God has left to me."—J.C. Howard

"I have met many deaf people—some educated by the oral method and some by the combined method, where signs are used. In every case those who have been educated by means of signs are the more intelligent, more independent, self-reliant, and have an air of being capable, competent and unafraid. They are happier and experience more real joy in life."—A.R. Spear

"In attempting to abolish signs as used as aids in educating the deaf, the unfortunate children are not only being deprived of their birthright, but a means of education is being taken from them."—A.R. Spear

"From the standpoint of a totally deaf person, proficient in speech and lip-reading, and with forty years' experience in the art, I can only say that lip-reading at its best is a matter of skillful guess work, and a sorry mess we sometimes make of it."—A.R. Spear

"The deaf do not object to speech and lip-reading. They know it is a great advantage to those who can attain to a working proficiency. The combined schools provide this as well as oral schools, and at the same time educate those

who cannot profit to any great extent by pure oral methods. This is so apparent it seems a waste of time to state it."—G.M. Teegarden

"I know the value of speech. I can speak well and read the lips well. But I plead for broadness as against narrowness. I plead for the child rather than for the method itself."—G.M. Teegarden

"You cannot eliminate the sign language. It is the natural language of the deaf. You may suppress its use to an extent, but in doing so you close an avenue to the mind and soul of the deaf-mute, and in so doing add to his losses."—G.M. Teegarden

"Nature hates force. Just as the flowing stream seeks the easiest path, so the mind seeks the way of least resistance. The sign-language offers to the deaf a broad and smooth avenue for the inflow and outflow of thought, and there is no other avenue for them like unto it."—G.M. Teegarden

"Under the best of circumstances, both the young and the adult deaf are heavily handicapped, and, in their instruction, no *method* which will aid in the smallest degree, to give them knowledge and power, should be excluded from the curriculum."—Alice C. Jennings

"It is a lamentable fact that, in matters relating to the deaf, their education and well-being, few if any take the trouble to get the opinion of the very people most concerned—the deaf themselves."—John H. Keiser

"If you try to suppress signs you will teach deceit, for the deaf will always use it on the sly. To deprive a deaf-mute of the sign language is like clipping a bird of its wings."—F. Maginn

These concerns led to the formation of a motion picture committee of the National Association of the Deaf during Veditz' administration. The sum of $5,000, a large sum in those days, was raised in short order, and filming of the old masters of sign began. The NAD recorded for posterity presentations in sign language by Edward Miner Gallaudet, John Hotchkiss, Edward Allen Fay, George W. Veditz, Robert McGregor, and other old masters. These films have been videotaped and are available for viewing at the Edward Miner Gallaudet Memorial Library at Gallaudet College.

With sign language under fire, it was obviously not a time when people sought the advice and opinions of deaf people. The education and welfare of the deaf was largely in the hands of hearing persons. It was rare indeed to find a deaf person serving on a school board or in an advisory capacity to a program that affected the welfare of the deaf. Few school administrators took counsel of deaf people, but one who did was Principal Enoch H. Currier of the New York School for the Deaf (Fanwood). When pressure was brought to bear on the Board of Directors of the school to switch to the pure oral method in 1912, Currier decided to seek the opinions of the leading deaf persons of the day. He received so many responses to his inquiry that he decided to publish them in a booklet entitled: *The Deaf: "By their fruits ye shall know them."* Those who responded to the invitation included professionals, businessmen, educators, members of the clergy, and a number of products of oral schools. Excerpts of some of their responses are printed elsewhere to give a feeling for the sentiments of the times. NYSD remained a combined method school.

On the other side of the coin, some oral products succeeded remarkably well. Mabel Hubbard Bell, the wife of Alexander Graham Bell, was deafened at the age of five years by scarlet fever. She attended Clarke School for the Deaf in Northampton, a school her father, Gardiner G. Hubbard, had helped to start. Mabel Bell was a skilled lipreader.

Latham Breunig, a 1935 graduate of the Clarke School for the Deaf, also deafened at the age of five years, earned a doctorate at Johns Hopkins University and became a statistician for the Eli Lilly Co. in Indianapolis. Breunig was the first chairman of the Oral

---

. . . the study of sociolinguistics made me realize that in order to study a language one must understand the people who use it.

—BARBARA KANNAPELL

Deaf Adult Section when it was organized within the Alexander Graham Bell Association, and he was the first deaf person to become president of that Association.

James C. Marsters was born deaf. He got his elementary education in a public school and attended the Wright Oral School in New York. He earned his BS degree at Union College in New York and attended Columbia University in New York City. Marsters earned his doctor of dental science (DDS) at the New York University College of Dentistry and later an MS at the University of Southern California. Marsters is a self-employed orthodontist in Pasadena, California. He has lectured in orthodontistry at USC. He holds a pilot's license and is active in an organization promoting telecommunications for the deaf.

Richard E. Thompson is another successful Clarke School graduate. Born deaf, Thompson earned an AB degree from Harvard *cum laude* in 1952 and a masters and a PhD in clinical psychology from Boston University. He was a member of the first National Advisory Committee for Education of the Deaf. He is a member of the Beverly School board. He was co-director of Psycho-Social Services for the Deaf at Newton Center before becoming director of the Massachusetts Office of Deafness. Now a skilled signer, he is very active in organizations of the deaf.

Barbara Ann Brauer was born deaf. She attended a residential school for deaf children in Michigan until the sixth grade when she was enrolled in the public school system. She earned her master's at Columbia University and a doctorate in clinical psychology at New York University. She is currently director of Mental Health Research in the Division of Research at Gallaudet College.

American Sign Language Comes Out of the Closet

And so it went through the decades until the 1960s. What took sign language so long to become acceptable again? Ignorance. Insensitivity. Cruelty. Pride. Well-meaning but overzealous and misguided intentions.

Slowly more and more people were beginning to realize that limiting a deaf child to a totally oral program did not guarantee success in speech and speech-reading skills. Researchers were beginning to find evidence that early use of sign language did not retard a deaf child's development of speech as many had thought it did. Other studies of deaf children of deaf parents who used sign language with their children showed that these children generally fared better academically, socially, and in the acquisition of written language than did those deaf children of hearing parents who did not use sign language.

The exposure of deaf people on television, a changing national mood towards disabled Americans, and the increasing articulateness and visibility of deaf leaders, were other factors. Another reason for sign language's acceptance was a man named Bill Stokoe.

In the mid-1950s Dr. William C. Stokoe, Jr. joined the Gallaudet College faculty as chairman of the English Department. He soon became fascinated by the language of signs, the leading means of communication used on campus. When he proposed a study of sign language, however, his colleagues surprisingly showed little interest. Some even thought that he was crazy to think of such an undertaking. Even deaf colleagues were indifferent. But, Stokoe persisted. In 1957 he started the Linguistics Research Program, an after-hours and summer research project. With two deaf assistants, Carl Croneberg and Dorothy Casterline, Stokoe began filming individuals giving presentations in sign language. Few of the participants understood what he was trying to do or the significance of his work, and most who took part in the experiments did so to humor him.

Next, Stokoe and his team spent thousands of hours carefully studying the signs captured on film. From these studies he noted familiar patterns emerging. He identified points of contrast, morphemes, and syntactical patterns, those necessary ingredients of a language. He was the first linguist to subject sign language to the tests of a real language, and he found that it withstood them all. When he published his initial findings in 1960, however, few people got excited or paid much attention. He was nearly alone in his belief that sign language, instead of being a collection of grotesque gestures, as many thought it was, was indeed a language in its own right.

In 1965 Stokoe, Casterline, and Croneberg published the results of their work in *A Dictionary of American Sign Language on Linguistic Principles*. In this book they presented signs of American Sign Language in symbols based on linguistic principles. (A revised edition, *Sign Language Structure*, followed in 1978.)

Stokoe's work, however, caught the attention and interest of other linguists in the United States and abroad. He had made sign language a legitimate and academically acceptable research topic. Other hearing linguists began studying it. A few deaf people also became interested in linguistics because of this work, entered degree programs in linguistics and began their own research related to American Sign Language. These studies overflowed into other academic disci-

Dr. Stokoe at work in his lab at Gallaudet College.

Gallaudet Today

plines—anthropology, sociology, psychology. In 1973 James Woodward completed his dissertation at Georgetown University on American Sign Language and became the first linguist to earn a doctorate in that subject.

These researchers found that American Sign Language, like other languages, undergoes change. They discovered that, contrary to popular belief, it has its own grammatical structure and that it can and does convey abstract concepts. Just because American Sign Language appears ungrammatical when it is translated word for word into English does not make it ungrammatical. Harry Markowicz, who studied both American Sign Language and French Sign Language and who has written many articles on the subject, explained that other spoken languages with different word orders from English also appear ungrammatical in word for word translations in English. Much of this research has found its way into print and has heightened interest in American Sign Language.

Stokoe defines American Sign Language as both a native and a natural language. A native language is the first language an individual learns to use for normal communication. It is believed that every human is born with a language capacity. An individual's native language depends on the language those around him are using and on his ability to receive all the signals of that language. ASL is usually the native language of those deaf and hearing children born of deaf parents in a home where sign language is the language used. In households where both ASL and English are used, many of these children grow up with two or more native languages equally exercising their native language capacity. These bilingual chil-

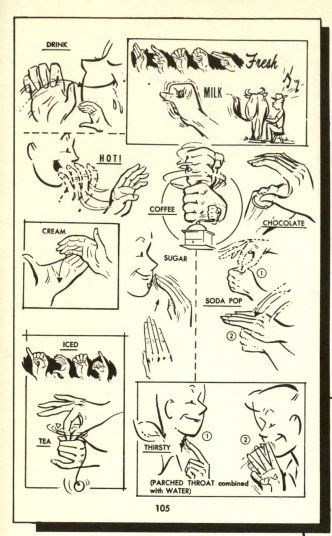

105

TALK WITH YOUR HANDS

WRITTEN AND ILLUSTRATED BY

David O. Watson

Winneconne, Wisconsin

Some illustrations from David Watson's book, *Talk With Your Hands*.

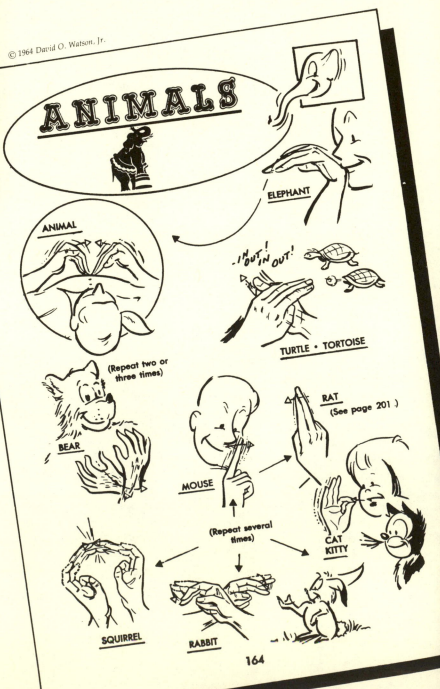

164

Silent Homage
(A Tribute to Interpreters)

The moving lips speak voicelessly—but hark:
The winging words fly from your fluttering hands;
And each, who dwells in silence, understands
How Dawn, the rosy-fingered, burns the dark
From shadow-worlds wherein the teeming brain
Lay, like a captive, in a dungeon-cell;
Your magic bursts the iron citadel,
And breaks the lock, and brings the light again!

Dear friend, how empty, vain and commonplace
Must seem this gratitude we offer you;
Yet now we render homage, as your due,
Remembering your patience, love and grace—
With twining fingers as you blithely go,
Daily, to fell our Walls of Jericho

—LOY E. GOLLADAY

dren are often intellectually advanced and academically superior to other children.

Stokoe describes a natural language as the language people of the world use in their everyday activities among themselves as well as for other purposes. A natural language is developed by its users, and it evolves over a period of time. He estimates that American Sign Language is the natural language of some 200,000 to 400,000 deaf Americans and deaf Canadians.

The discovery of American Sign Language as a true language has led to the identification of deaf culture as a rich, untapped field of study. Observed Carol Padden, a deaf linguistics student: "The culture of deaf people has not yet been studied in much depth. One reason is that, until recently, it was rare to describe deaf people as having a *culture.* . . ."

American Sign Language began to increase in popularity. Colleges, universities, high schools, private and public organizations, and agencies began offering courses in ASL. Deaf people suddenly found themselves in demand as teachers of their language. This interest and acceptance of sign language caught many deaf old timers by surprise. It has influenced the attitudes of deaf persons towards themselves, their language, their culture and made them take a closer look at their rights as American citizens.

In 1980 friends and colleagues of William C. Stokoe got together and secretly prepared a collection of essays in his honor. The book, *Sign Language and the Deaf Community: Essays in Honor of William C. Stokoe,* was published by the National Association of the Deaf and

presented to a surprised Stokoe at the NAD Centennial Convention. Royalties from the sale of the book will go into the William C. Stokoe Scholarship Fund to encourage continued research in the area of sign language.

Meanwhile, Bill Stokoe has found mastering sign language himself a tough subject. He is, as a colleague tactfully put it, "not a fluent signer." He continues to work on *his* sign language.

Sign Language Books

There appeared at the Convention of American Instructors of the Deaf meeting in Salem, Oregon, in the summer of 1961, a commercial artist from Winneconne, Wisconsin, named David Watson. Watson was from a deaf family—deaf parents, a deaf brother, and three deaf sisters. He had with him some sketches of animated signs which he had been preparing for a book. He wanted to know what the teachers at the convention thought of the drawings. To his surprise and delight everyone who saw them liked the drawings and encouraged him to complete his project. Inspired, Watson returned home to his drawing board and set to work. *Talk With Your Hands* was completed three years later. It was an instant success and within nine months the first run of 10,000 copies was sold out. His drawings appeared in two colors and showed the movement of signs. Wrote one customer: "Your book breathes." Watson has since produced a second volume and is at work on a third.

In 1963 Lottie Riekehof's *Talk to the Deaf,* L.M. Guillory's *Expressive and Receptive Fingerspelling for Hearing Adults* and Roger M. Falberg's *The Language of Silence* appeared. A year later Louie Fant's *Say It With Hands* rolled off the press. Much earlier—in 1909—J. Schuyler Long had produced *The Sign Language: A Manual of Signs* but, not since John W. Michael's *Handbook of Sign Language of the Deaf* which was printed in 1923 had there appeared a new book on sign language. These books opened the floodgate of many more sign language books that would appear during this decade and the next—more books on the subject than the country had ever seen. The list included hymnals, religious signs, flash cards, sign language games,

To know, once and for all, that our "primitive" and "ideographic gestures" are really a formal language on a par with all other languages of the world is a step towards pride and liberation.

—MERVIN D. GARRETSON

manuals for deaf-blind children, curriculum guides for teaching interpreters. *A Basic Course in Manual Communication* prepared by Terrence J. O'Rourke and published by the National Association of the Deaf appeared in 1970. It has sold almost one-half million copies since its release. By the end of the 1970s some 40 sign language-related books were on the market. Riekehof published a second book *The Joy of Signing*, and Fant has since published three more books *Ameslan: An Introduction to American Sign Language* (1972), *Sign Language* (1977) and *Intermediate Sign Language* (1980).

In 1980 T.J. Publishers brought out a package of materials for teaching American Sign Language. Written by Charlotte Baker and Dennis Cokely, it included a series of three student textbooks, two teacher's resource books on curriculum, methods and evaluation, and grammar and culture. A series of videotapes were also prepared to accompany the texts.

A Basic Course in American Sign Language by Tom Humphries, Carol Padden and Terrence J. O'Rourke also appeared that year.

The NAD Communicative Skills Program

The Rehabilitative Services Administration of the U.S. Department of Health, Education, and Welfare awarded a grant to the National Association of the Deaf in 1967 to begin a series of pilot sign language classes in the United States. Terrence J. O'Rourke, a deaf teacher of the deaf, was hired as director of this new Communicative Skills Program. Through this program thousands and thousands of persons have been introduced to sign language.

In 1972 the Graduate School at New York University began accepting American Sign Language as satisfying a language requirement. By the end of that year 38 other colleges were offering credit courses in manual communication.

In the 1970s the Communicative Skills Program began to focus more on improving the quality of the courses offered, and on assisting colleges, universities, and government agencies to begin sign language training programs of their own. In 1975 CSP formed the Sign Instructors Guidance Network (SIGN), a professional organization of sign language instructors, with evaluation and certification responsibilities. In 1977, CSP organized the first National Symposium on Sign Language Research and Teaching in Chicago. A second symposium was held in San Diego, California, in 1978 and a third in Boston in 1980.

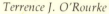

Terrence J. O'Rourke   *Roy Holcomb*

Terrence J. O'Rourke left the program in 1978 to start his own publishing business. He was succeeded by S. Melvin Carter, Jr. That year CSP added a program for training sign language instructors and doing curriculum development in the teaching of American Sign Language. Ella Lentz was hired as coordinator and assistant director of CSP. Through this program she works with sign language instructors in the ten Rehabilitation Services Administration regions, assisting them in upgrading their programs.

Edna Adler, a deaf consultant in the Office of Deafness and Communicative Disorders, Social Rehabilitation Services, Department of Health and Human Services, believes that this program "more than anything else helped remove the stigma of using sign language."

Total Communication Arrives

In the early 1960s, Dorothy Shifflett, a teacher with the Anaheim Union High School District in California and the mother of a deaf daughter, became disillusioned with the lack of progress her daughter was making through the oral approach. After contacts with deaf adults in the community, she switched to the combined system and began using a multi-approach to teaching deaf children in her school. She was influential in persuading teachers, parents, deaf and hearing children, and those who worked with deaf children to take classes in sign language. Deaf children were exposed to speech, speechreading, and auditory training as well as fingerspelling and signs. They were integrated with hearing children in physical education classes, during recess, and at lunch. Some attended classes for hearing children, including classes in Spanish and in band! One deaf boy was even included in the school's marching band. This approach did away with communication reservations, provided increased input to the deaf child, and stimulated his learning.

Mrs. Shifflett called her approach "The Total Approach." Although it was not the first time that deaf and hearing children had been integrated in a regular public school program and been taught sign language, it was a philosophy whose time had come. Dorothy Shifflett hired Herb Larson, a deaf teacher; he became one of the first deaf teachers to teach in the public school system outside a residential school in California.

In the fall of 1968 Roy Holcomb became the first area supervisor of the program for deaf students at the James Madison Elementary School. This school, with an enrollment of 800 hearing students, was part of the Santa Ana Unified School District in California. The program for deaf children was the oldest program of its kind in Orange County. The program's first teacher was Kathryn Fitzgerald, a relative of Edith Fitzgerald, inventor of the Fitzgerald Key. In 1968, the program consisted of six classes serving 34 deaf children from three to 12 years old.

Holcomb, a Texas School for the Deaf, Gallaudet College and California State University, Northridge product, and his teachers were aware that good communication was the key to a deaf child's successful learning process. They knew that once a child fell behind academically in his early years, he seldom, if ever, caught up. They wanted to provide each student with as much information as possible during these early formative years. They were interested in providing each student with a barrier-free communication environment and not in what they said were "theories as to what might be better for him in later life." They were interested in "real and genuine communication." They used the total approach at all levels at the school.

A year later Holcomb began using the term, "Total Communication." He widely publicized this system, and as other educators learned about it, they began adopting it and Holcomb became known as the "Father of Total Communication."

Roy Holcomb, who wears a hearing aid although he has a 90-decibel hearing loss, was one of the founders of the International Association of Parents of the Deaf and the author of *Hazards of Deafness*. (He once received a letter from the California State Credentials Department warning him that his job might be in jeopardy because of his deafness.) He was in demand as a speaker and was invited to serve on the advisory boards of at least six colleges that had programs for hearing impaired students. He is the recipient of numerous honors including the Dan T. Cloud Award (his wife, Marjorie, was also a recipient) given annually by the Center on Deafness at California State

University at Northridge. Gallaudet College awarded him an honorary Doctor of Laws degree. Eventually he left Santa Ana to become director of the Margaret S. Sterck School for the Deaf in Delaware.

The Maryland School for the Deaf was probably the first residential school to adopt officially the Total Communication philosophy and, under the leadership of Superintendent David Denton, became one of its strongest advocates. Margaret S. Kent, principal of MSD, defined Total Communication as "the right of every deaf child to learn to use all forms of communication so that he may have full opportunity to develop language competence at the earliest possible age." She and her colleagues at the Maryland School saw it as including "the full spectrum of language modes: child-devised gestures, formal sign language, speech, speechreading, fingerspelling, reading, and writing."

As it became increasingly used, Total Communication underwent modification, changes, and refinement. In 1976 an official definition of Total Communication was agreed on by members of the Conference of Executives of American Schools for the Deaf. The CEASD version read: "Total Communication is a philosophy requiring the incorporation of appropriate aural, manual, and oral modes of communication in order to insure effective communication with and among hearing impaired persons."

The pendulum was swinging back toward sign language. By 1976 two-thirds of the schools for the deaf in this country reported that they used Total Communication although many teachers in these schools could not sign well and made little or no effort to learn.

Manually Coded English Systems

The search to find a better way to teach English to deaf children has long eluded educators of the deaf. Special systems have been devised to assist in this process; they include the Barry Five Slate System, Wing's Symbols, and the Fitzgerald Key. (Both Wing and Fitzgerald were deaf.) Grammar textbooks used

Deaf people feel a strong identification with ASL since it is a part of their cultural background, but when they are involved in community activities, the use of another language allows them to interact with other deaf persons who are not Deaf.
—CAROL PADDEN

David A. Anthony

in public schools have been used and other teachers have had their own systems. English still remains a very difficult language for deaf students to master.

One spring day in 1962, David Anthony was reading a story about Basic English in *Life* magazine. The article told about a system created in the 1920s and 1930s by Charles K. Ogden, and Ivor A. Richards of Cambridge University. They had developed a list of 850 basic English words and rules for their use in an attempt to simplify English and make it easier for others to learn.

Born deaf and the son of deaf parents, Anthony knew first-hand the difficulties deaf children encounter in acquiring a working command of English. He was then a teacher of mentally retarded deaf children and adults at the Deaf Research Project at Lapeer State Home and Training School in Lapeer, Michigan.

Anthony, a graduate of Gallaudet College, saw weaknesses in the two traditional methods of teaching deaf children then in use. American Sign Language has a different grammatical structure and does not follow English syntax or word order. Speech and speechreading, on the other hand, were no better. While following the spoken English word order, lipreading involved too much guesswork; at best, only

about 40 percent of the spoken words are visible on the lips. Anthony knew, as did other educators, that a hearing child has a decided advantage in acquiring English. He is acoustically bombarded with words on a daily basis. He hears them on radio, television, in conversation with others, and at the dinner table. Deaf children, on the other hand, are shut off from such valuable, yet effortless, learning sources. Every single English word they learn has to be learned with an effort. Since deaf children cannot hear spoken English, Anthony wanted to find a way for them to see it as it is spoken. He thought that this Basic English list might be used to help his children. He realized that he had another problem: many of those words on the list had no signs. An idea was beginning to form in his mind.

David Anthony returned to Lapeer and discussed his idea with his colleagues there. They thought it had possibilities. The more he thought about it and discussed it the more sense it made. He proposed a system called Signing Essential English with the acronym SEE in keeping with his philosophy that to learn English deaf children must *see* it. This new sign system, developed largely by the inventiveness of his pupils, was the theme of his master's thesis at Eastern Michigan University where he was completing work on his degree in English.

In developing SEE, Anthony decided to use as little fingerspelling as possible. Every English word would have a distinct sign—even parts of a word (morphemes) would have a sign—and these signs would follow the spoken English word order. He developed signs for morphemes—those small units of meaning for words, prefixes (re-, com-, anti-, etc.), roots (-sist, -vail-, etc.), and suffixes (-ed, -ing, -ment, -ness, etc.)—so that it was possible to distinguish among, for example, *play, plays, playing, played, player,* etc. In SEE, a single word could have more than one sign. Take *boyishly*, for example. That word would be broken down into the morphemes: "boy," "ish," and "ly," and three different signs would be used in sequence. To deaf adults accustomed to American Sign Language who would normally fingerspell that word or use the signs "idea same" and "boy," Anthony's approach looked awkward and silly. Many felt that he was messing up sign language. But Anthony believed that if deaf children were to learn the term "boyishly," they would have to see it and that "idea same boy" was not the way the word was spoken or written. Breaking a word up into signs made it easier to understand than did fingerspelling it. Further, Anthony explained, "idea same boy" takes three signs to render, as does "boy" "ish," "ly."

370

SEE also uses the same sign for a word with different meanings. So, regardless of whether you run out of gas, run for election, or just plain run, the same sign is used for all three different versions. Anthony believes that a deaf child can figure out which meaning of the word is being used from the context of the sentence.

The scene next shifts to California where Anthony joined the teaching staff of the Brookhurst Junior High School in Anaheim. There a core group was formed to further develop Anthony's ideas. On Anthony's recommendation the group changed the name of his system to Seeing Essential English to play down the emphasis on signing so that the system would appeal more to parents. The members of this core group, besides Anthony, included Gerilee Gustason, Donna Pfetzing, Esther Zawolkow, and Dennis Wampler, among others. Gustason was deaf, having lost her hearing at the age of five. Pfetzing was the mother of a deaf daughter, a rubella baby, and a disillusioned oral proponent. Zawolkow was the daughter of deaf parents; Wampler was the son of deaf parents. Like Anthony, Gustason and Wampler were teachers. Pfetzing and Zawolkow were interpreters at Anthony's school. This group solicited reaction and input from many other deaf and hearing adults, parents, teachers, and interested persons. They began using the new system at their respective schools, refining it and adding to it. All of them were convinced that they were on the right track toward developing a system that would provide deaf children with a better way to develop better skills in written English.

About this time the members of the group began to disagree on some basic principles. Anthony believed that whenever necessary a new sign should be created. He also believed that each part of a word should have its own consistent sign. The others favored retaining as many traditional signs as possible. They also felt that excessive breaking up of words with signs was not the way to go. This disagreement led to a split, and two other visual English systems emerged.

Dennis Wampler felt that the signs should be presented in the symbols Stokoe had developed as opposed to descriptions or drawings of the signs. At the Starr King School in Sacramento, he developed the Linguistics of Visual English (L.O.V.E.) system. He also believed that a word must be signed the same way regardless of meaning, and he attempted to relate a sign to speech, sound, and spelling. His system was published but little more has been heard of it since then.

The third group involved Gustason, Pfetzing, Zawolkow. They called their system Signing Exact English or SEE II.

All three groups retained the same basic objective: to ease the acquisition of English by deaf children. All established principles to govern their systems and attempted to retain or modify existing signs which were unambigious. All three adhered to the sound/spelling/meaning criteria which Anthony had initially developed. They do not see their systems as a replacement for American Sign Language.

These visual English systems began to introduce many more initialized signs into our sign language. These initialized signs were formed by using the first letter of a word and a traditional sign, if one existed. Where no satisfactory sign existed, a new one was created. The use of initialized signs had been proposed earlier in the mid-1950s by Max N. Mossel, a mathematics teacher at the Missouri School for the Deaf, in a series of articles appearing in *The Silent Worker* entitled "Manually Speaking." Mossel proposed using the same sign and movement but changing the initialization. For example, the sign for "way" with the "r" letter became road, "s" became street,

This 1980 SEE II edition contains 455 pages of signs and descriptions.

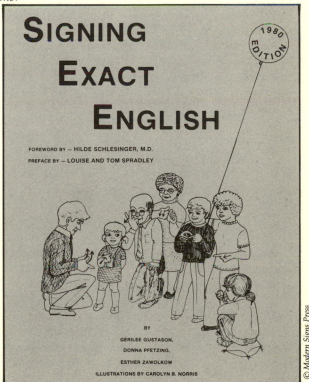

> . . . *a person can* **know** *and* **use** *English without being able to* **speak** *it.*

—BARBARA KANNAPELL

371

Messages using signs or fingerspelling such as this one emerged during the 1970s.

"p" became path, "l" became lane, and so on. His ideas did not catch on until the visual English systems began using them.

At about this time, Dr. Harry Bornstein, Barbara Kannapell, and Lillian Hamilton were working on a series of Signed English books for preschool deaf children at Gallaudet College.

Meanwhile, other manually coded English sign systems emerged.

In 1971 Anthony produced the first *S.E.E. Manual*. It had approximately 3,000 signs. In 1980 *Seeing Essential English: Codebreaker* and *Seeing Essential English: Elementary Dictionary* appeared. Anthony is one of the co-authors of both books.

A manual on *Signing Exact English* by Gerilee Gustason, Donna Pfetzing and Esther Zawolkow first appeared in 1972. It has since gone through many printings and three editions. Within four months of the appearance of the 1980 edition all 15,000 copies were sold out.

The proponents of these visual English systems believe their approach appeals to a larger number of parents of deaf children because it is easier for English speaking adults to learn to use signs following the spoken pattern of English than it is for them to learn American Sign Language. When visual English first appeared many deaf adults who lacked good English skills saw it as a wonderful opportunity for deaf children and regretted that it had arrived too late for them. But, in recent years, as it has been adopted by an increasing number of schools, an increasing resistance and negative attitude towards it has grown. This could stem, in part from those who see visual English as a threat to American Sign Language, who do not understand it and who are concerned about it "tarnishing" the beauty of American Sign Language. Some visual English signs have already found their way into American Sign Language. But, unlike American Sign Language, which linguists have identified as the natural language of deaf American people, visual English is an artificial language. Linguists who have studied languages for many years do not see an artificial language as a threat to a natural language, as long as it is not imposed on people and communities.

And Interest Grows . . .

This interest in sign language grew beyond some deaf old timers' wildest expectations. ASL became a popular language in the United States. (It has been erroneously reported as the third most widely used language in the country but actually it ranks lower than that.) Dr. Ross Stuckless of the National Technical Institute for the Deaf reported that by the late 1970s more hearing than deaf people had learned it.

Once I learned that ASL is my native language, I developed a strong sense of identity as a deaf person and a more positive self-image.

—BARBARA KANNAPELL

372

"The Sign Language Store" opened on Yoland Street in Northridge, California. Another store, "The I Love You Gift, Co," opened in Alexandria, Virginia. At these stores customers could buy wearing apparel, jewelry, school supplies, novelties, and miscellaneous other items with signs and fingerspelling or the I-Love-You symbol printed on them.

Posters and bumper stickers appeared in sign language or fingerspelling urging the public to "Stop Noise Pollution. Learn Sign Language," or "Let Your Fingers Do the Talkin'" or proclaiming "Total Communication—The right of every deaf child." Others advised: "I'm Not Ignoring You, I'm Deaf!" In response to the "Honk, if You Love Jesus" bumper sticker, another appeared with "Wave, if You Love Jesus."

"Keep Quiet," a crosswords cubes game with the manual alphabet on cubes, appeared on the market. Suzie L. Kirchner produced two books, *Play It By Sign* and *Signs for All Seasons: More Sign Language Games* which told how to play games in signs, pantomime, gestures, and fingerspelling. Pre-school readers, cookbooks, and song books in sign language and English came off the presses.

A song, "I Hear Your Hand," written by Mary Jane Rhodes, the mother of a deaf son, was signed on national television by Rita Corey. Deaf and hearing high school and college students and hearing interpreters formed sign-sing groups with such names as "Rock Gospel," "Deaf Awareness Troupe," "Singing Hands," "Breakthrough," "The Expressions," "Sing a Sign," "Vibrations," "Joyful Signs," and others and became popular local performing groups. Mitch Leigh's "The Impossible Dream," and Joe Brook's "You Light Up My Life," became two of the favorite songs used by deaf signers. The signed renditions of these songs touched the hearts of thousands.

Even chimpanzees and a gorilla got into the act. In 1966, Drs. R. Allen and Beatrice T. Gardner, a husband and wife research team at the University of Nevada, began teaching a young female chimp, named Washoe (signed "W" fanning the ear), sign language. The Gardners were interested in learning more about chimpanzees' behavior and capability to learn a human language. Since chimps do not possess the necessary vocal mechanisms to imitate human sound and since their hands closely resemble those of a human, the Gardners decided to experiment with signs. Washoe became the first chimp to converse with people in the language of signs. She learned 34 signs in 22 months and in four years knew 132.

Koko, the gorilla, learned enough signs to ask and respond to questions, to tell how she felt, and even to tell a lie. Francine Patterson, Koko's trainer, and a doctoral candidate at Stanford University at the time, became interested in the project when she learned about the Gardners' work with Washoe. Koko eventually developed a working vocabulary of 375 signs although she was recorded using as many as 645. Koko was pictured on the cover—she took the picture herself—of the October 1978 issue of *National Geographic.* The magazine printed a story of Patterson and her work with Koko entitled, "Conversations With a Gorilla." This interest in teaching chimps and apes sign language, of course, led to some wisecracks with oral-manual overtones. One went: "Which would you prefer: to be able to talk like a parrot or sign like a monkey?" In the hallway of a pure oral school was hung a picture of Washoe signing; under the picture was a handwritten note: "Do you want to be like her?"

The I-Love-You symbol which dates as far back as 1905 was resurrected and became universally popular. The king and queen of Sweden used it when visiting a school for deaf children recently. President Gerald Ford learned it when he was visited at the White House by Miss 1972 Deaf America, Ann Billington Bahl, and Miss 1974 Deaf America, Pam Young. While running for president, Jimmy Carter learned it on the campaign trail in Kansas City, Missouri, when he met a group of deaf people at one of his rallies. A picture of him using the symbol appeared in the national press. Following his election, *Time* magazine printed a color picture of him using the symbol during his inauguration walk down Pennsylvania Avenue in response to greetings from a crowd of deaf well-wishers. (Vice President Walter Mondale, following in an open car, unfamiliar with the symbol, but gamely trying to respond to the same group, was seen innocently waving an obscene gesture!)

Sign language classes spread. Some congressmen took classes at Gallaudet College; others hired teachers for themselves and their staffs. During the Carter administration, members of the White House security staff learned sign language. Deaf tourists to the White House were surprised to be asked in sign language if they had any questions. More churches began offering interpreted services. Government agencies, private industry, museums, and dinner theaters began offering interpreter services or sign language classes. Many police and fire departments trained their firefighters in basic signs so they could deal effectively with deaf persons in emergencies. The U.S. Park Service added interpreters to some of their regional historical tour sites and hired deaf guides. Some television networks began brief interpreted news programs for their deaf viewers and a few others employed deaf newscasters.

Washoe (above) is signing "sweet" for a lollipop and "hat" (right) for a woolen cap. Photos by R. A. and B. T. Gardner.

Moja, another chimp, signs "tree."

374

VOL. 154, NO. 4   OCTOBER 1978

NATIONAL GEOGRAPHIC

CONVERSATIONS WITH A GORILLA 438

DREAM ON, VANCOUVER 467

NEBRASKA'S SAND HILLS 493

DJIBOUTI, NEW NATION ON AFRICA'S HORN 518

AN AMERICAN RETRACES "TRAVELS WITH A DONKEY" 535

SUNKEN TREASURE OF ST. HELENA 562

OFFICIAL JOURNAL OF THE NATIONAL GEOGRAPHIC SOCIETY WASHINGTON, D.C.

NATIONAL GEOGRAPHIC OCTOBER 1978   GORILLA TALK VANCOUVER SAND HILLS DJIBOUTI DONKEY TREK TREASURE

By Koko© 1978 National Geographic Society

Koko, who knows 375 signs, is also a photographer. This self-portrait in a slightly wavy Plexiglass mirror appeared on the cover of the October, 1978 issue of National Geographic. *The project to teach Koko sign language was partly funded by the National Geographic Society.*

Political candidates began including interpreters with their television ads. Ex-Lax Pharmaceutical Company became one of the first to include an interpreter with their national television commercial. Among those who saw it was Alan Coren, editor of the British humor weekly *Punch*, who commented: "Just the other night in Boston, we saw an Ex-Lax ad for the deaf on the telly. Ah, thank God for America, where the deaf get constipated, too."

Deaf customers around the country were pleased to note the increase in number of business establishments that had a person who could sign. Store clerks at a Washington, D.C., area store began wearing "I Sign" buttons. Fifteen Sears stores in Orange County, California, hired Santa Clauses who could sign for the benefit of deaf children. Macy's in New York City provided interpreters for its Puppet Theatre. Pan Am Airlines accepted sign language as meeting a foreign language requirement in their stewardess training program, and many stewardesses on that airline began using signs to serve their deaf passengers better.

Participants attending the National Association of the Deaf convention at the Olympic Hotel in Seattle, Washington, in 1974 were greeted with cheerful "Good morning" signs, or asked if they would like some coffee by waitresses using signs in the hotel restaurant. Larry Peterson had taught some 40 hotel employees basic signs prior to the convention.

So many people were using simultaneous communication that at times deaf people could not tell if the stranger signing and mouthing words was a deaf or hearing person. Perhaps the biggest surprise of all was the announcement that both oral and manual interpreters would be provided at the Alexander Graham Bell Association convention being held in St. Louis in the summer of 1978.

Community Theatres of the deaf using deaf and hearing actors became popular in the late 1970s. By 1980 there were over 50 such theatrical groups around the country.

In 1974, "Sign Me Alice," was written by Gilbert Eastman, a deaf playwright. It was the first play of its kind. It was a delightfully funny play in sign language, a comedy spoofing sign language and the various sign systems of the day. George Detmold called it "the most popular play ever shown at Gallaudet; it had the

Oh, Signs! What crimes are committed in thy name! Thou art kicked and browbeaten; thou art proscribed and outlawed. They have taken away thy birthright, and thou feedest upon husks and thistles. Wert thou not so inherently vital, so necessary to the complete happiness of the deaf, thou had'st long since been wrapped in thy winding sheet.

—GROVER C. FARQUHAR
1920s

longest run, the largest audience, the greatest critical acclaim."

"Tales from a Club Room," another original play, premiered at the National Association of the Deaf centennial convention in Cincinnati, Ohio, in 1980. Written by Eugene Bergman and Bernard Bragg, it was performed with heavy emphasis on American Sign Language.

But oralism was not without its influence. Times had changed. As more and more people learned more about American Sign Language many teachers of deaf children and deaf adults realized that what they had been using in everyday conversation was not pure ASL, as they had thought, but a combination of ASL and English. Some called it "Pidgin Signed English" and others, "Manual English." Signing in an English context, of course, was nothing new. It was the labels that changed. Signing in an English context, in the 1940s for example was referred to as using the "correct language of signs" and called "Straight English." G. Dewey Coats who coined the term, "Manual English" in 1948, called its users "the hallmark of the better educated deaf person."

There remained, of course, those who preferred "pure" American Sign Language. They believed that, since it was their natural language, they had the right to use ASL at all times. They believed that deaf children should be taught ASL before attempts were made to teach them English, their second language. They believed that deaf children should be introduced to deaf culture as early as possible. Said one ASL proponent: "ASL is very much a part of a deaf person. If you want to change ASL or take ASL away from that person, you are trying to take his or her identity away." Some ASL militants even went as far as to call post-lingual deaf persons who spoke well and used sign simultaneously, "hearing deaf persons."

Today an increasing number of deaf persons sign, fingerspell, and speak or mouth words simultaneously when talking in mixed crowds. Maintaining tightly closed lips is no longer in vogue. The old sign language masters would have winced at such a sight.

A Quota International candidate for office caught the I-Love-You spirit with this cut-out campaign sticker.

Chapter 16

The 1970s

The Decade

HE 1970s was the decade of more awareness of deaf people, better understanding, and increased involvement. Interest in sign language continued to grow, legislation was passed benefitting deaf people, and more deaf people began standing up for their rights.

Deaf people became more involved in affairs influencing their lives. The Convention of American Instructors of the Deaf, the Alexander Graham Bell Association for the Deaf, and the Council on Education of the Deaf elected their first deaf presidents. Some schools for the deaf began adding deaf members to their governing boards.

Three deaf men—Dr. Harvey J. Corson (Louisiana), Dr. Roy Holcomb (Delaware), and Dr. Victor Galloway (Pennsylvania)—were picked as superintendents of state schools for the deaf. Elsewhere, deaf persons moved into administrative positions on state and national levels. Terrence J. O'Rourke became president, and Dr. Frank Bowe became executive director of a new national organization, the American Council for Citizens with Disabilities. Judith Tingley became program manager, Services for Deaf Persons in California, and Betty Broecker was named director of the Division of the Deaf in New Jersey. Alberta Smith became principal at the Tennessee School for the Deaf, and William Simpson became assistant superintendent at the North Carolina School for the Deaf in Greensboro. At Gallaudet College, two deaf men, Dr. Robert Davila and Dr. Thomas A. Mayes, were named vice presidents, and Dr. Mervin D. Garretson became special assistant to the president for advocacy. At the National Technical Institute for the Deaf Dr. T. Alan Hurwitz became an associate dean.

A Chair of Deaf Studies, named in honor of Dr. Powrie V. Doctor, was established at Gallaudet College. The number of deaf persons earning doctorates soared during the decade, and captioned television became a reality.

The spirit of the civil rights movement of the 1960s slowly began to catch on in the deaf community. Black Pride became Deaf Pride and Black Power became Deaf Power, although the latter was displayed more in a sense of jest than in a show of force. It depicted a person holding one hand over an ear indicating deafness and raising a clinched fist for power. As a group, deaf Americans still displayed much patience in demanding better services when compared to other minority groups, and in developing political clout. But, they were not idle. In Louisiana, they protested the selection of a school superintendent with no experience in the education of the deaf, and in New Jersey and Pennsylvania they picketed in support of the use of Total Communication at the schools for the deaf. In San Francisco and Washington, D.C., they joined forces with other disabled Americans at sit-ins to protest the delay in signing regulations for the Rehabilitation Act of 1973. Deaf actors also staged protests against producers who selected hearing actors to portray deaf persons in television films.

The terms "mainstreaming" and "hearing impaired" gained popularity during the decade. Mainstreaming—the placement of a deaf child in a regular

Ann Billington Bahl, Miss Deaf America, 1972-74, far right, teaches President Gerald Ford the universal sign for "I Love You," with assistance from Dr. Lottie Riekehof, Pam Young (Miss Deaf America 1974-76), and Senator Robert Griffin of Michigan.

public school—was simply a substitute for the old term, integration. Hearing impaired was a term that grouped deaf and hard of hearing individuals together under one name. When used in terms of statistics, it had an advantage, because it identified a much larger group. Some people, however, preferred it for different reasons. Some liked it because it did away with the word "deaf" which they found offensive and which they felt was too synonymous with "deaf-mute" and "deaf and dumb." Many deaf persons, however, did not care to use "hearing impaired" to describe themselves, preferring instead the word "deaf." Frederick C. Schreiber called it a "cop-out" and a term that "doesn't reflect the problem."

Lions International, which for years has assisted

There are only two kinds of people: Those who can't hear and those who won't listen.
—FREDERICK C. SCHREIBER

---

blind people through its fund-raising projects, added "Conservation of Hearing and Work for the Deaf" as a community service project. The Lions' interest in deafness was an outgrowth of the formation of the Alexandria-Potomac Lions Club in Virginia's District 24-A. The A-P Lions Club was the first club with a majority of deaf members. The club proposed the creation of the Helen Keller Memorial Fund for the Deaf, Inc., and it was approved by the Lions International body in 1971. More than a dozen clubs with deaf members have sprung up in the country since.

Quota International, a professional women's service club, started a "Shatter Silence" program to call attention to deafness. The organization began awarding scholarships to deaf students and started a national "Deaf Woman of the Year" award.

On May 5, 1970 the Gallaudet College faculty voted to accept "proficiency in the use of the simultaneous method" as an additional condition to the usual aca-

Shared Beauty

I cannot see a rainbow's glory spread
across a rain-washed sky when storm is over;
nor can I see or hear the birds that cry
their songs among the clouds, or through bright clover.
You tell me that the night is full of stars,
and how the winds and waters sing and flow;
and in my heart I wish that I could share
with you this beauty that I cannot know.
I only know that when I touch a flower,
or feel the sun and wind upon my face,
or hold your hand in mine, there is a brightness
within my soul that words can never trace.
I call it Life, and laugh with its delight,
though life itself be out of sound and sight.

—ROBERT J. SMITHDAS, LITT.D
The Deaf American

... a deaf actor not only brings power,
integrity, and reality to the portrayal of deaf
characters, but by their very presence in a
production can inspire new forms for the
theatre, new contexts for visual expression and
a unique approach to a variety of roles.

—ELIZABETH HOUSE
1979

demic requirements for obtaining tenure. The college began admitting a limited number of hearing students as special students on the undergraduate level. The first student admitted was 21-year-old Margaret Nagle, from Stephens Women's College in Columbia, Missouri. Nagle took courses in sign language translation for plays, stage production, and an independent course. She was inspired to seek admission to Gallaudet College when she saw a National Theatre of the Deaf production. Her experience on the Gallaudet campus changed her earlier ambition to become a lawyer in favor of becoming a teacher of the deaf.

Among the four persons awarded honorary degrees at the 1970 Gallaudet College commencement was Robert J. Smithdas, the first deaf and blind person in the United States to earn a master's degree. He earned

his MA 50 years after Helen Keller became the first deaf and blind person to earn a bachelor's degree. Smithdas was awarded an honorary Doctor of Letters degree. Smithdas was then director of Services for the Deaf-Blind at the Industrial Home for the Blind in New York. He is the author of *Life at My Fingertips,* an autobiography, and *City of the Heart,* a collection of his poetry. One of his poems, "Shared Beauty," appears in this chapter. In 1976 he was granted an honorary Doctor of Humanities degree by Western Michigan University in Kalamazoo, and in 1980, Johns Hopkins University awarded him a third honorary degree.

A Chicago hotel fire claimed the lives of two young students from the Illinois School for the Deaf. They had accompanied their Boy Scout troop to the city on an outing. Early in the morning a fire broke out in the hotel where they were staying, and, in an attempt to escape, they were overcome by smoke. The tragedy was worsened by the knowledge that, had they stayed in their rooms as the others did, they would most likely have lived.

Yerker Andersson of Washington, D.C., made history when he chatted over the telephone with a friend in Sweden. The occasion was a videophone satellite communications hook-up between the United States and Sweden. Andersson, who was born and grew up

Susan Davidoff, Miss Deaf America, 1976-78, appeared in "Sing a Sign" on national television with Vincent DiZebba.

C&P Telephone Co.

Bruce Hlibok in the "Runaways" at the Public Theatre in New York City.

379

You Have to be Deaf to Understand

By Willard J. Madsen

"You Have to be Deaf to Understand" was written by Willard J. Madsen, associate professor at Gallaudet College and a graduate of the Kansas School for the Deaf. Written in 1971, the poem first appeared in the *Dee Cee Eyes* and has since been reprinted in publications all over the country. It has received worldwide attention and has been translated into seven different languages.

What is it like to "hear" a hand?
You have to be deaf to understand.

What is it like to be a small child,
In a school, in a room void of sound—
With a teacher who talks and talks and talks;
And then when she does come around to you,
She expects you to know what she's said?
You have to be deaf to understand.

Or the teacher thinks that to make you smart,
You must first learn how to talk with your voice;
So mumbo-jumbo with hands on your face
For hours and hours without patience or end,
Until out comes a faint resembling sound?
You have to be deaf to understand.

What is it like to be curious,
To thirst for knowledge you can call your own,
With an inner desire that's set on fire—
And you ask a brother, sister, or friend
Who looks in answer and says, "Never mind"?
You have to be deaf to understand.

What it is like in a corner to stand,
Though there's nothing you've done really wrong,
Other than try to make use of your hands
To a silent peer to communicate
A thought that comes to your mind all at once?
You have to be deaf to understand.

What is it like to be shouted at
When one thinks that will help you to hear;
Or misunderstand the words of a friend
Who is trying to make a joke clear,
And you don't get the point because he's failed?
You have to be deaf to understand.

What is it like to be laughed in the face
When you try to repeat what is said;
Just to make sure that you've understood,
And you find that the words were misread—
And you want to cry out, "Please help me, friend"?
You have to be deaf to understand.

What is it like to have to depend
Upon one who can hear to phone a friend;
Or place a call to a business firm
And be forced to share what's personal, and,
Then find that your message wasn't made clear?
You have to be deaf to understand.

What is it like to be deaf and alone
In the company of those who can hear—
And you only guess as you go along,
For no one's there with a helping hand,
As you try to keep up with words and song?
You have to be deaf to understand.

What is it like on the road of life
To meet with a stranger who opens his mouth—
And speaks out a line at a rapid pace;
And you can't understand the look in his face
Because it is new and you're lost in the race?
You have to be deaf to understand.

What is it like to comprehend
Some nimble fingers that paint the scene,
And make you smile and feel serene
With the "spoken word" of the moving hand
That makes you part of the world at large?
You have to be deaf to understand.

What is it like to "hear" a hand?
Yes, you have to be deaf to understand.

Tim Medina on his "Total Communication News" program.

in Sweden, talked with a deaf shipyard employee in Tanum, Sweden. The event was arranged by the Communications Satellite Corporation to demonstrate the use of its new videophone. The videophone is a small television transmitter and receiver connected to an ordinary telephone.

In 1971 the legislature in Hawaii approved a bill granting disabled persons a personal state tax exemption of $5,000. In households where both husband and wife were disabled they could file for a deduction of $10,000. For the purpose of an extra exemption, deaf persons were defined as persons with a hearing loss of 82 decibels in the better ear. To claim the deduction, a certified audiogram had to accompany the form.

The Miss Deaf America Pageant was born during the 1970s. First to win the crown at the National Association of the Deaf convention in Miami, Florida, in 1972, was Ann Billington from Oklahoma who was running as Miss Gallaudet. Mary Pearce, Miss Deaf

Being deaf is an accident of nature, being indifferent is very often a deliberate choice of mankind. Of those two wounds in our society one at least is curable.
—RANDY AND NANETTE FABRAY MacDOUGALL

Mississippi, won the title in 1974 in Seattle, but when she elected to marry, she was succeeded by Pam Young, the runner-up. Susan Davidoff, Miss Deaf Maryland, held the crown from 1976 to 1978. Jackie Roth became the second Miss Deaf Maryland to win the crown in 1978. She held it for one year. She was succeeded by Debra Krause, Miss Deaf Pennsylvania and the first runner-up at the NAD convention in Rochester. Mary Beth Barber, Miss Deaf New York, won the title at the NAD Centennial Convention in Cincinnati.

The long dream of a home of its own finally became a reality for the National Association of the Deaf with the purchase of Halex House in Silver Spring, Maryland. The $640,000 modern three-story brick office building was formally dedicated on May 19, 1973.

Many will remember the 1970s as the decade of airplane hi-jackings, especially Jim Revells, who, as a young member of the Los Angeles Club of the Deaf, decided to have some fun on a flight to Oakland, California, where his team was to play the Oakland Club of the Deaf. Just before the plane departed, he took out his pad and pencil and wrote a note inquiring, "Will we go to Cuba?" and handed it to one of the stewardesses. The stewardess was not amused by his question and took the note to the pilot; the whole

---

Robert M. Greenmun
(1913-1970)

Robert M. (Mooers) Greenmun was a short, stocky man, with reddish blond hair and a ruddy complexion. Born September 27, 1913 in Binghamton, New York, he was deafened at the age of 12 and attended public school and the New York School for the Deaf at Malone.

For a while, following graduation from Gallaudet College, he was managing editor of *The Coolidge* (Ariz.) *News.* He began his teaching career in 1938 at the Ohio School for the Deaf. He taught at the New York School at Rome and at the Flordia School for the Deaf and the Blind. In Ohio he was an editor of *The Ohio Chronicle.*

Greenmun was elected secretary-treasurer of the National Association of the Deaf in Louisville, Kentucky, a post he held for 18 years—the longest term one person ever served as secretary-treasurer. He was an excellent pistol marksman and won several awards in national competition. He held an "expert" rating by the National Rifle Association. He was deputy sheriff in St. Johns County, Florida.

Greenmun was married to Rosalind Redfearn. They had one son.

He was killed when the car he was driving was struck by a train on April 11, 1970.

Gallaudet Alumni Newsletter

KRON-TV presents a regularly-scheduled newscast for the deaf, NEWSIGN, featuring Jane Wilk and Peter Wechsberg

8:25 AM WEEKDAY MORNINGS

Jane Wilk and Peter Wechsberg pioneered news reporting for the deaf community on KRON-TV in San Francisco.

team was required to disembark. The flight was held up while the player and his coach were thoroughly searched and questioned by FBI agents and airport personnel. Finally the players and their coach were allowed back on the plane, and the flight took off with an embarrassed but much wiser young man and his team.

At the beginning of the decade there was talk of making it possible for deaf students to enroll in law school. Wayne State University expressed interest in preparing deaf people for careers in law. Deaf college students with overall averags of ''B'' or better were encouraged to take the Law School Admission Test, and WSU offered to reimburse them for their interpreter's fees. By the end of the decade some 20 deaf students were attending law schools around the country.

Cynthia Saltzman delivering the morning news on WTOP-TV, Channel 9, in Washington, D.C.

In Texas, a law recognizing American Sign Language as a language and one that "may be taught in public schools in educational programs for both hearing and deaf students" was passed by the state legislature.

In New York City, Bruce Hlibok, a senior at the Horace Mann School in New York City, won a starring role in "Runaways," a social complaint musical being performed at the Public Theatre on Off-Broadway. The musical involved frustrated young people from 11 to 20 years old who supposedly came from broken homes (many did) or where parents were uncaring. The actors told the audience about themselves and acted out their stories. Hlibok had a speaking role which he delivered in sign language. An interpreter spoke for him. Christopher Sharp, writing in *Women's Wear Daily*, said Hlibok was the best reason for going to the production. The musical was eventually recorded on an album which included Hlibok's name, a unique place for a deaf person's name to appear!

In 1973 John A. Ensworth, a sixth grade teacher in Bend, Oregon, and the son of deaf parents, was selected National Teacher of the Year. He received his award at the White House in the presence of his mother, Mrs. Pat Nixon, and other dignitaries.

In 1974 Temple Deaf College opened in a vacant church in Kansas City with 13 students as the "country's only resident Bible College for the Deaf." The college was founded by the Rev. Harold L. Champion, the son of deaf parents. By 1978 the enrollment had grown to 50 and that year the college moved to a six-story building formerly used as a hospital.

In 1976 Louise Fletcher, the daughter of deaf parents, won an Oscar for her role in the movie, "One Flew Over the Cuckoo's Nest." On receiving her award on national television, she signed her acceptance and thanked her parents for "teaching me to have a dream."

When Washington, D.C., built a new subway system, blinking lights were installed along the edges of the platforms to warn deaf passengers and others of approaching trains. The transit system also installed telecommunications devices for deaf citizens so that they could call for information.

In August 1978 Department of Health, Education, and Welfare Secretary Joseph A. Califano, Jr. issued a memo to department heads instructing them to make DHEW meetings accessible to handicapped persons. It would be a bit presumptuous to expect a directive of this type to change years of oversight, but it did create an important awareness within higher government levels, and, as time passed, deaf government employees noticed an increased use of interpreters and more of their hearing co-workers taking classes in sign language. Another important step had been taken.

In 1979 the Supreme Court ruled that schools could not be forced to accept handicapped persons who are not able to meet essential physical requirements. The

---

Petra F. Howard
(1891-1971)

Petra Fandrem Howard was a person who "championed the cause of the deaf." She spent her lifetime serving deaf people in her home state and was the first director of the Minnesota Labor Bureau for the Deaf.

The Minnesota Bureau was established through the efforts of Anson R. Spear and was the first of its kind in the country. In 1930 the Bureau became part of the State Department of Vocational Rehabilitation. Through this relationship, the Bureau provided job placement, training, and other related services for deaf persons.

Petra Howard joined the newly established Bureau in 1915. One day while on the job in northern Minnesota, she received a call from a manufacturer in Minneapolis requesting 35 deaf workers for his plant by the next morning. She returned to the city and by midnight had rounded up 18 persons. By closing time the next day she had placed 33 men on the job.

Petra Fandrem became hard of hearing at the age of five years. She retained sufficient hearing to interpret for deaf persons. She acquired her education in the public school system, at the Minnesota School for the Deaf, and at Gallaudet College. She married Jay Cooke Howard, a deaf investment broker and the ninth president of the National Association of the Deaf; they had one son, Henry. The marriage ended in divorce.

Mrs. Howard's career spanned more than 40 years. She was president of the Minnesota Association of the Deaf, a member of the Board of Directors of the Gallaudet College Alumni Association, and exchange editor of *The Silent Worker*. On her retirement in 1960 she was awarded an honorary degree by Gallaudet College. She also received citations commending her work from President Dwight D. Eisenhower, Minnesota Governor Orville Freeman, and the Minnesota Association of the Deaf.

Born November 9, 1891, she died in a nursing home on March 5, 1971. She was 79 years old. A residential therapeutic center for deaf persons in St. Paul, Minnesota, is named for her.

decision was the outcome of a lawsuit filed by Frances Davis, a 46-year-old woman who suffered a severe hearing impairment. Davis had sought admission to a nursing college in North Carolina but was rejected because of her hearing impairment. She filed a suit based on Section 504 of the Rehabilitation Act of 1973 which requires institutions that receive federal aid to eliminate barriers that impede the admission of handicapped students. Davis argued the college was discriminating against her by refusing to admit her. The Supreme Court disagreed. In reversing a lower court's ruling, the Supreme Court stated that the law does not force schools to "accept handicapped persons who are not able to meet essential physical requirements." Many handicapped individuals, and those who work with disabled Americans, saw the ruling as a blow to equal opportunities.

There remained, of course, other negative aspects surrounding deafness, some of which seemed incred-

For one deaf man, captioned television arrived too late.

Paul Butler/Gallaudet Today

ible, considering the fact it was the 1970s, and it was assumed that there was a much more enlightened public. Some examples:

The term, "deaf-mute" continued to crop up in the press occasionally.

A deaf youngster in Chicago was shot and killed when he did not heed a landlord's command to stop. The youth and a friend had been surprised in a vacant apartment, had climbed out a window, and were on the run when he was shot.

In Los Angeles, a deaf couple, neither of whom could talk, lost their four-year-old daughter to a foster home by court order. At the first hearing the couple had no lawyer and did not know or understand what was going on. After the second hearing, the judge ordered the removal of the child to a foster home. A year later the couple learned through the grapevine about the Southern California Center for the Law and the Deaf and appealed for legal assistance. Their attorney, Allen King, blamed the court decision on the fact that they were deaf and could not provide "verbal stimulation" for their child. He also charged that the couple had been denied due process of law. Almost two years later a Superior Court judge ordered the child returned to her parents and directed the Public Social Services to work with the parents in meeting their daughter's speech needs.

Television and the Deaf Viewer

The development of television in mid-century largely brought disappointment to most deaf viewers. While sports events and "action" films (those programs with plenty of action and minimal dialogue) were popular with deaf people, most television programs were just another form of the "talkies" and were meaningless to anyone who could not understand the dialogue. Even the most skilled lipreaders could catch only scattered bits of information when a speaker's lips happened to be clearly visible on the screen.

The first efforts to make television understandable to deaf viewers were confined to interpreting programs into sign language. Interpreters were included in some news broadcasts and special programs from time to time.

In the late 1960s Malcolm J. Norwood began exploring the possibility of captioning television programs. Norwood was the deaf chief of the Media Services and Captioned Films Division of the Bureau of Education of the Handicapped (BEH), Office of Education, Department of Health, Education, and Welfare. He saw television as the most promising of all media for deaf people.

A survey was undertaken to see if hearing television viewers would be receptive to captions. This study found that ten per cent of the viewers in the sample population studied flatly rejected captioning. That amounted to about 20 million Americans which was more than the total number of hearing impaired Americans. The fact that a much larger segment of the population was receptive to captioning did not matter; it was obvious that open captioning would have a lengthy and tough fight to win acceptance and commercial networks would not want to take the risk. So,

Norwood decided to explore other alternatives; the outcome resulted in closed captioning.

In October 1971, BEH contracted with the WGBH Educational Foundation in Boston, Massachusetts, to produce a demonstration captioned television program for use by the Public Broadcasting Service. The following December, Norwood's office sponsored a national conference on television and the hearing impaired at the Southern Regional Media Center for the Deaf at the University of Tennessee in Knoxville. The National Bureau of Standards had developed a special broadcast device to transmit time signals on television for scientific purposes, called the NBS Time System. Broadcasters realized that this device could also be used to send captioned information and that the captions would be seen only by those viewers whose television sets were equipped with a decoder. At the Tennessee conference participants were shown a captioned version of *Mod Squad*, using the NBS system,

This Sears TeleCaption television set sold for about $520 when it first appeared on the market.

LET'S NOT GET TOO CASUAL ABOUT THIS THING.

Sears, Roebuck & Co.

385

broadcast by ABC-TV from its New York City studios. A second and similar demonstration followed at Gallaudet College some months later.

In 1973 the Public Broadcasting Service was given a contract by DHEW to do surveys, conduct research, and develop captioning technology. Gallaudet was sub-contracted by PBS to conduct a survey of hearing impaired persons in 12 cities and evaluate their attitude toward closed captions. The results of this report were later submitted by PBS as part of its petition to the Federal Communications Commission for the use of Line 21 for closed captions. (Line 21 is a portion of the lower television screen not normally used.)

In 1975 the Federal Communications Commission adopted a ruling to require television networks to provide visual captioning to warn hearing impaired persons in emergencies.

Through the efforts of the National Center for Law and the Deaf and Dr. Donald V. Torr, now assistant vice president for College Educational Resources at Gallaudet, changes were made in the copyright law to permit educational institutions for the hearing impaired to copy programs off-the-air for the purpose of captioning and rebroadcasting them over an institution's closed circuit television network.

The Caption Center at WGBH-TV

Meanwhile, the experiments at WGBH-TV were going very well. Out of their efforts, came the original open captioned version of the "French Chef" program broadcast over the Public Broadcasting Service in August and September 1972. But, once again, a need was identified in the deaf community for more access to public affairs and news programming. The challenge of producing a news program with captions is the time, effort, and equipment required to rebroadcast a news show in time for it still to be newsworthy. It had never been attempted before, but WGHB-TV decided to give it a try. WGBH-TV developed a system that enabled it, on December 3, 1973, to broadcast the first and only news program with open captions for hearing impaired audiences. This success led to the establishment of The Caption Center at WGBH-TV.

Each weekday evening, Caption Center staff members produce *The Captioned ABC News* program which WGBH then broadcasts at 11:00 p.m. Other PBS stations around the country pick up and air the program through the PBS network. To produce this program the staff, which includes deaf individuals, work under a pressing deadline. They tape the 6:30 p.m. ABC News, cut, rewrite, and edit the script to a sixth-grade

reading level, and to fit space limitations, time and insert the captions to fit the video portion of the program, ready for rebroadcast four and a half hours later. The staff also must add other material to replace the commercials shown during the regular program, since PBS is a public station and does not carry advertising. To fill these gaps WGBH includes sports results, weather reports, late-breaking news events, consumer reports, a chronicle of news related to deaf persons, and deaf heritage material.

The Caption Center has also produced such specials as captioning Richard M. Nixon's 21-minute second inaugural address, a weekly *Captioned ZOOM* program, an hour-long Miss Deaf America Pageant, and eight nightly reports on the XIII World Games for the Deaf played in Rumania. When the captions first appeared, a delighted viewer wrote WGBH-TV: "When I saw those captions it made me so happy I started yelling around the house 'Look. They gave me words!'"

By 1980 *The Captioned ABC News* was being broadcast over 142 public television stations. With continuing support from the Bureau of Education of the Handicapped and a recent grant from International Business Machines Corporation (IBM), *The Captioned ABC News* has been broadcast nationally on PBS since 1973.

National Captioning Institute

In 1976 the Federal Communications Commission agreed to reserve Line 21 on the television screen for the transmission of captions. That same year an independent, non-profit organization, the National Captioning Institute, was established with seed money from DHEW to caption regular and special television programs for showing through the closed captioning system. To launch this program, DHEW agreed to provide $3.5 million for the first year; $2.1

This NCI logo identifies television programs which have been captioned for deaf audiences.

Freda Norman, the Supersign Woman.

deaf and hearing-impaired Americans. I can announce today that we have completed long and complicated preparations which, by early 1980, should make it possible for the nation's deaf and hearing-impaired people to enjoy television through a system called closed captioning."

Closed captioning on television had arrived!

Television captioning arrived too late for one deaf man, however. Tired of waiting some 30 years for programs he could understand, a deaf Idahoan took his ax one day and smashed his television set to smithereens.

Other Developments in Television

An increasing number of stations began adding deaf actors or captions or sign language interpreters to some of their programs. *Sesame Street, Mr. Roger's Neighborhood, ZOOM, Making Things Work, Nova, Watch Your Child/The Me Too Show* were some of the programs which attempted to overcome the communications' barrier of deaf audiences.

Eventually, a few deaf newscasters broke into the highly-competitive field of news reporting and were given a few minutes on local television programs to present the news for the benefit of members of the deaf community. Following the lead of John Tubergen (see the 1950s), Jane Wilk and Peter Wechsberg teamed up and pioneered a live news program called NEWSIGN 4 in 1972. Their program was shown mornings over KRON-TV, Channel 4, in San Francisco. Cynthia Saltzman began appearing on WTOP-TV, Channel 9, in Washington, D.C. She had been recruited to report on severe weather conditions when a storm hit the area. The station received so much favorable response to the signed broadcast that Saltzman was retained to sign a regular five-minute news program every weekday morning.

A station in Portland, Oregon, recruited Henry Stack to present a five-minute news program over KGW-TV during a local break in the *Today Show*. Tim Medina had a popular "Total Communication News" program shown at lunch time on Channel 5, WTTG-TV, in Washington, D.C. Medina not only spoke and signed for himself, but visuals in the background and some captions on the screen made his program about as total as a news program could get. Gregg Brooks appeared regularly on a news program at Theta Cable

million the second year; $900,000 the third year; and $400,000 the fourth year. It was hoped that, after that, the Institute would become self-supporting.

Sears, Roebuck & Co. agreed to accept the responsibility for manufacturing and selling a captioning decoder at the lowest possible cost to deaf people.

Three major broadcasting systems—PBS, ABC, NBC—expressed intent to buy up to a total of 20 hours of captioned programs a week, most of it to be shown during prime time. One major network, CBS, decided not to participate in the new captioning program, choosing instead to cast its lot with a system called Teletext, which is still in the development stages in this country.

At 11 a.m. on March 23, 1979 DHEW Secretary Joseph A. Califano, Jr. made this announcement: "Today we celebrate a breakthrough for millions of

There is room in the world for deaf heroines aspiring to the heights.

—EDNA P. ADLER

TV in Los Angeles, and other stations in several states began interpreted news programs.

In December 1972 WMPB-TV in Maryland broadcast a three-hour program, *They Grow in Silence: An Evening on Deafness.* Produced jointly by WMPB-TV, Western Maryland College and the Maryland Center for Public Broadcasting, the program featured Dr. McCay Vernon, co-author of *They Grow in Silence,* and professor of psychology at Western Maryland College, and a panel of deaf persons and parents of deaf children. Telephone lines—including a teletypewriter—were made available so that viewers could call in and ask questions . . . many did. The program elicited so much response that WMPB-TV rebroadcast it a short time later.

In the late 1970s a group of deaf and hearing actors got together to form D.E.A.F. (Deaf Education and Artistics Frontiers) Media, Inc., in Oakland, California. With funding from the Bureau of Education of the Handicapped, Public Broadcasting Service, and the

Olivia Octopus found her extra hands helpful in communicating in sign language on the "Rainbow's End" television program.

D.E.A.F. Media, Inc.

It is presumed that teaching (deaf) people how to sign will influence speech negatively. Our data do not support this assumption. Yet this assumption still dominates the educational approach of many older teachers and it still inhibits the practice of manual communication in teacher training establishments.

Of course the earth is flat—we can believe our own eyes, can't we.

—DR. GEORGE MONTGOMERY
1970s

Charles Stewart Mott Foundation, this group produced a series of five half-hour programs called *Rainbow's End.* The programs unfold in a unique television studio in Anycity, U.S.A. where one of the leading characters, a quiet, shy secretary named Penny (performed by Freda Norman) transforms into Supersign (a "deaf" version of Wonder Woman) as the need arises and rushes to the rescue of a deaf person in distress.

Rainbow's End was designed by deaf professionals especially for hearing impaired children although it appeals to a much larger audience. It was developed to create a better self-image among deaf children, serve as role models (many of the actors are deaf), help develop language skills (one program about plurals, for example, shows an actor fingerspelling the same word with both hands), encourage family interaction, and create a better awareness of deaf people and their culture.

First aired in 1979, the program was so popular and the demand so great that it has since been broadcast three times nationally by PBS. The program won a local Emmy award for outstanding achievement in children's television programming. D.E.A.F. Media, Inc., has received awards for two other productions, *Silent Perspectives,* a program for deaf adults shown over KCSM-TV and *Eye Music,* shown on KOED-TV.

As the decade came to a close, deaf actors and actresses were appearing on television with increasing regularity. An estimated 40 million viewers saw deaf nine-year-old Jeffrey Bravin, son of deaf parents, star as Jonah in the CBS-TV Production, *And Your Name is Jonah.* Bravin performed with Actress Sally Struthers in the two-hour film-story about a young deaf boy misdiagnosed as mentally retarded.

Six-foot, 270-pound Lou Ferrigno, who acts as the Hulk in *The Incredible Hulk* CBS-TV series, has a 65-percent hearing loss caused by infection when he was three years old. A native New Yorker, Ferrigno grew up a shy, ashamed, and easily embarrassed youth and was called "Deaf Louie," according to press clippings. At the age of 16, he took up weight lifting and at 20 won the Mr. America contest. He has also won the Mr. Universe title twice.

Kevin V. Wieringen, a product of the Washington State School for the Deaf, appeared in *James at 15*. Alban Branton, a 17-year-old student at California School for the Deaf, Riverside, had a role in *Little House on the Prairie*.

Members of the National Theatre of the Deaf continue to appear regularly on the children's program, *Sesame Street*.

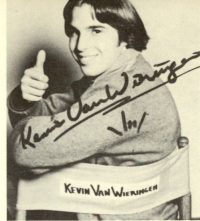

Kevin Van Wieringen on location in "James at 15."

Jeff Bravin in his role as Jonah.

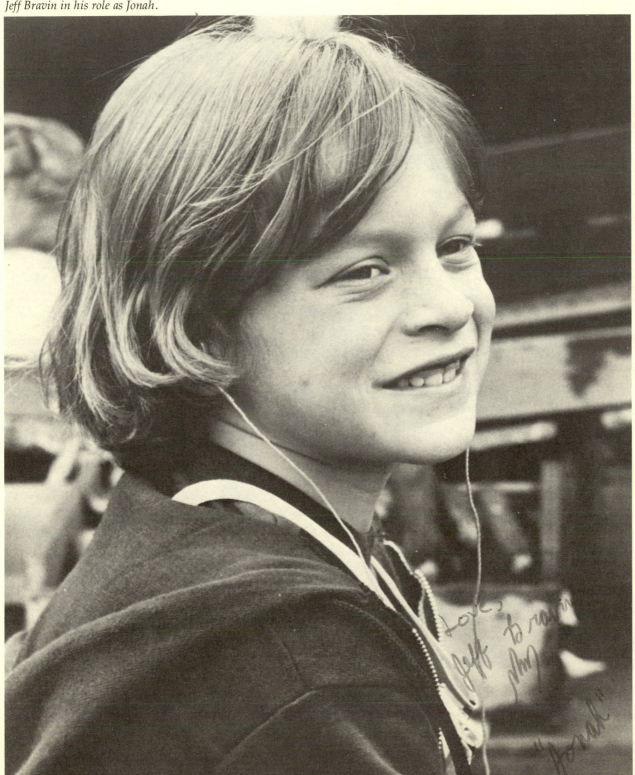

389

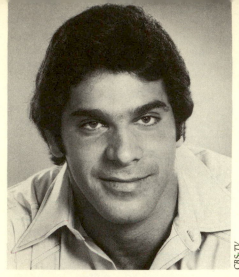

Lou Ferrigno, left, and as the "Hulk," below.

Rock Gospel

The reader did not want to believe the notice which appeared in the November 11, 1978 issue of the *Dee Cee Eyes,* but it was true. After almost a decade of interpreting religious and other songs in sign language, the item announced, the Rock Gospel group was folding.

Nine years previously two Gallaudet College chaplains, Father Rudolph Gawlik, a Catholic priest, and Pastor Dan Pokorny, a Lutheran minister, had teamed up with a local high school band, called "Edge," to present the first interpreted musical concert in the Gallaudet College auditorium. The two chaplains had no idea what they were getting into. The audience had never seen anything like it. They felt and loved every beat and before the evening was over there was not a person in the auditorium who had not been moved by the swaying, loud, rhythmic, vibrating

Rock Gospel

Rudy Gawlik, Donna Gadling, Dan Pokorny, Sharon Johnson, and Dennis Cokely, the hearing members of the Rock Gospel troupe. Below. Pam Minger and Dan Pokorny during a performance in Maryland.

Rock Gospel

beats. Rock Gospel was an instant success.

Yet, in spite of that success, the group nearly broke up in 1971. The high school musicians were leaving for college and Pokorny had the opportunity to participate in a one year's exchange program in Switzerland. Gawlik did not want the group to die so he recruited Pam Minger and Dennis Cokely, two Kendall School teachers, and kept it going. Using pre-recorded music, the trio performed in coffee houses doing folk songs and songs of war and peace. When Pokorny returned the following year the group teamed up with a new band called "The Sons of Thunder." This new group experimented with several visual innovations, including background slides, color, and designs. They cut a record, "Rock Gospel in Songs and Signs," and began accepting travel requests.

Trips to Edmonton, Alberta, and Winnipeg, Manitoba, Canada; Indianapolis, Pittsburgh, and Rochester followed. The Rock Gospel group appeared before mixed deaf and hearing audiences everywhere they went. Invitations were extended to appear on television in Indianapolis, and the group did a documentary for WTTG-TV in Washington, D.C. and were featured in a magazine write-up.

The group performed before the Seventh Congress of the World Federation of the Deaf in 1975 and at the White House Conference on the Handicapped in 1977. During its existence the group performed in 26 states, visited three Canadian provinces, made four videotapes and one record, and conducted numerous workshops at schools, clubs, and churches.

Wrote one deaf youngster following a performance: "I am happy I went. It made me feel good." Said another letter writer: "My heart was dancing." And, a third: "You won the heart of the deaf community."

Indeed, they had. No one else had ever before brought music on such a large scale so successfully to deaf audiences as did Rock Gospel.

Chair of Deaf Studies

In 1972 Gallaudet College established the Powrie V. Doctor Chair of Deaf Studies in memory of Professor Doctor. Dr. Doctor had been a member of the Gallaudet faculty for 43 years. He was chairman of the Department of Government and acting dean of the Graduate School when he died on July 31, 1971 in Paris, France, while attending the Congress of the World Federation of the Deaf.

Doctor grew up in Olathe, Kansas, hometown of the Kansas State School for the Deaf. (A library at the school is named for him.) His brother, Frank, was deaf and that influenced Doctor and their sister, Amy, to become teachers of the deaf. Doctor was editor of the *American Annals of the Deaf* for 20 years. He was a world traveller, known to thousands, and a writer and lecturer on the education of the deaf. Gallaudet's President Leonard M. Elstad called Doctor Gallaudet's goodwill ambassador.

One year appointments to the chair are reserved for a resident teacher-scholar in the field of education of the deaf, who has made or shows promise of making significant contributions to the field. The person selected receives a substantial salary and room and board on the campus. Specific duties include one colloquium lecture and one seminar course for each semester. Appointees are encouraged to contribute an original article to the *Annals*.

To date, six persons have held the Doctor Chair of Deaf Studies, the first being Leo M. Jacobs, a Gallaudet graduate and a high school mathematics teacher at the California School for the Deaf in Berkeley. Jacobs used the year to write *A Deaf Adult Speaks Out*.

The Rev. Steve L. Mathis, III, another Gallaudet graduate, principal of the Carver School for the Deaf in Gambrills, Maryland, and an Episcopal priest, was the second recipient. Mathis spent the year collecting and organizing Doctor's vast collection of writings and preparing a bibliography of Doctor's work. Mathis also worked on a biography of Doctor.

Dr. Hilde Schlesinger, a psychiatrist and project director of the Mental Health Service for the Deaf at the Langley Porter Neuropsychiatric Institute in California, was the third recipient. One of a few psychiatrists who are able to use sign language, she held the chair from January to August, 1976.

Richard G. Brill, superintendent of the California School for the Deaf, Riverside, held the chair in 1976-77. He spent the year studying the relationship between the education of deaf children and the concept of mainstreaming. His findings resulted in the publication of the book, *Mainstreaming the Prelingually Deaf Child*, in 1978.

Dr. Brill was followed by McCay Vernon, professor of psychology at Western Maryland College and co-author of *They Grow in Silence*. Dr. Vernon also serves as editor of the *American Annals of the Deaf*.

The sixth recipient of the chair is Lionel Evans, headmaster of the Northern Counties School for the Deaf at Newcastle-upon-Tyne in England. Dr. Evans is the first person from outside the United States to hold the chair.

Deaf Awareness Programs

One of the first Deaf Awareness programs—if not the first—took place in Colorado. Deaf Coloradoans, led by Jerome Moers, met with Governor John A. Love on November 10, 1972 to watch him sign a proclamation officially marking November 12-18, 1972 as Deaf Awareness Week. The purpose of the week was to make the public more aware of persons with hearing impairments and to dispel the myth that deaf people are not intelligent because they do not speak well. Moer's wife, Betty, appeared in a 30-second spot announcement on television throughout the week announcing the event. Moers predicted that other states would follow Colorado's example and begin observing a Deaf Awareness Week. And many did.

The success of the Deaf Awareness project was that it reached people on the local and state level. Suddenly neighbors and employees were learning that there were more deaf people in their midst than they realized. By 1975 Deaf Awareness Weeks had been proclaimed by governors and mayors throughout the country. No attempts were made to have a uniform nationwide date because it was felt by most that deaf awareness should be an on-going project. Libraries observed the event as did shopping centers and schools with displays and information distribution. Lions Clubs, Delta Zeta Sorority Chapters, the National Grange, the Red Cross, Jr. NAD Chapters, and others joined the event. One milk company printed a deaf awareness panel on 100,000 half-gallon milk containers for distribution. The Registry of Interpreters national office began assisting with the coordination of the project by offering Deaf Awareness mate-

Colorado Governor John A. Love greets Jerome Moers after proclaiming Deaf Awareness Week in 1972.

rials such as pins, decals, and bumper stickers. Through Quota International some public service announcement television spots were made as part of its "Shatter Silence" program.

At one high school teachers and students volunteered to wear ear plugs for a day in a "Deaf for a Day" program to experience some of the problems deaf people encounter. The Deaf Awareness program also included lectures by deaf persons.

In December 1974, Alice Hagemeyer initiated a Deaf Awareness Week at the Martin Luther King Memorial Library in Washington, D.C., where she worked. She arranged for deaf persons to speak at the program. Her motive was two-fold: to acquaint the public with deaf people and to acquaint deaf persons with the many varied services offered at the public library.

Hagemeyer's idea spread to other libraries and her leadership in the area eventually led to the establishment of a deaf section within the American Library Association. For her work in this area Alice Hage-

Alice Hagemeyer

Charles Shoup/Gallaudet College

...I think there ought to be more sign language and closed caption newscasts on television, and more visual aids for the deaf traveler at airline, rail or bus terminal.

—VICE PRESIDENT NELSON D. ROCKEFELLER

meyer was presented its President's Award by the National Association of the Deaf during the Centennial Convention in 1980.

More on Telecommunications

The teletypewriter which had come into use in the 1960s continued to gain popularity in the 1970s.

Insurance agents and stockbrokers added them to their homes or offices so that they could better serve deaf customers. As a result of some of these contacts with deaf people, businessmen began taking classes in sign language.

Western Union donated three teletypewriters which were installed in the new communications room in the United States Capitol Annex so that deaf people could call their senators and congressmen.

In Washington, D.C., the Washington Suburban Sanitary Commission added two around-the-clock telecommunications devices to serve deaf customers. One was installed in the customer service division and the other in the company's maintenance management radio room.

In Los Angeles, California, police nabbed six suspected thieves trying to break into some cars when John Seidel, a deaf New York Life insurance underwriter, awoke early one morning, and looking out his apartment window, saw the men, and became suspicious. He called police on his teletypewriter.

Prince George's County in Maryland added a teletypewriter to its Information Center when it opened Project Health Care for the Deaf at the County Health

Department headquarters to serve an estimated 46,000 hearing impaired and 8,000 deaf residents. By contacting the center, deaf residents are able to get information about all health services available in the county and to make appointments for any service delivered by the Health Department.

In Miami, Florida, National Airlines, Inc., became one of the first airlines to install teletypewriter services for its deaf customers. Initial response to the service was so enthusiastic that airline officials began considering the possibility of expanding the service statewide.

The Peter Bent Brigham Hospital in Boston added 24-hour services for deaf people in January 1979 when they installed telecommunication devices to serve the estimated 1,000 deaf persons in the New England area known to have their own telecommunications units. The hospital also began providing interpreter services for deaf patients in all areas of the hospital including ambulance service. That's not all. A TTY is located in the Peter Bent Brigham Hospital Emergency Room which can be used in cases of children's illnesses or poisoning to relay information to the Children's Hospital Medical Center or to the Massachusetts Poisoning Information Center or other emergency services.

Mt. Diablo Hospital Center in Concord, California, became accessible to the deaf community when the hospital's Volunteer Association donated a telecommunications device. Three employees of the hospital

I. Lee Brody of New Jersey with a Braille Phone Teletypewriter.

Shirley Glassman at the Radio-teletypewriter News Center in Philadelphia.

394

also learned sign language so they could better communicate with deaf patients.

But all was not roses. Ed Corbett, a deaf doctoral degree candidate in the new doctoral program at Gallaudet College, and an intern on the House of Representative's Education and Labor Committee, called the Office for Civil Rights on the teletypewriter one day to inquire about progress on Section 504 of the Rehabilitation Act of 1973. This office is responsible for implementing the section which attempts to prevent discrimination against handicapped individuals. To Corbett's shock and disbelief, he learned that *they* had no teletypewriter!

Hearing Ear Dogs

A deaf Minnesota lady contacted the Minnesota Society for the Prevention of Cruelty to Animals when her dog died. She had depended on that dog to act as her ears and tell her when someone was knocking on her door. The Society replaced the pet and within the next two years had also trained and placed six other hearing ear dogs. From this beginning was born a modest hearing ear dog program. On February 13, 1976, the program was formally turned over to the American Humane Association. Based in Englewood, Colorado, the program is under the direction of the Director of Animal Protection. A staff of six professionals with experience both in working with those who have hearing impairments and in animal training train the dogs. The administrator has a master's degree in the education of the hearing impaired.

The program, which depends on grants and contributions for its support, trains dogs in auditory awareness. The dogs are made available to the hearing impaired individuals at no cost. Dogs have been placed with hearing impaired persons all over the United States. The goal of the program is to place a dog with every hearing impaired person who wants one. To maintain the integrity of the program, the American Humane Association works closely with the National Association of the Deaf and other organizations for the hearing impaired.

Dogs are trained to tell their masters when the baby is crying or when there is someone at the door or to alert their deaf masters to a noise and direct them to the source. The dog will call attention to keys falling from a pocket, otherwise unheard, to smoke detector signals, and/or to sirens, alarm clocks, boiling water, etc.

The Society takes unwanted dogs and trains them to become ears for deaf persons. As their use became known, airlines began permitting trained hearing ear dogs passage on airlines in the USA. Officials predict that eventually hearing ear dogs will outnumber the 25,000 seeing eye dogs in the country.

Recipients of Honorary Degrees

Since its founding in 1864 when Gallaudet College awarded John Carlin an honorary Master of Arts degree, the college has awarded nearly 100 honorary degrees to deaf persons. Most of the recipients of these degrees are listed in *The Gallaudet Almanac.*

At least seven deaf persons are known to have been recognized for their noteworthy achievements by other colleges. Laurent Clerc was the recipient of three honorary degrees. He received degrees from Trinity College, Amherst College, and the University of Lyon in France. Gilbert Eastman believes that Clerc is the first deaf person in the United States (and possibly the world) to be awarded an honorary degree and probably the only one to receive three.

In 1860 Columbian College (now George Washington University) awarded James Denison an honorary Bachelor of Philosophy degree. Denison was the first teacher and, later, the first principal of the Kendall School for the Deaf.

John R. Gregg, the inventor of the Gregg Shorthand System, received a Doctor of Commercial Science degree from Boston University.

Frances Parsons became a world Total Communication ambassador during the 1970s. Here she is greeted at the Kwara State School for the Deaf in Nigeria. Gabriel Adepoju

> **As far as deaf people are concerned our civil rights are violated daily.**
>
> —FREDERICK C. SCHREIBER
> 1970s

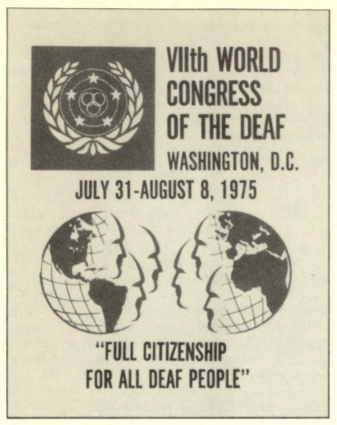

Poster announcing the Seventh World Congress of the Deaf which was held in Washington, D.C. in 1975.

George M. McClure, Sr., the well-known Kentucky School for the Deaf educator and editor, was awarded a Doctor of Literature degree by Centre College in 1934.

In 1947 Cadwallader Washburn received an honorary Doctor of Humane Letters degree from Bowdoin College in Brunswick, Maine.

In 1958, Seabury-Western Theological Seminary honored the Rev. Homer E. Grace, an Episcopalian priest, with a Doctor of Divinity degree.

Carthage College awarded Boyce R. Williams an honorary Doctor of Humane Letters degree in 1972.

Denison, McClure, Washburn, Grace, and Williams have also received honorary degrees from Gallaudet College.

...what you rightfully want is not to have everything done for you—but the opportunity to do for yourselves in shaping the society in which you live.

—VICE PRESIDENT NELSON D. ROCKEFELLER

Seventh World Congress of the World Federation of the Deaf

In 1975 the United States hosted the Seventh World Congress of the World Federation of the Deaf. It was held at the Washington Hilton Hotel in Washington, D.C., July 31 to August 8, 1975. The theme of the Congress was "Full Citizenship for All Deaf People." Over 3,000 deaf and hearing Americans in addition to participants from 70 other member nations attended the event.

There were eight major commissions each chaired by an international and a national president. These eight commissions dealt with arts and culture, communications, audiology, pedagogy, pyschology, social aspects of deafness, spiritual care, and vocational rehabilitation. Individuals from throughout the world were invited to present papers, and many did. Jack Ashley, the only deaf member of the British Parliament, was one of several VIPs who addressed the Congress.

Entertainment included performances by deaf theatrical groups from Sweden, Poland, Israel, Germany, and the United States.

During the week Gallaudet College had a convocation at which Vice President Nelson Rockefeller spoke. (He told those attending: "You want your views heard and I say, more power to you.") Honorary degrees were awarded to World Federation of the Deaf Bureau members D.K. Nandy of India, Ole Monk Plum of Denmark, and Cesare Magarotto of Italy. The Powrie V. Doctor Medallion (for international service to deaf people) was given to Quota International, the Rev. Thomas H. Sutcliffe of Great Britain, and Fritz Geisperger of West Germany.

Boyce R. Williams of the USA and Herbert Feuchte of West Germany making a presentation at the VIIth World Congress of the Deaf.

Resolutions were adopted by the different commissions. They called on all nations and the United Nations to give more attention to the needs of deaf persons; encouraged all countries with television systems to use captioned warnings in times of emergencies; urged more persons to learn International Sign Language; commended the United Nations Educational, Scientific, and Cultural Organization (UNESCO) for its sponsorship of the International Meeting of Experts on Education of the Deaf but took exception to two of the recommendations coming from this meeting which prohibit deaf teachers from teaching deaf children; affirmed the rights of deaf people to the same health services provided other people and recommended the involvement of those sensitive to the needs of deaf people when planning such services; encouraged increased efforts to educate hearing persons about deaf people; and strongly supported the concept of deaf people controlling their own organizations and being given the opportunity to assume leadership roles in programs serving deaf youth and adults, including rehabilitation and education programs.

If nothing more, the Congress itself set an example. The Congress was planned almost entirely by deaf people. Of the eight commissions, four were co-chaired by deaf persons. Five deaf individuals gave keynote addresses and 24 presented papers; nine responded to addresses; nine served as presiding officers of a session; and 14 others participated on panels. By comparison, a total of 10 deaf persons participated in the program of the previous Congress.

P.L. 94-142

Public Law 94-142—the "Education for All Handicapped Children Act of 1975"—was passed by the 94th Congress and signed into law by President Gerald Ford on November 29, 1975. It was landmark legislation for the handicapped because it charged the

The advent of Public Law 94-142 has and is causing great concern in the Deaf Community. We are afraid that the state will be fooled by the apparent economics that this law affords and rush to abolish special education programs and institutions for the deaf. We believe that, all things being equal, an integrated program—a mainstreaming program if you wish—is optional. But we know that all things are not equal.

—FREDERICK C. SCHREIBER
1970s

Overzealous and poorly informed groups have determined that the least restrictive educational environment for deaf children lies in wholesale mainstreaming in the regular public school system. We need to come to grips with this problem of naiveté about the unique communication barriers imposed by hearing loss. We need to work on amendments which will clarify the intent of this law and ensure that deaf children are not lost in the shuffle of this blanket legislation. The law must clearly state that most appropriate placement takes precedence over simplistic interpretations of the least restrictive environment.

—MERVIN D. GARRETSON

local, state and federal governments with the responsibility of guaranteeing that each handicapped American child would receive a free, appropriate public education. "Appropriate" was defined as placing the child in a program that best fit his needs as opposed to attempting to fit the child to a program.

The law called for the involvement of parents in the development of the child's individual education program (IEP), and guaranteed parents due process and the right to be heard, informed, and involved and to challenge decisions. It also guaranteed them the right to use their native tongue during school conferences or to have access to an interpreter.

The law assigned the local education agency (LEA) the responsibility of identifying all handicapped children within its area, evaluating their needs, developing their IEPs and recommending appropriate placement. Placement in the least restrictive environment was the desired option. The law also established a formula in which the federal government would pay a percentage of the costs of educating these handicapped children. The individual education plans were described as the heart of the law because they served as a form of blueprint for the child's education and provided a form of accountability. The law also encouraged the education agencies to employ handicapped persons wherever possible as they serve as role models.

Reaction to the law, and interpretations of its meaning, varied. Dr. McCay Vernon, the outspoken editor of the *American Annals of the Deaf* called it "the road to hell." He argued that the law was "grossly underfunded," which many agreed it was, and criticized the "naive assumption that mainstreaming is both feasible and desirable for the overwhelming majority of handicapped children." He pointed out that in most

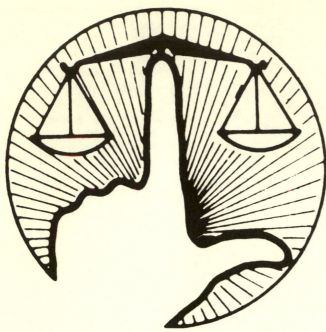

Logo of the National Center for Law and the Deaf.

states teachers of deaf children must take two additional years of graduate study above an undergraduate degree to qualify for certification to teach deaf children. "What can conceivably be the logic of expecting a regular public school teacher with little or no background in deafness to provide for the mainstreaming of one deaf child in a class of 25 to 40 hearing children, several of whom may also have major disabilities?" he asked. While conceding that the intent of the law was excellent, Vernon felt that "It pledges what it cannot deliver and for which it will not pay. It frequently feeds needs to deny the reality of a handicapped."

Some interpreted the "least restrictive environment" as meaning automatic placement of the majority of deaf children in the local public school, which it did not, and some gloomily forecast an impending doom for the special school. In some areas special schools experienced declines in enrollments. Others witnessed surges. Some individuals compared the law to the tip of an iceberg and pessimistically wondered about the amount of work and money that would be

---

The total subjection of a deaf child to a means of communication which he cannot understand in a school setting is not only unprofessional and usually ineffective, but it could well be viewed as a violation of the rights of another human being.

—DR. EDWARD C. MERRILL, JR.

---

required to achieve the law's mandate. National Association of the Deaf President Mervin D. Garretson called it a "Pandora's box of ambiguity and misrepresentation."

To help local education agencies determine the placement of deaf children, Gallaudet College suggested four principles be considered: 1) That deaf children have access to a wide variety of educational environments; 2) That they have access to all special services required for normal educational growth; 3) That the child and his parents have access to and freedom of choice of educational programs, and; 4) That the high cost of education of deaf children should not be a limiting factor. Gallaudet College cautioned that "the local education agency will find the cost of appropriate education services for deaf children usually equalling and often exceeding the per capita cost for the same quality of education offered by the special school."

As the 1970s drew to a close the full effect of P.L. 94-142 remained uncertain. It was too soon to tell, and it remained to be seen, what long range effects the law would have on deaf children.

National Center for Law and the Deaf

In October 1975 the National Center for Law and the Deaf was established as part of the Public Service Program at Gallaudet College. The Center was sponsored jointly by the National Law Center of George Washington University and Gallaudet College and funded in part by a grant from the Department of Health, Education, and Welfare. The Center is a walk-in legal clinic for deaf people. It works for better legislation for deaf people, challenges court rulings and conducts legal rights workshops dealing with police, landlord-tenant relations, consumer protection and other matters. Sy Dubow, a lawyer who specialized in public interest law, was hired as the Center's first legal director.

Within two years the Center had handled more than 300 cases. Noted one legal assistant, Liz Rennant: "More problems stem from communication failure than from outright discrimination." The existence of the NCLD encouraged a number of deaf students to enter law school. By 1980 there were 20 deaf students in law schools around the country.

Some legislation the Center supported or assisted in getting enacted included laws guaranteeing deaf people interpreters in state courts. By 1980 the NCLD reported that 48 states had some form of an interpreter law. The NCLD was involved in persuading the Federal Communications Commission to require television networks to include visual warnings in their emergency broadcasts. NCLD was successful in getting a change in the copyright law which permits educational institutions to reproduce television programs for captioning purposes. Staff members at the Center have been working on legislation and with public utility companies to get reduced telephone rates and better services for teletypewriter users. The Center was successful in fighting a Maryland ruling that would have required an interpreter to disclose information a deaf client had given his attorney. NCLD staff members plan legal workshops around the country to educate deaf people regarding their rights and work with members of the legal profession to make them more aware of the needs of deaf people and the problems they encounter in a legal setting.

In the summer of 1976 the members of the National Association of the Deaf voted to establish a Legal Defense Fund. The purpose of this fund is to have an impact on litigation on behalf of deaf people in fighting discrimination in areas of employment, education, social services, etc. The lawyer for the NAD Legal Defense Fund works closely with the National Center for Law and the Deaf staff.

Deaf Ph.D.s

The earliest known deaf American to earn a doctoral degree was Gideon E. Moore. He apparently suffered progressive deafness as a youth, and by the time he was 18 years old he was totally deaf. He attended the Bartlett School, a private school for deaf and hearing children in New York, and went on to Yale University where he graduated with honors in 1861. He entered Heidelberg University in Germany to study philosophy and chemistry. It was reported in *The Nation* that Moore was the first American to earn a Ph.D. *summa cum laude* from that university, no mean feat. On his return to this country he became a very successful chemist and assayer. (Moore had a younger deaf brother, Henry Humphrey, who became a successful artist.)

Once handicapped people have been accepted as citizens who are not different from any other person except that they have a greater challenge in life, we would see our handicapped friends move into a new world which holds them in high respect and which offers the dignity which they rightly deserve.

—DR. EDWARD C. MERRILL, JR.

I think we perceive among educators, rehabilitation personnel, and government people a developing sense of acceptance and attentiveness to what the NAD is seeking for the deaf population. This is evidenced by increasing involvement of deaf persons in affairs which concern ourselves.

—MERVIN D. GARRETSON

Edwin G. Nies became the second deaf person on record, and the first Gallaudet graduate, to earn a doctorate. Deafened in early childhood by spinal meningitis, Nies was educated at the Lexington School for the Deaf in New York City. Following graduation from Gallaudet College in 1911, he entered the University of Pennsylvania Dental School where he received his Doctor of Dental Surgery degree in 1914. He was a dentist for many years and, in later life, he became an Episcopal priest.

The Gallaudet Almanac, published in 1974, lists 23 deaf Americans who have earned the doctoral degree. (A "Deaf Ph.D." is defined as a person who was deaf at the time the degree was earned. The amount of hearing, of course, varies from individual to individual, but most individuals listed have little or no usable hearing.) Many others have earned a doctorate since the original list was compiled in 1974. (A current list of deaf doctoral degree holders appears in Appendix A.)

In 1938 Latham Breunig, a graduate of the Clarke School for the Deaf, earned a Ph.D. in chemistry at Johns Hopkins University. Breunig holds the distinction of being the first deaf president of the Alexander Graham Bell Association.

In 1952 James C. Marsters and Donald L. Ballantyne joined the list. Marsters earned his D.D.S. at New York University. He is a successful orthodontist in Pasadena, California. Ballantyne, who has been deaf since birth, earned his Ph.D. in biology at the Catholic University of America. Today he is professor of Experimental Surgery and chief of the Microsurgical Research and Training Laboratories at New York University. Richard E. Thompson, a Clarke School for the Deaf product, earned his Ph.D. at Boston University in 1964; the following year Thomas Mayes joined the list with a degree in Adult Education from Michigan State University. In 1969, Richard M. Phillips became the third Gallaudet graduate to earn a doctorate. Phillips majored in student personnel at the University of Maryland.

Deaf lawyers have appeared on the American scene since the early 1880s. Guilbert C. Braddock mentions

Deaf Persons with earned doctorates.

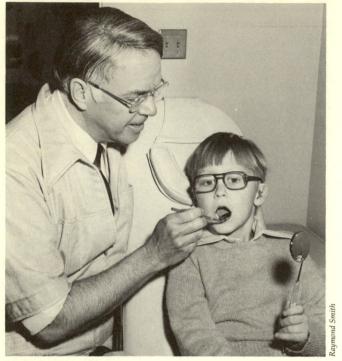

James C. Marsters

Raymond Smith

Robert R. Davila

Peter Moran/MSSD

William J. A. Marshall

MSSD

Steven K. Chough

Walter H. Wettschreck

Gerilee Gustason

Charles Shoup/Gallaudet Today

George Propp

Charles Shoup/Gallaudet Today

Richard M. Phillips

Charles Shoup/Gallaudet College

Donald L. Ballantyne

Rosa M. Razaboni, M.D.

400

Harvey J. Corson

Victor H. Galloway

Robert J. Lillie

T. Alan Hurwitz

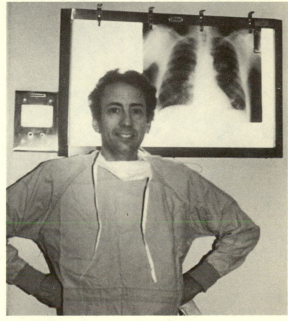

Nancy Kensicki

Frank Hochman

Malcolm J. Norwood

Edward Corbett

Thomas A. Mayes

401

Lowell J. Myers and Donald Lang.

four early deaf lawyers in his book, *Notable Deaf Persons:* Joseph G. Parkinson, Theodore A. Grady, Serrett Gittings, and W. S. Smith. James E. Gallagher, author of *Representative Deaf Persons,* names another, a New Yorker named Godfogle. Another deaf person, who was reported to have entered the legal profession in New York City, was William S. Abrams, deafened at six years of age and educated at the New York School for the Deaf (Fanwood). He was called "The Deaf and Dumb Lawyer," not a very complimentary title, but no doubt not the first one in that profession to be so called. A newspaper account tells about a deaf lawyer named N. B. Lutes who appeared before the Ohio Supreme Court to argue a case against the Tiffin National Bank. He is said to have lipread his wife during the proceedings. No mention, however, is made of any of the above persons earning a law degree.

Lowell J. Myers, who gained nation-wide attention for his legal work with Donald Lang, earned his law

degree at John Marshall Law School in 1956. Myers is the author of *The Law and The Deaf* published in 1964. John D. Randolph, a Gallaudet graduate, earned his law degree at Georgetown University Law School in 1960. In 1977, Robert Mather, a National Technical Institute of the Deaf graduate, earned his Juris Doctor degree at DePaul University.

During the 1970s the number of deaf persons earning doctorates in this country tripled, and there were more degree-recipients during that decade alone than during the previous ten decades. In 1972, 11 persons earned degrees—more than in any other single year.

In 1962, Raphael I. M. Price, who has been hard of hearing since birth, earned his M.D. at Jefferson Medical College. He is a plastic surgeon. Nansie Sharpless earned her Ph.D. in biochemistry at Wayne State University in 1970. An Oberlin College graduate, she became deaf when she was 14 years old. The first Gallaudet alumna to earn a doctorate was Betty G. Miller who received her Doctor of Education in Art Education degree at Penn State University in 1976.

John Schroedel, one of five deaf graduates to earn a doctorate at New York University, did so with distinction. He majored in sociology. The other NYU graduates include Allen Sussman (1973), Frank Bowe (1976), Robert L. Harris (1976), and Barbara Brauer (1979).

Six deaf persons who have earned doctorates come from other countries: Suleiman Bushnaq is from Trans-Jordan; Chuzo Okuda is from Japan; Peter Mba, Seth Tetteh-Ocloo, and James C. Agazie are from Nigeria; and Steven K. Chough is from South Korea.

Harvey Corson received his doctorate in Special Education at the University of Cincinnati in 1973. In 1977 he was named superintendent of the Louisiana School for the Deaf becoming one of the first prelingually deafened persons to become head of a residential school for the deaf in recent times.

Malcolm J. Norwood, Chief of Media Services and Captioned Films, U.S. Office of Education, picked up two degrees within a four-year period. He was awarded an honorary Doctor of Laws degree by Gallaudet College in 1972, and he earned a doctorate in Instructional Technology at the University of Maryland in 1976.

Robert R. Davila and Ronald E. Nomeland took advantage of a program for educators of the deaf offered by the U.S. Office of Education at Syracuse University. Davila earned his Ph.D. in Educational Technology in 1972 and Nomeland followed in 1973.

In 1979 Edward E. Corbett, a 1963 graduate of Gallaudet College, became the first deaf person to receive a doctorate from Gallaudet's new program in Special Education Administration.

Many of those persons earning degrees in the 1970s were recipients of financial assistance from the Gallaudet College Alumni Association Graduate Fellowship Fund. Established as a permanent endowment fund in 1968 with money raised by the Gallaudet alumni and their friends for the Gallaudet College Centennial Fund, this fellowship has given out over $100,000 in grants to doctoral degree candidates since.

The White House Conference

The White House Conference on Handicapped Individuals met at the Sheraton Park Hotel the week of May 23, 1977 to assess the problems and potentials of disabled Americans, generate a national awareness toward these individuals, and make recommendations to the President and the Congress which, if implemented, would enable handicapped individuals "to live their lives independently with dignity, and with full participation in community life to the greatest degree possible." The conference attracted close to 3,000 persons.

Approximately 800 of the delegates were themselves disabled. Coming from throughout the United States, they represented the 35 million American citizens who are handicapped. They were selected from more than 100,000 individuals who had participated in earlier state and regional conferences. Out of these conferences came a total of 24,000 recommendations from which 3,521 were selected for inclusion in the final conference report.

Over 50 hearing impaired delegates and 28 alternates participated in the conference. They were, according to Don G. Pettingill, one of the "most visible and positive groups present." Pettingill, who is deaf himself, was the logistics specialist for the conference and a liaison for the deaf participants on loan from the Gallaudet College Center for Continuing Education.

President Jimmy Carter addressed the participants at the closing session and at the end of his speech he signed "God bless you."

Deaf Jurors

Early in November, 1978, Sheldon Freedman, a deaf resident of Beverly, Massachusetts, was requested to appear for possible jury duty in the superior court in Lawrence. He appeared at the courthouse on the appointed day knowing that deaf persons were not se-

I am tired of meeting teachers of the deaf who do not know how to sign and who cannot understand what their students are saying. If I were preparing to teach in a German school, I would want to be sure I knew German.
—DR. GEORGE DETMOLD

lected as jurors but eager to prove that a deaf person was fully capable of serving on the jury. He took an interpreter with him.

To his surprise, no objections were raised to his serving on the jury because of his deafness. The judge did all he could to make Freedman comfortable as a member of the jury pool from which jurors are selected, and lawyers on both sides agreed that they would not challenge him because of his deafness.

Freedman's name was drawn from the pool and he became the ninth juror. The attorneys agreed to his selection and the judge moved him to the 14th chair so that he would have a better view of the courtroom and could see his interpreter, who sat just outside the jury box, better.

The court was all set to hear a motor vehicle accident case when the attorneys agreed on a settlement out of court and the case was dismissed. Freedman had come close to becoming the first known deaf juror to sit on a case.

In August 1979, John G. O'Brien, of Bellevue, Washington, was summoned for jury duty in a criminal case in Seattle, Washington. He jumped at the chance to serve. Like Freedman, he saw it as an opportunity to prove that a deaf person with a qualified interpreter could serve competently as a jurist. He was delighted when Judge T. Patrick Corbett agreed to furnish him with an interpreter and neither the prosecutor nor the attorney for the defense objected

A national conference on Scouting was held at the Model Secondary School for the Deaf in Washington, D.C. in 1979.

403

The main objective of SPECTRUM'S First Annual Focus on Deaf Artists Conference was to meet with deaf artists once again to re-evaluate the goals and aspirations and gain new direction according to the deaf artists' desires and needs. The Conference was held at beautiful Laos House near Lake Travis at Austin, Texas, from July 11 to 17, 1976.

THE LAOS HOUSE – FIRST SLEEPING UNIT

THE LAOS HOUSE – W JACK LEWIS LODGE

A new sign for SPECTRUM – FOCUS ON D
Conference experience inspired Doroth

IN ATTENDANCE

ELISABETH KRUSMARK
Austin, Texas
DOROTHY S. MILES
Northridge, California
JANE WILK
Washington, D. C.
TOMMIE RADFORD
Placeville, California
JOHN D. SMITH
San Francisco, California
SANDI NORRIS
Seabrook, Maryland
GEORGETTE DORAN
Washington, D. C.

ELIZABETH BAIRD
Newark, Delaware
CHARLES BAIRD
Newark, Delaware
CLARENCE RUSSELL, Jr.
Crofton, Maryland
JUAN HOFFMAN
Austin, Texas
PATRICK GRAYBILL
Waterford, Connecticut
DUANE HUGHES
Longview, Texas
BETTY G. MILLER
Washington, D. C.
(Co-Director, SPECTRUM)

and the following hearing:

NANCY CONNORS
Washington, D. C.
(interpreter)
PAT McMAHON
Austin, Texas
(Admin. Asst., SPECTRUM)
ELIZABETH T. YNDO
Austin, Texas
(Co-Director, SPECTRUM)
JANETTE NORMAN
Austin, Texas
(Co-Director, SPECTRUM)

Dot Miles, Tommie Radford, John D. Smith, Clarence Russell

Janette Norman, Pat McMahon, Chuck Baird

We began the first evening with an informal get-acquainted party followed the next morning with a brief introduction and report from the SPECTRUM Board of Directors. Each Director gave her background and how she became involved with SPECTRUM – FOCUS ON DEAF ARTISTS. A slide presentation showing the history of SPECTRUM accompanied the introduction. That afternoon was a successful attempt to harmonize the group with an "Art Therapy" Workshop led by hearing professional Myrna Baird.

Myrna Baird, Elisabeth Krusmark, Gigi Doran, Betty Miller

Clarence Russell, Sandi Norris, Elizabeth Baird

Patrick Graybill

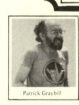

John Smith, Juan Hoffman

The Cook: Ruth Taylor

Nancy Connors, Chuck Baird, Myrna Baird

Elizabeth Baird, Gigi Doran, Dot Miles, Elizabeth Yndo

SPECTRUM
FOCUS ON DEAF ARTISTS

Illustrations by:
Betty G. Miller
& Pat McMahon
Photography by:
Butch Hancock
Layout by:
Elizabeth T. Yndo
Typography by:
Lane DeCamp

SPECTRUM Newsletter. October Issue. Vol. 1, No. 3.
SPECTRUM, Box 339, Austin, Texas 78767. Home Office at
611 "C" West 9th Street, Austin, Texas.
Phone (512) 472-2678 (Voice or TTY).
Directors: Betty Miller, Janette Norman, & Elizabeth T. Yndo
1976.

A "Consciousness of Abilities and Desires" Workshop was led by Betty G. Miller. Betty did field research in this area for her doctorate degree in Art Education. Junius Johnson generously donated his time and talent to the videotaping of Betty's session and the artists' interviews, which took place the following two mornings. These videotapes will become a permanent part of the SPECTRUM Video Tape Library.

Sandi Norris, Betty Miller, Elizabeth Baird, Tommie Radford, Gigi Doran

Junius Johnsto

Spectrum, Focus on Deaf Artists was started during the decade.

w out of our mutual sharing. The sign and the
s poem for signing and perform it for us.

SPECTRUM

Colors,
pure colors,
red, orange
 yellow, green
  blue
   purple deep, purple light —
each one alone
beautiful, strong and free —
 merge,
 blend,
into a clear
 white
 light,
shining that we may see
 the Sign.

Thus
let us unite —
each one alone a color
beautiful, strong and free —
join hands
finger by finger
blending
into a clear
 new
 light . . . .

 dark
errors, misunderstandings,
jealousies, frustrations
receding from
the light of our world,
 shining
that we may understand
 the Signs.

  Dorothy Miles
  July 13, 1976

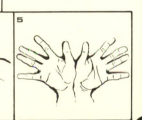

Juan Hoffman

Elisabeth Krusmark

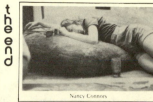

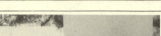

the end

Nancy Connors

he Workshop was followed by a reception for the Austin Community. This was the last formal activity, though a few people stayed on to visit and help with SPECTRUM. Everyone agreed that the Conference was very productive and a wonderful sharing experience. We are all looking forward to the next opportunity to come together again.

PATRICK GRAYBILL, from the National Theatre of the Deaf, led an Afternoon Workshop on Writing and Poetry, working with improvised exercises and inspirational "games." He also led a Children's Workshop, assisted by John D. Smith, his puppet 'Zela,' Chuck Baird & Juan Hoffman.

Chuck Baird & Patrick Graybill with workshop participants

John D. Smith with Zela and Patrick Graybill

Jane Wilks

The Newsletter

Early the next morning a work session began, discussion the function, style, and direction of the newsletter was an important instrument for keeping the Deaf Artists in touch with each other and that even though the actual printing will be done in Austin, different people from other parts of the country would take over writing and layout from time to time.

It also stated that a high standard of professionalism should be maintained in the photography, text, and illustrations. Several very good suggestions about content were given. One of those was for a special section for questions and answers.

Special Notice!

In the future, if you have any questions, problems, information you want to share with other artists or the SPECTRUM staff, send it to SPECTRUM — F.O.D.A. Newsletter, P. O. Box 339, Austin, Texas 78767.

Be sure to write on your letter permission for us to print it. Any other items or articles you'd like printed or wouldn't mind us printing should also have permission on them.

The discussion then moved on to the specific projects proposed for carrying out the Goals and Aspirations. The budget for each activity was looked at and discussed and priorities set that would later be made into resolutions at the Board of Directors meeting. This meeting was held July 16th.

SPECTRUM Priorities

FIRST, Do everything possible to engage DINI & Associates for the purpose of successfully funding SPECTRUM's present and future projects.

SECOND, The following projects are to be carried out concurrently:

Seek funding for the purpose of buying land which will be used as an investment under the guidance of a professional financial advisor until such time in the future that SPECTRUM — F.O.D.A. is prepared to build a permanent Arts Center and home office.

Procure the funds to bring Yacov Sharir to the United States and establish a professional company of deaf dancers, performances of which shall also be used to attract the interest of possible funding sources.

Expand current office staff and activities as a functioning professional deaf artists' clearinghouse, a sound base for administrating and coordinating future projects, and for continued production and growth of the SPECTRUM Newsletter.

THIRD, The following projects are to be carried out concurrently:

Implementation of the expanded Videotape Project, whose team members (with the exception of the road manager) will be deaf. The project will include selection and training of a video technical team, an interviewer, and a road manager.

Conduct annual SPECTRUM workshops for professional deaf artists.

FOURTH, Establish an artist-in-residence program in the form of workshops and classes to be conducted for children and students at Laguna Gloria or some other available facility.

FIFTH, Initiate a touring art show with the assistance of a major museum, the contents of which shall not be limited to visual arts but may include such things as videotapes of performing arts, visual deaf literature, and any other art form deemed feasible for travel.

Tommie Radford, Dot Miles, Charles Harker, Nancy Connors

Bernard "Tad" Lachowick, Tom Foster

Rainbow

Wednesday, July 14th, the deaf artists were presented lectures and discussions by the following people:
Wayne Gronquist, SPECTRUM Attorney.
Jim Roberson, SPECTRUM Accountant.
Tom Foster, owner of T.V. Images.
Sha Barr, representing the proposed Children's Project at Camp Trail.

The afternoon of July 13th, Charles Harker, the artist-architect of TAO Design Group, led a discussion which included tours of two of his unusual curvilinear structures and a film and slide presentation of the design & building process. The presentation was followed by a group discussion on the effect of movement in form on the deaf person. TAO Design Group is planning extensive research on psychology of space in the future and was very excited about this opportunity. The lecture was creatively interpreted by Dorothy Miles and Nancy Connors.

Exterior view, Earth House

Jim Roberson, Sha Barr

Wayne Gromquist, Nancy Connors

to his serving. The case involved a 22-year-old man charged with selling marijuana to an undercover man. O'Brien had no trouble participating in the deliberations and some jurors thought that the discussions were more orderly because of his presence. The case resulted in acquittal.

O'Brien's service as a deaf juror attracted the attention of the local media. A *Seattle Post-Intelligencer* editorial called it a victory for all deaf people, ". . . he has won a major battle in the war to secure for the deaf the privileges that the rest of us take for granted." A local weekly newspaper, however, opposed O'Brien's selection as a juror. It objected to the extra expense of hiring an interpreter, and questioned the qualifications of a deaf person to serve on jury duty. Said the *Seattle Sun:* "There are all kinds of things that deaf persons cannot do and it seems to us that jury duty, regrettably, is one of them."

Following the trial, O'Brien, who had previously been rejected for jury duty three times, was selected "Citizen of the Day" on August 30, 1979, in recognition of his contribution to the community.

In Oakland, California, Charles Beck, a graduate of St. Mary's School in Buffalo, New York, and a California resident, was summoned for jury duty but dismissed when it was found that he was deaf. Beck protested the discrimination and decided to fight the decision. He enlisted the help of the Deaf Counseling, Advocacy, and Referral Agency in Oakland and filed

a discrimination suit. The result was that the lawyers on both sides agreed to allow Beck to serve on the jury, accompanied by an interpreter.

Beck took his seat on the jury on October 25, 1979, to hear a case in which an Oakland man was to go to trial for soliciting a prostitute. The man was acquitted.

Homes for Elderly Deaf Persons

Three homes for elderly deaf citizens were constructed during the decade. Pilgrim Towers, a high-rise apartment building, was constructed in 1972 in Los Angeles, California. It offered apartments for the elderly at prices ranging from $77.50 to $121.50 a month.

In 1973 Tanya Towers, a project supported by the New York Society of the Deaf, opened in New York City.

Near the end of the decade another apartment building for deaf residents was completed in Westerville, Ohio. Comprising 107 units of one- and two-bedrooms, the building is the first of a three-phase apartment-nursing home complex called Columbus

John G. O'Brien serving on jury duty in Seattle, Washington.

John Holmberg

Columbus Colony in Westerville, Ohio.

Colony. This project, sponsored by the Ohio School for the Deaf Alumni Association, is eventually expected to accommodate 500 persons. Billed as the nation's first community for deaf, deaf-blind, and deaf-multihandicapped, the complex was formally dedicated on August 24 and 25, 1980.

The Gee Jay Show

The Gee Jay Show is about the closest thing to a deaf vaudeville show the deaf community has seen in recent years. It started out as the George Johnston Show, but Gary Olsen and Jr. National Association of the Deaf campers at Swan Lake Lodge in Pengilly, Minnesota, began referring to it as the Gee Jay (for G. J.) Show and the name stuck. The Gee Jay Show is a variety show consisting of slapstick humor, deaf jokes and skits, pantomimes, and dances. Songs with rhythmic beats are selected so that the mostly deaf audiences can join in with handclapping or foot stomping. The hour-and-a-half-long program usually climaxes with a special effect song rendition in which, for example, Johnston signs in silhouette behind a lighted screen. His show is very popular with deaf high school students and has a special appeal to many deaf audiences.

Most of Johnston's material is original and has been developed around the lives of deaf people. It identifies, satirizes, or pokes fun at the problems, contradictions, misconceptions, and ironies of deafness. His purpose is both to entertain and to teach.

Even schools do not escape Johnston's barbs as he performs, for example, a skit in which a deaf man meets a returning prisoner of war.

"You far, far jail?" inquires Johnston.

"Yes," nods the POW.

"You eat, eat, stink, lousy? How long?" asks Johnston.

"Yes," responds the POW, and holds up three fingers to indicate three years.

"Me same!" says Johnston. "Me 10 years deaf school!"

Skits are kept short and each has a punch line. Stage curtains are not used and one act follows another at a fast clip. All titles are displayed on placards. Johnston also likes to incorporate local talent or individuals into his act to give the presentation some local flavor.

407

George Johnston performing "Johnny B. Goode" at the Jr. NAD Camp in Pengilly, Minnesota.

One such local performer went on to establish his own one-man show. Johnston sees his show as an "everyday" thing. "Sometimes I see a joke or something absurd happen in life involving deafness and I put it into a skit." This is how his satire on oralism was developed. The scene opens in a home where the father of a deaf daughter, a strong oral advocate, repeatedly admonishes his daughter to speak and warns her never to use signs. Then, the father gets dressed and goes to work. His job? That of a football referee where he spends all afternoon signing: "Offside!"; "Clipping!"; "Interference!"; "Illegal Motion!", etc.

Another act may be a poke at deafness. Acting as a healer, Johnston sticks his finger in a deaf man's ear where, for comical effect, it becomes stuck. After a struggle, he finally gets his finger out and realizes that he has successfully restored the deaf man's hearing . . . only to leave him blind. Another may be that old, old favorite of deaf audiences where a deaf couple go to the movies and end up laughing or weeping at the wrong time much to the aggravation of those hearing persons around them.

Johnston has appeared on Dave Garroway's television program and on a David Brinkley Special. He has performed before national and state associations, clubs of the deaf, during sporting events, and at schools for the deaf. He has been a repeat performer at the Jr. NAD Camp. He has been met by a crowd at an airport, received standing ovations, been kissed and hugged by complete strangers, and received requests for repeat performances. Parents of deaf children have told him that he has opened their eyes.

George W. Johnston became deaf at the age of five years from scarlet fever. He graduated from the New Jersey School for the Deaf and Gallaudet College. While in college he won two best actor awards and was the first recipient of the Most Versatile Actor Award given by the college. He holds a master's degree in education from Catholic University and has completed all course work towards a doctorate in special education at the University of Cincinnati. A consultant with the Jersey City Board of Education, he resides in Plainfield, New Jersey, with his wife and two children.

Today, the imagination, the strength, and the relevance of Gallaudet College come largely from deaf people—the Gallaudet Legacy, if you will—who serve on the Board of Directors, in the administration, on the faculty of the College, and in almost every sector of our society.

—DR. EDWARD C. MERRILL, JR.

Milestones

Alice Jane McVan (1906-1970) was a researcher for 36 years at the Hispanic Society of America in New York City. She wrote numerous translations of Spanish poems and articles on Spanish subjects. A collection of her original poetry was published in 1953 under the title, *Tryst*. A second book, a study of Spain's major poets, entitled *Antonio Machado,* followed in 1959. Co-workers at the Hispanic Society and friends presented a bronze and glass display case to the Gallaudet College Library following her death. They requested that it be used to display works of deaf persons, a fitting tribute to the creative person that Alice Jane McVan was.

Dr. Harry Best (1880-1971), a hearing man, was the author of *Deafness and the Deaf in the United States* and about a dozen other books. He earned three master's degrees (one from Gallaudet College), a PhD, and a law degree. He was the recipient of three honorary degrees (one from Gallaudet College). A graduate of Centre College in Danville, Kentucky, locale of the Kentucky School for the Deaf, he taught in schools for the deaf in Nebraska, Washington, Alabama, and New York. He taught at the University of Kentucky for many years and was professor emeritus of Sociology at the time of his death on February 23, 1971.

Elizabeth English Benson (1904-1972) was the hearing daughter of deaf parents. Becoming a teacher of the deaf was a natural move for her. She joined the

Ben M. Schowe
(1894-1979)

Shortly after graduation from Gallaudet College, Ben M. Schowe joined Firestone Rubber and Tire Co. in Akron, Ohio, and began a career that would stretch over 40 years. He was hired as a placement officer responsible for recruiting deaf workers and became a labor economist and labor research specialist while retaining his responsibility for interviewing, placing, and counseling deaf employees. His experience in this work made him an authority on employment and the deaf worker. Schowe gave lectures and wrote extensively on this subject. Many of his articles received wide circulation. His writing appeared in *Factory Management and Maintenance, Employment Security Review*, and other publications. He wrote "Guidelines for the Employment of Deaf Workers," "The Deaf at Work," "Deaf Workers on the Home Front," and other articles that contributed to the removal of employment barriers for deaf people. His work was featured in "Successful Careers Out of Gallaudet College" in 1955.

Schowe was very active in organizations of the deaf. He was a member of the National Fraternal Society of the Deaf for 60 years and a leader in its Akron Division. He wrote a historical booklet for the NFSD. He was a member of the board of managers of Ohio's Home for the Aged and Infirm Deaf. He was president of the Gallaudet College Alumni Association from 1945 to 1950. During his administration, the Association became more involved with the college and began publication of the *Gallaudet Alumni Bulletin*.

As chairman of the National Association of the Deaf Industrial Committee, he was successful in getting the Works Progress Administration to rescind its refusal to hire deaf workers, and he persuaded a large insurance company to reconsider its policy of refusing to insure deaf employees, thus denying them employment, on a war-time government project in Missouri.

Born in Columbus, Indiana, Ben Marshall Schowe suffered progressive deafness during his youth. His hearing got worse as he got older and resulted in many embarrassing moments. He continued in public school until his second year in high school, received private tutoring, took correspondence courses, and attended, for one year, a small Virginia college, before transferring to Gallaudet College. He arrived on Kendall Green, in his own words, "a demoralized 19-year-old who knew no signs." He found life on the campus, however, "a real balm for my troubled soul." He was a very active undergraduate student. During his senior year, he was active in his fraternity, head senior, editor of the student publication, and president of the student athletic association. He graduated from Gallaudet in 1918.

Schowe saw himself as a maverick. He did not hesitate to disagree and speak his mind, often finding himself on the opposite side from the majority. He was a strong advocate for equal employment opportunities for deaf people at equal pay, and he resented the movement that would give deaf people an extra tax exemption. He saw it as a "degrading confession of weakness."

Schowe was appointed to the President's Committee on the Employment of the Physically Handicapped in 1959. He remained active in retirement and continued to write. His book, *Identity Crisis in Deafness*, was published in 1979, shortly before his death. Gallaudet College awarded him an honorary degree in 1951. He was an honorary member of the Conference of Executives of American Schools for the Deaf, and, in 1974, the Gallaudet College Alumni Association presented him its Laurent Clerc Award which recognizes outstanding contributions of a deaf person in the interests of deaf people.

Ben M. Schowe was married to a college classmate, Dorothy Conover. They had one son. Ben, Jr., who also has a hearing impairment, and is a teacher of the deaf. Schowe died on September 26, 1979, two days short of his 86th birthday, following a stroke and a long illness.

Gallaudet College faculty in 1926 and became dean of women in 1950. Her association with Gallaudet lasted 44 years. She was regarded as one of the most proficient interpreters of the deaf in the United States, and she was one of the founders of the Registry of Interpreters for the Deaf. She interpreted for such notables as President John F. Kennedy, President Lyndon B. Johnson, Francis Cardinal Spellman, J. Edgar Hoover, and many other well-known persons. She was a member of the Women's Army Corps, and during World War II she worked with deafened soldiers. In recognition of this service, a dormitory at the U.S. Army Medical Training Center at Ft. Sam Houston is named for her. A residence hall on the Gallaudet College campus is also named after her. Her parents, Harry and Minnie Benson, were teachers at the Maryland School for the Deaf. A gymnasium at MSD is named for her father. Her sister, Mary, was also a teacher of the deaf.

A penny postcard changed his life. As a youth, Norman C. Scarvie (1901-1973) suffered progressive deafness. The son of a minister, he considered himself a "cursed son of a servant of God," and he avoided people rather than endure their shouting. He led a lonely youth and spent much of his time in the northeastern Iowa woods hunting and trapping animals and mounting them. One day he received a postcard from J. Schuyler Long, the principal of the Iowa School for the Deaf. Long had learned of Scarvie's deafness and had written to invite the young man to enroll at ISD and prepare for matriculation to Gallaudet College. Scarvie had never heard of either school, but with his mother's encouragement he decided to forgo a winter of solo trapping in Minnesota and give school a try. Following his graduation from Gallaudet, he returned to ISD where he built a career as a distinguished educator. Hired first as a teacher, in 1943 he was promoted to vocational principal, becoming the second ISD graduate to become a principal. The first person was J. Schuyler Long—the man who had sent him that penny postcard.

Robert W. Horgen (1908-1979) was part-time director of the Wisconsin Association of the Deaf State Service Bureau from 1950 to 1971 and an employee of Madison Newspaper, Inc. for 35 years. As director of the bureau he edited the Association's publication, *The W.A.D. Pilot*, published a brochure on deaf workers, and undertook a special study of Wisconsin's rehabilitation problems associated with deafness. He served on the Governor's Committee of the Physically Handicapped, was a board member of HEAR, Inc., and a member of the State Advisory Board on the Education of the Deaf. He was an advisor to state

...all persons interested in the welfare of deaf citizens should endeavor . . . to develop policies which acknowledge deaf people as individuals and citizens, which insure their proper involvement in matters which affect their welfare as well as those of the common good, and which enable them to act on their constitutional rights.

—DR. EDWARD C. MERRILL, JR.

rehabilitation, education, employment, and welfare departments. Horgen was also very active in church and community affairs of the deaf. He died July 5, 1979.

Advertisements and announcements like this one appeared in the national press during the 1970s.

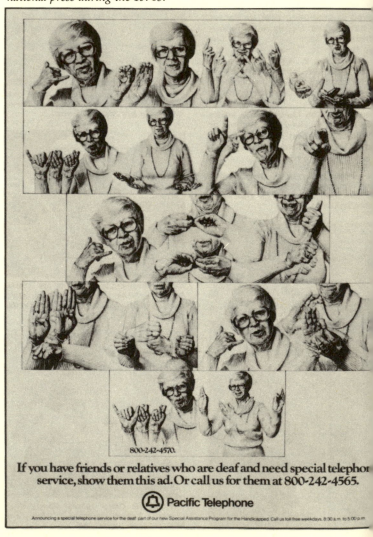

800-242-4570.

If you have friends or relatives who are deaf and need special telephone service, show them this ad. Or call us for them at 800-242-4565.

Pacific Telephone

Announcing a special telephone service for the deaf, part of our new Special Assistance Program for the Handicapped. Call us toll free weekdays, 8:30 a.m. to 5:00 p.m.

Deaf Like Me
Thomas S. Spradley and
James P. Spradley
Random House, New York 1978

In *Deaf Like Me*, parents, Thomas and Louise Spradley, tell of the nightmares they lived through upon learning that, while pregnant, Louise had been exposed to German measles. They are finally relieved of the anguish of waiting, hoping, and praying when their healthy daughter arrives. As time passes they begin to note, however, that something is wrong and their earlier worries and anxiety return. Finally they learn that their daughter, Lynn, is deaf. This discovery begins a long search for professional help to teach Lynn to talk and lipread, a route so many parents of deaf children, have taken. The Spradleys are led to the John Tracy Clinic in Los Angeles and begin faithfully following the pure oral approach. Talk, talk, talk to your child, they are told, and you will be rewarded one day, with speech, in return. So they talk and talk and talk to Lynn. They work with her faithfully, religiously. They do everything they are told, and more. They make every effort to help Lynn grasp the fundamentals of speech. But, Lynn does not talk back as spontaneously as they have been led to believe she will. The parents are cautioned that they must have patience . . . that it takes some deaf children longer to learn speech than others. Patience. If they persist, they are reminded, they will be rewarded. Doubts and anguish begin to set in when their daughter becomes frustrated at her inability to make herself understood. An emergency trip to the hospital when Lynn develops a case of spinal men-

ingitis makes the parents begin to realize that they have no means of communicating with their daughter, no way to share with her information about her illness, or to tell her why she must stay in the hospital. By chance, the father sees a deaf family on one of his visits to the hospital. He observes how freely they are communicating in sign language. Doubts again begin to set in.

While attending a parent-teacher meeting, called to look into the possibility of introducing a sign language class at their pure oral school, the father sees, for the first time, a postlingual deaf person speak and sign si-

multaneously. He begins to realize the enormity of the expectations he and his wife have placed on their small daughter to learn *their* spoken language. The Spradleys begin to question their right to deny their daughter the use of *her* native language—sign language.

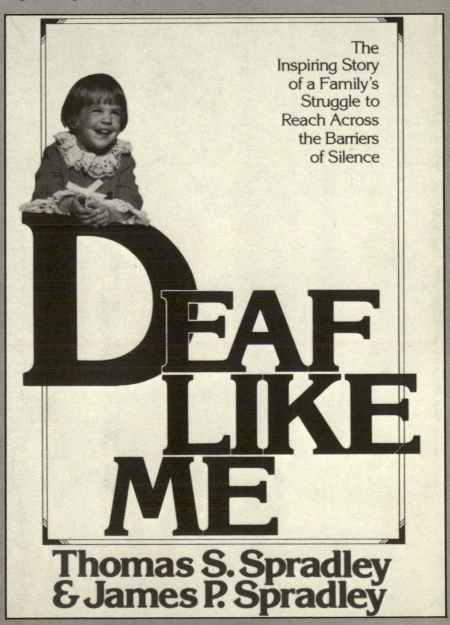

The
Inspiring Story
of a Family's
Struggle to
Reach Across
the Barriers
of Silence

DEAF LIKE ME

Thomas S. Spradley & James P. Spradley

The parents meet with a deaf couple, their interpreter, and the parents of another deaf child who have given up on the pure oral method and have learned sign language. Thomas Spradley is surprised that the deaf adult who spoke so well at the PTA meeting has difficulty lipreading him. And, for the first time, Spradley experiences the feeling of being left out when those around him converse in sign. He begins to understand how his daughter has felt in family gatherings, at the table, and on the many camping trips they have taken when she was completely shut off from the family conversations. Finally, the Spradleys decide to give sign language a try. They are amazed at the speed with which their daughter and hearing son, Bruce, learn sign language. Within three days mother and daughter have communicated to each other and understood those three magic words, "I love you," for the first time in their lives.

Sign language opens up a new world for them . . . a happier world . . . a world of reality, one they can accept.

The Spradleys have discovered the world of the deaf. They have come in out of the darkness. They no longer hold the false hope that some day their child will talk and lipread so well that she will fit effortlessly into the hearing world as they have been led to believe she would. Instead, they have discovered *her* world, the real world of the deaf, and by learning to communicate, have accepted it. It is a world where

communication is somewhat different than their own, but a world where a deaf person is recognized and accepted as an individual. Through self-acceptance, a deaf person is better prepared to cope in a hearing world.

Thomas, Louise, Lynn, and Bruce Spradley have finally found the best of both worlds.

Offspring of Deaf Parents

On these pages are but a few of the many children of deaf parents who became successful adults and led distinguished careers.

Owen C. Comp was a lieutenant aboard the U.S.S. Saratoga in the 1920s.

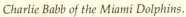
Charlie Babb of the Miami Dolphins.

413

Lon Chaney was a successful actor. He was known as "The Man of a Thousand Faces."

John S. Schuchman, Ph.D., is vice president for academic affairs at Gallaudet College.

Azie Taylor Morton is Treasurer of the United States. Her name appears on our currency.

Winfield McChord, Jr. is one of many sons of deaf parents who have headed a school for the deaf. He is superintendent of the Kentucky School.

Joseph J. Pernick is Chief Judge of Probate in Wayne County, Michigan.

A former Congressman from Texas, Homer Thornberry is Judge of the United States Court of Appeals, Fifth District.

Jim Stangarone is a career opportunities specialist at the National Technical Institute for the Deaf. Here he interprets for Lady Bird Johnson during NTID dedication ceremonies in 1974.

The Reality of Deafness

by Mervin D. Garretson

"The Reality of Deafness" was presented at the International Congress on Education of the Deaf in Hamburg, West Germany, in August, 1980. It appeared in the October, 1980 issue of The Deaf American. *Garretson is past-president of the National Association of the Deaf and special assistant to the president of Gallaudet College. Some excerpts:*

What does it mean to be deaf? What is the reality from within? How does the disability differ from the handicap? Is there a deaf culture? Does the deaf individual perceive the world differently from others? Is information processed visually actually identical to information processed auditorily? Do deaf persons follow "a different drummer"? Are there levels of social deafness? What is the deaf community? Just how much congruence should we expect between a deaf and a hearing person's viewpoint on the meaning of deafness and its ramifications?

Because most researchers do not live with hearing loss minute by minute, situation by situation, 24 hours a day, they do not experience the totality of deafness. Invariably their hypotheses or assumptions are formed from a hearing perspective so that the focus may be on an isolated aspect of deafness rather than a gestaltic whole. Some degree of tunnel vision and myopia may result in a pure-oralist fixation which excludes sign language and other forms of manual communication in favor of an overwhelming emphasis on speech and hearing. Completely disregarded are the felt needs of the deaf person who must cope both in his own circle and with the larger hearing majority.

It is no simple matter to present a composite of every deaf person's views on deafness. In spite of variations and nuances in individual interpretations of "the deaf experience" it may be possible to identify a generally common fabric that has physiological, psychological, and even philosophical significance for most deaf persons, whoever and wherever they may be.

From daybreak when greeted by a flashing light at bedside to the end of the day, each deaf person encounters all kinds of subtle little problems or inconveniences. Some of these incidents may be accepted humorously, but more often they are tolerated with patience and phlegmatism as everyday facts of life.

The nearly 1,000 "hazards" cited by Roy Holcomb (*Hazards of Deafness*, 1977) and others relate to household occurrences, frustrations inherent in traveling—be it by automobile, bus, train, or plane, to problems created by the telephone, TV, radio, hospitals, motels and hotels, elevators, appointments with doctors and dentists, experiences while shopping, ordering in a restaurant, the complexity of handling one's unheard native language with its changing idiom and syntax, the invariable frustrations involved in lipreading, in the attitude of other people, in situations arising from living in a world largely attuned to hearing, and all kinds of other minutiae which make up the realities of day-to-day existence in a world without meaningful sound.

To select at random a number of mundane recurrences: Although we may idly watch the evening news on television we never really know just what was announced until reading about it in the newspaper the next morning. Constantly lagging behind on current news flashes which most people receive on the radio, frequently on their morning drive to work. Un-

---

We need to be able to be what we are and to take pride in our successes and recognize our failures.

—FREDERICK C. SCHREIBER
1970s

---

awareness to the patter of rain until you step outside to go somewhere and perhaps find you've left the car windows down! Not hearing the drip from the kitchen faucet or the stuck toilet flusher and wondering why your water bill is so high. Moving from room to room all over the house seeking your wife because you can't call out to her . . . for those dwelling in three or four-story residences this can beat jogging for exercise!

Not being able to ring your family or friends unless they have a telecommunications device. Reaching a new city and trying to locate a deaf friend in the phone directory. Depending on a neighbor to call your doctor or dentist at the risk of your medical privacy. Wishing to respond to a "for sale" or "job opportunity" classified advertisement which lists only a phone number.

Having to purchase with your new automobile an expensive stereophonic radio which you never hear anyway. Encountering car trouble on the expressway or autobahn and wondering whether you will be understood on the roadside emergency phone. Riding in an automobile with a foursome of hearing friends and wondering about the conversation going on in front or back and all around you. It would be naive to assume that the person sitting next to you is going to mouth everything for your special benefit. The reality is otherwise.

And some of the vicissitudes of air travel. Some airports do not post flight departure and arrival times on closed-circuit TV, and may even have several flights leaving from the same gate, so you have to be on the alert to ensure boarding the right plane at the right time. Even though you notify the desk of your hearing impairment you continue to miss a flight now and then. Not hearing boarding announcements for the smoking or non-smoking section—which group goes first? And even once airborne not everything is smooth sailing (or flying). Announcements from the captain go unheard, and generally you are not even aware they have been made. Ordering cocktails from the stewardess, trying to understand her questions about destination, magazines, or is she offering me a pillow?

Once on the road we learn to forego a number of conveniences that others may take for granted, such as calling room service at the hotel or requesting the desk clerk to wake you up at a certain time. Or notifying the bellhop to take your luggage when checking out. Or more alarming, how does the deaf individual know when there is a fire warning? What if the hotel elevator balks midway between the 29th and 30th floor and you can't use the phone? Some deaf persons simply refuse to step on an elevator unless there are other people on it.

How about sitting in the waiting room of a doctor's crowded office wondering nervously when your name will be announced? And then the difficulty of reading his lips and his impossible hand-scribbling. The problem of ordering in a public restaurant because you are not sure of the noise level of the room and the waiter is unable to understand you. Inevitably you end up by pointing to the menu as one does in a foreign country.

Sitting at a lunch counter in a restaurant oblivious to the request of the stranger next to you for the salt and pepper and leaving the impression you are rude and insensitive. A passerby asks you for directions on the street; questions and conversations are thrown at you on trains and buses, on planes, in the subway, wherever you go. Taking a number in a store or barbershop for service and trying to figure out when your time comes up. Your pockets frequently jangle with change from purchases you have paid for with large bills because you are not sure you understood the exact price quoted by the salesperson.

The difficulties of mastering one's native language with its syntax and idiom, particularly English. Grateful for a community that knows sign language, where you can relax in your own culture and even be perceived as knowledgeable and expert in your own language. But the nagging tendency to feel inferior because it is different from the majority culture.

Running into a childhood friend whom you have learned to lipread quite well and becoming engaged in animated conversation. Another person comes along and soon your friend and the newcomer are talking at a fast clip, leaving you out cold. Attending banquets and large assembly meetings alone, without an interpreter, probably means you will spend the time observing the dress and mannerisms of different people around you or simply seek refuge in daydreams.

Except for a very few amazing lipreaders, usually assisted by a hearing aid, the deaf person soon learns his circle is restricted to close relatives, associates, and people tuned into deafness. Other than that, it's hit or miss. People tend to be misled by the "synthetic" or "intuitive" aspect of lipreading into assuming a great deal more than actually transpires. For example, when a deaf individual is accosted in the street by someone with an unlit cigarette, it's no big deal to figure the request is something like "got a light?" or "got a match?" Or when driving up to the Shell station for petrol, one anticipates such questions as "check your oil?" And at your initial visit to the doctor you are primed for such inquiries as "age?" "name?" "weight?" and "height?" Beyond that you will probably ask him to write down what he is saying.

While all deaf persons certainly recognize the importance of speech and speechreading development as necessary educational components, we soon encounter the limited reality of its application. Learning these skills does not necessarily ensure genuine participation in the mainstream. Definitely useful and desirable, oral skills need to be complemented with manual communication if one is to become a full person with every possible door accessible. Every lipreader faces a number of incontrovertible physical limitations. Speech articulation, for instance, has been measured at the rapid pace of 13 sound movements per second while the human eye can consciously see only eight or nine of these movements. The fact that the average person speaks at a rate of close to 200 words a minute, which is a great deal faster than the pace of a teacher of the deaf. A significant percentage of speech sounds are not visible on the lips, and with look-alike sounds and other problems lipreading becomes a tenuous art. These physical factors are aggravated by other obstacles such as poor lighting, shading and shadows, turning of the head, beards and mustaches, cigarettes and pipes, hand movements across the face, and so on.

Thus the rationale that pure-oral educational approaches prepare the deaf child for integration or mainstreaming into "the hearing world" tends to be something of a myth. As a matter of fact in the United States we are now training oral interpreters as well as manual interpreters. It is not unusual at a national convention, seminar, or forum to have as many as 20 or 30 deaf professionals following a manual interpreter and a couple of deaf adults sitting to one side with an oral interpreter because 1) they are unable to lipread the speaker or follow group discussions, and 2) they do not understand signs.

For these reasons, among others, we believe that the experiences of the deaf adult are important within the context of early education. Too many times parents and teachers tend to overlook the fact that a deaf child grows up into a deaf adult. Education of the hearing child is naturally geared to the needs of the adult hearing community. Strange as it may seem, education of the deaf has long centered around a concept of continuing childhood and the immediate desires of the parents. The reality is that the child will not long remain a child and eventually will confront adult needs and problems as a deaf person unless some miracle restores his hearing.

Most of us tend to separate deafness into two levels, the physiological and the psychological. The first relates to the simple fact of not hearing, to the disability itself. Because of advances in technology this aspect has received the most direct attention in the form of hearing aids, flashing lights for doorbells and alarms, telecommunication devices, captioned television, and other such devices. The second level, which is people or communication related, involves the actual handicap arising from the disability.

Practically all of the initial learning experiences of young hearing children are acquired through the auditory channel, saturated as they are with words and spoken language from every direction, including radio and television. This constant verbal bombardment is not taught but absorbed. The deaf child is at a distinct disadvantage from the beginning since there is an absence of the sound of daily living. He may grow up not fully participating in family discussions, may develop limited relationships with relatives, friends, and neighbors. He will face a constant filtering, delimiting, and lack of access to information. Such thinness of input frequently results in a poor grasp of the language of one's native country, an unawareness to social change and idiom and all of the other intangible nuances of the everyday dynamics of the hearing-oriented world. The lag which develops tends to become cumulative so that the deaf child gets farther and farther behind unless a more comprehensive communication

I am sometimes asked how it feels to be deaf. My answer is that most people have to adjust to a handicap of some sort, even if it's only being near-sighted, or freckle-faced, or weak in math, or unable to bowl ten strikes in a row. As a friend of mine once wrote, there are 215 million "handicapped" Americans.

My handicap feels perfectly normal because I've had it so long, and I've had to adjust to it. A reasonable sense of proportion plus the ability to laugh at one's self have been important assets.

—LOY E. GOLLADAY
1976

system is developed and the narrow social circle is expanded. Frequently the deaf person is a stranger in a strange land, a part of the furniture of a room, a physical presence in the mainstream, but not involved as a living, sharing human being.

What is the deaf community? Is it a homogeneous whole? Actually it is a microcosm of any community of people whose members follow all kinds of interests and intellectual pursuits. However, the deaf community knows no geography or boundaries, extending as it does over the borders of each country and across the seas through international sign. It may best be described as a linguistic community made up of both deaf and hearing people who are able to use some form of manual communication with or without speech.

The vast majority of deaf people tend to be bilingual, that is, we may acquire a modicum of knowledge of the language of our country, and also use sign language—be it German Sign Language, French Sign Language, Swedish Sign Language, or American Sign Language. We believe such a linguistic background to be necessary if we are, indeed, to play a living, participating role in a dynamic, and for us, bilingual and bicultural society. The alternative is half a life teetering on the edge of an uncertain communication barrier.

Because no one enjoys hovering on the fringe of a group, looking on with little or no understanding of the subject discussed, or simply acceptance as a marginal token, deaf people tend to organize their own clubs, regional or provincial organizations, and national associations of the deaf. In such a milieu we enjoy complete and equal access and are not relegated to the role of silent follower. Here the environment is normal and wholesome, and one's self concept is at an even keel. Similar rapport exists at international meetings of the Comité Internationale des Sports des Sourds (CISS) and the World Federation of the Deaf (WFD), where communication bridges are quickly developed through international sign.

Despite pejorative "ghetto" references by those unfamiliar with sign language, the international deaf community thrives today, alive and vibrant—an open-ended community with a great degree of valence into the large hearing mainstream. It may be the only truly international group that requires neither a translator nor an interpreter. And just as there is cultural integrity among certain ethnic and religious minorities, deaf persons take pride in their language and in the attainments of other deaf persons.

Chapter 17

The National Association of the Deaf

M. Kleberg

Frederick C. Schreiber

(1922-1979)
Executive Director
National Association of the Deaf

Endowed with a deep sense of social consciousness for the needs of grassroots deaf people, Frederick C. Schreiber was an action-oriented individual who has left a lasting impact on the lives of all of us, deaf and hearing alike. Brilliant, articulate, aggressive, and yet sensitive and blessed with a gift of humor, warmth, and peopleness, this human dynamo began early to gain those experiences which provided meaning and substance to his eventual national and international contributions.

Following his graduation from Gallaudet College in 1942, this native New Yorker entered the ranks of blue-collar workers in a war plant in Akron, Ohio, for the duration of World War II, taught briefly in Texas, tutored vocational rehabilitation clients in New York City, finally settling down as a linotypist for the U.S. Government Printing Office in Washington, D.C. All through these early years Fred actively participated in local clubs, Frat divisions, and community publications, all of which formed the real-life contact with the deaf community which enhanced his culminating work at the federal and world-wide level.

In 1964 he was elected to the Board of Directors of the National Association of the Deaf as secretary-treasurer, and two years later accepted the challenge of becoming Executive Director of this floundering and restructured sleeping giant with its extremely limited financial resources. At the time of his unexpected death on September 5, 1979, Fred had engineered the NAD into a fully solvent and powerful consumer organization with an annual budget of close to $2 million, its own national office building, and a staff of some 40 people. He had also made time to serve on countless advisory boards and on the Bureau of the World Federation of the Deaf.

Fighter and advocate for the rights of deaf persons, facilitator and developer, forceful, innovative, and creative, his legacy to the deaf community will long endure. Although he is no longer with us today, accolades honoring his many contributions continue to reach the National Association of the Deaf from the far corners of the world. The Gallaudet College Alumni Association is proud to honor one of its rarest and most impressive sons with the LAURENT CLERC AWARD—Frederick C. Schreiber.

This tribute to Dr. Schreiber was written by his good friend, Dr. Mervin D. Garretson. It was read at the presentation ceremony by a member of the Laurent Clerc Cultural Fund Committee of the Gallaudet College Alumni Association which presented the Laurent Clerc Award to Dr. Schreiber posthumously on April 12, 1980.

Presidents of the National Association of the Deaf

(Compiled by Rosalyn L. Gannon)

Name		Cause of Deafness/Age	State	Term
1. Robert P. McGregor	(1849-1926)	brain fever 7-8 years old	OH	1880-1883
2. Edwin A. Hodgson*	(1854-1933)	meningitis 18 years old	NY	1883-1889
3. Dudley W. George	(1855-1930)	Gradually became deaf 16 years old	IL	1889-1893
4. Thomas Francis Fox*	(1859-1944)	meningitis 12 years old	NY	1893-1896
5. Rev. Jacob M. Koehler	(1860-1932)	meningitis 10 years old	PA	1896-1900
6. James L. Smith*	(1863-1943)	meningitis 8-10 years old	MN	1900-1904
7. George W. Veditz	(1861-1937)	scarlet fever 8 years old	CO	1904-1910
8. Rev. Olof Hanson*	(1862-1933)	ears frozen 12 years old	WA	1910-1913
9. Jay Cooke Howard	(1872-1946)	unknown 7 years old	MN	1913-1917
10. Rev. James H. Cloud*	(1862-1933)	unknown 14 years old	MO	1917-1923
11. Arthur L. Roberts*	(1881-1957)	12 years old	IL	1923-1930
12. Franklin C. Smielau	(1870-1940)	6 years old	OH	1930-1933
13. William H. Schaub	(1894-1947)		MO	1933-1934
14. Marcus L. Kenner*	(1882-1969)	meningitis 10 years old	NY	1934-1940
15. Tom L. Anderson*	(1888-1966)	scarlet fever 12 years old	IA	1940-1946
16. Byron B. Burnes*	(1904-)	chicken pox 15 years old	CA	1946-1964
17. Robert G. Sanderson	(1920-)	spinal meningitis 11 years old	UT	1964-1968
18. Robert O. Lankenau	(1919-)	spinal meningitis 10 years old	OH	1968-1972
19. Don G. Pettingill	(1920-)	German measles 5 years old	MD	1972-1974
20. Jess M. Smith	(1919-)	diphtheria/scarlet fever 7 years old	IN	1974-1976
21. Mervin D. Garretson*	(1923-)	spinal meningitis 5 years old	MD	1976-1978
22. Ralph White	(1923-)	deaf at birth	TX	1978-1980
23. Gertrude S. Galloway	(1930-)	deaf at birth	MD	1980-1982

*Received honorary degree from Gallaudet College

City Elected	Years Served	School	College	Occupation
Cincinnati, Ohio	3	Ohio School for the Deaf	Gallaudet	Educator
New York, New York	6	Public School	Collegiate Institute	Editor/Educator
Washington, D.C.	4	Missouri School for the Deaf	Gallaudet	Educator
Chicago, Illinois	3	New York School for the Deaf	Gallaudet	Educator
Philadelphia, Pennsylvania	4	Pennsylvania School for the Deaf	Gallaudet	Minister
St. Paul, Minnesota	4	Minnesota School for the Deaf	Gallaudet	Educator
St. Louis, Missouri	6	Maryland School for the Deaf	Gallaudet	Educator
Colorado Springs, Colorado	3	Minnesota School for the Deaf	Gallaudet	Architect
Cleveland, Ohio	4	Minnesota School for the Deaf	Gallaudet	Investment Broker
Hartford, Connecticut Detroit, Michigan	6	Public School Illinois School for the Deaf	Gallaudet	Minister/Educator
Atlanta, Georgia Washington, D.C.	7	Kansas School for the Deaf	Gallaudet	NFSD official
Buffalo, New York	3	Ohio School for the Deaf	Gallaudet	Minister
(succeeded Smielau)	1	Missouri School for the Deaf		
New York, New York Chicago, Illinois	6	Lexington Avenue School		Businessman
Los Angeles, California	6	Colorado School for the Deaf	Gallaudet	Educator
Louisville, Kentucky; Cleveland, Ohio; Austin, Texas; Cincinnati, Ohio; St. Louis, Missouri; Dallas, Texas; Miami, Florida	18	Alabama School for the Deaf	Gallaudet	Educator
Washington, D.C. San Francisco, California	4	Utah School for the Deaf	Gallaudet	Supervisor, County Plat Office
Las Vegas, Nevada Minneapolis, Minnesota	4	Indiana School for the Deaf	Gallaudet	Chemist
Miami Beach, Florida	2	Idaho School for the Deaf	Gallaudet	Coord. Off Campus Programs
Seattle, Washington	2	Tennessee School for the Deaf Public High School	University of Tennessee	Educator
Houston, Texas	2	Colorado School for the Deaf	Gallaudet	Educator
Rochester, New York	2	Georgia School for the Deaf	Gallaudet	Educator/Rehab. Consultant
Cincinnati, Ohio	2	Kendall School, D.C.	Gallaudet	Educator

Presidents of the National Association of the Deaf, 1880-1980

Robert P. McGregor
OHIO

Edwin A. Hodgson
NEW YORK

Dudley W. George
ILLINOIS

Thomas F. Fox
NEW YORK

Rev. Jacob M. Koehler
PENNSYLVANIA

James L. Smith
MINNESOTA

George W. Veditz
COLORADO

Rev. Olof Hanson
WASHINGTON

Jay C. Howard
MINNESOTA

All photos unless otherwise identified from Gallaudet College Archives.

Rev. James H. Cloud
MISSOURI

Arthur L. Roberts
ILLINOIS

Franklin C. Smielau
OHIO

William H. Schaub
MISSOURI

Marcus L. Kenner
NEW YORK

Tom L. Anderson
IOWA

Byron B. Burnes
CALIFORNIA

Robert G. Sanderson
UTAH

Robert O. Lankenau
OHIO

425

Don G. Pettingill
MARYLAND

Jess M. Smith
INDIANA

Mervin D. Garretson
MARYLAND

Ralph White
TEXAS

Gertrude Galloway
MARYLAND

Frederick C. Schreiber
EXECUTIVE DIRECTOR
1966-1979

Albert T. Pimentel
EXECUTIVE DIRECTOR
1979-

Gary W. Olsen
ASST. EXEC. DIRECTOR
FOR STATE AFFAIRS
1978-

NAD members gather for their photo at the 25th anniversary convention in St. Louis, Missouri in 1904.

Highlights of the NAD Century
Compiled by Rosalyn L. Gannon

1850 New England Gallaudet Association of the Deaf organized.

1865 New York Association of the Deaf organized.

1876 Wisconsin Association of the Deaf organized.

1880 Deaf people representing twenty one states meet in Cincinnati, Ohio to organize the National Convention of Deaf-Mutes; 143 people attended; Edmund Booth chosen temporary chairman; A committee was selected to draw up a constitution and Robert P. McGregor of Ohio was elected first president; the formation of a Mute Colony was proposed but gained little support; Indiana Association of the Deaf organized.

1881 Iowa Association of the Deaf and the Pennsylvania Association of the Deaf organized.

1883 Second NAD convention held in New York City; Eighteen states were represented at this convention attended by 174 participants; members decided to raise funds for a statue in honor of Thomas Hopkins Gallaudet; the peddling issue surfaced; Edwin A. Hodgson of New York elected second president.

1884 Virginia Association of the Deaf organized.

1885 Minnesota Association of the Deaf organized.

1886 Texas Association of the Deaf organized.

1887 Michigan Association of the Deaf organized; $13,000 raised for the Gallaudet memorial.

1889 Third convention held in Washington, D.C.; Thomas Hopkins Gallaudet and Alice Cosgwell Memorial unveiled on the campus of the National Deaf-Mute College; Dudley W. George of Illinois elected third president; Constitution and by-laws adopted; Association objected to discrimination against the deaf in Civil Service and reference to schools for the deaf as "asylums"; Edwin A. Hodgson and Robert Patterson selected to represent the Association at first World's Congress of the Deaf in Paris.

1890 Arkansas Association of the Deaf organized.

427

th Convention and 3rd World Congress
of the Deaf

Buffalo, N. Y.   August 4th to 9th 1930

NAD Archives

1891   Kentucky Association of the Deaf organized.

1893   Fourth convention held in Chicago; NAD hosted second World's Congress of the Deaf; Thomas Fox of New York elected fourth president.

1894   Mississippi Association of the Deaf organized.

1895   Illinois Association of the Deaf organized.

1896   Fifth convention held in Philadelphia; Rev. Jacob M. Koehler of Pennsylvania elected fifth president. Julia Foley of Pennsylvania became the first woman elected to NAD Board.

1899   Sixth convention held in St. Paul, Minnesota; 166 members attended; Minnesota Governor Lind and Mayor Kiefer of St. Paul welcomed members to the city; Association goes on record in favor of the combined system of educating deaf children; Agreed to explore the establishment of school for the deaf in Alaska; The need of special religious instruction for the deaf brought to members' attention; James L. Smith of Minnesota elected sixth president.

1900   NAD incorporated in Washington, D.C.; Certificate of Incorporation signed by Amos G. Draper and Albert F. Adams of D.C. and Edwin A. Hodgson of N.Y.

1903   Washington Association of the Deaf organized and North Carolina Association of the Deaf organized.

1904   Seventh convention held in St. Louis during the Louisiana Purchase Exposition; Members expressed concern about trends in education of the deaf and voted to prepare and circulate information about the deaf and deafness to educators, legislators, parents and others; Resolution adopted calling for the expansion of vocational training in schools for the deaf; Association went on record supporting the establishment of schools for the colored deaf; George W. Veditz of Colorado elected seventh president; Missouri Association of the Deaf and Colorado Association of the Deaf organized.

1906   California Association of the Deaf organized.

1907   Eighth convention held in Norfolk, Virginia on the occasion of the Jamestown Ter-Centennial Exposition; The possibility of prohibition of intermarriage among deaf couples greatly concerned members; Resolution adopted to set up a $100,000 Endowment Fund; Committee appointed to meet with the

Members of the National Association for the Deaf and the World Congress of the Deaf at the 50th anniversary convention in Buffalo, New York 1930.

Civil Service Commission regarding discrimination against deaf workers; President Veditz became first NAD president to be re-elected.

1908   Louisiana Association of the Deaf organized.

1909   Utah Association of the Deaf and Kansas Association of the Deaf organized.

1910   Ninth convention held at Colorado Springs, Colorado; 520 members attended; President William H. Taft informed the NAD he had instructed the Civil Service Commission to remove all discrimination against the deaf; Deaf persons urged to vote for Taft; Olof Hanson of Seattle, Washington elected eighth president; Oklahoma Association of the Deaf and Georgia Association of the Deaf organized.

1911   South Carolina Association of the Deaf organized.

1912   Alabama Association of the Deaf organized.

1913   Tenth convention held in Cleveland; John D. Rockefeller invited members to a reception at his home; NAD unsuccessful in convincing the Nebraska State Legislature to repeal law requiring the exclusive use of the pure oral method; Jay C. Howard of Minnesota elected ninth president.

1915   Eleventh convention held in San Francisco during the Panama-Pacific Exposition; NAD continued fight against the Nebraska oral law; Supported bill introduced in Congress to establish a Bureau for the Deaf in the Department of Labor; Confronted with the problem of deaf peddlers as a result of increased unemployment; President Howard re-elected.

1916   North Dakota Association for the Deaf organized.

1917   Twelfth convention held in Hartford, Connecticut on the occasion of the centennial of the founding of the first permanent school for the deaf in America; Four deaf citizens represented France as goodwill ambassadors; NAD raised funds for three ambulances to help the French cause in World War I; Offered to recruit 1,000 deaf soldiers for President Theodore Roosevelt; Goodyear Tire and Rubber Company at Akron, Ohio and the Ford Motor Company at Detroit began employing many deaf workers; NAD continued fight against impostors; Association sent two representatives to the Convention of the American Academy of Opthalomology and Otolaryngology to present its case for the combined method; Supported the admission of deaf children to school at an earlier age than the customary age of eight; The Rev. James H. Cloud of Missouri elected tenth president; Florida Association of the Deaf organized.

1920   Thirteenth convention held at Detroit; 2,589 persons register; Deaf Americans sent over $700 in relief to the Austrian and Belgian deaf; NAD went on record protesting the practice of doctors who attempted to advise parents of deaf children about education; Fought quack doctors who claimed they could restore hearing; Urged legislation that would require doctors to report all cases of deafness to state boards of education; The Rev. James H. Cloud re-elected president.

1921   Oregon Association of the Deaf organized.

1923   Fourteenth convention held at Atlanta, Georgia, first in the deep south; George Washington University added course in the sign language to its curriculum; Arthur L. Roberts of Illinois elected eleventh president.

1926   Fifteenth convention held in Washington, D.C.; Dr. Percival Hall of Gallaudet College addressed the delegates; Members expressed concern about threats to their driving rights; Arthur L. Roberts re-elected president.

1930   Sixteenth convention held at Buffalo, New York during the fourth World Congress of the Deaf; Association observed 50th anniversary; Presented memorial of Charles Michael de l'Epée, the founder of the first free school for the deaf in the world to Le Couteulx St. Mary's Institution for the Deaf in Buffalo; NAD issued warning against attempts to restore hearing by airplane dives; Franklin C. Smielau of Ohio elected twelfth president; Arizona Association of the Deaf organized.

1931   Idaho Association of the Deaf organized.

1933   President Smielau resigned in April; William H. Schaub of Missouri succeeded him.

1934   Seventeenth convention held in New York City; Marcus L. Kenner of New York elected fourteenth president.

1937   Eighteenth convention held in Chicago; Members protested discrimination against the deaf in the Civilian Conservation Corps, the Social Security Administration and the Works Progress Administration; Supported sheltered workshops planned by the National Reconstruction Administration; President Franklin D. Roosevelt pledged his cooperation to increase Civil Service opportunities for deaf workers; President Kenner re-elected.

1939   Connecticut Association of the Deaf organized.

1940   Nineteenth convention held at Los Angeles, California; NAD sought for the first time to ascertain the special services offered to the deaf in vocational rehabilitation; Criticized the practice of day schools for "dumping" slow deaf pupils on residential schools while proclaiming their oral method superior; Tom L. Anderson of Iowa elected fifteenth president.

1941-45   President Anderson wired President Franklin D. Roosevelt that deaf people were available to the makers of war munitions since they could not be in combat; NAD established a "Victory Fund" and raised nearly $8,000, to purchase three clubmobiles for the American Red Cross to use for the comfort of fighting men on the European front; NAD fought a St. Louis court case in which a driver's license had been revoked on the grounds of deafness and the New York Legislature which required a doctor's approval before granting licenses to deaf drivers.

A copy of President Woodrow Wilson's note to NAD President Veditz.

Please give my warmest greetings to the convention and assure them that I shall do all I can to see that the utmost justice is done the deaf-mutes.

Woodrow Wilson

The White House,
Washington, D.C. Aug. 7, 1913.
George M. Veditz

FACSIMILE OF PRESIDENT WOODROW WILSON'S MESSAGE, CONVEYED THROUGH MR. VEDITZ, TO THE TENTH CONVENTION OF THE NATIONAL ASSOCIATION OF THE DEAF.

NAD Archives

NAD officers with Ohio Governor Lausche at the 75th anniversary convention in Cincinnati. Left to right: Robert M. Greenmun, Governor Lausche, LeRoy Duning, Byron B. Burnes, Marcus L. Kenner, G. Gordon Kannapell, and David Peikoff.

1946	Twentieth convention held in Louisville, Kentucky; Byron B. Burnes of California elected sixteenth president.
1949	Twenty-first convention at Cleveland, Ohio; NAD officials stressed the need for a permanent home office and a full-time staff; Cooperated with the Missouri Association of the Deaf to recognize Rhulin Thomas' coast-to-coast solo flight; Helped state associations in Michigan, Ohio, Texas, and Virginia fight for education reforms and the construction of new schools; Assisted deaf workers in their fight against Civil Service discrimination in post office employment; Appealed to the FBI for assistance in the passage of a bill to make interstate peddling a criminal offense; Undertook a movement to place two deaf professional baseball players, William Hoy and Luther Taylor, in the Hall of Fame at Cooperstown, N.Y.; President Burnes re-elected.

1950	First NAD home office opened in Chicago.
1953	Twenty-second convention held in Austin, Texas; Attacked a South Dakota editorial proposing a law to ban deaf drivers; Fought a plan to establish an oral day school in Washington, D.C. to supplant the Kendall School; Sought the support of the American Medical Association to combat misleading hearing aid advertisements; Sent a delegation to the World Federation of the Deaf in Rome, Italy; Burnes re-elected for third time.
1953	Opposed a Congressional proposal by Senator Jacob Javits of New York to grant an extra $600 income tax exemption to deaf persons.
1955	Twenty-third convention held at Cincinnati, Ohio; NAD received a $17,200 grant from the Office of Vocational Rehabilitation to undertake a national survey of occupations among the deaf; Supported a bill introduced in the

Marcellus Kleberg

Four NAD presidents gather at the dedication of Halex House in 1973. Left to right: Robert G. Sanderson, Robert Lankenau, Byron B. Burnes, and Don G. Pettingill.

Congress to provide captioned films for the deaf; Countered criticism on communication methods used at the Maryland School and Gallaudet College; Burnes re-elected for fourth term; Maryland Association of the Deaf organized.

1956 NAD reorganization meeting held at the Missouri School for the Deaf in Fulton.

1957 Twenty-fourth convention held in St. Louis, Missouri; NAD helped Georgia deaf get hearing test law for all drivers rescinded; Received additional grant of $30,000 to complete the occupational survey; President Burnes represented NAD at the Congress of the World Federation of the Deaf in Stockholm, Sweden; Encouraged the WFD to try for a consultative status to the United Nations; Burnes re-elected to fifth term.

1960 Twenty-fifth convention held in Dallas, Texas under newly re-organized by-laws; Minnesota became first association to pay quota under new system; Intensive membership drive launched; NAD recommended that the educational qualifications and salary levels for counselors and supervisors in residential schools be raised; Supported the members of the Iowa Association of the Deaf

in their fight against excessive use of the oral method and opposed the elimination of deaf teachers; Established the Jr. National Association of the Deaf; Burnes re-elected to sixth term.

1961 Ohio Association of the Deaf organized.

1962 Twenty-sixth convention held in Miami, Florida; NAD began convening on a biennial basis for the first time; Proposed the establishment of a council of organizations of the deaf.

1964 Twenty-seventh convention in Washington, D.C.; Registered smallest attendance of any NAD convention in modern times because of the Gallaudet College Centennial Celebration and the 1965 World Games for the Deaf; Assisted the Deafness Research Foundation promote its Temporal Bone Bank program; Began evaluating entertainment films for Captioned Films for the Deaf; *The Silent Worker* was renamed the *Deaf American*; Circulation reached 2400; Robert G. Sanderson of Utah elected seventeenth president; Home office moved from Berkeley, California to a suite on Eye Street in N.W. Washington, D.C. and placed under the management of Secretary-Treasurer Frederick C. Schreiber.

Halex House, the first Home Office building owned by the NAD. It is located in Silver Spring, Maryland.

1966 Twenty-eighth convention held in San Francisco; 2,000 people registered in spite of airline strike; Record budget of $51,000 adopted; Association voted to hire first full-time executive secretary; the Executive Board approved President's selection of Frederick C. Schreiber as the Association's first Executive Secretary; Feasibility study of including deaf youth into the Job Corps or the Office of Economic Opportunity undertaken; NAD developed joint workshop with the Registry of Interpreters of the Deaf; Established a cultural program to promote cultural activities among the deaf; Boyce R. Williams received the first NAD Distinguished Service Award.

1967 NAD received a grant of $75,000 from Vocational Rehabilitation Administration to conduct an international seminar on research in vocational rehabilitation; Received a grant of $48,000 to develop a sign language program; Terrence O'Rourke hired to direct the project; Provided legal help and raised over $3,000 to assist a deaf couple in a court adoption case in California; Home office doubled size; moved to new office containing seven rooms and about 1,600 square feet of space; Albert T. Pimentel appointed first Executive Director of the Registry of Interpreters for the Deaf; New Jersey Association of the Deaf organized.

1968 Twenty-ninth convention held in Las Vegas; Approved a 37½ hour work week for Home Office employees; hospitalization and life insurance policies added to staff's pay benefits; and increased Executive Secretary; salary to $17,000; persuaded federal Civil Service to give specifically written examination to deaf applicants for postal positions; Judge Sherman G. Finesilver received the Distinguished Service Award; Robert O. Lankenau elected eighteenth president; Registry of Interpreters and the Sign Language grants renewed; Grant for a nationwide census of the deaf received; Jr. National Association of the Deaf held first Convention at Gallaudet College in May.

1969 Supported Congressional legislation establishing the National Technical Institute for the Deaf and the Model Secondary School for the Deaf; Held first leadership workshop for deaf persons in Salt Lake City, Utah.

1970 Thirtieth convention held in Minneapolis; Workshops on "Rehabilitation and Adult-Youth," "Teacher Certification" and one on "Adult Education" included in convention; NAD employees reach 20 with annual payroll of $60,000; *Deaf American* circulation reached 4,600; Mary E. Switzer awarded third NAD Distinguished Service Award; Civil Service

agreed on NAD's request for especially designed written examinations for deaf applicants; Representatives voted to limit officers' terms to two years, delete one vice presidential position and add a president-elect position. The term of Board members was changed to four years and the number of Board members increased to eight persons; An award in memory of Robert M. Greenmun was established to be awarded on a biennial basis to a person who has done the most to help his fellow deaf men; A historic trans-ocean teletype phone conversation took place between officials of the Philippine Association of the Deaf and the National Association of the Deaf; Home Office announced the publication of a new book *A Basic Course in Manual Communication* compiled by Terrence O'Rourke; New Mexico Association of the Deaf organized.

1971 Executive Board decided to purchase Halex House in Silver Spring, Maryland a two-story building with 21,500 square feet costing $640,000; The Registry of Interpreters of the Deaf grant renewed for two-years, Emil S. Ladner hired as director of RID; *The Deaf American* circulation went over 5,000 mark for first time.

1972 Thirty-first convention held at Miami Beach, Florida; The Home Office began providing "on the job" office training for deaf students; President Lankenau reported on the meeting of the World Federation of the Deaf held under the auspices of the NAD in 1975; NAD staff increased to 28 full-time and 11 part-time employees; Publication division published seventh titles and a full time director was hired. A librarian was hired and a library was started; Jr. NAD published *The Jr. Deaf American* and the *Silent Voice*; Dr. McCay Vernon received the Distinguished Service Award; Ann Billington competing as Miss Gallaudet won the first Miss Deaf American title; Don G. Pettingill of Maryland chosen nineteenth president and Jess M. Smith elected first president-elect.

1973 Some 300 persons attended Halex House dedication; The architect and former owner presented a handsome walnut key to Immediate Past President Robert Lankenau; Two other former presidents, Robert G. Sanderson, the master of ceremonies and Byron B. Burnes, a speaker, participated in the program.

1974 Thirty-second convention held in Seattle, Washington; Jr. NAD Director Frank R. Turk reported 79 Junior NAD chapters; Editor Jess M. Smith reported that the circulation of *The*

Continued on page 436

Miss Deaf America

The selection of a Miss Deaf America was the outgrowth of a nationwide cultural program inaugurated at the 1966 National Association of the Deaf convention. A committee under the chairmanship of Douglas J.N. Burke organized a regional network with a chairman in each region directing cultural activities. Tournaments were held throughout the country in areas designated as physical, literary, spiritual, recreational, and home economics. Entrants in the national tournament first appeared at the Las Vegas convention in 1968 and 27 entrants went home with golden "NADDIES," (an award similar to the movie industry's Oscar and television's Emmy). In 1972 a contest to select Miss Deaf America was added to the talent program and Miss Ann Billington, who entered as Miss Gallaudet College, was chosen the first Miss Deaf America. Interest in the cultural program has waned over the years but the Miss Deaf America Pageant has grown and the number of contestants in the biennium program has increased.

Pam Young
MISS GALLAUDET
1974-76

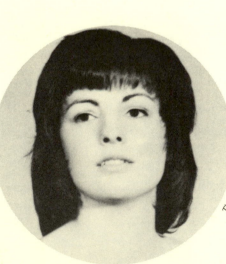

Mary Pearce
MISS DEAF MISSISSIPPI
SEATTLE, WASHINGTON
1974

Ann Billington
MISS GALLAUDET
MIAMI BEACH, FLORIDA
1972-74

Debra Krause
MISS DEAF PENNSYLVANIA
1979-80

Jackie Roth
MISS DEAF MARYLAND
ROCHESTER, NEW YORK
1978-79

Susan Davidoff
MISS DEAF MARYLAND
HOUSTON, TEXAS
1976-78

Mary Beth Barber
MISS DEAF NEW YORK
CINCINNATI, OHIO
1980-

435

Deaf American had reached 6,500; The National Census of the Deaf Population project completed *The Deaf Population of the United States* published that year; Grassroots Leadership Training Workshops offered as part of convention; Mary Pearce, Miss Deaf Mississippi, elected Miss Deaf America; NAD sponsored exhibit on deafness at President's Committee on the Employment of the Handicapped; Jess M. Smith of Indiana automatically elevated to presidency and Mervin D. Garretson of Maryland elected president-elect. Edna P. Adler, consultant at Social Rehabilitation Services received the Distinguished Service Award; Alaska Association of the Deaf organized.

1975 Massachusetts Association of the Deaf organized; Hosted the VIIIth World Federation of the Deaf Congress in Washington, D.C.

1976 Thirty-third convention held in Houston, Texas; NAD Board appointed Byron B. Burnes to write a history of the NAD for the approaching Centennial Convention; NAD budget neared $1.5 million dollars; President-elect Mervin D. Garretson of Maryland elevated to the presidency and Ralph White of Texas elected president-elect; Susan Davidoff, Miss Deaf Maryland, crowned Miss Deaf America; Established the NAD Legal Defense Fund; Began a joint Gallaudet College-NAD sponsored regional leadership training program for deaf persons in the U.S.A.

1977 Frederick C. Schreiber received honorary degree from Gallaudet College; Rhode Island Association of the Deaf organized.

1978 Thirty-fourth convention held in Rochester, New York; College credit courses offered to participants for the first time during a convention; The number of NAD employees reached thirty-three; Effort undertaken to have sign language taught in the public schools and accepted as a second language requirement in high schools and post-secondary institutions; Concern expressed about "mainstreaming" deaf children in public schools; Granted Bernard Bragg $2,000 to assist him in a world tour as an advocate for deaf persons' sign language and the involvement of deaf people in theatre; Opened a branch office in Indianapolis and hired Gary Olsen as Assistant Director for State Affairs; Governor Otis R. Bowen, M.D., Lieutenant Governor Robert Orr, and U.S. Senators Richard Lugar and Birch Bayh and William Hudnut III, Mayor of Indianapolis attended the open house. Ralph White of Texas automatically became president and Gertrude Galloway of Maryland president-elect; Jackie Roth of Maryland was the next Miss Deaf America; Wyoming Association of the Deaf organized.

1979 Begins publication of *The NAD Broadcaster* newspaper, Ed Carney chosen the publisher; Hired Lobbyist Jack Duncan as a Government Relations Officer; Frederick C. Schreiber died in a New York City hospital. Albert T. Pimentel hired as Executive Director.

1980 Centennial convention held in Cincinnati, Ohio.

Appendix A
Known Deaf Persons Who Have Been Ordained
(Dates of their ordination and birth and death.)

(A list of deaf clergymen was originally compiled by the Rev. Alexander MacLeod and published in the *American Annals of the Deaf* (Vol. 95, pp. 265-279, May 1950; Vol. 95, pp. 387-432, September 1950 and Vol. 96, pp. 363-381, January 1951). The list has been updated and additional information has been added by the author.)

Baptists

Rev. Phils W. Packward, 1880-90

Rev. John W. Michaels, 1905
(1850-1942)

Rev. Arthur D. Bryant, 1911
(1856-1939)

Rev. J. W. Gardner, 1914
(1884-1975)

Rev. Adolph O. Wilson, 1926
(1867-1939)

Rev. Carter E. Bearden, 1949
(1928-   )

Rev. Clifford P. Bruffey, 1952
(1930-   )

Rev. W. L. Asbridge, 1956
(1906-   )

Rev. Robert H. Boltz, 1961
(1938-   )

Rev. Jerry Jamison, 1972
(1949-   )

Rev. Ronnie B. Rice, 1974
(1957-   )

Rev. Gary Shoemaker, 1978
(1946-   )

Rev. Phillip Goldberg, 1978

Catholic

Rev. Thomas Coughlin, O.S.S.T., 1977
(1947-   )

Campbellite

Rev. A. H. Norris, 1911
(1877-1972)

Congregational

Rev. Samuel Rowe, 1878

Rev. John W. Chickering
(1831-1913)

Rev. Frank Read, 1883
(b. 1840)

Episcopalians

Rev. Henry Syle, 1883
(1846-1890)

Rev. Austin W. Mann, 1883
(1841-1911)

Rev. Jacob M. Koehler, 1887
(1860-1932)

Rev. G. Stanley Searing, 1892
(1859-1912)

Rev. Job Turner, 1891
(1820-1903)

Rev. James H. Cloud, 1893
(1862-1925)

Rev. Charles O. Dantzer, 1895
(1864-1924)

Rev. Oliver J. Whildin, 1901
(1869-1943)

Rev. Harry J. Van Allen, 1902
(1866-1919)

Rev. Franklin C. Smielau, 1902
(1876-1940)

Rev. George F. Flick, 1907
(1877-1951)

Rev. John H. Kent, 1908
(1878-1948)

Rev. George H. Hefflon, 1910
(1865-1926)

Rev. Brewster R. Allabough, 1911
(1861-1919)

Rev. Herbert C. Merrill, 1914
(1874-1945)

Rev. Hobart L. Tracy, 1915
(1867-1936)

Rev. Roma C. Fortune, 1918
(b. 1879)

Rev. Clarence W. Charles, 1920
(1866-1926)

Rev. Henry J. Pulver, 1922
(1895-1947)

Rev. Warren M. Smaltz, 1923
(b. 1895)

Rev. Homer E. Grace, 1924
(1890-1980)

Rev. J. Stanley Light, 1926
(1895-1963)

Rev. Guilbert C. Braddock, 1926
(1898-1972)

Rev. Collins S. Sawhill, 1927
(1857-1934)

Rev. Arthur O. Steidmann, 1928
(1883-1950)

Rev. Olof Hanson, 1929
(1862-1933)

Rev. Robert C. Fletcher, 1930
(1900-   )

Rev. Horace B. Waters, 1931
(1877-1938)

Rev. Gustav C. Meckling, 1937
(1903-   )

Rev. Georg Almo, 1939
(1902-   )

Rev. James C. Ellerhorst, 1942
(1914-   )

Rev. William M. Lange, 1943
(1909-   )

Rev. Arthur G. Leisman, 1943
(1895-1970)

Rev. Otto Berg, 1944
(1915-   )

Rev. Silas J. Hirte, 1950
(1920-   )

Rev. Edwin C. Nies, 1950
(1890-1973)

Rev. Steve L. Mathis, III, 1954
(1930-   )

Rev. Roger A. Pickering, 1963
(1931-   )

Rev. Jesse A. Pope, 1965
(1924-   )

Rev. Camille L. Desmarais, 1966
(1931-   )

Rev. Jay L. Croft, 1969
(1942-   )

Rev. James F. Alby, 1971
(1936-   )

Rev. Douglas Slasor, 1965
(1929-1980)

Rev. Thomas Rardin, 1978
(1952-   )

Rev. Roger G. Fielding, 1979
(1923-   )

Evangelical Alliance, The

Rev. Ezra C. Wyand, 1909
(d. 1919)

Lutheran Church Missouri Synod

Rev. William A. Ludwig, 1959
(1932-   )

Rev. Kjell O. Mork, 1977
(1944-   )

Rev. Robert Case, 1978

Rev. Laverne Maas, 1979

Lutheran Church of America

Rev. Edward F. Kaercher, 1929
(1903-1969)

Rev. Robert Collins, 1977

Methodists

Rev. Philip J. Hasenstab, 1890
(1861-1941)

Rev. Henry S. Rutherford, 1908
(b. 1874)

Rev. Daniel W. Moylan, 1912
(1869-1941)

*Rev. Samuel M. Freeman, 1920
(1856-1940)

*Rev. Frank C. Philpott, 1931
(1875-1948)

*assumed to be a member of that denomination

Presbyterian

Rev. Andrew C. Miller, 1927

United Brethen

Rev. Jasper Cross, 1890-95

438

Appendix B
Known Deaf Persons With Earned Doctoral Degrees
(Compiled by Rosalyn L. Gannon)

Year	Name	School	Age onset of deafness	Degree	College University	Major	Undergraduate Degree
1869	Moore, Gideon	Bartlett School NY	18 years	Ph.D.	Heidelberg U. (Germany)	Psychology, Chemistry	Yale U.
1914	Nies, Edwin W.	Lexington School	early childhood	DDS	U. of Pennsylvania	Dental Surgery	Gallaudet
1938	Breunig, Latham	Clarke School	5-7 years	Ph.D.	Johns Hopkins U.	Chemistry	Wabash College
1943	Steinbach, Howard L.		at birth	M.D.	St. Louis U.	Radiology	U.C.L.A.
1948	Vier, Marion C.	East H.S. Colorado	3 years	Ph.D.	U. of Colorado	Biochemistry	U. of Colorado
1949	Lillie, Robert J.	Wright Oral School	at birth	Ph.D	U. of Maryland	Animal Nutrition	Penn State
1952	Ballantyne, Donald L.	Canterbury Prep. School	at birth	Ph.D	Catholic U.	Biology	Princeton
	Marsters, James C.	Wright Oral School	at birth	DDS	New York U.	Dentistry	Union College
1954	Hawkins, Bruce	Classical H.S. Mass.	8 years	Ph.D	Princeton	Physics	Amberst College
1956	Myers, Lowell J.		12 years	J.D.	John Marshall Law School	Law	Roosevelt
1960	Randolph, John D.	Texas School and Fort Worth H.S. Texas	3 years	J.D.	Georgetown U. Law School	Law	Gallaudet
1962	Price, Raphael M.	self-educated	at birth	M.D.	Jefferson Med. College	Medicine	U. of Pennsylvania
1963	Weinberger, Myron		at birth	M.D.	Indiana U.	Medicine	Indiana U.
1964	Thompson, Richard E.	Clarke School Browne/Nichols School	at birth	Ph.D.	Boston U.	Clinical Psychology	Harvard U.
1965	Mayes, Thomas A.	Baker Oregon H.S.	6 years	Ph.D.	Michigan State U.	Adult Education	U. of Chicago
1967	Stibick, Jeffrey N. L.	Howey Academy, Texas	at birth	Ph.D	Catholic U.	Entomology	Rollins College
1969	Guertin, Ralph F.	Clarke School	7 years	Ph.D.	Yale	Theoretical Physc. Polytechis	Worcester Inst.
	Phillips, Richard M.	Arsenal Tech. H.S.	5 years	Ed.D	U. of Maryland	Student Personnel	Gallaudet
1970	Marshall, William J. A.	Catholic Schools, Mass.	13 months	Ed.D	U. of Illinois	Special Education	Stonehill
	Schowe, Ben M., Jr.	John R. Buchtel H.S.	7 years	Ph.D	Ohio State U.	Communications Sociology & Curriculum	Gallaudet
	Sharpless, Nansie S.	Westtown, Pa.	14 years	Ph.D	Wayne State U.	Biochemistry/ Chemistry	Oberlin College
	Stewart, Larry G.	Gladewater, Texas Public Schools	8 years	Ed.D	U. of Arizona	Education Rehab. Psychology	Gallaudet
1971	Bushnaq, Suleiman M.	Trans-Jordan	5 years	Ph.D	Catholic U.	Economics	Gallaudet
	Chatoff, Michael A.	Public Schools	22 years	LLM	N.Y.U. School of Law	General Law	Queens
	Doyle, Thomas D.	Bishop Lenghlin Mem. H.S., N.Y.	8 years	Ph.D	George Washington U.	Chemistry	Fordham, NY
	Johnson, Richard K.	Indiana School	12 years	Ed.D	U. of Arizona	Rehabilitation Administration	Gallaudet

Year	Name	School	Age onset of deafness	Degree	College University	Major	Undergraduate Degree
	Pachizarz, Judith	Sehlannon H.S. Il.	2½ years	Ph.D	St. Louis U.	Biochemistry/ Chemistry	Oberlin College
	Vescovi, Geno M.	St. Mary El. School	14 years	Ed.D	U. of Arizona	Counseling Psychology	Gallaudet
1972	Davila, Robert R.	California School (B)	8 years	Ph.D	Syracuse U.	Ed. Tech	Gallaudet
	Galloway, Victor H.	South Carolina	10-16 months	Ed.D	U. of Arizona	Rehab./Ed. Adm.	Gallaudet
	Gustason, Gerilee	San Bernardino	5-6 years	Ph.D	U. of Southern Calif.	Education	U. of S. California
	Hammerschlag, Paul E.		at birth	M.D.	Albert Einstein College	Otolaryngology	New York U.
	Jensema, Carl	Public School, Wis.	9 years	Ph.D	U. of Washington	Psychometrics Multi-Variate-Statistics	Wisconsin
	Kapp, Leon	Los Angeles H.S.	5 years	Ph.D	U. of Rochester	Biophysics	U. of California, Berkeley
	Mba, Peter	Nigeria	25 years	Ed.D	U. of Tennessee	Special Education	Gallaudet
	Propp, George	Nebraska School	15 years	Ed.D	U. of Nebraska	Education Administration	U. of Nebraska
	Stinson, Michael	Public School	3 years	Ph.D	U. of Michigan	Psychology	U. of Michigan
	Watson, Douglas	Arkansas School	8 years	Ph.D	Florida State U.	Counseling	Gallaudet
	Weiner, Michael	Overbrook H.S. Pa.	at birth	DDS	Temple U.	Dentistry	Muhlenberg
1973	Jordan, Irving King	Public School	21 years	Ph.D	U. of Tennessee	Psychology	Gallaudet
	Liebman, Jeffrey	Evanston Township H.S. Il.	at birth	Ph.D	U. of California, L.A.	Physiological Psychology	Oberlin College
	Mead, Richard	Hackley School, N.Y.	4 years	Ph.D	Harvard U.	Applied Math.	Harvard U.
	Nomeland, Ronald E.	Minnesota School	at birth	Ph.D	Syracuse U.	Education Technology	Gallaudet
	Snyder, James G.	Shaker Heights H.S.	unknown	DDS	U. of Iowa	Dentistry	Drake U.
	Sussman, Allen E.	P.S. 47, N.Y.	at birth	Ph.D	New York U.	Psychology	Gallaudet
	Teeteh-Ocloo, Seth L.	Nigeria	17 years	Ph.D	Southern Ill. U.	Special Education/ Administration	Gallaudet
1974	Corson, Harvey J.	Pennsylvania School	at birth	Ed.D	U. of Cincinnati	Special Education	Gallaudet
	Freeman, Jerome W.	Indiana School	7 years	Ed.D	U. of Tennessee	Curr. and Inst.	Gallaudet
	Preston, William		2 years	Ed.D	U. of Rochester	Medical Education	U. of Rochester
	Sanderson, Robert G.	Utah School	11 years	Ed.D	Brigham Young U.	Public School Adm.	Gallaudet
1975	Fleischer, Lawrence R.	Lexington, Fanwood Schools	at birth	Ed.D	Brigham Young U.	Public School Adm.	Gallaudet
	Golden, Emanuel	NY School (Fanwood)	at birth	Ed.D	Walden U.	Education	Gallaudet
	Goldstein, Inge F.	Evaliua de Rothschild, Jersualem	18 years	DPH	Columbia U.	Public Health	Wellesley
	Johnson, Verner C.	Evanston Township H.S. Ill.	at birth	Ph.D.	U. of Tennessee	Geology/ Geophysics	Southern Illinois U.

Year	Name	School	Age onset of deafness	Degree	College University	Major	Undergraduate Degree
	Okuda, Chuzo	Japan, Wisconsin School	4 years	Ph.D	Pennsylvania State U.	Mathematics	Gallaudet
1976	Bowe, Frank	Public School	3 years	Ph.D	NY City U.	Education Psychology	Western Maryland College
	Harris, Robert L.	Shorewood H.S. Wisc.	8 months	Ph.D	New York U.	Clinical Psychology	Lake Forest
	Hochman, Frank P.	P.S. 47, N.Y.	at birth	M.D.	Rutgers Medical School	Medicine	City College of NY
	Miller, Betty G.	Public School	unknown	Ed.D	Penn State U.	Art Education	Gallaudet
	Moore, Michael L.	Woodrow Wilson H.S., Texas	at birth	Ph.D	N. Texas State U.	Physical Chemistry	Gallaudet
	Norwood, Malcolm J.	American School	5 years	Ph.D	U. of Maryland	Inst. Technology	Gallaudet
	Schroedel, John G.	Public School	6 years	Ph.D	New York U.	Sociology	Gallaudet
1977	Humphries, Tom	Johnsonville H.S.	6 years	Ph.D	Union Graduate School	Cross Cultural Communication/ Language Learning	Gallaudet
	Kavic, Thomas A.		1 year	M.D.	U. of Pittsburgh School of Med.	Radiology	Franklin/Marshall
	Mather, Robert		at birth	J.D.	DePaul U. of Chicago	Law	NTID
	Reddy, Narasimha	Public School	15 years	Ph.D	U. of Wyoming	Biomedical Engineering	Osmania U.
1978	Agazie, James C.	Nigeria	4½ years	Ed.D	Atlanta U.	Adm./Super.	Gallaudet
	Bergman, Eugene	NY School (Fanwood)	7 years	Ph.D	George Washington U.	English Literature	Gallaudet
	Chough, Steven K.	South Korea	2½ years	D.S.W.	Columbia U.	Social Welfare	Gallaudet
1979	Babb, Richard L.	Michigan School	4½ years	Ph.D	U. of Illinois	Ed. Adm./Prog. Evaluation	Gallaudet
	Brauer, Barbara A.	Michigan School, Public School	at birth	Ph.D.	New York U.	Clinical Psychology	Oberlin College
	Corbett, Edward E., Jr.	Louisiana Public School	at birth	Ph.D	Gallaudet College	Spec. Ed. Adm.	Gallaudet
	Feder, Susan	Broowine H.S. Mass.	5 years	M.D.	Emory U. School of Med.	Psychiatry	Franklin/Marshall
	Hurwitz T. Alan	Central Institute, Public School	at birth	Ed.D	U. of Rochester	Curr./Teaching	Washington U.
	Kensicki, Nancy	Kent State High, Ohio	1½ years	D.A.	Catholic U.	English	Gallaudet
	Lang, Harry G.	Norwon H.S., PA.	15 years	Ed.D	U. of Rochester	Science Curriculum/ teaching	Bethany College
1980*	Goodstein, Harvey	NY School (Fanwood)	at birth	Ph.D	American U.	Math Education	Gallaudet
	Himmelstein, Jeffrey	Newton H.S., NYC	early childhood	Ed.D	Rutgers	Science Education	Long Island U.
	Johnson, Judith L.	S. Broward H.S., Fla.	at birth	Ed.D	Gallaudet	Spec. Ed. Adm.	Gallaudet
	Kannapell, Barbara	Indiana School	at birth	Ph.D	Georgetown U.	Sociolinguistics	Gallaudet
	Mapes, Herbert G.	Illinois School	5 years	Ph.D	American U.	Mathematics Ed.	Gallaudet
	Parks, Edwin	Ohio Public Schools	14 years	Ph.D	American U.	Organic Chemistry	Gallaudet

441

Year	Name	School	Age onset of deafness	Degree	College University	Major	Undergraduate Degree
	Robbins, Curt	New York Public Schools	at birth	Ph.D	U. of Maryland	Ed. Technology	Gallaudet
	Rosen, Roslyn	Lexington School	at birth	Ed.D	Catholic U.	Education Adm.	Gallaudet
	Howland, William	St. John's Prep. Mass.	at birth	Ph.D	McGill	Geog. Remote Sensing	U. of Vermont
	Rattner, Steven	Montgomery County H.S.	at birth	DDS	U. of Maryland	Dentistry	U. of Maryland
	Sutcliffe, Ronald E.	Iowa School	4 years	Ph.D	U. of Maryland	Adm. of Higher Education	Gallaudet

*Expect to receive degree in 1980 or soon afterwards

442

Jeff, Dixie, Rosalyn, Jack and Christy Gannon.

O. Gordon Banks

Writing a book is a long, drawn-out and tiresome process that greatly influences the lives of the writer's family and friends. It is a project which involves months and months of research. That means living with pockets full of notes, and with piles of paper, photographs, magazines and newspapers, books, etc. stacked and scattered everywhere throughout the house. And, on most piles is a scribbled note warning, "Do Not Touch!" The dining room table gets knocked out of commission because it becomes too cluttered with paper, typewriters and the like, to be used simply for eating.

Writing a book requires a great deal of sacrifice on the part of the author's family. It means that plans, outings, and fun activities take second place to "the book." Playing "Lion" (a family game) and horseback riding become less frequent. Broken toys remain broken and drippy faucets continue to drip. It means postponement of special events such as birthdays and Mother's Day and shortened or no holidays. Even the family dog gets neglected. In summer the grass grows to embarrassing heights and in winter, the snow does not get shovelled. Deadlines create worry, tension and loss of many nights' sleep and frequently the author exists only physically. His mind is elsewhere, prodding back in another era.

I have been fortunate, indeed, to have a patient, understanding and encouraging family. They have gamely lived through all this and have helped me so much in so many ways. Most importantly, they have helped me "keep the faith" and see this long project through to the finish. I could not have made it without them.

It is with love and appreciation that I acknowledge on this page my thanks to my family—my wife, Rosalyn, Jeff and Christy—for all the important contributions they have made to the completion of this book.

THE AUTHOR

About the Author . . .

Jack R. Gannon was born in the foothills of the Ozark Mountains of southern Missouri, into an environment of farming, woodworking and all things outdoors which he still considers the ingredients of perfect living.

Becoming deaf from meningitis at the age of eight, Jack entered the Missouri School for the Deaf in 1946 and graduated in 1954. There he found deaf people like himself, and they were an inspiration to him. The fine deaf teachers on the staff were especially impressive. He soon realized that they had encountered the same problems and roadblocks that awaited him, and they had attained outstanding success.

Through Grover C. Farquhar, Jack came to know the joys of creative writing, and he acquired a love for reading. It was Farquhar most of all who encouraged him in preparing for college. George Dewey Coats welcomed him into the fold, entrusting him with responsibilities without question, helping him develop qualities of leadership and independence. And it was Coats who instilled in him an appreciation of the NAD.

Jack went on to Gallaudet College and pursued his literary inclinations, editing *The Buff and Blue* and the 1959 *Tower Clock*. In his senior year he was student editor of the *Gallaudet Record*.

He graduated in 1959 and accepted a position as graphic arts instructor and coach at the Nebraska School for the Deaf, where he remained for nine years. He was co-founder of *The Deaf Nebraskan* and edited *The Nebraska Journal*. He held offices in state and local organizations of the deaf, and he wrote numerous articles, which soon made his name known throughout the land. In 1967, the eight-man football team he coached went through the season undefeated. Jack was named Coach of the Year by WTOP-TV of Omaha.

In 1968 Gallaudet College established for the first time a budgeted Alumni Office and Jack was chosen director of Alumni Relations and executive secretary of the Gallaudet College Alumni Association. The Alumni Office soon was combined with the Office of Public Relations to become the Office of Alumni and Public Relations in 1971, with Jack Gannon as director, a position he still holds. In this capacity Jack has participated in many leadership workshops and given many talks. He is in charge of one of the finest college publications in the United States, *Gallaudet Today*.

In 1977 Jack was asked by the NAD to write a book narrating the general history of the deaf population during the past century. He wrote an article

mentioning past events and developments during the century and concluded, "One could write a book."

The college granted him some time off from his duties on Kendall Green and he plunged into the monumental task of writing a book, *Deaf Heritage*. For two years he labored day and night gathering mountains of material, corresponding with countless contributors, and writing, writing, writing. The grass grew thick on his lawn and whiskers hung long from his chin as he burned the midnight oil night after night after night. To sustain him was one of the loveliest of families—his wife, Rosalyn, son Jeffery, 9, and daughter Christine, 7. Rosalyn was a constant help, searching for material, typing manuscript, and laying out pages, in addition to maintaining a comfortable and cozy home.

Jack did write a book! It will be an authoritative source of information for years to come. It is the most comprehensive account of the deaf community since Harry Best produced *Deafness and the Deaf in the United States* in 1943.

Byron B. Burnes
President Emeritus
National Association of the Deaf

444

Chapter Notes

The words identifying each quote are at the beginning of each sentence. For more information consult the Bibliography. Abbreviations used:

Annals—*American Annals of the Deaf*
DA—*The Deaf American*
DMJ—*Deaf-Mutes' Journal*
Fay Histories—*Histories of American Schools for the Deaf*
GAB—*Gallaudet Alumni Bulletin*
GAN—*Gallaudet Alumni Newsletter*
GT—*Gallaudet Today*
NDP—*Notable Deaf Persons*
SW—*The Silent Worker*

Prologue

pages xxi to xxiii

xxi *Diary of Laurent Clerc's Voyage from France to America in 1816.* xxii ibid.

Chapter 1—The Early Years

pages 1 to 58

1 totally deficient in: Fay Histories vol. 1 New York Institution p 10. died a victim: Braddock NDP p 64. 3 Every time I: Beauchamp "Causes of Deafness." creates self-respect: Fay Histories vol. 2 Texas Institution. 4 What Hath God: Collins. 5 No, I sometimes: Deaf Smith County Chamber of Commerce literature. So valant and: Huston p 132. 9 Are you deaf? Hazel Davis. 10 managed to get: Bass p 129. 12 It is absurd: Fay Histories vol. 1 Illinois School. This application: Fay Histories vol. 2 Clarke School. more through trail: ibid. 13 The Professors and: Fay Histories vol. 1 South Carolina Institution p 5. First colored pupils: ibid. second such pupils: ibid. 14 the more the: Fay Histories vol. 3 Mr. Knapp's School. 15 During the latter: ibid McCowen's School. a man blind: Braddock NDP p 7. 29 for the edification: SW 11/51 p 8. 30 Candidates for admission: Michigan School yearbook 1976. 31 carrying the torch: Fay Histories vol. 1 Mississippi Institution p 12. 36 a deaf but: Fay Histories vol. 2 Kansas Institution. 37 since we have: Lauritsen *History of the Minnesota School* p 157. 38 to grant and: Gallaudet College charter. 42 Christian school for: Bellhorn p 14. 47 brilliant mind and: newspaper clipping (no source). 48 the responses were: Fay Histories vol. 2 Northern New York Institution p 8. 50 Little did Congress: SW 11/53 p 11. when deaf administrators: Wolach p 1. 51 objections of the: Fay Histories vol. 2 North Dakota School p 5. 54 one of the: Bass History of the Hampton School p 2. the normal child: Central Institute brochure. 56 these two schools: MSSD Annual Report 1978.

Chapter 2—The 1880s

pages 59 to 74

62 to bring the: Burnes *The NAD Century* p 8. that deaf Massachusetts: news accounts of the day. could sway a: SW 10/27. the father and: Veditz "The Genesis of the NAD." 65 the velvet gauntlet: ibid. orator of the day: Loe p 21. 67 The motive of: ibid p 20. noted for his: Braddock NDP p 8. as we followed: SW 9/26/89. This statue does: Loe p 21. Like the gentle: Braddock NDP p 167. 68 The Yankees are: Bass *The History of Education . . .* p 80. Paleface papoose deaf: Braddock NDP p 139. performed a hundred: SW 9/88. 70 Whilst the game: Bass *The History of Education . . .* p 117. among adult deaf-mutes: SW 9/89. The frequent injury: SW 2/96. We wish the: SW 11/89. And may the: SW 4/89. 71 Victim No. 47: DMJ 12/11/84. 73 In the states: SW 6/90. by no means: SW 4/89.

Chapter 3—The 1890s

pages 75 to 92

75 highly probable: A. G. Bell *Upon the Formation . . .* p 12. Those who believe: ibid p 41. before the deaf: ibid p 45. 76 proving that a: ibid. the normal conditions: ibid p 47. There are other: Gillett SW 11/90. if their hearts: ibid. Those who oppose: SW 2/91. Either the man: ibid. 77 he comes in: Burnes *The NAD Century* p 110. 78 increase and diffusion: SW 5/95. comparatively fine lipreader: Ballin *The Deaf-Mute Howls.* a fluent talker: ibid. 80 body vigor and: SW 5/97. 81 The craze for: ibid. 82 probably the only: SW 2/93. 83 plenty of work: SW 11/94. 87 There are thousands: SW 1/93. 91 on alternate days: SW 1/96.

Chapter 4—Artists

pages 93 to 156

100 He is among: Staempfli. 105 perhaps the most: Little p 98. 125 explosive and a: Kowalewski "The Art of Frederick La Monto." 128

I'd like to: SW 1/3/80. The conditions of: ibid. 134 My brush is: SW 5/27. 136 something puzzles me: SW 11/25. 137 When I lost: artist's promotional brochure. 144 the father of: California School for the Deaf, Berkeley calendar 1972. 147 the lack of: Miller. 148 captured the very: ibid. 149 everything in the: ibid. 152 a courageous individual: Garvin p 57. 153 I love wood: Riverside City College flyer about the artist. 154 a credit to: letter from former employer Herbert F. Hilmer. Herbert's deafness was: ibid.

Chapter 5—The 1900s

pages 157 to 172

158 no deaf man: Mudgett DA 6/76. stared adversity in: ibid. 163 stretched a shoestrong: J. Frederick Meagher (no source). Lincoln-face who: ibid. 164 to aid in: DMJ 1/00. 166 a queer looking: J. L. Smith "The Deaf and the Automobile." Quite a number: ibid.

Chapter 6—The 1910s

pages 173 to 180

174 Your quick feet: Schauffler letter. I try to: SW 1/63 p 28. 175 fooling around with: Reilly. 178 The first and: ad promotion for Long's book. acknowledged everywhere: ad for *The Silent Worker*. 179 At this place: inscription on Fowler tablet, Guilford, Ct.

Chapter 7—The 1920s

pages 181 to 202

181 the first church: Grindrod letter 6/79. 183 Only a deaf: Braddock NDP p 112. as much a: ibid. My son. I: Koehler SW 11/27. 186 fraught with pithy: SW 11/48. brilliant, wise and: *History of All Angels' Mission* p 9. a loss to: ibid. 187 But really . . . when: parish newsletter 2/73. 189 because he did: *History of All Angels' Mission* p 11. 191 advocate religious and: National Council of Jewish Deaf brochure. It is always: *Ephpheta* 10/12. 194 cling to the: Glyndon p 351.

Chapter 9—The 1930s

pages 211 to 218

212 Oh, yeah, another: Kowalewski "Top of the Monument." 213 life began for: Vera Majella Larson Van Selus letter 2/16/78. I cannot think: *The Volta Review* (no date). 215 A cupped hand: *The Modern Silents* 2/39 p 7.

Chapter 10—The 1940s

pages 219 to 236

220 What's the matter: Malzkuhn interview. 222 It goes without: *The Washingtonian*. 223 had to be: Burnes *The NAD Century*. A gift from: ibid. one of the: *Our Heritage* p 71. The Associated Press: *The Silent Cavalier* 3/43. those bearing a: Best *Deafness and the Deaf*. This is a: *The Buff and Blue* 11/9/43. 228 in order to: *The Cavalier* 4-5/44. a valid difference: Coats GAB 6/48. Because most of: Burnes "A Tribute to Dewey Coats" DA 9/65 p 2. 229 an undenominational union: SW. 230 We are proud: Harry Jacobs 1949 AAAD program book. the maker of: J. H. McFarlane "George S. Porter" SW 9/48 p 4. 231 The future of: letter from Rosenfield to Schowe printed in the GAB 5/46 p 4. We want every: GAB Winter/47 p 2. Expanded to its: Annals 11/50 - 451. 232 Where would Gallaudet: Fusfeld GAB 4/47 p 6. and as we: ibid. An audiometer test: Elstad GAB Spring/48 p

7. 236 be satisfactorily taught: Buell Gallagher Report p 3. there is a: ibid p 17. first-rate National: ibid p i. The impact of: Orman letter 1/80. the most persuasive: Williams letter 2/80.

Chapter 11—Publications of the Deaf

pages 237 to 254

238 to educate deaf: Braddock NDP p 4. sententious and sensible: ibid p 5. devoted to the: letter in the Golladay Museum, American School for the Deaf. 239 a bright, lively: J. E. Gallaher p 55. 247 Constant employment will: Bass *History . . .* p 113. 248 the forms were: SW 9/48. Thereafter . . . it required: McClure "Reminiscences of a Centenarian" p 4. 250 It takes more: Meagher *The Washingtonian* 10/16/13. a fearless fighter: ibid. 251 one of the: Braddock NDP p 26. 252 one of the: ibid p 11. after a few: ibid. devoted to everything: ibid p 88. 253 only colored deaf: SW 8/90.

Chapter 12—The 1950s

pages 255 to 270

255 the genuine deaf: NAD leaflet. It is a: *Deaf-Mute Advance* 5/6/1874. Just why the: *The Frat* 6/46. 256 If we do: *The Frat* 3/49. Do not donate: *The Frat* 12/47 p 5. This card is: ibid. 259 No person can: *The Frat* 1-2/58. 261 a major contribution: SW. 262 what a strange: Annals 3/50. aggressiveness far beyond: *The Reporter* 12/12/57 p 4. 263 for help for: Burnes interview. an obvious need: SW 9/50. If you act: SW 3/51 p 14. Amazing New Medical: SW 1/51 p 7. Allen fashioned laws: Burnes *The NAD Century*. p 446. 270 Fancher's Band as: David Mudgett letter.

Chapter 13—Sports

pages 271 to 315

272 The item ascribes: Merrill letter 3/6/42. 272 But Zuppke . . . admits: Meagher *The Frat* 9/46. 273 Congrats, Eel; am: Meagher post card. 289 they were eagerly: Roy Stewart "How Wrestling came to Gallaudet." It was not: Letter from Thompson Clayton to Frank Turk 5/29/79. 290 I used to: Farquhar. 298 for the novel: Albert Berg "From My Reliquary of Memories." 299 ungrammatical, and at: SW 3/52 p 23. He made enemies: ibid. as prolific and: SW 4/56. 301 covered more territory: SW 12/51. 303 probably one of: ibid.

Chapter 14—The 1960s

pages 317 to 352

318 develop well-informed: *ICDA News* 7-8/62. to encourage, help: DA 9/64. 322 Soon the farm: Roy Stewart "In Memory of a Friend." Their splendid performance: Boyce Williams interview 10/1/80. 324 blue from head: Hofsteater "An Experiment in Pre-School Education." an expert with: ibid. to produce a: ibid. pull in your: Mudgett DA 2/65 p 7. We have lost: ibid. 329 Dad's *Time* has: Winfield McChord interview. 336 wanted beloved old: Burnes interview. 337 I had never: Nuernberger. We feel an: GT Winter/71 p 21. 338 a person who: ibid. 346 Pure art, drawn: NTD poster. Exciting, inventive, beautiful: ibid. you not only: NTD Fact Sheet. we are opposed: letter from Alexander Graham Bell Association to NBC-TV. bring enormous cultural: letter from David Hays. 348 America's great unknown: NTD Fact Sheet. fluid, delicate, powerful: ibid. A National Theatre: ibid. 352 People used to: Bragg interview.

Chapter 15—American Sign Language: Our Natural Language

pages 357 to 376

359 the noblest gift: Veditz "The Preservation of . . ." write well and: Little p 97. 361 We are friends: Burnes *The NAD Century* p 91. My object in: *The Deaf: . . .* p 60. what I am: ibid p 8. 362 The sign language: Burnes *The NAD Century* p 62. 363 The enemies of: ibid p 91. A new race: Veditz "The Preservation of . . ." 367 The culture of: *Sign Language and the Deaf Community* p 102. 369 theories as to: DA 4/69 p 9. the right of: DA 1/71 p 5. Total communication is: *Proceedings, Conference of Executives of American Schools for the Deaf 1976.* 376 Just the other: Gannon GT Spring/78 p 33. the most popular: GT Fall/74 p 31. the hallmark of: Coats *Annals* 3/48 p 124. ASL is very: *Sign Language and the Deaf Community* p 111.

Chapter 16—The 1970s

pages 377 to 417

378 cop-out . . . doesn't reflect: Schreiber quoted in the *Minnesota Tribune* (no date). proficiency in the: GAN 5/70. 383 may be taught: *Sign of Our Times* No. 57/80. country's only resident: Temple Deaf College promotion. championed the cause: Lauristen *History of the Minnesota School.* teaching me to: GAN 6/1/76. 384 accept handicapped persons: newspaper account of Davis case (no source). verbal stimulation: *Los Angeles Times* 2/25/78. 386 when I saw: WGBH-TV flyer. 387 Today we celebrate: HEW news release 3/23/79. 389 Deaf Louie: *National Enquirer* news clipping (no date). 392 I am happy: Rock Gospel collection of letters. 396 You want your: GT Fall/75. 397 the road to: Annals 12/78. 398 Pandora's box of: Garretson President's Report 1976-78. the local education: special issue on P.L. 94-142 GAN. more problems stem: *Denver Post* 1/9/77. 403 to live their: DA 4/77. 406 . . . he has won: *Seattle Post-Intelligencer* 8/79. There are all: *Seattle Sun* 8/79. 410 cursed son of: DA 3/67. 411-412 quotes from the book.

Bibliography

American Athletic Association of the Deaf (program books) March, 1947 and April, 1949.

Adler, Edna P. interview Washington, D.C.

"Administrative Leaders of the Pennsylvania School for the Deaf" The Mt. Airy World February-March, 1970.

"Agreement Reached on Captioned TV for Deaf People" *Wall Street Journal.*

Akin, E. Conley "Facts from the Past" *Tennessee Observer*
January, 1979.
February, 1979.
March, 1979.
April, 1979.
May, 1979.
January, 1980.

Alabama Churchman, The May, 1979.

Alber, Milda E. "Second School West of the Mississippi . . . The Iowa School for the Deaf" (unpublished paper).

Albronda, Mildred *The Magic Lantern Man: Theophilus Hope d'Estrella* T. J. Publishers, Inc. Silver Spring, Md. 1980.

Albronda, Mildred, and Dreyfus, Renee Beller *Theophilus Hope d'Estrella, 1851-1929* (pamphlet).

All Angels' Mission to the Deaf One Hundredth Anniversary 1859-1959 All Angels' Mission to the Deaf, Baltimore, Maryland 1959.

Allen, Frederick Lewis *Only Yesterday* Harper & Brothers, N.Y. 1957.

Allen, Laura "He SEEs Language" *The Dallas* (Tx.) *Morning News* February 29, 1976.

Alumni Newsletter (Gallaudet)
Vol. 1 No. 7 February, 1967.
Vol. 2 No. 3 January, 1968.
Vol. 4 No. 3 November, 1969.
Vol. 4 No. 4 January, 1970.
Vol. 4 No. 5 February, 1970.
Vol. 4 No. 6 March, 1970.
Vol. 4 No. 7 April, 1970.
Vol. 5 No. 2 November, 1970.
Vol. 5 No. 3 December, 1970.
Vol. 5 No. 6 March, 1971.

Vol. 5 No. 7 April, 1971.
Vol. 6 No. 1 October, 1971.
Vol. 6 No. 2 November-December, 1971.
Vol. 6 No. 3 January, 1972.
Vol. 6 No. 6 April, 1972.
Vol. 7 No. 1 October 1972.
Vol. 7 No. 2 November, 1972.
Vol. 7 No. 5 March, 1973.
Vol. 7 No. 8 May, 1973.
Vol. 14 No. 3 November, 1979.

"Alumnus Lectures on Orientation" *Gallaudet Record* February, 1959.

American Annals of the Deaf
Vol. 25 No. 4 October, 1880.
Vol. 82 No. 1 January, 1937.
Vol. 93 No. 1 January, 1948.
Vol. 93 No. 4 September, 1948.
Vol. 93 No. 5 October, 1948.
Vol. 95 No. 1 January, 1959.
Vol. 95 No. 2 March, 1950.
Vol. 95 No. 5 November, 1950.
Vol. 96 No. 1 January, 1951.
Vol. 96 No. 3 May, 1951.
Vol. 96 No. 4 September, 1951.

American Athletic Association of the Deaf Hall of Fame Records.

American Era, The April, 1968.

Anderson, Dave "Bonnie Sloan: Deafness Doesn't Matter A Lot" *New York Times News Service,* 1973.

Anderson, Dave "The Deaf Rookie" *New York Times News Service,* 1973.

Anderson, Tom L. "The Challenge to Leadership" *The Washingtonian* Vol. 51 No. 1, October, 1941 and Vol. 51 No. 2 November, 1941.

Anderson, Tom L. "Postwar and the Adult Deaf" *American Annals of the Deaf* Vol. 89 No. 4 September, 1944.

Anderson, Tom L. "What Industrial Education Has Done for the Deaf" *The Iowa Hawkeye* Iowa School for the Deaf, February 15, 1929.

Andrews, Chris "National Program to Help Deaf Launched Here" *International,* New York City Times Union, Rochester, N.Y. April 13, 1978.

Annual Report Gallaudet College 1910.

Anthony, David *S.E.E. Manual* Educational Services Division, Anaheim (Calif.) Union High School District 1971.

Anthony, David A. *Seeing Essential English: Code Breaker* Greeley, Coloraro, 1974.

Anthony, David A. *Seeing Essential English: Elementary Dictionary* Pruett, Boulder, Colorado 1978.

"Architect Marr" *The Silent Worker* April, 1929.

"Are Those Apes Really Talking?" *Time* March 10, 1980.

Atwood, Albert W. *Gallaudet College: Its First One Hundred Years* Intelligencer Printing Company, Lancaster, Pa. 1964.

Auerbach, Leon "Mr. and Mrs. Auerbach Represent Gallaudet College at 250th Anniversary of Abbe de l'Epée" *Gallaudet Alumni Bulletin* Vol. 7 No. 4 Fall, 1962.

Auerbach, Leon "The National Association of the Deaf—Then and Now" *The Deaf American* September, 1978.

Auerbach, Leon "Notable Persons From Fanwood" (unpublished paper) June 11, 1978.

Austin, James C. "Children's Stories in Signed English" *The Deaf American* Vol. 25 No. 8 April, 1973.

Authority, Media Services and Captioned Films (unpublished working paper).

Axling, P. L. "Labor Bureaus" *The Modern Silents* February, 1939.

Babbini, Barbara E. *Manual Communication: Fingerspelling and the Language of Signs* University of Illinois Press, Urbana, Ill. 1974.

Bacheberke's Inter-State Directory of the Deaf of Ohio, Indiana, Kentucky, Michigan Bacheberke, Cincinnati 1912.

Baker, Charlotte and Carol Padden *American Sign Language* T. J. Publishers, Inc., Silver Spring, Md. 1979.

Ballin, Albert *The Deaf Mute Howls* reprinted in *The Deaf Spectrum* Vol. 5 No. 5 & 6 May and June, 1974.

Ballin, Albert V. "Granville Redmond, Artist" *The Silent Worker* November, 1925.

"Ban the Sign-Language" *Deaf Carolinian* reprinted in *The Nebraska Journal* October, 1929.

Bancraft, Horace H. "Luther Taylor House Father at Illinois School for the Deaf One Time Big Leaguer" *The Illinois Advance.*

Barnett, Marian W. "The Handicapped Girl in Scouting" *Girl Scout Leader* November-December, 1972.

Bass, R. Aumon *The History of Education of the Deaf in Virginia* Virginia School for the Deaf and Blind, Staunton, 1949.

Bass, R. Aumon "History of the State School for the Deaf and the Blind, Hampton, Virginia" (unpublished paper) 1978.

Bass, R. Aumon *I Remember . . .* Friendship Sales, Richmond, Va., 1978.

Bass, R. Aumon "William C. Ritter Founder and Superintendent Hampton School for the Deaf and the Blind" (unpublished paper) February, 1978.

Bearden, Carter E. *The History of Southern Baptist Convention's Ministry to the Deaf* Home Mission Board, Atlanta, Ga. 1966.

Beauchamp, James B. "Causes of Deafness" (unpublished paper).

Beauchamp, James B. *History of the Kentucky School for the Deaf, Danville, Kentucky, 1923-1973* The Kentucky School for the Deaf Alumni Association, Inc., Danville 1973.

"Beggars' Symposium" *The Frat,* May, 1949.

Bell, Alexander Graham "Upon the Formation of a Deaf Variety of the Human Race" (a paper presented at the National Academy of Science on November 13, 1883 and later published in book format under the title of *Memoir: Upon the Formation of a Deaf Variety of the Human Race.)*

Bell, Ovid "Short History of Callaway Country" *History of Northeast Missouri* The Ovid Bell Press, Inc., Fulton, Mo. 1913.

Bellhorn, Walter "Detroit's Lutheran School for the Deaf" (Schools for the Deaf—Roy K. Holcomb) *The Silent Worker* Vol. 15 No. 11 July-August, 1963.

Bellugi, Ursula and Edward S. Kilma "The Roots of Language in the Sign Talk of the Deaf" *Psychology Today* No. 6 1972.

"Ben Marshall Schowe" *Successful Careers Out of Gallaudet College* Gallaudet College Press, Washington, D.C. January, 1955.

"Ben Marshall Schowe" *The Frat* September-October, 1979.

"Ben Marshall Schowe" *The Silent Worker* May, 1949.

Berg, Albert *From My Reliquary of Memories* Iowa School for the Deaf, Council Bluffs 1943.

Berg, Albert "Higher Education for the Deaf" *The North Dakota Banner* January, 1943.

Berg, Rev. Otto B. "History of St. Barnabas' Episcopal Mission" *The Deaf Episcopalian* Vol. 5A No. 2.

Best, Harry *Deafness and the Deaf in the United States* The Macmillan Company, N.Y. 1943.

Bevill, Robert E. and Larry Vollmar *Arkansas School for the Deaf, 125th Anniversary 1850-1975, History of Educational Services* (booklet) May, 1975.

"Bill to Establish a Department for the Deaf in the United States Bureau of Labor Introduced" *The Maryland Bulletin* reprinted in *The Washington Deaf Record* November, 1940.

Birth of the I.C.D.A. and Its Progress, The International Catholic Deaf Association.

Bjorlee, Ignatius, "The Deaf and the Automobile" Maryland School for the Deaf, Frederick 1940.

Blackburn, William "January 1, 1857: TSD" *The Lone Star* December, 1975.

Bleil, Christy "The Development of Sign Language" (unpublished paper) 1976.

"Bloch's One Man Show" *Gallaudet Today* Fall, 1975.

"Bloch's One Man Show" *One The Green* Fall, 1975.

Block, Mervin "Silent Rites Impressive" *The Chicago American* November 7, 1957.

Boatner, Edmund B. "Captioned Films for the Deaf" (unpublished paper) February 23, 1980.

Boatner, Maxine Tull *Voice of the Deaf* Public Affairs Press, Washington, D.C. 1959.

"Bobs, The Man" *The Frat* November-December, 1957.

Bonds, James D. "History of Football at the Illinois School for the Deaf" (unpublished master's thesis).

Boorum, Gail interview.

Bornstein, Harry "Signed English: A Manual Approach to English Language Development" *Journal of Speech and Hearing Disorders* March, 1974.

Boston Globe, The Boston, Ma. November 11, 1897.

Boston Recorder June 9, 1818 (Eastman's Clerc Collection).

Boughner, A. Brown *History of Hampshire County, W. Va.* H. W. Maxwell and H. L. Swisher, Morgantown, W. Va. 1897.

450

Bowe, Frank "Ben M. Schowe, Maverick from Akron" *The Deaf American* Vol. 25 No. 1 September, 1972.

Bowe, Frank and Martin Sternberg *I'm Deaf, Too: 12 Deaf Americans* National Association of the Deaf, Silver Spring, Md. 1973.

Bowe, Frank "The Incredible Story of Cadwallader Washburn" *The Deaf American* Vol. 23 No. 3 November, 1970.

Braddock, Guilbert C. *Notable Deaf Persons* Florence B. Crammatte, ed., Gallaudet College Alumni Association, Washington, D.C. 1975.

Braddock, Guilbert C. *The Silent Worker* September, 1888.

Bragg, Bernard interview Washington, D.C.

Brannon, Sheldon *Early History of the West Virginia Schools for the Deaf and the Blind, 1870-1970* Romney.

"Brief History of the Communicative Skills Program, A" *NAD Heritage* National Association of the Deaf, 1980.

"Brief History of Hereford and Deaf Smith County, A" (fact sheet) Deaf Smith County Chamber of Commerce, Hereford, Tex.

"Brief History of St. Mary's School for the Deaf, A" Buffalo, N.Y.

Brill, Richard G. *Mainstreaming the Prelingually Deaf Child* (A study of the Status of Prelingually Deaf Children in Various Patterns of Mainstreamed Education for Hearing Impaired Children) Gallaudet College Press, Washington, D.C. 1978.

Brown, Kitty "Soaps and the Handicapped" *Soap Opera Digest* September, 1978.

Brown, Robert S. *History of the Mississippi School for the Deaf* Gower Printing and Office Supply Co., Meridian, Miss. 1954.

Bruce, Robert V. *Alexander Graham Bell and the Conquest of Solitude* Little, Brown, Boston 1973.

Buckley, Tom "TV: Handicapped Parents" *The New York Times* April 5, 1978.

Buff and Blue, The February 21, 1940 and March, 1943.

Buff and Blue, The Founder's Number February, 1921.

"Building A Heritage—1858-1958" *The Alabama Messenger* Anniversary Number October, 1958.

Building of KDES, The, History and Prologue Kendall Demonstration Elementary School, (booklet) Washington, D.C.

"Buildings Dedicated on Frederick Campus *The Maryland Bulletin* October-November, 1976.

Burnes, Byron B. "Dr. Arthur L. Roberts" *The Silent Worker* Vol. 10 No. 4 December, 1957.

Burnes, Byron B. "Letter to the Editor" *The Cavalier* March, 1948.

Burnes, Byron B. *The NAD Century* History of the National Association of the Deaf (unpublished manuscript).

Burnes, Byron B. "A Tribute to Dewey Coats" *The Deaf American* Vol. 18 No. 4 December, 1965.

Burnes, Caroline and Catherine Ramger *A History of the California School for the Deaf, 1860-1960* California: School for the Deaf, Berkeley 1960.

Burnes, Robert L. "Everybody's Rooting for Bonnie" *Globe* November 24, 1973.

Burnett, John R. *Tales of the Deaf and Dumb with Miscellaneous Poems,* 1835.

"Butch Is A Lady" *The American Weekly* September 26, 1948.

Califano, Joseph A., Jr. (memorandum to department heads) August 16, 1978.

"Caption Center Completes Five Years of Programming for Hearing Impaired, The" *The Deaf American* December, 1978.

"Can Deaf Serve as Jurors?" *Seattle Sun* August, 1979.

"Captioned Films for the Deaf" (correspondence between Clarence D. O'Connor and Ben Hoffmeyer, February 19, 1980) The Edward Miner Gallaudet Memorial Library, Gallaudet College Washington, D.C.

"Captioned Films for the Deaf" (correspondence between Edmund B. Boatner and Mrs. Edward Gallaudet, December 2, 1949); and (between Edmund B. Boatner and Helen S. Kuigstere, November 15, 1950) The Edward Miner Gallaudet Memorial Library, Gallaudet College, Washington, D.C.

"Captioned Films for the Deaf" (Clarence O'Connor correspondence February 19, 1980 and February 28, 1980) The Edward Miner Gallaudet Memorial Library, Gallaudet College, Washington, D.C.

"Captioned Films for the Deaf" (John A. Gough correspondence February 26, 1980). The Edward Miner Gallaudet Memorial Library, Gallaudet College, Washington, D.C.

"Captioned Films for the Deaf" *The Gallaudet Almanac* 1974.

"Captioned Films to Expand" *The Frat* September-October, 1962.

"Captioned TV Demonstrated at Tennessee Conference" *The Deaf American* January, 1972.

"Captioning Television for the Deaf at WGBH, 1971-76" (unpublished report).

Carney, Edward C. interview Silver Spring, Md.

Carter, S. Mel, Jr. interview September 26, 1980 Silver Spring, Md.

"Carves a Career Despite Deafness" *Cleveland Plain Dealer* July 15, 1951.

"Case in Favor of Sign Language, The" *The New Yorker* December 13, 1958.

Casterline, Dorothy Sueoka interview Washington, D.C.

Cavalier, The (The Silent Cavalier)
 Vol. 1 No. 12 March, 1941.
 Vol. 1 No. 13 May, 1941.
 Vol. 2 No. 11 March, 1942.
 Vol. 3 No. 3 November, 1942.
 Vol. 3 No. 9 May, 1943.
 Vol. 3 No. 10 June, 1943.
 Vol. 4 No. 2 October, 1943.
 Vol. 4 No. 4 December, 1943.
 Vol. 4 No. 5 January, 1944.
 Vol. 4 No. 6 February, 1944.
 Vol. 4 No. 9 June, 1944.
 Vol. 8 No. 8 April, 1948.
 Vol. 9 No. 1 September, 1948.
 Vol. 9 No. 9 April, 1949.

Central Institute for the Deaf (brochure published by the school).

Chandler, Mrs. J. B. "Thomas Scott Marr, Architect" *The Silent Worker* June, 1929.

Cincinnati Commercial
 "Deaf Mutes' Convention" August 25, 1880.
 "A Quiet Convention" August 26, 1880.

Cincinnati Daily Gazette
 "Deaf Mute Convention" August 25, 1880.
 "A Silent Convention" August 26, 1880.
 "The Silent Convention" August 27, 1880.
 "The Silent Convention" August 28, 1880.

Cincinnati Enquirer
 "Sign Language 'Official' for Convention of Deaf" July 3, 1955.
 "Cincinnati Girl Chosen As Deaf Beauty Queen at Convention Outing" July 5, 1955.
 "Quiet Reigns In Convention Hall As Deaf Society 'Hears' Speakers" July 6, 1955.
 "Lausche Interpreter" July 8, 1955.

Cincinnati Times-Star
"Deaf Mutes' Convention" August 25, 1880.
"The Silent Congress" August 26, 1880.

Coats, G. Dewey "Manual English" *American Annals of the Deaf* March, 1948.

Collins, Allan C. *The Story of America in Pictures* Doubleday and Company, Inc., Garden City, N.Y. 1953.

Colorado Index, The March-April, 1974.

"Colorado Observes Deaf Awareness Week; First in Nation" *Town & County News* November 23, 1972.

Cooke, Guie C. "Pests to Exterminate" *The Washington Deaf Record* November, 1938.

Corbett, Ed "A Descriptive Study of Teachers of the Hearing Impaired in the United States, 1979" (unpublished doctoral dissertation) Gallaudet College.

Cornett, R. Orin "Definition of Cued Speech" (unpublished paper).

Cornett, R. Orin "Relationship of Cued Speech to Oral Communication, Signed English and ASL" (unpublished paper).

Cornett, R. Orin "The Use of Speech and Signs in Combination" (unpublished paper) October, 1978.

Conklin, Roy B. "Ask Deaf to Raise Funds for Planes" *The American Deaf Citizen* reprinted in *The Washington Deaf Record* Vol. 8 No. 10 April, 1942.

Crammatte, Alan B. interview Washington, D.C.

Crammatte, Alan B. "Kelly Stevens as Seen by a Friend" *Gallaudet Today* Summer, 1971.

Cranwill, Alfred "A Report of an Important Event in Lionism for the Deaf" *The Deaf American* October, 1972.

Creekmore, Betsy Beeler *Knoxville* The University of Tennessee Press, Knoxville 1958.

Cristina, Ray "If Language Has a Public Image . . . Then the Deaf Need a PR Agent" *Pitt* November, 1979.

Crowley, Susan "Man's Best Friend Provides An Ear to the World for the Deaf" *The Washington Post* February 8, 1979.

Cued Speech News Vol. 6 No. 2 May, 1978.

Daubenmier, Judy "Language Deaf Can S.E.E." *The Cedar Rapids* (Ia.) *Gazette* September 16, 1973.

Davis, Hazel "It Happened During the Civil War" (unpublished paper).

Deaf American, The
Vol. 17 No. 8 April, 1965.
Vol. 21 No. 8 April, 1969.
Vol. 23 No. 1 September, 1970.

"Deaf Awareness Week Promoted by IBMer" *IBM* Vol 3. No. 44 November 10, 1972.

"Deaf Boy Killed in Building Exit" Associated Press story reprinted in the *Deaf Westerner* May, 1978.

Deaf: "By Their Fruits Ye Shall Know Them," The (a collection of letters; booklet) The New York Institution for the Deaf (Fanwood) 1912.

"Deaf Child, The" *Bulletin* Vol. 1 No. 1 Gallaudet Press, Washington, D.C. March, 1951.

Deaf Churchman, The Vol. 52 No. 3 Summer, 1976.

"Deaf Colorado Gridder Honored by President" *The Denver Post* December 7, 1971.

"Deaf Couple Busy In War Production Work" *The Jacksonville* (Ill.) *Journal* September 17, 1943.

"Deaf Do Not Need to Peddle or Beg, The" *The California News* reprinted in the *Jersey School News* March-April, 1953.

"Deaf Hold-Up Victims Give D.C. Bandit the Big Jitters" *Times-Herald* Washington, D.C. April 25, 1941.

Deaf Independent of Massachusetts, The January-February, 1979.

"Deaf: Last Neglected Minority, The" *American Medical News* June 23, 1978.

Deaf Lutheran, The Vol. 65 No. 4 April, 1973.

"Deaf Man and the Police, The" *The Record* Michigan Association of the Deaf Vol. 12 No. 3 September, 1969.

"Deaf Man Helps Catch Six Burglars by Teletype" *The Silent News* March, 1980.

"Deaf Man Smashes TV" *The Silent Hoosier* Vol. 33 No. 10 June, 1978.

"Deaf-Mute Howls, The" *The Silent Worker* Vol. 41 No. 4 April, 1929.

"Deaf Mute Linotype Operators in Our State" *The Washingtonian* May 19, 1911.

Deaf-Mute Optic, The Vol. 7, No. 4 October 29, 1887.

"Deaf Mute Priests" *Ephpheta* October, 1912.

Deaf-Mutes Journal
August 2, 1880.
November 27, 1884.
January 3, 1918.

Deaf-Mutes' Journal, "Railroad Record for 1884" December 11, 1884.

Deaf New Mexican Vol. 9 No. 4 April, 1979.

"Deaf of Washington State and Employment, The" *The Washington Deaf Record* Vol. 5 No. 10 April, 1939.

"Deaf People Do Not Beg" *The West River* (S.D.) *Progress* June 1, 1939.

"Deaf Really Doing Their Part" *The Washington Deaf Record* Vol. 8 No. 10 April, 1942.

Deaf Smith County Chamber of Commerce literature Hereford, Tex.

"Deaf Wood Carver" (John Clarke) *The Washington Deaf Record* April, 1937.

"Death Takes Walter J. Krug Gallaudet Dean of Men" *Gallaudet Alumni Bulletin* Spring, 1962.

"Death Takes Walter J. Krug Gallaudet Dean of Men" *The Silent Worker* June, 1962.

"Dedication at Kansas School" *The Frat* January-February, 1962.

Dee Cee Eyes November 14, 1978.

Denton, David M. (memo re: Naming of Buildings) Maryland School for the Deaf, Frederick October 9, 1975.

Denton, David M. (memo to all departments) Maryland School for the Deaf, Frederick October 9, 1975.

Detroit Free Press July, 1953.

Diary of Laurent Clerc's Voyage from France to America in 1816 American School for the Deaf, West Hartford, Ct. 1952.

Dictionary of American Biography Vol. 8 1932-58.

Digest of the Deaf December, 1939.

Dillon, Thomas "The New Mexico School" *The Silent Worker* Vol. 6, No. 3 November, 1953.

Dillon, Thomas "The New Mexico School for the Deaf" *The New Mexico Progress* May, 1975.

"Disabled Americans: A History" *Performance* (Biennial Issue) Vol. 27 Nos. 5-6-7 November-December, 1976; January, 1977.

"Discontinuing *The Silent Worker*" *The Silent Worker* June, 1929.

Divine, Belle S. "A Deaf Victory Fund" *The Washingtonian* Vol. 51 No. 5 February, 1942.

"Dogs Help the Deaf" United Press International April 6, 1977 reprinted in *The Silent News* June, 1977.

Domich, Harold *John Carlin, A Biographical Sketch* (booklet) Gallaudet College, Washington, D.C. 1939.

"Donation of $1,000 and Five Acres Led to Establishment of School for Deaf and Blind" *The St. Augustine Record* August 23, 1964.

Doren, Charles Van ed., *Webster's American Biographies* G&C Merriam Company, Springfield, Mass. 1975.

"Dr. A. L. Roberts Passes Away" *The Illinois Advance*.

"Dr. B. M. Schowe Is Frequent Visitor" *Gallaudet Record* April, 1959.

"Dr. Harry Best's Survey" (Resolutions, Committee Report) *Gallaudet Alumni Bulletin* Winter, 1948.

"Dr. Moore Pays Us a Visit" *The Silent Worker* May 29, 1890.

"Dr. Tom L. Anderson, 78, Eminent Deaf Leader, Dies" *Alumni Newsletter* (Gallaudet) November, 1966.

"Dr. Schowe, Specialist In Labor Problems, Lectures" *The Buff and Blue* November, 1958.

Duncan, Susana "Nim Chimpsky And How He Grew" *New York* December 3, 1979.

Dunham, C. Allan "The Rochester School for the Deaf" (Schools for the Deaf—R. K. Holcomb) *The Deaf American* December, 1964.

"Dunn-McNary Plan to Aid Deaf Unemployed, The" *The Washington Deaf Record* July, 1935.

Earley, Sharon "Captioning at WGBH-TV" (unpublished report).

"Eastern Most School for the Deaf, The—The Governor Baxter School for the Deaf" (unpublished paper).

Echoes of Other Days Howard Glyndon (Laura C. R. Searing) Harr Wagner Publishing Co., San Francisco, Calif. 1921.

Eder, Richard "'Runaways' Move Up to Broadway" *The New York Times* May 15, 1978.

Edey, Maitland A., ed., *This Fabulous Century: Sixty Years of American Life* (Vol. 4, 1930-1940, and Vol. 5, 1940-1950) Time-Life Books, N.Y. 1969.

Edstrom, Eve "Lip Readers by Telescope Recorded Chats by Queen at Terp Grid Game" *The Washington Post* November 16, 1957.

Eighteenth Annual Report; The New York Institution for the Instruction of the Deaf and Dumb New York State 1836.

"E. L. Schetnan, Deaf, Successfully Conducts a Newspaper for Hearing People" *The Washington Deaf Record* Vol. 3 No. 8 February, 1937.

Elmer, L. A. "Sign Language" *The Silent Observer* December, 1947 reprinted in the *American Annals of the Deaf* 1948.

Elstad, Leonard M. "The Hard of Hearing and Gallaudet College" *Gallaudet Alumni Bulletin* Spring, 1948.

"Local Sculptor Achieves Success" *The Evening (D.C.) Star* June 12, 1930.

Evening Transcript, The Boston Mass. November 11, 1897.

Fabulous Century, 1870-1900, This Time-Life Books, N.Y.

"Faginism Rampant" *The Frat* March, 1949.

Falk, Charles J. "The Nebraska School for the Deaf" *The Silent Worker* February, 1957.

"Fatal Accident" *Deaf-Mutes' Journal* November 27, 1884.

Farquhar, Grover C. "Everett Ragan Honored at All-Sports Banquet" *The Missouri Record* April, 1954.

Fay, Edward Allen *Histories of American Schools for the Deaf* Vols. 1, 2 and 3 The Volta Bureau, Washington, D.C. 1893.

Fay, Edward Allen, ed., "School Items" *American Annals of the Deaf* Vol. 45 No. 4 June, 1900.

Fay, Edward Allen "The Classification of the Deaf and Some Indirect Causes of Deaf-Mutism" (unpublished address) Edward Miner Gallaudet Memorial Library Washington, D.C.

Fedo, Michael W. "Dogs Help the Deaf to Hear."

"Fifer Cadets, The" *The Deaf-Mute Advance* October 22, 1892.

"Film Fare" *The Silent Worker* Vol. 14 No. 6 February, 1962.

Finesilver, Sherman G. "They Can't Hear, But They Get the Message" *Traffic Safety* August, 1961.

Finesilver, Sherman G. "They Can't Hear, But They Get the Message" U.S. Dept. HEW, Office of Vocational Rehabilitation.

"First Deaf Juror in California, The" *San Francisco Chronicle* October 25, 1979.

"First School, The" *The Silent Worker* June, 1896.

Flint, Richard W., Andrea Herman and Kevin J. Nolan *Beverly School for the Deaf's One Hundred Years* 1876-1976 (booklet).

"Florida School for the Deaf and the Blind, Brief Historical Summary" (unpublished paper).

"For the Deaf: Destiny Rides Again" *The Silent Worker* Vol. 14 No. 4 December, 1961.

"For 105 Years Dr. George M. McClure, Sr. Led A Charmed Life" *Alumni Newsletter* (Gallaudet) November, 1966.

Fountains of Time: Master Plan of the Georgia School for the Deaf Barker & Cunningham, Architect, Cave Spring, Ga. 1972.

"Francis Green's Idea" *The Boston Globe* November 11, 1897.

Frisina, Robert D. "The National Technical Institute for the Deaf" *The Deaf American* October, 1968.

Fusfeld, Irving S. "On the Subject of Accreditation For Gallaudet College" *Gallaudet Alumni Bulletin*, Vol. 1 No. 3 April, 1947.

Fusfeld, Irving S. *Successful Careers Out of Gallaudet College*, Series 1 and 2 Gallaudet Press, Washington, D.C. 1956.

Fusfeld, Irving S. *Survey of the Maryland State School for the Deaf* School for Deaf Press, Frederick, Maryland, 1929.

Gallagher, Buell G. *The Federal Government and the Higher Education of the Deaf* Federal Security Administration, Washington, D.C. 1949.

Gallaher, James E. *Representative Deaf Persons of the United States of America* James E. Gallaher Publisher, Chicago, Ill. 1898.

"Gallaudet Aircraft Corporation" *Aircraft Year Book*.

Gallaudet Almanac, The Jack R. Gannon, ed., Gallaudet College Alumni Association, Washington, D.C. 1974.

Gallaudet Alumni Bulletin
Vol. 1 No. 1 May, 1946.
Vol. 1 No. 3 April, 1947.
Vol. 2 No. 2 Spring, 1948.
Vol. 2 No. 3 June, 1948.
Vol. 2 No. 4 October, 1948.
Vol. 3 No. 11 Fall, 1950.
Vol. 4 No. 3 January, 1955.
Vol. 5 No. 6 May, 1958.
Vol. 5 No. 6 March, 1959.
Vol. 5 No. 7 June, 1959.
Vol. 6 No. 1 Fall, 1960.
Vol. 7 No. 1 Fall, 1961.

Gallaudet Centennial Newsletter Gallaudet College Alumni Association, Washington, D.C.

Gallaudet Day: Program Material for December 10 Library Science Class at Gallaudet College 2nd ed. (booklet) Gallaudet Press, Washington, D.C. 1948.

Gallaudet, Edward M. "The Milan Convention" *American Annuals of the Deaf* January, 1881.

"Gallaudet is Making an Ass of Himself" General Dynamics ad in *Time* July 28, 1958.

"Gallaudet LD-4 Light Bomber Seaplane, The" *Aviation* March 15, 1919.

"Gallaudet Navy Seaplane, The" *Aerial Age Weekly* May 14, 1917.

"Gallaudet Statue, The" *The Silent Worker* September 26, 1889.

Gallaudet Today (Special issue on Communication) Winter, 1974/75.

Gallaudet Today
 Vol. 1 No. 3 Spring, 1971.
 Vol. 2 No. 1 Fall, 1971.
 Vol. 3 No. 1 Fall, 1972.
 Vol. 3 No. 2 Winter, 1972.
 Vol. 4 No. 4 Summer, 1974.
 Vol. 5 No. 2 Winter, 1974/75.
 Vol. 6 No. 1 Fall, 1975.
 Vol. 7 No. 1 Fall, 1976.
 Vol. 9 No. 1 Fall, 1978.

Gannon, Jack R. "And finally . . ." *Gallaudet Today* Winter, 1976 and Winter, 1978.

Gannon, Jack R. "The Nebraska School for the Deaf" *The Deaf American* May 1967.

Gantt, Dave "Library Services to the Deaf" (unpublished report) Lexington, Ky.

Garretson, Mervin D. interviews Washington, D.C., Silver Spring, Md., Rehoboth Beach, Del.

Garretson, Mervin D. "Milan Re-Visited" *Gallaudet Today* Winter, 1981.

Garretson, Mervin D. "President's Report, 1976-78" National Association of the Deaf, Silver Spring, Md. 1978.

Garretson, Mervin D. "The Veditz Genius" *The Silent Worker* May, 1951, and July, 1951.

Garvin, Donna-Belle "James Hosley Whitcomb, New Hampshire Silhouettist" *Historical New Hampshire* Spring-Summer, 1977.

Gaw, Albert C. *Legal Status of the Deaf, The* Press of Gibson Brothers, Washington, D.C. 1907.

George, James and Steve Mathis "Personalities In Brief" *The Buff and Blue* November 19, 1949.

Gertrude, Sister Rose "St. Mary's School" (Schools for the Deaf—R. K. Holcomb) *The Silent Worker* July, 1954.

Gilbert, Laura-Jean "Birth of a College, The" *Gallaudet Almanac*, 1974.

Gilbert, Laura-Jean "Deaf Missioner Retires July 31" *Washington Diocese* Summer, 1978.

Glyndon, Howard (Laura C. R. Searing) *Echoes of Other Days* Harr Wagner Publishing Co., San Francisco, Calif. 1921.

Goetter, Marie S. "The Centennial Story of NSD" *Nebraska School for the Deaf Centennial 1869-1969* Nebraska School for the Deaf Alumni Association 1969.

"Go to It!" *The Frat* December, 1947.

Goldsmith, Arthur "Navy Frogmen Learn a Silent Language" *This Week Magazine* May 21, 1961.

Golladay, Loy E. "Sign Language" (Letter to the editor) *The Chronicle of Higher Education* September 10, 1979.

Gordon, Robert A. "The Gallaudet D-1 and the Gallaudet Drive Aircraft" *Historical Aviation Album* 1966.

Goss, Maureen "Breaking the Sound Barrier" *PTR* January-February, 1979.

Gottlieb, Lynn "Jewish Deaf Community" *Second Jewish Catalog* Jewish Publication Society of America Philadelphia, Pa. 1976.

Gough, John A. "Captioned Films for the Deaf: The New Program" *The Volta Review* January 1963.

"Government Positions for Which the Deaf May be Considered" *NAD Bulletin* reprinted in *The Washington Deaf Record* November, 1939.

Grant, Joseph S. "Dr. A. L. Roberts; An Acknowledgement" *The Frat* January-February, 1958.

Graybill, Georgetta and Eugene Peterson "The Silent Angels of Mercy Hospital" *The Silent Worker* January, 1963.

Grayson, Ray "Hilbert Duning—Architect of Buildings and Successful Ventures" *The Silent Worker* September, 1950.

"Greeley Men Co-Author New Series for the Deaf" Book News, Pruett Publishing Co., Boulder, Colo.

Green, Eric "Extending Affirmative Action to Handicappers" *The National Center Reporter* Vol. 8 No. 3 September, 1978.

Greenmun, Robert M. "Peddlers" *The Frat* June, 1946.

Groce, Nora "Everyone Here Spoke Sign Language" *Natural History* June, 1980.

Gross, Henry *Missouri School for the Deaf and Dumb, A Sketch of Its History, Growth, and Present Facilities* (booklet) The Record Office 1893.

Guide to College/Career Programs for Deaf Students, A National Technical Institute for the Deaf and Gallaudet College, 1975.

Gussow, Mel "Stage: Inspired 'Runaways'" *The New York Times* March 10, 1978.

Gustason, Gerilee, Donna Pfetzing, and Esther Zawolkow *Signing Exact English* Modern Signs Press, Los Alamitos, California, 1980.

Hall, L. B. and R. T. Youngers, "The Oklahoma School" (Schools for the Deaf—R. K. Holcomb) *The Silent Worker* Vol. 6 No. 6 February, 1964.

Hamel, Clara A. "Scouting for Deaf Girls" *The Volta Review* May 23, 1939.

Hamilton, Robert H. *The Mystic Oral School, Past-Present-Future* (booklet) June, 1975.

Hampshire Review, The January 8, 1955 and January 26, 1955.

"Handed Note, Teller Feared It Was Holdup" *The Los Angeles Times* March 15, 1973.

Harris, William "Off and On Captive Adolescents" *The Soho Weekly News* March 23, 1978.

Hearing Dog, The The American Humane Association (brochure), Englewood, Colo.

"Hearings Before the Committee on Labor Subcommittee to Investigate Aid to the Physically Handicapped" House of Representatives, 78th Congress, Second Session September 12-14, 1944.

Helms, Dorothy *Interesting Deaf Americans* (unpublished manuscript).

HEW News (U.S. Dept. Health, Education, and Welfare) news release August 20, 1978.

Higgins, Francis C. "Eugene Elmer Hannan—American Deaf Sculptor" *On The Green*.

Higgins, Francis C. *On the Accomplishments of Some Deaf Men and Women* California School for the Deaf, Riverside 1965.

Hill, Troy E. "El Gaucho Writes:" *The American Deaf Sportsman* March, 1970.

454

"Hints to Deaf Mutes" *Deaf Mute* (Ill.) *Advance,* Vol. 5 No. 18, May 6, 1874.

"Historical Facts to Know" *50th Anniversary of N.J.S.D.—M.K.S.D. Alumni Association 1928-1978.* Marie Katzenbach School for the Deaf Alumni Association 1978.

"Historical Society Features Work of Deaf Artists Who Entered ASD Aged 51 When School Opened" *The American Era* January, 1961.

Historical Summary of the Gallaudet School for the Deaf, A 1879-1979 St. Louis, Mo. (unpublished paper) 1978.

History of the Boston School for the Deaf, The 75th Anniversary 1899-1974.

"History of Deaf Missions" (fact sheet) Council Bluffs, Ia. 1977.

"History of the Louisiana State School for the Deaf 1852-1972" (unpublished paper).

Hodgson, Edwin A. *Facts, Anecdotes and Poetry Relating to the Deaf and Dumb* Deaf-Mutes' Journal Print, New York City, 1891.

Hofsteater, Howard T. "An Experiment in Pre-school Education" *Bulletin* Vol. 8 No. 1 Gallaudet Press, February, 1959.

Hofsteater, Howard T. "A Tribute to Roy J. Stewart, Alumnus Semper Fidelis" *Gallaudet Alumni Bulletin* Spring, 1963.

Holcomb, Roy K. *Hazards of Deafness* Joyce Media, Inc., Northridge, Calif. 1977.

Holcomb, Roy K. "Thumbnail History of Total Communication" (unpublished paper) 1978.

Holycross, Edwin Issac *The Abbe de l'Epée and Other Early Teachers of the Deaf* Edwin Isaac Holycross, Columbus, Oh. 1913.

"Home for the Aged and Infirms" *American Annals of the Deaf* Vol. 93 No. 5, November, 1948 and Vol. 95 No. 4, September, 1950.

"Home" *The Ranch Hand* Vol. 6 No. 5 and 6 May-June, 1978.

Hoosier, The Centennial Number, 1843-1943 Indiana School for the Deaf, Indianapolis, Indiana.

"How the Handicapped Use Metro" *Metro Memo Tabloid* Issue No. 71 September, 1979.

"How the 'Kingdom' Got Its Name" *The Missouri Record* January, 1972.

"How the Queen Saw An Odd New Game—And What She Said" *Life* October 28, 1957.

Howard, Jay Cooke "Michigan Deaf Leader Advocates Labor Bureau for the Deaf" *The Modern Silents* November, 1937.

Howard, Petra M. "Minnesota's Bureau for the Deaf" *The Silent Worker* Vol. 2 No. 2 October, 1949.

Howson, J. W. "The Argonaut" (about Theophilus d'Estrella) *The Silent Worker* February, 1928.

Huston, Cleburne *Deaf Smith: Incredible Texas Spy* Texian Press, Waco, Tex. 1973.

"I Want to Help Deaf People Get A Piece of the Rock" *Prudential Outlook* Second Quarter, 1978.

ICDA News, The International Catholic Deaf Association July/August, 1962.

Illinois Advance, The
Vol. 56 No. 2 November 23, 1923.
    January, 1942.
    February, 1946.
    October, 1952.

"In memory of Francis Green" *Evening Transcript,* Boston November 11, 1897.

Indiana School for the Deaf Information Handbook for Parents, Indianapolis 1977.

"Industrial Education of the Deaf, The" *The Silent Worker* October 28, 1928.

"Inimitable Harry Rosenfield of Federal Security Agency, The" *Gallaudet Alumni Bulletin* Vol. 2 No. 4 Winter, 1948.

"International Catholic Deaf Association, The" (brochure).

"Iowans Act" *The Frat* July, 1949.

"It's The Law" *Signs for Our Times* Linguistics Research Laboratory Gallaudet College No. 57 1980.

Jacobs, Leo M. *A Deaf Adult Speaks Out* Gallaudet College Press, Washington, D.C. 1974.

Jacobson, Casper B. "The Automobile and Deaf Drivers" *The Silent Worker* October, 1954.

"James F. Meagher" *The Modern Silents* March, 1938.

Jeffres, Janet and Margaret Barley *Speechreading* Chas. Thomas Publishers, Springfield, Ill. 1971.

Johnson, Elizabeth H. "Ability of Pupils to Understand Communication" *American Annals of the Deaf* March, 1948 and May, 1948.

Johnson, William A. "Former I.S.D. Teachers at Girl Scout Council Dinner" *The Illinois Advance,* November, 1960.

Jones, John W. *One Hundred Years of History in the Education of the Deaf in America and its Present Status* State School for the Deaf, Columbus, Oh. 1929.

Jones, Lillian R. "The Louisiana State School" (Schools for the Deaf—R. K. Holcomb) *The Silent Worker* Vol. 4 No. 3 November, 1951.

Jones, Ray. L. *Telephone Communication for the Deaf: Speech Indicator Manual* Northridge, Calif.

Jordan, Jerald interview, Silver Spring, Md.

Juliette Low and the Girl Scouts Girl Scouts of the United States of America, New York 1960.

"Junior National Association of the Deaf" (unpublished paper).

Kansas City Times, The June 26, 1953 and September 28, 1960.

"Kansas School Honors Our Late Grand President, Arthur L. Roberts" *The Frat* November-December, 1961.

Kansas School for the Deaf Archives, Olathe, Kansas.

Kelley, Lillian "Gar and Randy . . . Friends Share 'Ears'."

Kelly, Kevin "'Runaways' Near Miss for Elizabeth Swados" *The Boston* (Mass.) *Globe* March 24, 1978.

Kelly, Ronett E. "Governor Baxter State School for the Deaf" (Schools for the Deaf—R. K. Holcomb) *The Deaf American* February, 1967.

Kendall, John "Deaf Couple Fail to Regain Custody of Their Daughter" *Los Angeles Times* February 25, 1978.

Kendall School for the Deaf, The April, 1943, (booklet).

Kennedy, Shawn G. "For Deaf Student, One Teacher" *The New York Times* December 2, 1979.

Kentucky Standard, The May 5, 1932.

Kirkley, James R. "The Colorado School for the Deaf and the Blind" (Schools for the Deaf—R. K. Holcomb) *The Deaf American* April, 1965.

Klima, Edward S. and Ursula Bellugi "Poetry Without Sound" *Human Nature* October, 1978.

Koehler, Rev. J. M. "Ordinations of Deaf Men" *The Silent Worker* November, 1927.

Kohl, Herbert R. *Policy Study 1: Language and Education of the Deaf* New York Center for Urban Education 1966.

Kowalewski, Felix A personal sketch *The California Palms* February, 1975.

Kowalewski, Felix "Hillis Arnold: American Deaf Sculptor" *The Deaf American* Vol. 25, No. 3 November, 1972.

Kowalewski, Felix "Robert Freiman, Artist of Two Worlds" *The Deaf American* Vol. 26, No. 3 November, 1973.

Kowalewski, Felix "The Art of Frederick La Monto" *The Deaf American* Vol. 23, No. 7 March, 1971.

Kowalewski, Felix "Top of the Monument" (unpublished paper).

Kroll, Jack "Babes Up in Arms" *Newsweek* March 27, 1978.

Kruger, Art Sports Collection.

"Lad, Deaf for 8 Years, Wins D.C. Prize in Essay Contest" *The Washington Star* May 20, 1930.

Lane, Harlan "Notes for a Psycho-History of American Sign Language" *The Deaf American* September, 1977.

"Lars M. Larson" *The Wisconsin Times* Vol. 18 No. 26 March 26, 1896.

"Last Farewell, A" *The Frat* November-December, 1957.

Lauritsen, Wesley *History of the Minnesota School for the Deaf, Faribault, 1863-1963*. Minnesota School for the Deaf, Faribault 1963.

Lauritsen, Wesley "Mrs. Petra Howard Honored Upon Retirement" *The Silent Worker* Vol. 12 No. 6 February, 1960.

Lauritsen, Wesley "The Minnesota School for the Deaf" *Then and Now, A History of Rice County and Faribault, Minnesota.*

Lavos, George "The Michigan School" (Schools for the Deaf—R. K. Holcomb) *The Silent Worker* Vol. 6 No. 9 May, 1954.

Lederer, Joseph *A Follow-up Report on: Policy Study 1 Language and Education of the Deaf by Herbert R. Kohl* Center for Urban Education, N.Y. 1968.

"Legal Defense Fund Report" National Association for the Deaf February, 1979.

"Legislative Program of the American Federation of the Physically Handicapped, Inc." American Federation of the Physically Handicapped, Inc., Washington, D.C. 1954.

Leisman, Rev. A. G. "In Memoriam: Arthur Laurence Roberts" *The Frat* November-December, 1957.

Lemonds, Cherry and Pam Moss *Choosing A Job . . . Information About Deaf People and Their Jobs* Southern Regional Media Center for the Deaf The University of Tennessee, Knoxville 1974.

Lentz, Ella interview September 26, 1980 Silver Spring, Md.

Lewis, Arthur H. "World's Safest Drivers" *Ford Times* March, 1948.

Levy, Richard C. "TV Opens Line to the Deaf" *Parade* July 8, 1979.

Life October 22, 1948.

LinWeber, Ralph E. *American Deaf Softball Guide* Baseball Research Bureau, Toledo, Oh. 1961.

LinWeber, Ralph E. *Graduation Classes of the Ohio School for the Deaf, 1869-1949* Ralph E. LinWeber Publisher, 1950.

Litchfield, Kendall D. "One-Hundred Fifty Years—A Long Time Young!" New York School for the Deaf, White Plains, N.Y. 1967.

Little, Nina Fletcher "John Brewster, Jr., 1766-1854." *Connecticut Historical Society Bulletin* October, 1960.

Lodato, Antoinette "Lena" "A Historical Summary of the Gallaudet School for the Deaf" (unpublished paper) December, 1978.

Loe, Elva F. "The Story of the Thomas Hopkins Gallaudet Statue by Daniel Chester French" *The Gallaudet Almanac* 1974.

Long, Dr. J. Schuyler "History of the Sign Language" *The Modern Silents* Vol. 2 No. 11 December, 1938.

Long, J. Schuyler *The Sign Language* Robert Henderson, Des Moines, Ia. 1918.

Long, Mrs. E. F. "Stray Straws" *Representative Deaf Persons of the United States of America*, by James E. Gallaher *The Silent Worker* February, 1910.

"Lou's A Big Man in Spirit, Too!" *Looking Good*, CBS Fall Preview Spectacular 1979.

Lougue, Sister Maria Kostka *Sisters of St. Joseph of Philadelphia: A Century of Growth and Development, 1847-1947* The Newman Press, Westminister, Md. 1950.

Ludwig, William A. correspondence. (information on deaf Lutherans) The Edward Miner Gallaudet Memorial Library, Gallaudet College Washington, D.C.

Lunde, Anders S. and Stanley K. Bigman *Occupational Conditions Among The Deaf: A Report on a National Survey Conducted by Gallaudet College and the National Association of the Deaf* Gallaudet College Washington, D.C. 1959.

MacNeil, Ben Dixon *The Hattersman* John F. Blair, Winston-Salem, N.C. 1958.

Madsen, Willard J. "Walter John Krug—A Living Legend Lives On" *Our Heritage* D.C. Chapter, Gallaudet College Alumni Association 1964.

"MFA Tours for Deaf" *Houston* (Tex.) *Post* November 2, 1979.

Malzkuhn, Eric interview Washington, D.C.

Manson, Rev. Alexander MacLeod "The Work of the Protestant Churches for the Deaf in North America 1815-1949" *American Annals of the Deaf* May, 1950 and September, 1950.

Margulies, Lee "TV Reviews: When a Parent is Embarrassing" *Los Angeles Times* April 5, 1978.

Markowicz, Harry *American Sign Language: Face and Fancy* Public Service Programs Gallaudet College Washington, D.C. 1977.

Marra, William J. "KSD Traces History to Philip A. Emery" The Olathe Historical Society, Olathe, Kan.

Mary, Sister, S.S.J. "St. Mary's School for the Deaf" (Schools for the Deaf—R. K. Holcomb) *The Deaf American* July, August, 1967.

"Mass in Language of Signs" *The ICDA News* Vol. 15 No. 2 March-April, 1966.

"Master Plays Violin Made by Deaf Man, Pronounces Workmanship 'Very Acceptable'" *The Washingtonian* January, 1968.

Maxwell, H. W. and H. L. Swisher *A History of Hampshire County, West Virginia.*

May, Florence Lewis "Cadwallader Washburn An Appreciation" *Gallaudet Alumni Bulletin* June, 1954.

McCanner, Hazel K. "The Hessian Barracks' A Witness to History" Maryland School for the Deaf, Frederick 1976

McCanner, Hazel K. "History of MSD—The First 100 Years" *The Maryland Bulletin.*

McChord, Winfield interview, Danville, Ky.

McChord, Winfield "The Role of Women in the History and Development of the Kentucky School for the Deaf" *The Kentucky Standard* December, 1977.

McClure, George M. "Reminiscences of a Centenarian" *The Nebraska Journal* Vol. 91 No. 2 November, 1961.

McClure, George M. "The First State School for the Deaf" *American Annals of the Deaf* March, 1923.

McClure, William J. correspondence (information on the McClure family) Edward Miner Gallaudet Memorial Library College Washington, D.C.

McEwen, Charles "Portrait Painter's Works Emerge Like Photographs" *The Silent News* February, 1974.

McFarlane, J. H. "George S. Porter" *The Silent Worker* Vol. 1 No. 1 September, 1948.

McFarlane J. H. "The Alabama School" *The Silent Worker* Vol. 3 No. 10 June, 1951.

McSweeney, John M. ed., *The Mt. Airy World 1820-1938* Pennsylvania School for the Deaf April, 1938.

Meagher, J. Frederick "Francis P. Gibson" *The Illinois Advance.*

Meagher, J. Frederick postcard to Paul D. Hubbard Marra Museum Kansas State School for the Deaf, Olathe.

Meagher, J. Frederick *The Frat* January, 1938.

Meagher, J. Frederick "The Spotlight" *The Frat* March, 1947.

Meagher, J. Frederick "Fifty Deaf Marksmen Dead" *The Washingtonian* Vol. 24 No. 10 February 17, 1916.

"Member of Class of '40 is Television Newscaster" *Gallaudet Alumni Bulletin* Vol. 5 No. 6 Winter, 1959.

Merrill, Edward C., Jr. "New Measures of Credibility: Universal Rights and Progress in Education of the Deaf" *Gallaudet Today* Vol. 6 No. 1 Fall, 1975.

Merrill, Herbert C. letter to Paul D. Hubbard, March 6, 1942 Marra Museum Kansas State School for the Deaf, Olathe.

Merrill, Stephen E. "Master Etcher of His Times, Cadwallader Washburn, Now of Brunswick, Continues His Creative Art at 88" *The Brunswick (Me.) Record,* June 24, 1954.

Metro Round-Table Newsletter St. Louis, Mo. February, 1979.

Meyers, Lewis M. "Centennial 1870-1970," *The Oregon Outlook* November, 1970.

Michigan School for the Deaf Yearbook Flint 1976.

"Midwest Tournament" *The Modern Silents* March, 1938.

"Milepost" (about Dr. Harry Best) *Gallaudet Alumni Newsletter* April, 1971.

Mindrum, Beverly "40 Years of Work With Deaf" *Minneapolis Tribune.*

Minnesota Sets Pace in Aiding the Deaf" *The Washingtonian* October, 1915.

Missouri Deaf-Mute Record February 27, 1888.

"Missouri School for the Deaf During the Civil War, The" *The Missouri Record* January, 1972.

Model High School for Deaf (Hearing before the Committee on Labor and Public Welfare, United States Senate, Eighty-ninth Congress) U.S. Government Printing Office, Washington, D.C., 1966.

"Model Secondary School for the Deaf" *Annual Report* Washington, D.C. 1978.

Modern Silents, The Vol. 3 No. 1 January, 1939.

Moeller, Rev. F. A., S. J. "The Appeal of the Deaf Mute" *First American Catholic Missionary Congress,* 1908.

Moeller, Rev. F. A., S. J. "Education of the Catholic Deaf Mute" *N.C.W.C. Review* August, 1931.

"Mom and Dad Can't Hear Me" (letter from Daniel Wilson, producer, to Taras B. Denis) April 11, 1978. The Edward Miner Gallaudet Memorial Library, Gallaudet College Washington, D.C.

Moore, Carol Ann "Getting Around Town" *Greeley (Colo.) Tribune* March 23, 1977.

Moores, Donald P. *Educating the Deaf* Houghton Mifflin Company, 1978.

Morris Broderson The University of Arizona Museum of Art, Tucson 1975.

Morristown (N. J.) *Daily* September 2, 1953.

Mossel, Max "Manually Speaking" *The Silent Worker*
Vol. 8 No. 8 April, 1956.
Vol. 8 No. 9 May, 1956.
Vol. 8 No. 10 June, 1956.
Vol. 8 No. 11 July 1956.

"Movie Captioned for the Deaf Closes" *The New York Times* June 6, 1979.

"Mrs. Gallaudet Dies; Widow of Aviator" (newspaper clipping, no source) 1973.

Mudgett, David E. "Howard T. Hofsteater, 1909-1964" *The Deaf American* February, 1965.

Mudgett, David E. "Howard Tracy Hofsteater—1909-1964" *Gallaudet Alumni Bulletin* Vol. 8 Nos. 1 & 2 Fall, 1964 and Winter, 1965.

Mudgett, David E. "The NFSD Story: Diamond Jubilee 1901-1976" *The Deaf American* Vol. 28 No. 10 June, 1976.

Murphy, Fred "Visitor's Register Tells Interesting KSD Story" (newspaper clipping, no source).

Myers, Lowell J. *The Law and the Deaf* edited by Max Friedman Department of Health, Education, and Welfare Vocational Rehabilitation Administration Washington, D.C. 1967.

"N.A.D. Gift" *The Washington Deaf Record* Vol 10 No. 9 March, 1944.

NAD State Association Handbook Gary Olsen, ed., National Association of the Deaf, Silver Spring, Md.

"National Association of the Deaf" *The Exceptional Parent* December, 1979.

"National Center on Deafness" California State University at Northridge (brochure) 1980.

"National Congress of Jewish Deaf" (flyer).

National Observer, The
Vol. 14 No. 2 September, 1953.
Vol. 14 No. 4 November, 1953.
Vol. 14 No. 5 December, 1953.
Vol. 14 No. 6 January, 1954.
Vol. 14 No. 12 July, 1954.
Vol. 16 No. 2 September, 1955.
Vol. 16 No. 5 December, 1955.
Vol. 15 No. 12 July, 1955.
Vol. 16 No. 4 November, 1955.
Vol. 16 No. 8 March, 1956.
Vol. 16 No. 9 April, 1956.
Vol. 16 No. 11 June, 1956.
Vol. 16 No. 12 July, 1956.

"National Technical Institute for the Deaf, The" *The Deaf American* April, 1969.

National Theatre of the Deaf (program books) 1967, 1978, 1979 and NTD fact sheet.

Nebraska Journal, The
Vol. 93 No. 6 March, 1964
Vol. 94 No. 4 January, 1965.
Vol. 94 No. 5 February, 1965.
Vol. 94 No. 6 March, 1965.
Vol. 95 No. 1 October, 1965.
Vol. 95 No. 2 November, 1965.
Vol. 95 No. 3 December, 1965.
Vol. 95 No. 8 May, 1966.

Nelson, W. Dale "New Legal Hope for the Deaf" *The Sunday Denver Post* January 9, 1977.

"New Building at VSDB Dedicated" *The Virginia Guide* May, 1968.

"New Career Frontier is Opened for the Deaf" *Sarasota Herald-Tribune* July 16, 1976.

"New Jersey Division of the Deaf" Annual Report Fiscal Year 1979.

New Mexico Progress, The Santa Fe, New Mexico May, 1975.

"New Telecaption TV Set Has Closed-Captioning Electronics for Hearing-Impaired *News from Sears* (news release) July 15, 1980.

New York Journal of the Deaf, The 1939.

New York Missionary, The February, 1973.

New York Times, The April 22, 1979.

New release G-3 Gallaudet College Washington, D.C.

North American Review April, 1867.

North Dakota Banner, The March-April, 1936 and January, 1943.

Norwood, Malcolm J. "A Review of Media Services and Captioned Films" (A paper presented at the Symposium on Research and Utilization of Educational Media for Teaching the Deaf) Lincoln, Neb. April 2, 1974.

Norwood, Malcolm J. interview February 10, 1980 New Carrollton, Md.

Norwood, Malcolm J. "Media and Technology: It's Impact Educationally and Socially on the Deaf in the United States" (A paper presented at the International Congress on the Education of the Deaf, Tokyo, Japan) August 25-29, 1975.

Norwood, Malcolm J. "Media Horizons" *Proceedings of the Forty-Sixth Meeting of the Convention of American Instructors of the Deaf,* Indiana School for the Deaf, Indianapolis, Ind. June 24-29, 1973.

Norwood, Malcolm J. "New Horizons for the Deaf" *School Life* January, 1963.

Norwood, Malcolm J. "The Second Decade" *Symposium on Research and Utilization of Educational Media for the Deaf* March 17-19, 1969.

"Not for Sale" *Globe-Gazette*, Mason City, Ia. November 8, 1947.

Nuernberger, Donald "Nubby" "The Christensen Adoption Story" *The Deaf American* January, 1968.

O'Brien, John G. interview Washington, D.C. and Seattle, Washington.

"Off Broadway" *The New Yorker* March 20, 1978.

"Official Announcement to the Deaf of America" *The Washington Deaf Record,* Vol. 8 No. 3 September, 1941.

Official Program: CISS/VIII World Winter Games for the Deaf Lake Placid, N.Y., USA February 2-8, 1975.

Ohio Chronicle, The Vol. 84 No. 15 January 19, 1952.

"Old Gym, The" *The Missouri Record* February, 1970.

"Old Masters of the Sign Language" *The Deaf American* September, 1964.

"Oldest Organization of Deaf Being Sought; We Think It's New England Gallaudet Association" *The American Era* April, 1968.

Olson, Lucile *Heritage of the Wisconsin School for the Deaf* Delavan, Wisconsin.

On The Green July 7, 1980.

"On the Run" *The Frat* August, 1949.

One Hundred Twenty-fifth Anniversary of St. Mary's School for the Deaf Buffalo, N.Y. 1853-1978.

"One Hundred Years of the Indiana State School for the Deaf" *The Hoosier* Centennial Number 1943.

Oral Deaf Adults Section Handbook Alexander Graham Bell Association for the Deaf, Inc. Washington, D.C. 1977.

Oregon Outlook, The February, 1928.

Orman, James N. interview Washington, D.C.

Orman, James N. "The President's Message" *Gallaudet Alumni Bulletin*, Vol. 7 No. 8 Winter, 1964.

O'Rourke, Terry J. interview, Silver Spring, Md.

Our Heritage: Gallaudet College Centennial: 1864-1964 D.C. Chapter, Gallaudet College Alumni Association Graphic Arts Press, Washington, D.C. 1964.

"Out of the Past" *The Companion* February, 1978.

Pach, Alexander L. "With The Silent Workers" *The Silent Worker* July, 1922.

Panara, Robert F., Taras B. Denis, and James H. McFarlane *The Silent Muse: An Anthology of Prose and Poetry by the Deaf* Gallaudet College Alumni Association, Toronto, Canada 1960.

Panara, Robert F. "The Deaf Writer in America From Colonial Times to 1970" *American Annals of the Deaf* September and November, 1970.

Panara, Robert F. "Total Communication for the Deaf" *Rehabilitation Record* January-February, 1971.

"Pardon My Intrusion . . ." *The Missouri Record* November, 1960.

Patterson, Francine "Conversations With a Gorilla" *National Geographic* Vol. 154 No. 4 October, 1978.

Pearl Harbor and the USS Arizona Memorial: A Pictorial History Richard A. Wisniewski, ed., Pacific Basin Enterprises, Honolulu 1977.

Peet, Dr. Elizabeth "Cadwallader Washburn" *Gallaudet Alumni Bulletin* June, 1952.

Peet, Dr. Elizabeth "Our Hall of Fame" *Gallaudet Alumni Bulletin* March, 1952.

Peikoff, David interview, Washington, D.C.

PSAD News, The Pennsylvania Society for the Advancement of the Deaf May, 1949.

Petersen, Eugene W. "The Magic of A Penny Postal Card" *The Deaf American* Vol. 19 No. 7 March, 1967.

Peterson, Edwin G. "Should the Deaf Be Allowed to Drive?" *The Companion* Minnesota School for the Deaf Vol. 64 No. 13 April 6, 1939.

Pettingill, Don G. "White House Conference On Individuals" *The Deaf American* April, 1977 and July-August, 1977.

"PL 94-142 and Deaf Children" (special issue) *Gallaudet Alumni Newsletter.*

"Plea in Sign Language" *Kansas City Times* June 21, 1949.

Porter, Sarah H. "Suppression of Signs by Force" *American Annals of the Deaf* Vol. 39 1894.

Post-Star Glenn Falls, N.Y. July 22, 1977.

Powers, Helen *Signs of Silence, Bernard Bragg and the National Theatre of the Deaf* Dodd, Mead & Company, N.Y. 1972.

"Pres. Oliver in Charge of N.A.D. Victory Fund in State" *The Washington Record* Vol. 8 No. 10 April, 1942.

Proceedings, First Triennial Reunion of the Indiana School for the Deaf Graduates and Former Pupils August 24-26, 1886.

Proceedings of the Workshop on Community Development Through Organizations of and for the Deaf Alan B. Crammatte and Loel F. Schreiber, eds., Office of Vocational Rehabilitation, Department of Health, Education, and Welfare Washington, D.C. 1961.

"Professional Counseling Services to the Deaf" Family Service of Prince George's (Md). County, Inc. (letter and brochure).

Propp, George "Community Development Through Organizations of and for the Deaf" *The Nebraska Journal* Vol. 90 No. 8 May, 1961.

Raindrop, The: A Collection of Entertaining Stories for Young People, The Alexander Graham Bell Association for the Deaf Washington, D.C. 1975.

458

Reaching Out . . . to Wisconsin's Hearing Impaired Citizens The Final Report of the Governor's Committee on Problems of Deaf and Hard of Hearing People, 1979.

Recent Developments in Manual English (papers presented at a Special Institute sponsored by the Department of Education) Gallaudet College Washington, D.C. 1973.

Reed, John S. "Deaf Telephone Users: Their Fingers Do the Talking" (magazine article, no source).

Reed, Richard D. interview Fulton, Mo. 1979.

Reed, Richard D. "Missouri School for the Deaf" *The Missouri Record* January, 1972.

Reed, Richard D. "MSD's Kentucky Connection" *The Missouri Record*.

Reilly, Henry R. "The Might-Have-Been Story of Gallaudet" *The Rhode Islander* November 29, 1959.

Reporter, The December 12, 1957.

Reports: "Tour and Observations of Schools for the Deaf in North America" by Dr. Eric Stanley Greenaway and "International Congress on the Modern Educational Treatment of Deafness" by Mrs. Phyllis Watson Canadian Association of the Deaf, Ontario, Canada, 1958.

Rhode Island School (unpublished paper).

Rhodes, Mary J. "From a Parent's Point of View" *The Deaf American* Vol. 23 No. 6 February, 1971.

Richards, Rev. Ray "The Silent Faith" *The Catholic Connection* June, 1978.

Ridgeway, James "'Dumb' Children" *The New Republic* August 2, 1969.

Riser, Catherine "Alabama School for the Deaf" (Schools for the Deaf—R. K. Holcomb) *The Deaf American*, Vol. 18, No. 5 January, 1966.

Roe, W. R. *Peeps into the Deaf World* Derby Bemrose & Sons Limited, 1917.

Rome (N.Y.) *Register* reprinted in *The Silent Worker*, Vol. 5, No. 7 October, 1892.

Rosenfield, Harry N. "Federal Agent Outlines ABC of College Survey" (letter to editor) *Gallaudet Alumni Bulletin* May, 1946.

Rothrick, May U. ed., *The French Broad-Holston County; A History of Knox County Tennessee* The Knox County History Committee, East Tennessee Historical Society 1946.

St. Louis Cardinals *Press Book*, 1973 and 1974.

"Santa Ana Unified School District Program for the Deaf" *The Deaf American* April, 1969.

Sawyer, Leonard A. *The Liberty Ships* Cornell Maritime Press, Cambridge, Md. 1970.

Schneider, W. F. "Anent the N.A.D." *The Washingtonian* May 5, 1911.

Schowe, Ben M. "Extra Exemption?" (letter to the editor) *The Frat* May-June, 1962.

Schowe, Ben M. "The Silent Powerhouse" *The American Deaf Sportsman* Vol. 1 No. 3 September, 1969.

Schowe, Ben M. "Guidelines for the Employment of Deaf Workers" *Employment Security Review*.

Schowe, Ben M. "Handicapped?" Office of Vocational Rehabilitation, Federal Security Agency, Washington, D.C.

Schowe, Ben M. "Reflections in the Mirror" *The Michigan Mirror* March, 1946.

Schowe, Ben M. "The Deaf in Industry" Gallaudet College *Bulletin* Vol. 4 No. 2 October, 1955.

Schowe, Ben M. "These Deaf-Mutes Are Good Factory Workers" *Factory Management and Maintenance* McGraw Hill Publishing Co., Inc. August, 1946.

Schowe, Dr. B. M. "A Confession of Faith" *The Silent Worker* September, 1956

Schowe, Dr. B. M. "Self-Security and the Humble Heart" *The Frat* September-October, 1959.

Schreiber, Herb "Deaf 'Hijacker' Nabbed!" *The Washingtonian* April, 1972.

Schreiber, Frederick C. "Home Office Notes" *The Deaf American*.

Schroedel, John "Unity and Progress Achieved by Council" *Alumni Newsletter* (Gallaudet) Vol. 3 No. 8 May, 1969.

Schunhoff, Hugo F. "The Bountiful Sixties: Prelude to Accountability" *The California News* April, 1971.

Science September 5, 1890, October 31, 1890.

"Scoop, A Palpable Scoop!, A" *The Reporter* December 12, 1957.

Scott, Judith Marra "St. Joseph's School for the Deaf New York Archdiocese 1869-1979."

"Seeing Essential English (SEE) Program Aids Deaf" *Rocky Mountain News* June 11, 1972.

Senate Document No. 287 1846.

"Senate Passes Captioned Film Library Bill; Now in House Committee on Education and Labor" *The American Era* reprinted in *The Utah Eagle* January, 1958.

75th Anniversary Edition, The: The North Carolina School for the Deaf 1894-1969 Morganton 1969.

Shales, Tom "Mom and Dad Can't Hear Me" *The Washington Post* April 5, 1978.

Shaposka, Bert "James N. Orman: Great Moral Courage and Perserverance in the Cause of the Deaf Man" *The Deaf American* May, 1965.

Shaposka, Bert *The NAD Story* National Association of the Deaf.

Shaposka, Bert "Tom L. Anderson: The Guiding Philosophy In the Life of a Conscientious Public Servant" *The Deaf American*, November, 1966.

Sharp, Christopher "Runaways" *Women's Wear Daily* March 13, 1978.

"Short History of Cameron Methodist Church of the Deaf, A" (program book) May 8, 1960.

Siger, Leonard "The Silent Stage" *Johns Hopkins Magazine* Vol. 12 No. 1 October, 1960.

"Sign-Language Classes for Teachers of the Deaf" *The Ohio Chronicle* December 2, 1939 reprinted in *The Washington Deaf Record* January, 1940.

Sign Language and the Deaf Community; Essays in Honor of William C. Stokoe, Charlotte Baker and Robbin Battison, eds., National Association of the Deaf, Silver Spring, Md. 1980.

"Sign Language, The" *The Deaf-Mute Optic* Vol. 6 No. 19 February 12, 1887.

"Sign Language, The" *The Sign* Vol. 6 No. 3 October 6, 1893.

Silent Cavalier, The March, 1941.

Silent Hoosier, The March 16, 1916, June 1, 1945 and June, 1978.

"Silent Learning: At Innovative College, Deaf Students Receive A Full Campus Life" *Wall Street Journal* May 8, 1976.

Silent News, The July, 1978.

Silent Worker, The
Vol. 2 No. 6 November, 1888.
Vol. 2 No. 10 January, 1889.

Vol. 2 No. 13 April, 1889.
Vol. 2 No. 14 May, 1889.
Vol. 3 No. 16 September, 1889.
Vol. 3 No. 22 1890.
Vol. 3 No. 23 May, 1890.
Vol. 3 No. 24 June, 1890.
Vol. 4 No. 26 November, 1890.
Vol. 4 No. 27 December, 1890.
Vol. 4 No. 29 February, 1891.
Vol. 4 No. 31 April, 1891.
Vol. 4 No. 36 November, 1891.
Vol. 4 No. 37 December, 1891.
Vol. 5 No. 1 February, 1892.
Vol. 5 No. 8 November, 1892.
Vol. 5 No. 10 January, 1893.
Vol. 5 No. 11 February, 1893.
Vol. 6 No. 2 October, 1893.
Vol. 6 No. 4 December, 1893.
Vol. 6 No. 5 January, 1894.
Vol. 6 No. 6 February, 1894.
Vol. 6 No. 7 March, 1894.
Vol. 6 No. 10 June, 1894.
Vol. 7 No. 2 October, 1894.
Vol. 7 No. 3 November, 1894.
Vol. 7 No. 5 January, 1895.
Vol. 7 No. 8 April, 1895.
Vol. 8 No. 5 January, 1896.
Vol. 8 No. 9 October, 1896.
Vol. 9 No. 9 May, 1897.
Vol. 10 No. 5 January, 1898.
Vol. 15 No. 7 March, 1903.
Vol. 15 No. 10 June, 1903.
Vol. 16 No. 3 December, 1903.
Vol. 34 No. 10 July, 1922.
Vol. 35 No. 7 April, 1923.
Vol. 37 No. 4 January, 1925.
Vol. 39 No. 5 February, 1927.
Vol. 1 No. 6 February, 1949.
Vol. 2 No. 1 September, 1949.
Vol. 2 No. 7 March, 1950.
Vol. 3 No. 1 September, 1950.
Vol. 3 No. 2 October, 1950.
Vol. 3 No. 3 November, 1950.
Vol. 3 No. 4 December, 1950.
Vol. 3 No. 5 January, 1951.
Vol. 3 No. 6 February, 1951.
Vol. 3 No. 7 March, 1951.
Vol. 3 No. 8 April, 1951.
Vol. 3 No. 9 May, 1951.
Vol. 3 No. 10 June, 1951.

Silent Worker, The (revived)
Vol. 4 No. 4 December, 1951.
Vol. 4 No. 11 July, 1952.
Vol. 5 No. 1 September, 1953.
Vol. 6 No. 6 February, 1954.
Vol. 9 No. 10 June, 1957.
Vol. 11 No. 8 April, 1959.
Vol. 11 No. 9 May, 1959.
Vol. 13 No. 7 March, 1961.
Vol. 15 No. 11 July-August, 1963.
Vol. 16 No. 1 September, 1963.
Vol. 16 No. 2 October, 1963.
Vol. 16 No. 6 February, 1964.
Vol. 16 No. 8 April, 1964.
Vol. 16 No. 9 May, 1964.
Vol. 16 No. 11 July-August, 1964.
Vol. 17 No. 1 September, 1964. (*The Silent Worker* renamed *The Deaf American*)

Deaf American, The
Vol. 17 No. 2 October, 1964.

Vol. 17 No. 3 November, 1964.
Vol. 17 No. 4 December, 1964.
Vol. 19 No. 5 January, 1967.
Vol. 19 No. 7 March, 1967.
Vol. 19 No. 8 April, 1967.
Vol. 19 No. 9 May, 1967.
Vol. 19 No. 10 June, 1967.
Vol. 21 No. 2 October, 1968.
Vol. 21 No. 8 April, 1969.
Vol. 23 No. 4 December, 1970.
Vol. 24 No. 3 November, 1971.
Vol. 24 No. 9 May, 1972.

Silent World Philadelphia, Pa. June 23, 1892.

"Sloan Likely to Start at Tackle for Big Red" *Columbia Missourian* September 12, 1973.

"Sloan Makes Cards' Cut, Otis Acquired" Springfield, Mo. newspaper clipping September 13, 1973.

Smith, Jack "A Mission for the Deaf" *Performance* February, 1973.

Smith, Jess M. "George Dewey Coats" (The Editor's Page) *The Deaf American* Vol. 18 No. 1 September, 1965.

Smith J. L. "The Deaf and the Automobile" *The Maryland Bulletin* January, 1923.

Smithdas, Robert J. "Shared Beauty" *The Deaf American* Vol. 26 No. 10 June, 1974.

Somers, Claire "Hearing-Impaired Count Gains on Several Fronts" *Arise* March, 1978.

Somers, Claire "Oscar Show Creates a Controversy Among Deaf Actors" *Accent on Living* Fall, 1978.

South Carolina School for the Deaf and the Blind, The—One Hundredth Anniversary (booklet) 1849-1949.

South Dakota Advocate, The December, 1929.

Spradley, Thomas S. and James P. Spradley *Deaf Like Me* Random House, N.Y. 1978.

Sparks, William B. (promotional materials).

"Statement by Joseph A. Califano, Jr., Secretary of Health, Education, and Welfare" *HEW News* March 23, 1979.

"Statistics of Deaf Drivers" *Ohio Motor Travel* reprinted in *The Washington Deaf Record* February, 1939.

Stem, Carolyn "The Junior NAD Story" Jr. NAD Convention program book 1968.

Stevens, Kelly H. "Henry Humphrey Moore, a Retrospect" *The Silent Worker* May, 1927.

Stewart, Larry G. "A Truly Silent Minority" *The New York Times* March 16, 1972.

Stewart, Roy J. "About the N.A.D. Lecture Films in the Sign Language" (letter to a friend) November, 1964.

Stewart, Roy J. "Gallaudet College Alumni Association Films" (unpublished report).

Stewart, Roy J. "How Wrestling Came to Gallaudet College" (unpublished paper).

Stewart, Roy J. "In Memory of a Friend" *Gallaudet Alumni Bulletin* Spring, 1963.

Stokoe, William C., H. Russell Bernard and Carol Padden "An Elite Group in Deaf Society" *Sign Language Studies* 12 Gallaudet College.

Stone, Alice V. "Oral Education, A Challenge and a Necessity" *The Volta Review* May, 1968.

Stone, Mary E., and Joseph P. Youngs, Jr. "Catholic Education of the Deaf in the United States" *American Annals of the Deaf* Vol. 93, No. 5 November 1948.

Sugiyama, William T. interview Hyattsville, Md.

"Summary of Dr. Harry Best's Survey Report" *Gallaudet Alumni Bulletin* Winter, 1948.

Sunday Star, The (D.C.) June 8, 1956.

"Survey Advisory Committee Confers With Dr. Best" *Gallaudet Alumni Bulletin* May, 1946.

"Survey Shows Deaf Automobile Drivers Far Superior to Others" *Philadelphia Bulletin* reprinted in *The Modern Silents* October, 1937.

Swaim, Robert L., Jr. "Deaf Performer in an Off-Broadway Musical *The Silent News* March, 1978.

Swain, Robert L., Jr. "John Brewster, Jr., 18-19th Century Deaf Artist, Accorded Recognition" *The Deaf American* Vol. 20, No. 5 January 1968.

Swaim, Robert L., Jr. "Why the Language of Signs is Being Taught to a Chimpanzee at the University of Nevada" *The Deaf American* September, 1968.

Swanborough, Gordon and Peters M. Bowers "Gallaudet D-1, D-4" *United States Navy Aircraft Since 1911* Funk & Wagnalls, N.Y. 1968.

"Tale of Two Names: Deaf Smith and XIT, A" (booklet) Deaf Smith Feedyards, Inc. Amarillo, Tex.

Taub, Peter B. "Interception of the 50" *Times-Union* August 7, 1975.

"Tabular Statement of Schools for the Deaf in the United States, 1850-1948" *American Annals of the Deaf* Vol. 93 No. 1 January, 1948.

"Technical School for the Deaf, A" *The Silent Worker* Vol. 5 No. 7 October, 1892.

Teegarden, G. M. "The Future of the Deaf" *Colorado Index* Vol. 21 No. 3 October 6, 1894.

Teich, Howard and Raleight Pinskey "HELP! Fire Safety for the Deaf" *Firehouse* August, 1978.

Telephone Communication for the Deaf: Speech Indicator Manual San Fernando Valley State College, Northridge, Calif.

"Television and Deaf Persons: An Update" *Gallaudet Today* (special issue) Vol. 8 No. 3 Spring, 1978.

"Television and the Deaf" *Gallaudet Today* (special issue) Vol. 4 No. 2 Winter, 1973.

"Thanks, Boys" *The Frat* December, 1947.

Third Biennial Report of the Board of Trustees of the School for Defective Youth of the State of Washington 1892.

Thom, John L. "Deaf Artist Turns to Local Scenes After Travels Abroad" *Morning Advocate* Baton Rouge, La. March 12, 1939.

"Thomas H. Gallaudet Afloat, The" *The Silent Cavalier* Vol. 4 No. 3 November 15, 1943.

Tingley Judy, ed., *Silent Voices: Literary Issue of the Junior Deaf American* The Marie H. Katzenbach School for the Deaf, West Trenton, N.J. 1968.

"Town of Canajoharie" *Frothingham's History of Montgomery County* (N.Y.)

Turk, Frank R. interview Washington D.C.

Turner, William W. "The Causes of Deafness" *American Annals of the Deaf* June, 1868.

"TV News With a Difference" *Prime Time* Vol. 4 No. 12 December, 1973.

"TV Signs On!" *Gallaudet Today* Vol. 9 No. 2 Winter, 1979.

Understanding Language Through Sign Language Research Academic Press, New York.

"Uneducated Deaf-Mute, The" *The Silent Worker* Vol. 5 No. 7 October, 1892.

"Unique Health Project for Deaf is Launched" (news release) Prince George's (Md.) County May 24, 1978.

Van Selus, Vera Majella Larson (letters to Ann Bennett February 11, 1978, March 2, 1978 and April 7, 1978) New Mexico School for the Deaf Library.

"U.S. Senate Inaugurates New Teletypewriter Communication System for the Deaf" *Western Union News Bureau* October 24, 1978.

Utah Schools for the Deaf and the Blind Ogden, Utah (brochure).

Vasnick, Andrew interview Washington, D.C.

Veditz, George W. "The Preservation of the Sign Language" (from a videotape in the Edward Miner Gallaudet Memorial Library, Gallaudet College).

Veditz, George W. "The Genesis of the National Association" *Deaf-Mutes' Journal* June 1, 1933.

Vernon, McCay and Hugh Pickett "Mainstreaming" *The Banner* North Dakota School for the Deaf December, 1979 and January, 1980.

Vernon McCay "The Road to Hell" (editorial) *American Annals of the Deaf* December, 1978.

"Videotape Made Here Will Help PAA Flight Attendants Work With Their Deaf Passengers" *Pacific Business News,* Honolulu, Hawaii May 7, 1979.

Vinson, Emery E. "The Prayer of the Deafened" *Oregon Outlook* February, 1928.

Wagner, William *Reuben Fleet and the Story of Consolidated Aircraft* Aero Publishers, Inc., Fallbrook, Calif. 1976.

Waindel, Gerald "Signing—An International Language" *Inside Interior* February, 1977.

Walsh, Rev. David interview Washington, D.C. 1979.

Washington Post, The March 29, 1979 and May 5, 1979.

Washingtonian, The February 15, 1912, October 16, 1913 and March, 1971.

Webster's Biographical Dictionary G. & C. Merriam Company, Springfield, Mass., 1976.

West Virginia Tablet, The March, 1932.

"What Experience Taught Them" *New York Journal of the Deaf* reprinted in *The Washington Deaf Record* February, 1939.

"What One Station is Doing: WGBH-TV" *Gallaudet Today,* Winter, 1973.

Whisman, Charley interview Indianapolis, Ind. 1977.

Whisman, Charley "Highlights of the History of the Indiana School for the Deaf" The *Silent Hoosier* September, 1978.

White, Warren "Deaf People Are Lobbying, Group Claims" Rochester (N.Y.) *Democrat and Chronicle* July 3, 1978.

White, Warren "Deaf Have Political 'Death Wish'" Rochester (N.Y.) *Democrat and Chronicle* July 2, 1978.

"Who's Who in the Deaf World" *The Silent Worker,* Vol. 37 No. 4 January, 1925.

Wiest, Oliver "ISD Stunned by Chicago Tragedy" *Jacksonville* (Ill.) *Courier* January 27, 1970.

William J. Marra interview Olathe, Kan. May, 1979.

Williamson, Dick "His Talents Wouldn't be Denied" *The American-Statesman,* Austin, Tex. June 6, 1971.

Williamson, Hugh P. "Fulton's History Told in Tales of 'Kingdom of Callaway'" (Chamber of Commerce publication).

461

Wilson, Carol "A Natural" High Point (N.C.) *Enterprise* February 4, 1979.

Wilson, George C. *Deaf Like Me* Grand Blanc Printing and Publishing, Grand Blanc, Mich. 1977.

Wolach, Marvin "Mr. and Mrs. NMSD Retiring" *The New Mexico Progress* Vol. 67 No. 9 May, 1975.

Wood, Willard H. "Jones Mervin Vestal Heads North Carolina Deaf Labor Bureau" *The Modern Silents* May, 1938.

Wood W. H., Sr. *The Forgotten People* St. Petersburg, Florida Dixie Press, St. Petersburg, Fla. 1973.

Woodward, James "Historical Bases of American Sign Language" (A paper presented at the Rochester Conference on Sign Language and Neurolinguistics, September, 1976) published in *Understanding Language Through Sign Language Research* Academic Press, N.Y. 1978, Patricia Siple, editor.

"WPA Job Handed Deaf Man After Field Agent Tells 'em" *The American Deaf Citizen* reprinted in *The Washington Deaf Record* December, 1938.

"W.P.A. Situation, The" *The Washington Deaf Record* Vol. 4 No. 11 May, 1938.

World Book Encyclopedia, The.

VIIth World Congress of the World Federation of the Deaf (program book) July 31-August 8, 1975.

"Yesterday-Today" (program book) Kansas School for the Deaf, Olathe 1961.

"Your Navy in Hawaii" Navy Bicentennial, 1775-1975 (U.S. Navy pamphlet) 1975.

"You Need More Than Just A Magic Marker" *Prime Time* Vol. 3 No. 9 September, 1973.

Yount, William R. *An Introduction to Ministry with the Deaf* Broadman Press, Nashville, Tenn. 1976.

Index

Abrams, William S., 402
Accessible to handicapped persons, 383
Actors and Actresses, 350, 351, 352, 353
Acuna, Angel, 54, 301-02
Adams, Samuel A., 186
Adams, Sara T., 82
Adams, Wayman, 140
Adler, Edna P., 338, 368
    quoted, 387, 406
Adoption, 337
Aerial Medication, 92
Agazie, James C., 402
Agricultural Research Service, 120
Akron Goodyear Silents, 42
Alabama, 7
Alabama School for the Deaf. See Schools
Alaska-Yukon-Pacific Exposition, 36
Albronda, Mildred, 111, 145
    and her books, The Magic Lantern Man: Theophilus Hope d'Estrella; Douglas Tilden: Portrait of a Deaf Sculptor, 145
Alexander Graham Bell School. See Schools
Allen, Gordon L., 265, 266
Allen, George H., 253
Allen, Gordon B., 246
Allen, Harry Van, 187
Allen, Joe, 278, 282
Allen, R., 373
Alphabet cards, 256, 259
Altizer, Rueben S., 244
Amateur Athletic Union boxing tournament, 224
America, 157
American Athletic Association of the Deaf, 296-297, 300
    AAAD Bulletin, 300

AAAD Hall of Fame, 297, 305-07 (ill.); athlete of the year (ill.) 309-10; coaches, 308; old timers, 308; sports leaders-writers, 308
American Antiquarian Society, 247
American Deaf Softball Guide, 295-96
American Federation of the Physically Handicapped, 223, 230
American Indians, 148
American School for the Deaf. See Schools
American Sign Language, 359, 367, 372, 376, 383, "Comes out of the closet," 364; native and natural language, 365, 367; popularity, 367
American Water Color Society, 113
Anderson, Tom L., 31, 42, 223, 326
Andersson, Yerker, 379, 381
Andrewjeski, Lilly G., 265
Annual Staff and Teachers' Salaries, 74
answering services, 325, 326
Anthony, David A., 370-72
    S.E.E. Manual, 372
Archibald, Orson, 164-66
Architects
    Duning, Hilbert C., 154
    Hanson, Olof, 155
    Marr, Thomas S., 156
Arden, T. G., 69 (See also George M. Teegarden)
Argo, William K., 21
Ariadna Hall, 28
Arizona School for the Deaf and the Blind. See Schools
Arnold, Hills, 94
    and his sculpture "Abraham and Isaac," 94; "Crucifix of Christ," 94; "The Lord is My

Shepherd," 95; "Mother Ann and Child," 95
Art schools
    Academy of Design, New York, 144
    American Academy of Arts, Chicago, 133
    Ateliex Louis Bilocal and Academie Colorossi, Paris, 140
    Buffalo Art Center School, 125
    Circulo Belles Artes, Madrid, 140
    Corcoran School of Art, 100, 118, 123, 140
    Ecole des Beaux Arts, 134
    Flint Institute of Arts, Michigan, 123
    Hopkins Art Institute, San Francisco, 82
    Julien Academy, 136
    Maryland Institute, College of Art, 115, 130
    New York School of Fine and Applied Arts, 123, 140
    Phoenix Art Museum, Arizona, 100
    San Francisco Art Association's School of Design, 110, 136
    Trenton School of Industrial Arts, 140
    articulation, 11, 15, 20
Artists
    Arnold, Hillis, 94-95
    Bloch, David, 96-99
    Brewster, John, 104-05
    Broderson, Morris, 93, 100-103
    Carlin, John, 106-07
    Clarke, John L., 108-09
    d'Estrella, Theophilus, 110-12
    Freiman, Robert J., 113-14
    Frisino, Louis, 115-17
    Hannan, Eugene E., 118-19
    Hughes, Regina O., 120-22
    Kowalewski, Felix, 123-24

463

LaMonto, Frederick, 125-26
LeClercq, Charles J., 127-28
Miller, Betty, 129-32
Miller, Ralph R., 133
Moore, H. Humphrey, 134-35
Redmond, Granville, S., 136
Sparks, William B., 137-39
Stevens, Kelly H., 140-42
Tilden, Douglas, 143-46
Washburn, Cadwallader L., 147-50
Whitcomb, James H., 151-52
Wood, Tom, 153
Ashbridge, W. L., 191
Associations, 76
Associations of/for the Deaf, 59
　Alexander Graham Bell Association
　　for the Deaf, 261, 318, 323, 346
　American Humane Association, 395
　Binghampton Civic Association of
　　the Deaf, 256
　California Association of the Deaf,
　　55, 337
　Dixie Association of the Deaf, 166
　Empire State Association, 256, 263
　Ephphatha Conference of Workers
　　Among the Deaf, 188
　Episcopal Church's Conference of
　　Church Workers Among the
　　Deaf, 184, 188
　Gallaudet College Alumni
　　Association, xiii, 16, 41, 50, 59,
　　137, 184, 231, 263, 339, 341
　　first major disagreement over the
　　　direction, 317;
　　centennial gift, 317;
　　Graduate Fellowship Fund, 317;
　　　403;
　　permanent alumni office, 317
　Gallaudet College Athletic
　　Association, 289
　Hebrew Association of the Deaf,
　　New York, 191
　Hebrew Association of the Deaf,
　　Philadelphia, 191
　Indiana Association of the Deaf, 179
　Jr. National Association of the Deaf,
　　29, 318, 407
　　awards, 319
　　committee of establishment, 319
　　conventions, 319, 320
　　involved in raising funds,
　　　planning deaf awareness
　　　programs, 320;
　　Youth Leadership Conference,
　　　320·
　Michigan Association, 263
　Missouri Association of the Deaf,
　　196
　Montana Association of the Deaf,
　　51
　New England Gallaudet
　　Association of the Deaf, 44, 59
　New York Society of the Deaf, 406
　Ohio School for the Deaf Alumni

　　Association, 407
　Oklahoma Association of the Deaf,
　　266
　Ontario Association of the Deaf,
　　339
　Texas Association of the Deaf, 243,
　　261
　Texas Fine Arts Association, 141
　Virginia Association of the Deaf,
　　244
　Wisconsin Association of the Deaf,
　　29
　Wisconsin Association of the Deaf
　　State Service Bureau, 410
Antencio, Bernie, 288
Athletes, deaf, 229-30
　deaf, black, 282, 302
　deaf, contributions, 272, 276
　deaf, on hearing teams, 299-303
Atwood, Ralph H., 46
audiophones, 15
Auerbach, Hortense, 323, 340
Auerbach, Leon, 62, 323
Augusta, Mary (ship), xxi
Augustin, Roscoe, and his invention
　(back reliever), 170
Austin Peay State College, 279-80
automobile, 166

Babb, Charlie, 410
Babbidge, Homer, quoted, 318
Backus, Levi S., 238
Bahl, Ann Billington, 373, 378, 381
Ball, Danford E., 22
Ballantyne, Donald L., 399
Ballard, Melville, 39, 45, 239
Ballin, Albert, 78, 136, 254
　his portrait, Issaac Lewis Peet, 78;
　　painting, Reverend Thomas
　　Gallaudet, 78; his book, *The
　　Deaf Mute Howls*, 78, 254
Ballin, David, 78
Bancroft, Anne, 346, 348
Baptists, 190
Barbee, General Elias, 20
Barbee, Lucy (daughter), 20, 21
Barber, Laura, 287
Barnes, John, 8
Bartlett, David Ely, 7, 134
Bartletts' School, Mr. See Schools
Barton, Raymond R., 198
Basch, Jay J., 20
Baseball, 292-96
　deaf professional players, 291
　hand count, origin of, 272
Basilica of the Assumption, 191
Basketball, 282-86
　basketball, coaches, 303
　basketball players, professionals,
　　303
　deaf teams with 20 + season
　　victories (chart), 284

first black tournament player, 282
Gallaudet, 282
　girl's teams (ill.), 285
　prep All-Americans, 286
　prep All-American Selection Board
　　Members, 286
　prep coach of year (chart), 284
　tournaments, 282-85, 296-97, 300,
　　303
Bass, Mary (wife), 22
Bass, R. Aumon, 10, 22, 54, 170
　and his alarm clock, 170
Bastick, Mrs. J., 92
Battle of Leesburg and Edward's
　Ferry, 31
Battle of San Jacinto, 4, 5
Baxter Family, 45
Baxter, Percival P., 45
Baynes, Harry L., 34, 39
Beamer, H. C., 52
Bearden, Carter C., 190, 193
　and his books—*Handbook for the
　　Religious Interpreters for the Deaf*,
　　191; co-author—*A Manual of
　　Religious Signs*, 191; *Sing Praise,
　　a Hymnal for the Deaf*, 191;
　　*The History of Southern Baptist
　　Convention's Ministry to the
　　Deaf*, 191
Bearden, Carter, Jr., 193
Beauchamp, James B., 3, 21, 216, 250
Beck, Charles, 406
Belcher, Don, 198
Belinda, Johnny, 261
Bell, Alexander Graham, 12, 32, 45,
　58, 59, 75-79, 325
　''Upon the Formation of a Deaf
　　Variety of the Human Race,''
　　75
Bell, Henry, 39
Bell, Mabel Hubbard, 78, 364
Bellevue House, 63
Benedictine Monks, 359
Bennett, George W., 82
Bennett, Hester Parsons, 254
　Road Girl, 254
Benoit, J.B.A., 167, 170
　and his horseless carriage, 170
Benson, Elizabeth E., 39, 319, 409, 410
Benson, Harry, 39
Benson, Mary, 39
Berg, Albert, 70, 298, 299
Berg, Rev. Otto, 186, 250
Berg, Tom, 297
Bergman, Eugene and Bernard Bragg,
　play, *Tales from a Club Room*, 376
Bergman, Eugene and Trenton
　Batson, 254
　The Deaf in Literature: An Anthology,
　　254;
　The Deaf Experience, 254
Bernard Picture Company of New
　York, 137
Berger, Harold O., 304

Berkeley, William M., 10
Berry, Rev. Thomas B., 47
Berry, Senator of Faribault, 37
Best, Harry,
  Blindness and the Blind in the United States, 224
Best, Harry, 224, 231, 409
  book, *Deafness and the Deaf in the United States*, 409
Best Survey, 231
  reaction to, 234-36
Beverly School for the Deaf. See Schools
Bicycle, 215
  "All About the Gears," 81
  bicycle clubs, 81
  bicycle luggage carrier rack, 170
  bicycling, 80, 81
  "Care of a Bicycle, The," 81
  "Eclipse," 81
  "Some truths About a Bicycle," 81
Bilger, Charles, 37
bill, 179
Billbergia regina, 121
bill requiring teletypewriter, 3, 27
  Special note, 327
Birck, Ruth, 36
Birck, Vernon S., 36
Bishop, Dr. Milo E., 58
Black students, 14
Blansit, Alice, 171
Blinking lights, 325, 383
Bloch, David, 96, 97
  and "Bloch playing card," 96;
    "Accident," 97; "Bringing
    Wreaths for the Mourning
    Family," 98; "Contrast," 98; "A
    Long Beam Holds Up the
    Traffic," 99; "Carrying Wares,"
    99; "Progress," 99
Bloxham, Gov. W. D., 49
Board of Trustees, 90
Boatner, Dr. Edmund B., 227, 267, 268
Boatner, Maxine Tull, 318
Bohli, Robert A., 44
Boland, John A., 41
Bolling, Colonel William, 1, 22, 73
Bolling School. See Schools
Boltz, Robert H., 191
Books, by, about deaf people,
  A Basic Course in American Sign Language (Humphries, Padden, O'Rourke), 368
  A Basic Course in Manual Communication (O'Rourke), 250, 368
  Antonio Machado (McVan), 409
  A Sign Directory (Long), 178
  Badge of Honor, The (Ulmer), 250
  Biography of Spring Street in Los Angeles, The (Swigart) 215
  Bits of History (Crane), 16

Centennial History of the Kentucky School for the Deaf, A (Fosdick), 20
Common Signs of the Deaf, 178
Deaf and Dumb, Facts, Anecdotes and Poetry, The (Hodgson), 65, 90
Deaf Like Me (Spradley and Spradley), 411
Deaf Mute Howls, The (Ballin), 78
Deaf Persons in Professional Employment (Crammatte), 50, 254, 320, 340
Deafness (Wright), 254
Dictionary of American Biography, 28
Dictionary of American Sign, Language on Linguistic Principles, A (Stokoe, Casterline and Croneberg), 365
Dictionary of Idioms for the Deaf, A, 318
Directory of American Artists (Fielding), 136
Douglas Tilden: Portrait of a Deaf Sculptor (Albronda), 145
First State School for the Deaf, The (McClure), 21
Forgotten People, The (Wood), 254
Great Truths Simply Told (Weed), 90
Green Pavilions (Muse), 26, 254
Handbook of Sign Language of the Deaf (Michaels), 190, 367
Handicapping America (Bowe), 254
Hazards of Deafness (Holcomb), 209, 210, 216, 217, 218
Histories of American Schools for the Deaf (Fay), 78
History of the California School for the Deaf, (Burnes, Ramger), 36
History of Education of the Deaf in Virginia (Bass), 22
History of the Kentucky School for the Deaf (Beauchamp), 21
I am Deaf, Too (Bowe and Sternberg), 254
Language of Silence, The (Falberg), 367
Law and the Deaf, The (Myers), 254, 402
Magic Lantern Man: Theophilus Hope d'Estrella, The (Albronda), 111
Mainstreaming the Prelingually Deaf Child (Brill), 392
Manual for the Printer's Apprentice, (Hodgson), 65
Marriage of the Deaf (Fay), 77
No Sound (Wiggins), 254
Notable Deaf Persons (Braddock), 185, 402
"Notes on America," (Dickens), 73
Paddle Your Own Canoe (Emery), 44
Raindrop, The, 67, 69
Rehabilitating America (Bowe), 254
Representative Deaf Persons (Gallagher), 44

Sign Language and the Deaf Community: Essays in Honor of William C. Stokoe, 365
Sign Language Structure (Stokoe, Casterline and Croneberg), 365
Sign Language, The, A Manual of Signs (Long), 29
Signing Essential English (Gustason, Pfetzing, Zawolkow), 370-72
Signing Exact English (Anthony), 370, 371
Silence, Love, and Kids I Know (Smith), 250
Silent Muse, The (Panara, MacFarlane, Denis), 250
Sound of the Stars (Parsons), 254
Straight Language for the Deaf, (Fitzgerald), 227
They Grow in Silence (Vernon and Mindel), 388, 392
To Her I Love (Sowell), 250
Tryst (McVan), 409
Valley Forge (Sullivan), 254
Who's Who in America, 137, 141
Booth, Edmund, 31, 42, 62, 67, 73, 251
Booth, Frank W., 42
Borglum, Gutzon, 118
Bornstein, Dr. Harry, 372
Bowe, Frank G., 254, 402
  books, *I am Deaf, Too*, 254;
    Handicapping America, 254;
    Rehabilitating America, 254
Bowling, 282
  associations, 282
  deaf, perfect game, 282
Boxers, professional, 290-92
boxing, welterweight contenders, 291
Braddock, Rev. Guilbert C., 67, 68, 136, 183, 185, 186, 244, 251, 252, 399
  and his book, *Notable Deaf Persons*, 185, 402
Bradley, Joe G., 253
Bragg, Bernard 16, 346, 349
  "The Quiet Man," 349
Braidwood, John, 1
Braidwood, Thomas, 5
Brant, Samuel, 45
Branton, Alban, 3, 89
  acted in "Little House on the Prairie," 389
Brauer, Barbara Ann, 364, 402
Bravin, Jeffrey, 388, 389
  acted in "And Your Name Is Jonah," 388
Bray, Mrs. W. J., 54
Brenner, Henry, 44, 299, 301
Breunig, H. Latham, 318, 327, 364, 399
Brewington, Emma, 174
Brewster, John, 16, 104, 359
  and his paintings, "Girl in Green," 104; "Boy With Finch," 105

Bridgman, Laura, 39, 73, 362
Brightman, W. J., 82
Brill, Richard G., 44, 246, 392
    and his book, *Mainstreaming the
        Prelingually Deaf Child*, 392
Broderson, Morris, 93, 100, 125
    and his paintings, "Self-Portrait
        with Sound of Flowers," 93;
        "Lizzie's Dream," 100; "Tribute
        to Winslow Homer," 101;
        "Lament for Ignacio Sanchez
        II," 102; "Home of Sanchez
        Mejias," 103; "Thoreau," 103
Brody, I. Lee, 394
Broecker, Betty, 377
bronze copy of the original model of
        the Thomas Hopkins Gallaudet
        and Alice Cogswell Statue, 141
Brown, Alfred L., 282
Brown, Eli, 92
Brown, James S., 23, 29
Brown, Melvin, 53
Brown, Rev. John G., 39
Brown, Thomas J., 170
    and his invention—a device for
        holding an ironing table, 170
Brown, Tince, 53
Browning, Orville H., 6
Bruce, Joseph, 193
Bruffey, Clifford P., 191
Brunson, Albert W., 253
Bryant, Arthur D., 39, 191
Buckingham, Tom, 288
Buildings named for deaf people.
        See also memorials
    Argo-McClure Hall, 21
    Ariadna Hall, 28
    Ballard House, 39
    Barbee Hall, 21
    Beauchamp Hall, 21
    Benson Gymnasium, 39
    Birck Hall, 36
    Brewster Gymnasium, 16
    Brown, Ola Mary Cafeteria, 23
    Clerc Hall, 21, 39
    Cogswell Hall, 39
    Crandall Hall, 36
    Crutchfield Hall, the Vocational
        Building, 25
    Deer Hall, 50
    Denison House, 32, 39
    Divine Hall, 50
    Drake House, 39
    Durian Vocational Building, 16, 261
    Emery Hall, 37
    Fosdick Hall, 21
    Fowler Hall, 39
    Frederick Hall, 39
    Gross Hall, 28
    Howson Gymnasium, 36
    Hughes Gymnasium, 39
    Hunter Gymnasium, 50
    Kastner Hall, 29

Krug Hall, 39
    Lewis Dormitory, 33
    Lindstrom Hall, 36
    MacDonald Hall, 50
    Middleton Hall, 21
    Nevil Vocational School, 20
    Northrop Hall, 50
    Norton Hall, 36
    Peterson Dormitory, 58
    Pope Complex, 49
    Roberts Hall, 36
    Robinson Hall, 28
    Rockwell Gymnasium and
        Auditorium, 261
    Runde Hall, 36, 223
    Smith Hall, 38
    Stanfill Vocational Building, 23
    Stevens Hall, 30
    Stewart Gymnasium, 30
    Tilden Vocational Building, 36
    Thomas Athletic Facility, 21
    Thornberry Hearing and Speech
        Center, 33, 39
    Underhill Gym, 24
    Washburn Arts Center, 39
    Watson Hall, 50
    Willard Unit, 23
    Zieske Vocational Wing, 31
Bunn, Luther, 244
Burdett, Kenneth C., 48
Burdick, Eulalia, 260
Bureau of the Deaf, proposed, 219
Bureau of Education of the
        Handicapped (BEH), 385
Burnes, Byron B., 34, 42, 205, 222,
        230, 246, 250, 263, 266, 267, 328,
        330, 331, 338
Burnes, Caroline Hyman 36, 319
Burns, S. Robey, 25, 296, 298, 300
Burt, Colonel Erasmus R., 9, 31
Bushnaq, Suleiman, 402
Butch, dog entertainer, 225-27, (ill.)
        226
Butler, Gwendol, 320
Butler, Ray, 52
Brittons, 260
Byouk, Louis M., 43

Cahen, Herman, Julius, brother, 341
Caldwell, Dr. William 34
Calhoun, Mr., 41
Califano, Secretary Joseph A., 383,
        387
California School for the Deaf. See
        Schools
Cameron, Virginia, 189
Candle lighter, 170
Captioned Films for the Deaf, 266-68,
        317
Carlin, John, 11, 15, 20, 21, 39, 68, 106

and his oil painting, "Laurent
        Clerc," 106, 107
Carlos, Don, 70
Carlton, Cora, 49
Carnegie Medal, 179
Carnegie Medal Winners, 213
Carney, Edward C., 22, 337, 339
Carrell, Owen G., 253
Carrett, Julius, 3, 7
Carrithers, I. C., 92
Carter, President Jimmy, 373, 403
Carter, S. Melvin, Jr., 368
Case, Robert, 188
Casey, Arietta Robertson, 41
Casterline, Dorothy, 365
Castle, Dr. William E., 58
catarrhal deafness, 92
Catholic, 191
causes of deafness, 184
Census, 1
Central Institute for the Deaf. See
        Schools
Central New York Institution for
        Deaf-Mutes. See Schools
Central New York School for the
        Deaf. See Schools
Chair of Deaf studies 377, 392
    Powrie V. Doctor Chair of Deaf
        Studies, 392
Chamberlain, William M., 238, 252
Chamberlayne, Hartwell M., 10
Champion, Rev. Harold L., 383
Chaney, Lon, 414
Chapin, E. L., 41
Chaplin, Charlie, 136
Chapman, Senator of Minnesota, 73
Charles, C. W., 178
Charter, 12
Cherry, Ladislaw S., 160, 163, 250,
        338
Chicago and Eastern Illinois Railroad
        Line, 82
Chicago Club of the Deaf, 261
Chicago Day School for the Deaf. See
        Schools
Chicago Tribune, 263, 264
Chidester, Holdridge, 41
Children of deaf parents, 76
Chopin, Paul, 118
Chough, Steven K., 402
Christensen Case, The, 337
Christensen, Wayne and Madeline,
        337
Christ Methodist Church for the Deaf,
        189
Christian Deaf Fellowship, 229
Christmas, 91
Chronology, xxv-xxxi
    NAD, 427
    sports, 273
Churches
    All Angels' Mission to the Deaf, 186
    All Soul's Church for the Deaf in
        Philadelphia, 47, 183, 185

American Lutheran Church, The, 188
Ashbury Methodist Church, 189
Bethlehem Lutheran Church in Omaha, 188
Calvary Baptist Church, 4, 191
Cameron Methodist Church, 189
Crusselle-Freeman Mission at St. Mark's Methodist Episcopal Church, 189
Grace Episcopal Church, 185
Grace Methodist Church, 189
Latter Day Saints Church, 189
Lutheran Church, The, 42, 229
Lutheran Church of the Missouri Synod, 6
Ogden Branch for the Deaf, 189
Our Saviour Lutheran Church for the Deaf, 188
St. Ann's Church, New York City, 90, 181, 185
St. Matthew Lutheran Church, 193
St. Stephens Church, 181, 183
St. Thomas Mission for the Deaf, 46
Silent Berean Congregation of the Union Avenue Christian Church, 193
Chesboros, Ebenezer, 28
Churchill, Winston, 28
Cincinnati Day Public School for the Deaf. See Schools
Cincinnati Reds, 87
Civil Service Commission, 223
Civil War, The, 7, 24, 27, 28, 29, 31, 33, 37, 40
Clark, Matthew, 26, 33
Clark, Mr. and Mrs. Asa, 26
Clark, Pomeroy B., Mrs., 35
Clarke, John, 12
Clarke, John L., 108
and his wood carving, panel, 108; carved panels, 109
Clarke School for the Deaf. See Schools
Classroom Humor, 208
Clatterbuck, Marvin B., 41
Clayton, Thompson, 289
Clerc, Laurent, xxi, xxii, xxiii, 2, 11, 16, 17, 20, 21, 32, 39, 68, 238, 323, 359
Clerc, Mrs., 59
Cleveland Day School for the Deaf. See Schools
Cleveland, President Grover, 70
Cleveland Printing Company, 82
Cloud, Daniel, 46
Cloud, Rev. James H., 45, 46, 87, 165, 179, 183-84, 240, 276
Clubs for/of the Deaf, 76, 81
Mascia Club for the Deaf, The, 256
Coaches, deaf of hearing teams, 298-99
Coats, G. Dewey, 28, 228, 265, 266, 376

Cocke, General John, 23
Cogswell, Alice, xxii, 67
Cogswell, Dr. Mason, xxii, xxiii, 16
Cokely, Dennis, 391, 392
Coleman, Edwin, 92
Coleman, Thomas H., 49
Colleges and Universities
Appalachian State University, 24
Arizona University, 47, 54
Baylor, 190
Boston University, 364, 395
Bowdoin College, 148, 396
California State University, Northridge, (CSUN), 44, 56
California University, 35, 36, 100, 110, 144
Carnegie Institute, Pittsburgh, 100
Carthage College, 396
Centre College, 2, 20, 21, 396
Chicago University, 54
Cincinnati University, 154
Columbia, 32, 364
Community College, 317
Delgado College, 317
Delgado Junior College, 58
DePaul University, 402
Eastern Michigan University, 370
Gallaudet College, 4, 11, 17, 20, 22, 29-34, 36-57, 62, 69, 70-71, 79, 82, 84-85, 113, 118, 120-123, 129, 137, 141, 147-149, 153, 156, 163-165, 175, 180, 189, 190-191, 214, 244, 252, 267, 317-318, 334, 362, 365, 373, 392
accreditation 38, 232-233, 236;
admission-hearing students on the undergraduate level, 379;
admission practices, 232;
alumni, 232, 236;
Best Survey of, 233-234;
early student body, 233;
expansion of, 230-236;
Gallagher Survey of, 235-236;
government study of, 230, 231;
graduate school, 38;
history, 38-39
mace, 323
Georgetown University Law School, 402
George Washington University, 395, 398
Gregg College, 169
Harvard University, 364
Hebrew Union College, 191
Hogarth Business University, 82
John Marshall Law School, 402
Johns Hopkins University, 36, 364, 399
Louisiana State University, 29, 30, 140
Lenoir Rhyne College, 24
Maryland University, 262

Massachusetts Institute of Technology, 147, 156
Minnesota University, 91
Missouri University, 91
Mount St. Joseph College, 318
Naval Academy, 215
Nevada University, 373
New York University, 402
New York University College of Dentistry, 364
Ohio Mechanics Institute, 154
Rhode Island University, 44
Rochester Institute of Technology, 56
St. Paul Technical Institute, 58
San Fernando Valley State College, California, 47
Seabury-Western Theological Seminary, 396
Seattle Community College Washington, 58
Southern California University, 364
Temple Deaf College, 383
Tennessee, University of, 38
Union College, 364
University of North Carolina, Chapel Hill, 247
University of Pennsylvania Dental School, 399
Wayne State University, 382
Western Maryland College, 388
Western Pennsylvania University, 69
Westminster College, 28, 54
Yale University, 22
College degrees, 11
Colombo, LeRoy, 286
Colorado School for the Deaf and the Blind. See Schools
Colored department, 14
Columbia River, 50
Combined system, 15, 65, 79, 359
Coming Men, 157
Common Weeds of the U.S., 121
Community Colleges, 58
Comp, Owen C., 410
Confederate soldiers, 31
Conference of Executives of American Schools for the Deaf, 52, 318, 323
Conference of Principals of American Instructors of the Deaf and Dumb, 63, 79. See also Conference of Executives of American Schools for the Deaf
congenitally deaf, 75, 76
Connecticut Asylum for the Education and Instruction of Deaf and Dumb Persons, Hartford. See American School for the Deaf
Connecticut Chapter, 340
Constan, Benjamin, 136
Constance, Helen, 119
Contreras, Jesus, 288

Convention of American Instructors of the Deaf, 16, 42, 50, 69, 248, 267, 318, 323
Cooke, W. D., 23
Corbett, Edward E., 3, 38, 395, 402
Corbett, Judge T. Patrick, 403
Cordano, Waldo, 277
Coren, Alan, 376
Corey, Patricia, 267
Cornett, R. Orin, 334-35
correspondence course, 55
Corson, Harvey J., 20, 30, 377, 402
Coughlin, Thomas, 35, 191, 192
Council of Organizations Serving the Deaf, 317, 336-37
Craig, Douglas, 39, 214
Craig, Sam B., 40
Craig, William N., 40
Crammatte, Alan B., 50, 230, 244, 250, 254;
    and his book, *Deaf Persons in Professional Employment*, 50, 254, 320, 340
Crammatte, Florence B., 244
Crandall, Henry B., 35, 36
Crane, John E., 16
Crane, Myron L., 82
Cranwill, Alfred, 337
Creager, Harry T. Athletic Field, 39
Croneberg, Carl, 365
Crow, Arthur, 27
Crusselle, W. F., 189
Crutchfield family, 25
Cued Speech, 334-35
Culberton, George, 198, 202
"cures," 92
Currency for the state, 8
Currier, Enoch H., 363
    quoted; 363
Curtis, Paul S., 37, 294-95
Cuscaden, Scott, 42

Dachau Concentration Camp, 96
Dallas Pilot Institute for the Deaf, 229
Dallas Times-Herald, 141
Dalton, Governor John N., 23
Dantzer, Charles, 183
Davidoff, Susan, 379, 381
    T.V. program, *Sign A Song*, 379
Davila, Robert, 33, 56, 377, 402
Davis, Cecil B., 31
Davis, Ed, 193
Davis, Frances, 384
Davis, Joshua, 9, 10
Deaf Administrators, 338
deaf athletes, "Five Iron Men," 223-24
deaf athletes, WWII, 223
Deaf Awareness, 393
Deaf Bowler, The 282
deaf boxer, 224
Deaf: 'By Their Fruits Ye Shall Known Them,' The, 363, 364

deaf citizens, 256
deaf clergy, 181
deaf customers, 376
Deaf Driver, The, 166, 228
deaf drivers, rights of, 259, 260
Deaf Education and Artistics Frontiers (D.E.A.F.) Media, Inc., 388
deaf education, gov't role in, 233, 236
deaf ghettos, 360
Deaf Heritage, 193
deaf inventors, 170
deaf jurors, 403
Deaf, Legislation affecting, 219, 227, 228, 229, 236, 260, 261, 267
deaf-mutes, 384
Deaf-Mutes Union, 164
deaf needs; television, tornado warnings, 262
deaf newspapermen, 251
deaf nurses, 173
Deaf people, 359; awareness, 377
Deaf Persons in Professional Employment, 50
Deaf Persons in the United States Who Have Earned a Pilot's License, 201
Deaf Ph.Ds, 399
    Appendix, 437
deaf pilots, 195
deaf policeman, 82
deaf power, 377
deaf pride, 377
deaf principals or superintendents, 87
deaf, publications of the, 231
Deaf Smith County, 5
Deaf Smith, Erastus, 4, 5
deaf soldiers, 10
deaf students, educational needs of, 236
deaf teachers, 76, 228, 361
    refused to hire, 361
deaf, teaching methods, 227
"Deaf Variety of the Human Race," 75
Deaf World, Our (humor), 203
deafness, advantages of, 228
Deafness, Causes of, 2, 3, 219, 297, 300
deafness, types of, 236, 359
deCistue, Isabella, 134
Dedication, ix
Delgado, Gilbert, 267
Deegan, William J., 292, 294
Deer, Dewey, 50, 265
Deitch, Solomon, 158
deLeon, Pedro Ponce, 359
de l'Epée, Abbé Charles Michel, xxi, bust, 91; 323
"Denison Fraction Teacher," 32
Denison, James, 32, 65, 395
Denominational Schools
    Archbishop Ryan Memorial Institute, Philadelphia, 6
    Boston School for the Deaf, Randolph, Mass., 6

Chinchuba Institution for the Deaf, Marroro, La., 6
DePaul Institute in Pittsburgh, 6
Ephphetha School, Chicago, 6
German Evangelical Lutheran Deaf-Mute Institution, Detroit, 6
Le Couteulx St. Mary's School for the Deaf, Buffalo, 5, logo, 18; 33
Lutheran School for the Deaf, 6, 42
Marial Consilia Deaf-Mute Institution, Carondelet, Mo., 5
St. Francis Xavier School, Baltimore, 6
St. Joseph's School for the Deaf, Milwaukee, 6
St. Joseph's School for the Deaf, New York City, 6
St. Joseph's School in Oakland, Calif., 6
St. Mary's School in St. Paul, Minn., 6
St. Rita School for the Deaf, Cincinnati, Oh., 6
Department of Health, Education, and Welfare, 320, 383, 386, 398
Depression, The, 211
Desmarais, Rev. Camille, 185, 186
d'Estrella, Theophilus Hope, 35, 82, 110, 136, 144
    and his pictures, "The Opening Gate," 110; "A Rebuke," 111; "A Mischievous Knowing Glance," 112; "Wisteria Garden," 112
Detmold, George, 376
Deuel, Harold, 288
de Zubiaurres brothers, 118
de Zubiaurres, Valentin, 140
Diamond Head School. See Schools
Dickens, Charles, 73
Dickerson, L. B., 190
Dickenson, Sidney E., 170
Dictionary of American Biography, 194
Dictionary of Idioms for the Deaf, A, 318
Dillon, Florence, 50
Dillon, Thomas J., 50, 338
discrimination, 211
District of Columbia, Washington, 7
Divine, Belle, 50
Divine, Louis, 50
Dix, Harry P., 295
DiZebba, Vincent, 379
Dobson, Chester, 32
Dobson family, The, 32
Dobson, Mary, 32
Dobyns, J. R., 9
Doctor, Amy, 392
Doctor, Frank, 392
Doctor, Powrie V., 322, 392. See also Chair of Deaf Studies, 377, 392
doctorate degree, first earned, 7
Domich, Harold J., 250, 331
Donald, Dora, 47

Donnelly, R. A., 83
doorbells for the deaf, 221
Dougherty, George T., 28, 62, 170, 214
Douglas, Ranald, 82
Downes, Noah, 39, 303
Downey, Jack, 54
Drake, Harley D., 39, 191, 322
Drake, Race F., 22, 23
Draper, Amos G., 39, 43
Driggs, Burton W., 54
driving rights, 169
Dubow, Sy, 398
Dundon, Edward, 292
Duning, Hilbert, 22, 154, 265
 and his buildings—Indian Hill
 Church, 154; Upham Hall,
 Miami University, 154;
 Women's Dormitory, Miami
 University, 154
Duning, LeRoy, 154, 265
Durian, Walter, G., 16, 261
Duval, William W., 341
Dwyer, John E., 82
Dyer, Louis A., 43

Eakins, Thomas, 135
Earliest women superintendent, one
 of, 47
Eastern Iowa School for the Deaf. See
 Schools
Eastman, Gilbert, 395
 and his play, "Sign Me Alice," 376
Echols, Nate, 282
Economically Important Foreign Weeds,
 Potential Problems in the United
 States, 121
Ederle, Gertrude, 297
Edington, Wallace, 244
Edison, Thomas A., 215
education of blind deaf students, 91
Education of deaf children, early
 attempts, 1
Edward Miner Gallaudet Memorial
 Library, 236
Eiler, Laura, 123
elimination of the term, "mute," 62
Elizabeth, Queen, 262
Elkins, Gertrude, 157, 158
Elkins, Wilson H., 262
Elliott, Richard, 65
Elms, Constance Hasenstab, 189
elocution, 9
Elstad, Leonard M., 38, 231, 233 (ill.),
 259; quoted, 342
Emanuel, Ed., 200
Emery, Philip A., 36, 44, 170, 252
 and his book, Paddle Your Own
 Canoe, and Who Killed Cock
 Robin, 44
Engelsman, Bernard, 12
Englehardt, Philip, 90

Ensworth, John A., 383
Estrada, Alfred, 288
Eugene Meyer Foundation, 236
Evan, Alex, 212
Evans, Clifford U., 196
Evans, Gilbert, 199, 202
Evans, Lionel, 392
Evansville, Indiana School for the
 Deaf. See Schools
Eversaul, George H., 213
"Experiment in Television," 346

Fahr, Morris, 202
Falberg, Roger M., 367
 and his book, The Language of
 Silence, 367
Fancher, Frederick G., 25, 269, 270
Fannin, O. P., 26
Fant, Louie J., 195, 367, 368
 and his books, Ameslan: An
 Introduction to American Sign
 Language, 368; Intermediate Sign
 Language, 368; Say It With
 Hands, 367; Sign Language, 368
"Fanwood," 16
Fanwood Quad club, 87
 and Quadities, 87
Farquhar, Grover C., 28, 250
 quoted, 227, 231, 376
father of sculpture on the West Coast,
 144
Fay, Barnabas M., 30
Fay, Edward A., 30, 77
 book, Histories of American Schools
 for the Deaf, 78
Federal Communications Commission
 law, 386; placement, 398
Federal troops, 31
Ferrigno, Lou, 388, 389, 390
 and his role as the Hulk in The
 Incredible Hulk, CBS-TV series,
 388
Feuchte, Herbert, 396
Fifer Cadets of Illinois, The, 79, 80
Fifer, Governor of Illinois, 80
films, 173
Finch, Marion, 174
Fine, Dr. Peter J., Infirmary, 39
Finesilver, Sherman G., 169
fingerspelling, 11, 78, 359, unusual
 uses of, 225-227
fire department, 91
Firsts
 first American to earn a Ph.D.
 summa cum laude from Heidelberg
 University, 399
 Firsts Among Deaf Pilots, 200
 first and only school located on an
 island, Maine, 45
 first Boy Scout troop in a school for
 the deaf in the U.S., 44

first Catholic school for the deaf in
 the U.S., 5
first chairman of the Oral Deaf
 Adult Section of Alexander
 Graham Bell Association, 364
first chapter to kick off the
 Centennial Fund Drive, 340
first chimp to converse with people
 in the language of signs, 373
first church exclusively for deaf
 people in this country, 181
first deaf and blind person in the
 U.S. to earn a masters degree,
 379
first deaf black basketball
 tournament player, 282
first deaf black person to graduate
 from the Kansas School, 70
first deaf black teachers, 3
first deaf-blind person to be
 educated in this country, 39
first deaf-blind person to earn a
 bachelor's degree, 379
first deaf Catholic priest in the
 U.S., 35
first deaf children to receive formal
 classroom instruction in
 America, 1
first deaf editor of a newspaper on
 record in the country, 238
first deaf man ordained as a priest
 in this country, 181
first deaf man ordained in the
 history of Methodism, 189
first deaf man to publish a book in
 this country, 254
first deaf person in the U.S. (and
 possibly the world) to be
 awarded an honorary degree
 and probably the only one to
 receive three, 395
first deaf person known to win a
 Carnegie Medal for heroism,
 215
first deaf person to become
 president of Alexander
 Graham Bell Association, 364
first deaf person to earn a degree
 from Gallaudet College, 45
first deaf person to receive a
 certificate from the University
 of Cincinnati, 154
first deaf person to receive a
 doctorate from Gallaudet
 College, 402
first deaf pilot to fly solo across the
 United States, 196
first deaf professional actor-mime
 to gain national attention in the
 U.S., 349
first deaf professional baseball
 player, 292
first deaf professional to be

appointed to a federal
government position, 338
first deaf student to enroll at the
University of California, 110
first deaf superintendent, 68
first deaf teacher at the Virginia
School for the Deaf and the
Blind, 68
first deaf teacher in the U.S., 16
first deaf woman to earn a degree
from Gallaudet College, 51
first Division for the Deaf, 51
first Eastern Schools for the Deaf
basketball tournament, 48, 285
first editor of *The Buff and Blue,* 249
first efforts by a television station to
reach deaf, audiences, 262
first Episcopal Church in Jefferson
County, 185
first executive director of Council of
Organizations Serving the
Deaf, 337
first executive director of
Telecommunications for the
Deaf, Inc., 327
first female member of the National
Fraternal Society for the Deaf,
158
first female to hold a national NFSD
office, 158
first four-week Youth Leadership
Development Camp at Pine
Lake Lodge, 320
first free school for the deaf in the
world, 118, 323
first Gallaudet College graduate to
earn a doctorate, 399
first Girl Scout troop in a school for
the deaf in the U.S., 25
first hearing student admitted to
the undergraduate level at
Gallaudet College, 379
first holder of the Dr. Doctor Chair
of Deaf Studies, 36
first in Hillsboro, Tex., to have a
printing press run by
electricity, 253
first instance in which a deaf man
coached a hearing college
team, 70
first Jr. National Association of the
Deaf convention, 319
first legal director of National
Center for Law and the Deaf,
398
first licensed deaf male pilot in the
world, 196
first linguist to earn a doctorate in
American Sign Language, 365
first linguist to subject sign
language to the tests of a real
language, 365
first magazine of the deaf, 252
first National Symposium on Sign

Language Research and
Teaching, 368
first national Youth Leadership
Conference, 320
first newspaper Pueblo ever had,
252
first ordained deaf Baptist Minister,
22
first periodical printed exclusively
for deaf persons, 238
first permanent public school for
the deaf in America, 16
first person from outside the U.S.
to hold the chair of Deaf
Studies, 392
first play of its kind, 376
first president of the Little Paper
Family, 248
first president of the National
Association of the Deaf, 22
first president of Registry of
Interpreters of the Deaf, 328
first pure oral school in the U.S., 12
first regional basketball
tournament, 283
first "safe bicycle" in Pittsburgh,
215
first school for handicapped
children in the Western
Hemisphere, 16
first school for the deaf newspaper,
247
first school for the deaf publication
in this country, 245
first school for the deaf west of the
Appalachian Mountains, 1
First state school for deaf and blind,
6
first state-supported school for the
deaf, 1, 20
first state to provide an institution
for deaf blacks, 14
first state to provide an institution
for the education of black deaf
children, 24
first student from Kentucky to enter
Gallaudet College, 251
first teacher of the Kendall School
for the Deaf, 395
first time that the World Games for
the Deaf were played on
American soil, 318
first vocational program among
schools for the deaf, 20
first weekly newspaper for the
deaf, 239
first woman pilot in South Dakota,
47, 195
first women admitted to Gallaudet
College, 38
first women superintendents, one
of, 54
first World Games of the Deaf 5
medal winner (swimming), 286

*Fisherman's Guide to North America,
The,* 115
Fishing in Maryland, 115
fishing permit stamps, 115
Fitzgerald, Edith, 29, 170, 227
and her invention, "The Fitzgerald
Key," 170;
and her book, *Straight Language for
the Deaf,* 227
"Fitzgerald Key, The," 29, 170, 227
Fitzpatrick, Hilton "Fitzy," 291
Five Civilized Tribes, 52
Five dollar bill, Deaf Smith, 4
Fletcher, Estelle, 184
Fletcher, Louise, 184, 185, 383
Fletcher, Rev. Robert C., 34, 184, 186
Flick, Rev. George F., 185
Flint, F. H., 253
Float, Jeffrey, 287
Florida School for the Deaf and the
Blind. See Schools
Flournoy, John J., 26, 73
Flying Parson, The, 185
Foltz, Edward S., 37, 265, 282
Football, 276-282
Deaf All-Americans, high school,
278
Gallaudet, 276, 277, 279, 280
"Goodyear Silents," 278, 280-281,
303
football huddle, origin of, 272
inter-school competition, 277
NFL teams with deaf players, 279
professional, 278
state champions, 277
undefeated teams, 277, 278 (chart)
winningest seasons, 277
Ford, Henry, quoted, 220
Ford, President Gerald, 373, 378
Ford Times, 169
Forest Park, 54
Foreword, xiii
Fort Gibson, 52
Fort Monroe Workshop, 323
Fort Vancouver, 50
Fosdick, Charles P., 20, 21
Fowler, Dr. Edmund P., 212
Fowler, Major, 37
Fox, Thomas F., 16, 62, 239, 264, 265,
276
Francisco, "Pancho" Villa, 171
Fraternal Insurance Society, 157
Freedman, Sheldon, 403
Freedom Train, 1976, 160
Freeman, Rev. Samuel, 189
Freiman, Robert J., 113
and his paintings, "Self-portrait,"
113; "Rosemarie Louit," 114;
"Garconnet de St. Paul de
Vence," 114; "Prince Doon
Thai of Laos," 114
French, Daniel Chester, 65, 67
and the statue of Thomas Hopkins
Gallaudet and Alice Cogswell,

67; bust of Garfield, 65-67
French Government, 77
French Royal National Institute for the Deaf, 323
French Sign Language, 359, 365
French, William M. DeCoursey, 42, 50
Frisina, D. Robert, 28, 57
    quoted, 323, 334
Frisino, Louis, 39, 115
    and his paintings—"Canvasbacks," 115; "Red Fox," 116; "Chesapeake Bay Retriever with Goose," 116; "Brown Trout," 116; "Rainbow Trout," 116; Pintails," 117; "Labrador Retriever with Pintail," 117; Golden Retriever with Hen Mallard, 117
Fuller, Dalton, 37
Fuller, Sarah, 15
Fulton, Mo., 266
Funkehouse, William 293
Fusfield, Irving S., 184

Gadling, Donna, 391
Gallagher, Buell G., 235
Gallagher's Survey, reaction to, 236
Gallaher, James E., 44, 240
    and his book, Representative Deaf Persons, 44
Gallaudet Aircraft Corporation, 175
Gallaudet airplane, 175
Gallaudet College Alumni Reunion, 74
Gallaudet College, name changed to, 236
Gallaudet College Signed English, 133
Gallaudet Conference, The, 31
Gallaudet Day School for the Deaf. See Schools
Gallaudet Drive, The, 177
Gallaudet, Edson, F., 175
Gallaudet, Edward Miner, 32, 38, 45, 65, 67, 68, 91, 119, 164, 175, 191
Gallaudet Memorial Statue, 66
Gallaudet, Sophia Fowler, 179
Gallaudet, Rev. Thomas, 46, 165, 181, 186, 323
Gallaudet, Thomas Hopkins, 6, xxi, xxii, 6, 7, 16, 17, 31, 32, 38, 43, 44, 48, 51, 65, 90, 238, 359
Galloway, Gertude (Scott), 33, 39
Galloway, Victor H., 47, 377
Galvan, John, 36
Gamblin, Rudolph, 299
games, 373,
Gannon, Jack R., xiii, 42, 250, 339; about the author, 442
Gannon, Rosalyn L., 422, 427, 441
Gardner, Beatrice T., 373
Gardner, J. W., 191
Garfield, President James A., 65

Garnett, Alexander Y.P., 8
Garretson, Mervin D., xix, 42, 51, 246, 250, 265, 319, 322, 337, 338, 339, 377, 398, 421
    quoted, 397, 399;
    "The Reality of Deafness," 415-417
Garvin, Donna-Belle, 152
Gates, Elizabeth W., 152
Gawlik, Rudolph, 391, 392
Gazly, John H., 31
Geary, John H., 51, 87
General Assembly, 23, 24
Gee Jay Show, 407, 408
George, Dudley Webster, 62, 251
George, James G., 251
Georgia School for the Deaf. See Schools
"German Method, The," 12, 15
gestures, 136
Geyer, Gust, 82
Giangreco, C. Joseph, 40
Gibbs, Betty Sue, 137
Gibson, Francis, P., 158, 160, 163
Gibson Hotel, 63
Gill, Martin, 82
Gillett, Phillip G., 76, 79, 189
Girl Guides, 195
Girl Scouts, 195
Glassman, Shirley, 394
Glyndon, Howard, 194. See also Laura C. R. Searing
Gobbles, Edward, 279
Goldberg, Phillip, 191
Gold Rush, The, 136
Golladay, Loy E., museum, 16; 41, 58, 250, 367
    and his poetry, "Ten Fingers, Have I," 325; "Silent Homage," 367
    quoted, 417
Gooding, Frank R., 53, 54
Goodson, John H., 247
"Goodson Printing Office," 10
Goodwin, E. McKee, 23
Gough, John A., 267, 268
Government Printing Office, 223
Governor Baxter School for the Deaf. See Schools
Grabill, Wilson H., 29
Grace, Rev. Homer E., 186, 396
Grady, Theodore, 35, 36, 83
Graham, Dr. Alice A., 173
Grant, Leon, 302
grants, 2
Graves, Peter, 265
Gray, Arlie, 52
Great Depression, The, 158
Greeley, Horace, 238
Green, Francis, 1
Greenberger, David, 44
Greenmum, Robert, 263, 265, 331, 381
Gregg, John R., 169, 395
    and his pamphlet—"Light-Line Phonography!" 169; Gregg shorthand, 169, 395; Gregg

Publishing Co., 169; Gregg College, 169
Griffing, Wendell, 52
Griffing, W. Ted, 52, 250, 265, 340
Gross, Bernard, 199
Gross, Henry, 28
Grosvenor, Mrs. Gilbert, 261
Grow, Charles B., 21
Guild of Natural Science Illustrators, 121
Guillory, L. M., 367
    and her book, Expressive and Receptive Fingerspelling for Hearing Adults
Gunson, B. F., 83
Gustason, Gerilee, 371
    and her book, Signing Essential English, 370, 371

Hagemeyer, Alice, 393, 394
Hahn, Lillian, 246
Haight, Henry, 70, 170
    and his incubator for hatching baby chicks, 170; thermostat, 170
Hairston, Eugene, "Silent," 291
Halex House, 327
Hall, Mrs. Ethel Taylor, 42
Hall, Gillian, 286
Hall, Percival, 38, 230, 232, 233
Hall, Mrs. Tommy G., 193
Hamilton, Lillian, 372
Hanau, Jean, 140
Hannan, Eugene E., 34, 118, 119
    and his work, statue of de l'Epée, 34, 118; bust of the Rev. Thomas Gallaudet, 119; bust of the Rev. Thomas Hopkins Gallaudet, 119; bust of Edward M. Gallaudet, 119
Hanson, Agatha Plaza, 39
Hanson, Olof, 31, 38, 39, 50, 51, 87, 155, 276
    and his buildings, Washington School for the Deaf, 156; North Dakota School for the Deaf; a boy's dormitory at the Kendall School; a building for the State School for Feeble-minded; a residence for Dr. J. L. Noyes, 156
Harper, Robert S., 260
Harris, Glenn I., 51
Harris, Robert I., 402
Harte, Bret, 35
Hartford School. See American School for the Deaf
Hasenstab, Rev. Philip J., 163, 179, 189, 276
Hauser, Jean C., 200
Hawes, Wealthy, 28
Hayes, Governor Rutherford B., 22

Hays, A. Dudley, 41
Hays, David, 346, 348, 349
    quoted, 356
Hazards of Deafness, 209, 210, 216, 217, 218
hearing aids, 212
hearing aids, misleading
    advertisements, 263, 264
Hearing Ear Dogs, 395
hearing impaired, term, 377, 378
Hearn Manual Labor School. See
    Georgia School for the Deaf
Hefflon, Rev. George H., 185
Heidelberg University, 399
Hellers, Peter N., Jr., 157
Helms Foundation Hall of Fame, 297
Herbert, C. G., 178
Herdtfelder, August P., 41
heredity, 76
Higgins, Francis C., 191
Hill, Wells L., 43, 252
Hilliard, Ethel M., 54
Hilmer, Herbert F., 154
Hines, Rudolph, 39
Hirsch, Samuel, 346
His Busy Hour, 78
Hispanic Society, 409
Hlibok, Bruce; his role in "The
    Runaways," 379, 383
Hodgson and Son, architects, 155
Hodgson, Edwin A., 16, 62, 65, 67, 77, 87, 155, 239, 264
    and his book, *The Deaf and Dumb, Facts, Anecdotes and Poetry*, 65, 90
Hoffmeyer, Ben E., quoted, 256
Hofsteater, Howard T., 324
Hogan, J. H., "Voices, Voices," 87
Hoge, Rev. James, 22
Holcomb, Roy, 33, 47, 209-10, 368.
    See also, *Hazards of Deafness*
Holman, Joe, 156
"Hollow of the Moon, The" (Terry), 254
Holter, Henry, 244
Home Circle, 252
Homes for the Aged, Infirm Deaf
    Persons
    Columbus Colony, 406-07
    Gallaudet Home, 70, 165
    Home for the Aged, Moultrie, Florida, 166
    New England Home, 165
    Ohio Home for the Aged and Infirm Deaf, 22
    Pilgrim Towers, 406
    Tanya Towers, 406
Home for Little Children Who Cannot
    Hear in West Medford, Mass., 15
honorary degrees, deaf recipients of, 395
Hoover, President, 170
Horgen, Robert W., 29, 322, 338, 410

Horse Railroad Company, 70
Hoskins, Rev. I. H., 92
Hotchkiss, John B., 16, 39, 239
Houston, General Sam, 4, 5
Howard, Jay C., 38, 211, 212
    quoted, 363
Howard, Petra F., 211, 244, 383
Howe, Samuel G., 12, 73
Howlett, John H., 253
Howson, James W., 36, 265
Hoy, William E., 87, 272, 292; baseball team, 293
Hubbard, Gardiner G., 12, 364
Hubbard, Mabel, 12
Hubbard, Paul D., 36, 37; athletic field 272; 276, 299
Hudson's Bay Company, 50-51
Huff, Kenneth, 328
Hughes, Frederick H., 39, 120
Hughes, Regina Olson, 120, 121
    and her scientific illustrations,
        "Tribrito a una Planto, Dioscorea Composita," 120;
        "Daubentonia Puncicea D.C. Coffee weed," 120; "Brucea antidysenterica Mill," 121;
        "Stokesia laevis," 122
humor, 203
Humphrey, Henry, 399
Humphrey, Ozias, 134
Humphries, Tom, Padden, Carol and
    O'Rourke, Terrence, *A Basic Course in American Sign Language*, 368
Hunt Institute of Botanical
    Documentation, Carnegie-Mellon University, 121
Hunter, William S., 50
Huntingdon, Bishop, 183
Hurburt, Jim, 261
Hurd, Uel, 37
Hurt, Alvis L., 253
Hurwitz, T. Alan, 377
Hutchinson, Meda (Scott), 33

Idaho School for the Deaf and the
    Blind. See Schools
Ijams, Rev. W. E., 31
Illinois School for the Deaf. See
    Schools
"The I love You Gift, Co.," 373
I-Love-You Symbol, 373
Imparo, Frank, 288
Indian hostilities, 37
Indiana School for the Deaf. See
    Schools
Ingle, Truman L., 261
Ingram, Monroe, 70
insurance protection, 157
integration, 14, 76
Intermarriages, 73, 75, 76

International Congress of the Deaf, 16, 165
International Congress on Education
    of the Deaf, 359
International Convention in Milan, 63
interpreters, 193,
    Free lance interpreters, 328
    paid interpreters, 328
    services, 373
Introduction, xix
inventors, 215
Iowa, 7
Iowa School for the Deaf. See Schools

Jackson, Margaret E., 244
Jackson, President Andrew, 32, 152
Jacobs, Harry M., 246
Jacobs, John A., 2, 7, 9
Jacobs, Leo M., 36, 246, 254, 392
    and his book, *A Deaf Adult Speaks Out*, 36; 254, 392
Jacobs, Monroe, 270
Jaimie, Don, 135
Jamison, Jerry, 191
Jancik, Francis, 170
    and his invention, lifter, 170
Jenkins, Weston, 240
Jennings, Alice C., quoted, 363
Jochem, Charles M., 48
John Tracy Clinic, The. See Schools
Johns, H. L., 3
Johnson, Alphonso, 43, 49
Johnson, Armanda A., 3
Johnson, Herschel, 52
Johnson home, 34
Johnson, Howard H., 40, 41
Johnson, Joseph Henry, Sr., 33
Johnson, President Lyndon B., 58, 96, 319
Johnson, Mrs. Lyndon B., 57
Johnson, Richard O., 23
Johnson, Sharon, 391
Johnson, William P., 26
Johnston, George, 407, 408
Jones, David, 82
Jones, Ray L., 57
Jordan, Jerald M., 318, 320, 330, 331
Judaism, 191

Kaercher, Edward, 189
Kannapell, Barbara, 372
    quoted, 364, 371, 372
Kannapell, George G., 265
Kansas School for the Deaf. See
    Schools
Kastner, August C., 29
Katz, Lee, 337
Katzenbach, Mrs. Marie H., 47
Keiser, John H., quoted, 363

Keith, William, 136
Keller, Helen, 165, 261, 379
Kendall, Amos, 4, 32, 38, 191
Kendall Demonstration Elementary
    School. See Schools
Kendall Green, 38, 175, 214, 220. See
    Gallaudet College
Kendall School. See Kendall
    Demonstration Elementary
    School
Kennedy, Jonathan R., 42
Kenner, Marcus L., 205, 328
Kentucky School for the Deaf. See
    Schools
Kerr, Rev. John Rice, 28
Kerr, William D., (son) 20, 27, 28
Kihm, George, 293
King, Alphonso, 135
Kingdom of Callaway, The, 28
Kline, Donald, 123
Klingensmith, Gary, 301
Knapp, Frederick, 14, 15
Knight of the Order of King Charles
    the Third, 135
Knoxville's City Hall, 8
Koch, Harold, 288
Koehler, Rev. Jacob M., 46, 47, 183,
    186, 187
Koko, 373, 375
Kolander, Ray, 52
Kowalewski, Felix, 94, 95, 212
    and his painting, "Chapel Hall,"
        123; "Apres le Bal, "124
Koziar, Stephen W.,
    and his poetry, "On The Edward
        Miner Gallaudet Statue," 333;
        "Glad Recompense," 336
Kraus, Rev. George, 193
Krug, Walter J., 39, 320, 338
Kruger, Art, 49, 277, 282, 284, 286,
    289, 297, 300, 311-315, (ill.) 301
    quoted, 299
Kubis, John, 29
Kuhns, Rev. H. W., 41, 42

Labor Bureaus, 211
Lahn, Nathan, 37
Lambrecht, Jeff, 278
Lamoreaux, Alfred J., 252, 253
LaMonto, Frederick, 125, 126
    and his work, "The Ten
        Commandments," 125; "Death
        in the Afternoon," 125; "Helen
        Keller's Breakthrough," 126;
        "Lady Godiva," 126; "Leda
        and the Swan," 126
Land grants, 2
    Kentucky, 2
    New York, 2
    Pennsylvania, 2
Lang, Donald, 402
Lange, Paul, 87

Lange, Rev. Canon William M., 187,
    264
Larson, Herbert C., 29
Larson, Lars M., 29, 44, 49, 50, 62, 63,
    87, 213
Lashbrook, Charles, 250
Laurens, Jean Paul, 136
Laurent Clerc Award, 421
Lauritsen, Wesley, 38, 51, 170, 244,
    250
    and his athletic schedule book, 170
LaVor, Martin, quoted, 383
Lawrence, D. H., 213
Lawrence, Ivan, 337
Layton, George, 50
Leagues
    Art Student's League, New York
        City, 118, 147
    League of American Pen Women,
        121
    Southern States Art League, 141
    Washington Art League, 123
LeClercq, Charles J., 81, 82, 83, 84,
    91, 127, 128
    and his engraving work, "Niagara"
        and "Erie," 81; and his
        illustrations, "Recycling," 127;
        Scenes along the route to Kye
        Beach," 127; Scenes along the
        bicycle trail, 128; Scenes from
        the Trenton Area, 128; Scenes
        from the pen of Charles
        LeClercq, 128
LeCouteulx Institution for the Deaf.
    See St. Mary's School
Le Couteulx, Louis, 34
Le Couteulx St. Mary's Benevolent
    Society for the Deaf, 34
Leech, Dr., 87
legislation, 256
Leisman, Rev. Arthur G., 29, 185
    and, the flying parson, 185; and his
        poem, "The Deaf Minister,"
        187
Leiter, Caroline M., 261
Leitner, George M., 292, 294
Lentz, Ella, 368
l'Epee, Abbe de, 359
Levine, Edna S., 346, 348, 349
Lewis, Arthur H., 169
    and his article, "World's Safest
        Drivers," 169
Lewis, Emily, 33
Lewellyn, Thomas Carlton, 22,
    "Father of the Mason-Dixon
    Basketball Tournament," 22, 285
Lexington School for the Deaf. See
    Schools
Liberty Bicycles, The, 86
library, 266
Library of Congress, 148
Life, 262
Light, Rev. J. Stanley, 185
"Light-Line Phonography!" 169

Lindberg, Charles A., 195
Lindstrom, Annie, 36
Lindstrom, Thure A., 41, 261
Linguistics of Visual English
    (L.O.V.E.), 371
Linotype, 83, 88, 89
Lions, The, 378
    Helen Keller Memorial Fund for the
        Deaf, Inc., 378
Lippincott, Almon Miner, 196, 199,
    201
Lippitt, Mrs. Henry, 44
Lippitt, Jeanie, 44
Lincoln, Abraham, 6, 11, 38
LinWeber, Ralph E., 22, 295-296
Little Paper Family, The, 247, 248
    LPF editors, 249, 250
Little Theatre of the Deaf, 356
Lloyd Parks, 28
Loe, Elva, 67
Logan, James H., 67, 68, 69
    and, The Raindrop, 67
London Daily Telegraph, 28
London, Danny, 260
Long, Mr. and Mrs. Ellsworth, 52
Long, J. Schuyler, 31, 32, 178, 215,
    240, 250, 410
    and his books, A Sign Directory, 178;
        The Sign Language: A Manual of
        Sign Language, 367
    quoted, 236
Los Angeles Club of the Deaf, 295
Louisiana, 7
Louisiana School for the Deaf. See
    Schools
Love, James Kerr, 75
Love, Governor John A., 393
Low, Juliette Gordon, 195
Lowell, Edgar L., 327
Lowery, 52
Lowman, Alto M., 39, 51
Lowman, Rex, 250, 338
    book, Bitterweed, 250
    poem, "Bitterweed," 338
Lucania, the steamship, 82
Ludwig, William A., 188
Lutes, N. B., 402
Lutheran Church in America, 188
Lutheran Church—Missouri Synod,
    188
Lutheran School for the Deaf. See
    Schools
Lynch, Thomas, 294
Lynn, Mrs. Ollie S., 178, 179
Lyons, Don, 302-3

MacDonald, Della, 50
MacDougall, Randy and Nanette
    Fabray, quoted, 381
MacIntire, Rev. Thomas, 23
Madero, President, 148

Madsen, Willard J.,
    poem, "You Have to be Deaf to
        Understand," 250, 380
Maginn, F., quoted, 363
mainstreaming, 266
    term, 377-78

Malone, Charlie, 82

Malzkhun, Eric, 220
Manley, Prof. Basil, 92
Mann, Rev. Austin A., 69, 183

manual communication, 359

Manual English, 228
Manual training program, 79
Marceau, Marcel, 349
Marguesas Islands, 148
Mariano, Lou, 301
Markowicz, Harry, 365
Marr, Thomas S., 35, 39, 82, 156
    and his designs, the Methodist
        Publishing House, the baseball
        grandstand, and the Tennessee
        School for the Deaf, 156
Marra, William J., 35, 36
Marsden, Robert T., 27
Marshall, Archie, 39
Marshall, Catherine A., 246
Marshall, Charles, 25, 42
Marshall, Marvin, 224
Marsters, James C., 364, 399
Marty, John J., 32
Mary and Belle (schooner), 82
Maryland Duck stamp, 115
Maryland School for the Deaf. See
    Schools
Masher, Willie, 170
    and his invention, "Mute's
        Telephone," 170
Massey, Leslie, 265
Mather, Robert, 402
Mathis, Rev. Steve L.
    quoted, 416
Mayes, Julia, 341
Mayes, Tom, 341, 377, 399
Mba, Peter, 402
McCarthy, Mrs. Marie, 260
McChord, Winfield, 21, 414
McClure, George M., Sr., 21, 28, 59,
    248, 250, 329, 396
McClure, William C., 21, 28
McClure, William J., 21, 28
McCord, William S., 24
McCowen, Mary T., 15
McCreery, Thomas, 22
McDaniel, Lemuel, 137
McFarland, Rev. W. O., 50
McFarlane, James H., 34, 230, 246
McGinley, Bernard, 304
McGray, F., 82
McGregor, Robert P., 22, 43, 45, 62,
    240
    the first NAD president, 43

McLean, James, 23
McVan, Alice Jane, 409
    books, Tryst, 409; Antonio Machado,
        409
Meagher, J. Frederick, 160, 163, 230,
    246, 285, 286, 289, 299
    quoted, 272
Medina, Tim, "Total Communication
    News" WTTG-TV, Channel 5,
    387
Menfort, Mr., 31
Memorials to deaf people. See also
    Buildings
    Bust of Laura Bridgman, 39
    Clerc Street, 32
    Craig, Douglas Street, 39
    Creager, Harry T. Athletic Field, 39
    Deaf Smith County, 5
    Dobson Street, 32
    Draper, Amos G. Street, 39
    Fine, Dr. Peter J. Infirmary, 39
    Golladay Museum, 16
    Hanson, Agatha Plaza, 39
    Hotchkiss Athletic Field, The, 39
    Hubbard, Paul D., football field, 36,
        272
    Long, J. Schuyler, Street, 32
    Lowman, Alto M., Street, 39
    Marra Museum, (ill.) 35, 36
    McCord Student Union Building 24
    Neesam, Frederick J. Athlete Field,
        29
    Roberts, Arthur L., Memorial
        Library, 161
    Roberts, Earl, Athlete Field, 31
    see also
    Gallaudet College Hall of Fame, 39
    see also
    National Fraternal Society of the
        Deaf Hall of Fame, 162
Menchel, Robert S, 44
Mercer County, New Jersey
    Wheelmen Club, 81
Mercy Hospital, 173
Mergenthaler, Ottmar, 83
Merklin, Arthur, 265
Merrill, Edward C., Jr., 38, 137, 342
    quoted, 398, 399, 408, 410
Merrill, Frances, 342
Merrill, Rev. Herbert C., 184, 187
Merriman, Randy, 38
Methodist, 189
Meyers, David, 331
Mexican revolution, 148
Michaels, John W., 22, 27, 70, 190,
    191, 285, 367
    and his book, Handbook of Sign
        Language of the Deaf, 190, 367
Michigan School for the Deaf. See
    Schools
Middleton, Daniel, 21
Middleton, Mildred, 21
Milan resolution, 359

Miles, Dorothy,
    poem, "Gestures," 250
Milestones in Sports, 273-75
Milford, John, 54
military company, 79
military tactics, 79
military uniforms, 260
Miller, Betty G., 129, 130, 131, 133,
    402
    and her work, "Bell School," 129;
        "Education for the Deaf," 130;
        "Education for the Deaf," 130;
        "Ameslan Prohibited," 131;
        "Lipreading," 132
Miller, Eugene, 288
Miller, Gladys, 133
Miller, John S., 165
Miller, Ralph R., 133
    and his illustrations, "I want to be a
        farmer;" "Stores;" "Mealtime
        at the Zoo;" "Tommy's Day;"
        "The Three Little Pigs;" "Little
        Red Riding Hood;"
        "Goldilocks and the Three
        Bears," 133
Mills, John A., 28
Minger, Pam, 391, 392
Mingus, Daniel, 47
Minnesota Institute for the Deaf and
    Dumb. See Minnesota School for
    the Deaf
Minnesota School for the Deaf. See
    Schools
Mission Helpers of the Sacred Heart,
    53
Mississippi River, 140
Mississippi School for the Deaf. See
    Schools
Missouri School for the Deaf. See
    Schools
Mitchell, DeWitt, 2
M. and M. Karolik Collection, 152
Model Secondary School for the Deaf.
    See Schools
Moehle, Billie, 158
Moeller, Harold, 53
Moers, Betty, 393
Moers, Jerome, 393
Moja, (ill.) 374
Molohon, Henry A., 25
Monaghan, Bilbo ("Mule"), 31, 227,
    278, 279, 282
Mondale, Vice President Walter, 373
Monroe, Colonel James, 16
Monroe, Fanny, 16
Monroe, President James, 16
Montana School for Deaf and Blind.
    See Schools
Montez, Lee, 277
Montgomery County Phoenix, 238
Montgomery, George, quoted, 388
Monument, 179
Moore, Frederick A., 37, 285
Moore, Gideon, E., 7, 399

Moore, Henry H., 70, 134, 135
  and his paintings, "Mother and
    Daughter," 134; "Portrait of a
    Titled Lady," 134; "The
    Acrobats," 135; "In a Japanese
    Garden," 135
Moore, Jos., M.D., 92
Moore, Mike, 285
Morgan, Mabel McDaniel, 52
Mork, Kjell Omahr, 188
Morrow, Robert D., 28, 54
Morse, Samuel F.B., 4
Moskowitz, Charles, 226, 244
Mose, Thomas L., 156
Mossel, Max N., 196, 261, 371
Mott, Charles Stewart Foundation,
  341, 388
  produced "Rainbow's End," 388
Mount Airy School. See Schools
Mt. Diablo Hospital Center, 394
Mount, Joseph, 27, 36, 251, 252
Mouton, Hershel, 53
Moylan, Daniel W., 189
Murphy, Fred R., 256
Muse, Helen E., 26
  book, *Green Pavilions*, 254
Muskie, Senator Edmund, 268
Museums

  Abby Aldrich Rockefeller Folk Art
    Center, 16
  American—Anderson Galleries,
    New York, 123
  Art Gallery, Riverside City College,
    153
  Art Institute in Chicago, 118
  Bognar Galleries, Los Angeles, 125
  Connecticut Museum, New Britain,
    113
  Hirshhorn Museum and Sculpture
    Gardens, 100
  Kenneth Taylor Galleries,
    Nantucket, 113
  Laguna Beach Art Festival, 125
  Long Beach Museum of Modern
    Art, 125
  Metropolitan Museum of Art, New
    York City, 148
  Montana Historical Society
    Museum, Helena, Montana,
    108
  Musée Municipal de St. Paul de
    Vence, France, 113
  Museum of Fine Arts, Boston, 104,
    113, 152
  National Gallery, 123
  New Hampshire Historical Society,
    151, 152
  Pasadena Art Museum, California,
    100
  Riverside Art Center and Museum,
    123
  Roerich Museum, New York, 123,
    141

San Diego Fine Arts Gallery, 125
San Francisco Palace of Fine Arts,
  123
Smithsonian Institution, 121
Stanford University Museum of
  Art, 100
Walt Disney Studios, Burbank,
  California, 123
Mudgett, David, 158
Mudo, El, 171
Mute, The, 171
Mute's Telephone, 170
Myers, Lowell J., 254, 402
  book, *The Law and The Deaf*, 254,
    402
Mystic Oral School. See Schools
"My Third Eye" (play), 354, 355, 356

Nack, James, 254
Nagle, Margaret, 379
Napoleon, 77
  and the Volta Prize, 77
Nation, The New York, 70
National Association of the Deaf, xiii,
  16, 21, 22, 26, 28, 31, 33, 34, 35,
  36, 38, 42, 47, 48, 54, 59, 60-61,
  62, 69, 77, 79, 81, 118, 164, 169,
  179, 196, 246, 256, 260, 263, 259,
  264, 269, 317, 319, 327, 337, 338,
  339, 362, 367, 376, 395, 399
  Assistant Executive Director for
    State Affairs, 426
  Communicative Skills Program, 368
  Deaf America, Miss, 381, 434, 435
  Diamond Jubilee, 265, 328
  "Dollar a Month Plan," 228
  Endowment Fund, 263
  Executive Director, 426
  first home office, 328
  "Fulton Tontine," 265
  Halex House, 381
  "Highlights of the NAD Century,"
    427
  "Knights of the Flying Fingers,"
    228
  Knights of the Flying Fingers
    Awards, 328
  Legal Defense Fund, 399
  NAD in the 40s, 222-223, 224
  NAD's Committee on Industrial
    status, 79
  Officers of, 1940s, 222, 229
  "Order of the Georges," 228, 328
  Presidents of the NAD, 422, 423,
    424, 425, 426
  Problems faced in 50s, 263
  Reorganization plans, 264-266
  WW II Red Cross Clubmobile, 223,
    (ill.) 221
National Academy of Science, 75
National Agricultural Library, 121
National Airlines, 394

National Arboretum, 121
National Arts Club, New York City,
  169
National Captioning Institute, 386
  Logo, 386
National Center for Law and the
  Deaf, 386, 398, 399
  Logo, 398
National Congress of Jewish Deaf, 191
National Convention of Deaf-Mutes.
  See National Association of the
  Deaf, 62
National Deaf-Mute College, 11, 42,
  65, 70, 79, 82. See also Gallaudet
  College
National Fraternity Society of the
  Deaf, 30, 33, 36, 157, 158, 159,
  160, 163, 259, 339
  and awards, 161; Board of
    Directors, 163; "Carry on"
    Motto, 163; Diamond, Jubilee,
    158
  Divisions
    Chicago #1, 157; McKinley Lodge
      #922, 157; Jacksonville,
      Illinois, 160; Mobile, 160;
      Toronto, 160;
    Division of the year, 162; divisions,
      160; *The Frat*, 160; Frater of the
      year, 162; Grand Presidents of
      the NFSD, 161; Hall of Fame,
      160; Home Office, 159-160;
      Membership, 157, 160;
      Membership, women, 157;
      scholarships, 160; seal, 161;
      volunteer awards, 160
National Geographic, 373, 375
National Leadership Training
  Program, 317
National Observer, The, 346
National Poultry Exhibition, 170
National Registry of Professional
  Interpreters and Translators for
  the Deaf. See Registry of
  Interpreters of the Deaf
National Royal Institution for the
  Deaf, Paris, xxi
National Technical Institute for the
  Deaf, 28, 41, 56, 57, 317, 372, 334,
  335, 338
  history, 57
national television programs, 356
National Theatre of the Deaf, 16, 317,
  338, 346, 349, 350, 351, 352, 353,
  354, 389
"Natural Method," 15
Nebraska School for the Deaf. See
  Schools
Neesam, Frederick J., 29, 158, 282
Negro students, 13
Nelson, Edith M., 39
Netusil, Anton J., 31
Nevil, George W. Vocational School,
  20

Newcomb, Elliott, 267, 268
New England Industrial School for
    Deaf Mutes. See Beverly School
    for the Deaf
New Jersey School for the Deaf. See
    Marie H. Katzenbach School for
    the Deaf
Newman, Lawrence, 318, 319
    quoted, 328, 337, 403
    Award for Creative Writing, 318
    California Teacher of the Year, 318
New Mexico School for the Deaf. See
    Schools
Newsam, Albert, 20
News-Tribune, 82
New York Daily News, The, 177
New York Giants baseball team, 37
New York Institution for the
    Improved Instruction of Deaf
    Mutes. See Lexington School for
    the Deaf
New York School for the Deaf. See
    Schools
New York Tribune, 83
New Yorker, The, 238
Nies, Edwin W., 187, 399
Ninety Nines, 195
Nodine, Mary Hart, 44
Nomeland, Ronald E., 33, 402
Nordyke, Benajah R., 36
normal deaf person, 360
Normal Department, 38. See also
    Gallaudet College Graduate
    School
Norman, Freda, The Supersign
    Woman, 388
Norris, Arthur, Jr., 285
North American Decoy, 115
Northampton, 12
North Carolina Bureau, 211
North Carolina School for the Deaf.
    See Schools
North Dakota School for the Deaf.
    See Schools
Northern, T.Y., 223
Northrop, Helen, 50
Norton, Frances, 36
Norwood, Malcolm J., 41, 267, 268,
    338, 385, 402
Nostrand, Jacob Van, 33
Nun, 179

Oakland Daily Times, 36
Oates, Sammy, 301
O'Brien, John G., 403, 406
occupations, 81, 82
Ocloo, Seth Tetteh, 402
O'Connor, Dr. Clarence, 267
Offspring of deaf parents, 410
Ogden, Kate, 156
Ohio Federation of Organizations of
    the Deaf, 22

Ohio Institution for the Education of
    Deaf and Dumb. See Ohio School
    for the Deaf
Ohio School for the Deaf. See Schools
Oklahoma School for the Deaf. See
    Schools
Okuda, Chuzo, 402
Oldest journal devoted to the
    education of the deaf in the
    world and in America, 238
Olsen, Gary, 407
O'Neil, Kitty, (ill.) 297; 297-98
O'Neill, Eugene, 346
O'Neill Theatre Center, 346, 348
Ontario Camp for the Deaf, 160
Ontario School for the Deaf. See
    Schools
"Operation lipread," 262
Oppenheimer, Ben, 170
    and his invention, rubber cap, 170
oral, aural and lipreading method,
    179
Oral Deaf Adult Section of the
    Alexander Bell Association, 318,
    327
oral deaf people, 318
Oral Education, 11
"oral failures," 361
oralism, 173, 193
oral philosophy, 360
    reasons for, 360
Oregon School for the Deaf. See
    Schools
Orman, James, N., 16, 236, 265, 338,
    341
Orman Plan, The, 265, 266
O'Rourke, Terrence, 338, 368, 377
    A Basic Course in Manual
    Communication, 250, 368
Orrill, Louis B., 33, 261
Osaka School for the Deaf. See
    Schools
Overland Monthly Magazine, 111

Pach, Alexander L., 68, 82, 158
Packard, Philip W., 191
Padden, Carol, 367
    quoted, 369
Padden, Melinda Chapel, 319, 320
Paden, Dale, 170
    and his invention, vise-grip pliers
    and pipe wrench, 170
Palmer, Howard, 321
    as "Othello," 321
Panama-Pacific Exposition, 136
Panara, Robert F., 58, 262
    quoted 342, 360
pantomime, 136
Papalia, Anthony, 325
    poem, "Now the Deaf Are Doing
    It!"

"Pard," Museum at Hill City, South
    Dakota, 195
Paris Salon, 36, 87, 137, 144
Paris Universal Exhibit, 135
Park, Grace Coleman, 49
Parkinson, Joseph B., 239
Parks, Ray, 279
Parks, Roy, 28
Parsons, Frances M., 254, 395
    Sound of the Stars, 254
Patterson, Francine, 373
Patterson, Robert, 22, 87
Payne, Edward T., 195
Paxton, May, 173, 174
Paxton, Pollard, 170
    and his invention, a toy cart with
    two figures on top, 170
Pearce, Mary, 381
Pearl Harbor, 219-220
Peddling, 255, 256
    "The Deaf Do Not Beg," 255, 256;
    efforts to stem peddling, 256;
    legislation to control, 256;
    peddlers, 256, 257, 259; reasons
    for, 255, 257; resentment of,
    257, 258, 263
Peet, Elizabeth, 69
Peet Family, the, 78
Peet, Harvey Prindle, 16
Peet, Isaac L., 65, 90
Peet, Mary Toles, 254
    poem, "Verses," 254
Peikoff, David, 232, 250, 339-341, 263
Penn, Arthur, 348
Penn, W. E., 92
Pennsylvania Institution for the Deaf
    and Dumb. See Pennsylvania
    School for the Deaf
Pennsylvania School for the Deaf. See
    Schools
percent of deaf teachers, 3
Perkins, Mr. & Mrs. Gilman H., 44
Perkins Institution, 73
Pernick, Joseph J., 414
Pershing, General John, 172
Peter Bent Brigham Hospital, 394
Peters, Frosty, 279
Petersen, Nick, 42, 282
Peterson, Donald, 331
Peterson, Edwin G., 51
Peterson, Peter N., 51, 58
Pettingill, Don G., 54, 246, 319, 403
Pfetzing, Donna, 371
Phi Kappa Zeta, 121
Philadelphia Phillies, 87
Philadelphia Record, The, 169
Phillips, Richard M., 39, 212, 250, 338,
    399
Phoenix Day School for the Deaf,
    The. See Arizona School for the
    Deaf and the Blind
Physical education, 70, 179
Pictorial Corporation of America, 137
Pidgin Signed English, 376

Pierce, Curtis, 71
Pimentel, Albert, 339
Pintner, Rudolph, quoted 235
P.L. 85-905, 267
P.L. 86-276, 318
P.L. 94-142
   bill, 397
   term, 397
Players' Guide, 349
Poetry by deaf poets
   "Belle Missouri," by Howard Glyn-
      don, 7, 28
   "Bitterweed" by Rex Lowman, 338
   "A Deaf Man's Prayer," by Emery
      Edwin Vinson, 182
   "Deaf Minister, The," by A. G.
      Leisman, 187
   "Glad Recompense," by Stephen
      W. Koziar, 336
   "On His Deafness," by Robert F.
      Panara, 269
   "On The Edward Miner Gallaudet
      Statue," by Stephen W.
      Koziar, 333
   "Pests to Exterminate," by Guie C.
      Cooke, 213
   "Shared Beauty," by Robert J.
      Smithdas, 379
   "Silent Homage," by Loy E.
      Golladay, 367
   "Ten Fingers Have I," by Loy E.
      Golladay, 325
   "They Say I'm Deaf," by Saul N.
      Kessler, 269
   "Voices, Voices," by J. H. Hogan, 87
   "You Have to be Deaf to
      Understand," by Willard J.
      Madsen, 380
point system, 160
Pokorny, Dan, 391, 392
Poncar, Robert, 278
Poore, Mrs. H. T., 54
Pope, Alvin E., 47, 48
Pope, Artemus W., 49
Pope, Verle A., 49
population, 59
Porter, George S., 48, 83, 90, 230, 240,
   242
posters and bumper stickers, 373
Potter, Maurice, (ill.) 293
Price, Raphael I. M., 402
priest, Episcopalian, 7
Prince, Edmund M., 179, 213, 215
Prince George's County, Maryland,
   394
Pritchard, Alva Dean, 49
Professional Rehabilitation Workers
   Among the Deaf, 317
programs, 7
   integrated, 7
   mainstreaming, 7
Prologue, xxi
Propp, George, 42, 208, 251, 265
   "Proppaganda," 251

Publications, deaf, 230, 286
   American Annuals of the Deaf, 16, 21,
      24, 30, 75, 77, 79, 239, 392, 397
   American Deaf Citizen, The, 242
   American Deaf News, 244
   America Era, The, 41, 250
   Anamosa Eureka, The, 62, 251
   Art in America, 105
   Association Review, The. See *The
      Volta Review*
   Baltimore News-American, 115
   Boston Journal, 71
   Buff and Blue, The, 249, 250
   California News, The, 250
   Cavalier, The, 230, 231, 242, 244,
      250. See *The Silent Cavalier*
   Colorado Index, 248
   Companion, 38, 248, 249, 250
   Daily Bulletin, 81
   Deaf, The, 270
   Deaf American, The, 49, 71, 123, 158,
      300, 246, 247
   Deaf Churchman, The, 186, 250
   Deaf Lutheran, The, 188
   Deaf-Mute, The, 62, 246, 247, 255
   Deaf-Mute Casket, The, 24, 246, 247
   Deaf-Mutes' Companion, 238
   Deaf-Mutes' Journal, The, 16, 65, 71,
      87, 164, 240, ill, 239
   Deaf-Mutes Times, The, See also *The
      Silent Worker*, 71, 20, 230, 240
   Deaf Nebraskan, The, 250
   Deaf Oklahoman, 52, 250
   Deaf Spectrum, The, 246
   Dee Cee Eyes, The, 247
   Digest of the Deaf, 244
   Empire State News, 247
   Ephpheta, 191
   Frat, The, 160, 185, 247, 250, 255,
      286
   Gallaudet Almanac, The, 254, 395
   Gallaudet Alumni Bulletin, 231, 232,
      250
   Gallaudet Alumni Newsletter, 232,
      247, 250
   Gallaudet Guide, 238
   Gallaudet Record, 250
   Gallaudet Today, 250
   Goodson Gazette, 247
   Illinois Advance, The, 247, 341
   Iowa Hawkeye, The, 31, 250
   Junior Deaf American, The, 319
   Kansas Star, The, 70
   Kentucky Deaf-Mute, 251. See *The
      Kentucky Standard*
   Kentucky Standard, The, 21, 178, 247,
      250
   Lincoln Silent Club News, 247
   Little World, The, 20
   Lone Star, The, 33
   Mexico (N.Y.) Independent, 239
   Michigan Mirror, The, 83, 247
   Mission Lane, 186
   Missouri Record, The, 250, 256

   Modern Silents, The, 242, 243
   Mt. Airy World, The, 20, 239
   NAD Broadcaster, The, 246
   National Exponent, The, 83, 239, 240,
      242
   National Gazette, 48
   National Observer, The, 244
   Nebraska Journal, The, 208, 247, 250
   New York Journal of the Deaf, The,
      239, 286. See *The Deaf-Mutes'
      Journal*
   North Dakota Banner, The, 250
   NTID Focus, The, 247
   Ohio Chronicle, The, 178, 247
   Powell Publications, 248
   Radii, 238
   Radii and Phoenix, 238
   Ranch Hand, The, 246
   Register, The, 250, 252
   Silent Broadcaster, The, 244
   Silent Cavalier, The, 244. See *The
      Cavalier*
   Silent Hoosier, The, 250
   Silent Missionary, The, 186
   Silent News, The, 246
   Silent News-Letter, The, 186
   Silent Optimist, The, 160
   Silent Success, The, 160
   Silent Worker, The, 48, 71, 73, 81, 83,
      86, 90, 123, 160, 165, 178, 185,
      230, 239, 240, 242, 243, 246,
      249, 250, 261, 262, 328, 371. See
      The Deaf American
   Silent World, The, 20, 73
   Southerner, The, 244
   Sports Parade, The, 244
   Texas Mute Ranger, The, 33
   Virginia Guide, The, 247
   Volta Review, The, 178, 212, 247
   W.A.D. Pilot, The, 247, 410
   West Virginia Tablet, The, 41, 250
   Ye Silent Crier, 247
Puccini, Giacamo, 346
   "Gianni Schicci," 346
pupils, number of (1940), 219
pure oral method, 3, 15, 20, 65, 78
pure oral schools, 12, 359
Purtell, Senator Williams, 267

Queen Christina of Spain, 135
Quigley, Howard M., 318
Quinn, James H., 37
Quota International, 378
   Deaf Woman of the Year Award,
      378; "Shatter Silence"
      program, 378, 393; Scholarship
      awards, 378

Racha, Philip, 82
Racycle, The, 86

Rafferty, Dwight L., 250
"Rainbow's End," 388
Rakow, J. Pierre, 267
Ramger, Catherine Marshall, 36
Ramger, Harold, 330, 331
Randles, Archie R., 51
Randolph, John D., 402
Rath, Emil, 50
Rath, Gunnar, 244
Rattan, Everett, 290
Ravn, Alden, 53, 220
Records. See sports records
Redmond, Carrie Ann Jean, 136
Redmond, Granville S., 35, 36, 136
    and his paintings, "A Winter Scene
        on the Seine," 136; "Low
        Tide," 136
Redmond, Seymour, 87
    and his painting, "The Winter
        Evening," 87
Reed, John, 247
Regensburg, O. H., 239, 240
Registry of Interpreters for the Deaf,
    317, 327, 328, 410
Regulations, 180
Reid, F. L., 42
Reinke, Rev. August P., 188, 193
Religion, 193
Relihan, Maurice, 41
Renaissance, 77
residential schools, 76, 78, 219, 361
Resolution at Milan, Italy, 63
Revells, Jim, 381
Rhode Island School for the Deaf. See
    Schools
Rhodes, Allison Phidel, 225
Rhone, Court Judge Bayard, 337
Rice, Ronald P., 286
Richardson, Katherine B., 173
Richardson, Scott James, 337
Richardson, Suzanne, 341
Richmond (Ky.) Messenger, 251
Rider, Edward, C., 49
Rider, Henry C., 48, 63, 65, 87, 239
Riekehof, Lottie, 367, 378
    Talk to the Deaf, 367; The Joy of
        Signing, 368
Riggs, Mrs. Bess M., 190
Ringle, John, 37, 277
Ripley's Believe It or Not cartoons, 222,
    164, 213, 215, 222, 224, 227, 229,
    231, 260, 293, 298
Ripley, Robert, 226
Ritchie, William, 92
Ritter, William C., 22, 54
Roberts, Arthur L., 33, 36, 163, 250,
    258, 259
    quoted, 244
Roberts, Earl, 31
Roberts, Kathy, 193
Robinson, Warren, 28, 79
Rochester Method, The, 44
Rochester School for the Deaf. See
    Schools

Rockefeller, Abby Aldrich
    Folk Art Center, 104, 105
Rockefeller, John D., 108, 179
Rockefeller, Vice President Nelson D.
    quoted, 393, 396
Rock Gospel, 391, 392
Rockwell, Walter, 16, 261
Rogers, Harriet B., 12
Romero, Emerson, 266, 267, 170
    and his inventions, wake-up alarm,
        clocks with built-in lamps,
        baby cry signals, doorbell
        lights, vibrators and buzzers,
        170; Vibralarm Service, 170
Rood, Marvin S., 41, 250
Roosevelt, President Teddy, 69
Rose Cottage, 13
Rosson, Lester G., 295
Roth, Jackie, 381
Roy, William B., 262
Ruge, Wilbur J., 203, 205, 206, 207
Runde, Winfield S., 36, 223
runners, deaf, 304
Russell, Joe, 277
Russo-Japanese War, 148
Rutherford, Rev. Henry, 189
Ryan, Archbishop Memorial Institute
    for the Deaf. See Schools

St. John's Institute. See Schools
St. Joseph's Institution. See Schools
St. Mary's School. See Schools
St. Thomas Mission for the Deaf, 184
Saltzman, Cynthia, 382, 387
Sanders, Oscar, 261
Sanderson, Robert G., 48, 328, 330,
    331
    quoted, 318, 322, 331, 386
Santa Anna, General Antonio de, 4, 5
Santa Claus, 91
Saunders, L. W., 31, 91
Savinsky, Frederick, 286
Scarvie, Norman G., 31, 410
Schetnan, Enoch L., 253
Schick, Eugene, 250
Schlesinger, Hilde, 392
Schlieff, Wayne, 220
Schneider, Mrs. O. A., 193
Schoneman, Frederick W., 341
Schools for the deaf
    Alabama School for the Deaf, 39,
        70, 91, 137, 171, 277
        history, 33-34
    American School for the Deaf, xxii,
        20, 32, 41, 68, 73, 75, 79, 82,
        151, 183, 238, 251, 252, 267,
        268, 276, 277, 286, 318, 359
        history, 16
    Alexander Graham Bell School, 301
    Arizona State School for the Deaf

    and the Blind, 47, 48, 63, 277,
        301
        history, 54
    Arkansas School for the Deaf, 19,
        26, 46, 51, 91, 165, 190, 282,
        285, 287, 288
        Civil War, 8
        history, 26-27
    Bartlett's School, Mr., 183
        history, 7
    Beverly School for the Deaf,
        Massachusetts
        history, 46
    Bolling School, Cobbs, Virginia
        history, 1
    California School for the Deaf,
        Berkeley, 33, 43, 82, 83, 87,
        100, 123, 136, 144, 276, 285,
        303, 317
        history, 35-36
    California School for the Deaf,
        Riverside, 123
        history, 55
    Central Institute for the Deaf
        history, 54
    Central New York School for the
        Deaf, 49
    Chicago Day School for the Deaf,
        36, 170
        history, 44
    Cincinnati Day Public School for
        the Deaf, 22
        history, 43
    Clarke School for the Deaf, 227,
        364, 399
    Cleveland Day School for the Deaf,
        51
    Colorado School for the Deaf, and
        the Blind, 2, 51, 188, 277, 278,
        282, 288, 301
        history, 42-43
    Columbia Institution for the Deaf
        and Dumb, 38
        Civil War, 9; history, 32. See also
            Gallaudet College
    Columbia Institution for the
        Instruction of the Deaf, and
        Dumb, 4. See also Gallaudet
        College
    Diamond Head School, Hawaii
        history, 53; Pearl Harbor, 219-20
    Eastern Iowa School for the Deaf
        history, 50
    Evansville, Indiana School for the
        Deaf
        history, 48
    Florida School for the Deaf and the
        Blind, 52, 53, 70
        history, 49
    Gallaudet Day School for the Deaf,
        St. Louis, 165, 184
        history, 45-46
    Georgia School for the Deaf, 73, 91
        Civil War, 9; history, 26

Governor Baxter School for the
Deaf, Portland, Maine
history, 45
Idaho School for the Deaf and the
Blind
history, 53
Illinois School for the Deaf, 31, 46,
53, 70, 75, 76, 79, 80, 90, 133,
136, 189, 195, 227, 276, 277,
278, 279, 282, 285, 294, 295, 296
causes of deafness, 2; Civil War,
8; history 6, 25-26
Indiana School for the Deaf, 6, 50,
52, 70, 90, 164, 165, 179, 298
history, 23
Iowa School for the Deaf, 30, 40,
47, 54, 91, 277, 283, 294, 299
history, 31-32
John Tracy Clinic, The, Los Angeles
history, 55
Kansas State School for the Deaf,
35, 42, 44, 46, 52, 70, 91, 119,
170, 276, 277, 283, 293, 294,
295, 299
history, 36-37
Kendall Demonstration Elementary
School, 40, 45, 56, 118, 267
history, 32-33
Kentucky School for the Deaf, 28,
59, 81, 84, 288
Civil War, 7, 9; history, 1-2, 5, 20-
21
Lexington School for the Deaf, 12,
267
Louisiana School for the Deaf, 20,
52, 70, 277, 278
history, 29-30
Marie H. Katzenbach School for the
Deaf, 70, 81, 90, 91, 164, 193,
285, 294
history, 47-48
Maryland School for the Deaf, 44,
47, 303
history, 39
Michigan School for the Deaf, 32,
45, 123, 157, 160, 277
history, 29-31
Mill Nick Manor School, Lutheran
School for the Deaf, 261
Minneapolis Day School for the
Deaf, 38, 51, 52
Minnesota School for the Deaf, 5,
50, 51, 70, 147, 156, 198, 276,
277, 288, 362
history, 37-38
Mississippi School for the Deaf, 91,
164, 277, 278, 279, 282
history, 31
Missouri School for the Deaf, 51,
70, 196, 276, 277, 288, 371
history, 27-28; uniforms, 21
Model Secondary School for the
Deaf, Washington, D.C., 285,
317

history, 56
Montana School for Deaf and Blind
history, 51
Mount Airy School, 15, 91, 304
Mystic Oral School, 285
Nebraska School for the Deaf, 15,
32, 47, 50, 277, 282, 283
history, 41-42
New Mexico School for the Deaf,
29, 44, 63, 213, 285
history, 49-50
New York Institution for the
Instruction of Deaf and Dumb,
New York City, 1, 28, 81
See also, New York School for
the Deaf, Fanwood
New York School for the Deaf,
Fanwood, 22, 30, 33, 35, 37, 41,
43, 44, 46, 47, 48, 51, 53, 65, 78,
81, 90, 91, 123, 151, 240, 260,
269, 277, 299, 363
causes of deafness, 2; history, 16-
17
New York State School for the
Deaf, Rome, 81, 91
history, 43-44
North Carolina Institution for the
Deaf and Dumb and Blind in
Raleigh, 8, 90
North Carolina School, Central,
Greensboro
history, 24
North Carolina School, Eastern,
Wilson
history, 24
North Carolina School for the Deaf,
Morganton, 277, 279, 285, 288
history, 23-25
North Dakota School for the Deaf,
38, 44, 52
history, 50-51
Northern New York School for the
Deaf
history, 48
Ohio School for the Deaf, 3, 44, 62,
82, 154, 292, 293, 296, 362
history, 22
Oklahoma School for the Deaf, 277
history, 52
Ontario School for the Deaf, 277
Oregon School for the Deaf
history, 41
Osaka School for the Deaf in Japan,
261
Pennsylvania School for the Deaf,
15, 17, 30, 39, 70, 90, 156, 189,
277, 288
history, 20, 46-47
Rhode Island School for the Deaf,
285, 299
history, 44-45
Rochester School for the Deaf, New
York

history, 44
St. John's Institute, Milwaukee, 118
St. Joseph's Institution, 91
St. Mary's School, Buffalo, New
York, 118, 125, 282
history, 34-35
South Carolina School for the Deaf
and Blind, 47, 49
history, 13, 26
South Dakota School for the Deaf,
283
history, 47
Sterck, Margaret, School for the
Hearing Impaired in Delaware,
33
Tennessee School for the Deaf, 171,
193, 276, 277, 285
Civil War, 8; history, 23
Texas School for the Deaf, 28, 53,
140, 190, 261, 277, 286, 299,
301, 399
history, 33
Utah Schools for the Deaf and the
Blind, 54, 63, 91
history, 48-49
Virginia State School for the Deaf at
Hampton
history, 54
Virginia School for the Deaf and the
Blind, 40, 50, 54, 279, 285
history, 22
Washington State School for the
Deaf, 41, 285
history, 50
West Virginia School for the Deaf
and the Blind, 123, 179, 267,
291
history, 40-41
Western Pennsylvania School for
the Deaf, Edgewood, 165
history, 39-40
Wisconsin School for the Deaf, 31,
79, 277, 282
history 28-29
Schools for Deaf Blacks, 14
Georgia, 14
North Carolina, 14
South Carolina, 14
Schools founded by deaf persons, 19
schools, residential, 76, 78, 219, 361
school seals and logos through the
years, 18
Schools used by armed forces, 8
Columbia Institution, 8
Georgia, 8
Louisiana, 8
Mississippi, 8
Missouri, 8
Tennessee, 8
Virginia, 8
Schowe, Ben M. Sr., 231, 341, 250, 409
Schreiber, Frederick C., 247, 269, 317,
331, 378, 421
quoted, 325, 378, 395, 397, 415

479

Schreiber, Loel F., 230, 246
Schroeder, Anton, 38, 170
  and his invention, candle lighter,
    170
Schroedel, John, 250, 402
Schuchman, John S., 414
Schulman, Walter M., 246
Schunoff, Hugo F., 317
  quoted, 320, 328, 335
Schyman, William, (ill.) 301, 303
Scientific America, The, 170
Scott, Judge A. A., 337
Scott, Mary Agnew, 54
Scott, Roger, 33
Scranton Oral School. See
    Pennsylvania School for the
    Deaf, Scranton
Scurlock, George H., 79
seals, logos
  Caption Center, The, 384
  National Association of the Deaf,
    419
  National Captioning Institute, 386
  National Center for Law and the
    Deaf, 398
  National Fraternal Society of the
    Deaf, 161
  schools, 18
Searing, Laura C., 28, 67, 194, 254.
    See also Howard Glyndon
Searing, Rev. Stanley, 165
Sears, Roebuck and Co., 387
  decoder, 387
Seaton, Charles D., 41
Seattle Exposition, 136
Seely, Perry E., 55
Seidel, John, 394
Seixas, David G., 17, 20
Seminaries
  Columbia Theological, 191
  Lutheran Theological, 189
  New Orleans Baptist, 190
  Virginia Theological Seminary,
    Alexandria, 22
Separate departments for black and
    white students, 14
Shanklin, George, 170
Sharp, Mrs. I. F., 92
Sharpless, Nansie, 402
Sheehan, Cardinal Lawrence, 191
Sheridan Circle, 119
Sherman, Eleanor E., 244
Shifflett, Dorothy, 368
Shipman, Eldon, 28
Shipman, Ernest, 28, 168
Shoemaker, Gary, 191
Sicard, Abbe, 359
Signing Essential English (SEE), 370,
    371
Signing Exact English (SEE II), 371, 372
Sign Instructors Guidance Network
    (SIGN), 368
Sign Language, 12, 15, 65, 78, 79, 173,
    179, 183, 193, 318, 346, 348, 356,

359, 360, 361, 364
  attempts to suppress, 361, 362; best
    way to educate deaf children,
    361; change, 365; classes, 373,
    383; controversy, 346; enemies,
    363; filming, 364, 365;
    interpreters, 388; outlaw of,
    362; reasons for change of
    opinion, 365; songs, 221
"Sign Language Store, The," 373
silent films, 136, 262
silent press, the, 238
Silent Wheelmen, The, 80
Silent Worker, The, contributors to, 230
silhouettist, 151
Silver, Alton, 191, 262
Simmons, Mrs. M. M., 189
Simpson, Delos A., 45, 46
Simpson, Howard W., 47
Simpson, James, 47, 87
Simpson, William, 10, 377
Sipek, Richard F., 25, 292, 295, (ill.)
    293
Sisters of Loretto, The, 5
Sister Patricia, Bridget Hughes, 179
Sisters of St. Joseph, 5, 34
Skinner, George E., 37
Skinner, William L., 164
Sloan, Bonnie, 279, (ill.) 302
Sloyd system, 163
Smaltz, Warren M., 265
Smith, Alberta, 377
Smith, Glenn, 289, 290, 299
Smith, Hadley W., quoted, 272, 279,
    286
Smith, James L., 37, 38, 81, 166, 248,
    250, 276, 361, 362
Smith, Jess, 265, 327
Smith, Jim M., 246
Smith, Linwood, 250
  book, *Silence, Love, and Kids I Know,*
    250
Smith, Michael J., 252
Smith, Williams S., 41
Smithdas, Robert J., 379
  books, *City of the Heart,* a collection
    of his poems, 379; *Life at My
    Fingertips,* autobiography, 379;
    poem, "Shared Beauty," 379
Smithsonian Institute, 175
Society for the Promotion of Church
    Work Among the Deaf, The, 186
softball, tournament, 297
Sollenberger, Earl, 254
  poem, "Along With Me," 254
songs, 373
Sorolla, Joaquin, 147
South Carolina School for the Deaf
    and Blind. See Schools
South Dakota School for the Deaf.
    See Schools
Southern Baptist Convention, 190
Southern Baptist Ministry to the Deaf,
    190

Southern California Center for the
    Law and the Deaf, 384
Sowell, James W., 250
  collection of poetry, *To Her I Love,*
    250
space experiments, 330, 331
Sparks, Bill, 34
Sparks, William B., 137
  and his portraits, 138, 139; portrait
    of Dr. Edward C. Merrill, Jr.,
    139
Spartanburg High School, South
    Carolina, 47
speak and lipread, 12
Speaker, Lillie, 174
Spear, Anson R., 38, 50, 51, 87, 265
  quoted, 363
Spear-Heywood Envelope Company,
    51
"Spear Safety Envelope," 51
Spear Safety Envelope Company, 51
Speckhardt, G., 42
Spectrum, Focus on Deaf Artists, 404-
    405
speech, 79
speech and sign language, 79
speech and speech reading, 359
"Speed Demon, The," H. Berger, 304
Spellman, John, 44
Sports, achievements in 1940s, 227
Sports, milestones, 273-275
Sports Records
  National Deaf American Swimming
    (Men short course (25 yards),
    313; National Deaf American
    Swimming Records (women)
    short course (25 yards), 314;
    National Deaf America Track
    and Fields (men), 313; National
    Deaf America Track and Fields
    Records (women), 314; Schools
    for the Deaf Regional
    Basketball Tournament
    Champions, 311; California,
    312; Central, 312; Eastern, 311;
    Eastern II, 311; Mason-Dixon,
    312; Midwest, 312; New
    England, 311; World
    Swimming Records (men)
    Long Course (50 meters), 314;
    World Swimming Records
    (women) long course (50
    meters), 315; World Track and
    Field Records (men), 315;
    World Track and Field Records
    (women), 315
Spotlight, in *The Frat,* 160
Spradley, Thomas S. and James P.
    Spradley, 411
  book, *Deaf Like Me,* 411
Spy, 9
Stack, Archie, 50, 220
Stack, Henry, 387
  KGW-TV in *the Today Show,* 387

Stalling, Rev. John W., 229
Stanford, Rev. John, 1, 16
Stangarone, Jim, 414
State Board of Education, 53, 90
State Legislature, 20, 22, 23, 25, 28,
    29, 30, 31, 33, 37, 40, 41, 42, 47,
    48, 49, 50, 51, 55
Statue of General Philip H. Sheridan,
    118
Statue of Thomas Hopkins Gallaudet
    and Alice Cogswell, 65, 67
Stephenson, Reubin C., 82, 87, 292,
    294
Sterck, Margaret School. See Schools
Sterling, James, 196
Sternberg, Martin L. A., 254
    I am Deaf, Too, 254
Stevens, Clyde, 30
Stevens, Kelly H., 33, 140, 141, 142
    and his paintings, "Oaks, Levee
        Road," 140; "I looked over
        Jordan," 141; "Zinnia in White
        Pitcher," 142; "Basque Boy in
        Red Cap," 142 and
        "Enchantment," 142
Stevens, Bishop William Bacon, 183
Stevenson, William E., 41
Stewart, Ellen Pearson, 33
Stewart, James, 30, 249
Stewart, Joanna S., 69
Stewart, Larry, 33
Stewart, Roy J., 33, 173, 289, 336
Stewart, Roy and Ellen, 322
Stickles, Frederick, 82
Stirling, James, Jr., 196
Stokoe, Casterline and Croneberg
    *A Dictionary of American Sign
        Language on Linguistic Principles,*
        365; *Sign Language Structure,*
        365
Stokoe, William C., 365, 367
    book, *Sign Language and the Deaf
        Community: Essays in Honor of
        William C. Stokoe*
    Linguistics Research Program, 365
Stokoe, William C. Scholarship Fund,
    367
Stout, John M., 69
    and deaf trick bicycle rider, 69
Strachan, Paul, 230
Strassler, Barry, 327
Strong, Charles K. W., 65
Struthers, Sally, 388
Stuckless, Ross, 372
Studebaker, Elizabeth, 36
Students, hard of hearing, 232
Sugiyama, Bill, 219
Sugiyama, Randy, 42
Sullivan, Frank B., 160, 163
Sullivan, James A., 186, 254
    book, *Valley Forge,* 254
Sullivan, Lottie, 42
Sunny Clime, 27
Supalla, Clarence, 246

Sussman, Allen, 402
Sutton, Yancey, 301
Swaim, Dean, 41
Swett, Margaret, 46
Swett, Nellie, 46
Swett, William B., 46
swimmers, deaf, 286-87
Switzer, Mary E., 337, 338, 346
Syle, Henry, 7, 39, 47, 181, 183, 186

Taft, Lorado, 118
Tate, George, 28, 157
Tate, James, N., 28
tax exemption, 381
Taylor, Luther H., 25, 37, 260, 292,
    293, 294, 295, (ill.) 271
Teachers, deaf, 7
Teachers, deaf black, 3
teachers of hearing students, 82
technical education, 79
Technical Vocational Institute, 317
Teegarden, George, M., 39, 40, 67,
    68, 69, 78
    quoted, 233, 363
Teitelbaum, Bernard, 40
Telecommunications for the Deaf,
    Inc., 327
telegraph, 4
telephone, 59, 323
teletypewriters, 325, 326, 394, 395
    GA, 325; SK, 325
Teletypewriters for the Deaf, Inc., 325
Television, 193, 262, 269, 384-389
    ABC-TV, 386, 387
    Caption Center, The, 386
        producers of the Captioned ABC
            News programs, 386
    CBS-TV, 388
        producers of, "And Your Name
            Is Jonah," 388; TV series,
            "The Incredible Hulk," 388
    closed captioning, 387
    deaf viewer, 384
    KCSM-TV, 388
    KGW-TV, 387
    KOED-TV, 388
    KRON-TV, Channel 4, San
        Francisco, 387
    Line 21, 386
    NBC-TV, 387
    NBS Time System, 385
    PBS-TV, 386, 387
    "Television Chapel," 193
    WGBH-TV; 386
    WMPB-TV
        Three-hour program, "They
            Grow in Silence: An Evening
            on Deafness," 388
    WTOP-TV, Channel 9, 382, 387
    WTTG-TV, Channel 5, 387, 392

Tellier, Daniel, Jr.
    and his invention, door alarm, 170
Tellinghuisen, Karen, 35
Temporal Bone Bank, 343
Ten Oldest Educational Publications
    of the Deaf Still Being Published,
    239
Tennessee School for the Deaf. See
    Schools
Territorial Asylum for the Deaf and
    Dumb. See New Mexico School
    for the Deaf, 49
Territorial Legislature, 50, 53
Territorial School for the Education of
    the Deaf. See Oklahoma School
    for the Deaf
Terry, Howard L., 244, 254
    his poem, "The Hollow of the
        Moon," 254
Texas, 4, 5, 7
Texas Institute for Deaf, Dumb and
    Blind Colored Youth. See Texas
    School for the Deaf
Texas School for the Deaf. See
    Schools
Theatre of Signs, 356
Thomas, Sr., Charles A., 21
Thomas, Rhulin A., 196, 197, 230
Thompson, Richard E., 46, 364, 399
Thornberry, Homer, 414
Thornton, William, 1
Tice, Merlin, 200
Tilden, Douglas, 35, 36, 82, 87, 136,
    143, 144, 145, 146
    and his sculpture, "Admission
        Day," 36, 145; "The Ball
        Player," 36, 87; "The Bear
        Hunt," 36, 87, 143-144;
        "California Volunteers," 36;
        "Father Junipero Serra," 36;
        "The Football Player," 146;
        "The Mechanics," 144, 145;
        "The National Game," 144;
        "Senator Stephen M. White,"
        260; "The Tired Boxer," 87,
        144; "The Young Acrobat," 87
Tilden Park, 144
Tillinghast, Edward M., 54
Tillinghast, E. S., 47, 51, 54
Tillinghast, Edward W., 47
Tillinghast, Hilda, 47
Tillinghast, J. A., 51
Timon, Right Rev. John, 5, 6, 34
Tingley, Judith, 377
TJ Publishers, Inc., 145, 250, 368
Tooton, W. V., 71, 72
tornado warning, 262
Torr, Donald V., 386
Total Communication, 368
Tracy, Mrs. John, 55
Tracy, Mrs. Spencer, 323
"Tragedy of Deafness, A.," by James
    Beauchamp, 216
train deaths, 71

transcontinental railroad linked the
    nation, 59
Transcript, 252
True, Mary, 45
Truman, George W., 196
Truman, President, 196
Trundle, Henry C., 341
Trundle, John A., 39
Tubergen, John, 261, 262
Tuck, Louis C., 16, 41, 186
Turk, Frank, 319; quoted, 277
Turner, Job, 22, 68, 183
Turner, William A., 75
Turner, Rev. W. W., 75
Tyler, Rev. Joseph D., 22, 68

Ulmer, Thomas A., 41, 250
    autobiography, *The Badge of Honor*,
        250
Underhill, Odie, 24
United States Centennial Exhibition,
    70
U.S. Congress, 56, 57
U.S. Government Printing Office, 153
U.S. Saving Bonds, 160
U.S.S. Rhodes (ship), 225
U.S.S. Thomas Hopkins Gallaudet
    (ship), launched, 224; named,
    224; career 224-225; (ill.) 225
Universities. See Colleges
Utah Schools for the Deaf and the
    Blind. See Schools

Van Buren Administration, 32
Vasnick, Andy, 349
Vaughan, Major General Harry, 196
Veditz, George W., 39, 42, 62, 77,
    240, 265, 276, 359, 363, 364
Veditz, Mrs. George W., 42
Vernon, McCay, 388, 392, 397, 398
    co-author of *They Grow in Silence*,
        388, 392
Vestal, James M., 211
videophone satellite communications,
    379, 381
Vinson, Emery Edwin
    poem, "A Deaf Man's Prayer," 182
Virginia School for the Deaf and
    Blind. See Schools
Virstein, Jimmie, 289
Vocational Rehabilitation Service, 317,
    320
vocational training programs, 91, 211,
    247
"Voices, Voices," (Hogan), 87
Volta, Alessandro, 77

Volta Bureau, 42, 67, 77, 78, 261
"Volta Fund," 77
Volta Prize, 77

Wait, Selah, 25
Walker family, The, 13, 26
Walker, N. E., 13
Walker, Rev. Newton P., 13, 26
Wall, Robert Carr, 170, 215
    and his invention, bicycle luggage
        carrier rack, 170
Walter, Jean, 261
Wampler, David, 371
Ward, Augustus M., 26
War of Methods, The, 359. See also
    sign language
Warshawsky, Leonard B., 160, 286
Washburn, Cadwallader L., 39, 147,
    148, 149, 150, 182, 396
    and his etchings, "Where Boats
        Beach," 147; "Berber Khalife,"
        148; "The Matriarch," 148;
        "Antonio Viale," 149; "A
        Bedouin Girl," 150; "Hopi
        Indian Tribesman," 150;
        "Bronze Dragon in Front of
        Temple," 150; "Sacred Well,"
        150
Washington Evening Star, 196
Washington, Gary, 301
Washington Monument, The, 212
Washington Post, The, 262
Washington State Capitol, 136
Washington State School for the
    Deaf. See Schools
Washington Suburban Sanitary
    Commission, 394
Washoe, 373, 374
Waterstreet, Edmund, 29
Watson, Abbie, M., 254
Watson, Angelia, 171, 172
Watson Children, The, 172
Watson, David, 171, 172, 366, 367
    his book, *Talk With Your Hands*, 366,
        367
Watson, Edna, 172
Watson, James, 54
Weaver, Ben, 168
Weaver, Ralph, 168
Weaver, Reuben S., 167
Wechsberg, Peter, 382, 387; news
    program, *NEWSIGN*, 387
Weed, George, M., 90
    and his book, *Great Truths Simply
        Told*, 90
Weeks, William H., 362
Weitbrecht, Robert, 198
Wenger, Arthur, 48
Wenger, Ray, 48
Western Union, 394
Westervelt, Zenas F., 44

West Virginia School for the Deaf and
    the Blind. See Schools
Wettschreck, Walter, 197
WGBH Educational Foundation,
    Boston, 385
"What Hath God Wrought?," 4
Wheeler, Ned C., 48
Whildin, Rev. Oliver J., 186
Whistler, James, 147
Whitcomb, James H., 151
    and his silhouetts, "Elizabeth
        (Whitcomb) Gates," 151;
        "James Hosley Whitcomb," 152
White, Bill R., 246
White, Bishop William, 20
White, B. R., 230
White, George, 348
White, Harriet T. See Mrs. W. J. Bray
White, Harry, 62
White, Henry C., 48, 54, 63
White House Conference, The, 403
White, Ralph H., xiii, 26
Whitt, Alonzo, 288
Who's Who listing, 249
Wieringen, Kevin V., 389
    in *"James at 15,"* 389
Wiggins, Julius, 246, 254
    book, *No Sound*, 254
Wilk, Jane, 382, 387
    news program, *NEWSIGN*, 387
Wilkins, Bill, 197
Wilkinson, Warring, 34
Willard, William, 23
Willhite, Nellie Zabel, 47, 195
Williams, Boyce R., 29, 47, 211, 229,
    236, 267, 320, 322, 330, 338, 346,
    396
William, Edward E., 92
Williams, George C., 82
Williams, Mel, 339
Williams, Thomas S., 288-89
Willigan, Martin, 303, (ill.) 302
Wilson, Rev. Adolph O., 190, 191, 215
Wilson, Harriet, 154
Wilson Signature, 430
Winecoff, Edgar M., 244
Wing, George, 16, 170
    and his, "Wings's Symbols," 16,
        170
Wing's Symbols, 16, 170
Winston, Bickerton family, 341
Wisconsin School for the Deaf. See
    Schools
Wright, Harold, 200
Wright, Jennie, 47
Wolach, Marvin, 50
"Women of the Year." See Phi Kappa
    Zeta
Wood, Elizabeth, 48
Wood, Tom, 153
    and his work, 153
Wood, Willard H., 244, 254
    book, *The Forgotten People*, 254

482

Woodbury, Max W., 189
Woodward, John W., 26, 27, 359, 365
Woodward, Virginia (wife), 27
World Congress of the Deaf, 214, 396
World's Fair, 87, 165
    New York, 100; St. Louis, 36, 42
World Games for the Deaf, 286, 287,
        296, 300
Work Progress Administration, 211
World War II,
    assembly line workers, 222
    discrimination against Japanese
        students, 222
    deaf draftees, 220
    financial support for, 222

NAD financial support for, 223
    prices before, 219
    postwar years, 227
    sports during, 224
    the war effort, 220-222
Wrestling, 287-290
    Gallaudet, 287 (ill.), 288-289
    outstanding, 290, 303
    National AAU Champions, 289
    tournaments, 287-8
Wright, David, 254
    Deafness, 254
Wurdemann, Frank, 84, 167
Wyman, Jane, 261

Yates, Fred P., 22, 23
Yates, Leo A., 23
yellow fever, 70
Yolles, Lawrence, 229, 263
Young, Pam, 373, 378, 381
Youngblood, Mrs. S. H., 193

Zachariasen, William, 279
Zawolkow, Esther, 371
Zieske, Paul, 31
Zimble, Nathan, 27, 287, 288 (ill.) 286
    quoted, 303